Our Life in the Church

Teacher's Manual

Our Life in the Church

Teacher's Manual

Faith and Life Series
Revised Edition
BOOK EIGHT

Ignatius Press, San Francisco
Catholics United for the Faith, Steubenville

Director of First Edition: The late Rev. Msgr. Eugene Kevane, Ph.D.
Assistant Director and General Editor of First Edition: Patricia Puccetti Donahoe, M.A.
First Edition Writers: Sister Mary Ann Kirkland, I.H.M., Sister Mary Catherine Blanding, I.H.M., and Sister Mary Theresa Wynne, I.H.M.

Revision Writers: Colette Ellis, M.A. and Matthew Ramsay
Director and General Editor of Revision: Caroline Avakoff, M.A.
Editor of Revision: Christopher Bess

Catholics United for the Faith, Inc. and Ignatius Press gratefully acknowledge the guidance and assistance of the late Reverend Monsignor Eugene Kevane, former Director of the Pontifical Catechetical Institute, Diocese of Arlington, Virginia, in the production of the First Edition of this series. The First Edition intended to implement the authentic approach in Catholic catechesis given to the Church through documents of the Holy See and in particular the conference of Joseph Cardinal Ratzinger on "Sources and Transmission of Faith." The Revised Edition continues this commitment by drawing upon the *Catechism of the Catholic Church* (Libreria Editrice Vaticana, 1994, 1997). Excerpts from the English translation of the *Catechism of the Catholic Church* for use in the United States of America copyright © 1994, United States Catholic Conference, Inc.—Libreria Editrice Vaticana. English translation of the *Catechism of the Catholic Church*: *Modifications from the Editio Typica* copyright © 1997, United States Catholic Conference, Inc.—Libreria Editrice Vaticana. Used with permission.

Scripture quotations are from the Holy Bible, Revised Standard Version, Catholic Edition. Old Testament © 1952; Apocrypha © 1957; Catholic Edition, incorporating the Apocrypha © 1966; New Testament © 1946; Catholic Edition © 1965, by the Division of Christian Education of the National Council of the Churches of Christ in the United States of America. All rights reserved.

Contents

Introduction to the *Faith and Life* Revised Edition

The *Faith and Life* series, which includes a student text, Teacher's Manual, and *Activity Book* for grades 1–8, has been used in schools and parishes across the country since its original publication in 1987. This revision of the original series continues our commitment to the faithful transmission of the teachings of the Roman Catholic Church by emphasizing the importance of Scripture and the *Catechism of the Catholic Church.*

The Student Textbook:

The *Faith and Life* student texts have undergone minimal revision. The beautiful and inspiring religious artwork has been maintained, for faith has inspired art for centuries, and religious art has, in turn, inspired our faith. Art is a valuable educational tool, especially in the teaching of religious truths to children, for it offers a visual image in addition to the oral and written word. Art can also be a source of meditation for students and teachers as they investigate the paintings, discuss the religious imagery, and come to understand the beautiful symbols and the artistic expressions they communicate.

New vocabulary in all the grades is now indicated by bold type, and each definition can now be found both within the chapter and in the glossary.

The questions provided for memorization in each chapter have been expanded and carefully revised for age-appropriateness. In addition, relevant references to the *Catechism of the Catholic Church* are indicated next to every question. Each chapter now opens with an appropriate Scripture passage, and relevant Bible verses are quoted throughout. These changes demonstrate the Scriptural foundation of the faith as well as the significance of the new *Catechism of the Catholic Church* for the Church as a fruit of Vatican Council II. Common Catholic prayers have been inserted both in the text and also in an expansive list of prayers at the back of the student text.

The Teacher's Manual:

The *Faith and Life* Teacher's Manuals are the most heavily updated and expanded aspects of this extensive revision process. Useful information previously provided in the supplemental Resource Binders of the original series has been incorporated into the new Teacher's Manuals, thus eliminating the need for individual binders.

Each chapter of the Teacher's Manuals begins with a list of important references to the *Catechism of the Catholic Church* and Scripture passages that support the chapter lessons. This is followed by a clear and succinct summary of the doctrine discussed in the following four lessons. This summary may be used as a guide for once-a-week catechism or CCD classes.

The revised Teacher's Manual provides a full week of detailed lesson plans for each chapter with four days of teaching and one day of review and assessment. Each color-coded lesson clearly indicates the teaching aims and materials necessary for that day. Optional craft materials, songs, appendix pages, and additional video and book resources are also included. The lesson plans themselves are designed to be guides in teaching even the most complex truths of the faith with age-appropriate examples.

Comprehensive chapter quizzes and optional unit tests can be found in Appendix A. Appendix B contains additional activities, resources for group projects, and black-line pages for making copies for the class.

One entirely new addition to the revision is the "Catholic Culture and Tradition" box found on the second page of each lesson. These boxes include supplemental materials for the teacher, information on the lives of the saints, explanations of terms, descriptions of Church traditions and rituals, relevant citations, suggestions for activities, additional resources, and prayers.

Once-a-Week Lesson Plans:

To assist Parish and CCD Programs, "once-a-week lesson plans" can be formulated by using the summary boxes for doctrinal content from the chapter introductory page and the italicized sections throughout the four lessons. A recommended format is as follows: read the entire chapter, use a lesson plan consisting of the italicized sections, which cover the necessary material and doctrines with sufficient development, then spend time reinforcing the material with the memorization of questions, vocabulary, and prayers. The quizzes can then be sent home for family reinforcement and review. The unit quizzes can still be administered in class once a month to assist the teacher in monitoring the students' progress.

The Activity Book:

The *Faith and Life* Activity Books have been significantly expanded to include one activity for each lesson, that is, four activities per chapter. The goal was to offer the teacher a wide variety of reinforcement tools in a separate text without losing the interest of the students. In the final grades the activities focus on comprehension and synthesis of the ideas expressed, as students are encouraged to make their own, both intellectually and actively, what they have been taught.

The *Faith and Life* series, revised edition, aspires to aid teachers and parents (the primary educators) in transmitting the truths, doctrines, wealth of traditions, and cultural richness of the Roman Catholic Church.

For Teachers and Catechists

Text and Grade Level

The eighth grade student text, *Our Life in the Church*, focuses on the nature and history of the Church, and the universal call to holiness of all her members. Eighth graders are more able to abstract, think, and reflect. While building upon these adolescent abilities, the goal of this text is to give students a generous and wholehearted love for the Church based on a clear understanding of her divine nature and the treasures contained therein. Finally, special emphasis is made of the various vocations to which students may be called, particularly the priesthood and religious life, that they may begin to develop a readiness to serve God as he desires.

Catechesis: Nature and Purpose

Catechesis is the systematic instruction of children, young people, and adults into the Catholic faith and the teachings of the Church with the goal of making them into Christ's disciples (cf. CCC 5). It is the handing-on of Christ's message to his people. The *General Catechetical Directory* describes catechesis as a form of ministry of God's Word, "which is intended to make men's faith living, conscious, and active, through the light of instruction" (GCD 17; 1971).

The Catechist: God's Instrument

To be a catechist is to be God's instrument. Every catechist has a responsibility to teach the fullness of the truth faithfully, while witnessing to those entrusted to his care. A fervent sacramental life and regular prayer life are the catechist's best personal preparation. Any instructor can use textbooks and teaching tools, learn various methods for effective classroom participation, and develop lesson plans to facilitate an academic environment. But nothing is as important as witnessing through your words and deeds and petitioning God for the on-going formation and spiritual growth of the students. No matter how much knowledge you impart to your students, you should recognize that you merely plant the seeds of faith that God himself must cultivate in their souls.

John Paul II states in *Catechesi Tradendae*: "at the heart of catechesis we find . . . the Person of Jesus of Nazareth . . . in catechesis it is Christ . . . who is taught . . . and it is Christ alone who teaches . . ." (CT 5,6). Religious education must always be centered on the triune God and on Christ himself. God chose to reveal himself throughout salvation history, through his creation, the prophets, the Scriptures, and most perfectly in the Person of Jesus Christ. This revelation, preserved faithfully through Sacred Scripture and Tradition, has been entrusted to the Church that every catechist is called to serve.

Catechesis in today's ministry is often coupled with evangelization—a first hearing of the good news of salvation. Through catechesis, you should guide your students to seek, accept, and investigate profoundly the Gospel so that they in turn may become witnesses of Christ. The new *Catechism of the Catholic Church*, together with Sacred Scripture, provides catechists with the tools necessary to achieve this.

The Role of Parents: The First Catechists

The family provides the first and most important introduction to Christian faith and practice for any child, since parents are the primary educators of their children. Instruction in the faith, which begins at an early age, should include not only the parents' good Christian example, but also a formation in prayer and an explanation and review of what students have learned from religious instruction and attending liturgical events.

Parental cooperation is very important to a teacher's success as a catechist. You should try to involve parents in their children's instruction. Discuss with them the program and methods you are using, consult them about better ways to teach their children, and ask for assistance if problems arise. Let parents know that you are there to help them fulfill their duties in forming and educating their children in Christ (cf. GCD 78, 79).

Methodologies

The *General Catechetical Directory* provides an overview of various successful methodologies you may find useful. Knowledge can be transmitted through prayer and liturgy, through words and deeds, or through texts and activities, but the students learn it primarily from you, the catechist.

Induction and Deduction:	Inductive methods serve well in the presentation of facts and in considering and examining those facts in order to recognize their Christian meaning. Induction is the process of reasoning from a part to a whole, from particular to general principles. It is not independent of deductive methods, which reason from the general to the particular and include interpretation and determining cause and effect. These two methods, taken together, aid in the students' understanding of the unity of the faith, the inter-relation of topics, and most importantly their practical applications.
Formulas:	Expressing thoughts or ideas succinctly and accurately in a memorable form allows for ease of memorization and better understanding of a topic. In the early stages of education, memorization should be utilized more frequently since children first need language to communicate meaning. In theology, semantics are very important, for Christians have died for their faith and schisms have occurred because of word use (e.g., the *Filioque* in the Nicene Creed). Such formulas also provide a uniform method of speaking among the faithful.
Experience:	Personal experience is reflective and practical, and it transforms abstract theories into applicable and memorable concepts. Catechists should use concrete examples in class and encourage their students to judge personal experience with Christian values.
Creativity:	Creative activities enable students to meditate upon and express, in their own words, the messages they have learned.
Groups:	In catechesis the importance of group instruction is becoming more apparent. Groups aid the social and ecclesial formation of students, and they foster a sense of Christian co-responsibility and solidarity.

The *Catechism of the Catholic Church*: An Important Tool

Today's classrooms are filled with children who have various needs and backgrounds. Complicated by an atmosphere of religious indifference, religious hostility, and an apparent absence of Catholic culture, knowledge, and meaningful practice, your catechetical work becomes especially valuable. One important tool that belongs to all the faithful is the *Catechism of the Catholic Church*, which is divided into four sections: the Creed, the Sacraments, the Moral Life, and Prayer.

The Creed:	The Creed is a summary of the faith and the Church's baptismal promises. As a public profession of faith, Catholics find in it their identity as members of Christ's Mystical Body. This is the faith handed down from Christ to the apostles and to the entire Church.
Sacraments:	The seven sacraments are outward signs instituted by Christ to confer grace. Active participation in the sacramental life of the Church, such as attending Mass prayerfully and faithfully, should be encouraged from a young age.
The Moral Life:	The moral life does not limit; instead it provides the boundaries that define the Catholic identity and allow for proper love of God and neighbor. A right moral life is man's gift to God, a response to his unconditional love. Every Catholic should be an example to others.
Prayer:	Prayer unites a person with God (through words, actions, silence, and presence), and it should be encouraged and put into practice from early childhood. There are many forms of prayer, but each brings the soul closer to God.

The *Faith and Life* Teacher's Manual provides much of what you will need to be an effective catechist, but it will only be fruitful depending on how you utilize it and how you teach and minister the Word of God to your students. Take very seriously your responsibilities as a catechist. Frequently call upon Christ as his witness and disciple to help you hand on his message. Persevere and draw near to God, bringing your students with you.

Additional material may be found at www.CatecheticalResources.com and www.Domestic-Church.com.

CHAPTER ONE
CHRIST'S ABIDING PRESENCE

Catechism of the Catholic Church References

Christ's Presence in the Church: 669, 787–96, 823
Call of the Twelve: 638–44, 763–65, 863, 857
Church as Divine: 772–73, 932
Church as Human: 672, 824, 853
Church's Origin, Foundation, and Mission: 758–69, 778
Community: 770–71
Hierarchy of the Church: 771, 871–87, 914, 934
Holy Spirit and the Church in the Liturgy: 1091–1109, 1112
Christ Founded the Church: 424, 726

The "Keys of the Kingdom": 551–53, 567
Mission of the Apostles: 858–60, 869
Mystery of the Church: 770–76, 779–80
Paschal Mystery in the Church's Sacraments: 1113–34
Pentecost: the Holy Spirit and the Church: 731–41, 746–47, 767–68
Presence of Christ in the Eucharist: 1373–81, 1410, 1418
Presence of Christ in the Liturgy: 1084–90, 1111

Scripture References

Incarnation: Lk 1:26–45
Public Ministry: Mt 3:13–17; 26:17–47
Crucifixion: Mt 26:47—27:66
Resurrection: Jn 20:1–31
Founding of the Church: Mt 3:13–19; 16:13–20;
      Jn 21:10–19

Ascension: Acts 1:1–12
Sending of the Holy Spirit: Acts 1:13—2:4
Emmaus: Lk 24:1–35
Mystical Body: 1 Cor 12:12–27

Summary of Lesson Content

Lesson 1

Jesus suffered, died, and rose from the dead as an act of love for us.

Jesus promised to be with us until the end of the age.

Jesus is present in the Word of God, in the People of God, and, most especially, in the Eucharist.

The Father and the Son sent the Holy Spirit for the life of the Church, which continues Jesus' mission in the world.

Lesson 2

Christ founded his Church. This founding is recorded in Scripture.

The Church is both divine and human. She is divine in her origin and life. She is human in her hierarchy and membership.

Lesson 3

The Church requires a structure in order to function well. This structure includes hierarchy, membership, rules, and organization. In her structure, the Church is human.

Lesson 4

Through, with, and in the Church, Christ is present.

Christ founded the Church. The Church is divine.

LESSON ONE: ABIDING PRESENCE

Aims

The students will learn that Jesus suffered, died, and rose from the dead as an act of love for us.

They will learn that Jesus promised to be with us until the end of the age. He is present in the Word of God, in the People of God, and, most especially, in the Eucharist.

They will learn that the Father and the Son sent the Holy Spirit for the life of the Church, which continues Jesus' mission in the world.

Materials

- *Activity Book*, p. 1

Optional:
- "The Church's one foundation," *Adoremus Hymnal*, #560

Begin

Discuss reasons we know that Jesus cared enough for us not to leave us as orphans. Have the students give biblical, historical, and personal examples of ways we know that Christ remains present with us.

What do these examples tell us about God's love for man and for us, specifically?

CHAPTER 1

Christ's Abiding Presence

According to the riches of his glory he may grant you to be strengthened with might through his Spirit in the inner man, and that Christ may dwell in your hearts through faith . . . to him be glory in the church and in Christ Jesus to all generations, for ever and ever. Amen.

Ephesians 3:16–17, 21

"I will not leave you desolate; I will come to you" (Jn 14:18).

These overwhelming words of Our Lord Jesus at the Last Supper ring in our ears as they have rung through the ages. Christ suffered the agony of his Passion and the ignominious death on the Cross because of his love for us. He said, "Greater love has no man than this, that a man lay down his life for his friends" (Jn 15:13). He died to save us from sin and to show us the way to glory through taking up our daily crosses. He wanted to lift us up to himself.

But what would happen after Jesus' death, Resurrection and final Ascension into heaven? His friends feared what would happen. Would he leave only a memory of those days when his friends and disciples so keenly felt the joy of his presence among them? Imagine what it would be like if you had been among them and known him.

The disciples on the road to Emmaus said to each other after Jesus parted from them, "Did not our hearts burn within us while he talked to us?" (Lk 24:32). That question shows something of the mysterious power his words and his presence must have had. Was this loving holy presence of Jesus to be gone for ever from the earth? No, Jesus Christ himself said, "I am with you always, even to the close of the age" (Mt 28:20).

Abiding Presence

A good father does not forget his children when he goes away. He wants to make sure that they will be taken care of in his absence. Jesus' love for us was so great that it did not stop even with dying for each one of us personally. He wanted to continue to take care of us.

How did Jesus provide for us? How is he with us always?

The words to the apostles "I will not leave you orphans" were immediately preceded by the promise that the Holy Spirit would be sent to them. God the Father would send "the Spirit of Truth," also called the Spirit of Love, or the Fire of Love, who would be the soul of his Church. Christ has left us that Church. Christ is the eternal Shepherd and has appointed a

11

Develop

1. Read paragraphs 1–6 (up to "Christ Founded His Church").

2. Review the saving events of Christ's life. The students must understand the significance of these events
- Incarnation: Lk 1:26–45
- Public Ministry: Mt 3:13–17; 26:17–47
- Crucifixion: Mt 26:47—27:66
- Resurrection: Jn 20:1–31
- Founding of the Church: Mt 3:13–19; 16:13–20; Jn 21:10–19
- Ascension: Acts 1:1–12
- Sending of the Holy Spirit: Acts 1:13—2:4
The students may dramatize these stories or create a story board including these stories.

3. Read the story of Emmaus from the Gospel of Luke (Lk 24:1–35). Help the students to recognize Emmaus as a pre-figuration of the first Mass (Liturgy of the Word = Christ explaining the Scriptures, Liturgy of the Eucharist = Christ recognized in the breaking of the bread).

4. The Catechism of the Catholic Church *says that in the most Blessed Sacrament of the Eucharist the Body, Blood, Soul, and Divinity of Jesus is truly present (CCC 1374). Have the students recite the various ways that Christ is present to his Church. Spend time explaining the real presence of Christ in the Eucharist. Visit the tabernacle of your Church for prayer time.*
- *Discuss each of the ways Christ is present, and have the students give examples.*
- *Discuss Christ's presence in other churches. Do other churches experience the presence of Christ in each of these ways?*

Name:_____

Christ's Abiding Presence

Answer the following questions in complete sentences.

1. How much did Jesus love us?
   <u>Jesus loved us so much that he suffered and died for us.</u>

2. What did he mean when he said he will not leave us orphans?
   <u>When Jesus said that he would not leave us orphans he meant that he would be with us always by being present in the Eucharist and by sending his Holy Spirit to guide the Church.</u>

3. Who did Jesus and God the Father send to us?
   <u>Jesus and God the Father sent us the Holy Spirit.</u>

4. Why did Christ found a Church?
   <u>Christ founded a Church to continue his presence on earth and to shepherd his people.</u>

5. What does it mean for you to be a member of Christ's Church?
   <u>To be a member of Christ's Church means that each member plays a vital role and adds to the overall harmony.</u>

Reinforce

1. Have the students work on *Activity Book*, p. 1.

2. Give the class time to work on the Memorization Questions and Words to Know from this chapter.

3. Visit the Blessed Sacrament in your church. Spend time in prayer before Our Eucharistic Lord.

4. Have the students write a response to Christ's gift of his abiding presence.

5. Discuss the need for the Holy Spirit, who is the soul of the Church. It is through the work of the Holy Spirit that Christ's truths are taught faithfully, that Christ is made present in his sacraments, and that we are inspired to be united with Christ in prayer.

Conclude

1. Teach the students to sing "The Church's one foundation," *Adoremus Hymnal*, #560.

2. End class by praying the Act of Faith.

Preview

In the next lesson, the students will learn about the Church that Jesus founded.

PRAYER TO THE HOLY SPIRIT
by Saint Augustine

Breath in me, O Holy Spirit, that all my thoughts may be holy.

Act in me, O Holy Spirit, that my work may be holy.

Draw my heart, O Holy Spirit, that I may love but what is holy.

Strengthen me, O Holy Spirit, to defend all that is holy.

Guard me, O Holy Spirit, that I may always be holy.

NOTES

_____
_____
_____
_____
_____
_____
_____
_____
_____
_____
_____
_____

LESSON TWO: CHRIST'S CHURCH

Aims

The students will learn that Christ founded his Church. This founding is recorded in Scripture.

They will learn that the Church is both divine and human. She is divine in her origin and life. She is human in her hierarchy and membership.

Materials

• *Activity Book*, p. 2

Optional:
• "The Church's one foundation," *Adoremus Hymnal*, #560

Begin

Discuss the students' understanding of the Church. What is the "Church"? Answers may include:
• Building
• Community
• World-wide organization
• Channel of grace
• Mystical Body of Christ, etc.
Learn the students' knowledge-base, so that it may be broadened and built upon.

chief shepherd and other shepherds to represent him in the care of his flock.

Christ Founded His Church

It is recorded in the Gospels that many times Christ spoke of the Church in parables or implicitly. But twice he spoke of her explicitly.

1. First Christ said to Peter in front of the other apostles, "You are Peter, and on this rock I will build my church, and the powers of death shall not prevail against it" (Mt 16:18). What did he mean when he said he will build *his*

Church? He obviously meant what he said. He said so with some emphasis and solemnity.

2. In another passage Jesus says that, if disputes and grievances cannot be settled charitably among those involved, they should be brought to the Church and the Church will make the ultimate decision about the argument. If then the offender "refuses to listen even to the church, let him be to you as a Gentile and a tax collector" (Mt 18:17). In other words in the mind of Christ, the Church was to be the final judge and arbiter of whatever questions might arise among his followers.

12

Develop

1. Read paragraphs 7–9 (to "The Church Has a Structure").

2. Discuss how Jesus founded his Church (Mt 16:18–19). Note especially:
• *She is founded upon a profession of faith*
• *Peter was established as the visible head of the Church (Pope)*
• *Jesus specifically used the word, "Church"*
• *The Church has a power that extends to heaven and is stronger than the powers of hell*
• *The Church will last until the end of time (indefectibility)*

3. Jesus directs his followers to take their grievances with one another to the Church—the Church will act as mediator and judge. This shows that the Church has authority. (Optional: You may discuss the role of the Church in governing her people. How many of her rules for governing are

recorded in canon law? (Canon law is is the ecclesiastical law or the law of the Church.)

4. Discuss the role of the apostles in the Church. They were entrusted with continuing the work of Christ. As the first bishops, they were to teach, sanctify, and govern. This role is still upheld by all bishops. (Optional: you may discuss how the apostles were male, and thus those who receive the Sacrament of Holy Orders all must be male.)

5. Discuss and make a chart on the board (or have the students record a chart in their books) showing how the Church is both human and divine.

6. Discuss the role of the Holy Spirit in guiding the Church: in her teachings, in her governance, in her sacramental life, in her saints and prayers, etc.

Name:_____

The Church of Christ

Answer the following questions in complete sentences.

1. In Matthew 16:16–19, what does Jesus mean when he says he will build his Church?

   When Jesus said he will build his Church, he meant that the Church is built by God and is of divine, not human, origin. She will have the presence and guidance of the Holy Spirit.

2. What role would Peter have in this Church?

   Peter would be leader of the Church.

3. Why do you think Jesus gave his authority to Peter in front of the other apostles?

   Jesus gave his authority to Peter in front of the apostles so that all would know that the authority came directly from Jesus.

4. In Matthew 18:17, Jesus speaks again of his Church. What role will the Church have according to this passage?

   The Church has the role of final judge and arbiter.

5. Is the Church merely a human institution?

   The Church is not merely a human institution, but of divine origin and led by God.

6. Is the Church only divine?

   The Church is both divine and human since it is also made up of human beings.

Reinforce

1. Have the students work on *Activity Book*, p. 2.

2. Give the class time to work on the Memorization Questions and Words to Know from this chapter.

3. Break the students into two groups to discuss and dramatize the two explicit mentionings of the Church.

4. Discuss the role of the Church and her authority (and how it differs from civil authority). You may use examples of:
   - Divorce vs. annulment
   - Moral issues, e.g., abortion
   - Saint Thomas More and his martyrdom because of his obedience to the Church above Henry VIII.

It is important for the students to understand that sometimes society does not subscribe to God's authority—even though God's authority is ultimate and binding to all.

Conclude

1. Lead the students in singing "The Church's one foundation," *Adoremus Hymnal*, #560.

2. End class by praying the Act of Faith.

Preview

In the next lesson, the students will learn about the structure of the Church.

THE CHURCH OF CHRIST

Human	Divine
Exists in time	Infallible
Exists on earth	Spotless
Made up of men	Eternal
Her members may sin	Universal
	Founded by Jesus

PRAYER TO THE HOLY SPIRIT
traditional

Come Holy Spirit, fill the hearts of your faithful.
R/ *And enkindle in them the fire of your love.*

Send forth your Spirit and they shall be created.
R/ *And you will renew the face of the earth.*

LESSON THREE: STRUCTURE

Aims

The students will learn that the Church requires a structure in order to function well. This structure includes hierarchy, membership, rules, and organization. In her structure, the Church is human.

Materials

- *Activity Book*, p. 3

Optional:
- "The Church's one foundation," *Adoremus Hymnal*, #560

Begin

What would a school be like without a principal? What about a class without students or a school day without a schedule or rules of discipline?

Discuss the need for societies to have structure: leaders, hierarchy, members, rules, and organization. This need for structure is the same in the Church.

In both these passages Jesus clearly speaks of his intention to begin his Church. He in fact continues immediately after both these declarations to say to his apostles, "Whatever you bind on earth shall be bound in heaven . . ." (Mt 16:19; 18:18). This is an almost shocking statement. Christ here was actually giving power over heaven, to a select group of twelve apostles. It was a divine authority that he gave them.

So we see that the Church was willed, founded and built by Christ. He said, "I will build my Church." The Church is therefore of divine origin. She is different from any other society or community. No other human society can claim the presence and guidance of the Holy Spirit. The Church is not man-made nor merely human. This is why we call the Church a supernatural mystery.

The Church Has a Structure

Her members are human, to be sure. And God who understands and provides for our needs, made us to live together in community. "It is not good that man should be alone" (Gen 2:18). He also takes into account the universal characteristics of human societies: for instance, that a society needs leaders, a hierarchy (or assistant leaders), members, rules, and some kind of organization. Without these, societies would become chaotic. It belongs to the nature of things that societies cannot function without structure. We see this in a family or in a sports team.

Or take the example of an orchestra. There is a conductor. Then there is the first violinist, who leads the string section, while the clarinetist leads the woodwinds. It is also necessary to have all sorts of instruments, not just one or one kind. Some—for example, the cymbals—may seem to have an insignificant role. But what would it sound like at the crucial moment without them? They are truly necessary for the music to sound complete.

Using the example of an orchestra as a comparison to the Church we can say that the structure of the whole orchestra, the conductor, the various leaders, the players, and the instruments are absolutely necessary for the sake of the music. The music cannot come through harmoniously without a structure. On the other hand, they would all be mute without the music. The music is the soul of the whole thing. So it is with the Church. The Holy Spirit—the Spirit of Truth, the Spirit of Love—is, as it were, the music. He is the very soul of the Church. So Christ has promised us this heavenly music, the Holy Spirit sent by the Father, coming through the structure of the institutional Church. In the case of the Church, the fundamental structure itself is willed by Christ.

13

Develop

1. Read paragraphs 10–12 (up to "Christ's Church").

2. Compare the Church with an orchestra using paragraphs 11 and 12, and the Chalk Talk at right. You may further this analogy by asking the students how these elements of orchestral music can be related to the Church:
- *Composer*
- *Conductor*
- *Various instruments*
- *Music*
- *Silence*
- *Practice*
- *Audience*

3. There are many different models of the Church. Discuss the model of the Mystical Body of Christ. Read together 1 Cor 12:12–27. What role do the students have in the Mystical Body (together and individually)?

4. Discuss each of the following questions:
- *Who is the leader of the Church? (Christ)*
- *Who is in the hierarchy? (Pope, Cardinals, Bishops, Priests, Religious, Laity.) Discuss the distinctions of and the complementarity of these roles.*
- *Who are members of the Church? (Communion of Saints: saints and angels in heaven, the souls in purgatory, the faithful on earth)*
- *What are the rules of the Church? (Moral Life: Ten Commandments, Precepts, Corporal and Spiritual Works of Mercy, Virtues, Canon Law, etc.)*
- *What is the organization of the Church? (The Universal Church is divided into dioceses governed by bishops)*

Have the students name examples of each of the above-mentioned elements of the Church structure.

Name:_____

Church Structure

Using the analogy of an orchestra, explain the structure of the Church.

<u>Answers will vary.</u>

_____
_____
_____
_____
_____
_____
_____
_____
_____
_____
_____
_____
_____
_____
_____
_____
_____
_____
_____
_____

Reinforce

1. Have the students work on *Activity Book*, p. 3.

2. Give the class time to work on the Memorization Questions and Words to Know from this chapter.

3. The students may research different models for the Church, including: the Vineyard, Sheepfold, Ark, Mother, Bride, etc. Have the students apply the qualities of the structure of the Church to these models and present their findings to the class.

4. Discuss the respect we should have for the Church as well as her members and clergy.

5. Discuss the importance of every member in the Church. Have the students write ways that they can contribute to the life of the Church.

Conclude

1. Lead the students in singing "The Church's one foundation," *Adoremus Hymnal*, #560.

2. End class by praying the Act of Faith.

Preview

In the next lesson, the students will learn about Christ's relationship with his Church.

CHALK TALK: MATTER AND FORM OF THE CHURCH

NOTES

_____
_____
_____
_____
_____
_____
_____
_____
_____
_____
_____
_____

LESSON FOUR: HIS CHURCH

Aims

The students will learn that through, with, and in the Church, Christ is present.

They will learn that Christ founded the Church and that the Church is divine.

Materials

- *Activity Book*, p. 4

  Optional:
  - "The Church's one foundation," *Adoremus Hymnal*, #560

Begin

We know that the Church was founded by Christ in order to continue his saving mission. His work is carried out by the members of his Church, the guidance of the Holy Spirit, and with his help. Christ founded the Church, Christ's work is done in the Church, and the Church leads us to encounter Christ. The Church is truly Christ's.

Christ's Church

Through, with, and in the Church, Christ Our Lord is present. She is *his* Church. She is not someone's idea of what is needed, or the decision of some group that it would be a sensible thing to found a community and elect leaders. She is not a mere human construction, something created by man which can be reorganized at will. It is Christ himself who has founded his Church and divinely appointed his apostles and their successors. He has called each one of us through baptism to play a vital role as a living member of the Church. It is through the Church that we receive the sacraments. It is through the Church that we receive the Holy Eucharist, which is the amazing gift of his presence among us.

In this section of the book we will study this Church of Christ in detail—what she is, what she teaches, her order, her members and what, in brief, has been her history.

Q. 1 **What is the Church?**
The Church is the community of disciples, who, through the Holy Spirit, profess the faith of Jesus Christ, participate in his sacraments, and are united in communion with the pastors he has appointed (CCC 815).

Q. 2 **Who founded the Church?**
The Church was founded by Jesus Christ, who gathered his faithful followers into one community, placed her under the direction of the apostles with Saint Peter as her head, and gave her himself as perfect Sacrifice, the sacraments, and the Holy Spirit, who gives her life (CCC 763–66).

14

Develop

1. Read paragraphs 13 and 14 (to the end of the chapter).

2. Read Eph 5:21–32. Discuss this passage and how the relationship of a husband and wife is modeled after Christ and the Church. What does this reveal about Jesus' love for his Church and the members of his Church? Explain that this is why the Church is referred to as "She" or the Bride of Christ and mother of all. This is also why women religious symbolize the Church as bride and mother.

3. Discuss how the Church is different from any human institution:
- *Her members cannot vote on what they believe*
- *Her members cannot save themselves*
- *She is not created by man*
- *She must be submissive to Christ and his teachings (found in Scripture and Tradition) in faith, morality, and practice or discipline*

- *She is living*
- *The life of grace is dispensed through her*

4. Discuss how the Church is similar to human institutions:
- *We can be active in the Church*
- *She gathers in buildings, has human leadership, and has human needs (there are bills to pay, etc.)*

5. Discuss the importance of recognizing both elements of the Church (human and divine). Discuss the following scenarios:
- A priest is caught stealing money. What does this say about the Church and her teachings?
- Some theologians or bishops want to change a moral teaching; e.g., make homosexual activity morally good; or change a doctrine; e.g., make Mary a person of the Trinity. What can we say about this?

Name:_____

Understanding Christ's Church

Read the following Bible verses and write a brief paragraph on what they teach us about the Church.

1 Corinthians 12:27—13:13

Answers will vary.

Ephesians 5:21–33

Reinforce

1. Have the students work on *Activity Book*, p. 4.

2. Give the class time to work on the Memorization Questions and Words to Know from this chapter and to prepare for the quiz.

3. *The students should understand that, though the members of the Church (even in the hierarchy) are sinful persons, the Church herself is guided by the Holy Spirit. The Holy Spirit uses the members of the Church to do the work of Christ. This does not mean that when members of the Church sin they do the work of Christ; rather, we are all sinners, but we are still called to do Christ's work. The Church is protected from erroneous teachings in matters of faith and morals. However, there have been "dark times" in the Church. We must remember that our faith is in Christ and his teachings, not in the individual members of the Church.*

Conclude

1. Lead the students in singing "The Church's one foundation," *Adoremus Hymnal*, #560.

2. End class by praying the Act of Faith.

Preview

In the next lesson, the students' understanding of the material covered in this chapter will be reviewed and assessed.

SAINT JOAN OF ARC

From 1337 to 1453, France and England fought a series of battles now known as the Hundred Years War. England was trying to take land on the European continent and France was fighting back. Things were not going well for France. Their prince, the Dauphin, wasted his time at court and made no attempt to fight back as the English conquered city after city. In 1412, a French peasant girl named Joan of Arc was born. Growing up, she was renowned for her holiness and charity, spending many hours in prayer and giving food, and even her bed, to poor travelers who came through her village. When she was fourteen, Saint Michael, Saint Catherine, Saint Margaret, and others appeared and spoke to her. Gradually they began to reveal to her that she had a special mission from God: she was to save France. As a poor peasant girl who could not read or write, she was naturally afraid, but by the time she was seventeen she presented herself before the Dauphin, who gave her command of a small army and sent her to save the city of Orleans which was under siege by the English. Saint Joan's troops saved Orleans and went on to free many cities from the English. Soon the Dauphin was crowned King Charles VII. But the war was not over and Saint Joan was later captured and sold to the English. While she was being interrogated, the English asked her about her understanding of the Church and she answered "Christ and the Church are One!" In the end, the English burnt her at the stake, but in 1920, she was canonized by Pope Benedict XV.

CHAPTER ONE
REVIEW AND ASSESSMENT

Aims

The students' understanding of the material covered in this chapter will be reviewed and assessed.

Materials

- Quiz 1, Appendix, p. A-1

Optional:
- "The Church's one foundation," *Adoremus Hymnal*, #560

Review

1. The students should have a good understanding of the life of Christ, his works, and his mission.

2. The students should know how Christ is present in his Church.

3. The students should know that Jesus founded the Church to continue his work—to teach, sanctify, and govern his people.

4. The Church is human and divine. The students should be able to explain this mystery and distinguish between the human and divine elements of the Church.

5. The students should understand Christ's relationship with the Church.

6. The students should understand their role in the Church.

Name: _____

Christ's Abiding Presence   **Quiz 1**

Part I: Answer in complete sentences.

1. How do we know that Jesus intended to found the Church? Why did he found the Church?
   We know that Jesus intended to found the Church because he told us he would build her. He founded the Church to continue his presence on earth and to shepherd his people.

2. How is the Church human?
   The Church is human because she is made up of and run by human beings.

3. How is the Church divine?
   The Church is divine because she is of divine origin and led by God.

4. How is Christ present in the Church?
   Christ is present through, with, and in the Church. She is his Church and founded by Christ who appoints the apostles and his successors and calls each of us through Baptism to play a vital role as a living member of the Church. It is through the Church that he makes us holy.

5. What is your role in the life of the Church?
   Answers will vary.

Faith and Life • Grade 8 • Appendix A   *A - 1*

Assess

1. Distribute the quizzes and read through them with the students to be sure they understand the questions.

2. Administer the quiz. As they hand in their work, you may orally quiz the students on the Memorization Questions from this chapter.

3. After all the quizzes have been handed in, review the correct answers with the class.

Conclude

1. Lead the students in singing "The Church's one foundation," *Adoremus Hymnal*, #560.

2. End class by praying an Act of Faith.

CHAPTER TWO
THE BIRTH OF THE CHURCH

Catechism of the Catholic Church References

Apostles: 726, 731–32, 830, 1076
Church's Origin, Foundation, and Mission: 758–69, 778
Covenant with Noah: 56–58, 71
David and the Prayer of the King: 2578–80, 2594
Deposit of Faith: 84, 97, 175
Deposit of Grace: 2003
God Forms His People, Israel: 62–63, 72, 218, 2077
God's Promise to Abraham: 705–6, 762
Jesus' Mission of Salvation: 456–60
The "Keys to the Kingdom": 551–53, 567
"The Kingdom of God Is Very Near": 541–42, 567
Last Supper: 610–11, 621
Mission of the Apostles: 858–60, 869
Names and Images of the Church: 751–57, 777

Old Law: 1961–64, 1975, 1980–82
Pentecost: the Holy Spirit and the Church: 731–41, 746–47, 767–68, 1076
Priesthood in the Old Covenant: 1539–43
Proclamation of the Kingdom of God: 543–46
Promise of a Redeemer: 410–12, 420–21
Revelation of God's Plan of Salvation: 51–53, 68
Salvation History: 51–67
Stages of Revelation: 54–55, 69–70
Ten Commandments, Path to the Kingdom of Heaven: 1724
The Twelve Apostles: 551–53
Typology and the Unity of the Old and New Testaments: 128–30, 140
Unity of the Church: 813–22, 866

Scripture References

Pentecost: Acts 2:1–11
Protoevangelium: Gen 3:15
Noah: Gen 9:8–11
Abraham: Gen 17

Moses: Ex 3–25
Levitical Priesthood: Ex 28:40; 30:22–33
Davidic Covenant: 2 Sam 22; 23:1–7
Sending of Disciples: Mt 21:1–9; Mk 6:1–13; Lk 10:1–9

Summary of Lesson Content

Lesson 1

Jesus promised to send the Holy Spirit. The Nicene Creed professes "we believe in the Holy Spirit . . . who proceeds from the Father and the Son."

The Holy Spirit descended upon the apostles at Pentecost.

Pentecost is the "birthday" of the Church.

Lesson 2

Throughout salvation history the plan for the Church is visible through God's relationship with man and the development of a hierarchical community of believers bound to God in a covenant.

God's revelation tells us his will and his truth.

God revealed himself gradually until fully revealing himself in Christ.

Lesson 3

Jesus Christ is God the Son, the Second Person of the Holy Trinity, become man. He is true God and true man.

Jesus made the Church present by his presence, his teaching, and the formation of his followers. Jesus chose Saint Peter to be the head of the apostles and his visible representative after the Ascension.

Lesson 4

Jesus entrusted the mission of his Church to the apostles. The Church is to manifest herself to the world and bring all men to Christ.

The Holy Spirit descended upon the apostles (leaders of the Church) to empower their work.

Jesus is with his church today and will be until the end of time.

LESSON ONE: PENTECOST

Aims

The students will learn that Jesus promised to send the Holy Spirit. The Nicene Creed professes "we believe in the Holy Spirit . . . who proceeds from the Father and the Son."

They will learn that the Holy Spirit descended upon the apostles at Pentecost.

They will learn that Pentecost is the "birthday" of the Church.

Materials

- *Activity Book*, p. 5

Optional:
- "Christ is made the sure foundation," *Adoremus Hymnal*, #561

Begin

Read Jesus' promise to send the Holy Spirit in Jn 14:26 and 15:26. What do these two passages tell us? Who sends the Holy Spirit? Who is the Holy Spirit? Look up Is 11:2. What are the gifts of the Holy Spirit? What, therefore, can we determine about people who exhibit these gifts?

CHAPTER 2

The Birth of the Church

"But the Counselor, the Holy Spirit, whom the Father will send in my name, he will teach you all things, and bring to your remembrance all that I have said to you."

John 14:26

The words above, taken from the last discourse of our Lord on the night before he died, contain his promise to send the Holy Spirit to give life to his Church. In the second chapter of the Acts of the Apostles we find St. Luke's account of this great event.

The descent of the Holy Spirit upon the apostles is called **Pentecost** and is considered the "birthday" of the Church. On this day the Holy Spirit appeared—in the form of tongues of fire—to the small community of Jesus' followers who had gathered in the upper room in Jerusalem—the first members of the Catholic Church. The Holy Spirit gave them the grace to preach the Good News of Jesus Christ so that the Church might increase and spread as Our Lord had commanded.

Pentecost was, however, only the final step in God's plan to establish his Church on earth. For thousands of years God had been preparing for this moment when his Church would finally be manifested to the world. There were, in fact, three stages in the establishment of the Church. It was prefigured in the Old Testament, made present during Christ's life on earth, and made manifest to the world on Pentecost.

The beginnings of the Church can be found in the promises God made to Adam after the Fall. God made further promises to Noah after the flood. In fact, the ark, which saved Noah and his family from the waters of the flood, is a symbol of the Church.

With Abraham and the formation of the chosen people, the origins of the Church become more clear. At this stage, God made a covenant with Abraham and his descendants to be their protector. This was the beginning of the "**ekklesia**"—the people set apart—that they might become holy. (Ekklesia is the Greek word for "assembly." It is the word used in the New Testament for the Church. God calls together the "assembly" of his people, the Church, through his word.)

As we follow the history of the chosen people—the Jews—we see even more clearly the early stages of the Church. When Moses led his people out of Egypt God renewed his covenant (now with the whole people), making them into a true nation. Now they began to worship God through a formal religion, with special ceremonies and a certain code of moral behavior, namely, the Ten Commandments. They

15

Develop

1. Read paragraphs 1–3.

2. Review the Holy Trinity, covering these points:
- *One God*
- *Three distinct Persons who share in the divine nature*
- *Equality of three Persons*
- *First Person: Father (Creator)*
- *Second Person: Son (Redeemer). The Second Person becomes Man in the Divine Person of Jesus Christ*
- *Third Person: Holy Spirit (Sanctifier)*
- *Father begets Son (Son eternally begotten of the Father)*
- *Father and Son send Holy Spirit (Holy Spirit proceeds from the Father and the Son)*

3. Review the Holy Spirit. How is he depicted in art? What are symbols of the Holy Spirit? Where do we see the Holy Spirit in Scripture? What is the role of the Holy Spirit in the Church? What role did the Holy Spirit have in the writing of the Scriptures and in prophetic messages from God?

4. Read the account of the descent of the Holy Spirit at Pentecost and the events occurring immediately thereafter (Acts 2:1–47).
Questions:
- *What were the apostles like before Pentecost? After?*
- *Why did Saint Peter say they were not drunk?*
- *How were the people from different countries able to understand the apostles?*
- *Why did the preaching of Saint Peter affect so many? What happened?*
- *Why can we say that Pentecost is the birthday of the Church?*

5. Review the concept of the "birthday of the Church." Is Pentecost the first day of the Church? (No, just as life begins at conception but the birth occurs nine months later.)

Name:_____

The Birth of the Church

Answer the following questions in complete sentences.

1. What did Jesus promise during his last discourse?
   Jesus promised that he would send his Holy Spirit to teach and to bring remembrance to all he did on earth.

2. Who gives life to the Church?
   The Holy Spirit gives life to the Church.

3. Explain why Pentecost is called the "birthday" of the Church?
   Pentecost is called the "birthday" of the Church because that is the day that Jesus sent his Holy Spirit to give life to the Church.

4. What gift did the Holy Spirit give the followers of Jesus who gathered in the upper room?
   In the upper room, the Holy Spirit gave the followers of Jesus the gift to preach and spread the Good News.

5. Was Pentecost the beginning of God's plan for the Church? Explain your answer.
   No. Pentecost was not the beginning of God's plan for the Church. He had been preparing man for his Church since the Fall of Adam and Eve.

6. Read all of Acts 2 and write what happened after the descent of the Holy Spirit.
   Answers will vary.

Reinforce

1. Have the students work on *Activity Book*, p. 5.

2. Give the class time to work on the Memorization Questions and Words to Know from this chapter.

3. The students may create Trinity projects by doing one of the following:
   • Research the Church's teachings on the three Divine Persons
   • Find the three Divine Persons in the parts of the Mass; with their findings, the students should reveal what we can know about each Person
   • Find depictions of the Holy Trinity or the Divine Persons in art and describe what these works reveal about the Trinity and each Person
The students should write reports or make presentations to the class.

Conclude

1. Teach the students to sing "Christ is made the sure foundation," *Adoremus Hymnal*, #561.

2. End class by praying the Prayer to the Holy Spirit.

Preview

In the next lesson, the students will learn about prefigurements of the Church.

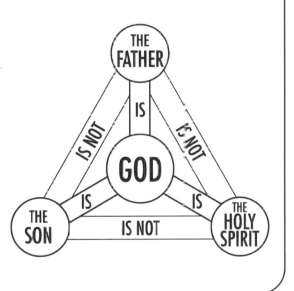

THE HOLY TRINITY

"In the Father and with the Father, the Son is one and the same God."
—CCC 262

"With them, the Sprit is one and the same God."
—CCC 263

NOTES

_____
_____
_____
_____
_____
_____
_____
_____
_____
_____
_____
_____
_____
_____

LESSON TWO: PREFIGUREMENTS

Aims

The students will learn that throughout salvation history the plan for the Church is visible through God's relationship with man and the development of a hierarchical community of believers bound to God in a covenant.

They will learn that God revealed himself gradually until fully revealing himself in Christ. God's revelation tells us his will and his truth.

Materials

- *Activity Book*, p. 6

Optional:
- "Christ is made the sure foundation," *Adoremus Hymnal*, #561

Begin

Discuss the word *ekklesia*, a Greek word meaning "assembly." It is from this word that "church" is derived. The Church is an assembly of believers who come together for worship. They are called together by God. God does not need a Church, but he established one for our good. We need a community for our beliefs—why? For support, to "keep us honest" (accountability), to safeguard and pass on teachings, to provide rites and traditions which assist us in expressing our faith, etc.

16

Develop

1. Read paragraphs 4–9 (to the end of the Heb 1:1–2 quote).

2. Have the students break into groups and read the following stories from the Bible:
- *Adam and Eve: Gen 1:1—3:15*
- *Noah: Gen 6:1—9:11*
- *Abraham: Gen 22:1–18*
- *Moses: Ex 19:1—20:22*
- *Levitical Priesthood: Ex 28:40; 30:22–33*
- *David: 2 Sam 6:1—7:17 (2 Sam 22:1—23:7)*
- *Prophets: e.g., Jeremiah: Jer 31:31–40; 32:36–40*

Each student should:
- Make a presentation on his passage (drama, art, or report)
- Explain how his passage shows God's plan for the Church (reveals prefigurements) including: covenant, congregation, worship, law, structure (hierarchy), human/divine elements

3. Create a timeline on the board as the various presentations are made, showing God's plan for the Church coming to fruition. Mark key figures and events and identify the New Testament figures and events they foreshadow.

4. The students should make their own timelines or booklets on "Old Testament Types of the Church," adding art (either pictures they find or their own renditions) of the events prefiguring the Church. They should add notations explaining the significance of these events in the development of the Church. They may also add responses of faith recorded in each significant event.

5. Discuss with the students:
- *Why did God want a Church?*
- *Why didn't God just implement a Church without the prefigurements and development?*
- *How can we know the Church is what God wants?*

Name:_____

The Church in God's Plan

Answer the following questions in complete sentences.

1. Write about God's plan for the Church in the events of the following people's lives.

Adam and Eve:
He promises that he will put enmity between the woman and the devil and her seed will crush his seed.

Noah: *God made a covenant with Noah and every living creature that never again would a flood destroy the earth. The ark is a symbol of the Church.*

Abraham: *God made a covenant to set apart and protect Abraham and his descendants.*

Moses: *God renewed his covenant and formed the Israelites into a true nation with a religion.*

David: *God renewed his covenant and formed a kingdom with David as king.*

Jesus: *Jesus laid the foundation for his Church by his death, Resurrection and Ascension and by sending his Holy Spirit.*

Apostles: *Jesus gave his apostles his authority and power to spread the Gospel to all men.*

2. Define the Greek word *ekklesia* and explain how it relates to the Church.
Ekklesisa is an assembly. God calls all men to his "assembly", in his Church in order that they may be made holy.

6   *Faith and Life Series • Grade 8 • Chapter 2 • Lesson 2*

Reinforce

1. Have the students work on *Activity Book*, p. 6.

2. Give the class time to work on the Memorization Questions and Words to Know from this chapter.

3. The students may dramatize events of the Old Testament that prefigure the Church.

4. Each student or group of students can make presentations on the Old Testament types for the Church This can be set up as a "Church fair," in which the students take time to visit the various presentations, and you may ask questions regarding the ways the Old Testament types relate to the Catholic Church. Award a prize for the best presentation.

5. Show depictions of the Old Testament types as found in the Sistine Chapel ceiling.

Conclude

1. Lead the students in singing "Christ is made the sure foundation," *Adoremus Hymnal*, #561.

2. End class by praying the Prayer to the Holy Spirit.

Preview

In the next lesson, the students will learn about Jesus establishing the Church.

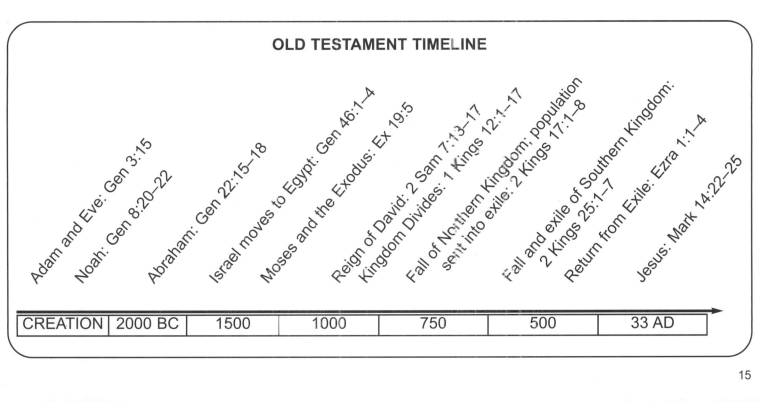

OLD TESTAMENT TIMELINE

Adam and Eve: Gen 3:15 • Noah: Gen 8:20–22 • Abraham: Gen 22:15–18 • Israel moves to Egypt: Gen 46:1–4 • Moses and the Exodus: Ex 19:5 • Reign of David: 2 Sam 7:13–17 • Kingdom Divides: 1 Kings 12:1–17 • Fall of Northern Kingdom; population sent into exile: 2 Kings 17:1–8 • Fall and exile of Southern Kingdom: 2 Kings 25:1–7 • Return from Exile: Ezra 1:1–4 • Jesus: Mark 14:22–25

CREATION	2000 BC	1500	1000	750	500	33 AD

LESSON THREE: JESUS

Aims

The students will learn that Jesus Christ is God the Son, the Second Person of the Holy Trinity, become man. He is true God and true man.

They will learn that Jesus made the Church present by his presence, his teaching, and the formation of his followers. Jesus chose Saint Peter to be the head of the apostles and his visible representative after the Ascension.

Materials

• *Activity Book*, p. 7

Optional:
• "Christ is made the sure foundation," *Adoremus Hymnal*, #561

Begin

The Old Testament prefigurements of the Church were fulfilled when Jesus established the Church in the New Testament. Jesus, as the head of the Church, was prefigured by each of these stories. Discuss:
  • *Adam and Eve: Jesus is the New Adam*
  • *Noah: Jesus, through the Church (ark) saves man*
  • *Abraham: Jesus is the Son (Isaac) offered to God*
  • *Moses: Jesus gives the New Law*
  • *Levitical Priesthood: Jesus is the High Priest*
  • *David: Jesus is the head of the Church*
  • *Prophets: Jesus fulfills their prophecies*

---

now prefigured what Peter said of the Christian Church. They were a "chosen race, a royal priesthood, a holy nation, God's own people . . ." (1 Pet 2:9).

In the laws of the Old Covenant we can see the Church prefigured. This chosen race, a people set apart, was established with a sacred priesthood to celebrate their Liturgy. This worship of God was a corporate act, that is, the action of the whole people. At the head of the chosen race was God himself, but on earth Moses was his representative. Under Moses there was a hierarchical structure. Aaron and his sons were priests and all other priests would come from their descendants, members of the tribe of Levi. All of this was so that this "church" could fulfill its purpose—to make the people holy.

Later in their history God formed his people into a kingdom, renewing his covenant with David, who foreshadowed the eternal King—Christ. This chosen people was now firmly established, with God as King and David as God's earthly **vicar**, or representative, a foreshadowing of the relationship of Christ and the Pope as the visible head of his Church.

God continued to reveal himself and his will to the people through the prophets. Through these prophets God prepared this chosen race for the coming of the Savior, through whom the Church would be firmly established.

"In many and various ways God spoke of old to our fathers by the prophets; but in these last days he has spoken to us by a Son, whom he appointed the heir of all things, through whom also he created the world" (Heb 1:1–2).

When the Son of God became a man and made his dwelling among us, the Church was actually established on earth. Christ laid the foundations as he preached during his public life. First he chose twelve disciples, called apostles, who were to be the leaders of the Church. They were from different backgrounds: some were uneducated—simple fishermen; another was educated and held a position in the government—a tax collector. Jesus spent a great part of his time teaching and forming this group of specially chosen men, the Twelve Apostles. To the multitude he taught in parables, but to the Twelve he spoke directly, "To you has been given the secret of the kingdom of God, but for those outside everything is in parables" (Mk 4:12). His intention clearly was that they would be carriers of his message: "Follow me and I will make you become fishers of men" (Mk 1:17).

One of the apostles, Peter, was chosen by Our Lord to be the leader of all and to be Jesus' representative on earth. After Peter demonstrated great faith, Our Lord said to him, ". . . . you are Peter, and on this rock I will build my church, and the powers of death shall not prevail against it. I will give you the keys of the kingdom . . ." (Mt 16:18–19). By giving Peter the "keys" Our Lord signified the authority that was given to Peter.

At the Last Supper, the night before he died, Our Lord prayed for unity in his Church. He prayed "not . . . for these only, but also for those who believe in me through their word, that they may all be one. . ." (Jn 17:20–21). He also promised to send them the Holy Spirit so

Church Teaching

"The origin and growth of the Church are symbolized by the blood and water which flowed from the open side of the crucified Jesus" (LG, 3).

17

Develop

1. Read paragraphs 10–14 (up to "The last instruction of Our Lord.")

2. Review the Church's teachings on Jesus Christ, including:
  • *Jesus is God the Son, the Second Person of the Trinity, made man (Incarnation = God made man)*
  • *Jesus is true God and true man*
  • *As God Jesus is equal with the Father*
  • *As man, Jesus is like us in all things but sin*
  • *Jesus is the mediator between God and man*
  • *Jesus is the Savior—he redeemed us by his life, death, and Resurrection. He is the pleasing sacrifice of atonement to the Father on behalf of man. He is the perfect victim and the perfect priest. We know his sacrifice was accepted because of the Resurrection*
  • *Jesus taught with the authority of God and gave us the New Law*
  • *Jesus performed many miracles, which teach us about God and are signs of Jesus' Divinity*

• *Jesus instituted the sacraments to confer the grace that he won upon the Cross to mankind. With the life of grace, we can live forever with God in heaven*

3. Discuss the importance of Saint Peter and his possession of the keys to the Kingdom of Heaven. Keys are a sign of authority given to a lead steward in the absence of the master. The steward then makes decisions on behalf of the master and acts on his behalf until the master returns.

4. Discuss the deposit of grace. It is the treasury of grace won by Christ's death and Resurrection, dispensed through the Church.

5. The deposit of faith is the truths revealed by our Lord during his life on earth. The apostles were entrusted to teach it in its entirety without error (with the help of the Holy Spirit).

Name:_____

Jesus Founds the Church

Answer the following questions in complete sentences.

1. Briefly explain how God established the Church during each of the three stages listed below:

   Old Testament times:
   God chose a people, set them apart and established a sacred priesthood to celebrate their liturgy. He set up a hierarchical structure for the people.

   Life and death of Jesus:
   Jesus chose the apostles as leaders, taught them about his kingdom, gained merits for the Church by his death and sent the Holy Spirit to guide his Church. He also commissioned the apostles to baptize all nations.

   New Testament days of the apostles:
   The apostles spread the Gospel to all men and nations.

2. Explain the Deposit of Grace. How do we receive it?
   The Deposit of Grace refers to the graces of salvation won by Our Lord by his death and Resurrection. We receive it through the sacraments.

3. Explain the Deposit of Faith. How do we receive it?
   The Deposit of Faith is the truth revealed by Jesus Christ in his public life and after his Resurrection, but before his Ascension. It is handed on to us through the apostles and their successors.

Reinforce

1. Have the students work on *Activity Book*, p. 7.

2. Give the class time to work on the Memorization Questions and Words to Know from this chapter.

3. Have the students write an essay entitled, "How Jesus Founded His Church and Provided for Her Needs."

4. *The students should research the twelve apostles. They should know their names, life works, places they brought the Gospel, and ways they died. The students may write "interviews" with apostles. They may be creative with their writing, but their work should honestly reflect the lives of the apostles.*

Conclude

1. Lead the students in singing "Christ is made the sure foundation," *Adoremus Hymnal*, #561.

2. End class by praying the Prayer to the Holy Spirit on p. 5.

Preview

In the next lesson, the students will learn about the mission of the Church.

NOTES

_____
_____
_____
_____
_____
_____
_____
_____
_____
_____

LESSON FOUR: MISSION

Aims

The students will learn that Jesus entrusted the mission of his Church to the apostles. The Church is to manifest herself to the world and bring all men to Christ.

They will learn that the Holy Spirit descended upon the apostles (leaders of the Church) to empower their work.

They will learn that Jesus is with his Church today and will be until the end of time.

Materials

• *Activity Book*, p. 8   Optional:
                                    • "Christ is made the
                                       sure foundation,"
                                       Adoremus Hymnal,
                                       #561

Begin

Discuss how the Church continues the work of Christ:
- *She passes on his teachings*
- *She dispenses his grace, especially through the sacraments*
- *She calls a community together for worship*
- *She cares for the members of this community*

---

that they might recall all that Jesus had taught them and be able to teach his message. Through these words Jesus made it clear that his Church was to continue after his death.

When Our Lord ascended into heaven, the basic structure of the Church was complete. By his death he merited for us the graces of salvation. We call this the **deposit of grace**, which is dispensed to us through the sacraments of the Church.

The truths that Our Lord revealed during his three years of public life and during the forty days after the Resurrection were given in a special way to the apostles so that they might teach others. This we call the **deposit of faith**.

The last instruction of Our Lord to the apostles, according to St. Matthew's Gospel, mandated the mission of his Church. On the day of the Ascension Our Lord told his followers, led by St. Peter and the apostles, "Go therefore and make disciples of all nations, baptizing them in the name of the Father and of the Son and of the Holy Spirit, teaching them to observe all that I have commanded you; and lo, I am with you always, to the close of the age" (Mt 28:19–20). The Church, in other words, must manifest herself to the world and bring all men to Christ.

Ten days later, while the leaders of the Church were gathered in prayer, this manifestation began. The Holy Spirit, promised by Our Lord, descended upon them, and they were filled with the Spirit of Love and Truth, who gave them the grace to go forth and preach. On this day Peter, as the leader of the Church, preached his first sermon to the Jewish pilgrims gathered in Jerusalem, urging them to be baptized. "Those who received his word were baptized, and there were added that day about three thousand souls" (Acts 2:41). At this point the Church began her mission to the world.

Since that first Pentecost, the Church has grown and spread into every part of the world. The same Church that was prefigured in the Old Testament, formed by Christ, and manifested to the world on Pentecost still exists today, leading men to God. The Church was finally established as "a chosen race, a royal priesthood, a holy nation. . . . Once you were no people, but now you are God's People" (1 Pet 2:9–10).

Words to Know:
    Pentecost   ekklesia   vicar
    deposit of grace   deposit of faith

Q. 3   *Why did God choose one people from among all nations?*
God chose one people from among all nations to provide a witness of his promise to them (CCC 60).

Q. 4   *Why did Jesus Christ institute the Church?*
Jesus Christ instituted the Church so that men might have in her a secure guide and the means of holiness and eternal salvation (CCC 775–76).

Q. 5   *What is Pentecost?*
Pentecost is the event of the descent of the Holy Spirit upon Mary and the apostles fifty days after Easter. It is the birthday of the Church (CCC 731, 737).

18

Develop

1. Read paragraphs 15–17 (to the end of the chapter).

2. Discuss the Great Commission.
- *What is the difference between an apostle and a disciple?*
- *Where is the Good News to be proclaimed?*
- *Is the instruction merely to baptize? Why must we also teach?*
- *What are the apostles to teach?*
- *Do we see this reflected in the work of bishops (to teach, sanctify, and govern)?*
- *How does Christ remain until the close of an age?*
- *How have the apostles fulfilled this Great Commission? How does it continue in this day?*

3. Review the events of Pentecost. It is important that the feast of Pentecost brought people from all over the world to Jerusalem. Read Mt 21:1–9; Mk 6:1–13; and Lk 10:1–9. Disciples were sent ahead of Christ to places where he would go to bring the Good News. This way, the people were pre-

pared to recognize him. After Pentecost, the newly baptized would return to their homes and live the Christian life, speaking of the great events at Pentecost. This would prepare the way for the apostles to come and bring the Good News and found churches in their lands.

4. Reviewing the missionary work of the apostles, show on a map the places where they proclaimed the Good News. Show how the Church then spread all over the world. You may discuss the missionary Church today. Missionaries still go to places such as China, Russia, Africa, etc. to bring the Gospel to the people there.

5. Review how the Church was prefigured, formed by Christ, and manifested to the world on Pentecost. The Church has been growing ever since!

Name:_____

Fishers of Men

Write a brief essay on what Jesus meant when he called his apostles to be "fishers of men." How can you be a fisher of men, too?

<u>Answers will vary.</u>

_____
_____
_____
_____
_____
_____
_____
_____
_____
_____
_____
_____
_____
_____
_____
_____
_____
_____
_____
_____

Reinforce

1. Have the students work on *Activity Book*, p. 8.

2. Give the class time to work on the Memorization Questions and Words to Know from this chapter and to prepare for the quiz.

3. *Direct your students to make charts, collages, or posters centering on the three stages in the establishment of the Church: prefiguration, presence, and manifestation.*

4. Have the students create a world map, coloring the places where the apostles brought the Gospel and where various missionaries brought the Gospel throughout time, spreading the Church to the whole world.

Conclude

1. Lead the students in singing "Christ is made the sure foundation," *Adoremus Hymnal*, #561.

2. End class by praying the Prayer to the Holy Spirit

Preview

In the next lesson, the students' understanding of the material covered in this chapter will be reviewed and assessed.

THE APOSTLES AFTER PENTECOST

- Simon Peter: first Pope; traveled to Antioch, Corinth, and finally Rome. He was crucified in Nero's Circus on the Hill of Vaticanos around AD 64.
- Andrew, brother of Peter: traveled to Greece as a missionary. He was martyred by being tied to a cross. Even while hanging on the cross, he continued to preach to the people who came to see him until his death.
- James the Greater, son of Zebedee: martyred under Herod soon after Pentecost (Acts 12:1–2).
- John, son of Zebedee: leader of the churches in Asia; settled in Ephesus in AD 97. He was exiled to the prison island of Patmos during the persecution of Domition. He was later released and returned to Ephesus where he died.
- Philip: traveled to Greece to preach and was crucified during the persecution of Domition.
- Bartholomew: preached in India and Armenia. He was flayed and beheaded in Armenia by King Abanopolis.
- Thomas: preached to the Parthians, Medes, and Persians; then traveled to India and was martyred.
- Matthew: unknown, may have traveled to Ethiopia or Persia.
- James the Lesser, son of Alphaeus: first Bishop of Jerusalem. He was martyred by the Jews there around AD 62.
- Jude Thaddeus: traveled to Persia with Saint Simon and was martyred there.
- Simon the Cananean: traveled to Persia with Saint Jude and was martyred there.
- Judas Iscariot: betrayed Christ. He committed suicide soon after.

CHAPTER TWO
REVIEW AND ASSESSMENT

Aims

The students' understanding of the material covered in this chapter will be reviewed and assessed.

Materials

- Quiz 2, Appendix, p. A-2

Optional:
- "Christ is made the sure foundation," *Adoremus Hymnal,* #561

Review

1. The students should have a strong understanding of the Trinity, the Holy Spirit, and Jesus Christ.

2. The students should know why Pentecost is considered the birthday of the Church. They should understand the significance of Pentecost in the spreading of the Church throughout the world.

3. The students should understand the prefigurements of the Church and Christ in the Old Testament. They should know that Christ is the head of the Church.

4. The students should know how Jesus founded his Church and provided for all her needs in structure, grace, and faith.

5. The students should understand the terms deposit of faith and deposit of grace.

6. The students should understand the Great Commission. They, too, are called to bring the Good News to others.

Name: _____

The Birth of the Church   Quiz 2

Part I: Define the following terms.

Deposit of grace: <u>all the grace necessary for salvation which Jesus merited for us by his death</u>

Deposit of faith: <u>the content of revelation entrusted to the Church by Jesus Christ and handed on through Scripture and Tradition by the apostles and their successors</u>

Pentecost: <u>the "birthday" of the Church; the day that Jesus sent his Holy Spirit to give life to the Church</u>

Vicar: <u>a representative; one serving as an agent for someone else</u>

Ekklesia: <u>Greek word for "assembly" which is used in the New Testament for the Church</u>

Part II: Explain how God established the Church during each of the three stages listed below.

1. Old Testament:
   <u>The Church is prefigured in the Old Testament in the promises God made to Adam and Eve after the Fall, to Noah after the flood, to Abraham and the formation of the chosen people, in the covenant made with Moses, and later in the kingdom established in David.</u>

2. Life and death of Jesus Christ:
   <u>Jesus laid the foundation for his Church during his public life and by his death, Resurrection, and Ascension into heaven. After his Ascension he sent the Holy Spirit to the leaders of his Church.</u>

3. New Testament days of the apostles unto the present:
   <u>Jesus gave his apostles and their successors his authority and power to spread the Gospel to all men.</u>

A - 2   *Faith and Life • Grade 8 • Appendix A*

Assess

1. Distribute the quizzes and read through them with the students to be sure they understand the questions.

2. Administer the quiz. As they hand in their work, you may orally quiz the students on the Memorization Questions from this chapter.

3. After all the quizzes have been handed in, review the correct answers with the class.

Conclude

1. Lead the students in singing "Christ is made the sure foundation," *Adoremus Hymnal,* #561.

2. End class by praying the Prayer to the Holy Spirit.

CHAPTER THREE
THE NATURE OF THE CHURCH

Catechism of the Catholic Church References

Apostolic Succession: 77–79, 861–62, 869
Charity: 1822–29, 1844
Christ's Missionary Mandate in the Church: 849–56, 868
Christian Holiness: 2012–16, 2028–29
Church as Apostolic: 811–12, 857–65, 869, 935
Church as Catholic: 811–12, 830–56, 868, 870
Church as Holy: 811–12, 823–29, 867
Church as One: 811–22, 866
Church as the Body of Christ: 787–96, 805–8
Church's Hierarchical Constitution: 871–96, 934–39
Church's Origin, Foundation, and Mission: 758–69, 773
Corporal Works of Mercy: 2447
Deposit of Faith: 84, 97, 175
Ecclesial Ministry: 874–79

Episcopal College and Its Head, the Pope: 880–87
    Task of Teaching: 888–92
    Task of Sanctifying: 893
    Task of Governing: 894–96
Jesus' Mission of Salvation: 456–60
Last Judgment: 1038–41, 1059
Liturgical Traditions and the Catholicity of the Church: 1200–3, 1208
Liturgy and Cultures: 1204–7
Names and Images of the Church: 751–57, 777
Pope and Bishops: Successors to Peter and the Apostles: 861–62, 880–87, 935–38
Proclamation of the Kingdom of God: 543–46
Vocation of the Laity: 782–86, 898–913, 940–43

Scripture References

Mustard Seed: Mk 4:30–32
Sheepfold: Jn 10:1–10
Vineyard: Mt 21:33–43
Bride: Rev 21:9;19:7; 22:17;
    Eph 5:23–33

Building: 1 Cor 3:9; Eph 2:19,22
Flock: Is 40:11; Ex 34:11
Field: 1 Cor 3:9
Kingdom: Jn 14:2; Mt 3:2; 5:1–12
Parable of the Sower: Lk 8:5–15

Leaven in Bread: Mt 13:33
Treasure: Mt 6:21; 13:44
Pearl: Mt 13:46
Net: Mt 13:47
Mystical Body: 1 Cor 12:12–31

Summary of Lesson Content

There are many images for the Church in the New Testament, including Kingdom, mustard seed, sheepfold, vineyard, building, bride, Mystical Body, ark, mother, fish net, pearl, treasure, leaven in bread.

Lesson 3

The Church is catholic in the fullness of her means of salvation, truth, and revelation. The Church is catholic because she is universal, without limit of time, race, or membership.

The Church is apostolic in her original leaders, the apostles, and in her Pope and the Sacrament of Holy Orders, passed through apostolic succession. The Church is apostolic in her teaching, passed from Christ, through the apostles, to all Christians.

Lesson 2

The Church is one in doctrine, teaching, worship, liturgy, sacrifice, and government under the Vicar of Christ.

The Church is holy in her origin because her founder is Christ, who is holy and the source of holiness. The Church is holy because of the work of the Holy Spirit. The Church is holy in her members.

Lesson 4

Jesus Christ fulfilled his mission on earth for all men in all times. He established the Church to continue the work of his mission (salvation for all men) and to communicate his grace to all men. This work, dispensing grace, is continued through the Church, especially in the sacraments.

The Church governs Christians, while guarding and faithfully transmitting the faith.

LESSON ONE:
MODELS OF THE CHURCH

Aims

The students will learn that there are many images for the Church in the New Testament, including: Kingdom, mustard seed, sheepfold, vineyard, building, bride, Mystical Body of the Church, ark, mother, fish net, pearl, treasure, leaven in bread.

Materials

- *Activity Book*, p. 9

Optional:
- "O Love, who drew from Jesus' side," *Adoremus Hymnal*, #562

Begin

Explain that there are many images or models for the Church. They are not perfect, however. They are meant to help us better understand the great mystery of the Church. Each model gives us some insight. Today, we will learn some of these models.

CHAPTER 3

The Nature of the Church

He is the head of the body, the church; he is the beginning, the first-born from the dead, that in everything he might be pre-eminent.

Colossians 1:18

"By her relationship with Christ, the Church is a kind of sacrament or sign of intimate union with God, and of the unity of all mankind" (LG, 1).

We have seen that the Church is a society that was carefully formed by God and began its mission at Pentecost. This society is composed of those baptized persons who profess the faith taught by Jesus Christ and handed down by his apostles and their successors. The members participate in the sacraments given to us by our Lord, and are united with their bishops under the leadership of the Pope.

In order to understand the nature of the Church more fully, we need to examine three significant points: (1) the Church as the Mystical Body of Christ, (2) the marks of the Church, and (3) the reasons Christ established his Church.

Images in the New Testament

Many images used in the New Testament help us to understand the Church. A number of these arise from Our Lord's own words. Christ frequently spoke of the Kingdom that will be established on earth and finally completed in heaven. Several parables, like that of the mustard seed, use this image, showing us how the Kingdom will grow and flourish on earth, or how the wicked and the just will live together in the world but will finally be separated at the end of time. If we reflect on this image, we can see how it pertains to the Church.

In other places Christ uses the image of the sheepfold. We, the faithful, are the sheep, led by human shepherds on earth but most perfectly by the Good Shepherd, Christ himself. In still other places our Lord uses the images of the vineyard, a building, and his bride to represent the Church. How would these be images of the Church? You may need to use your New Testament to help you.

The Mystical Body of Christ

One of the most beautiful images is that of the Church as the **Mystical Body of Christ**. The roots of this image can also be found in the words of Christ. When Our Lord was speaking of the Last Judgment, he told us that we would be judged in part on the basis of our charity toward others—feeding the hungry, clothing the naked, giving drink to the thirsty, and so on. He concludes by saying, "Truly, I say to you, as you did it to one of the least of these my brethren, you did it to me" (Mt 25:40). In other words, we serve Christ by serving others.

19

Develop

1. Read paragraphs 1–14 (up to "Marks of the Church").

2. Direct your students to research in the Bible the various images for the Church:
- *Mustard Seed: Mk 4:30–32*
- *Sheepfold: Jn 10:1–10*
- *Vineyard: Mt 21:33–43*
- *Building: 1 Cor 3:9; Eph 2:19,22*
- *Bride: Rev 21:9;19:7; 22:17; Eph 5:23–33*
- *Flock: Is 40:11; Ex 34:11*
- *Field: 1 Cor 3:9*
- *Kingdom: Jn 14:2; Mt 3:2; 5:1–12*
- *Sower and Seed: Lk 8:5–15*
- *Leaven in Bread: Mt 13:33*
- *Treasure: Mt 6:21; 13:44*
- *Pearl: Mt 13:46*
- *Net: Mt 13:47*
- *Mystical Body: 1 Cor 12:12–31*

3. Have the students write explanations of the models of the Church. They may explain the strengths and the weaknesses of these models, create images, and present their reports to other students.

4. The students may create their own images for the Church. Discuss these images and their efficacy.

5. The students may make a collage of images of models of the Church.

6. Discuss the Church as sacrament. Like of the seven sacraments, the Church is instituted by Christ and confers his grace.

Name:_____

Creation

Explain the following images of the Church. You may read Matthew 13:24–50; 18:12–14; 20:1–16; 22:1–10.

Kingdom: <u>Answers will vary.</u>

Mustard Seed:

Wicked and Just:

Sheepfold:

Treasure:

Net:

Bride:

Mystical Body:

Reinforce

1. Have the students work on *Activity Book*, p. 9.

2. Give the class time to work on the Memorization Questions and Words to Know from this chapter.

3. Have the students research, write, and present reports on the models of the Church.

4. Give the students an opportunity to draw/make collages of the models of the Church.

5. Discuss the students' ideas of images for the Church.

6. Discuss how these images should help them to understand the Church and increase their faith.

Conclude

1. Teach the students to sing "O Love, who drew from Jesus' side," *Adoremus Hymnal*, #562.

2. End class by praying an Our Father.

Preview

In the next lesson, the students will learn about the first two marks of the Church: one and holy.

SAINT PAUL

Apostle to the gentiles and one of the greatest missionaries the Church has ever known, Saint Paul began his involvement with the Church in a strange way: persecuting it. The first mention of Saint Paul in the Bible is his participation in Saint Stephen's martyrdom, and soon after he begins the first persecution of the Church. However, even when persecuting the Church, Saint Paul contributed to her missionary work. The Christians in Jerusalem "were scattered" but they "went about preaching the word" (Acts 8:1). They had to flee Jerusalem, but they used their flight as an opportunity to spread the Word as Jesus had commissioned them to do. Paul continued to persecute the Church until his famous encounter with Our Lord on the road to Damascus (Acts 9). From that point on he became a fervent follower of Christ, first becoming involved with the Church in Antioch and then going on three great missionary journeys through Israel, Palestine, Asia Minor, Greece, and all the way to Rome. His epistles inspired many churches and make up a large part of the New Testament. In his Letter to the Corinthians, Saint Paul describes his conversion and mission: "Last of all, as to one untimely born, [Christ] appeared also to me. For I am the least of the apostles, unfit to be called an apostle, because I persecuted the church of God. But by the grace of God I am what I am, and his grace toward me was not in vain" (1 Cor 15:8–10).

LESSON TWO: ONE, HOLY

Aims

The students will learn that the Church is one in doctrine, teaching, worship, liturgy, sacrifice, and government under the Vicar of Christ.

They will learn that the Church is holy in her origin because her founder is Christ, who is holy and the source of holiness. The Church is holy because of the work of the Holy Spirit. The Church is also holy in her members.

Materials

- *Activity Book*, p. 10

  Optional:
  - "O Love, who drew from Jesus' side," *Adoremus Hymnal*, #562

Begin

Discuss common marks, such as brand names, imprints on silver, or stamps on fine china. A mark identifies something. So, too, there are four marks of the Church to identify the true Church of Jesus Christ. Read the Nicene Creed and have the students list the marks: one, holy, catholic, and apostolic. We will discuss these four marks in the next two lessons.

In another place, when Jesus sent the disciples out to preach in his name, he said, "He who hears you hears me, and he who rejects you, rejects me . . ." (Lk 10:16). From both of these passages, we see that Christ in some way identifies his followers—the Church—with himself.

There is another passage (Acts 9:1–5) in which the words of Christ are recorded. Not long after Pentecost a man named Saul of Tarsus was fanatically hounding and pursuing the early Church. "I persecuted the Church of God," he later admitted (1 Cor 15:9). One day on the road to Damascus he was knocked off his horse by a light from heaven and heard mysterious words. A voice said, "Saul, Saul, why do you persecute me? . . . I am Jesus of Nazareth, whom you are persecuting." How was it that Saul (later St. Paul) was persecuting Christ by persecuting his Church? Did it amount to the same thing? What was meant by these words?

For the rest of his life St. Paul would think about these words telling him that Christ and

20

his Church are one. This was such a great mystery that its meaning seemed inexhaustible. He later developed this image of the Church as the Body of Christ in his first letter to the Corinthians (1 Cor 12:12–31), his letter to the Ephesians (Eph 1:22–23, 4:4, 5:23–33), and in many other letters.

Our physical bodies have many different parts, which are arranged so that they can work together. All of these parts—eyes, ears, hands, feet, heart, lungs, and so on—form *one* body, and each part must work for the good of the whole. If one part of the body suffers, the other parts share in this pain, while the healthy parts must come to the assistance of the sick parts. If one part—such as an infected limb—threatens the health of the whole body, it may need to be removed.

As St. Paul tells us, the same is true of the Church. The individual members of the Church must help their fellow members. A sin committed by one member hurts the whole. One saint lifts up the whole. "If one member suffers, all suffer together; if one member is honored, all rejoice together" (1 Cor 12:26). Sometimes it is even necessary to remove one member from the Church in order that the whole may remain healthy.

Furthermore, each of the many organs of the body has its own specific function and is arranged in some kind of order. Each has its own task. The eye cannot and should not want to do what the ear does. The hand cannot and should not want to do what the feet do. The same is true of the Church. In the unity of the Body of Christ there is a diversity of members. There are many individuals in the Church occupying special positions and exercising special functions, but all are united in one whole under Christ. The head of this Body is Christ. St. Paul reminds us, "He is the head of the body, the Church . . ." (Col 1:18). It is Christ who unites this Body and whose life we share.

Develop

1. Read paragraphs 15–23 (up to "Catholic").

2. Review that Jesus prayed for the unity of the Church at the Last Supper (Jn 17:1–26). Discuss this passage. What does it mean?

3. How is the Church one?
- *Faith (doctrines, creeds, and moral teachings)*
- *Worship, liturgy, and sacraments*
- *Sacrifice of the Mass (which is the same sacrifice as that of the Cross)*
- *Membership in the Mystical Body*
- *Government (one divine authority, Magisterium [Pope and Bishops in union with him], rules)*

4. How is the Church holy?
- *Her origin is holy—Jesus Christ (founder of Church)*
- *Her purpose is holy: to teach and sanctify*

- *Her teachings are holy and her means of grace (sacraments) are holy*
- *Her members, who accept the life of grace (saints), are holy*
- *The Holy Spirit is the life of the Church*

5. Using the Chalk Talk at right, discuss how the Church is holy, although not all of her members are. You may discuss current issues in the Church (if there are any) or create a fictitious scenario to help the students understand that even when the members of the Church are not holy (even priests or the Pope) the Church is still holy.

6. Discuss ways that the students can promote the unity and sanctity of the Church. Ideas may include:
- Oneness: Pray for unity of Christians, learn the faith, pray for the Pope, do works of charity
- Holiness: Receive Penance and Communion, live a moral life, pray to the Holy Spirit, learn about the saints

Name:_____

The Marks of the Church I

Explain the following marks of the Church.

The Church is One:

Answers will vary.

_____
_____
_____
_____
_____
_____
_____
_____
_____
_____

The Church is Holy:

_____
_____
_____
_____
_____
_____
_____
_____
_____
_____
_____
_____
_____

10   *Faith and Life Series • Grade 8 • Chapter 3 • Lesson 2*

Reinforce

1. Have the students work on *Activity Book*, p. 10.

2. Give the class time to work on the Memorization Questions and Words to Know from this chapter.

3. Have the students work on a project. Assign them to do one thing to promote the unity of the Church and one thing to promote the sanctity of the Church. They should write about their experiences in a journal.

4. Have the students begin a presentation on the four marks of the Church. They may create a poster, write a report, or create a video explaining each of the four marks of the Church.

Conclude

1. Lead the students in singing "O Love, who drew from Jesus' side," *Adoremus Hymnal*, #562.

2. End class by praying an Our Father.

Preview

In the next lesson, the students will learn about the Church as catholic and apostolic.

CHALK TALK: THE CHURCH, HUMAN AND DIVINE

NOTES

_____
_____
_____
_____
_____
_____
_____
_____
_____
_____
_____

LESSON THREE: CATHOLIC, APOSTOLIC

Aims

The students will learn that the Church is catholic in the fullness of her means of salvation, truth, and revelation. The Church is catholic because she is universal, without limit of time, race, or membership.

They will learn that the Church is apostolic in her original leaders, the apostles, and in her Pope and the Sacrament of Holy Orders, passed through apostolic succession. The Church is apostolic in her teaching, passed from Christ, through the apostles, to all Christians.

Materials

- *Activity Book*, p. 11

Optional:
- "O Love, who drew from Jesus' side," *Adoremus Hymnal*, #562

Begin

Begin class by praying the Nicene Creed. Review the first two marks of the Church:
- One: in belief, worship, and government
- Holy: in means, members, origin, purpose, and sacraments

Today, we will learn how the Church is catholic and apostolic.

The Church lives from Christ, in Christ, and for Christ. Christ lives with her and in her. As members of the Church, we are joined together by the Holy Spirit who is present throughout the Church.

The Pope is the *visible* head of the Church, representing Christ. The bishops with the Pope teach, sanctify, and rule in the name of Christ. The priests and deacons assist in this work. Lay people, who make up the bulk of the Church, have their special tasks within the Body of Christ. They may, for instance, be the hands that take care of children in their families or help the poor. They may be the feet that go to visit the sick. They may be the tongues that teach their children the ways of God or spread the Word of God to others in the world. They may be defenders of the faith, like St. Thomas More. Each one has his special vocation, and all work for the one Body of Christ. All are called to holiness.

Again, the individual parts of the body form one living organism, which requires nourishment to grow and mature. The Body of Christ, like the human body, must be nurtured constantly by the graces that are received through the sacraments.

Calling the church a "body," however, is not just a figure of speech. The Church is truly the Mystical Body of Christ. *Mystical* here means spiritual. It is also called mystical to remind us of the supernatural character of this society, which is both human and divine. Unlike purely human organizations, the ultimate purpose of the Church is salvation. The goal is heaven. The Church includes the souls in heaven and those in purgatory. The Church helps us to know, love, and serve God in this life so that we can be united with him for ever in the next.

Marks of the Church

The Church, as we have seen, is a visible institution made up of human beings united with Christ as the invisible head. Since the earliest centuries, Christians have believed that there are four signs, or *marks*, by which the true Church can be recognized. These marks are included in the Nicene Creed: "We believe in one holy catholic and apostolic Church."

Let us now examine what each of these four marks means.

One

The *unity* in the Church is striking and is probably the clearest of the marks. This unity is found in three areas.

First, there is the unity of belief. The Church teaches the same doctrines everywhere and always. Throughout the world the members of the Church profess this one faith. The clearest statements of this faith are in the creeds, particularly the Apostles' Creed and the Nicene Creed. There is also unity of moral teaching, based on the Ten Commandments and the teachings of Jesus Christ. These doctrinal and moral beliefs have through the ages always been and will always remain the same.

Second, the Church is one through her unity of worship and Liturgy. There is one sacrifice, the Mass, by which all members are united in worshipping God. The Church is united also in receiving the Eucharist and other sacraments, by which all share in the life of Christ. While there is absolute unity in the *essentials* of worship, there is rich variety in the rituals and ceremonies that surround them, as we shall see later in our studies.

Third, there is unity of government in the Church. All members submit themselves to one divine authority, Christ. Christ promised us that there would be ". . . one flock, [and] one shepherd" (Jn 10:16). The shepherd is Christ, and he is represented by his Vicar on earth, the Pope. The bishops, successors of the apostles, are shepherds. The Pope is the su-

---

Develop

1. Read paragraphs 24–27 (sections titled "Catholic" and "Apostolic.")

2. We are called Catholics. Why are we not called merely Christians like members of Protestant denominations? Catholic is one of the four marks of the Church. "Catholic" means "universal." How is this seen in our Church? We have the fullness of Christ's truth and revelation:
- This is found in Scripture and Tradition
- This is safeguarded and taught by the Magisterium

This faith (and Church) is for all people of all places:
- If we go to Europe, Asia, South America, or Timbuktu the faith will be the same. The Mass will be the same, we have the same Pope, etc.

The faith (and Church) is for all times:
- Jesus didn't just save the people in his time but established the Church so that all people can know him and his salvation until the end of time

3. How is the Church apostolic?
- The Church originated with the apostles (upon whom Christ built his Church)
- The Church is still ruled by the successors of Peter and the apostles (Pope and bishops)
- Holy Orders can be traced back to the apostles, meaning they have the powers necessary to continue Jesus' saving work (e.g., hear confessions and absolve sins, consecrate the Eucharist, etc.) This is called apostolic succession. You may use the Chalk Talk at right to explain this.
- The Church professes the faith and doctrine taught by the apostles, called the deposit of faith. The deposit of faith was entrusted to the Church by Christ.

4. Discuss how the students can promote the universality and apostolicity of the Church:
- Universality: pray for missionaries, pray with your family
- Apostolicity: pray for the Pope, pray for priests

Name:_____

The Marks of the Church II

Explain the following marks of the Church.

The Church is Catholic:

Answers will vary.

_____
_____
_____
_____
_____
_____
_____
_____
_____

The Church is Apostolic:

_____
_____
_____
_____
_____
_____
_____
_____
_____
_____
_____
_____
_____

Reinforce

1. Have the students work on *Activity Book*, p. 11.

2. Give the class time to work on the Memorization Questions and Words to Know from this chapter

3. Have the students work on a project. Assign them to do one thing to promote the universality of the Church and one thing to promote the apostolic nature of the Church. They should write about their experiences in their journals.

4. The students should continue working on their presentations of the four marks of the Church. They may create posters, write reports, or create videos.

Conclude

1. Lead the students in singing "O Love, who drew from Jesus' side," *Adoremus Hymnal*, #562.

2. End class by praying an Our Father.

Preview

In the next lesson, the students will learn why Jesus founded the Church.

CHALK TALK: APOSTOLIC SUCCESSION

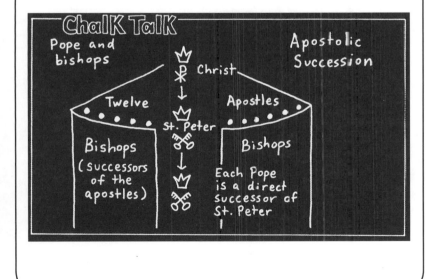

NOTES

_____
_____
_____
_____
_____
_____
_____
_____
_____
_____
_____

LESSON FOUR:
WHY A CHURCH?

Aims

The students will learn that Jesus Christ fulfilled his mission on earth for all men in all times. He established the Church to continue the work of his mission (salvation for all men) and to communicate his grace to all men. This work, dispensing grace, is continued through the Church, especially in the sacraments.

They will learn that the Church governs Christians, while guarding and faithfully transmitting the Faith.

Materials

- *Activity Book*, p. 12   Optional:
  - "O Love, who drew from Jesus' side," *Adoremus Hymnal*, #562

Begin

Review how Christ established the Church during his time on earth:
- He was born into the world
- He taught and performed miracles, revealing God and his will for mankind
- He called disciples and apostles to live the Good News
- He suffered, died, and rose from the dead, restoring the life of grace to all men
- He founded the Church as the means of grace

---

preme shepherd, and he, together with them, rules the Body of Christ. Christ knew that any community needed a leader to survive, so he appointed Peter to be his visible representative. It is Peter's successor and those bishops in union with him who now govern the Church. We are united to our bishop, and he in turn is united to the Pope.

Holy

The second mark of the Church is *holiness*. The Church is holy in her origin, first of all, because her Founder, Jesus Christ, is holy and is the source of all holiness. The Church is holy also in her purpose, which is the sanctification and salvation of all her members. She has all the means at her disposal to make her members holy. Her sacraments are also holy because they lead to holiness.

Finally, the Church is holy in those of her members who open themselves to grace, God's life, which is given by the Holy Spirit. Throughout history, the Church has been manifested in the holiness of many men and women who have wholeheartedly accepted Christ and his Church. These *saints*, both canonized and uncanonized, are living proofs that the Church

is holy. Christ said, "By their fruits you shall know them." We can see the fruits of the Church in her saints.

It is important to remember that the holiness of the Church does not mean that all members of the Church are holy. Far from it, unfortunately. Most of us fall far short of holiness and many times even fall into sin. In fact, our Church history reveals that there have been many who have led "unholy" lives. But sin is the result of imperfections in our human nature, not in the nature of the Church herself. Despite our failures we must always strive to imitate the holiness of our Founder.

Catholic

The third mark of the Church is that she is **catholic**, or universal. The Church is called catholic because she possesses the fullness of Christ's truth and revelation, and also because she is for all men at all times and in all places. She is not limited to one race or nation. Her members include both the rich and the poor, the educated and the uneducated, the young and the old. The Church founded by Jesus Christ, unlike the pagan religions at the time, was meant to include every human being.

22

Develop

1. Read paragraphs 28–33 (to the end of the chapter).

2. Review the powers that the apostles were given in order to continue the work of Christ:
- *The power to consecrate the Eucharist (given at the Last Supper)*
- *The power to forgive sins (given after the Resurrection)*
- *Authorization to baptize in the name of the Father, Son, and Holy Spirit (Great Commission).*
- *The power to govern and teach*

Can the students think of other powers given to continue the work of Christ? For example, God gives us the power of the Holy Spirit and his gifts to serve God according to his will, the power to heal and cast out demons, the power Confirm, etc.

3. Mt 16:19 records the great power and authority given to Peter: "Whatever you bind on earth shall be bound in heaven, and whatever you loose on earth shall be loosed in heaven." What does this mean?

- *The Church has the authority to judge what is necessary for salvation and sanctification*
- *The power of the Church is real and binding*
- *There is a great responsibility on behalf of the Church to work according to the will of God.*

4. Discuss that it may be easy now to be followers of Christ and faithful to the teachings of the Church, but it may not always be so. Because our world is troubled with sin, often people we know and love are tested with circumstances that make it difficult to follow the Church (e.g., homosexuality, contraception, fornication, and abortion). When we are confronted with choices that we find difficult or confusing, it is important that we turn to the Church and accept her guidance.

Name:_____

Why the Church?

Answer the following questions in complete sentences and find Bible passages to support your answers.

1. Why did Jesus Christ found the Church?
   <u>Jesus Christ was only on a part of this earth for a short time. So to reach all men everywhere for the rest of time, he established the Church to continue and spread the Gospel.</u>

2. How does the Church continue Jesus's work?
   <u>The Church continues Jesus's work by spreading the Gospel and administering the sacraments.</u>

3. What did Jesus entrust to Peter and the apostles?
   <u>Jesus entrusted Peter and the apostles with the power and means to carry out his mission.</u>

4. What power did the apostles receive at the Last Supper?
   <u>The apostles received the power to govern and teach at the Last Supper.</u>

5. What power did the apostles receive after the Resurrection?
   <u>The apostles received the power to forgive sins after the Resurrection.</u>

6. What were they commanded to do on the day of the Ascension?
   <u>The apostles were commanded to baptize and spread the Word to all nations.</u>

12   *Faith and Life Series • Grade 8 • Chapter 3 • Lesson 4*

Reinforce

1. Have the students work on *Activity Book*, p. 12.

2. Give the class time to work on the Memorization Questions and Words to Know from this chapter and to prepare for the quiz.

3. Have the students write essays on why we need the Church. These essays may be recorded in their journals.

4. Discuss how we encounter Christ in his Church —that every sacrament is an encounter with our Lord. We are united with him in the Liturgy and in prayer, we listen to God in the readings from the Scriptures, and we are most blessed with his presence in the Eucharist.

Conclude

1. Lead the students in singing "O Love, who drew from Jesus' side," *Adoremus Hymnal*, #562.

2. End class by praying an Our Father.

Preview

In the next lesson, the students' understanding of the material covered in this chapter will be reviewed and assessed.

THE CHURCH: GUIDE TO A MORAL LIFE

Man's final end is the vision of God in heaven. If we are to attain that end, we must act in a way that leads us to that goal. But how are we to know which actions are right? God has given us several sources to help us to make that decision. First, there is the natural law and a conscience in every man. Using reason and our conscience, we can determine right from wrong. But since the fall, we are sometimes mistaken. We may see things other than God as our final end, and even with the proper end, our conscience needs to be well formed. To help us in our weakness, God has revealed his Law to us. He began with the Ten Commandments and the Old Testament Law. This Law was fulfilled in Jesus and is now given to us by the Church. Following the Church's rules is the surest path to heaven.

NOTES

_____
_____
_____
_____
_____
_____
_____
_____
_____
_____
_____
_____

This mark has become more evident as the Church has grown over the centuries. The Church has spread throughout many nations according to the command of Christ. And through her missionary work, the Church continues to manifest this mark of universality.

Apostolic

The final mark of the Church is that she is **apostolic**. This means that the Church originated with the apostles, upon whom Christ built his Church. We have already seen how Christ chose the Twelve to be the foundation of his Church. Apostolicity also refers to the fact that the Church is still ruled by the legitimate successors to Peter and the apostles, namely, the Pope and the bishops. In other words, the mark of apostolicity is made clear by the fact that authority in the Church can be traced in an unbroken line back to the apostles.

The Church is also apostolic in the sense that she professes the same doctrine taught by the apostles, the deposit of faith given to the Church by Christ. This deposit of faith remains the same in all essentials. Thus the Church is founded on the apostles and the teaching given to them by Our Lord.

Why the Church?

We have seen that Christ founded the Church, his Mystical Body, and identified her by four unique and visible signs. But why did he establish this Church? Understanding this will give us a more complete grasp of the nature of the Church.

To begin with, Our Lord was on earth for only a short time. In order to offer salvation to all men, not just those living in Palestine two thousand years ago, he established his Church to continue his work. By his death Our Lord merited sufficient graces to save all men. He then entrusted to Peter and the apostles the power and the means necessary to carry out the work of salvation. Our Lord himself gave the apostles the task of administering the sacraments.

At the Last Supper, for example, they were given the power to celebrate the Holy Eucharist. After the Resurrection, they received the power to forgive sins. And on the day of the Ascension, they were directed to baptize in the name of the Persons of the Trinity.

So that the Church could carry out this mission of sanctification, Christ also gave the Church the powers to govern and to teach. The power to govern is necessary so that our weakened wills will have the guidance and support needed to follow Christ and his commands. This power was indicated when Christ told first Peter, and later all of the apostles, ". . . whatever you bind on earth shall be bound in heaven, and whatever you loose on earth shall be loosed in heaven" (Mt 16:19). The Church, then, has the power from Christ to be the final judge determining what is necessary for salvation and sanctification.

Finally, the Church has the power from Christ to teach, so that we may know the truths that Christ has revealed to us. The Church safeguards us from false teaching. We have already seen that Christ instructed his apostles to go forth and teach what he had taught them. This work is carried on primarily by the successors of the apostles, the Pope and the bishops, and those who share in their authority.

In the next chapter we will consider in more detail the teaching mission of the Church and especially the sources of her teaching. In later chapters we will consider the governing and sanctifying missions of the Church.

Words to Know:
Mystical Body of Christ   catholic   apostolic

23

Q. 6 *What are the means of holiness and of eternal salvation that are found in the Church?*

The means of holiness and of eternal salvation which are found in the Church are the sacraments, prayer, spiritual counsel, and good example (CCC 1692).

Q. 7 *Which is the Church of Jesus Christ?*

The Church of Jesus Christ is the Catholic Church, which alone is one, holy, catholic, and apostolic as Jesus willed her to be (CCC 811).

Q. 8 *How is the Church one?*

The Church is one in her origin from God; in her founder Jesus Christ; and in her life of the Holy Spirit; and also one in her faith, in the sacraments, and in her pastors (CCC 813, 815).

Q. 9 *How is the Church holy?*

The Church is holy through her founder Jesus Christ and his Holy Spirit, as well as through her holy faith (CCC 823).

Q. 10 *How is the Church catholic?*

The Church is catholic, or universal, in that she was instituted for all men, is suitable for all men, and has extended over the whole world (CCC 836).

Q. 11 *How is the Church apostolic?*

The Church is apostolic in that she was founded on the apostles and continues in their teaching, sacraments, and authority, through their successors, the bishops (CCC 857).

24

CHAPTER THREE
REVIEW AND ASSESSMENT

Aims

The students' understanding of the material covered in this chapter will be reviewed and assessed.

Materials

- Quiz 3, Appendix, p. A-3
- "O Love, who drew from Jesus' side," *Adoremus Hymnal*, #562

Review

1. Review various images of the Church. The students should be able to explain the model of the Mystical Body for the Church.

2. Consider the four marks of the Church. The students should be able to explain the meaning of each of the four marks:
   - One
   - Holy
   - Catholic
   - Apostolic

3. The students should know how and why Jesus founded the Church.

4. The Church is necessary for our salvation. The students should be able to explain why we need the Church for our own salvation.

Name: _____

The Nature of the Church   Quiz 3

Part I: Explain the four marks of the Church using examples.

One: <u>The Church is one in unity of belief, worship, and Liturgy and in unity under Christ. Examples will vary.</u>

Holy: <u>The Church is holy in her origin, purpose, and in her members who open themselves to grace.</u>

Catholic: <u>The Church is catholic because she has the fullness of Christ's truth and is for all men at all times and in all places.</u>

Apostolic: <u>The Church is apostolic in that she originated with the apostles and professes the same doctrine as the apostles, and she continues to be led by the legitimate successors of Peter and the apostles.</u>

Part II: Explain how the Church is the Mystical Body of Christ.
<u>Answers will vary but should be based on student text.</u>

Assess

1. Distribute the quizzes and read through them with the students to be sure they understand the questions.

2. Administer the quiz. As they hand in their work, you may orally quiz the students on the Memorization Questions from this chapter.

3. After all the quizzes have been handed in, review the correct answers with the class.

Conclude

1. Lead the students in singing "O Love, who drew from Jesus' side," *Adoremus Hymnal*, #562.

2. End class by praying an Our Father.

CHAPTER FOUR
THE TEACHING CHURCH

Catechism of the Catholic Church References

Apostolic Succession: 77–79, 861–62, 869
Apostolic Tradition: 75–76, 96
Church's Task of Teaching: 888–92, 939
Creeds: 185–97
Deposit of Faith: 84, 97, 175
Doctors and Theologians: 236, 2033, 2038
Ecumenical Councils: 884
Encyclicals: 2033, 2049–50
Fathers of the Church and Catechesis: 8
Holy Spirit as Interpreter of Scripture: 109–14, 137
Inspiration and Truth of Scripture: 105–8, 136
Heritage of Faith Entrusted to the Whole Church: 84, 98
Magisterium of the Church: 85–87, 100
Dogmas of Faith: 88–90
Fathers of the Church: 8, 688

Supernatural Sense of Faith: 91–93, 101
Growth in Understanding the Faith: 94–95
Jesus Christ as the Fullness of all Revelation: 65–67, 73
Mystery of Faith: 42, 50, 158, 206, 230, 234, 237, 1066
New Testament: 124–27, 139, 515
Old Testament: 121–23
Relation between Tradition and Holy Scripture: 80–83, 96–97
Revelation: 51–73
Revelation of God as Trinity: 238–48, 261–64
Revelation of God's Plan of Salvation: 51–53, 68
Sacred Deposit of the Word of God: 78, 80–84, 95
Sensus Fidei: 889, 911
Stages of Revelation: 54–55, 69–70
Ways of Knowing God: 31–38, 46–48, 286

Scripture References

God's Revelation: Eph 1:4–5; 1:9; 2:18; 2 Pet 1:4

Deposit of Faith: 1 Tim 6:20

Summary of Lesson Content

Lesson 1

Public revelation began with Abraham and ended with Saint John the Evangelist.

The sacred deposit of the Word of God was inspired by God and entrusted to the Church. There is one deposit of the Word of God, and from it flow Sacred Scripture and Sacred Tradition.

Lesson 2

The Apostolic Fathers were instructed by the apostles.

Creeds are formulations of the faith, written as summaries for the faithful transmission of the faith.

Ecumenical councils (gatherings of all the bishops in union with the Pope) are called to clarify Church teaching.

Lesson 3

As Catholics, we are blessed with Fathers and Doctors of the Church. Church Fathers are holy teachers of the faith from the first eight centuries AD. Church Doctors are saintly theologians and teachers of later centuries.

Popes have also written documents on the faith. Some of these documents are decrees from amongst the Fathers and the teachings of Christ, called encyclicals.

The *sensus fidei* is the testimony of what the faithful have believed over the centuries and what saints have thought, meditated upon, and believed.

Lesson 4

The deposit of faith was completed with the death of Saint John; however, our understanding of the deposit of faith has developed over the last two millennia. This growth in the Church's understanding is called the development of doctrine, which is the gradual unfolding of the meaning of the truths Christ has revealed to us.

LESSON ONE: REVELATION

Aims

The students will learn that public revelation began with Abraham and ended with Saint John the Evangelist.

They will learn that the sacred deposit of the Word of God was inspired by God and entrusted to the Church. There is one deposit of the Word of God and from it flow Sacred Scripture and Sacred Tradition.

Materials

- *Activity Book*, p. 13

  Optional:
- "Glorious things of thee are spoken," *Adoremus Hymnal*, #563

Begin

Tell the students a story about how you became a religion teacher and why you enjoy teaching. Instruct the students to take out a paper and pencil and write about what you told them. They may share with one another to be sure the information they record is accurate. Explain how you gave them the entire oral report (Tradition) and they recorded it as accurately as they could (Scripture). As well-written as their reports may be, we may discover more information (such as how you told the story, your intention in telling the story, etc.) through discussion with the teacher/class (Magisterium).

CHAPTER 4

The Teaching Church

They asked him, "Teacher, we know that you speak and teach rightly, and show no partiality, but truly teach the way of God."

Luke 20:21

"This gospel was to be the source of all saving truths and moral discipline. This was faithfully done: it was done by the apostles who handed on, by the spoken word of their preaching, by the example they gave, by the institutions they established, what they themselves had received" (DV, 7).

As we have already seen, Our Lord left to the Church the *deposit of faith*. His final command to the apostles was to teach all that he had instructed them. He relied on his apostles and their successors to carry his message to the world. This is made known to us today through the living voice of the Church—the Pope, the bishops, the priests—even the laity. Each of these conveys to us the message of Christ, especially the clergy, who are, by their office, the representatives of Christ. The Church bases her teaching on the deposit of faith revealed to us by God. Before we look at the source of this teaching we should first consider what is meant by *revelation*.

What Is Revelation?

Revelation literally means to "draw back the veil" or to uncover. God is primarily a mystery to us. On our own we can have only a lim-

ited knowledge of him. However, God has unveiled some of the mysteries about himself so that we might come to know and love him. He has helped us to know who he is and what he expects of us.

In other words, revelation is the communication by God to man of the truths about himself that he wants man to know but that man could never uncover on his own. These truths are known as doctrines or teachings of our faith.

God did not reveal these truths about himself all at once but only gradually with the passing of time. The process of public revelation began with Abraham and ended with the death of the last apostle, St. John.

The first phase of God's revelation can be found in the Old Testament. Because this revelation took place long before the birth of Christ, we call it "pre-Christian" revelation. If we look at the Old Testament, we can see that God gradually revealed more about himself as the centuries passed.

This revelation was completed when God fully showed himself to us by becoming man and living among us. This phase is known as "Christian" revelation. It contains the truths revealed by Jesus Christ to his apostles. These

25

Develop

1. Read paragraphs 1–10.

2. Define revelation. Revelation literally means "to unveil" something. God revealed himself and his teaching to man because we could not have discovered these truths on our own (in time and without error). Just as a teacher explains things clearly to his students to help them learn and understand, so too, God reveals himself so that we can understand God revealed himself gradually through salvation history and perfectly in the Divine Person of Jesus Christ.

3. The first phase of revelation occurred in the Old Testament. It is called "Pre-Christian" revelation. During this time, God revealed his existence as the one true God. He also revealed his plan for salvation. This phase of revelation was fulfilled in God's perfect revelation of himself in becoming man (Jesus Christ). This phase is known as "Christian" revelation. Christian revelation contains the truths revealed by Jesus

Christ to his apostles. These truths include the most important mysteries of our faith. Among them are the Trinity, the Incarnation, and the Eucharist.

4. The Word of God is inspired by God (and perfectly revealed in Christ, who is the Word made Flesh). It has been communicated to us in two ways:
- *Sacred Scripture: the word of God put down in writing under the breath of the Holy Spirit*
- *Sacred Tradition: the entirety of the Word of God entrusted to the apostles by Christ and the Holy Spirit*

These two sources of revelation are closely connected and must be kept together for proper understanding of the truths of God and their faithful transmission. The Word of God is entrusted to the Teaching Church, called the Magisterium (the Pope and the bishops in union with the Pope), to safeguard and faithfully transmit it to God's people.

Revelation

Answer the following questions in complete sentences.

1. Who comprises the teaching Church?
   The teaching Church is comprised of the Pope, bishops,
   priests and laity.

2. What is revelation?
   Revelation is communication
   by God to man regarding
   the truths about himself.

3. When did public revelation begin and end?
   Public revelation began with Abraham and ended with St.
   John.

4. Where can revelation be found?
   Revelation can be found in the Old Testament and in the
   New Testament.

5. Who is the source of revelation?
   The Word of God is the source of revelation.

6. How are Scripture and Tradition bound together?
   Scripture and Tradition are bound
   together by the Word of God,
   from which they both flow.

Faith and Life Series • Grade 8 • Chapter 4 • Lesson 1   13

Reinforce

1. Have the students work on *Activity Book*, p. 13.

2. Give the class time to work on the Memorization Questions and Words to Know from this
chapter.

*3. Discuss the end of public revelation with the
death of Saint John the Evangelist. Because public revelation was fulfilled in Christ, there is no
more revelation necessary. Saint John the Evangelist was the last first-hand witness of these
truths, which he recorded in his Gospel and in
the Book of Revelation.*

4. You may teach about the synoptic Gospels.
Matthew, Mark, and Luke share similar stories
and likely shared information in writing their
texts. Although there are some differences, these
do not discredit their writings or the truths contained therein. They provide various perspectives
on the same teachings for different audiences.

Conclude

1. Teach the students to sing "Glorious things of
thee are spoken," *Adoremus Hymnal*, #563.

2. End class by leading the students in praying
the Nicene Creed.

Preview

In the next lesson, the students will learn about
the Early Church.

CHALK TALK: SOURCES OF REVELATION

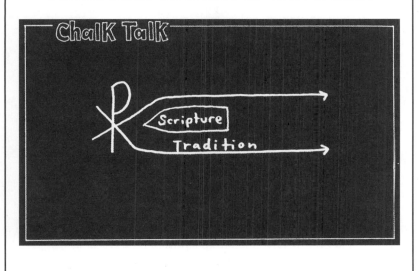

Scripture ⟷ **Tradition**

Magisterium

"It is clear, therefore, that sacred tradition,
Sacred Scripture and the teaching authority of the Church, in accord with God's
most wise design, are so linked and joined
together that one cannot stand without the
others, and that all together and each in its
own way under the action of the one Holy
Spirit contribute effectively to the salvation
of souls."

—*Dei Verbum* 10

LESSON TWO: EARLY CHURCH

Aims

The students will learn that the Apostolic Fathers were instructed by the apostles.

They will learn that creeds are formulations of the faith, written as summaries for the faithful transmission of the faith.

They will learn that ecumenical councils (gatherings of all the bishops in union with the Pope) are called to clarify Church teaching.

Materials

- *Activity Book*, p. 14

Optional:
- "Glorious things of thee are spoken," *Adoremus Hymnal*, #563

Begin

The apostles were taught by Christ. They were witnesses to his life, deeds, miracles, teachings, death, Resurrection, and Ascension. They were Christ's closest followers, who knew him and his revelation most intimately. They passed on what Christ taught to disciples. Some recorded their knowledge in the Gospels to ensure its transmission.

Note: Can we have Scripture without Tradition? No! Scripture comes from Tradition.

26

Develop

1. Read paragraphs 11–17.

2. The apostles trained disciples in all that they knew to be revealed by Christ (many of these disciples were bishops in the Early Church). The leaders of the Church were very faithful in transmitting the truths of Christ carefully and in their entirety. The immediate disciples of the apostles are called the Apostolic Fathers.

3. Review that Sacred Scripture and Sacred Tradition (the Word of God) was entrusted to the apostles (the leaders of the Church) and, therefore, was entrusted to the Church to safeguard, interpret, and faithfully transmit.

4. In the Early Church there was some confusion over various teachings and thus clarification was needed. Christians turned to the Teaching Church (which has the duty to safeguard, interpret, and faithfully transmit the truth). The

Magisterium (Teaching Church) is the Pope and the bishops in union with him. They gathered together in what is called an ecumenical council. This has certain requirements:
- *Universal invitation (all bishops invited)*
- *Sufficient representation (most bishops attended)*
- *Papal authorization (Pope has the last word, and if the bishops are not in union with the Pope, they do not have authority)*

Some doctrines clarified in ecumenical councils are: the Trinity, the Incarnation, the Eucharist, Mary as Mother of God.

5. From some of the councils, in which Church teaching was clarified and our understanding of doctrine summarized, creeds were written to summarize our faith and ensure that it is faithfully transmitted. Examples are the Apostles' Creed, the Nicene Creed, the Nicene-Constantinople Creed, and the Athanasian Creed.

Creeds and Councils

Answer the following questions in complete sentences.

1. What is a creed?
   A creed is a statement of belief.

2. What is the Apostles' Creed?
   The Apostles' Creed is the earliest summary of the Church's beliefs.

3. What is the Nicene Creed?
   The Nicene Creed is an expansion and explanation of the Apostles' Creed. It was formed at the Council of Nicea.

4. Why were creeds written?
   Creeds are written to explain more fully, and in better detail, some of our doctrines.

5. What is an ecumenical council?
   An ecumenical council is a gathering of bishops from all over the world to discuss Church matters under the authority of the Pope.

7. What is discussed at ecumenical councils?
   Normally, controversies over doctrine are discussed and more completely and accurately stated at ecumenical councils.

14   *Faith and Life Series • Grade 8 • Chapter 4 • Lesson 2*

Reinforce

1. Have the students work on *Activity Book*, p. 14.

2. Give the class time to work on the Memorization Questions and Words to Know from this chapter.

3. *Have the students write summaries of the ecumenical councils and their primary teachings. Each student can research a different council and make a presentation for the other students. Be sure the students understand the importance and teachings of the first seven ecumenical councils.*

4. The students may research different creeds and compare them.

Conclude

1. Lead the students in singing "Glorious things of thee are spoken," *Adoremus Hymnal*, #563.

2. End class by leading the students in praying the Nicene Creed.

Preview

In the next lesson, the students will learn about the writings of the Church.

EARLY ECUMENICAL COUNCILS

- First Nicaea, 325: affirmed that Jesus is true God (same substance as the Father).

- First Constantinople, 381: affirmed the divinity of Holy Spirit.

- Ephesus, 431: proclaimed Mary *Theotokos* (God bearer) and affirmed the unity of Jesus as one Divine Person, even in the womb of Mary.

- Chalcedon, 451: affirmed that Jesus is one Divine Person with two natures: human and divine.

- Second Constantinople, 553: affirmed Church teaching on the Trinity and the Incarnation.

- Third Constantinople, 680–681: affirmed that Jesus has two wills, human and divine, along with his two natures, and that the human will, although separate, submits in all things to his divine will.

- Second Nicaea, 787: affirmed that worship is due to God alone and that we can venerate saints, relics, and sacred images.

LESSON THREE: CHURCH WRITINGS

Aims

The students will learn that the writings of the Fathers and Doctors of the Church are testimonies to the teachings of the Church. Church Fathers were recognized as special writers of faith. Church Doctors are saintly theologians and teachers of later centuries.

They will learn that Popes have also written documents on the faith. Some of these documents are decrees or expressions of the teachings of Christ, called encyclicals. The *sensus fidei* is the testimony of what the faithful have believed over the centuries and what saints have thought, meditated upon, and believed.

Materials

- *Activity Book*, p. 15

  Optional:
  - "Glorious things of thee are spoken," *Adoremus Hymnal*, #563

Begin

It is important for the Church to document what she believes. Often the Church is of one accord. However, there are times when new movements of thought that are contrary to the truths of our faith are made popular. We must refer to the documents of the Church in order to understand the truths of our faith. For example, neo-gnosticism occasionally re-surfaces in an immoral culture, but referring to Church writings, we can be protected from error.

---

revelations include the most important mysteries of our faith. Among them are the Trinity, the Incarnation, and the Eucharist.

Source of Revelation

"God graciously arranged that the things he had once revealed for the salvation of all peoples should remain in their entirety, throughout the ages, and be transmitted to all generations" (DV, 7). This sacred deposit of the Word of God has been entrusted to the Church.

There is only one single sacred deposit of the Word of God, but from it flow both Sacred **Tradition** and Sacred **Scripture**, the Bible. It is important to recognize that Tradition and Scripture are bound closely together and communicate one with the other. "Sacred Scripture is the speech of God as it is put down in writing under the breath of the Holy Spirit. Tradition transmits in its entirety the Word of God which has been entrusted to the apostles by Christ the Lord and the Holy Spirit" (DV, 9). By means of Tradition, the books of the Bible are known to the Church, and the Scriptures are more thoroughly understood and interpreted.

Sacred Scripture, the Bible, is the written Word of God. It is made up of a collection of books written at various times by different men who wrote under God's inspiration. As we know, the Bible is made up of the Old Testament, which contains pre-Christian revelation, and the New Testament, which contains Christian revelation.

The New Testament, however, does not contain all that Jesus did and said. In fact, the various books of the New Testament were not even begun until some twenty or thirty years after the death of Christ. The apostles began to preach the message of Christ first, and only later were some of these teachings committed to writing. Scripture itself testifies to the fact that the Gospels do not include all of Jesus'

words. At the end of his Gospel, St. John says, ". . . there are also many other things which Jesus did; were every one of them to be written, I suppose that the world itself could not contain the books that would be written" (Jn 21:25).

What Jesus taught his apostles was passed on to their disciples. For example, St. Polycarp of Smyrna, St. Ignatius of Antioch, and St. Clement of Rome all lived during the last part of the first century and the beginning of the second century. Because they were personally taught by the apostles, they are known as **Apostolic Fathers**. Their writings contain some of Jesus' teachings that are not explicitly found in the New Testament.

Over the centuries many varied and contradictory interpretations of the Bible have arisen. Who had the authority to decide which was the right one? It is important to note that the Church—which, as we have seen was given authority by Christ (Mt 16:19) to settle all disputes on earth—is the interpreter of Sacred Scripture. She is the custodian (or guardian) of Scripture and Tradition because she was promised the guidance of the Spirit of Truth.

The Second Vatican Council says, "Sacred Tradition and Sacred Scripture make up a single deposit of the Word of God, which is entrusted to the Church" (DV, 10).

Creeds

An important written expression of Tradition is found in the *creeds*, or statements of belief, of the Church. These creeds are summary statements of the main doctrines proposed for belief by the Church. The earliest of these dates back to very early times and is called the *Apostles' Creed*.

The *Nicene Creed*, formulated at the council of Nicaea in the fourth century, is an expansion and explanation of the Apostles' Creed. In the first creed, and in fact in the early days of

27

Develop

1. Read paragraphs 18–23 (up to "Development of Doctrine").

2. Discuss the Church Fathers. They are saintly Christian writers of the early centuries of the Church, who are recognized as special witnesses of the faith. They often wrote against heresies (false teachings) or helped people to better understand the faith. Have the students read the list of the Fathers provided at right.

3. Discuss the Doctors of the Church. They are saintly theologians and teachers of later centuries of the Church, whose writings are outstanding in guiding the faithful at all times. There are three women Doctors of the Church (Saint Thérèse of Lisieux was recently named as such). A list is provided on p. 41 of this manual.

4. The Pope, by himself, can teach on matters of faith and morals. Often popes write encyclicals—letters sent to the

bishops and the faithful, expressing the teaching of the Church on matters of faith and morals and other timely subjects.

5. Another form of Church Tradition is the sensus fidei. *This is the testimony of the faithful. It records what they believed over the centuries, what saints have thought, meditated upon, believed, etc. Included in this testimony are the actions and prayers of the faithful. The whole body of the faithful who have an anointing from the Holy Spirit cannot err in matters of the faith. This, however, is not limited to any one time, but through all times and in all places. This is an important body of testimony for the Church.*

6. Assign each student a Father/Doctor of the Church to research. Each student should make a presentation of his findings.

Name:_____

Our Heritage of Faith

Write descriptions of the Fathers and Doctors of the Church below:

Fathers of the Church:

Answers will vary.

_____

_____

_____

_____

_____

_____

_____

_____

_____

_____

Doctors of the Church:

_____

_____

_____

_____

_____

_____

_____

_____

_____

_____

_____

Faith and Life Series • Grade 8 • Chapter 4 • Lesson 3   15

Reinforce

1. Have the students work on *Activity Book*, p. 15.

2. Give the class time to work on the Memorization Questions and Words to Know from this chapter.

3. Each student should research a different Father or Doctor of the Church and present his findings to the other students.

4. Have the students think of an example of the *sensus fidei* and its importance in the Church. (Marian doctrines are a good example.)

5. Each student should choose an encyclical and explain it to the class.

Conclude

1. Lead the students in singing "Glorious things of thee are spoken," *Adoremus Hymnal*, #563.

2. End class by leading the students in praying the Nicene Creed.

Preview

In the next lesson, the students will learn about the development of doctrine.

MAJOR CHURCH FATHERS

St. Ambrose of Milan	St. Hilary of Poitiers
St. Athanasius	St. Ignatius of Antioch
St. Augustine of Hippo	St. Irenaeus of Lyons
St. Basil the Great	St. John Chrysostom
St. Benedict of Nursia	St. John of Damascus
St. John Cassian	St. Julius I
St. Clement of Alexandria	St. Justin Martyr
St. Clement I	St. Leo the Great
St. Cyprian of Carthage	Novatian
St. Cyril of Jerusalem	Origen
Eusebius of Caeserea	St. Peter Chrysologus
St. Gregory of Nyssa	St. Polycarp
St. Gregory the Great	Rufinus of Aquileia
Hermas	Tertullian

NOTES

_____

_____

_____

_____

_____

_____

_____

_____

_____

_____

_____

_____

LESSON FOUR:
DEVELOPMENT OF DOCTRINE

Aims

The students will learn that the deposit of faith was completed with the death of Saint John; however, our understanding of the deposit of faith has developed over the last two millennia. This growth in the Church's understanding is called the development of doctrine which is the gradual unfolding of the meaning of the truths Christ has revealed to us.

Materials

- *Activity Book*, p. 16

Optional:
- "Glorious things of thee are spoken," *Adoremus Hymnal*, #563

Begin

Review the deposit of the Word of God and its communication through Sacred Scripture and Sacred Tradition. This is entrusted to the teaching Church, the Magisterium.

Review the Apostolic Fathers, councils, and creeds that help us to clarify our beliefs and transmit them to the faithful.

Review other Church writings as means of understanding our faith throughout time and in all places.

---

the Church, most doctrines were stated in plain and simple language. Over the years questions and difficulties arose concerning many of these doctrines. The later creeds, particularly the Nicene, were written to explain more fully some of these doctrines.

Councils

A second written expression of Tradition is found in the statements of the Ecumenical Councils of the Church. A Church council is a gathering of all the bishops—under the authority of the Pope—to discuss matters of concern to the Church. We call them *ecumenical*, meaning whole or worldwide, because they involve all the bishops. Over the centuries councils have frequently been called in response to controversies over basic doctrines of the faith. The councils have given the Church the occasion to explain more completely and accurately certain beliefs.

The earliest controversies were over the Trinity and the human and divine natures of Christ. The Council of Nicaea addressed these questions. It is evident that when there was a controversy there had to be an arbiter (or umpire) to decide what the true teaching was. Later councils addressed questions about which books were in fact inspired and thus to be included in the Bible, the nature and number of the sacraments, and the nature of the Church. The decisions of these councils clarify or define the teaching of the Church.

The lists that follow contain some of the most important of the Fathers and Doctors of the Church.

FATHERS OF THE CHURCH

St. Ambrose	St. Jerome
St. Augustine	St. John Chrysostom
St. Basil the Great	St. John Damascene
St. Benedict	St. Leo the Great
St. Cyprian	St. Paulinus of Nola
St. Gregory the Great	St. Polycarp
St. Ignatius of Antioch	

DOCTORS OF THE CHURCH

St. Albert the Great	St. Francis de Sales
St. Alphonsus Liguori	St. John of the Cross
St. Anselm	St. Peter Canisius
St. Bernard of Clairvaux	St. Robert Bellarmine
St. Bonaventure	St. Teresa of Avila
St. Catherine of Siena	St. Thérèse of Lisieux
	St. Thomas Aquinas

28

Develop

1. Read paragraphs 24–25, as well as the inset box on Cardinal Newman (to the end of the chapter).

2. Explain that the deposit of faith was completed with the death of Saint John; however, our understanding of the deposit of faith has developed over the last two millennia. This is called the development of doctrine: the gradual unfolding of the meaning of the truths that Christ revealed to us. To demonstrate this, explain that we all know our mothers. However, we grow in our understanding of their love through the sacrifices they make and their displays of this love (e.g., affection, gifts, ongoing support, etc.). As we grow older, we also learn about our parents' relationship (how they met, how they fell in love, etc.) and who they are individually (hobbies, dreams, etc.). Although our understanding of our parents is growing, they have not changed (and in some way we already knew these things). We simply learned to communicate or articulate what we already knew: this person we

call mom is the same person who dreams of her child's wedding and children, loves her spouse and children, etc. All of this is what we mean by "mom" or "dad."

3. The development of doctrine relies upon the sources of revelation as interpreted by the Magisterium, upon the Apostolic Fathers, Fathers and Doctors of the Church, and the sensus fidei.

4. Review the box on Cardinal Newman in the Student text. The students should appreciate the importance of his work on the development of doctrine.

5. Have the students make their presentations on the Fathers and Doctors of the Church. They may dress up for their presentations, or play a game, such as name that Doctor or Father.

Name:_____

Development of Doctrine

Answer the following questions in complete sentences.

1. What is *sensus fidelium*?
   <u>Sensus fidelium means "the sense of the faithful" and
   refers to what the faithful have believed over the
   centuries.</u>

2. What is *sensus fidei*?
   <u>Sensus fidei is the fact that the faithful cannot err
   in matters of belief.</u>

3. What are encyclicals? Do these change Church teaching?
   <u>Encyclicals are letters by the Pope to bishops and the
   faithful expressing the teaching of the Church on faith,
   morals, social responsibilities and other important topics.</u>

4. Explain the development of doctrine. Do the truths of the Church change?
   <u>The development of doctrine is the gradual unfolding of the
   meaning of many things Christ revealed to us, making
   explicit what was already understood implicity. The truths
   of the Church do not change.</u>

5. Using the example of the Immaculate Conception, explain the process of the
   development of doctrine.
   <u>Answers will vary.</u>

Faith and Life Series • Grade 8 • Chapter 4 • Lesson 4

Reinforce

1. Have the students work on *Activity Book*, p. 16.

2. Give the class time to work on the Memorization Questions and Words to Know from this chapter and to prepare for the quiz.

3. The students may study the Immaculate Conception as an example of the development of doctrine.

Conclude

1. Lead the students in singing "Glorious things of thee are spoken," *Adoremus Hymnal*, #563.

2. End class by leading the students in praying the Nicene Creed.

Preview

In the next lesson, the students' understanding of the material covered in this chapter will be reviewed and assessed.

DOCTORS OF THE CHURCH
(all are saints)

Albert the Great	Gregory the Great
Alphonsus Liguori	Hilary of Poitiers
Ambrose of Milan	Isidore of Seville
Anselm of Canterbury	Jerome
Anthony of Padua	John Chrysostom
Augustine of Hippo	John Damascene
Basil the Great	John of the Cross
Venerable Bede	Lawrence of Brindisi
Bernard of Clairvaux	Peter Canisius
Bonaventure	Peter Damian
Catherine of Siena	Robert Bellarmine
Cyril of Alexandria	Teresa of Avila
Cyril of Jerusalem	Thérèse of Lisieux
Francis de Sales	Thomas Aquinas

NOTES

_____
_____
_____
_____
_____
_____
_____
_____
_____
_____
_____
_____

_____
_____
_____
_____
_____
_____
_____
_____
_____
_____
_____
_____
_____
_____
_____
_____
_____
_____
_____
_____
_____
_____

Fathers and Doctors of the Church

The writings of the *Fathers* and *Doctors* of the Church are also written records of witnesses. The **Fathers of the Church** are saintly Christian writers of the early centuries of the Church who are recognized as special witnesses of the faith. Among the more well-known are the following: St. Athanasius, a bishop during the late third century who defended the doctrine that Christ was both God and man against the Arian heresy; St. Augustine, a bishop of the fourth century who converted after leading a life of great sin and became one of the greatest theologians in the Church; and St. Jerome, a monk and a scholar during the fourth century who translated the Bible into Latin, the common language of the people at that time.

The **Doctors of the Church** are the saintly theologians and teachers of the later centuries whose writings are outstanding in guiding the faithful at all times. One of the foremost among these is the great Dominican St. Thomas Aquinas, who lived in Italy during the thirteenth century. Three women are included among the Doctors: St. Teresa of Avila, St. Catherine of Siena, and St. Thérèse of Lisieux. To help you understand more about the Fathers and Doctors, you might want to choose one from the list at the end of the chapter and read about his life.

The writings and decrees of individual Popes are another expression of the teachings of Christ. Some of these are known as **encyclicals**, letters sent by the Pope to the bishops and the faithful, expressing the teaching of the Church on matters of faith, morals, social responsibility, and other important topics.

There is also the "**sensus fidelium**". Literally, this phrase means "the sense of the faithful." This testimony is from what the faithful have believed over the centuries and what the saints have thought, meditated, and believed, and from the actions, prayers, etc. of the faithful.

The Church teaches us that the "whole body of the faithful who have an anointing that comes from the Holy One cannot err in matters of belief. This characteristic is shown in the supernatural appreciation of the faith (*sensus fidei*) of the whole people, when, 'from the

CARDINAL NEWMAN

John Henry Cardinal Newman was born in England in 1801. He was an Anglican scholar who founded the Oxford Movement in England in order to reform the Anglican Church. In many sermons, lectures, and books, Newman expounded the "Anglo-Catholic" position. One of his most important works was a book entitled *On the Development of Christian Doctrine*, in which he discussed how the Church's understanding of her Faith deepens over time. His discussion of this question was the most complete treatment of it up until that time.

Eventually John Henry Newman was led to the true Church of Christ through his studies and his writings. Toward the end of his life he was made a cardinal of the Church by Pope Leo XIII.

29

_____
_____
_____
_____
_____
_____
_____
_____
_____
_____
_____
_____
_____

bishops to the last of the faithful' they manifest a universal consent in matters of faith and morals" (LG, 12).

Development of Doctrine

One last point remains to be made here about the teaching of the Church. Although the deposit of faith was completed with the death of the last apostle, St. John, our understanding of it has developed over the last twenty centuries. We call this the **development of doctrine**. This is the gradual unfolding of the meaning of many things that Christ revealed to us. It is this development of doctrine that we find in the councils of the Church, the writings of the Fathers and Doctors, and the practical experience of the faith among the faithful of the Church. Since the Holy Spirit, who continues to guide the Church, is the Spirit of Truth, any further development can never be—and never has been—in contradiction to any previous doctrine. One example to illustrate this is the definition of the doctrine of the Immaculate Conception of Our Lady. This doctrine is hinted at in Scripture ("Hail, full of grace," Lk 1:28), was defended by some of the Doctors of the Church, and was part of the *sensus fidelium* for centuries. Yet it was not officially declared until 1854, by Pope Pius IX. It was not a new revelation, but rather an unfolding of one doctrine over time. Something that is implicit in a doctrine becomes explicit, or it can be the logical consequence of a doctrine.

In this chapter we have discussed the sources of the Church's teaching. In the next chapter we will consider the authority of the Church, first, as it pertains to matters of doctrine and the teaching of the Church and, second, as it pertains to matters of discipline, the governing of the Church.

Words to Know:

revelation   Tradition   Sacred Scripture   Apostolic Fathers   Fathers of the Church   Doctors of the Church   encyclical   *sensus fidelium*   development of doctrine

---

Q. 12   *What is the Apostles' Creed?*
The Apostles' Creed is the summary and profession of faith in the chief mysteries and other truths revealed by God through Jesus Christ (CCC 187, 194).

Q. 13   *What is a mystery?*
A mystery is a truth revealed by God which is beyond our reason (CCC 237).

_____

_____

_____

_____

_____

_____

_____

_____

_____

_____

_____

_____

_____

_____

_____

_____

_____

_____

_____

_____

_____

Q. 14 *What are the chief mysteries of faith that we profess in the Creed?*

The chief mysteries of faith that we profess in the Creed are the Holy Trinity and the Incarnation, Passion, death, and Resurrection of Jesus Christ (CCC 189–90).

Q. 15 *What is the deposit of faith?*

The deposit of faith is all that is contained in Sacred Scripture and Sacred Tradition, handed on in the Church from the time of the Apostles, and from which the Magisterium draws all that it presents for belief as being revealed by God (CCC 84–86).

Q. 16 *What is the development of doctrine?*

The development of doctrine is the growth in understanding of God's revelation through the study and prayer of believers and the teaching of the Magisterium (CCC 66, 94).

Q. 17 *What is the sensus fidei?*

The *sensus fidei* is a supernatural appreciation of the faith shown by universal consent in matters of faith and morals, as expressed by the whole body of the faithful under the guidance of the Magisterium (CCC 92–93, 889).

Q. 18 *What is an ecumenical or general council?*

An ecumenical or general council is a gathering of all the bishops of the world with the consent of the Pope, to exercise their collegial authority over the universal Church (CCC 884).

Q. 19 *What is an encyclical?*

An encyclical is a pastoral letter written by the Pope and sent to the whole Church to express Church teaching on some important matter. (CCC 892).

31

_____

_____

_____

_____

_____

_____

_____

_____

_____

_____

_____

_____

_____

_____

_____

_____

Name: _____

The Teaching Church   Quiz 4

Part I: Matching.

1. _D_ Men personally taught by the Apostles
2. _G_ Letter written by the Pope about Church teaching
3. _A_ Communication by God to humanity
4. _I_ Growing in our understanding of God's revelation
5. _B_ The written Word of God
6. _C_ Teachings of Jesus passed on to his followers
7. _J_ The Teaching Church
8. _H_ Testimony of what Christ's followers have believed
    for centuries
9. _E_ Holy teachers/theologians of Christian doctrine
10. _F_ Christian writers of the early days of the Church

a. Revelation
b. Scripture
c. Tradition
d. Apostolic Fathers
e. Doctors of the Church
f. Fathers of the Church
g. encyclical
h. _sensus fidei_
i. development of doctrine
j. Magisterium

Part II: Answer in complete sentences.

1. Why do we need Sacred Scripture, Tradition, and the Magisterium?
   We need Sacred Scripture, Tradition and the Magisterium because from
   Sacred Scripture and Tradition flow the sacred deposit of the Word of
   God. They are sources of God's revelation to man, which is safeguarded
   by the Magisterium, the custodian of Scripture and Tradition.

2. Who are the Fathers and Doctors of the Church? Name one Father or Doctor and explain what
   he has done for the Church.
   The Fathers of the Church are Christian writers of the early centuries
   whose writings and teachings are the earliest expressions of the
   Tradition of the Church. Doctors of the Church are saints whose
   writings are acknowledged by the Church for their enduring theological
   and spiritual value.

3. What is an ecumenical council? Why are they important? Give the name, date, and significance of two ecumenical councils.
   An ecumenical council is a gathering of all the bishops throughout the
   world—with the consent of the Pope—to discuss matters of concern
   to the Church. They are important because they more completely and
   accurately explain our beliefs.

_A - 4_   _Faith and Life • Grade 8 • Appendix A_

Assess

1. Distribute the quizzes and read through them with the students
to be sure they understand the questions.

2. Administer the quiz. As they hand in their work, you may orally
quiz the students on the Memorization Questions from this chapter.

3. After all the quizzes have been handed in, review the correct
answers with the class. Repeat steps 1–3 for the unit test.

Conclude

1. Lead the students in singing "Glorious things of thee are spoken," _Adoremus Hymnal_, #563.

2. End class by leading the students in praying the Nicene Creed.

Aims

The students' understanding of the material covered in this chapter and unit will be reviewed and
assessed.

Materials

- Quiz 4, Appendix,
  p. A-4

- Unit 1 Test, Appen-
  dix, pp. A-5–A-6

Optional:
- "Glorious things of
  thee are spoken,"
  Adoremus Hymnal,
  #563

Review

1. The students should understand God's revelation. They must know the definition of revelation,
the periods of revelation, the sources of revelation, and to whom revelation has been entrusted.

2. The students should be able to identify the
Apostolic Fathers, the Church Fathers, and the
Doctors of the Church.

3. The students should be able to write out one of
the Church's creeds from memory.

4. The students should know the number of councils. They should know from memory the names,
dates, and doctrines taught in the first seven
councils.

5. The students should be able to give a biography
of either a Father or Doctor of the Church.

6. The students should be able to explain encyclicals, the _sensus fidei_, and the development of
doctrine.

CHAPTER FIVE
CHURCH AUTHORITY: TEACHING, GOVERNING

Catechism of the Catholic Church References

Bishops: 881, 883, 886, 891
Church's Hierarchical Constitution: 871–96, 934–39
Ecclesial Ministry: 874–79
Episcopal College and Its Head, the Pope: 880–87
    Task of Teaching and the Gift of Infallibility:
    888–92
    Task of Governing: 894–86
Heritage of Faith Entrusted to the Whole Church: 84–98
Hierarchy: 879, 911
Magisterium of the Church: 85–87, 100, 889–91
    Dogmas of Faith: 88–90

Freedom from Error: 889–91
Growth in Understanding the Faith: 94–95
Infallibility: 891, 2035
Man's Freedom: 1730–48
Mystery of Faith: 42, 50, 158, 206, 230, 234, 237, 1066
Pope and Bishops: Successors to Peter and the Apostles:
861–62, 880–87, 935–38
Precepts of the Church: 2041–43
Primacy of Pope: 832, 891, 2035
Supernatural Sense of Faith: 91–93, 101

Scripture References

The Truth Will Make You Free: Jn 8:32
Infallibility: Jn 14:26

Jesus Gives the Church Governing Authority: Mt 18:15–18

Summary of Lesson Content

Lesson 1

The primacy of Peter is reflected in the hierarchy of the Church. The Bishop of Rome is the Vicar of Christ, above the other bishops (successors of the apostles). The hierarchy shares in the duties of teaching, sanctifying, and governing the Church.

Lesson 3

Infallibility is a charism given by the Holy Spirit (the Spirit of Truth) to protect the Church from error. Infallibility is exercised in ordinary and extraordinary ways to protect the Church from error in matters of salvation (faith and morals). The Pope alone, and the bishops in union with him, share the charism of infallibility. This charism is exercised by the Magisterium.

Lesson 2

Freedom is found in the assent to the true and the choice of the good. The Church is the greatest promoter of freedom for she identifies the true and the good and she is infallible in matters of faith and morals (all that is necessary for salvation).

Lesson 4

The Church has authority in matters of discipline. She has the right and duty to formulate rules for her members (for their good). These rules do not pertain to our beliefs, but to our actions. These rules are changeable under the direction of the Magisterium. As Catholics, we are bound to obey the Church's proper authority.

LESSON ONE: HIERARCHY

Aims

The students will learn that the primacy of Peter is reflected in the hierarchy of the Church. The Bishop of Rome is the Vicar of Christ, above the other bishops (successors of the apostles). The hierarchy shares in the duties of teaching, sanctifying, and governing the Church.

Materials

- *Activity Book*, p. 17   Optional:
  - "Faith of our fathers!" *Adoremus Hymnal*, #603

Begin

Begin class with a review of the Sacrament of Holy Orders:

- *Instituted by Christ at the Last Supper with the words "Do this in remembrance of me"*
- *Matter: man*
- *Form: prayer of ordination*
- *Minister: bishop*
- *Three degrees: bishop, priest, and deacon*

CHAPTER 5

Authority in the Church: Teaching and Governing

Let every person be subject to the governing authorities. For there is no authority except from God, and those that exist have been instituted by God.

Romans 13:1

We have already seen that Christ gave his apostles a supernatural authority. He also said very solemnly: "All authority in heaven and earth has been given to me. Go therefore and make disciples of all nations. . ." (Mt 28:18–19). He thus commissioned the apostles to teach and govern his Church, with Peter at their head.

The Pope and the bishops as their successors form the Church's hierarchy. A **hierarchy** is a ranking of those in authority. This ranking in the Church comes to us from Christ. The basic structure was laid down by him and, as the Church grew, the structure was expanded and developed.

At the head of this hierarchy is the **Pope**, the successor of St. Peter, the bishop of Rome, and the visible head of the universal Church. The Pope has **primacy**, or the "first place," in the Church. He holds the primary authority to teach, govern, and sanctify all members of the Church. The Pope is the visible head of the Church. He represents Christ, the invisible head.

United with the Pope in governing the Church are the successors of the apostles, the bishops. With the Pope the bishops are the most important authorities and teachers in the Church. Each **bishop** is a shepherd, deriving his authority from Christ, and he is responsible for governing the local church, one portion of the whole flock.

This is a pastoral work to which they dedicate themselves. It is important for us to understand that in governing they are performing a great service for our salvation. The shepherds are serving their flock, following the example of humble service which was given when Jesus washed the feet of his disciples. In fact, one of the Pope's titles is *Servus Servorum Dei*, which means "servant of the servants of God."

The Pope and the bishops exercise their authority whenever they teach the faithful in their care. Our Lord commanded his apostles to teach all that he had taught. Consequently, the bishops as their successors are fulfilling Our Lord's command when they exercise their teaching office.

32

Develop

1. Read paragraphs 1–6 (up to Freedom, Authority, and Truth).

2. Christ had a supernatural authority. We know this by his power to perform miracles, forgive sins, and reveal God. We can see it in his plan for salvation and by his Resurrection. He said that all authority on heaven and earth had been given to him. Using this authority, he founded the Church upon the apostles.

3. The Church has a hierarchy: the Pope and bishops in union with him. This ranking comes from Christ. He provided the original hierarchical structure which has developed over time with the needs of the Church.

4. The Pope is the head of the hierarchy. This is called the primacy of Peter, since the Pope is the successor of Peter. He holds the primary authority to teach, govern, and sanctify all

members of the Church. He is thus the visible head of the Church, representing Christ (the invisible head) on earth.

5. United with the Pope are the bishops (successors of the apostles). Each bishop has his authority from Christ, as well, and is responsible for governing a local church (diocese).

6. Priests and deacons, although they share in the Sacrament of Holy Orders, are dependent upon their bishop, and they are his representatives to the parishes in his diocese. They share in the teaching, sanctifying, and governing ministry of the bishop, though it is not their own. This is why they promise obedience to the bishop in their ordinations.

7. Have the students discuss their duty of obedience to the legitimate authorities of the Church. Who are these authorities? How is this authority exercised?

Name:_____

Authority in the Church

Answer the following questions in complete sentences.

1. With what authority did Christ institute the Church?

   <u>Christ instituted the Church with his own authority.</u>

2. What authority did he give to his apostles?

   <u>Christ gave his apostles a supernatural authority to teach all that he had taught.</u>

3. What did Jesus commission his apostles to do?

   <u>Jesus commissioned his apostles to make disciples of all nations.</u>

4. Who forms the hierarchy of the Church?

   <u>The Pope and bishops form the hierarchy of the Church.</u>

5. Who is the Pope? What is Papal Primacy?

   <u>The Pope is the Bishop of Rome, successor to Saint Peter and the visible head of the Church.</u>

6. How is he *Servus servorum Dei*?

   <u>The Pope is Servus servorum Dei since he governs us in humble service.</u>

7. Who are the bishops?

   <u>The bishops are successors of the apostles. They are shepherds who govern a portion of the local church.</u>

Faith and Life Series • Grade 8 • Chapter 5 • Lesson 1　　17

Reinforce

1. Have the students work on *Activity Book*, p. 17.

2. Give the students time to work on the Memorization Questions and Words to Know.

3. Have the students write letters to their bishop, thanking him for his service to all in the diocese.

4. The students should research the Pope and learn about his work for the Church. They may research different popes throughout Church history to see their important role in the salvation of mankind.

Conclude

1. Teach the students to sing "Faith of our fathers!" *Adoremus Hymnal,* #603.

2. End class by leading the students in the prayer to Saint Michael the Archangel.

Preview

In the next lesson, the students will learn about infallibility.

SERVUS SERVORUM DEI

The office of the papacy has many titles. We may refer to the man who holds it as Pope, Bishop of Rome, Vicar of Christ, Supreme Pontiff, Successor of Peter, Holy Father, etc. Another traditional title is *Servus Servorum Dei*, which is Latin for Servant of the Servants of God. Pope Gregory the Great (540–604) was the first to use this title commonly. It refers to the humility of the office, and reminds us that we are servants of God and that God instituted the papacy to help us on our way to him. Just like Jesus, Christ's Vicar is here "not to be served but to serve" (Mt 20:28).

NOTES

_____

_____

_____

_____

_____

_____

_____

_____

_____

_____

_____

LESSON TWO: FREEDOM

Aims

The students will learn that freedom is found in the assent to the true and the choice of the good. The Church is the greatest promoter of freedom, for she identifies the true and the good and she is infallible in matters of faith and morals (all that is necessary for salvation).

Materials

• *Activity Book*, p. 18   Optional:
                      • "Faith of our fathers!"
                       Adoremus Hymnal,
                       #603

Begin

Write on the board: INFALLIBILITY
   I. What it is not:
      A. Perfect judgment on everything
      B. Impeccability
   II. What it is:
      A. Extraordinary
         1. *Ex Cathedra*
         2. Ecumenical Councils
      B. Ordinary
         1. Encyclicals
         2. Synods
Leave this visible for the next lesson also.

Freedom, Authority, and Truth

Freedom is one of the values we most cherish. It is given to us by God and belongs to human dignity. The Church is the great defender of human freedom. You might think that because there is a teaching authority in the Church, you have less freedom. We have to think whether we mean freedom *from* reality or freedom *within* reality. Many people confuse the two. It would, for instance, be foolish to ignore the reality of the law of gravity and in the name of freedom walk off the roof of a tall building. You want to live in reality, which means you want to know the truth. By knowing the truth, you will be truly free.

It is a gift of God's mercy to have an authority whose teaching, inspired by the Holy Spirit, is truth. Christ said: "The truth will make you free" (Jn 8:32).

Free from Error

Because the teachings of Jesus Christ showed the way to eternal salvation, it is extremely important that they remain in their essentials free from error. And so, Our Lord promised the Church, ". . . I am with you always, to the close of the age" (Mt 28:20). He also promised to send the Holy Spirit, who ". . . will teach you all things, and bring to your remembrance all that I have said to you" (Jn 14:26).

With these and other words Our Lord left his Church with the great gift of **infallibility**. Infallibility means that the constant teaching of the Church about matters of faith or morals, as contained in the deposit of divine revelation, will be free from error. This infallibility was given to the whole Church for our benefit so that we could have certainty of truth. If we reflect briefly on the history of the Church, we will see that, even in times of great confusion, the Church's teaching remained essentially unchanged. Why? There is only one explanation —the Holy Spirit given to the Church by Christ has protected and guided the teaching authority of the Church.

Infallibility belongs to the whole Church, which means that the true Church of Christ can never teach a doctrine that is contrary to what Christ taught. But infallibility also belongs in a special way to the legitimate authorities of the Church—the Pope and the bishops. Whenever

33

Develop

1. Read paragraphs 7–11 (up to Infallibility of the Pope).

2. Explain to the students that freedom is found in truth. Use the example of a web of lies: If you tell one lie, you often will tell many lies, or need an accomplice to verify your lie, etc. True freedom is an assent to the true and the choice of the good. We can only serve one master—we must choose God's way. In choosing the good and the true, it becomes easier to avoid sin. In this we are truly free from sin/evil and free for God. This is what is meant by "The truth will make you free" (Jn 8:32).

3. God the Father and God the Son sent the Holy Spirit—the Spirit of Truth—"who will teach you all things, and bring to your remembrance all that I have said to you" (Jn 14:26). In this promise, Christ's Church is given the great gift of infallibility—the gift of freedom from error (for truth). Infallibility ensures that the constant teaching of the Church about matters of faith and morals, as contained in the deposit of divine revelation, will be free from error. This gift is given to the Church so we can have certainty of truth and the means of salvation.

4. Infallibility ensures that the true Church of Christ can never teach a doctrine that is contrary to what Christ taught. It belongs in a special way to the authorities of the Church (the Magisterium).

5. Infallibility is a protection from error in teaching on matters of faith and morals. It does not mean that the Pope or the Pope and bishops together can make up anything and that it will be true. Infallibility is not to be confused with impeccability or sinlessness. The leaders of the Church are not sinless—although they should strive for holiness and be an example for the rest of the Church.

Free from Error

Answer the following questions in complete sentences.

1. Why is it so important that Church teachings remain free from error?
   It is so important that Church teaching remain free from error because she teaches us the way to salvation.

2. What is infallibility?
   Infallibility is the gift of the Holy Spirit that protects the Church from teaching error in matters of faith and morals.

3. Does obedience to the Church make one more or less free? Explain.
   Obedience to the Church makes one more free because we are living in reality. We should always strive to understand the teachings of the Church but if we do not, we must trust that the Lord knows what he is doing and that it is for our good.

18   *Faith and Life Series • Grade 8 • Chapter 5 • Lesson 2*

Reinforce

1. Have the students work on *Activity Book*, p. 18.

2. Give the students time to work on their Memorization Questions and Words to Know.

3. The students should look up passages from Scripture that discuss the gift of infallibility.

4. The students should consider the true exercise of freedom. It is found in the Christian way of life, including the moral life. Just as a DVD player comes with a user's manual—the rules of the device—so too, the moral life has rules for us to follow. If we choose to follow them, we will be free to live in union with God. We can break the rules; we can put a slice of bologna in a DVD player —it fits! This action breaks the rules of the manual and the DVD player. So, too, we can break God's Commandments, but we will harm ourselves and others breaking our union with God. The effects of sin make it harder for us to live in that union.

Conclude

1. Lead the students in singing "Faith of our fathers!" *Adoremus Hymnal,* #603.

2. End class by leading the students in the prayer to Saint Michael the Archangel.

Preview

In the next lesson, the students will learn about the exercise of infallibility.

FREEDOM FOR THE TRUTH

"When you were slaves of sin, you were free in regard to righteousness. But then what return did you get from the things of which you are now ashamed? The end of those things is death. But now that you have been set free from sin and have become slaves of God, the return you get is sanctification and its end, eternal life."   —Rom 6:20–22

"The law of the Spirit of life in Christ Jesus has set me free from the law of sin and death."   —Rom 8:2

"Where the Spirit of the Lord is, there is freedom."   —2 Cor 3:17

"For freedom Christ has set us free; stand fast therefore, and do not submit again to a yoke of slavery."
                                                                                                                                               —Gal 5:1

"Live as free men, yet without using your freedom as a pretext for evil; but live as servants of God. Honor all men. Love the brotherhood. Fear God."   —1 Pet 2:16

LESSON THREE: INFALLIBILITY

Aims

The students will learn that infallibility is a charism given by the Holy Spirit (Spirit of Truth) to protect the Church from error. Infallibility is exercised in ordinary and extraordinary ways to protect the Church from error in matters of salvation (faith and morals). The Pope and the bishops in union with him share the charism of infallibility. This charism is exercised by the Magisterium.

Materials

- *Activity Book*, p. 19

Optional:
- "Faith of our fathers!" *Adoremus Hymnal,* #603

Begin

Today, we will learn the two exercises of infallibility. Review why we need the gift of infallibility. We need infallibility to protect us from error, so that we may live in the freedom of God in his truth.

Review the chart written on the board from the previous lesson.

the bishops in union with the Pope teach or proclaim a matter of faith or morals as something which must be definitively held, these teachings are infallible. They are protected from error. The bishops with the Pope reaffirm in their own dioceses the constant and certain teachings of the Church on matters of faith and morals.

Infallibility of the Pope

Infallibility also belongs in an even more special way to the successor of St. Peter, the Pope. When the Pope speaks alone is he always infallible? Obviously not. He is infallible in very definite circumstances. For instance, he is infallible when the following conditions—which are called extraordinary—are met: (1) The Pope must be speaking on matters of faith or morals; (2) he must be speaking to the *whole* Church, not a particular group or segment of the Church; (3) he must be speaking **ex cathedra** (literally, from the chair of authority),

34

which means he is speaking as Pope, not merely as a bishop or member of the Church; and (4) he must be intending to use his authority to pronounce an unchangeable decision.

The doctrine of papal infallibility has been accepted, at least implicitly, by the Church from the beginning. It follows from Christ's promise to St. Peter making him the head of the Church. To preserve effectively the teachings of Christ, St. Peter and his successors would need this guarantee from Christ. It was not, however, *defined*, or officially declared a dogma of the Church, until 1870 at the First Vatican Council. (This represents an example of the *development of doctrine*, which we discussed in the last chapter.) Pius IX exercised this authority when he defined the doctrine of the Immaculate Conception in 1854, *before* Vatican I. Pius XII used this gift when the doctrine of Our Lady's Assumption was declared in this manner in 1950.

Thus two Popes, almost a century apart, defined on their authority a dogma of faith, one definition coming before and one after the dogma of papal infallibility itself was defined. This illustrates an important point. A formal, infallible definition, either by the Pope himself or by an ecumenical council of the Church, introduces no new teaching, no new doctrine. The Pope is not infallible because a general council said so; on the contrary, a general council could say so only because the Pope *is* infallible and the Church has always believed it. Our Lady's Immaculate Conception and Assumption are not true because a Pope declared them so; a Pope could declare them so only because they *are* true and the Church has always believed them. Such pronouncements are simply formal and final definitions of doctrines always held by the Church.

It is important to note two things about papal infallibility. First, not everything the Pope says is infallible. He must be speaking accord-

---

Develop

1. Read paragraphs 12–17 (up to "The Church Governs").

2. The Church's infallibility in teaching is exercised by the extraordinary and the universal and ordinary teaching office (Magisterium) of the Church. The extraordinary Magisterium is exercised in two ways.

- By the Pope alone, when teaching *ex cathedra*, defines a matter of faith or morals as something to be held by the whole Church. This teaching is infallible. Two recent examples of such infallible papal teaching are the definitions of the dogmas of the Immaculate Conception and the bodily Assumption of Mary. On December 8, 1854, Pope Pius IX defined as revealed by God that Mary was conceived without original sin (Immaculate Conception). On November 1, 1950, Pope Pius XII defined as revealed by God the truth that Mary was assumed body and soul into heaven (Assumption of Mary).

- By an ecumenical council when defining matters of faith and morals. An ecumenical council is a meeting of all the bishops, in union with the Pope. The Council of Nicaea (325) is an example of an ecumenical council that taught in an infallible manner. It infallibly declared the Son, as God, to be equal with the Father.

3. The universal and ordinary teaching office or Magisterium is infallible when the bishops, united with the Pope and each other, all teach that the matter of faith or morals is to be held definitively by all members of the Church.

Name:_____

Magisterium

Answer the following questions in complete sentences.

1. Explain the following:

   Extraordinary Magisterium:

   The Extraordinary Magisterium refers to the formal exercise of the teaching office of the Pope and the bishops.

   Ordinary Magisterium:

   The Ordinary Magisterium refers to the normal, regular exercise of the Church's teaching office.

2. Define the following words.

   Ex cathedra:

   Ex cathedra is when the Pope alone, intending to use his authority, defines or proclaims a doctrine of faith or morals. We are bound to believe this. Literally it means "from the chair of authority".

   Doctrine:

   Doctrines are those elements which are essential beliefs of our faith.

   Synod:

   A synod is a meeting of some bishops with the Pope to discuss the doctrinal and pastoral needs of the Church.

   Magisterium:

   The Magisterium is the teaching office of the Church.

3. Write a paragraph on the infallibility of the Pope. Include the four conditions an infallible papal teaching must have.

   Answers will vary.

Faith and Life Series • Grade 8 • Chapter 5 • Lesson 3   19

Reinforce

1. Have the students work on *Activity Book*, p. 19.

2. Give the students time to work on their Memorization Questions and Words to Know.

3. Have the students dramatize exercises of infallibility, both ordinary and extraordinary:
   • Pope teaching *ex cathedra*
   • Ecumenical council

Conclude

1. Lead the students in singing "Faith of our fathers!" *Adoremus Hymnal*, #603.

2. End class by leading the students in the prayer to Saint Michael the Archangel.

Preview

In the next lesson, the students will learn about the governing Church.

NOTES

_____
_____
_____
_____
_____
_____
_____
_____
_____
_____
_____

LESSON FOUR: GOVERNING

Aims

The students will learn that the Church has authority in matters of discipline. She has the right and duty to formulate rules for her members (for their good). These rules do not pertain to our beliefs, but to our actions. These rules are changeable under the direction of the Magisterium. As Catholics, we are bound to obey the Church's proper authority.

Materials

- *Activity Book*, p. 20

Optional:
- "Faith of our fathers!" *Adoremus Hymnal*, #603

Begin

Review that the Church's authority was given to her by Christ himself. This authority is exercised in teaching and government.

Read Mt 18:15–18 as an example of Jesus giving the Church a governing authority—binding in heaven and on earth.

---

ing to the conditions laid down. It follows that his private opinions or statements, even those on faith or morals, are not infallible. It is only when he speaks as the Vicar of Christ that he can speak infallibly. Second, infallibility should not be confused with sinlessness, or **impeccability**, on the part of the Pope. The Pope is a human being and, like all of us, he can sin. We have been blessed recently with Popes whose personal holiness is great; in fact, one of them, Pius X, is a canonized saint. Thus, we sometimes expect sinlessness in the Pope and confuse this notion with infallibility.

Magisterium

The teaching office, or duty, of the Church, known as the **Magisterium**, is exercised in two ways: extraordinary and ordinary. The *Extraordinary Magisterium* refers to the solemn and formal exercise of the teaching office of the Pope and the bishops and it is always authoritative. It is infallible when the Pope alone *ex cathedra*, or an ecumenical council of the bishops of the world with the Pope, defines or proclaims a doctrine of faith or morals. We have already seen that both of these are rare; there have been twenty-one general councils in approximately two thousand years, and not every one of these councils has proclaimed infallible doctrine.

The *Ordinary Magisterium* refers to the normal, regular exercise of the Church's teaching office, and it, too, is always authoritative. For this, various forms of communication have been used throughout history. In our times we see the ordinary magisterium used in encyclical letters of the Pope, statements from a **synod** (a meeting of some bishops with the Pope), and individual instruction from bishops to the faithful in their dioceses.

Although the bishops, taken individually, do not enjoy the privilege of infallibility, they do, however, proclaim infallibly the doctrine of Christ. . . .

When, even though dispersed throughout the world but preserving for all that amongst themselves and with Peter's successor the bond of communion, in their authoritative teaching concerning matters of faith and morals, they are in agreement that a particular teaching is to be held definitively and absolutely (LG, 25).

The Church Governs

In our consideration of the Church's authority so far we have been concerned with matters of *doctrine*. Doctrines of our faith are those elements that are the essential beliefs of our faith. The creeds contain many of these doctrines. But the authority of the Church is not limited to matters of doctrine, on faith and morals. The Church also has authority to govern her members. This authority is exercised in matters of *discipline*. The Church, like any so-

> ". . . If I ask anyone: 'Would you rather have your joy in truth or in falsehood?' he would say: 'In truth', with just as little hesitation as he would say that he wants to be happy. And certainly the happy life is joy in truth, which means joy in you, who are truth, God, *my light, health of my countenance, my God*."
>
> —St. Augustine, *Confessions*, bk. X, chap. 23

35

Develop

1. Read paragraphs 18–24 (to the end of the chapter).

2. The Church teaches doctrines and moral laws that come from God. She also needs to create rules to help her members believe what God has revealed and to obey God's laws. These rules are sometimes called disciplines of the Church. Examples include:
- Days of fast and abstinence
- Holy days of obligation
- The length of the Eucharistic fast

3. Doctrine concerns things revealed by God. Doctrines revealed by God cannot be changed, even by those in authority in the Church. Examples include:
- Beliefs about the Trinity, the Incarnation, and the Primacy of Peter and his successors
- The Ten Commandments
- The matter and form of the sacraments

4. Disciplines of the Church may change, depending on the needs of the Church. Examples of disciplines that have changed include:
- The option of receiving Holy Communion in the hand or on the tongue, rather than only on the tongue
- The language in which Holy Mass is celebrated

5. As Catholics, we should obey the authorities of the Church in matters of doctrine (faith and morals) and discipline. We should obey Church authorities as we would Christ himself. We should strive to understand the Church's teaching and laws and to follow them. Use the analogy of soldiers in an army, or football players obeying a coach. We should have trust that those in authority know what is best for us and try to understand the reasons for what they tell us. We should be united with Church authorities in pursuing what is good.

Name:_____

The Church Governs

Answer the following questions in complete sentences.

1. What are doctrines of our faith?

   <u>Doctrines of our faith are those elements that are essential</u>
   <u>beliefs of our faith.</u>

2. How does the Church exercise her authority in discipline?

   <u>The Church exercises her authority in discipline by form-</u>
   <u>ulating rules for her members which are for their good.</u>
   <u>These rules do not pertain to our beliefs but to our action.</u>

3. Why do we follow the Church's rule on fasting?

   <u>We follow the Church's rule on fasting because we believe</u>
   <u>the Church should direct us in such matters for our spiritual</u>
   <u>good.</u>

4. What are other examples of Church authority in discipline?

   <u>Other examples of the Church's authority in discipline are</u>
   <u>the Church's law that requires us to particate in Mass on</u>
   <u>certain Holy Days and the rules concerning certain liturgical</u>
   <u>rites.</u>

5. What is obedience?

   <u>Obedience is when we comply with the will of another who</u>
   <u>has the authority to command us.</u>

6. How must the faithful in the Church act like players on a football team?

   <u>Answers will vary.</u>

20   *Faith and Life Series • Grade 8 • Chapter 5 • Lesson 4*

Reinforce

1. Have the students work on *Activity Book*, p. 20.

2. Give the students time to work on the Memorization Questions and Words to Know and prepare for the quiz.

3. Have the students research examples of unchanging doctrine (note that the development of doctrine does not change doctrines, but further defines what is known) and changing disciplines.

4. The students should choose and research a topic (faith, morals, or discipline) that they find difficult to understand, embrace, or explain to others. They should be able to explain why we must be obedient to the Church's authority.

Conclude

1. Lead the students in singing "Faith of our fathers!" *Adoremus Hymnal,* #603.

2. End class by leading the students in the prayer to Saint Michael the Archangel.

Preview

In the next lesson, the students' understanding of the material covered in this chapter and unit will be reviewed and assessed.

NOTES

_____
_____
_____
_____
_____
_____
_____
_____
_____
_____
_____

ciety, has the right and the need to formulate rules for her members for their own good, to lead them to holiness of life. These rules do not pertain to our beliefs but to our actions.

If we look at some of our Church disciplines we can see how the Church governs us. For example, the Church tells us that we may not eat meat on Ash Wednesday or the Fridays of Lent. This is a matter of discipline and not part of our creed. But we follow this rule because we believe that the Church should direct us in such matters for our spiritual good. Another example is the Church law that requires us to *fast* (abstain from eating), except for good reason, for one hour before receiving Holy Communion. Other examples of the Church's authority to govern are the obligation to participate in Mass on certain Holy Days and the rules concerning certain liturgical rites. Can you think of others? Each of these laws is a legitimate use of the Church's governing power to ensure that Christ's Church and her members will remain strong.

One further point should be made about the distinction between matters of discipline and matters of doctrine. Matters of doctrine are those things in our faith that have been revealed to us by God and thus cannot be changed by us. They cannot even be changed by those in authority in the Church. But matters of discipline are those practices that have developed over time, laws made by the proper authorities, and thus they can be changed by them. This has happened in the past and may well happen again.

Obedience

We, as faithful Catholics, have an obligation to respond properly to the Church's authority. We have an obligation to believe the doctrines of the faith if we wish to be members of the Church. We will never completely understand the great mysteries of our faith. They are rich in meaning and above us, and we must strive to learn more about them, to love them, to study them, and to exercise the virtue of faith.

In matters of discipline we must be *obedient*. Obedience means that we should comply with the will of another who has the authority to command us. We have already seen that the Church has such authority from Christ. Remember that the Church speaks for Christ; the obedience and respect that we show to Christ's representatives are the same obedience and respect we would show to Christ himself.

There may be times when a particular Church law seems unclear or unwise to us. What do we do then? The following analogy will help you understand. The captain of an army is in a position of authority, and the rest of the company must listen to him and obey him when he gives orders. In fact, they trust him to make decisions wisely. While they must understand the orders, it is not necessary that they understand why he makes a particular

Prayer

"Almighty and eternal God, you guide all things by your word, you govern all Christian people. In your love protect the Pope you have chosen for us. Under his leadership deepen our faith and make us better Christians. We ask this through Christ our Lord. *Amen.*"

(General Intercessions for Holy Week)

36

order at a certain time. The other soldiers try to understand why an order is made, but if they cannot, they assume that the captain knows what he is doing. In order to win the battle they must follow his directions.

The faithful in the Church must act like soldiers in an army. We should strive to understand the spirit that animates the law and then obey it. If we cannot understand it right away, we must presume that those in authority do. This is not blind obedience, for we have first tried to understand and then submitted ourselves to those who do. We should try to understand the Church's laws and to obey them in a spirit of charity. The authority of the Church comes from Christ, who told his apostles that his power was being given to them.

Words to Know:
hierarchy Pope primacy bishop infallibility *ex cathedra* impeccability Magisterium synod

Q. 20 *Who is the Pope?*
The Pope is the successor of Saint Peter, the bishop of Rome, the visible head of the entire Church, and the Vicar of Jesus Christ, who is the invisible head of the Church (CCC 882).

Q. 21 *What do the Pope and the bishops united with him constitute?*
The Pope and the bishops united with him constitute the teaching body of the Church, called the Magisterium (CCC 888–89).

Q. 22 *Can the Pope teach error when he defines matters of faith and morals?*
No, the Pope cannot teach error when he defines matters of faith and morals because he has the gift of infallibility (CCC 891).

Q. 23 *Can the Pope and the bishops united with him teach error when they define matters of faith and morals?*
No, the Pope and the bishops united with him cannot teach error when they define matters of faith and morals; they are infallible because "the Spirit of truth" (Jn 15:26) assists the Church continually and protects her from error (CCC 889).

Q. 24 *What is infallibility?*
Infallibility is the gift of the Holy Spirit that protects the Church from teaching errors in matters of faith and morals (CCC 890–91).

37

Q. 25 *How is the Ordinary Magisterium exercised?*
The Ordinary Magisterium is exercised when, in matters of faith and morals, there is a definitive position taught by the Church through the Pope or the bishops in union with the Pope. (CCC 88, 883, 892).

Q. 26 *How is the Extraordinary Magisterium exercised?*
The Extraordinary Magisterium is exercised in two ways: 1) when the Pope, as Supreme Pontiff of the Church, gives an authoritative universal teaching on matters of faith and morals, and 2) when all the bishops in union with the Pope give an authoritative universal teaching on matters of faith and morals through an ecumenical council (CCC 884, 891).

38

Name:

Authority in the Church: Teaching and Governing **Quiz 5**

Part I: Using the definitions below, write in the correct term.

1. Ex Cathedra — Said of the Pope when he speaks "from the chair" to bind the whole Church in matters of faith and morals

2. Immaculate — This word means to be without sin.

3. Magisterium — The extraordinary and ordinary teaching of the Church.

4. Pope — This man is the successor of the Apostle Peter and the representative of Jesus Christ on earth.

5. Hierarchy — The various levels of authority in the Church.

6. Council — The meeting of some bishops with the Pope.

7. Bishop — The "Shepherd" of a geographical area called a diocese.

8. Infallibility — A protection from teaching error in matters of faith and morals.

9. Ecumenical Council — A universal gathering of bishops with the Pope to define Church teaching.

10. Obedience — Submission to the authorities of the Church in matters of doctrine and discipline.

Part II: Answer in complete sentences.

1. Explain what true freedom is. Does submitting to Church authority enhance or restrict our freedom?

   True freedom is living in reality and having control over one's actions. Submitting to Church authority enhances freedom because when we follow the Church's teachings, we are living in reality. We should always strive to understand the teachings of the Church but if we do not, we must trust that the Lord knows what he is doing and that it is for our good.

2. Can a bishop alone teach infallibly? Explain.

   The only bishop who can alone teach infallibly is the Bishop of Rome, the Pope. When bishops in union with the Pope teach or proclaim on matters of faith or morals, they teach infallibly.

Aims

The students' understanding of the material covered in this chapter will be reviewed and assessed.

Materials

- Quiz 5, Appendix, p. A-7

  Optional:
  - "Faith of our fathers!" *Adoremus Hymnal* #603

Assess

1. Distribute the quizzes and read through them with the students to be sure they understand the questions.

2. Administer the quiz. As they hand in their work, you may orally quiz the students on the Memorization Questions from this chapter.

3. After all the quizzes have been handed in, review the correct answers with the class.

Conclude

1. Lead the students in singing "Faith of our fathers!" *Adoremus Hymnal*, #603.

2. End class by leading the students in a prayer for the Pope.

Review

1. The students should be able to explain the hierarchy of the Church and the primacy of Peter.

2. The students should understand the authority of the Church to teach and govern.

3. The students should have a sound understanding of true freedom.

4. The students should be able to explain infallibility and know how it is exercised.

5. The students should understand the difference between doctrine and discipline.

6. The students should understand their responsibility of obedience to the Church.

CHAPTER SIX
THE VISIBLE HIERARCHICAL CHURCH

Catechism of the Catholic Church References

Apostolic Succession: 77–79, 861–62, 869
Church's Hierarchical Constitution: 871–96, 934–39
Church's Origin, Foundation, and Mission: 758–69, 773
Diocese: 833
Ecclesial Ministry: 874–79
Episcopal College and Its Head, the Pope: 880–87
Mission of the Apostles: 858–60, 869
Obedience: 144–49, 176
Pope and Bishops: Successors to Peter and the Apostles: 861–62, 880–87, 935–38

Priesthood of the Old Covenant: 1539–43
Sacrament of Holy Orders: 1536–1600
Sacrament of Orders in the Economy of Salvation: 1539–53, 1590–92
Structure of the Church: 1556–59
Three Degrees of the Sacrament of Holy Orders: 1554–71, 1593–96
The Twelve Apostles: 551–53
Unique Priesthood of Christ: 1544–45

Scripture References

Matthias: Acts 1:15–26

Summary of Lesson Content

Lesson 1

Christ gave the Church the mission to evangelize all nations, implying the need for successors. In the Bible, the selection of Matthias to replace Judas reveals that the apostles understood this and began using the powers entrusted to them by Christ.

The Council of Jerusalem demonstrates the Church's authority and is an early exercise of infallibility.

Lesson 3

Priests and deacons share in the bishop's power and authority to meet the needs of the members of the diocese in specific parishes.

Lesson 2

The Church is divided into dioceses. Each diocese is led by a bishop, whose role is to teach, sanctify, and govern.

An archbishop is charged with an important diocese, usually the oldest in a geographical area.

The Pope is the bishop of the diocese of Rome.

Lesson 4

Monsignors and cardinals are positions of honor bestowed by the Pope.

The Pope is elected from the college of cardinals, many of whom serve him in the curia.

LESSON ONE: APOSTOLIC

Aims

The students will learn that Christ gave the Church the mission to evangelize all nations, implying the need for successors. In the Bible, the selection of Matthias to replace Judas reveals that the apostles understood this and began using the powers entrusted to them by Christ.

They will learn that the Council of Jerusalem demonstrates the Church's authority and an early exercise of infallibility.

Materials

- *Activity Book*, p. 21

- List of all Popes, Appendix, pp. B-1–B2

Optional:
- "God of our fathers, whose almighty hand," *Adoremus Hymnal*, #625

Begin

Have the students imagine that they are the apostles. They recognize that they cannot go to all ends of the earth: they are aging and will need others to replace them. What would they look for in selecting a new "apostle" or bishop? The students should consider their criteria and have mock interviews for the position.

CHAPTER 6

The Visible Hierarchical Church

And they cast lots for them, and the lot fell on Matthias; and he was enrolled with the eleven apostles.

Acts 1:26

We have seen that Christ founded his Church and willed her basic structure. He built her on Peter. "You are Peter, and on this rock I will build my church" (Mt 16:18). Our Lord himself gave us the outlines of the Church's hierarchy. As is mentioned numerous times in the Gospels, Christ chose twelve apostles, and he gave them the power to carry on his work —teaching, governing, and through the sacraments sanctifying the faithful. He said to the apostles,

Whatever you bind on earth shall be bound in heaven and whatever you loose on earth shall be loosed in heaven (Mt 16:19).

Successors to the Apostles

Christ gave the apostles the mission of evangelizing all nations. Since *all* nations could evidently not be evangelized by the apostles during their lifetime, Jesus was of course addressing all those who would be their successors down through the centuries.

The apostles also understood him in this way, because immediately after the Ascension, as recorded in the Acts of the Apostles (1:15–26), Peter stood up and told the disciples that he and they must choose someone to replace Judas. They chose Matthias. Thus they began to exercise their power to bind and loose by electing the first successor to an apostle.

Christ in his wisdom chose this structure. He knew that the Church, like any society, would need authority to govern. Without it the Church would be in chaos. In the Old Testament we also see a certain amount of structure among the chosen people. There were different tribes with clearly defined territories, and, sometimes, special functions. For instance, priests came only from the tribe of Levi. There were leaders chosen not by men but by God, such as Abraham, Moses, and David. In the New Testament, which is the fulfillment of the Old, we see the establishment of a hierarchical Church, with divine authority. It is important to realize that the Church is not a federal union or democracy where majority opinion prevails, a corporation where managerial skills are uppermost, or an organization where efficiency is first. The Church may use human wisdom, but she is far above human wisdom. She is supernatural in her essential structure. God says, "As the heavens are higher than the

39

Develop

1. Read paragraphs 1–7 (up to Church Structure).

2. Discuss how Matthias was selected to replace Judas. Read Acts 1:15–26. What were the apostles' requirements for Judas' replacement? How was Matthias selected? (How was God seen in this decision-making process?) You may dramatize these events. Other questions you may ask include:
- *How did the apostles have the authority to choose another apostle?*
- *What does it mean that Matthias was enrolled with the other apostles? (Ordination to fullness of Holy Orders)*

3. In the Old Testament, we see instructions for God's chosen people. How? (twelve tribes, levitical priesthood, God called specific leaders, etc.)

4. Why can we call the Church a theocracy? God is her head, and she has his authority, which directs the life of the

Church. She is not run by elections or popular opinion; she is not a corporation. This means that we cannot work our way up the hierarchical chain, we cannot change doctrine depending upon our opinion or fancy, and a majority of bishops cannot make decisions that are contrary to the teachings of Christ. Christ is the head of his Church.

5. Review apostolic succession using the Chalk Talk on p. 27 of this manual.

6. Using the Chalk Talk at right, show how the Church hierarchy was foreshadowed in the Old Testament.

7. Using Appendix pp. B-1–B-2 (list of all popes), show how the Pope is the successor of Peter and that this chain is unbroken from the time of Christ.

Name:_____

Successors of the Apostles

Answer the following questions in complete sentences.

1. Who did Jesus establish as the head of his Church?
   <u>Jesus established Peter as head of the Church.</u>

2. What role did the other apostles have in the hierarchy of the Church?
   <u>The other apostles had the role of teaching, governing, and sanctifying the faithful through the sacraments.</u>

3. How did St. Peter know that he was to choose a successor for Judas?
   <u>St. Peter knew he should choose a successor to Judas because he knew Christ wanted all nations at all times to receive his message. Thus, Christ wanted successors for his apostles.</u>

4. Why did Jesus establish a hierarchical structure for his Church?
   <u>Jesus established a hierarchical structure because he knew the Church would need his authority to govern.</u>

5. Compare the structure of the Church with the structure of the Jewish religion in the Old Testament.
   <u>Answers will vary.</u>

6. Is the Church human? Is the Church supernatural?
   <u>The Church may use human wisdom, but she is far above human wisdom. She is supernatural in her essential structure.</u>

7. How did the authority of the apostles get passed on to other bishops, including our bishops today?
   <u>The apostles passed on their authority to bishops, making them their successors. The bishops today have received this same power.</u>

Faith and Life Series • Grade 8 • Chapter 6 • Lesson 1   21

1. Have the students work on *Activity Book*, p. 21.

2. Give the students time to work on their Memorization Questions and Words to Know.

3. Have each student research a different Pope and make a presentation about him for the class. The students may dress-up in costume or create posters in order to add interest to their presentations.

Conclude

1. Teach the students to sing "God of our fathers, whose almighty hand," *Adoremus Hymnal*, #625.

2. End class by leading the students in the Prayer for Vocations below.

Preview

In the next lesson, the students will learn about Church structure.

PRAYER FOR VOCATIONS
by Pope John Paul II
from the 40th World Day of Prayer for Vocations, May 11, 2003

Mary, humble servant of God most high,
the Son to whom you gave birth has made
   you the servant of humanity.
Your life was a humble and generous
   service.

Let the young people of the third millenium
look to you, young daughter of Israel,
who have known the agitation of a young
   heart
when faced with the plan of the Eternal
   God.

Make them able to accept the invitation of
   your Son
to give their lives wholly for the glory of
   God.

Make them understand that to serve God
   satisfies the heart,
and that only in the service of God and his
   Kingdom
do we realize ourselves in accordance with
   the divine plan,
and life becomes a hymn of glory to the
   most holy Trinity. *Amen.*

CHALK TALK: DECISION-MAKERS FOR CHRIST

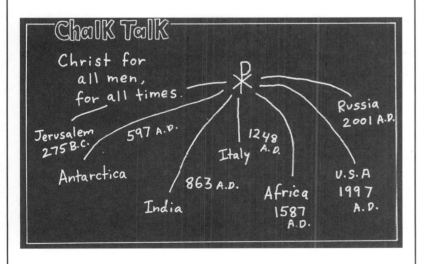

63

LESSON TWO:
CHURCH STRUCTURE

Aims

The students will learn that the Church is divided into dioceses. Each diocese is led by a bishop, whose role is to teach, sanctify, and govern.

They will learn that an archbishop is charged with an important diocese, usually the oldest in a geographical area.

They will learn that the Pope is the bishop of the diocese of Rome.

Materials

- *Activity Book*, p. 22

Optional:
- "God of our fathers, whose almighty hand," *Adoremus Hymnal*, #625

Begin

Today, the successors of the apostles are more numerous than twelve. In order for the Good News to reach all nations, many bishops were needed—to teach, sanctify, and govern the Church in each land. Today there are thousands of bishops and dioceses around the world (see box at right).

earth, so are my ways higher than your ways and my thoughts than your thoughts" (Is 55:9).

As we have seen, this hierarchical Church started to function at the very outset, after Christ's Ascension.

Later in the Acts we find the account of the Council of Jerusalem (Acts 15). At this council several of the apostles and other leaders of the early Church met to solve certain questions concerning the gentile members of the Church. Both of these incidents show us that the apostles understood Our Lord's command for them to build up the Church.

The apostles received from Christ the fullness of his powers which they, in turn, passed on to the bishops, their successors. In the early Church each bishop was responsible for the Christians in a particular area. As the Church grew, the apostles passed on their power to other men, increasing the number of bishops. It is this same power that the bishops today have received, making them the successors of the apostles.

Church Structure

Today the Church is spread throughout the world and is divided into various *dioceses*. A

40

diocese is a particular community of the faithful, usually established by geographic area. At the head of each diocese is a bishop, whose role is to teach, govern, and sanctify the faithful in his care. Some bishops have received the title of *archbishop*. An archbishop is the head of an important diocese—usually the oldest in a particular area. His diocese is then called an *archdiocese*. The archbishop has the same power and responsibility as a bishop. All of the bishops are united under the bishop of Rome—the Pope, who is the Vicar of Christ on earth. Just as Peter had authority over the other apostles, the bishop of Rome has the authority to lead the other bishops and to teach the entire Church.

As the Church continued to grow in the early days, other men—deacons and priests—were appointed and given a share in his powers by the bishop. This is still true today. Because the bishop cannot personally care for all the people within his diocese, the territory is further divided into *parishes*. The bishop then delegates his authority and the power to celebrate some of the sacraments to the *priests* in charge of these parishes. Each parish is headed by a *pastor*, who usually has one or more assistants to help him care for the spiritual

Develop

1. Read paragraph 9 (the first paragraph of Church Structure).

2. Remind the students that the Church is divided into geographical regions called dioceses. The Pope is the bishop of the diocese of Rome. What is your diocese?

3. Explain that an archdiocese is an important diocese, usually the oldest in a given area. Its leader is called an archbishop. The archbishop has the same duties as a bishop. Using the Chalk Talk, at right, explain the similarities and differences between a diocese and an archdiocese (and between bishops and archbishops).

4. Review the role of the bishop: to teach, sanctify, and govern. The bishop has the fullness of the Sacrament of Holy Orders. He is able to celebrate all seven sacraments: Baptism, Penance, Eucharist, Matrimony, and Anointing of

the Sick. He is the ordinary minister of Confirmation. Only a bishop can ordain men to Holy Orders.

5. Every bishop must report to the Pope. They work together in ministering to the needs of the Church.

6. You may discuss how a bishop is selected. A Papal Nuncio offers names to the Pope and the Pope himself selects the bishop.

7. Review that the Pope is called the Vicar of Christ (Christ's representative) on earth. He has the authority over all other bishops. He teaches, sanctifies, and governs the entire Church. What a tremendous responsibility!

Name:_____

Church Structure from the Bible

Read the following Bible verses and write a brief paragraph about the institution of Church structure.

Matthew 13:16–17; 16:13–20:

<u>Answers will vary.</u>

_____
_____
_____
_____
_____
_____
_____
_____
_____

Acts 6:2–6; 15:1–35:

_____
_____
_____
_____
_____
_____
_____
_____
_____
_____
_____
_____

Reinforce

1. Have the students work on *Activity Book*, p. 22.

2. Give the students time to work on their Memorization Questions and Words to Know.

3. Have your students research the history of your diocese. They should know important dates, historic sites/churches, the history of bishops, etc.

Conclude

1. Lead the students in singing "God of our fathers, whose almighty hand," *Adoremus Hymnal*, #625.

2. End class by leading the students in the Prayer for Vocations.

Preview

In the next lesson, the students will learn about priests and deacons.

CHALK TALK: CHURCH HIERARCHY

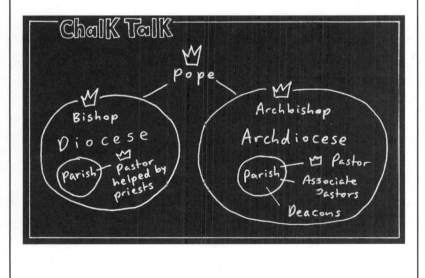

DIOCESES WORLDWIDE

Australia: Dioceses, 31; Bishops, 58
Brazil: Dioceses, 250; Bishops, 415
Canada: Dioceses, 75; Bishops, 82
Egypt: Dioceses, 12; Bishops, 16
England: Dioceses, 19; Bishops, 36
Ireland: Dioceses, 26; Bishops, 50
Japan: Dioceses, 16; Bishops, 26
New Zealand: Dioceses, 6; Bishops, 12
Philippines: Dioceses, 69; Bishops, 119
Poland: Dioceses, 41; Bishops, 121
Scotland: Dioceses, 8; Bishops, 9
South Africa: Dioceses, 25; Bishops, 37
USA: Dioceses, 194; Bishops, 278

LESSON THREE: ASSISTANTS

Aims

The students will learn that priests and deacons share in the bishop's power and authority to meet the needs of the members of the diocese in specific parishes.

Materials

- *Activity Book*, p. 23

Optional:
- "God of our fathers, whose almighty hand," *Adoremus Hymnal*, #625

Begin

Review the role of the bishop in his diocese. Ask questions to demonstrate the bishop's need for assistance, such as:

- Can the bishop celebrate all the masses in his diocese on Sunday?
- Can the bishop teach all people their religion?
- Can the bishop visit all the sick people in his diocese to ensure they receive the Anointing of the Sick?
- Can the bishop decide how every parish spends its budget?
- Can the bishop make sure every person receives dignified Christian care?

---

needs of the parishioners. As a pastor (which comes from the Latin word for shepherd), he is to lead and serve the flock entrusted to his care. The pastor's work is one of service. Christ asked the shepherds to give their very lives for those in their care. Like the bishops, priests share in the priesthood of Christ, principally by celebrating Mass and forgiving sins. They do not, however, have the power of the bishop to ordain others to the priesthood. The priest also shares in the teaching office of the bishop when he preaches at Mass or instructs the faithful of his parish.

There are also *deacons*, whose role is to assist the bishop. They, like priests, are usually assigned by the bishop to work in a parish and help in the care of the faithful. The deacon is ordained by the bishop but does not have the power to say Mass. He can administer the Sacrament of Baptism and witness marriages for the Church. He also shares in the teaching office of the bishop through his preaching. The deacon may also help the priest by visiting the sick, counseling the bereaved, or practicing other works of mercy in the diocese.

Some priests and bishops are made cardinals with the job of electing the Pope and being his closest advisors. Some priests are given the honorary title monsignor. These two groups are not steps within the sacrament of Holy Orders as the others are. **Monsignor** is an honorary title given by the Pope to many priests. The office of **cardinal** is also an honor bestowed by the Pope. At the present time most cardinals are chosen from among the bishops of the Church, although at other times in history some were priests or even laymen. The primary function of the cardinals is to elect the Pope, who has for many centuries been elected from among the *college of cardinals*.

In addition to this, the cardinals assist the Pope in the *curia*. The **curia** consists of the many administrative and judicial offices by which the Pope directs the Church. We might think of it as similar, in some ways, to the President and his various cabinet offices. Each of the curial offices is usually headed by one of the cardinals, although some may be headed by a bishop or priest.

Not all of these offices in the Church are essential. Since the bishops have the fullness of Christ's priesthood, they can provide for all of our spiritual needs. Without the bishops we would not have the sacramental life, which Our Lord gave us for our salvation. This simple structure may have been enough for the early Church. However, now that the Church has grown so large, those who assist the bishops—priests and deacons—make it possible for many more people to receive the graces of Christ.

Just as the authority of the Church comes from Christ, so Christ gave to his Church the power to sanctify. In the next chapter we will look at those sacraments that both sanctify us and incorporate us into the Church.

Words to Know:
diocese   monsignor
cardinal   curia

41

Develop

1. Read paragraphs 9–10 (the second and third paragraph under Church Structure).

2. The bishop cannot possibly meet every need in his diocese and he needs help. By ordaining men to the priesthood, he shares his power and authority to ensure that his Catholic community is being cared for.

3. Review the priesthood. Every parish has a pastor or administrator to care for its needs. Sometimes a parish has parochial vicars or associate pastors to help the pastor/ administrator in serving the parish. The priests can ordinarily celebrate five of the seven sacraments (Baptism, Penance, Eucharist, Matrimony, and Anointing of the Sick). A priest needs permission to celebrate Confirmation. A priest cannot confer Holy Orders, only a bishop can. A priest shares in the teaching office of the bishop by giving instruction in his parish (e.g., through the homily), or overseeing instruction in his parish (e.g.,

CCD program). A priest has administrative duties in the parish (e.g., caring for the building, recording sacraments). He must be a careful steward who is responsible to the bishop.

4. A deacon may be permanent or transitional. A permanent deacon may be married when ordained (but if he should become widowed he must remain celibate). A transitional deacon will become a priest and cannot marry in the Latin Rite. Deacons can baptize and celebrate weddings and funerals. A deacon does not have the power to forgive sins or to consecrate the Eucharist. He is, however, to be a servant at the altar and an ordinary minister of Communion. Deacons share in the teaching ministry of the Church through reading the Gospel and giving homilies. A deacon has a special care for the poor, counseling and practicing works of mercy for the diocese.

5. The students may research holy priests and deacons.

Name:_____

Worldwide Organization of the Church

Answer the following questions in complete sentences.

1. What is a diocese? What is your diocese?
   A diocese is a particular community of the faithful, usually established by geographical area.

2. Who is the head of each diocese and what is his role?
   The head of each diocese is the bishop. His role is to teach, govern, and sanctify the faithful under his care.

3. What powers does the bishop give to priests and deacons?
   The bishop gives his priests the power to celebrate the sacraments and to share in his teaching authority. The deacons also receive the power to celebrate some of the sacraments and also to share in the teaching office of the bishop through preaching.

4. What is a parish? What is a pastor?
   A parish is a territory which is part of the diocese. A pastor is head of a parish.

5. What is a parishioner?
   A parishioner is a member of a parish.

6. What is a monsignor? What is a cardinal?
   A monsignor is an honoring title given by the Pope to a priest. A cardinal is an honoring title bestowed on a priest by the Pope.

7. What is the Curia?
   The Curia is the administrative and judicial offices by which the Pope directs the Church.

Faith and Life Series • Grade 8 • Chapter 6 • Lesson 3   23

Reinforce

1. Have the students work on *Activity Book*, p. 23.

2. Give the students time to work on their Memorization Questions and Words to Know.

3. Assign each student to interview a different priest, deacon, or seminarian in your diocese about his vocation, ministry, and ordination (plans for ordination). They should ask at least ten good questions and prepare a report.

4. Have a priest, deacon, or bishop visit your class to discuss his vocation. Be sure your students have written questions in advance and that they are focused. You may want to provide the questions ahead of time to your guest.

Conclude

1. Lead the students in singing "God of our fathers, whose almighty hand," *Adoremus Hymnal* #625.

2. End class by leading the students in the Prayer for Vocations.

Preview

In the next lesson, the students will learn about other roles in the Church.

THE SACRAMENT OF HOLY ORDERS

• Matter: laying on of bishop's hands on a man

• Form: prayer of the bishop

• Minister: bishop

• Effects: confers indelible spiritual seal; configures recipient to Christ to act as his representative as priest, teacher, and pastor (priest, prophet, and king); actual graces particular to vocation; for priests: ability to confer Sacraments of the Eucharist, Penance, Confirmation, and Anointing of the Sick; for bishops: ability to confer Sacrament of Holy Orders.

NOTES

_____
_____
_____
_____
_____
_____
_____
_____
_____
_____
_____

LESSON FOUR:
HONORARY ROLES

Aims

The students will learn that monsignors and cardinals are positions of honor bestowed by the Pope.

They will learn that the Pope is elected from the college of cardinals, many of whom serve him in the curia.

Materials

- *Activity Book*, p. 24

- Vestments, Appendix, pp. B-3–B-4

Optional:
- "God of our fathers, whose almighty hand," *Adoremus Hymnal* #625

Begin

Review the three degrees of Holy Orders. You may review the matter, form, minister, effects, degrees, and faculties of each degree. Be sure the students know there are only three degrees (e.g., Pope is not another degree).

Q. 27 *Who are the chief pastors of the Church?*
The chief pastors of the Church are the Pope and the bishops in union with him (CCC 862, 880).

Q. 28 *What is the Sacrament of Holy Orders?*
Holy Orders is the sacrament by which a man is configured to Christ and is given the power to continue the apostolic ministry as a bishop, priest, or deacon (CCC 1536).

Q. 29 *Who confers the Sacrament of Holy Orders?*
The bishop confers the Sacrament of Holy Orders (CCC 1576).

Q. 30 *How does the bishop confer the Sacrament of Holy Orders?*
The bishop confers the Sacrament of Holy Orders by imposing hands and praying that the Holy Spirit be sent upon the man receiving Holy Orders (CCC 1573).

42

Develop

1. Read paragraphs 11–14 (to the end of the chapter).

2. Review the definition of monsignor. It is an honorary title given by the Pope to priests who have given faithful service in the promotion of the Church, often in the service of education, founding a parish, or serving on committees for the good of the Church.

3. Review the role of a cardinal. Most always, cardinals are selected by the Pope from among the bishops. The primary function of the cardinals is to elect the Pope, who has for many centuries been elected from the College of Cardinals.

4. Review the process in electing a Pope. When a Pope dies (or is no longer active as Pope) a conclave is called and all the cardinals from around the world gather at the Vatican. They meet in the Sistine Chapel to elect a new Pope. During this time, black smoke is seen coming from a chimney to indi-

cate that the conclave is in session. The cardinals cannot meet with people from the outside world and must prayerfully elect a new Pope. When the new Pope is elected, white smoke rises from the chimney.

5. If possible, watch a video on the election of a Pope. Let the students understand the tradition of this process and the anticipation the Church feels between popes. Have the students pray for the Pope and for the leadership of the Church.

6. Cardinals also serve by working in the curia. The curia are the different judicial offices by which the Pope directs the Church (like branches of government). See the list of curia, at right, and the important works they do.

Name:_____

Visible Church Hierarchy

Complete the crossword puzzle using the clues below.

In founding his Church, Our Lord accomplished the fulfillment of the (9 down) Testament. He gave (7 across) to his apostles, declaring that sins which were forgiven on (2 down) would be forgiven in (1 across) . In the (15 down) , we read that the apostles selected successors, the bishops, to carry on Christ's (16 across) .

Today the Holy Father leads the Church in union with the bishops of the world and is assisted by the cardinals who make up the (5 down) .

The bishops, as shepherds, (8 down) , govern, and (17 across) the people. To assist them in these tasks, they confer (12 across) on (6 down) and (10 across) through the Sacrament of Holy (11 down) , each according to his own particular (3 across) in the Body of Christ.

Pastors perform their priestly duties in the (14 across) community. Deacons serve the people of God by preaching and performing works of (13 down) . (4 down) people are also called to participate in the evangelical mission of the Church in their families, work places, and neighborhoods.

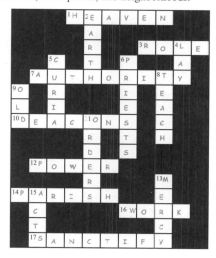

Faith and Life Series • Grade 8 • Chapter 6 • Lesson 4

1. Have the students work on *Activity Book*, p. 24.

2. Give the students time to work on their Memorization Questions and Words to Know and prepare for the quiz.

3. The students should learn the number of cardinals and the number who can participate in a conclave. How many different popes have elevated these cardinals to their office? Why is this important? How might this influence the future leadership of the Church?

4. *Look at pictures of the different degrees of Holy Orders and offices in the Church and discuss their vestments—similarities, differences, proper titles, colors. (See Appendix, pp. B-3–B-4 for help.)*

Conclude

1. Lead the students in singing "God of our fathers, whose almighty hand," *Adoremus Hymnal* #625.

2. End class by leading the students in the Prayer for vocations.

Preview

In the next lesson, the students' understanding of the material covered in this chapter and unit will be reviewed and assessed.

THE CURIA

In the Apostolic Constitution *Pastor Bonus*, Pope John Paul II defined the Roman Curia as "the complex of dicasteries and institutes which help the Roman Pontiff in the exercise of his supreme pastoral office for the good and service of the whole Church and of the particular churches. It thus strengthens the unity of the faith and the communion of the people of God and promotes the mission proper to the Church in the world" (I 1). A large part of the Curia are the sacred congregations which oversee various aspects of Church life. The following is a list of some of the congregations:

- *Congregation for the Doctrine of the Faith*; protects the Church from heresy and promotes her true doctrine
- *Congregation for Divine Worship and the Discipline of the Sacraments*; works with the Congregation for the Doctrine of the Faith to promote and regulate the Church's liturgy, especially the sacraments
- *Congregation for the Oriental Churches*; deals with issues affecting the Eastern Catholic churches
- *Congregation for the Causes of Saints*; oversees everything leading to canonization and beatification of those being considered for canonization

CHAPTER SIX
REVIEW AND ASSESSMENT

Aims

The students' understanding of the material covered in this chapter will be reviewed and assessed.

Materials

- Quiz 6, Appendix, p. A-8
- "God of our fathers, whose almighty hand," *Adoremus Hymnal*, #625

Review

1. The students should understand that Christ instituted the hierarchical Church. The apostles implemented the hierarchical structure from the earliest days after the Ascension.

2. The students should know the degrees of Holy Orders.

3. The students should know the history of their diocese and a biography of a priest.

4. The students should know what monsignors and cardinals are.

5. The students should understand how the Pope is elected to office.

Name:

The Visible Hierarchical Church — Quiz 6

Part I: Define the following terms.

Diocese: <u>the part of the Church over which a bishop has authority</u>

Monsignor: <u>a title of honor given to certain members of the clergy</u>

Cardinal: <u>a title of honor bestowed by the Pope. Cardinals' main function is to elect a Pope</u>

Curia: <u>the body of officials who assist a bishop (diocesan curia) or the Pope (the Roman curia) in governing a diocese or the universal Church</u>

Bishop: <u>successors of the apostles who have received the fullness of the priesthood and are the spiritual leaders of the Christians in their diocese</u>

Priest: <u>someone who is chosen to pray and offer sacrifice to God on behalf of others</u>

Vicar of Christ: <u>a representative; one serving as an agent for someone else</u>

Part II: Explain why the apostles selected other apostles/bishops. How was Matthias chosen?

<u>The apostles selected other apostles because they needed successors in order for them to be able to fulfill the Lord's command to teach all men at all times and places. They chose Matthias by picking straws.</u>

A - 8 — *Faith and Life • Grade 8 • Appendix A*

Assess

1. Distribute the quizzes and read through them with the students to be sure they understand the questions.

2. Administer the quiz. As they hand in their work, you may orally quiz the students on the Memorization Questions from this chapter.

3. After all the quizzes have been handed in, review the correct answers with the class.

Conclude

1. Lead the students in singing "God of our fathers, whose almighty hand," *Adoremus Hymnal*, #625.

2. End class by leading the students in the Prayer for Vocations.

CHAPTER SEVEN
SACRAMENTS OF INITIATION

Catechism of the Catholic Church References

Baptism: 1213–74, 1275–84
Bearing Witness to the Truth: 2471–74, 2506
Church as One: 811–22, 866
Church as the Body of Christ: 787–96, 805–8
Confirmation: 1285–1314, 1315–21
Eucharist: 1322–1405; 1406–19
Fruits of Communion: 1391–1401, 1416
Grace: 1996–2005, 2021–24

Liturgical Traditions and the Catholicity of the Church: 1200–1203, 1208
Liturgy and Cultures: 1204–6, 1207
Martyrdom: 2473–74, 2506
Rites: 1203, 1125
Sacraments of Christian Initiation: 1212, 1275
Signs of Bread and Wine in the Eucharist: 1333–36, 1412

Scripture References

Baptism:
  Necessity of Rebirth: Jn 3:5
  Institution by Christ: Mt 28:18–20
  Meaning and Effect: Rom 6:3–11; Gal 2:19–20;
  3:14, 26–29; Eph 1:3–5; 2:4–10; Col 1:14; 2:9–13;
  3:1–3; 1Pet 1:3–5
Eucharist:
  Bread of Life: Jn 6:35–59
  Roots in Passover: Ex 12:1–28,
  Melchizedek's Offering: Gen 14:18

Priesthood of Christ: Heb 8–10
Multiplication of Loaves and Fish: Jn 6:1–15
Last Supper: Mt 26:26–28; Mk 14:22–25; Lk 22:7–20
Emmaus: Lk 24:13–53
Meaning and Effects: 1 Cor 10:16–17
Confirmation:
  Jesus Gives Apostles the Holy Spirit: Jn 20:22
  Pentecost: Acts 2:1–11; 8:14–17; 9:17–19; 10:5;
  Tit 3:4–8

Summary of Lesson Content

Lesson 1

The sacraments are the ordinary means by which the Catholic Church confers grace.

The Sacraments of Initiation include: Baptism, Eucharist, and Confirmation. These sacraments bring us into the Church and give us full participation in her.

Baptism is the door to the other sacraments. By Baptism, we are freed from sin, filled with grace, and made members of the Church.

Lesson 2

The Eucharist is the source and summit of our faith. The Eucharist is Christ really and truly present, Body, Blood, Soul, and Divinity, under the appearances of bread and wine.

The Eucharist is nourishment for our souls and unites us with the Mystical Body of Christ.

Lesson 3

Confirmation is the sacrament whereby we receive the fullness of the Holy Spirit. It enables us to confess our faith and bear witness to it.

By Confirmation, we are made full members of the Church and are given the grace for the duties and responsibilities of full membership.

Lesson 4

A rite is a common way of practicing the faith by a particular group of Catholics.

The rites are of ancient origin and can be traced back to the apostles. They reflect the cultures, languages, and histories of various places and peoples.

All the Catholic rites are united under Christ and his Vicar on earth, the Pope.

LESSON ONE: INITIATION

Aims

The students will learn that the sacraments are the ordinary means by which the Catholic Church confers grace.

They will learn that the Sacraments of Initiation include: Baptism, Eucharist, and Confirmation. These sacraments bring us into the Church and give us full participation in her.

They will learn that Baptism is the door to the other sacraments. By Baptism, we are freed from sin, filled with grace, and made members of the Church.

Materials

- *Activity Book*, p. 25   Optional:
  - "Sing praise to our Creator," *Adoremus Hymnal*, #500

Begin

Begin by reviewing the definition of a sacrament: an outward sign instituted by Christ that confers grace. It is important to review that grace was lost after the Fall by Adam and Eve. Man could not redeem himself (and restore grace to himself). The gates of heaven were closed and could only be opened by the death and Resurrection of Christ, who is the perfect sacrifice of atonement. Christ gave the Church and the sacraments as channels of his grace, so that we may participate in the rewards he won for us on the Cross.

CHAPTER 7

The Church Sanctifying: Sacraments of Membership

Now you are the body of Christ and individually members of it.

1 Corinthians 12:27

"And the Word became flesh and dwelt among us, full of grace and truth; we have beheld his glory, glory as of the only Son from the Father. . . . And from his fullness have we all received, grace upon grace" (Jn 1:14, 16).

To help us understand the Church's role in the dispensation of grace let us consider for a moment the parable of the Good Samaritan. You may already be familiar with this parable, but today we will look at it in a slightly different light.

A man was going down from Jerusalem to Jericho, and he fell among robbers, who stripped him and beat him and departed, leaving him half dead. Now by chance a priest was going down that road; and when he saw him he passed by on the other side. So likewise a Levite, when he came to the place and saw him, passed by on the other side. But a Samaritan, as he journeyed, came to where he was; and when he saw him, he had compassion, and went to him and bound up his wounds, pouring on oil and wine; then he set him

on his own beast and brought him to an inn, and took care of him. And the next day he took out two denarii and gave them to the innkeeper, saying, "Take care of him; and whatever more you spend, I will repay you when I come back" (Luke 10:30–35).

We know that Our Lord told this parable in answer to a question about who is our neighbor. This parable teaches us a lesson about real charity. However, it seems that Our Lord also

43

Develop

1. Read paragraphs 1–8 (up to the section on the Eucharist).

2. Read Lk 10:30–35. (It is important that the students learn to read from the Bible.) The students may dramatize this reading and make it into a modern-day parable.

3. Discuss Saint Augustine's interpretation of this passage. Review how this relates to what was covered in the Begin Section. You may review the necessity of the sacrifice of Christ for the salvation of mankind.

4. Look up the following biblical passages on Baptism:
  - Necessity of Rebirth: Jn 3:5
  - Institution by Christ: Mt 28:18–20
  - Meaning/effect: Rom 6:3–11; Gal 2:19–20; 3:14, 26–29; Eph 1:3–5; 2:4–10; Col 1:14; 2:9–13; 3:1–3; 1 Pet 1:3–5

5. Review the matter, form and minister:

- *Matter: pouring of water three times (or triple immersion)*
- *Form: N. I baptize you in the Name of the Father and of the Son and of the Holy Spirit. Amen.*
- *Minister: usually a priest or deacon, but in case of an emergency, anyone can baptize.*

6. Review the rite and symbols used in the rite of Baptism. Review the effects of Baptism (washes away sin, gives grace, makes us members of the Church, confers an indelible sacramental seal on the soul).

7. Baptism of blood refers to those who die for the faith without being baptized and are united with Christ by their witness. Baptism of desire refers to the explicit desire of catechumens to be baptized.

8. Have each student research his own Baptism.

Name:_____

Baptism

Write an essay summarizing the Church's teaching on Baptism. Be sure to include whether we must be baptized in order to be saved and enter heaven.

Answers will vary.

_____
_____
_____
_____
_____
_____
_____
_____
_____
_____
_____
_____
_____
_____
_____
_____
_____
_____
_____
_____
_____
_____
_____
_____

Reinforce

1. Have the students work on *Activity Book*, p. 25.

2. Give the students time to work on their Memorization Questions and Words to Know.

3. Have the students renew their baptismal promises, then bless themselves with holy water (a reminder of Baptism and a profession in the faith we believe).

4. The students may make posters or compose poems demonstrating their understanding of the Parable of the Prodigal Son.

5. The students may write letters or prayers to Christ, thanking him for his sacrifice and gift of grace. These letters or prayers may be recorded in journals.

Conclude

1. Teach the students to sing "Sing praise to our Creator," *Adoremus Hymnal*, #500.

2. End class by leading the students in the Profession of Faith.

Preview

In the next lesson, the students will learn about the Holy Eucharist.

RITE OF BAPTISM

The minister immerses the candidate in water or pours water on his head three times, while saying: "N., I baptize you in the Name of the Father, and of the Son, and of the Holy Spirit."

SYMBOLS

- Water: cleanses as we are cleansed from sin.
- Chrism: reminds us that we share in the threefold ministry of Christ as priest, prophet, and king.
- Candle: we should receive the light of Christ.
- White garment: we are pure and clothed in Christ.

NOTES

_____
_____
_____
_____
_____
_____
_____
_____
_____
_____

LESSON TWO: EUCHARIST

Aims

The students will learn that the Eucharist is the source and summit of our faith. The Eucharist is Christ really and truly present, Body, Blood, Soul, and Divinity, under the appearances of bread and wine.

They will learn that the Eucharist is nourishment for our souls and unites us with the Mystical Body of Christ.

Materials

- *Activity Book*, p. 26   Optional:
  - "Sing praise to our Creator," *Adoremus Hymnal*, #500

Begin

Review that the Eucharist is both the celebration of the Mass and the sacrament celebrated at the Mass.

The Mass makes present the saving mysteries of Christ, so that we may participate in them. The teachings of Christ, the Last Supper, the Crucifixion, Resurrection, and Emmaus are all made present at the Mass.

The Mass is both the sacrifice of Christ and the meal of the Bread of Life—Christ present, really and truly Body, Blood, Soul, and Divinity under the appearances of bread and wine.

had a deeper message in mind about grace and the sacraments. As the fourth-century bishop St. Augustine explained in one of his sermons, this parable teaches us about our salvation.

Let us suppose that the man who is traveling from Jerusalem to Jericho is Adam, who also represents the whole human race. He was "robbed"—by the devil—of his riches, that is, the life of grace. Just as the man was left half-dead by the side of the road, the human race is weak, fallen, and without the many gifts God intended for us. Most importantly, after the Fall we were unable to attain salvation. The priest and the Levite signify the priests and the prophets of the Old Covenant, who were unable to restore us to supernatural life. Finally, the Samaritan pouring oil and wine on the man's wounds represents Christ, who "pours out" graces through the sacraments to heal our spiritual wounds.

We can see how man can find his salvation through the Church (represented by the inn) and how the bishops in union with the Pope continue the work of Christ until he comes again.

44

Sacraments of Initiation

The main purpose of all the sacraments is to give us grace and bring us to salvation. However, three of these sacraments are also important to our life as members of the Church. In fact, Baptism, Holy Eucharist, and Confirmation are the sacraments by which we are fully incorporated into the Body of Christ. These sacraments are sometimes called **sacraments of initiation**, since they bring us into the Church and give us full participation in her. They also signify our unity in the Body of Christ.

Baptism

Baptism frees us from original sin and fills us with divine life—sanctifying grace. We receive the Holy Spirit, who then lives in us. It makes us children of God and heirs to the Kingdom of heaven. This sacrament unites us with Christ in a special way, giving us an invisible seal, or mark, which can never be taken away.

Yet the effects of Baptism goes far beyond our own personal lives. Baptism makes us members of the Mystical Body of Christ. In St. Paul's letter to the Corinthians he tells us, "For by one Spirit we were all baptized into one body . . . and all were made to drink of the one Spirit" (1 Cor 12:13). So Baptism makes us members of the Church and unites us closely with all those who have been baptized in Christ.

The next sacrament we will discuss is the Eucharist, which in itself is the most important of the sacraments. First of all, it is a source of spiritual food. This aspect of the Eucharist was prefigured in many ways in the Old Testament—for example, when the manna in the desert nourished the Israelites for many years. In the New Testament, after the multiplication of the loaves and the fishes, Our Lord spoke to his disciples about the "Bread of Life:"

Develop

1. *Read paragraphs 9–12 (up to the section on Confirmation).*

2. Read Jn 6:35–69. Discuss the lessons this passage teaches us about the Eucharist: it is Christ truly present: Body, Blood, Soul, and Divinity; it is a promise of eternal life.

3. Read from the Bible the following passages about the
- Eucharist: Roots in Passover: Ex 12:1–28
- Melchizedek's Offering: Gen 14:18
- Priesthood of Christ: Heb 8–10
- Multiplication of Loaves and Fish: Jn 6:1–15
- Last Supper: Mt 26:26–28; Mk 14:22–25; Lk 22:7–20
- Emmaus: Lk 24:13–53
- Meaning and Effects: 1 Cor 10:16–17

4. *Review the matter, form, and minister:*
- *Matter: Bread and Wine*

- *Form: the Eucharistic Prayer within the liturgy, with its institution narrative: "This is My Body . . . This is My Blood"*
- *Minister: ordained priest*

5. *Jesus is present Body, Blood, Soul, and Divinity under the appearance of bread alone, or under the appearance of the wine alone, and in each of their parts (e.g., if a consecrated host is broken, Jesus is entirely present in each of its parts; Jesus, himself, is not broken).*

6. *Review the steps to worthy Communion: be in the state of grace, observe the Eucharistic fast, and know whom we are about to receive—then receive reverently. The effects of a worthy Communion include: union with Christ, increase in the life of grace, cleansing of venial sins and preservation from future sins, union among members in Church, a strengthening of our commitment to the poor.*

The Divinity of Jesus

Explain how the Eucharist is:

1. A meal: *Answers will vary.*

2. A sacrifice:

3. A communion:

4. The greatest act of worship:

5. The same sacrifice as the Cross:

6. A memorial:

7. The New Covenant:

8. Jesus:

26   *Faith and Life Series • Grade 8 • Chapter 3 • Lesson 2*

Reinforce

1. Have the students work on *Activity Book*, p. 26.

2. Give the students time to work on their Memorization Questions and Words to Know.

3. Have the students study the parts of the Mass. Be sure they know by heart all the responses of the Mass.

4. The students should research their First Communions, finding pictures and documents.

5. Take the students to pray before the Blessed Sacrament. If possible arrange for adoration and benediction.

Conclude

1. Lead the students in singing "Sing praise to our Creator," *Adoremus Hymnal*, #500.

2. End class by leading the students in the Profession of Faith.

Preview

In the next lesson, the students will learn about Confirmation.

TITLES FOR THE EUCHARIST

- Lord's Supper
- Breaking of the Bread
- Memorial
- Holy Sacrifice
- Holy and Divine Liturgy
- Sacred Mysteries
- Blessed Sacrament
- Holy Communion
- Bread of Angels
- Bread from Heaven
- Medicine of Immortality
- Holy Things for the Holy
- Bread of Life

For an explanation of most of these titles, see the *Catechism of the Catholic Church,* 1328–1332.

NOTES

_____
_____
_____
_____
_____
_____
_____
_____
_____
_____
_____

LESSON THREE: CONFIRMATION

Aims

The students will learn that Confirmation is the sacrament whereby we receive the fullness of the Holy Spirit. It enables us to confess our faith and bear witness to it.

They will learn that by Confirmation, we are made full members of the Church and are given the grace for the duties and responsibilities of full membership.

Materials

• *Activity Book*, p. 27

Optional:
• "Sing praise to our Creator," *Adoremus Hymnal*, #500

Begin

Often we misunderstand Confirmation. We are not "getting" something in this sacrament like in the others—we already received the life of grace, the indwelling of God, the Holy Spirit and his gifts, the virtues, etc. In Confirmation, we receive the outpouring of the Holy Spirit and his gifts that were given to us in Baptism. In Confirmation, we become full members of the Church, empowered to use these gifts for the building up of the Church.

Baptism is also the gateway to all the other sacraments. Once we have become part of the Church we are able to receive from her the graces dispensed through the other sacraments.

Jesus said to them, "I am the Bread of Life; he who comes to me shall not hunger, and he who believes in me shall never thirst. . . . Your fathers ate manna in the wilderness, and they died. This is the Bread which comes down from heaven, that a man may eat of it and not die. I am the living Bread which comes down from heaven; if any one eats of this Bread, he will live for ever; and the Bread which I shall give for the life of the world is my Flesh. . . . Truly, truly, I say to you, unless you eat of the Flesh of the Son of Man and drink his Blood, you have no life in you; he who eats my Flesh and drinks my Blood has eternal life, and I will raise him up on the last day" (Jn 6:35, 49–51, 53–54).

Our Lord tells us here of the necessity to nourish the life of grace born in us through Baptism. Just as our bodies require nourishment, we must "feed" the life of grace through reception of the Eucharist, the *Flesh* and *Blood* of which Our Lord speaks.

Furthermore, the sacrament of the Eucharist is both a cause and a sign of the unity of the Church. The Eucharist causes first our union with Christ and through him our union with one another. All those who receive Christ are truly united through this sacrament. St. Paul affirms this also, in his letter to the Corinthians, when he says, "Because there is one bread, we who are many are one body, for we all partake of the one bread" (1 Cor 10:17). It is this union with Christ and his Body that is signified by the words *Holy Communion*.

Even the elements of bread and wine chosen by Our Lord for this sacrament signify the very unity that it brings about. Just as many grains of wheat make up the one loaf of bread, and many grapes produce the one cup of wine, so too many Christians are joined into the one Body of Christ through the Eucharist.

Confirmation

The third sacrament of initiation is Confirmation. Confirmation is the sacrament in which we receive the fullness of the Holy Spirit. This enables us to profess and confess our faith as strong and perfect Christians and soldiers of Jesus Christ.

Although we receive the Holy Spirit at Baptism, Confirmation completes what is begun in Baptism and has been nourished through the Eucharist. The new life of grace that we receive, usually as infants, is strengthened in us at Confirmation. At Baptism we were spiritual infants in the Church; at Confirmation we become spiritual adults.

We know from our experience that, as we grow older, we take on more and more responsibilities. When you become an adult, you will have to bear the responsibilities of citizenship —voting, paying taxes, and perhaps fighting to defend your country.

The same is true in the Church. As adult Christians we have the responsibility to bear witness to Christ. This means that we must live

45

Develop

1. Read paragraphs 13–19 (up to Rites in the Church).

2. Help the students make the connections between the three Sacraments of Initiation:
Confirmation completes what is begun in Baptism and strengthened in the Eucharist. Baptism is like birth, Confirmation is like maturation. Our parents profess our faith for us as infants, we profess it every time we receive Communion ("Amen"), and publicly profess it for ourselves at Confirmation. Our parents give us a baptismal name and we take a confirmation name.

3. Read these biblical passages about Confirmation:
• Jesus gives apostles the Holy Spirit: Jn 20:22
• Pentecost: Acts 2:1–11
• Acts 8:14–17; 9:17–19; 10:5; Tit 3:4–8

4. Review the matter, form, and minister of Confirmation:

• *Matter: laying on of hands and anointing with chrism*
• *Form: N. be sealed with the Gift of the Holy Spirit. Amen.*
• *Minister: bishop (although he may delegate a priest)*

5. Review the effects of Confirmation:
• *Unites us more closely to Christ*
• *Increases in us the gifts of the Holy Spirit*
• *Perfects our bond with the Church*
• *Gives us strength to spread and defend the faith*
• *Imprints indelible mark on the soul*

6. Traditionally, confirmandi take a Confirmation name. It reflects the individual's choice of a saintly patron. A confirmandi may choose a saint of either gender, or may qualify a name, e.g., Joseph—Josephine. In taking the name of a saint, one claims the patronage of this saint, beseeching his intercession, and choosing to follow his example of holiness.

Confirmation

Answer the following questions in complete sentences.

1. Why do we need Confirmation if we receive the Holy Spirit at Baptism?
We need Confirmation as well as Baptism because Confirmation completes what is begun at Baptism. It seals or confirms the baptized into the faith.

2. What responsibilities do you take on in the Church when you are Confirmed?
You take on the responsibilities of being a witness to Christ, living for him in your daily life, and defending and spreading the faith.

3. What does it mean to be a "soldier of Christ"? What is our armor?
To be a "Soldier of Christ" means that we must spread and defend our faith. Our armor is of God: the sacraments and sacramentals, as well as what St. Paul refers to in Ephesians.

4. How can we continue to strengthen our faith?
We can continue to strengthen our faith through reading, instruction, prayer, and the sacraments.

5. Unscramble the names of the gifts and fruits of the Holy Spirit. Underline the gifts and circle the fruits.

OYJ	Joy	TDYEOSM	Modesty
EEPAC	Peace	GELDKONWE	Knowledge
RREEAFFOHTLDO	Fear of the Lord	FGREINSUNOGLF	Long Suffering
ITYPE	Piety	TAPIEENC	Patience
HSCATITY	Chastity	GOSOSDEN	Goodness
HAIRTCY	Charity	TINOCNECEN	Continence
DUNRETNGDASNI	Understanding	LDSENISM	Mildness
WMISDO	Wisdom	TITORFUDE	Fortitude
SSKNDEIN	Kindness	LIDEFTIY	Fidelity
NOUSCEL	Counsel		

Faith and Life Series • Grade 8 • Chapter 7 • Lesson 3   27

Reinforce

1. Have the students work on *Activity Book*, p. 27.

2. Give the students time to work on their Memorization Questions and Words to Know.

3. The students should write reports on their patron saints.

4. If students are already confirmed, have them make a presentation on their experience of Confirmation.

5. *Have the students write their plan for their lives as Catholics. They should include descriptions of ways they will live their faith, spread their faith, defend their faith, and support their faith with ongoing education and formation, etc. These reports should reflect the duties assumed in Confirmation.*

Conclude

1. Lead the students in singing "Sing praise to our Creator," *Adoremus Hymnal*, #500.

2. End class by leading the students in the Profession of Faith.

Preview

In the next lesson, the students will learn about Catholic rites.

HOLY OILS

These oils are usually blessed by the bishop at the Chrism Mass on Holy Thursday.

- **Oil of Catechumens:** olive or vegetable oil; used at Baptism; also poured with chrism into the baptismal waters when they are blessed at the Easter Vigil.

- **Sacred Chrism:** olive or vegetable oil mixed with balm; used for Baptism, Confirmation, Ordinations of priests and bishops, and for the dedication of churches and altars.

- **Oil of the Sick:** olive or vegetable oil; used for the Sacrament of the Anointing of the Sick.

FROM THE CATECHISM

"Anointing, in Biblical and other ancient symbolism, is rich in meaning: oil is a sign of abundance and joy; it cleanses (anointing before and after a bath) and limbers (the anointing of athletes and wrestlers); oil is a sign of healing, since it is soothing to bruises and wounds; and it makes radiant with beauty, health, and strength.... The pre-baptismal anointing with the oil of catechumens signifies cleansing and strengthening; the anointing of the sick expresses healing and comfort. The post-baptismal anointing with sacred chrism in Confirmation and ordination is a sign of consecration."
—CCC 1293–1294

LESSON FOUR: RITES

Aims

The students will learn that a rite is a common way of practicing the faith by a particular group of Catholics.

They will learn that the rites are of ancient origin and can be traced back to the apostles. They reflect the cultures, languages, and histories of various places and peoples. All the Catholic rites are united under Christ and his Vicar on earth, the Pope.

Materials

- *Activity Book*, p. 28
- Icons, Appendix, p. B-5

Optional:
- "Sing praise to our Creator," *Adoremus Hymnal*, #500

Begin

Catholic means universal. Often, even within our own diocese, we can see variations in the Mass. Sometimes the music is different or churches vary in architectural style. The Mass might be celebrated in different languages (e.g., Latin, English, or another language). These variations all occur within our own rite (the Latin rite). There are, however, other Catholic Churches which celebrate with a different rite—the Eastern rite Catholic churches. Today we will learn about them.

---

for Christ in our daily lives, defend Christ and our faith when it is challenged, and perhaps even die as *martyrs*. The graces of Confirmation prepare us to meet these challenges.

The notion of defending our faith led many of the Church Fathers to speak of Confirmation making us *soldiers of Christ*. St. Paul uses this idea when he writes to the Christians in Ephesus, encouraging them to be strong in their faith:

> Therefore take the whole armor of God, that you may be able to withstand in the evil day, and having done all, to stand. Stand therefore, having girded your loins with truth and having put on the breastplate of righteousness; . . . above all taking the shield of faith, with which you can quench all the flaming darts of the evil one. And take the helmet of salvation, and the sword of the Spirit, which is the word of God (Eph 6:13–14, 16–17).

We must pray then that we use the gift of the Holy Spirit to strengthen and defend our faith always.

As members of the Mystical Body united through these sacraments we have obligations to live as part of Christ's Church. We must ac-

cept the teachings of the Church and follow the laws that she has wisely set down.

We must also continuously strengthen our faith through reading and instruction. We know that Confirmation is usually preceded by an intense period of instruction preparing us for our place as adult Christians. However, growth in knowledge and understanding of our faith should not end here. Just as most of us continue our secular education in an informal way after completing school, we must continue our education in our faith. We must strive to deepen our understanding so that we may draw closer to God and our eternal goal.

Rites in the Church

With these three sacraments comes full membership in the Church. But the way the sacraments are celebrated may vary. This is because the Catholic Church is composed of various *rites*. Here a **rite** refers to a common way of worship and of practicing the faith by a particular group of Catholics.

These rites are ancient in origin, and all of them can be traced back, in some way, to the days of the apostles. When the apostles set out

---

Church Teaching

"The Holy Catholic Church, which is the Mystical Body of Christ, is made up of the faithful who are organically united in the Holy Spirit by the same faith, the same sacraments and the same government. They combine into different groups, which are held together by their hierarchy, and so form particular churches or rites. Between those churches there is such a wonderful bond of union that this variety in the Universal Church, so far from diminishing its unity, rather serves to emphasize it. For the Catholic Church wishes the traditions of each particular church or rite to remain whole and entire, and it likewise wishes to adapt its own way of life to the needs of different times and places" (OE, 2).

46

Develop

1. Read paragraphs 20–27 (to the end of the chapter).

2. Have the students point out what distinguishes the different rites: culture, language, history of different places and people.

3. Discuss what we have in common with the various Catholic rites:
- *We share the same faith—given to us by Christ*
- *We share the same liturgical symbolism*
- *We share in the same understanding of the mysteries of God*
- *We share in holiness—though it may be expressed in different forms*
- *We share in the same organization of the Church, with the Pope as the head of the Church*
- *We share in the same sacraments (all seven)*

4. Create a chart comparing the Latin rite and the Byzantine rite, using examples found in the text.

5. Use the Chalk Talk, at right, to help the students understand the similarities and differences.

6. Have the students look at some icons of the Eastern rite and study their beauty and symbolism. Optional: Have the students create an icon, using traditional colors and symbolism.

7. If possible, visit a Byzantine church and stay for Liturgy. Discuss the similarities and differences in the Liturgy. You may have an Eastern rite priest/deacon come and visit your class to discuss his rite and share some of his traditions.

Name:_____

Different Rites

I. Compare the Roman and the Byzantine rites in the chart below.

ROMAN RITE	BYZANTINE RITE
Answers will vary.	

II. Answer the following questions in complete sentences.

1. Where did the different rites come from?
   The different rites came from the various ways the liturgy was celebrated in different parts of the world. In the days of the apostles, as the Church grew, priests celebrated Mass according to the customs of their nation.

2. Do all rites share the same essential teachings?
   Yes. All rites share the same essential teachings.

3. Do all the various Catholic rites have the same Pope?
   Yes. The various Catholic rites have the same Pope.

28   *Faith and Life Series • Grade 8 • Chapter 7 • Lesson 4*

Reinforce

1. Have the students work on *Activity Book*, p. 28.

2. Give the students time to work on their Memorization Questions and Words to Know and prepare for the quiz.

3. Have the students research the history of the different rites. They should also know the current patriarchs.

4. The students should study Eastern rite saints, or the Eastern Doctors of the Church and some of their teachings.

Conclude

1. Lead the students in singing "Sing praise to our Creator," *Adoremus Hymnal*, #500.

2. End class by leading the students in the Profession of Faith.

Preview

In the next lesson, the students' understanding of the material covered in this chapter and unit will be reviewed and assessed.

CHALK TALK: CHURCH RITES

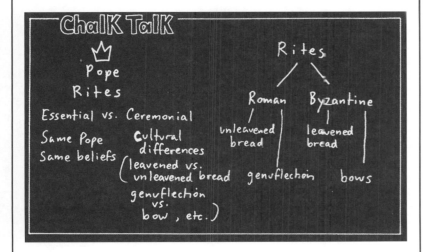

THE CHURCHES OF THE ONE CHURCH

Western: Roman

Eastern:

Armenian
• Armenian
Chaldean
• Chaldean
• Syro-Malabar
Antiochian
• Syrian
• Maronite
Alexandrian
• Coptic
• Ethiopian

Byzantine
• Bulgarian
• Greek
• Hungarian
• Melkite
• Romanian
• Slovak
• Ukrainian
• Albanian
• Russian

to "teach all nations," they had received the Holy Spirit and were well-grounded in the doctrines of the faith. But they had not yet settled on the precise forms for the various ceremonies. In fact, these ceremonies developed over a long period of time and reflected the cultures, languages, and history of the various places where the gospel was preached.

As the Church grew, each bishop celebrated Mass and administered the sacraments according to the customs of the city where he lived. Certain cities eventually exercised more influence than others on the surrounding countryside. Of course, Rome, as the center of both the Roman Empire and the Church itself, was the most important. Constantinople (modern-day Istanbul in Turkey) was the center of the eastern half of the empire and became quite important too.

In the Church today there are several different rites. The largest of these—and the one with which you are probably most familiar—is the *Roman rite*, which is used throughout the Western world. It is called "Roman" because the ceremonies originally come from the diocese of Rome. The second-largest rite is the *Byzantine rite*. This rite comes from the ceremonies of the church in the city of Byzantium, or Constantinople—the eastern part of the old Roman Empire. There are also several smaller rites whose origins can be found in other Eastern parts of the world.

These rites are all united under Christ and his Vicar on earth—the Pope. All who belong to them are members of the Catholic Church. The fundamental beliefs are the same, but the expression of those beliefs and the ceremonies vary according to the different cultural origins. To help you understand, let us look at a few differences between the Roman rite and the Byzantine rite.

In the Roman rite, *unleavened* bread is used for the Eucharist, while Byzantine Catholics use *leavened* bread. While Roman-rite Catholics traditionally genuflect before the Blessed Sacrament, Byzantine-rite Catholics have always bowed as a sign of respect. Members of the Roman rite make the Sign of the Cross from left to right; members of the Byzantine rite do so from right to left. The churches of the Byzantine rite are decorated with *icons*. An **icon** is a painting of Our Lord, Our Lady, or the saints, often created on wood and decorated with gold and jewels. The churches of the Roman rite often contain statues in addition to other kinds of images. You will not usually find statues in a Byzantine church.

As you can see, the differences are not in essential beliefs. Both reverence the Eucharist as the Body and Blood of Christ, even though respect is shown to this great sacrament in different ways. This variety enriches the Church, but it also points back to its unity, since all are part of *one* Church.

We have seen that it is through her sacramental life that the Church sanctifies her members. In the next chapter we will consider the form of the Church's worship.

Words to Know:
sacraments of initiation   rite   icon

47

Q. 31 *What is Baptism?*

The Sacrament of Baptism takes away original sin and fills our soul with sanctifying grace. It makes us Christians, that is, followers of Jesus Christ, sons of God, and members of the Church (CCC 1213).

Q. 32 *What is the matter of Baptism?*

The matter of Baptism is water (CCC 1228, 1239).

Q. 33 *What is the form of Baptism?*

The form of Baptism is the following words: "I baptize you in the Name of the Father and of the Son and of the Holy Spirit." (CCC 1240).

Q. 34 *Who is the minister of Baptism?*

The ordinary minister of Baptism is a bishop, priest, or deacon, but in case of necessity anyone can baptize, provided he has the intention of doing what the Church intends (CCC 1256).

Q. 35 *How is Baptism given?*

Baptism is given by immersing a person in water or pouring water on his head three times while saying, "I baptize you in the Name of the Father and of the Son and of the Holy Spirit" (CCC 1239–40).

Q. 36 *What effects does Baptism produce?*

Baptism makes the baptized person a child of God and a member of the Church by removing original sin and any personal sin, bestowing the life of grace, marking the baptized person as belonging to Christ, and enabling him to receive the other sacraments (CCC 1279–80).

_____

_____

_____

_____

_____

_____

_____

_____

_____

_____

_____

_____

_____

_____

_____

_____

_____

_____

_____

_____

_____

_____

Q. 37 *Does Baptism change us?*

Yes, Baptism transforms us spiritually, causing us to be born into a new life as adopted children of the Father, members of Christ's body, and temples of the Holy Spirit (CCC 1265, 1279).

Q. 38 *If Baptism is necessary for all men, is no one saved without Baptism?*

Without Baptism, no one can be saved. For those who have not been baptized through no fault of their own, the Baptism of blood, which is martyrdom for Jesus Christ, or Baptism of desire (desire for Baptism), brings about the benefits of the Sacrament of Baptism (CCC 1257–60).

Q. 39 *Why can Baptism be received only once?*

Baptism can be received only once because it impresses a permanent spiritual mark upon the soul, which distinguishes a person as Christ's own forever (CCC 1246, 1272).

Q. 40 *What is this permanent spiritual mark?*

The permanent spiritual mark impressed upon the soul at Baptism is a distinctive spiritual mark that will never be taken away (CCC 1272).

Q. 41 *What does this permanent spiritual mark do?*

The mark impressed upon the soul at Baptism sets one aside as belonging to Christ (CCC 1272).

Q. 42 *What are the duties of one who is baptized?*

One who is baptized has the duties of following the teachings of Jesus Christ as found in his Church, including believing the faith of the Church, receiving the sacraments, and obeying the Church's pastors (CCC 1273).

_____

_____

_____

_____

_____

_____

_____

_____

_____

_____

_____

_____

_____

_____

_____

_____

Q. 43 *What is the Eucharist?*

The Eucharist is the sacrament that contains the Body, Blood, Soul, and Divinity of our Lord Jesus Christ, under the appearances of bread and wine (CCC 1333).

Q. 44 *Is the same Jesus Christ present in the Eucharist who was born on earth of the Virgin Mary?*

Yes, the same Jesus Christ is present in the Eucharist who was born on earth of the Virgin Mary (CCC 1373–75).

Q. 45 *What is the matter of the Eucharist?*

The matter of the Eucharist is bread made with wheat and wine made of grapes (CCC 1333).

Q. 46 *What is the form of the Eucharist?*

The form of the Eucharist are these words of Jesus Christ: "This is my Body. . . This is the cup of my Blood" (CCC 1339).

Q. 47 *Who is the minister of the Eucharist?*

The minister of the Eucharist is a priest (CCC 611, 1337).

Q. 48 *When did Jesus Christ institute the Eucharist?*

Jesus Christ instituted the Eucharist at the Last Supper, when he consecrated and changed bread and wine into his Body and Blood and distributed it to the apostles, commanding them to "do this in memory of me" (CCC 1337, 1339).

Q. 49 *Why did Jesus Christ institute the Eucharist?*

Jesus Christ instituted the Eucharist to be the permanent memorial of his Passion, death and Resurrection, spiritual food, and the means by which he is ultimately united with the faithful (CCC 1382).

50

NOTES

Q. 50 *How long does Jesus Christ remain within us after Communion?*

After Communion, Jesus Christ remains physically within us as long as the Eucharistic species remains (about 15 minutes) (CCC 1377).

Q. 51 *Is Jesus Christ present in all the consecrated Hosts in the world?*

Yes, Jesus Christ is present in all the consecrated Hosts in the world (CCC 1373, 1377).

Q. 52 *Why is the Most Holy Eucharist kept in churches?*

The Most Holy Eucharist is kept in churches so that the faithful may receive it in Communion, have it for Eucharistic devotion, and recognize it as the perpetual assistance and presence of Jesus Christ in the Church (CCC 1378–79).

Q. 53 *What is the Sacrament of Confirmation?*

The Sacrament of Confirmation makes us more perfect Christians and soldiers of Christ. Confirmation is the sacrament by which God strengthens our faith through the Holy Spirit, sends us out as witnesses of Jesus, and seals our membership in the Catholic Church with the seven gifts of the Holy Spirit (CCC 1285).

Q. 54 *What is the matter of Confirmation?*

The matter of Confirmation is the anointing with sacred chrism (CCC 1293, 1297).

Q. 55 *What is the form of Confirmation?*

The form of Confirmation is the following words: "Be sealed with the gift of the Holy Spirit" (CCC 1300).

51

Q. 56 *Who is the minister of Confirmation?*
The ordinary minister of Confirmation is a bishop, although a priest may receive special facilities to administer the Sacrament of Confirmation (CCC 1313).

Q. 57 *How does the bishop administer Confirmation?*
The bishop administers Confirmation to the one being confirmed by anointing him with chrism on the forehead, which is done by the laying of hands, and through the words, "Be sealed with the gift of the Holy Spirit" (CCC 1299–1300).

Q. 58 *How does Confirmation make us more perfect Christians?*
Confirmation makes us more perfect Christians and witnesses of Jesus Christ by giving us an abundance of the Holy Spirit, his grace and his gifts, which confirm and strengthen us in faith and in the other virtues (CCC 1303).

Q. 59 *What dispositions should a person who is going to be confirmed have?*
A person who is going to be confirmed should be in the grace of God and ought to know the principal mysteries of our faith. He should approach the Sacrament with devotion, aware that by being confirmed he is being consecrated to God and marked with the Holy Spirit (CCC 1309–10).

Q. 60 *What does the sacred chrism signify?*
Sacred chrism signifies that he who is confirmed is consecrated to God and marked with the Holy Spirit (CCC 1293–95).

Q. 61 *What does the anointing on the forehead in the form of a cross signify?*
The anointing on the forehead in the form of a cross signifies that the confirmed person, as a brave witness of Jesus Christ, should not be ashamed of the Cross nor fear enemies of the faith (CCC 1295–96).

52

NOTES

85

Q. 62 *What are the duties of one who is confirmed?*
One who is confirmed has the duties of witnessing to and defending the faith, and continuing to live his baptismal promises.

Q. 63 *What are the seven gifts of the Holy Spirit?*
The seven gifts of the Holy Spirit are: wisdom, understanding, counsel, knowledge, piety, fortitude, and fear of the Lord (CCC 1831).

Q. 64 *What are the fruits of the Holy Spirit?*
The fruits of the Holy Spirit are: charity, joy, peace, patience, kindness, goodness, continence, mildness, fidelity, self-control, modesty, and chastity (CCC 1832).

53

Name:

The Church Sanctifying: Sacraments of Membership Quiz 7

Part I: Fill in the chart.

SACRAMENT	MATTER	FORM	MINISTER	EFFECTS
Baptism	Water	Words "I Baptize you in the Name of the Father and of the Son and of the Holy Spirit."	Priest/Deacon/ Bishop	Removes original sin and bestows the life of grace
Confirmation	Anointing with Sacred Chrism	Words "Be sealed with the gift of the Holy Spirit."	Bishop	Makes us more perfect Christians and witnesses to Jesus Christ
Eucharist	Bread and Wine	Words "This is My Body...This is the cup of my Blood."	Priest	Strengthens us and is spiritual food

Part II: The following sentences describe aspects of Baptism, Eucharist, and Confirmation. Indicate the sacrament described by each sentence.

1. Baptism   This is the very first sacrament a person receives.
2. Confirmation   In this sacrament, we become Spirit-filled soldiers of Christ.
3. Eucharist   This sacrament is food for the soul, without which it would die of spiritual starvation.
4. Baptism   Through the water and words of this sacrament, we become brothers and sisters of Jesus Christ.
5. Confirmation   When we receive this sacrament, we are said to have become adult or more mature Christians.
6. Baptism   This sacrament is the "gateway" to all the other sacraments.
7. Eucharist   This sacrament is unique in that it is Jesus truly present Body, Blood, Soul and Divinity.
8. Confirmation   This sacrament brings with it a special responsibility to witness to Jesus and the Gospel, and to defend our faith.
9. Eucharist   This sacrament does not put an indelible mark on your soul.

Part III: Briefly describe some of the similarities and differences between the Eastern and Western Rites.

Answers will vary.

Faith and Life • Grade 8 • Appendix A   *A - 9*

Aims

The students' understanding of the material covered in this chapter will be reviewed and assessed.

Materials

- Quiz 7, Appendix, p. A-9
- "Sing praise to our Creator," *Adoremus Hymnal* #500

Assess

1. Distribute the quizzes and read through them with the students to be sure they understand the questions.

2. Administer the quiz. As they hand in their work, you may orally quiz the students on the Memorization Questions from this chapter.

3. After all the quizzes have been handed in, review the correct answers with the class.

Conclude

1. Lead the students in singing "Sing praise to our Creator," *Adoremus Hymnal*, #500.

2. End class by leading the students in the Profession of Faith.

Review

1. The students should understand that Christ is the source of all grace. Christ dispenses his grace through the Church and specifically through the sacraments.

2. The students should know the Sacraments of Initiation. They should be able to give the matter, form, minister, and effects of each Sacrament of Initiation.

3. The students should know that there are different rites in the Catholic Church. They should know what these rites have in common with the Latin rite, and how they differ.

CHAPTER EIGHT
THE CHURCH SANCTIFYING: WORSHIP

Catechism of the Catholic Church References

Advent: 524, 1095
Christmas Mystery: 525–26, 563
Easter as Central Christian Feast: 638, 1169
Forms of Penance in Christian Life: 1434–39
Lent: 540, 1095, 1438
Liturgical Seasons: 1163–65
Liturgical Year: 1168–73, 1194

Liturgy: 1066–75
Liturgy as the Work of the Trinity: 1077–1109, 1110–12
Liturgy of the Hours: 1174–78, 1196
Pentecost: the Holy Spirit and the Church: 731–41, 746–47, 767–68
Preparations for Christ's Coming: 522–24
Sanctoral in the Liturgical Year: 1172–73, 1195, 2030

Scripture References

Liturgy: Eph 1:9; 2:4; 3:9, 16–17

Summary of Lesson Content

Lesson 1

The ends of worship are praise and adoration, thanksgiving, contrition, petition and intercession.

The Liturgy is the official public worship of the Church. The Liturgy differs from private devotion.

The three elements that make up Liturgy include: the Mass, the sacraments, and the Divine Office, or the Liturgy of the Hours.

Lesson 2

The liturgical year is divided into seasons symbolized by different colors.

The liturgical year parallels the life of Christ and is based upon the major feasts of Christmas, Easter, and Pentecost.

Lesson 3

Advent celebrates the coming of Christ. Christmas is the celebration of the birth of Christ, the Incarnation, and is an anticipation of the Second Coming. Christmas includes Epiphany—the revelation of Christ to the gentiles—and ends with the Baptism of Christ.

Lent is a time of penance, recalling the preparation for Christ's public ministry. Holy Week celebrates the Passion of Christ. Easter celebrates the Resurrection. It begins with the vigil and ends on Pentecost.

Lesson 4

Pentecost celebrates Christ's gift of the Holy Spirit to the Church.

The remaining time in the Church year is called Ordinary Time. During this time, the Church reflects upon the mysteries celebrated and on Christian growth through the teachings of Christ.

Other feasts include: Holy Days of Obligation, Sunday feasts, and feasts of Mary and the saints.

LESSON ONE: WORSHIP

Aims

The students will learn that the ends of worship are praise and adoration, thanksgiving, contrition, petition and intercession.

They will learn that the Liturgy is the official public worship of the Church. The Liturgy differs from private devotion.

They will learn that the three elements that make up the Liturgy include: the Mass, the sacraments, and the Divine Office, or the Liturgy of the Hours.

Materials

- *Activity Book*, p. 29   Optional:
  - "To Jesus Christ, our sov'reign King," *Adoremus Hymnal*, #480

Begin

Review the four ends of worship:
- *Praise and Adoration*
- *Thanksgiving*
- *Contrition (sorrow for sin)*
- *Petition & Intercession*
Ask the students how these ends are exemplified in worship as they know it.

CHAPTER 8

The Church Sanctifying: Worship

And I heard every creature in heaven and on earth and under the earth and in the sea, and all therein, saying, "To him who sits upon the throne and to the Lamb be blessing and honor and glory and might for ever and ever!"

Revelation 5:13

"The Liturgy is the summit toward which the activity of the Church is directed; it is also the fount from which all her power flows" (SC, 4).

Men have worshipped their Creator since the beginning of the world. Long before Christianity, many civilizations had elaborate forms of public worship that had been established for centuries. These pagan peoples recognized the need to offer something to their Creator in return for the many benefits that they had received. They also recognized that this worship should be public, since so many of their blessings were received in common. The great civilization of Greece, which rose to prominence in the centuries immediately preceding the coming of Christ, was one that practiced public worship.

The word "liturgy" comes from the Greek and means "public work." Originally, this referred to any public act, especially those done by the wealthy for the benefit of the rest of society. It was understood that people who had benefited were bound to make some return

from these benefits. The wealthy would often sponsor plays or some other work for the whole society. By extension, the word was transferred to acts of worship, since the wealthy would often support these as well. As we will use the word here, **liturgy** means the Church's official public worship. This worship of God must be performed both as individuals and as a people. The Liturgy differs from our private devotions and prayers in being public and in having an external and a formal aspect. It is the action of Christ and his entire Church, rather than the action of an individual. Christ said, "Where two or three are gathered together in my name, there am I in the midst of them" (Mt 18:20).

Through the Liturgy we, the Mystical Body of Christ, are united with Christ in his priestly role to give honor and praise to God. It is proper that the Church as a whole people should do this, since the Church as a whole people was given the graces necessary for salvation. The Liturgy allows us as a whole people to offer to God the highest praise possible, since in it we unite ourselves with Christ in praising the Father. It also adds a new dimension to prayer,

54

Develop

1. Read paragraphs 1–7 (up to The Liturgical Year).

2. Review the definition of the Liturgy (have a student find it in the text). The public worship of God is performed both by individuals and as a people. Three elements make up the Liturgy:
- *The Mass (and celebration of the Eucharist)*
- *The sacraments*
- *Liturgy of the Hours (also called the Divine Office)*

3. Review that the Mass is the perfect form of the Liturgy, since in the Mass we join most perfectly to Christ who offers himself to the Father. We can participate in the Mass most perfectly by receiving Holy Communion worthily.

4. The sacraments are the Liturgy. They are special channels of grace, given to us by Christ. Sacraments make it possible for us to live the life of grace.

5. The Liturgy of the Hours is prayed by every bishop, priest, deacon, and religious throughout the world. Many lay people also pray the the Liturgy of the Hours, which is also known as the Divine Office. The Liturgy of the Hours is the prayer of the Church. It is made up of psalms, instructions, Scripture, hymns, and writings of the saints. It is prayed throughout the day and reflects the liturgical year.

6. Private devotion is different from the Liturgy. The Liturgy is a sign of the unity of the Church. Therefore, there are fixed rules for its proper celebration. Private devotions are the pious practices of individuals. Although they may be celebrated in public or in community, they do not form part of the Liturgy of the Church, and they are not necessary for salvation. Some examples may include: novenas, devotions, such as those to the Sacred Heart or the Infant of Prague, or prayers to a saint.

Name:_____

Worship

Answer the following questions in complete sentences.

1. What does "liturgy" mean?
   Liturgy means the Church's official public worship.

2. How does the Liturgy differ from private devotions?
   The Liturgy differs from private devotions because it is public and has external and formal aspects.

3. How are we united to Christ in his priestly role through the liturgy?
   We are united to Christ in his priestly role through the Liturgy because the Liturgy is the action of Christ and his entire Church.

4. What are the three elements to liturgy? Explain them.
   1. The Sacrifice of the Mass is where we perfectly join with Christ's offering of himself to the Father and are nourished with his Body in the Eucharist.

   2. In the sacraments, we receive God's grace and are able to partake in the supernatural life.

   3. In the recitation of the Divine Office, we sanctify our day with prayer and unite our prayer with the prayer of the Church.

5. How can the Liturgy be a sign of the unity of the Church?
   The Liturgy can be a sign of the unity of the Church by being uniformly celebrated throughout the entire world.

6. Why do we have rituals?
   We have rituals to ensure that the Liturgy is reverent, dignified, and worthy of being offered to God.

Faith and Life Series • Grade 8 • Chapter 8 • Lesson 1   29

Reinforce

1. Have the students work on *Activity Book*, p. 29.

2. Give the students time to work on their Memorization Questions and Words to Know.

3. *Discuss why the Liturgy is governed by rules:*
   • *For its proper and universal celebration*
   • *To protect its dignity and to maintain reverence*
   • *For valid celebration (e.g., to ensure the sacraments are efficacious)*

4. Have a religious, priest, or deacon visit the class to explain the Liturgy of the Hours. Make copies for your entire class and pray vespers.

5. You may review the parts of the Mass and the rites of the sacraments. You may review the symbols of the seven sacraments. Have the students make posters depicting the symbols of the sacraments.

Conclude

1. Teach the students to sing "To Jesus Christ, our sov'reign King," *Adoremus Hymnal*, #480.

2. End class by leading the students in the Morning Offering.

Preview

In the next lesson, the students will learn about the liturgical year.

CHALK TALK: PRAYER OF THE CHURCH

NOTES

_____
_____
_____
_____
_____
_____
_____
_____
_____
_____
_____

LESSON TWO:
LITURGICAL YEAR

Aims

The students will learn that the liturgical year is divided into seasons symbolized by different colors.

They will learn that the liturgical year parallels the life of Christ and is based upon the major feasts of Christmas, Easter, and Pentecost.

Materials

- *Activity Book*, p. 30
- Liturgical calendar

Optional:
- "To Jesus Christ, our sov'reign King," *Adoremus Hymnal*, #480

Begin

God is outside of time, since he created the sun, moon, and stars, which we use to measure time. God is eternal, but his creation is finite. God's plan for salvation has occurred in time. Miraculously, God the Eternal Son, in the fullness of time, became man. This very act sanctified time, making it a means to holiness. We can imitate Christ's life on earth and prepare for the end of time when Jesus will come again in glory (Jesus' life, death, and Resurrection).

since we join in the heavenly chorus of the Communion of Saints, who all belong to the Church. Praying in community lifts up our hearts and increases charity.

Three elements make up the Liturgy: (1) the Eucharist, that is, the Holy Sacrifice of the Mass, (2) the sacraments, and (3) the Divine Office, or Liturgy of the Hours. Each time the Mass is offered, the perfect Sacrifice of Calvary, that is, the whole Paschal mystery, the Passion, death, and Resurrection of Christ, is renewed on our altars. The Mass, then, is the most important element, since it is here that we join most perfectly with Christ offering himself to the Father. We can take part in the Mass most perfectly by worthily receiving the Body and Blood of Christ in the Sacrament of the Eucharist. In the Eucharist, we are nourished with the Body of Christ and, in this way, we become more fully the Body of Christ.

The remaining six sacraments make up the second element of the Liturgy. These are the special channels of God's grace, given to us by Jesus Christ and enabling us to participate in the supernatural life. Over the centuries the prayers and ceremonies that accompany the sacraments have changed, but the essential form was established by Christ himself.

Finally, the public worship of the Church is carried out by the daily recitation of the Divine Office, or Liturgy of the Hours. The Liturgy of the Hours is a prayer of praise composed of Psalms, prayers, instructions, and readings from Scripture and the writings of the saints. These are divided into segments called "hours," each of which is to be prayed at certain times during the day. This enables us to sanctify the entire day by praising God. Priests and other religious have a special obligation to recite, say, or sing the Office, but it is prayed by many lay people as well.

In order that the Liturgy may truly be a sign of the unity of the Church, the Church has laid

down certain fixed and universal rules for its proper celebration. In this way, Catholics all over the world can join together in one act of public worship. These rituals also ensure that the Liturgy is reverent, dignified, and worthy of being offered to God.

The Liturgical Year

Our natural lives are governed to a great extent by the natural rhythm of the seasons. As the year passes, our lives are affected by the sea-

55

Develop

1. Read paragraphs 8 and 9 (up to Advent and Christmas).

2. The liturgical year cycles through different seasons just like the natural year. The liturgical year, however, parallels the life of Christ. It is based upon the central mysteries of his life. The Church year begins with Advent, which is a preparation for the coming of Christ at Christmas—the celebration of the Incarnation and Nativity of our Lord. The liturgical year follows the public life of Christ, through Lent, up to the Passion and death of Our Lord, and his Resurrection at Easter. The liturgical years celebrates his Resurrection, his Ascension, and the sending of the Holy Spirit at Pentecost. We re-enter Ordinary Time to continue growing in the path of holiness, shown to us by Christ, and in the life of grace given to us through his Church.

3. The liturgical year has a calendar, colored with different colors to symbolize the different seasons of Advent,

Christmas, Lent, Easter, and Ordinary Time. Show the students a liturgical calendar and have them make and decorate calendars of their own. Include in this calendar the liturgical seasons, solemnities and feasts, Holy Days of Obligation, and their patron saints' days.

4. The readings of the Mass reflect the liturgical year (e.g., readings on the Nativity of Christ at Christmas, on the Passion during Holy Week, etc.). There are three liturgical cycles to the readings (which means in three years, the Church goes through the entire Bible if you include daily Masses).

5. The Church gives each year a theme or title of honor. Discuss this year's title and have the students make a poster or banner based upon this theme.

6. Discuss the attributes of Christ found in paragraph 8 of the student text.

Name:_____

Liturgical Year

Make a pie chart of the Liturgical Year. Use the proper liturgical colors.

Compare the Liturgical Year to the natural (seasonal) year.

<u>Answers will vary.</u>

_____
_____
_____
_____
_____
_____
_____
_____
_____
_____

30   *Faith and Life Series • Grade 8 • Chapter 8 • Lesson 2*

Reinforce

1. Have the students work on *Activity Book*, p. 30.

2. Give the students time to work on their Memorization Questions and Words to Know.

3. The students may work on their liturgical calendars.

4. The students should write meditations upon one of Jesus' attributes.

5. Have the students parallel the liturgical year with the natural year.

Conclude

1. Lead the students in singing "To Jesus Christ, our sov'reign King," *Adoremus Hymnal*, #480.

2. End class by leading the students in the Morning Offering.

Preview

In the next lesson, the students will learn about Advent, Christmas, Lent, and Easter.

NOTES

_____
_____
_____
_____
_____
_____
_____
_____
_____
_____
_____
_____

LESSON THREE: CHRISTMAS, EASTER; LENT AND ADVENT

Aims

The students will learn that Advent celebrates the coming of Christ. Christmas is the celebration of the birth of Christ, the Incarnation, and is an anticipation of the Second Coming. Christmas includes Epiphany—the revelation of Christ to the Gentiles—and ends with the Baptism of Christ.

They will learn that Lent is a time of penance, recalling the preparation for Christ's public ministry. Holy Week celebrates the Passion of Christ. Easter celebrates the Resurrection. It begins with the vigil and ends on Pentecost.

Materials

- *Activity Book*, p. 31

Optional:
"To Jesus Christ, our sov'reign King," *Adoremus Hymnal*, #480

Begin

Using the inset box, at right, review the liturgical colors and their symbolism.

Discuss where we see the liturgical colors in the Church (vestments, altar cloth, etc.). These colors should help us to remember the season and remind us of the focus of the season.

---

sons in nature. As we pass from one season to another, we must change our clothing, our activities, and even the food we eat. We also notice that the colors in nature change as we move from one season to another, for example, the changing colors of the leaves in autumn. The life of the Church is similar to this pattern in nature. The Church year is divided into seasons as well. As we move from one season to another, our spiritual lives and activities change, just as our natural lives and activities change with the passing of the seasons. As in nature we see the colors change with the seasons, so too, in the Church's year we see a change in colors. This Church year is known as the **liturgical year**. Each division, or season, of the year has its own special prayers for the Mass and the Divine Office. The mysteries of God are so great and inexhaustible that we will always have to continue to grow in understanding and love. Since we are unable to grasp Christ's revelation all at once, our Mother the Church shows us one facet at a time rhythmically during the whole liturgical year. The person of Jesus has so many varied aspects—such as mercy, gentleness, majesty, justice, authority, tenderness, severity, compassion, sorrow, serenity, love, peace, and many more—that we will never come to the end of the mystery that is Jesus, and thus never finish praising him.

The liturgical year is based upon the three major feasts of Christmas, Easter, and Pentecost. (See the diagram on page 58.) These feasts celebrate the principal events in the history of our salvation: the Incarnation, that is, the second Person of the Trinity becoming man; the Redemption, that is, the suffering, death, and Resurrection of Our Lord; and Pentecost, that is, the descent of the Holy Spirit upon the apostles, which is the birthday of the Church. Of these three feasts, Christmas and Easter are especially important, and thus they require periods of preparation as well as peri-

56

ods of celebration. Easter is the most important, and therefore the periods of preparation and celebration are longer. Let us now look at the seasons of the liturgical year.

Advent and Christmas

The liturgical year begins on a Sunday in late November or early December, four weeks before Christmas, with the season of Advent. Advent is the penitential season of preparation that precedes the feast of Christmas. The word *Advent* comes from the Latin word that means "coming."

During Advent the Church meditates on both past and future events. In the centuries before Christ, God's chosen people awaited and kept themselves prepared for the birth of a Savior. Likewise, we prepare ourselves to celebrate Christmas, the feast of his first "coming" among us. During this period, we also contemplate the *Second* Coming of Christ at the end of the world. The Liturgy of Advent prepares us for this event as well.

Advent is a season of penance, since this is the best way to prepare our hearts for Christ. The readings and prayers in the Mass and the Divine Office focus upon this idea and help us to meditate on the two comings of Christ. We hear in the Gospel, for example, the message of John the Baptist about repenting in order to prepare for the Messiah's coming. We also hear the words of Isaiah on a similar theme.

Despite this penitential theme, Advent retains a sense of joyful expectation, since the coming of the Savior is an event of great joy. We should rejoice, since the Savior was in fact born among us. On the third of the four Sundays of Advent, the Church particularly reminds us of this through the liturgical readings and prayers. This Sunday is called "Gaudete Sunday," taken from the Latin word meaning "rejoice."

Develop

1. Read paragraphs 10–14 (up to Lent and Easter).

2. Discuss Advent. When does it begin? It begins four full weeks before Christmas. Advent means "coming." It is a time of waiting and watching. It is a time of preparation for the coming of Christ. During Advent, we prepare for three comings:
- *The Nativity of Jesus*
- *The coming of our Lord into our hearts (conversion)*
- *The Second Coming of Christ at the end of time*

How do we celebrate Advent? What does the color tell us? Purple is a color that symbolizes penance. The Advent color is a blueish purple like the sky just before dawn. During Advent, we should prepare ourselves for the coming of Christ. We should do penances such as fasting, almsgiving, and receiving the Sacrament of Penance. As such, Advent is a time of joyful anticipation—Jesus is coming! We focus on this joyful anticipation, especially on Gaudete Sunday. Gaudete means "rejoice." The color for this Sunday is rose.

4. Christmas begins with Mass on December 24. The season of Christmas includes the Nativity, Epiphany, and the Baptism of Christ. The emphasis is on Christ coming into the world (at his birth, to the Gentiles, and into public ministry).

5. Read paragraphs 15–18 (up to Pentecost).

6. Lent is forty days (not counting Sundays), like Jesus' forty days in the desert. This is a time of penance: fasting, abstinence, almsgiving, works of charity, and receiving the Sacrament of Penance. Holy Week recounts the Passion of Christ. Lent ends with the Resurrection of Christ, which is celebrated during the Easter season.

Name:_____

Liturgical Seasons: Christmas and Easter

Answer the following questions in complete sentences.

1. What are we preparing for during Advent?
    We are preparing for the coming of Christ during Advent.

2. Why is Advent a season of penance?
    Advent is a season of penance because that is the best way to prepare our hearts for Christ.

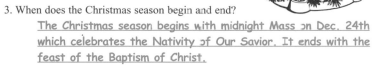

3. When does the Christmas season begin and end?
    The Christmas season begins with midnight Mass on Dec. 24th which celebrates the Nativity of Our Savior. It ends with the feast of the Baptism of Christ.

4. What do we celebrate during Christmas?
    During Christmas we celebrate the birth of Our Savior.

5. What do the forty days of Lent represent?
    The forty days of Lent represent the forty days Jesus spent in the desert preparing for his public life.

6. During Lent, what does the Church urge us to do? During Lent, the Church urges us to do penance in reparation for our sins.

7. What is special about Holy Week?
    Holy Week is special because we remember the events leading up to Our Lord's Passion and death.

8. When does Easter Season begin?
    Easter Season begins on Holy Saturday with Easter Vigil Mass.

9. How long is the Easter Season?
    The Easter Season is fifty days in length.

Faith and Life Series • Grade 8 • Chapter 8 • Lesson 3   31

Reinforce

1. Have the students work on *Activity Book*, p. 31.

2. Give the students time to work on their Memorization Questions and Words to Know.

3. *Break the students into groups to research different customs and Catholic traditions:*
   • *Advent—Jesse tree, Advent wreath, Advent log, etc.*
   • *Christmas—Christmas tree, Christmas cookies, exchange of gifts, Epiphany celebrations, etc.*
   • *Lent—fasting/abstinence rules, volunteering at a soup kitchen, etc.*
   • *Easter—Easter eggs, feast, Easter bonnets, etc.*
   Each group should make a presentation for all the other students.

4. The students should reflect upon and write prayers for each liturgical season.

Conclude

1. Lead the students in singing "To Jesus Christ, our sov'reign King," *Adoremus Hymnal*, #480.

2. End class by leading the students in the Morning Offering.

Preview

In the next lesson, the students will learn about Pentecost, Ordinary Time, and other feasts in the liturgical year.

LITURGICAL COLORS

	GREEN	RED	WHITE	PURPLE	ROSE
Meaning	Life, Hope	Fire, Love, Blood	Purity, Joy	Sorrow, Penitence	Joy
Use	Masses during Ordinary Time	Masses for Martyrs, Pentecost, Passion	Masses for Jesus, Mary, Virgins, Confessors, Easter, and Christmas	Masses during Advent and Lent; Masses for the dead	Gaudate Sunday in Advent; Laetare Sunday in Lent

LESSON FOUR: PENTECOST AND ORDINARY TIME

Aims

The students will learn that Pentecost celebrates Christ's gift of the Holy Spirit to the Church.

They will learn that the remaining time in the Church year is called Ordinary Time. During this time, the Church reflects upon the mysteries celebrated and on Christian growth through the teachings of Christ. Other feasts include: Holy Days of Obligation, Sunday feasts, and feasts of Mary and the saints.

Materials

- *Activity Book*, p. 32
- Missals

Optional:
- "To Jesus Christ, our sov'reign King," *Adoremus Hymnal*, #480

Begin

You may choose to begin the class reviewing the significant events of Holy Week by the Easter Triduum. Easter is the most important celebration of the Church year, and the students really need to understand the great mysteries that are recalled at Easter. You may use a missal to review these liturgies, the events they celebrate, and the readings that accompany them.

The season of Advent ends with the midnight Mass on December 24, as the Church begins her celebration of the great feast of Christmas. This feast celebrates the nativity of our Savior and is the beginning of the Christmas season. In contrast to Advent, this is a season of great joy. It includes the feast of the Epiphany, when we celebrate the revelation of Christ to the Gentiles, represented by the three wise men, and it ends with the feast of the Baptism of Christ.

Lent and Easter

The next season of the year is the season of preparation for the feast of Easter. It is called Lent and begins on Ash Wednesday. The ashes we receive on that day remind us of our own mortality. The Lenten season lasts for forty days, a little more than six weeks. The forty days represent the forty days Jesus spent in the desert preparing for his public life. In the Liturgy of Lent the Church urges us, through the readings and prayers, to do penance in reparation for our sins. We can do this through fasting, self-denial, almsgiving, and other good works.

Since this season is so closely linked to the suffering and death of Our Lord, the Liturgy does not express the sense of expectant joy that permeated the Advent season. Nevertheless, the Church does set aside the fourth Sunday in Lent to express our anticipated joy in Christ's Resurrection. This Sunday is called "Laetare Sunday," taken from another Latin word, meaning "rejoice."

The final week of Lent, Holy Week, is particularly important. During this week we concentrate on the events leading up to the Crucifixion of Our Lord. The Gospels that record the Passion of Christ are solemnly read, and the other prayers and readings directly focus on these events.

The season of Lent ends with the solemn announcement of the Resurrection of Our Lord Jesus Christ at the Easter Vigil Mass on Holy Saturday evening. At this Mass we begin our celebration of the feast of Easter and the Easter season. The Easter season is marked by a sense of triumphant joy, since Jesus has overcome death and risen from the dead. This season lasts for fifty days, concluding with the third major feast of the liturgical year, the feast of Pentecost.

Pentecost

Pentecost is the feast that celebrates the presence of the Holy Spirit in the Church. Just as the Holy Spirit spoke through the prophets in the Old Testament, Our Lord promised to his apostles at the Last Supper that he would send the Holy Spirit to guide his Church. ". . . the Holy Spirit . . . will teach you all things and bring to your remembrance all that I have said to you" (Jn 14:26). This promise was ful-

> ### Prayer
> "It is truly right that with full hearts and minds and voices we should praise the unseen God, the all-powerful Father, and his only Son, Our Lord Jesus Christ."
>
> (Easter proclamation: *Exsultet*)

57

Develop

1. *Read paragraph 19 (Pentecost).*

2. *Review the events of Pentecost. This is the great celebration of the birthday of the Church. It occurs fifty days after Easter (ten days after the Ascension. This feast reminds us of the Holy Spirit, who gives life to the Church. The color red reminds us of the fire of the Holy Spirit.*

3. *Read paragraphs 20 and 21 (Ordinary Time).*

4. *Look on a liturgical calendar and see which times are Ordinary Time and how much of the Church year is Ordinary Time. The color of Ordinary Time is green—a sign of life and growth. During this time, we are to reflect upon the teachings of Christ and grow in holiness.*

5. *Read paragraphs 22–29 (to the end of the chapter).*

6. *Teach the students the Holy Days of Obligation. You may use the chart at right as a guide. Be sure the students understand what each day celebrates. They should memorize the dates of the Holy Days of Obligation.*

7. Review the three significant events that occur toward the end of the liturgical year: Trinity Sunday, Corpus Christi, and Christ the King. Discuss celebrations that are associated with these feasts such as Eucharistic Procession, Crowning of Christ, etc.

8. Many feasts celebrate the lives of Christ, Mary, and the saints. Most feast days are dedicated to the honor of a saint. Have the students look up their patron saints' feast days.

9. Review the vestments used during liturgical celebrations. If possible, look at your priest's vestments and admire the quality, color, and imagery used in their decoration.

Name:_____

Ordinary Time and Feast Days

Answer the following questions in complete sentences.

1. What is Pentecost and when is it celebrated during the Liturgical Year?
   <u>Pentecost is the feast on which we celebrate the birth of</u>
   <u>the Church and the coming of the Holy Spirit to the</u>
   <u>apostles. It is celebrated during the Easter Season.</u>

2. When is Ordinary Time?
   <u>Ordinary Time is the time between Christmas and Lent and</u>
   <u>Easter and Advent.</u>

3. What does the Church reflect upon during Ordinary Time?
   <u>During Ordinary Time, the Church reflects upon the</u>
   <u>mysteries of Christmas and Easter.</u>

4. List the Liturgical Colors and what they symbolize.
   <u>Purple symbolizes penance and sorrow.</u>
   <u>White symbolizes joy and glory.</u>
   <u>Green symbolizes life.</u>
   <u>Red symbolizes blood and fire.</u>
   <u>Rose symbolizes joy in the midst of penance.</u>
   <u>Black symbolizes mourning.</u>

5. Into what three main groups can we divide the other feasts that occur during the Liturgical Year? For each group, explain what they are and give some examples.
   1. <u>Holy Days (examples will vary)</u>

   2. <u>Sunday feasts.</u>

   3. <u>Feasts of the saints and Our Blessed Mother.</u>

HOLY DAYS OF OBLIGATION

These are special feast days on which the Church requires us to go to Mass. We celebrate six holy days of obligation in the United States:

- The Immaculate Conception—December 8
- Christmas—December 25
- Mary, Mother of God—January 1
- The Ascension of Jesus—Forty days after Easter*
- The Assumption of Mary—August 15
- The Solemnity of All Saints—November 1

*   The bishops' conference may transfer this feast to the following Sunday

Reinforce

1. Have the students work on *Activity Book*, p. 32.

2. Give the students time to work on their Memorization Questions and Words to Know and prepare for the chapter and unit quizzes.

3. Review the different symbols for the Holy Spirit and ways they may be applied to Pentecost.

4. Review any particular local devotions celebrated on specific Holy Days of Obligation or feast days.

5. *Give the students time to memorize the Holy Days of Obligation. Review their obligation to attend Mass on those days.*

Conclude

1. Lead the students in singing "To Jesus Christ, our sov'reign King," *Adoremus Hymnal*, #480.

2. End class by leading the students in the Morning Offering.

Preview

In the next lesson, the students' understanding of the material covered in this chapter and unit will be reviewed and assessed.

NOTES

_____
_____
_____
_____
_____
_____
_____
_____
_____
_____
_____

filled on the first Pentecost, and our celebration of this feast reminds us of this great gift.

Ordinary Time

There remains the time in the liturgical year that falls between Christmas and Lent and between Easter and Advent. This time is called ordinary time, since it is not marked by one of the principal events of our faith. "Ordinary," however, does not mean unimportant. This time allows us to reflect more deeply on the mysteries that we have just celebrated and to develop our love for God more fully. Certain Sundays and Holy Days during this time are also set aside to commemorate other significant elements of our faith or events from the life of Our Lord and Our Lady.

The diagram that follows will help us to see these seasons of the year more clearly.

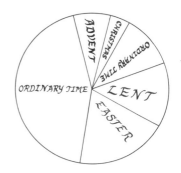

Other Feasts

Now that we have seen the basic framework for the liturgical year, we will fill it in with some of the feasts that occur throughout the year. We can divide these into three main

58

groups: (1) Holy Days, (2) Sunday feasts, and (3) feasts of the saints and Our Blessed Mother. The Church has set aside several days out of the year to commemorate certain significant events in our faith. In the United States, six of these feasts are Holy Days of Obligation, that is, days on which we are obliged to attend Mass. They are: (1) the Immaculate Conception of Our Lady (December 8); (2) Christmas (December 25); (3) the Solemnity of Mary, the Mother of God (January 1); (4) Ascension (forty days after Easter); (5) the Assumption of Our Lady (August 15); and (6) All Saints' Day (November 1). As you can see, these feasts occur throughout the liturgical year, except during the season of Lent.

Several great feasts of the Church are celebrated on Sundays throughout the year. Like the Holy Days, these special Sundays are found throughout the liturgical seasons. During the Christmas season we celebrate the *Feast of the Holy Family*, the model for all families, on the Sunday after Christmas. In the United States the *Feast of the Epiphany* is celebrated on the Sunday closest to January 6. On the following Sunday we celebrate the *Baptism of Jesus*, which marked the beginning of his public life.

In the ordinary time after Pentecost we celebrate two other great mysteries of our faith: the Trinity (on *Trinity Sunday*) and the Eucharist (on the *Feast of Corpus Christi)*. Finally, the liturgical year ends with the *Feast of Christ the King*, which reminds us to look ahead to the time when Christ will come in glory and reign as our King.

In addition to Sundays and Holy Days, there are many weekdays throughout the liturgical year that are set aside as special commemorations. Several recall events from the life of Our Blessed Mother. Others honor the saints as great examples of the Christian life. On these days we should call upon Mary and the saints to pray to God on our behalf.

Return to the diagram to see how the feasts fit into the liturgical year. As you have already seen, the colors of the liturgical year change. We see this most clearly in the **vestments**—the special garments worn by the priest and other ministers for celebrating the Liturgy—but also in other decorations in our churches. The three major colors are purple, white, and green. These are used at particular times during the various seasons of the year. *Purple* symbolizes penance and sorrow, so it is used during the seasons of Advent and Lent. *White* symbolizes joy and glory, so it is used at Christmas and Easter. *Green* symbolizes life and hope, so it is used during the ordinary time, when we should be filled with hope.

Three other colors are used less frequently, but also serve to remind us of what we are celebrating. First among these is *red*, which symbolizes fire and blood. It is used on the feast of Pentecost for the Holy Spirit, who was symbolized by fire. It is also used when we celebrate the Passion of Our Lord, the feasts of the martyrs, the feasts of apostles, and the feasts of the evangelists. *Rose* is symbolic of joy in the midst of penance and is used on Laetare and Gaudete Sundays. As we have seen, these Sundays occur during the penitential seasons and are days of rejoicing. Finally, the color *black* is a symbol of mourning. It may be used for Masses for the dead or All Souls' Day.

Thus, we have seen how the Church provides us with a beautiful and meaningful way of worshipping God throughout the year. It enables us to reflect on the key mysteries of our faith and the lives of Our Lord and his Mother as we go from season to season. In order to unite ourselves more perfectly with our fellow Christians, our prayers should reflect the themes so beautifully set forth for us by the Church. Thus, our entire prayer life will become a more perfect form of worship to be given to Almighty God.

Words to Know:

Liturgy   liturgical year   vestments

Church Teaching

"The sacred liturgy is the public worship which Our Redeemer as Head of the Church renders to the Father, as well as the worship which the community of the faithful renders to its Founder and through him to the Heavenly Father. It is, in short, the worship rendered by the Mystical Body of Christ in the entirety of its head and members" (MD).

59

_____
_____
_____
_____
_____
_____
_____
_____
_____
_____
_____
_____
_____
_____
_____
_____
_____
_____
_____
_____
_____
_____
_____
_____
_____

Q. 65   *What is liturgy?*
Liturgy is the priestly work of Jesus Christ, including the public participation of the People of God in his work. This includes the celebration of the Mass, the other sacraments, and the Liturgy of the Hours (CCC 1069–71).

Q. 66   *What is the liturgical year?*
The liturgical year is the cycle of feasts that surround the life and mysteries of Christ's work on earth. The seasons are Advent and Christmas, Lent and Easter, Pentecost and Ordinary time (CCC 1168–71).

Q. 67   *Why does the Church celebrate feasts of saints and martyrs?*
When the Church celebrates feasts of saints and martyrs, she proclaims the Paschal Mystery in those who have suffered and have been glorified with Christ and raises them up as examples (CCC 1173).

Q. 68   *What is the Liturgy of the Hours?*
The Liturgy of the Hours is the prayer of the Church. It is devised so that the whole course of the day and the night is made holy by the praise of God (CCC 1174–78).

60

_____
_____
_____
_____
_____
_____
_____
_____
_____
_____
_____
_____
_____
_____
_____

Name: _____

The Church Sanctifying: Worship   Quiz 8

Part I: Answer in complete sentences.

1. What is liturgy?
   Liturgy is the Church's official public worship.

2. List and explain the three elements of liturgy:
   1. The Sacrifice of the Mass is where we perfectly join with Christ's offering of himself to the Father and are nourished with his Body in the Eucharist.

   2. The sacraments are the means by which we receive God's grace and are able to partake in the supernatural life.

   3. The recitation of the divine office is how we can sanctify our day with prayer and unite our prayer with the prayer of the Church.

Part II: Fill in the chart describing the use and symbolism of the liturgical colors.

	GREEN	RED	WHITE	PURPLE	ROSE
Used for (masses and seasons)	Ordinary Time	Pentecost, feast days of martyrs	Christmas, Easter, certain saint days	Advent and Lent	Gaudete Sunday, Laetare Sunday
Symbolizes	life	blood and fire	joy and glory	penance and sorrow	joy in the midst of penance

_A - 10_   _Faith and Life • Grade 8 • Appendix A_

Aims

The students' understanding of the material covered in this chapter and unit will be reviewed and assessed.

Materials

- Quiz 8, Appendix, p. A-10

- Unit 2 Test, Appendix, pp. 11–12

Optional:
- "To Jesus Christ, our sov'reign King," _Adoremus Hymnal_ #480

Review

1. The students should be able to distinguish between the Liturgy of the Church and private devotion. The students should know the three elements of the Liturgy: the Mass, the sacraments, and the Liturgy of the Hours.

2. The students should understand the structure of the liturgical year and how it parallels the life of Christ. The year focuses on significant events from Christ's life including:
   - Christmas (prepared for with Advent)
   - Easter (prepared for with Lent)
   - Pentecost
   The rest of the year includes Ordinary Time and feast days.

3. The students should know the liturgical colors and their significance.

4. The students should know the Holy Days of Obligation.

Assess

1. Distribute the quizzes and read through them with the students to be sure they understand the questions.

2. Administer the quiz. As they hand in their work, you may orally quiz the students on the Memorization Questions from this chapter.

3. After all the quizzes have been handed in, review the correct answers with the class. Repeat steps 1–3 for the unit test.

Conclude

1. Lead the students in singing "To Jesus Christ, our sov'reign King," _Adoremus Hymnal_, #480.

2. End class by leading the students in the Morning Offering.

CHAPTER NINE
MARY, MOTHER OF THE CHURCH

Catechism of the Catholic Church References

Annunciation: 484–86, 494, 509–11, 723, 2676
Assumption: 966, 974
Consequences of Original Sin: 55–58, 399–400, 402–9, 416–19
Devotion to the Blessed Virgin: 971
Immaculate Conception: 490–93, 508
Intercessory Prayer of Mary: 969, 975
Mary as Eschatological Icon of the Church: 972, 975
Mary as Mother of the Church as Our Mother: 963–70, 973–74
Mary's Consent: 494, 511

Mary's Divine Motherhood: 495, 509
Mary's Predestination: 488–89
Mary's Virginity: 496–507, 510
Meditation on the Rosary: 2705–8, 2723
New Eve: 487–11
Obedience of Mary's Faith: 148–49
Original Sin: 388–90, 396–401, 415
Perpetual Virginity: 496–507
Prayer in Union with Mary: 2617–19, 2622
Prayers of Intercession: 2634–36, 2647

Scripture References

Annunciation and Visitation: Lk 1:26–56
Joseph's Dream: Mt 1:18–24
Jesus Gives Mary as Our Mother: Jn 19:26-27

The Fall: Gen 3
Wedding at Cana: Jn 2:1–11

Summary of Lesson Content

Lesson 1

The Annunciation was the announcement to Mary that God chose her to be the Mother of God.

Mary is the New Eve, the mother of all who live according to the life of grace.

Jesus gave Mary to his followers to be our mother. She is the mother of the Church.

Lesson 2

Because of Mary's assent to be the Mother of God, she was given several privileges. The first of these is the Immaculate Conception.

Mary was conceived without original sin. The grace won by Christ on the Cross was applied to Mary in anticipation of this saving event. In this way, Mary could be the perfect vessel for the Son of God. Mary was given the life of grace from the moment of her conception.

Lesson 3

Mary was given the privilege of perpetual virginity. This means that Mary was a virgin before the conception and birth of Christ, during these events, and after these events.

As perpetual virgin, Mary represents the Church, our pure and holy mother of all on earth.

At the end of her earthly life, Mary was assumed, body and soul, into heaven. She did not experience the corruption of the grave.

Lesson 4

The Litany of Loreto gives honor to Mary. Her titles remind us of the great honors bestowed upon Mary.

Mary is a powerful intercessor and the Mediatrix of Grace.

LESSON ONE: MOTHERHOOD

Aims

The students will learn that the Annunciation was the announcement to Mary that God chose her to be the Mother of God.

They will learn that Mary is the New Eve, the mother of all who live according to the life of grace. Jesus gave Mary to his followers to be our mother. She is the mother of the Church.

Materials

- *Activity Book*, p. 33
- Images of Mary

Optional:
- Rosary kits
- "Hail, holy Queen enthroned above," *Adoremus Hymnal*, #530

Begin

Begin the class by looking at various images of Mary. There are many images and titles for Mary. Have each student choose his favorite image or title for Mary to research. You may use the Litany of Loreto at the back of the student text for some examples. The students should understand that all of these different titles describe the same Mary—they are simply different perspectives of the same woman, describing one of her attributes, an apparition, a patronage, etc.

CHAPTER 9

Mary—Mother of the Church

When Jesus saw his mother, and the disciple whom he loved standing near, he said to his mother, "Woman, behold, your son!"

John 19:26

". . . the angel Gabriel was sent from God to a city of Galilee named Nazareth, to a virgin . . . and the virgin's name was Mary. And he came to her and said, 'Hail, full of grace, the Lord is with you! . . . Do not be afraid, Mary, for you have found favor with God. And behold, you will conceive in your womb and bear a son, and you shall call his name Jesus. . . .' And Mary said, 'Behold, I am the handmaid of the Lord; let it be done to me according to your word.' And the angel departed from her" (Lk 1:26–28, 30–31, 38).

These words from St. Luke describe the **Annunciation** and mark the first reference in the Gospels to Mary, the mother of Our Lord. It is appropriate that we should first see her in this scene, since our salvation depends in a great way on this event. Mary was not forced to become the Mother of God. God announced to her through his messenger Gabriel that she had been chosen for this role. Yet his choice required her consent. This consent is beautifully and simply given by Our Lady in her words, "Let it be done to me according to your word."

At the moment of Mary's **fiat** (the Latin word for "let it be done") the "Word became flesh." In other words, the Son of God was conceived in her womb. Mary freely accepted God's will for her and gave life to the Son of God so that we might share in his divine life. Thus, our very salvation depended upon Mary's obedience to the will of God.

The New Eve

Mary's importance for our redemption is reflected in the title frequently given to her by the Fathers of the Church—the "new Eve." Christ has been called the "new Adam," because by his death he undid the harm done by Adam, the first man. So, too, we can speak of Mary and compare her to Eve. "Eve" means "the mother of all the living." Eve helped to bring sin into the world by tempting Adam. Mary, however, helped to bring salvation from sin by listening to and accepting the invitation of God and then becoming the Mother of God. Eve brought death into the world, but Mary brought life—eternal life through Christ. Mary's faith and obedience to God's will will correct Eve's pride and disobedience of God's command. Mary, by submitting herself perfectly to God's will, returned to mankind what had been lost to us through original sin.

61

Develop

1. Read paragraphs 1–6 (up to Privileges Given to Mary).

2. Read Luke 1:26–56. This includes the Annunciation and Visitation. The students may dramatize these events and discuss the following questions:
- *How did the angel greet Mary? Why?*
- *What did Gabriel tell Mary? Why did Mary ask how this would be possible? How would this be possible?*
- *Did Mary consent? How did she show her consent?*
- *Why did Gabriel tell Mary that Elizabeth was with child?*
- *Why did Mary go to Elizabeth? Would this have been easy for Mary?*
- *Mary was betrothed, not married. What would it have meant for Mary to be expecting a baby while not married in that time period? Mary was likely about age 14. What difficulties might Mary have faced? Read Mt 1:18–24 to see how Joseph handled this news.*

3. Mary's fiat—"Let it be done"—reminds us how we should respond to God's will in our lives.

4. "The Word was made flesh." This reminds us that Jesus is true God and true man and that he took his human nature from Mary. It also reminds us how Jesus is made present in the Eucharist—God is made present among us in the Blessed Sacrament.

5. Compare Mary and Eve. Point out how Mary is the New Eve—the mother of all living according to the order of grace.

6. From Jn 19:26–27, we can see how Jesus gave Mary to John, his beloved disciple. John represents all of us—we are to receive Mary as our mother. Just as John receives Mary into his home, how can we receive Mary into our homes and hearts? Mary is the mother of Jesus. The Church is his body and so, by extension, Mary is the Mother of the Church.

Name:_____

Mary: Mother of the Church

Answer the following questions in complete sentences.

1. Why does Mary have an important role in salvation?

   <u>Mary has an important role in salvation</u>
   <u>because at the moment of her fiat the</u>
   <u>Son of God was conceived in her womb.</u>

2. What is the Annunciation?

   <u>The Annunciation refers to the event when</u>
   <u>God announced to Mary through his</u>
   <u>messenger Gabriel that she had been</u>
   <u>chosen to be the Mother of God.</u>

In the chart below, compare Mary and Eve. Remember that Mary is the New Eve.

EVE	MARY
Made without original sin	Made without original sin.
Received life from the rib of Adam	Received life from her parents.
Had Sanctifying Grace	Had Sanctifying Grace.
God asked something of her	God asked something of her.
Eve listened to the voice of the angel of lies	Mary listed to the angel Gabriel.
Eve disobeyed God and offered the forbidden fruit to Adam	Mary said "yes" and conceived the Son of God.
Sin, death, darkness, and all the effects of sin entered the world	Grace, life, and light and all the effects of life enter the world.
A woman and her seed were promised to redeem the world	The promise is fulfilled.
Called Mother of the Living	Called Mother of God and all Christians.

Faith and Life Series • Grade 8 • Chapter 9 • Lesson 1   33

MARY AND EVE

EVE	MARY
Formed from the rib of a man	Immaculately conceived
"She took some of its fruit and ate it."	"I am the handmaid of the Lord."
"The man called his wife 'Eve'."	"Hail, full of grace."
Mother of all the living	Mother of the Church, "Woman, behold your son."

LOVING MOTHER OF THE REDEEMER

Loving mother of the Redeemer,
gate of heaven, star of the sea,
assist your people who have fallen,
yet strive to rise again.

To the wonderment of nature,
you bore your Creator,
yet remained a virgin after as before.

You who received Gabriel's joyful greeting,
have pity on us poor sinners.

LESSON TWO: IMMACULATE MARY

Aims

The students will learn that because of Mary's assent to become the Mother of God, she was given several privileges. The first of these is the Immaculate Conception. Mary was conceived without original sin. The grace won by Christ on the Cross was applied to Mary in anticipation of this saving event. In this way, Mary could be the perfect vessel for the Son of God. Mary was given the life of grace from the moment of her conception.

Materials

- *Activity Book*, p. 34
- Our Lady of Lourdes, Appendix, p. B-6
- Saint Catherine Labouré, Appendix, p. B-7

Optional:
- "Hail, holy Queen enthroned above," *Adoremus Hymnal*, #530

Begin

Teach the students that what we know and believe about Mary is based upon what we know and believe about Christ. Every grace that Mary received was won by Christ upon the Cross, but it was given to Mary in anticipation of her great work in salvation history. For example, we know that Jesus was truly human, but without sin. His human nature was taken from Mary, so Mary had to be without sin. We find evidence of this in Scripture. Mary's purity has been the belief of the Church since the beginning. The Church has defined these beliefs as true.

Mary, Our Mother

As Eve was the physical mother of the human race, Mary is our spiritual Mother. While hanging on the Cross, Our Lord spoke to Mary and the apostle John. He said to Mary, "Woman, behold your son!" And then he turned to John and said, "Behold, your mother!"

(Jn 19:26–27). These words were not meant only for Our Lady and St. John, but for all of Jesus' followers. Jesus gave his own Mother to all of us. When Jesus said he would not leave us orphans, he also meant to leave us his Mother. Her care for us is evident in many ways. We call Mary "Our Blessed Mother." Like any mother, Mary has a special love for every one of her children. She leads us into her Son's presence. She watches over each and shares in each one's joys and sorrows. In turning to Mary, as we would to our own mother on earth, we draw closer to God.

In addition to being a spiritual Mother to each of us as individuals, Mary is also the Mother of the whole Church. As Mary was the Mother of Christ's physical body, she is also the Mother of his Mystical Body—the Church —of which we are members through our Baptism.

Mary's role in our redemption goes beyond giving birth to Christ. Her cooperation in God's will began at the Annunciation and continued to the foot of the Cross. There, Mary willingly accepted the death of her Son and joined with him in that suffering. The graces that Christ won for us come to us through Mary. It is for this reason that we can say, "to Jesus, through Mary."

Privileges Given to Mary

Because Mary was chosen by God to be the Mother of his divine Son, he gave to her several *privileges*. Three of these are: (1) freedom from original sin, (2) complete and per-

> ### Prayer
> "Mary, Mother of Grace, Mother of Mercy, shield me from the enemy and receive me at the hour of my death."
>
> (Enchiridion, 61)

62

Develop

1. Read paragraphs 7–11 (up to Perpetual Virginity).

2. Review original sin and its effects, using the chart at right. The students may dramatize the Fall and/or read the account of the Fall in Gen 3.

3. Mary was free from original sin. It was fitting for the Mother of God to be without stain, as she was the vessel of God, who gave flesh to his Son. Just as we must be free from mortal sin and filled with grace when we receive Holy Communion, so too, Mary was free from original sin and all personal sin to bear the Son of God within her womb.

4. We can say that Mary was the Tabernacle of God, the new Ark of the Covenant. What an honor! So, too, when we receive Our Lord in Communion, we are living tabernacles. Jesus dwells within us.

5. The doctrine of the Immaculate Conception was formally taught by the Church on December 8, 1854 by Pope Pius IX. This is an example of development of doctrine and papal infallibility. The Feast of the Immaculate Conception is celebrated by the Church on December 8th, and it is a Holy Day of Obligation. Under this title, Mary is the patroness of the United States of America.

6. You may review the apparition of Mary at Lourdes to Saint Bernadette (see Appendix, p. B-6 for the story). This apparition confirms the Church's teaching on the Immaculate Conception. Have the students act out the events of Lourdes.

7. Discuss Saint Catherine Labouré and the Miraculous Medal. Discuss Mary's appearances to Saint Catherine and her desire for the medal to be struck and distributed (see Appendix, p. B-7). Give the students miraculous medals.

Name:_____

Free from Original Sin

Answer the following questions in complete sentences.

1. What is original sin, who has it, and what does it do to our souls?
   Original sin is the fallen state of human nature which affects
   every person born into the world.

2. Why does Mary not have original sin and what is this great privilege called?
   Mary does not have original sin because God wished her to
   be worthy to be the Mother of God. This great privilege is
   called the Immaculate Conception.

3. When was this doctrine infallibly defined? By whom?
   This doctrine was infallibly defined on December 8, 1854 by
   Pope Pius IX.

4. How did Mary confirm this doctrine?
   Mary confirmed this doctrine four years later when she
   appeared at Lourdes to St. Bernadette and said, "I am the
   Immaculate Conception."

5. When do we celebrate this mystery and feast?
   We celebrate this mystery and feast day on December 8.

34   *Faith and Life Series • Grade 8 • Chapter 9 • Lesson 2*

Reinforce

1. Have the students work on *Activity Book*, p. 34.

2. Give the students time to work on the Memorization Questions and Words to Know from this chapter.

3. *Have the students write an essay on how Jesus came to us through Mary and Mary's role in salvation. We can thus call her the co-redemptrix. (Co-redemptrix does not mean equal to the Redeemer, Jesus, it means that she cooperated in the work of redemption; e.g., a co-pilot is not the pilot, but helps a pilot in the flight of a plane.)*

4. You may view images of the Basilica of the National Shrine of the Immaculate Conception in Washington, D.C.

Conclude

1. Lead the students in singing "Hail, holy Queen enthroned above," *Adoremus Hymnal*, #530.

2. End class by praying Loving Mother of the Redeemer.

Preview

In the next lesson, the students will learn about Mary's perpetual virginity and the Assumption.

EFFECTS OF ORIGINAL SIN

	ORIGINAL NATURE	FALLEN NATURE	ANTIDOTES OF GRACE
Intellect	Illuminated by God	Ignorance	Faith
Will	Loving obedience	Malice	Spiritual combat and charity
Passions	Spontaniously loves the good	Weak/disordered	Spiritual combat and charity
Body	No suffering or death	Suffering and death	Hope of resurrection

LESSON THREE: MARY'S GIFTS

Aims

The students will learn that Mary was given the privilege of perpetual virginity. This means that Mary was a virgin before the conception and birth of Christ, during these events, and after.

They will learn that Mary, as a perpetual virgin, represents the Church, our pure and holy mother of all on earth. At the end of her earthly life, Mary was assumed, body and soul, into heaven. She did not experience the corruption of the grave.

Materials

• *Activity Book*, p. 35

Optional:
• "Hail, holy Queen enthroned above," *Adoremus Hymnal*, #530

Begin

Mary is a model for all of us. Discuss how the students should imitate Mary and her virtues. Discuss the motto: To Jesus through Mary. What does this mean? It has been said that the most perfect way for us to go to Jesus is the same way he came to us: through Mary. Consecration to Mary means we entrust ourselves to Mary and her patronage, believing that she will bring us, our prayers, and our needs to her Son and perfect them in presenting them in union with hers.

---

petual virginity, and (3) freedom from having body and soul separated until the end of the world.

Because Mary was chosen by God to be the Mother of his divine Son, he gave to her several *privileges*. Three of these are: (1) the Immaculate Conception, (2) complete and perpetual virginity, and (3) the Assumption of Mary into heaven, body and soul.

Free from Original Sin: The Immaculate Conception

We know that all human beings have inherited original sin from our first parents, Adam and Eve. When they sinned, they lost for themselves—and for us—the great gift of *sanctifying grace*, God's life in our souls. While we are not personally responsible for original sin, we bear the effects—especially being weak and easily tempted to sin.

Because God wished Mary to be worthy to become the Mother of God, she was created free from all sin, including original sin. God prepared Mary so that she would be worthy to carry the Son of God in her womb. In the same way, the ark of the Covenant was built in the Old Testament to be a fitting receptacle for the written Word of God. God instructed the people, through Moses, that the ark should be built of a rare wood and elaborately decorated with gold. In this way it would be an appropriate symbol of God's presence. How much more fitting was it, then, that God should prepare Mary, who would contain the Word of God himself, not just a symbol of God's presence. Mary is, then, the "new Ark of the Covenant."

Besides Our Lord, Mary is the only human being who was created without original sin. As the poet Wordsworth so beautifully put it, "she is our tainted nature's solitary boast." From the moment of her conception in the womb of her mother, St. Anne, Mary was filled with divine life. Because she was without original sin, she was free from our weakness and inclination to sin. She truly was, as the archangel Gabriel said, "full of grace." This great privilege is called the **Immaculate Conception**.

This doctrine has been taught by the Church but was not formally defined until December 8, 1854, by Pope Pius IX. This was an occasion when papal infallibility was invoked. Our Lady herself confirmed this doctrine four years later. When she appeared to St. Bernadette in the grotto at Lourdes, she identified herself by this title. When asked who she was, Mary replied, "I am the Immaculate Conception."

The feast of the Immaculate Conception, celebrated on December 8, has become a Holy Day of Obligation since the doctrine was defined. This feast is particularly important for Catholics in the United States, for it is under this title that Mary was declared patroness of our country.

Perpetual Virginity

A second great privilege given to Mary was that of **perpetual virginity**. Perpetual virginity means that Mary was always a virgin: before the conception and birth of Christ, during the birth, and after the birth of Christ.

While Our Blessed Mother is mentioned only a few times in the Gospels, her virginity is explicitly mentioned by both St. Luke and St. Matthew. In St. Luke's Gospel, Mary tells the angel that she is a virgin. The angel confirms this. In St. Matthew's Gospel, Joseph confirms the fact that he is not the father of the Child in her womb. They are both told that the Child is conceived of the Holy Spirit.

And Mary said to the angel, "How can this be, since I have no husband?" And the angel said to her, "The Holy Spirit will come upon you; therefore the child to be

63

Develop

1. Read paragraphs 12–16 (up to Mary in our Lives).

2. The perpetual virginity means just that—Mary was a virgin before, during, and after the conception and birth of Jesus. This doctrine was formally defined at the Second Council of Constantinople in 553. Perpetual virginity is twice referenced in Scripture:
• *Gabriel said Mary would conceive by the Holy Spirit—for she knew not man.*
• *Gabriel had to encourage Joseph to take Mary as his wife, since he knew he was not the father of the child she was carrying, but that this child was conceived by the Holy Spirit.*
This teaching reminds us that Mary and Joseph lived celibately, even during their marriage. They are models of purity and celibacy for religious, and of chastity for all marriages.

3. Mary, as virgin and mother, is a model of the Church.

Mary is the mother of all God's children born by the life of grace, yet the Church is the pure and spotless Bride of Christ.

4. One of the effects of original sin is death and corruption of the body. Mary, free from original sin, did not experience this effect. Mary's Assumption is a sign of hope for all Christians, as we believe in the resurrection of the body and life everlasting. The Assumption of Mary was defined November 1, 1950 by Pope Pius XII. The feast is celebrated August 15 and is a Holy Day of Obligation.

5. The Eastern Rite teaches that, at the end of Mary's life, she fell asleep in the Lord and was assumed to heaven bodily. The Latin Rite does not state whether Mary died or rested in the Lord. The teaching of the "sleeping of Mary" is called the dormition, and is not contrary to the Church's teaching on the Assumption of Mary.

Name:_____

More Privileges of Mary

Answer the following questions in complete sentences.

1. What is Mary's perpetual virginity?
   Mary's perpetual virginity is the fact that Mary was a virgin before, during, and after the birth of Christ.

2. How do we know that St. Joseph is not Jesus' father?
   We know that St. Joseph is not Jesus' father because the Bible tells us so. If Jesus is the Son of God, God is his Father, not a man.

3. Which creeds teach Mary's perpetual virginity?
   Mary's perpetual virginity is taught in the Nicene and Apostles' Creeds.

4. What is the Assumption of Mary?
   The Assumption of Mary is the doctrine that Mary was assumed into heaven body and soul.

5. When was the doctrine of the Assumption declared infallibly?
   The doctrine of the Assumption was declared infallibly on November 1, 1950.

6. When do we celebrate this feast?
   We celebrate the Assumption on August 15.

Reinforce

1. Have the students work on *Activity Book*, p. 35.

2. Give the students time to work on the Memorization Questions and Words to Know from this chapter.

3. Discuss the religious life and its value. It is a life dedicated solely to Christ, anticipating union with Christ forever in heaven. Religious life is a living witness on earth of Christ's heavenly promise for his followers. The vow of chastity/celibacy not only indicates that one will not marry, but that his heart will be fixed on Christ.

Conclude

1. Lead the students in singing "Hail, holy Queen enthroned above," *Adoremus Hymnal*, #530.

2. End class by praying Loving Mother of the Redeemer.

Preview

In the next lesson, the students will learn about the role of Mary in our lives.

SAINT LOUIS MARIE DE MONTFORT

Saint Louis de Montfort lived and died around the beginning of the eighteenth century. Ordained a priest when he was twenty-seven, he worked in hospitals and gave missions to the poor until being named a missionary apostolic by Pope Clement XI. He then devoted himself entirely to traveling throughout France and giving missions to the poor. At these missions, he brought many lapsed Catholics and Protestants back to the Church. He focused especially on devotion to the Rosary and total consecration to Jesus through Mary. As he wrote in *True Devotion to the Blessed Virgin,* "All our perfection consists in being conformed, united, and consecrated to Jesus Christ; and therefore the most perfect of all devotions is, without any doubt, that which the most perfectly conforms, unites, and consecrates us to Jesus Christ. Now Mary, being the most conformed of all creatures to Jesus Christ, it follows that of all devotions, that which most consecrates and conforms the soul to Our Lord is devotion to his holy Mother. The more a soul is consecrated to Mary, the more it is consecrated to Jesus Christ." According to Saint Louis, just as Jesus came to us through Mary in the Incarnation, we can go to Jesus through Mary by consecrating ourselves to her and trusting her to bring us to her Son. True devotion to Mary always leads to true devotion to Christ.

LESSON FOUR: MEDIATRIX

Aims

The students will learn that the Litany of Loreto gives honor to Mary. Her titles remind us of the great honors bestowed upon Mary.

They will learn that Mary is a powerful intercessor and the Mediatrix of Grace.

Materials

- *Activity Book*, p. 36

Optional:
- "Hail, holy Queen enthroned above," *Adoremus Hymnal*, #530

Begin

Pray the Litany of Loreto found at the back of the student text with the students. Explain each of the titles for Mary in this prayer.

The Litany of Loreto is a petition to Mary for her prayers. Intercessory prayer is an important part of our faith. We ask others to pray for us and in union with us. We are not worshipping Mary by praying to her; rather, we are asking her to take our prayers to Jesus. In this way, it would be more accurate to say we pray to Jesus through Mary.

---

born will be called holy, the Son of God" (Lk 1:34–35).

When his mother Mary had been betrothed to Joseph, before they came together she was found to be with child of the Holy Spirit; . . . an angel of the Lord appeared to him in a dream saying, ". . . that which is conceived in her is of the Holy Spirit . . ." (Mt 1:18, 20).

Mary's virginity is given further testimony in the creeds. In the Apostles' Creed, we proclaim our belief in Jesus Christ, who "was conceived by the power of the Holy Spirit, born of the Virgin Mary. . . ." Similar statements are found in the Nicene Creed, as well as in many other prayers. This doctrine was formally defined at the Second Council of Constantinople in 553 A.D.

Mary's Assumption into Heaven

The third great privilege of Our Lady that we will discuss here is Mary's **Assumption**. The Assumption means that Mary was taken, at the end of her earthly life, body and soul to heaven. When we die, we know that our soul is separated from our body, and so we are not complete. We must wait until the end of the world for God to restore our bodies, in a glorified state, to us. This is one of the consequences that we bear because of original sin. Since Mary was conceived without original sin, it is fitting that God chose to spare the Mother of his Son this consequence of it.

Like the doctrine of the Immaculate Conception, the doctrine of Mary's Assumption has been part of the Church's belief from the beginning. Since about the fifth century, the Eastern rites of the Church have celebrated the feast of the Assumption on August 15. However, it was not until 1950 that this doctrine was formally defined. On November 1 of that

64

year, Pope Pius XII infallibly defined this doctrine. The feast of the Assumption, celebrated on August 15, is now a Holy Day of Obligation.

Mary in Our Lives

"Mary has by grace been exalted above all the angels and men to a place second only to her Son, as the most holy Mother of God who was involved in the mysteries of Christ; she is rightly honored by a special cult in the Church" (LG, 66).

In the Litany of Loreto (see the Appendix), we proclaim Mary as the Queen of angels and the Queen of saints. She has been exalted by God above all other creatures and now holds a place second to her Son, Christ, the King. Why should Mary be placed above even the angels? She has earned this honor because of her role in our salvation and her fullness of grace since the beginning of her life.

Because of Mary's place at the right hand of her Son, she should receive the proper veneration from us. We do not adore Our Lady, since adoration, or divine worship, is reserved for God alone. Rather, we **venerate** her (honor her) above all other creatures because of her special place in our salvation. We believe that she is "full of grace" and as such is "blessed among women." Because of her place, it is fitting, as she herself proclaimed, that "all generations will call [her] blessed" (Lk 1:48).

In honoring Mary we also recognize that she is, as St. Pius X wrote, "our sure way to Christ." As our Mother, Mary will **intercede** in heaven for us, as she did for others when she was on earth. Recall the story of Our Lord's first public miracle. Jesus and his disciples, together with Mary, were at a wedding in Cana. The host ran out of wine, and Mary turned to her Son, asking him to do something about it. And,

Develop

1. Read paragraphs 17–22 (to the end of the chapter).

2. Mary is a powerful intercessor. She brings our prayers and prays on our behalf before her Son. We see from the Wedding of Cana that Our Lord answers the prayers of his mother. Together read this passage: Jn 2:1–11. Discuss the following questions:
- *What was the need at the wedding? Whose need was it?*
- *Why did Mary turn to her Son?*
- *What did Jesus tell Mary? Did he answer her prayer?*
- *What was Mary's advice to the servants? How can we follow this advice?*
- *What was the quality of the wine? What does this say about God's generosity in answering his mother's prayers?*

3. Discuss that Jesus is the one Mediator between God and man. Sometimes Mary is referred to as the Mediatrix of Grace. This means that all grace won by Christ is obtained

for us through Mary. If Jesus is the source of all grace and he came to us through Mary, then we can say that Mary is the Mediatrix. This is a parallel teaching to the title of Co-redemptrix.

4. What should a relationship with a mother be like? What confidence should we have in Mary? Discuss ways the students can develop their relationship with Mary.

5. Teach the students that we do not adore or worship (latria) Mary, for this is reserved for God alone. We honor (dulia) the saints for the glory this gives God, in recognizing his work in his servants. Mary is the greatest of the saints and the foremost example of God's goodness. We reserve the highest devotion (hyperdulia) for Mary alone, because of her unique sanctity.

Name:_____

Mary in our Lives

Answer the following questions in complete sentences.

1. Why is Mary queen of the angels and saints (and heaven and earth!)?
   Mary is the queen of angels, saints, heaven, and earth because of her critical role in our salvation and because she has received the fullness of God's grace.

2. How did she earn this title?
   She earned this title because God has exalted her above all other creatures, and she holds a place at the Son's right hand.

3. Why does Mary receive veneration from us?
   Mary receives veneration from us because of her role in our salvation and because Jesus wants us to honor his mother.

4. What did Pope St. Pius X tell us about Mary?
   Pope St. Pius X told us that Mary is "our sure way to Christ" and that she will intercede for us.

5. What does it mean for Mary to intercede for us?
   To say that Mary will intercede for us means that she will pray to Jesus on our behalf.

6. What is the Litany of Loreto? Explain this prayer.
   The Litany of Loreto is a series of invocations to the Blessed Virgin containing many titles of Our Lady which we can meditate on.

36   *Faith and Life Series • Grade 8 • Chapter 9 • Lesson 4*

Reinforce

1. Have the students work on *Activity Book*, p. 36.

2. Give the students time to work on the Memorization Questions and Words to Know from this chapter and to prepare for the quiz.

3. Each of the students should choose a title of Mary from the Litany of Loreto and artistically depict Mary under this title.

4. Have the students write prayers of consecration to Mary.

5. Teach the students the Rosary and all of the mysteries shown in the chart at the bottom of this page. Have the students write meditations on each mystery.

Conclude

1. Lead the students in singing "Hail, holy Queen enthroned above," *Adoremus Hymnal*, #530.

2. End class by praying Loving Mother of the Redeemer.

Preview

In the next lesson, the students' understanding of the material covered in this chapter will be reviewed and assessed.

THE MYSTERIES OF THE ROSARY

The Joyful Mysteries
The Annunciation
The Visitation
The Nativity
The Presentation
The Finding in the Temple

The Sorrowful Mysteries
The Agony in the Garden
The Scourging at the Pillar
The Crowning with Thorns
The Carrying of the Cross
The Crucifixion

The Glorious Mysteries
The Resurrection
The Ascension
The Descent of the Holy Spirit
The Assumption
The Coronation

The Luminous Mysteries
The Baptism of Christ in the Jordan
The Wedding Feast at Cana
The Proclamation of the Kingdom of God
The Transfiguration of Our Lord
The Institution of the Holy Eucharist

as we know, Jesus granted her request; he would not refuse his Mother.

This episode teaches us an important lesson. Mary will continue to intercede with Jesus for her children. And Jesus, as he did at Cana, will listen to her pleas for us. Let us remember, then, to turn to Mary in prayer, asking her to give us through her Son the graces we need:

"O Mary, conceived without sin, pray for us, who have recourse to thee."

The Litany of Loreto: Our Lady's Litany

A litany is a form of prayer consisting of a series of petitions, each of which is followed by a fixed response. The litany begins by in-voking the Persons of the Trinity and concludes with invocations of the Lamb of God. The body of the litany consists of petitions corresponding to a particular theme. The litanies that are formally recognized by the Church are the litanies to the Holy Name, the Sacred Heart, the Precious Blood, the Blessed Virgin, St. Joseph, and the saints.

The litany of the Blessed Virgin, known as the Litany of Loreto, is a series of invocations of the Blessed Virgin, each with the response, "Pray for us." It contains many beautiful titles of Our Lady and provides us with much to meditate. As you read and say this ancient prayer, which you will find in the Appendix, think about the meaning of each of Mary's titles.

"For behold, henceforth all generations will call me blessed; for he who is mighty has done great things for me. . . ."

(Lk 1:48–49)

Church Teaching

"This motherhood of Mary in the order of grace continues uninterruptedly from the consent which she loyally gave at the Annunciation and which she sustained without wavering beneath the Cross. . . . Taken up to heaven she did not lay aside this saving office but by her manifold intercession contin-ues to bring us the gifts of eternal salvation. By her maternal charity, she cares for the brethren of her Son, who still journey on earth surrounded by dangers and difficulties, until they are led into their blessed home" (*LG*, 62).

65

LITANY OF THE LORETO

Lord, have mercy on us.
Christ, have mercy on us.
Lord, have mercy on us.
Christ, hear us.
Christ, graciously hear us.
God the Father of heaven,
have mercy on us.
God the Son, Redeemer of the world,
have mercy on us.
God the Holy Spirit,
have mercy on us.
Holy Trinity, One God,
have mercy on us.

Holy Mary, *pray for us.**
Holy Mother of God,
Holy Virgin of virgins,
Mother of Christ,
Mother of divine grace,
Mother most pure,
Mother most chaste,
Mother inviolate,
Mother undefiled,
Mother most amiable,
Mother most admirable,
Mother of good counsel,
Mother of the Church,
Mother of our Creator,
Mother of our Savior,
Virgin most prudent,
Virgin most venerable,
Virgin most renowned,
Virgin most powerful,
Virgin most merciful,
Virgin most faithful,
Mirror of justice,
Seat of wisdom,
Cause of our joy,
Spiritual vessel,
Vessel of honor,
Singular vessel of devotion,
Mystical rose,
*Pray for us is repeated after each invocation.

Tower of David,
Tower of ivory,
House of gold,
Ark of the covenant,
Gate of Heaven,
Morning star,
Health of the sick,
Refuge of sinners,
Comforter of the afflicted,
Help of Christians,
Queen of Angels,
Queen of Patriarchs,
Queen of Prophets,
Queen of Apostles,
Queen of Martyrs,
Queen of Confessors,
Queen of Virgins,
Queen of all Saints,
Queen conceived without original sin,
Queen assumed into heaven,
Queen of the most holy Rosary,
Queen of peace,

Lamb of God, who take away the sins of the world, *spare us, O Lord.*
Lamb of God, who take away the sins of the world, *graciously hear us, O Lord.*
Lamb of God, who take away the sins of the world, *have mercy on us.*

Pray for us, O holy Mother of God.
That we may be made worthy of the promises of Christ.

Let us pray: Grant, we beseech Thee, O Lord God, unto us Thy servants, that we may rejoice in continual health of mind and body; and, by the glorious intercession of blessed Mary ever Virgin, may be delivered from present sadness, and enter into the joy of Thine eternal gladness. Through Christ our Lord. *Amen.*

Words to Know:

Annunciation Fiat Assumption
Immaculate Conception
perpetual virginity   venerate intercede

66

NOTES

_____
_____
_____
_____
_____
_____
_____
_____
_____
_____
_____
_____
_____
_____
_____
_____
_____
_____
_____
_____
_____
_____
_____

Q. 69 *What is the Immaculate Conception?*

The Immaculate Conception is the gift of God by which Mary was preserved from original sin, from the moment of her conception, by the merits of Jesus Christ (CCC 491).

Q. 70 *What does it mean to say that Jesus was born of the Virgin Mary?*

To say that Jesus was "born of the Virgin Mary" means that by the power of the Holy Spirit, Jesus was conceived in the womb of Mary without a human father (CCC 496, 499).

Q. 71 *What is the Assumption of Mary?*

The Assumption of Mary is a gift from God, given to Mary at the end of her earthly life, whereby she was taken up into heaven body and soul (CCC 966).

Q. 72 *Why is it proper to say that Mary is the Mother of God?*

It is proper to say that Mary is the Mother of God because she is the Mother of Jesus Christ, the Second Person of the Holy Trinity, true God and true Man (CCC 495).

Q. 73 *Do Catholics worship Mary?*

Catholics do not worship Mary, but venerate (honor) her as a model of faith and the greatest of all the saints (CCC 971).

_____
_____
_____
_____
_____
_____
_____
_____
_____
_____
_____
_____
_____
_____

Name:

Mary—Mother of the Church   Quiz 9

Part I: Define the following terms.

Annunciation: <u>the event of the angel Gabriel announcing to the Blessed Virgin</u>
<u>that she would be the Mother of God and her responding yes</u>

Fiat: <u>a Latin word meaning "let it be done"; it is the Latin translation of Mary's</u>
<u>words to the angel Gabriel when she was asked to be the Mother of God</u>

Immaculate Conception: <u>Mary's conception free of the stain of original sin</u>

Perpetual Virginity: <u>the doctrine that Mary was always a virgin: before, during,</u>
<u>and after the birth of Christ</u>

Part II: Answer in complete sentences.

1. Do Catholics pray to Mary? Do we worship her? Explain.
   <u>Catholics do pray to Mary. We do not worship Mary. (We only worship</u>
   <u>God.) We venerate Mary because of her role in our salvation and</u>
   <u>because Jesus wants us to honor his mother.</u>

2. Choose and explain a title of Mary.
   <u>Answers will vary.</u>

Part III: Fill in the blanks and true or false.

1. Mary is called the new <u>Eve</u> just as Jesus is called the new <u>Adam</u>.

2. When Jesus said, "Behold your son," he made Mary our spiritual <u>mother</u>.

3. Mary has been called our sure <u>way</u> to Jesus, and she will help us reach heaven by her
   <u>prayers</u>.

4. <u>False</u> The phrase "Immaculate Conception" refers to the time when Jesus first began
   to live within the womb of Mary.

5. <u>True</u> Mary's "Assumption" means that she is now in heaven with both her body and
   her soul.

Faith and Life • Grade 8 • Appendix A   A - 13

Aims

The students' understanding of the material covered in this chapter will be reviewed and assessed.

Materials

- Quiz 9, Appendix p. A-13

  Optional:
  - "Hail, holy Queen enthroned above," *Adoremus Hymnal,* #530

Review

1. The students should be able to explain the following:
   - Annunciation
   - Visitation
   - Immaculate Conception
   - Virginal Conception
   - Assumption
   - Coronation of Mary

2. The students should be able to name the Marian dogmas.

3. The students should understand how Mary is an intercessor. They should be able to define Co-redemptrix, Mediatrix of Grace, and New Eve.

4. The students should know the mysteries of the Rosary.

5. The students should understand what consecration to Mary means.

6. The students should be able to explain one of the titles of Mary from the Litany of Loreto.

Assess

1. Distribute the quizzes and read through them with the students to be sure they understand the questions.

2. Administer the quiz. As they hand in their work, you may orally quiz the students on the Memorization Questions from this chapter.

3. After all the quizzes have been handed in, review the correct answers with the class.

Conclude

1. Lead the students in singing "Hail, holy Queen enthroned above," *Adoremus Hymnal,* #530.

2. End class by praying Loving Mother of the Redeemer.

CHAPTER TEN
THE COMMUNION OF SAINTS

Catechism of the Catholic Church References

Angels: 328–36, 350–52
Canonized Saints: 828
Christian Holiness: 2012–16, 2028–29
Church as the Body of Christ: 787–96, 805–8
Communion in Spiritual Goods: 949–53, 961
Communion of Saints: 946–62
Heaven: 1023–29, 1053
Intercessory Prayers: 956
Mystical Body of Christ: 779–805

Patron Saints: 2683–84
Prayer for the Dead: 1032, 1055
Prayers of Intercession: 2634–36, 2647
Purgatory: 1030–32, 1054
Sacrifice: 2099–2100
Saints: 686–88
Saints as Companions in Prayer: 2683–84, 2692–93
Saints as Patrons: 2156

Scripture References

Where Two or Three Are Gathered: Mt 18:20
Paul on the Saints: Rom 8:28; 15:25; Phil 1:1; Col 1:2; 12;
2 Cor 2:2; Eph 1:1

The Souls in Heaven: Rev 7:9–12

Summary of Lesson Content

Lesson 1

The Communion of Saints refers to the members, both living and dead, of Christ's Mystical Body. This includes the faithful on earth, the holy souls in purgatory, and the angels and saints in heaven.

The Church Militant refers to those who are united to Christ on earth. They are militant in their pursuit of eternal life with God in heaven. This is also called the Pilgrim Church (journeying toward heaven). We are united with each other in charity and prayer.

Lesson 3

The Church Triumphant includes those united with Christ who already share in the eternal glory of heaven: the angels and saints. They are models of holiness and intercessors on our behalf.

Canonized saints are those recognized by the Church for their holiness on earth. The Church infallibly declares that the saints are in heaven. We may turn to them for intercessory prayer.

Lesson 2

The Church Suffering refers to the holy souls who died in the state of grace, and are being purified and prepared for heaven in purgatory. The Church Suffering is also called the Church Penitent.

The souls in purgatory suffer purification. The greatest suffering is the holy longing for union with God in heaven. We can assist these souls with our prayers and indulgences.

Lesson 4

Patron saints are saints we choose to honor. We seek their intercession. They are models of holiness, entrusted with the prayers of those under their patronage.

LESSON ONE: CHURCH MILITANT

Aims

The students will learn that the Communion of Saints refers to the members, both living and dead, of Christ's Mystical Body. This includes the faithful on earth, the holy souls in purgatory, and the angels and saints in heaven.

They will learn that the Church Militant refers to those who are united to Christ on earth. They are militant in their pursuit of eternal life with God in heaven. This is also called the Pilgrim Church (journeying toward heaven). We are united with each other in charity and prayer.

Materials

- *Activity Book*, p. 37
- Litany of the Saints, Appendix, pp. B-8–B-9

Optional:
- "For all the saints," *Adoremus Hymnal*, #590

Begin

Begin class by discussing intercessory prayer. In the last chapter, we learned that Mary intercedes on our behalf before the throne of her Son. We also pray for people, for example, during the prayers of the faithful at Mass. Sometimes we ask others to pray for our needs and intentions as well. Intercessory prayer reminds us that "where two or three are gathered in my name, there am I in the midst of them" (Mt 18:20).

CHAPTER 10

The Communion of Saints

And he who searches the hearts of men knows what is the mind of the Spirit, because the Spirit intercedes for the saints according to the will of God.

Romans 8:27

"Exactly as Christian communion between men on their earthly pilgrimage brings us closer to Christ, so our community with the saints joins us to Christ, from whom, as from its fountain and head, issues all grace and the life of the People of God itself" (LG, 50).

We have seen that the Church is the Mystical Body of Christ with Christ as its head and Mary as its Mother. We who have been baptized in Christ are the members. Membership in the Mystical Body is not limited to those living on earth. Since Baptism leaves us with a permanent character that can never be taken away, those who die faithful to their baptismal promises are still part of the Mystical Body. We use the term **Communion of Saints** to refer to the Church in this sense—as including her members both living and dead.

The term *saint* is used in various ways. In the widest sense, it means "holy one;" all those who have been baptized share in the holiness of Christ. More specifically, saints are those who have died and are with God in heaven. In the strictest sense, the term refers to those who have been officially declared by the Church to be in heaven—those we call *canonized saints*. The union of these saints is based on our common possession of the life of grace and is expressed through the exchange of spiritual goods. Thus the Communion of Saints includes all of the faithful who are united in Christ—the faithful on earth, the souls in purgatory, and the *blessed*, or saints, in heaven.

The Church Militant

The first part of the Communion of Saints is the faithful on earth. We are known as the **pilgrim Church** since we are journeying (on a pilgrimage) to heaven. Sometimes we also refer to this group as the **Church Militant**. This indicates the "fight," or "struggle," that we on earth must constantly wage against sin and temptation.

Our unity is one of love. We are asked by Christ to carry one another's burdens, to serve each other, to help especially the least among us by the corporal and spiritual works of mercy. This is also done in a special way through prayers for each other. We frequently ask others to pray for us, or we join with them in praying for a particular need.

Intercessory prayer, prayer on behalf of another person, has long been a part of our religious heritage. In the *Old Testament* we often

69

Develop

1. Read paragraphs 1–5 (up to The Church Suffering).

2. The Communion of Saints refers to the Church—all those, living and dead, who are united with Christ—including: the Church Militant, those baptized and united with Christ through the Church; the Church Suffering, those who died in the state of grace and are being prepared for heaven through the purification of Purgatory; and the Church Triumphant, those who share in the eternal glory of heaven. Since we are all members of the Mystical Body of Christ, we are in relationship with one another and must work together for the building up of God's kingdom. One way we do this is through prayer. Using the Chalk Talk at right, show how the Church prays for her members and who benefits from those prayers.

3. Discuss the term "saint." It refers to those who are holy—those who are in the state of grace. We can be assured that those in heaven and purgatory are in the state of grace. We must always strive to live in the state of grace. This is life's spiritual battle, a fight we have against sin and temptation. This is why we are called the Church Militant

4. *The unity of the Church and her members is one of love. We are called to serve one another with acts of charity, works of mercy, and prayers. Have the students give examples of each. Review the Works of Mercy:*

Corporal Works
- *Feed the hungry*
- *Give drink to the thirsty*
- *Clothe the naked*
- *Shelter the homeless*
- *Visit the sick*
- *Visit the imprisoned*
- *Bury the dead*

Spiritual Works
- *Counsel the doubtful*
- *Instruct the ignorant*
- *Admonish the sinner*
- *Comfort the sorrowful*
- *Forgive injuries*
- *Bear wrongs patiently*
- *Pray for the living and the dead*

Name:_____

The Church Militant

Answer the following questions in complete sentences

1. What is the Church Militant?

   The Church Militant is the pilgrim Church on earth, journeying towards heaven.

2. What is the Church Militant fighting?

   The Church Militant is fighting sin and temptation.

3. How is the Church Militant united in love?

   The Church Militant is united in love by praying, serving one another, and carrying our crosses with love.

4. How do we partake in intercessory prayer?

   We partake in intercessory prayer by praying for others and asking them to do the same for us.

Faith and Life Series • Grade 8 • Chapter 10 • Lesson 1

37

Reinforce

1. Have the students work on *Activity Book*, p. 37.

2. Give the students time to work on the Memorization Questions and Words to Know from this chapter.

3. *Look up the following passages, in which St. Paul uses the term "saints": Rom 8:28; 15:25; Phil 1:1; Col 1:2, 12; 2 Cor 2:2; Eph 1:1. Let the students discuss the meaning of the word saint in each of these passages.*

4. Have the students depict the Mystical Body of Christ (the Church) with all her members.

5. *Discuss the help the students can receive from the holy souls and the saints. What duty do we have to the holy souls and the saints? What duty do we have to the Church Militant?*

Conclude

1. Teach the students to sing "For all the saints," *Adoremus Hymnal*, #590.

2. End class by praying the Litany of the Saints.

Preview

In the next lesson, the students will learn about the Church Suffering.

CHALK TALK: PRAYERS OF THE CHURCH

Chalk Talk

Church Triumphant

Prays for / Prays to

prays for / prays to

Church Militant (Pilgrim) ← prays for / prays for → Church Suffering

NOTES

_____
_____
_____
_____
_____
_____
_____
_____
_____
_____
_____

119

LESSON TWO: CHURCH SUFFERING

Aims

The students will learn that the Church Suffering refers to the holy souls who died in the state of grace and are being purified and prepared for heaven in purgatory. The Church Suffering is also called the Church Penitent.

They will learn that the souls in purgatory suffer purification. The greatest suffering is the holy longing for union with God in heaven. We can assist these souls with our prayers and indulgences.

Materials

- *Activity Book*, p. 38
  Optional:
- "For all the saints," *Adoremus Hymnal*, #590

Begin

Explain the need for purgatory. Use the example of making an apple pie. We gather the good apples (those that have not rotted), peel them, core them, and cut out the blemishes. It is these apples that make it into the pie. The souls in heaven are the apples that made it into the pie. Some souls are "rotten"—those who chose to die in unrepentant mortal sin. Those who are in the state of grace, but have venial sin temporal punishment due to sin, must be purified before they can enter heaven. God is merciful to care for and accept these souls!

see the leaders and prophets of Israel pray to God for their people. When Our Lord was on earth we heard him pray to his Father for his disciples at the Last Supper. He also encouraged them to pray for one another and for those who would persecute them. In his letters, St. Paul often asks the people to pray for him and mentions his own prayers for them. For example, in his letter to the Christian community in Rome he says ". . . without ceasing I mention you always in my prayers" (Rom 1:9). The Fathers and Doctors of the Church also frequently exhort us to pray for one another. In the Liturgy today the Church encourages us as well. In the *Prayer of the Faithful* at the end of the Liturgy of the Word, we pray expressly for the Church and the needs of her members.

The Church Suffering

Prayer for one another does not end with death. While those in heaven do not need our prayers, those in purgatory do, and we, the Church Militant, can and should pray for them as well. These souls in purgatory represent the second part of the Communion of Saints and are known as the *Church Penitent* or **Church Suffering**.

When we die we do not all necessarily go straight to heaven. Those who do go directly to heaven love God perfectly and have no trace of sin left on their souls. Most of us, however, who die in the state of grace, still have some venial sins on our souls, or may not have sufficiently atoned for past sins, and some punishment due to sin may still be necessary.

The souls in this imperfect state not only need to be cleansed, but they want to be cleansed as well. They know that they are not yet prepared to be in the presence of God. Recalling one of Our Lord's parables may help us understand this:

70

The Kingdom of heaven may be compared to a king who gave a marriage feast for his son, . . . when the king came in to look at the guests, he saw there a man who had no wedding garment; and he said to him, "Friend, how did you get in here without a wedding garment?" And he was speechless (Mt 22:2, 11–12).

Just as the man who came to the wedding feast was required to have the proper garment, so we must be spotlessly clothed to enter the Kingdom of Heaven. If we are not we will, like the guest at the wedding, be "speechless" before our heavenly King.

Those souls who need to be cleansed and purified before seeing God go to *purgatory*. Purgatory is a place of temporary suffering that cleanses the soul and makes it worthy to see God. The Church's teaching on purgatory is very consoling. Though we are sinful, God in his mercy gives us a chance to make up for these venial sins, and for the punishment still due for our confessed mortal sins. The principal suffering in purgatory is not seeing God. Even though the souls in purgatory really do suffer they are filled with peace because they are assured that they will be with God soon. They no longer fear for their salvation. They know that they are being made ready for heaven.

The souls in purgatory, however, are unable to do anything for themselves to shorten their time there. They depend on us, the Church Militant, to help them. We can do this by offering prayers for them, particularly the Mass, as well as offering other charitable acts. We can also offer our own sufferings here on earth for these souls.

Our Catholic practice of praying for those who have died is rooted in God's revelation to the Jews. In the *Old Testament*, the book of Maccabees tells the story of Judas Maccabeus, who lived in the second century before Christ.

Develop

1. Read paragraphs 6–15 (up to the Church Triumphant).

2. God in his justice judges every soul at the moment of his death. Every sin must be reconciled with God. We choose our eternal destination by the life we live. We choose heaven by living in the state of grace. We choose hell by rejecting God and his grace through mortal sin or rejecting Baptism. Some souls are in the state of grace, but they are not yet perfected—they need purgatory. It is not because God is mean or cruel that we have purgatory—it is because of his merciful love. To enter heaven, we must be perfect, as our heavenly Father is perfect. We often have imperfections on our soul, venial sin or punishment due to sin, that must be purified before we may enter heaven. God could see even the slightest imperfection and reject a soul; instead, he sees the life of grace and gives us purgatory that we may be purified and live with him forever in heaven.

3. Purgatory is a state of purification. It is a time of suffering. However, every soul in purgatory knows it will be united with God in time—it does not fear for its salvation. It is saddened that it is not yet with God, but it is peaceful knowing that it is being made ready for heaven.

4. The souls in Purgatory cannot relieve their own sufferings or speed up their purification. The saints in heaven and the faithful on earth can pray for the holy souls in purgatory, asking God to grant eternal rest unto them. We can assist them with our prayers and by obtaining indulgences for them. It is a common practice to have a Mass said for a deceased person. We have a great duty to pray for the souls in purgatory. It is pious to pray for the souls who have no one to pray for them or for the next soul to be released from purgatory.

5. Discuss All Souls' Day, celebrated November 2nd.

Name:_____

The Church Suffering

Answer the following questions in complete sentences.

1. What is the Church Suffering?
   The Church Suffering is the holy souls in purgatory.

2. Who goes to purgatory? Why? What happens there?
   Those who die in a state of grace but who still have venial sin on their souls, or who have not sufficiently atoned for past sins, go to purgatory. They go to purgatory because they are not yet prepared for heaven and need to be purified. In purgatory, souls temporarily suffer so that their souls may be cleansed and they may be made worthy to see God.

3. What does Matthew 22:2–12 teach us about purgatory?
   Mt 22:2-12 teaches us that we must be completely pure to enter the Kingdom of Heaven.

4. What is the principal suffering in purgatory? Are the souls also full of peace? Why?
   The principal suffering in purgatory is not seeing God. Yes, the souls in purgatory are full of peace because they are assured that they will be with God soon and know they are being prepared for heaven.

5. Can souls in purgatory help themselves? Discuss a passage from the Bible that tells us what we should do for the Church Suffering.
   The souls in purgatory cannot help themselves. The book of Maccabees tells us that we should pray and sacrifice for the dead.

6. When do we pray for the dead during the Liturgy? How else can we pray for the dead?
   We pray for the dead during the Eucharistic prayer at Mass. We can also pray for the dead by remembering them at Mass and offering sacrifices for them.

38   *Faith and Life Series • Grade 8 • Chapter 10 • Lesson 2*

Reinforce

1. Have the students work on *Activity Book*, p. 38.

2. Give the students time to work on the Memorization Questions and Words to Know from this chapter.

3. Have the students create a family tree and pray for their deceased family members.

4. Visit a cemetery and pray for the souls of the faithful buried there.

5. The class may work on obtaining indulgences for the holy souls.

6. The students should write intercessory prayers to the holy souls, asking them to pray for us, and remember us when they are in heaven.

Conclude

1. Lead the students in singing "For all the saints," *Adoremus Hymnal*, #590.

2. End class by praying the Litany of the Saints.

Preview

In the next lesson, the students will learn about the Church Triumphant.

PARTIAL AND PLENARY INDULGENCES

The Pope or bishops in union with him can grant indulgences. When Jesus died on the Cross, he paid the price for all our sins. Therefore, when we receive an indulgence, the Church opens for us the Treasury of the Church (the infinite merits of Christ and the saints) to obtain from God the remission of our temporal punishment. There are two types of indulgences:

- Partial indulgences remit some of the temporal punishment due to sin. They can be granted by bishops.

- Plenary indulgences remit all of the temporal punishment due to sin. They can only be granted by the Pope.

When granting an indulgence, the Church will ask us to do some good work, such as going on a pilgrimage to a certain place or praying special prayers. Along with that, we must receive the Sacraments of Penance and Eucharist, pray for the Holy Father, and be free from all attachment to sin. We should receive indulgences whenever we can and thank God for his mercy and forgiveness. See the *Catechism of the Catholic Church*, 1471–1479.

LESSON THREE: CHURCH TRIUMPHANT

Aims

The students will learn that the Church Triumphant includes those united with Christ who already share in the eternal glory of heaven: the angels and saints. They are models of holiness and intercessors on our behalf.

They will learn that canonized saints are those recognized by the Church for their holiness on earth. The Church infallibly declares that the saints are in heaven. We may turn to them for intercessory prayer.

Materials

- *Activity Book*, p. 39

Optional:
- "For all the saints," *Adoremus Hymnal*, #590

Begin

Discuss this quotation: "The greatest tragedy in life is not to be a saint." Ask the students what this means. Ask them who can be saints. When do we start being saints? How do we face the struggles we have when pursuing sanctity?

Perhaps some of the students know people who they think are saints on earth and in heaven. Why do they think they are saints? How can we imitate them?

After a battle, it was discovered that some of his dead soldiers who were good men had sinned before their deaths. Judas Maccabeus then had prayers and sacrifices offered to God for these men: ". . . it was a holy and pious thought . . . he made atonement for the dead, that they might be delivered from their sin" (2 Macc 12:45).

In this passage God reveals to us that our prayers can help those who have died. It was also the belief of the early Christians and is part of Tradition. In many ancient Christian tombs we find inscriptions which encourage prayers for those who are buried there.

Because prayer for those who have died is so important, the Church sets aside one day each year on which the whole Church prays for the souls in purgatory. This is All Souls' Day and is celebrated on November 2. The month of November is dedicated to prayers for those who have died, particularly our own family members and friends.

We should not forget the souls in purgatory during the remainder of the year, particularly at Mass, during the Eucharistic prayer when we pray for the dead. But we should try to do this at other times as well. For example, many Catholics add the following short prayer to their prayer before or after meals:

"May the souls of the faithful departed, through the mercy of God, rest in peace. *Amen*."

There are other things as well that can help us remember to pray for those who have died. Often holy cards are distributed at funerals. The purpose of these cards is to remind us to pray for the person who has died. As pictures in our homes remind us to think of our family members who have died, so, too, these holy cards remind us of them. We should keep them some place where they can remind us to pray for the faithful departed.

The Church Triumphant

The blessed in heaven can also pray for the souls in purgatory, as well as for us on earth. They are the third part of the Communion of Saints—the **Church Triumphant**. Those in the Church Triumphant have completely conquered sin and now share in eternal glory, even before the resurrection of their bodies.

Among the blessed in heaven are the **canonized saints**, whom the Church has officially declared to be in heaven. As we have seen, the most important among these is Our Lady. There are also many other souls who have reached heaven—perhaps some of our own relatives and friends—and deserve to be called saints as well. We do not know for certain who they are, but the Church honors them with a feast each year—the feast of All Saints on November 1.

All these are saints in glory with Christ, who, shining like stars in the firmament, are "standing before the throne and before the Lamb" (Rev 7:9). We are ultimately united with them in our love and union in Christ, and in the grace he gives us. In our prayers, especially in the Liturgy of the Church, we join their heavenly chorus in the glorification of God, saying:

Blessing and glory and wisdom and thanksgiving and honor and power and might be to our God for ever and ever! *Amen* (Rev 7:12).

We are not just praying alone, each member of the Church by himself. We are united in a community of incomparable grandeur, in a victorious union of love. This great community lifts us up and generates fruits of grace in us.

We partake in this Communion of Saints, and we can turn to the saints for help, just as we turn to other members of the Church on

71

Develop

1. Read paragraphs 16–18 (to the end of Rev 7:12).

2. When we think of heaven, we often think of angels, canonized saints, and family members. We might think of them as being very far away. We might think that heaven is boring. On the contrary, Saint Thérèse of Lisieux taught that the souls of the faithful departed are very close, and that those in heaven are working very hard for the life of the Church to bring greater glory to God.

3. When we are at Mass, all the angels, saints, and holy souls are gathered around the altar to worship God and gain benefits from the graces of this spiritual treasure. We must remember to pray for the holy souls and to ask the saints to pray with and for us at Mass. We are all united in the Holy Mass and, intimately, in the reception of Holy Communion.

4. Among the blessed in heaven are canonized saints. These are people who lived holy lives on earth and whom the

Church recognizes and declares infallibly to be in heaven. The Church elevates them as models of holiness and seeks their intercession in prayer. The most important of these saints is Mary.

5. Using the box at right, explain the canonization process to the students.

6. Discuss the feast of All Saints' Day, celebrated on November 1. Have the students research their patron saints, dress up, and have a saints party during the next lesson. During this party, have each student make a presentation on his saint. You may do this in the form of a game, such as "Name that Saint." They should prepare questions about their saints for this game. They may make costumes using symbols associated with their saints.

Name:_____

The Church Triumphant

Answer the following questions in complete sentences.

1. What is the Church Triumphant?
   The Church Triumphant is the saints in heaven.

2. Who are the canonized saints?
   The canonized saints are those whom the Church has officially declared to be in heaven.

3. How do we honor the Church Triumphant during the Liturgy?
   We honor the Church Triumphant during the Liturgy by joining in their chorus of praise and giving glory to God.

4. How are we united with them?
   We are united with them through love. Since we are all sons of God, we are their brothers and sisters in Christ.

5. How can we turn to the saints for help?
   We can turn to the saints for help by praying to them and speaking to them just like friends.

6. When we venerate the saints, do we also honor God? Why?
   Yes. When we venerate the saints, we also honor God because his life shines through them. Just as we give honor to an artist when we admire his work, we honor God when we venerate the saints who are his handiwork.

7. When did the Church start devotion to the saints?
   The early Church started devotion to the saints when she began to honor the apostles and martyrs.

Reinforce

1. Have the students work on *Activity Book*, p. 39.

2. Give the students time to work on the Memorization Questions and Words to Know from this chapter.

3. The students should begin working on their presentations (and making costumes) for their saint party.

4. Discuss the traditions of All Saints' and All Soul's Day, as celebrated by Catholics.

Conclude

1. Lead the students in singing "For all the saints." *Adoremus Hymnal*, #590.

2. End class by praying the Litany of the Saints.

Preview

In the next lesson, the students will learn about patron saints.

CANONIZATION PROCESS

There are three levels to pass through on the road to canonization: Venerable, Blessed, and Saint.

Venerable: During the first stage of the canonization process, the life of the person to be canonized is investigated. All of his writings are gathered and carefully studied, and his friends, family, and acquaintances are interviewed. The local bishop then creates a file of the person's life and writings and submits it to the Vatican, where officials examine the file. If they determine that the candidate's life expressed heroic virtue, he is proclaimed "Venerable" and receives the title, "Servant of God."

Blessed: The only way to become a Blessed is for a miracle to be attributed to the Servant of God's intercession. If a miracle occurs that seems to be from his intercession, a group of theologians and scientists examines the case. They must determine two things: whether it is in fact a miracle (scientifically unexplainable), and whether it can be attributed to his intercession. Once the miracle has been approved, the person may be "Beatified," which means they have been proclaimed "Blessed."

Saint: The final stage requires a second miracle. Upon the acceptance of a second miracle, the Blessed can be "canonized." This means that the Pope has proclaimed him a saint. At this point, his name can be added to the liturgical calendar and he can be venerated by the faithful all over the world.

LESSON FOUR: PATRONS

Aims

The students will learn that patron saints are saints we choose to honor. We seek their intercession. They are models of holiness, entrusted with the prayers of those under their patronage.

Materials

- *Activity Book*, p. 40   Optional:
  - "For all the saints," *Adoremus Hymnal*, #590

Begin

At Confirmation, we often choose a patron saint, whose name we take as a Confirmation name. We choose this saint to intercede on our behalf, to be our example, and to care for us on our journey to heaven. We often choose a saint whose story we like or who touches our life in some way; in other ways, the saint chooses us. If we pray hard and are attentive to the Spirit's promptings, we will see that our selection of a patron saint is not an arbitrary matter, but one guided by Providence.

---

earth. We ask them to intercede with God for us, just as we might ask a friend here to do the same.

We should remember that we are not worshipping the saints, but praying to God *through them*. The saints are truly united with us through Christ and want to help us. St. Thérèse of Lisieux remarked before her death that she would "spend her heaven doing good upon earth." And this is what the saints do when we turn to them.

We are also honoring God when we venerate the saints. The saints are masterpieces of God's grace. Grace has triumphed in them and the devil has been conquered. In venerating them we honor God, whose life shines forth in them.

Devotion to the saints goes back to the early days of the Church. The early Christians began to honor the apostles after their deaths, and later the martyrs were included as well. Gradually, the practice was extended to other holy men and women. The Church recognized their holiness and saw that they could be examples to the faithful. The saints show us that we can reach heaven, and they show us the way.

The saints came from all walks of life—some were married with families, some were priests or religious sisters or brothers, some were kings or queens, some were rich and oth-

ers poor. Yet, they all had their complete devotion to God in common. Since their lives were so different, it is not surprising that we might find the life of one saint more interesting or helpful to us than another. One often develops a devotion to a particular saint.

For example, the people of one country may have a devotion to a particular saint whose life was intimately connected with their nation. St. Patrick spread the Catholic faith throughout Ireland, and because of this he is the **patron saint** of Ireland. St. Thomas More was a great lawyer and statesman in England. He is the patron saint of all lawyers and also the patron saint of all laypeople because he served God as a layman. We might also have a special devotion to the saint for whom we were named.

Because the lives of the saints are such important examples for us, in the next two chapters we will briefly examine a few of them. This will also give us a chance to see something of the history of the Church as we look at the times in which they lived.

Words to Know:

Communion of Saints   pilgrim Church
Church Militant   intercessory prayer
Church Suffering   Church Triumphant
canonized saint   patron saint

72

Develop

1. Read paragraphs 19–26 (to the end of the chapter).

2. Review that we do not worship saints. However, we do venerate them. What are some ways we honor the saints and recognize their holiness? We honor saints in relics, images, icons, medals, novenas, paintings, songs, etc.

3. Saints come from all walks of life. Have the students give examples of married saints, religious saints, priestly and single saints, old saints, young saints, rich and poor saints. Their lives are very different, but they all have love of God in common. The students should discuss their patron saints, if they have chosen some, and why they were attracted to those particular saints. Encourage the students to consider seriously the challenges the saints faced, their holy lives, their teachings, their deaths, etc.

4. Discuss patron saints. They can also be entrusted with the patronage of groups of people, countries, schools, etc. For

example, Saint Patrick is the patron of Ireland and Saint Luke is the patron of artists.

5. When we choose a saint as a patron, we are entrusting ourselves to his care and prayers. We hope to follow his example of holiness and obtain the same reward.

6. The students should celebrate their saint party. They should play a game or make presentations on their saints.

7. You may discuss the liturgical calendar and the feasts of the saints. We usually celebrate a saint's feast on the anniversary of his death, since this is his "birthday" into heaven! You may review the liturgical colors associated with various feasts, e.g., red for martyrs.

Name:_____

Definitions

Define the following words using the student text.

Communion of Saints: <u>The Communion of Saints is all the faithful,</u> <u>who form the Body of Christ and share in all the good that</u> <u>exists and is done in that Body.</u>

Church Triumphant: <u>The Church Triumphant is the saints in heaven.</u>

Church Suffering: <u>The Church Suffering is the souls in purgatory.</u>

Pilgrim Church: <u>The pilgrim Church is the Church on earth,</u> <u>journeying toward heaven.</u>

Church Militant: <u>The Church Militant is the same as the pilgrim</u> <u>Church. However, the Church Militant emphasizes the aspect</u> <u>of the Church on earth fighting sin and temptation.</u>

Intercessory Prayer: <u>Intercessory prayer is prayer on behalf of</u> <u>another person.</u>

Canonized Saint: <u>A canonized saint is someone the Church has</u> <u>officially declared to be in heaven.</u>

Mystical Body of Christ: <u>The Mystical Body of Christ is the Church in</u> <u>all her members with Christ as head and Mary as mother.</u>

All Souls' Day: <u>All Souls' Day is on November 2 and is the day the</u> <u>Church sets aside to remember and pray for the souls in</u> <u>purgatory.</u>

All Saints' Day: <u>All Saints' Day is on November 1 and is the day we</u> <u>honor all the saints.</u>

40   *Faith and Life Series • Grade 8 • Chapter 10 • Lesson 4*

Reinforce

1. Have the students work on *Activity Book*, p. 40.

2. The students may work on the Memorization Questions and Words to Know from this chapter and prepare for the quiz.

3. Give the students time to celebrate their saints and to make their presentations on them.

4. The students can make a saints calendar, marking their favorite saints' feast days, so that they will remember to pray to them. They may decorate their calendars with religious art, prayer cards, medals, etc.

Conclude

1. Lead the students in singing "For all the saints," *Adoremus Hymnal*, #590.

2. End class by praying the Litany of the Saints.

Preview

In the next lesson, the students' understanding of the material covered in this chapter will be reviewed and assessed.

SAINT PIO OF PIETRELCINA

Padre Pio joined the Order of the Capuchins at the age of sixteen and was ordained a priest seven years later. His life was full of many amazing mystical graces. There are many accounts of the saint bilocating and of healings attributed to his prayer, and he reportedly was visited by angels and souls from purgatory. In confession, he had the ability to read souls, that is, he would know the sins of the penitent without being told. Also, he had the gift of knowing exactly what to say to penitents, be it encouragement or reproach, to bring them closer to God. People came from all over the world to confess to the saint who spent as many as twelve hours in the confessional each day. But some of his miracles caused him great suffering. In 1918, as Saint Pio was praying before a crucifix, he received the stigmata, the wounds of Christ, on his hands and feet. These wounds were very painful and Saint Pio lost huge amounts of blood every day. In humility, he tried to hide the wounds and is commonly pictured wearing gloves, but his stigmata were well known. Also, he was reportedly visited by the devil who attacked him physically and spiritually. However, the saint persevered in holiness and, with God's help, overcame any difficulties that came his way. Padre Pio loved to celebrate Mass and his Masses could go on for hours. During Mass, it seemed that his wounds became even more painful, but he endured it all out of love for God. Saint Pio died on September 23, 1968 at the age of eighty-one.

Q. 74 *What does "Communion of Saints" mean?*
The Communion of Saints means that all the faithful, living and dead, share in all the good that exists and is done in the universal Church (CCC 947).

Q. 75 *Do the blessed in heaven and the souls in purgatory form a part of the Communion of Saints?*
The blessed in heaven and the souls in purgatory form a part of the Communion of Saints because they are joined to each other and with us through charity, because those in heaven intercede for us, and those in purgatory gain our assistance by our prayers (CCC 955–58).

Q. 76 *Who are the saints?*
The saints are holy people who are in heaven (CCC 957–58).

Q. 77 *Why should we pray to the saints as well as to God?*
We should pray to the saints as well as to God because God wills to help us through the prayers of others, including the saints, who are very holy and close to him (CCC 956).

Q. 78 *Why are the angels, the saints, and Our Lady powerful intercessors with God?*
The angels, saints, and Our Lady are powerful intercessors with God because they are closely united to Christ in heaven (CCC 956, 2674).

73

Name: _____

The Communion of Saints   Quiz 10

Part I: Define the following terms.

Communion of Saints: <u>the relationship that exists between all of the members of the Church, whether they are in heaven, in purgatory, or on earth</u>

Pilgrim Church: <u>the Church on earth, journeying toward heaven</u>

Canonized Saint: <u>someone the Church has officially declared to be in heaven</u>

Intercessory Prayer: <u>prayer on behalf of another person</u>

Purgatory: <u>a state after death of temporary suffering that cleanses and purifies the soul and makes it worthy to see God</u>

Part II: Answer in complete sentences.

1. How is the communion of saints a community of prayer?
   <u>The communion of saints is a community of prayer because all the souls in heaven pray for those on earth and those in purgatory. The souls in purgatory pray for those on earth. And those on earth pray for others on earth and for the souls in purgatory.</u>

2. How can you honor or venerate a saint?
   <u>You can honor or venerate a saint by praying to him, learning about him, and following his example.</u>

3. Why should you pray for the dead?
   <u>You should pray for the dead because the dead are unable to do anything for themselves and rely upon us for help. Also Scripture tells us it is a holy thing to do.</u>

4. What is the Church Militant fighting?
   <u>The Church Militant is fighting temptation and sin.</u>

_A - 14_   _Faith and Life • Grade 8 • Appendix A_

Aims

> The students' understanding of the material covered in this chapter will be reviewed and assessed.

Materials

> • Quiz 10, Appendix, p. A-14
>
> Optional:
> • "For all the saints," _Adoremus Hymnal_, #590

Assess

> 1. Distribute the quizzes and read through them with the students to be sure they understand the questions.
>
> 2. Administer the quiz. As they hand in their work, you may orally quiz the students on the Memorization Questions from this chapter.
>
> 3. After all the quizzes have been handed in, review the correct answers with the class.

Conclude

> 1. Lead the students in singing "For all the saints," _Adoremus Hymnal_, #590.
>
> 2. End class by leading the students in the Litany of the Saints.

Review

> 1. The students should be able to explain the Communion of Saints.
>
> 2. The relationship and unity between the members of the Communion of Saints (who can pray for and assist others) should be understood by the class.
>
> 3. The students should understand and define: Church Militant, Church Suffering, and Church Triumphant.
>
> 4. The students should know what a canonized saint is, what a patron saint is, and what a living saint is.

CHAPTER ELEVEN
SAINTS: THE FIRST THOUSAND YEARS

Catechism of the Catholic Church References

Apostles: 77–79, 857–60, 1506, 1724
Christ's Missionary Mandate in the Church: 849–56, 868
Christian Holiness: 2012–16, 2028–29
Consecrated Life: 914–16, 944–45
Consecration and Mission: 931–33
Eremetical Life: 920–21

Heresies: 817, 2089
Jesus as True God and True Man: 464–70, 480–83
Martyrdom: 2473–74, 2506
Mission of the Apostles: 858–60, 869
Missionary Work: 849, 855, 859–59
Monasteries: 914–16, 925–27, 944–45

Scripture References

Pentecost: Acts 2:1–4
Great Commission: Mt 28:19

Summary of Lesson Content

Lesson 1

The early Church grew and spread due to the preaching of the apostles, as Christ had commissioned them.

The first three hundred years after the life of Christ were a time of Christian persecution. The martyrs witnessed to the truths of Christ and his Church.

Lesson 2

Constantine legalized Christianity and ended Roman persecutions.

Heresy is the denial of a doctrine of the faith. The early Church faced the problem of heresies such as Arianism.

Doctors and Fathers of the Church worked to protect the Church from heresy and error.

Lesson 3

Monasteries are communities of people committed to serving Christ. Monks are bound by vows of poverty, chastity, and obedience. They are responsible for the spreading of Christianity, Christian education, Christian witness, and prayer.

Lesson 4

Other challenges facing the Church included Islam, schism, and corruption of the clergy.

Schism is a refusal to submit to the Pope or the Church, which is subject to him.

Many of the clergy in the Church became corrupt. As the Roman Empire collapsed, the clergy assumed civil responsibility, exercising both spiritual and temporal power.

LESSON ONE: APOSTLES AND MARTYRS

Aims

The students will learn that the early Church grew and spread due to the preaching of the apostles, as Jesus had commissioned them.

They will learn that the first three hundred years after the life of Christ were a time of Christian persecution. The martyrs witnessed to the truths of Christ and his Church.

Materials

- *Activity Book*, p. 41

Optional:
- "From all thy saints in warfare," *Adoremus Hymnal*, #592

Begin

Review the beginning of the Church at Pentecost (Acts 2:1–4). Three thousand believers were baptized and went back to their homelands with the Good News of Salvation. Review also Christ's great commission to the apostles, sending them to all nations (Mt 28:19). The apostles had the great responsibility of missionary work, to bring the Good News and Baptism to all nations.

CHAPTER 11

Saints in Our History: The First Thousand Years

For this reason, because I have heard of your faith in the Lord Jesus and your love toward all the saints, I do not cease to give thanks for you, remembering you in my prayers. . . .

Ephesians 1:15–16

About two thousand years have elapsed since the founding of the Church and its birth on Pentecost. As we have seen, it began as a small community, but like the mustard seed in the parable, it has grown and spread throughout the world. During that time it has faced many difficulties and weathered many storms. Yet the Church has survived and is today the same Church of which Our Lord spoke when he said to Peter, ". . . on this rock I will build my church, and the powers of death shall not prevail against it" (Mt 16:18).

The Church could not have survived without the constant guidance and protection of the Holy Spirit. In order to preserve the Church God has raised up many holy men and women who are today recognized as *saints*. With God's help they have been able to put their various talents and personalities in the service of the Church's special need.

The virtuous lives of these saints are still a source of example and inspiration for us today. Let us now look at a few periods in the Church's history as they are reflected in the lives of some of her greatest saints.

74

"And his gifts were that some should be apostles, some prophets, some evangelists, some pastors and teachers, for the equipment of the saints, for the work of ministry, for building up the body of Christ, until we all attain to the unity of faith and of the knowledge of the Son of God" (Eph 4:11–13).

Apostles and Martyrs

The early days of the Church were marked by the apostles carrying out Our Lord's command: "Go therefore and make disciples of all nations" (Mt 28:19). This *missionary* activity manifests the Church's universality. We have seen that right after Pentecost Peter went out to preach, and by the end of the day three thousand persons were baptized. He was imprisoned, suffered, labored, performed miracles in the name of Jesus, and continued to preach and speak with authority.

Later he went to Antioch and finally to Rome, where he stayed for the rest of his life. Peter thus became the first bishop of Rome.

Develop

1. Read paragraphs 1–13 (up to Fathers and Doctors of the Church).

2. Review the lives of the apostles and where their missionary work took them (see box at right). You may "interview the apostles." Have the students play the parts of the apostles, discussing the work, hardships, and joys of going out to all nations. Questions might include:
- *Where did you go?*
- *Were you well received?*
- *What challenges did you face? (E.g., travel, language, culture.)*

3. Compare the missionary work of Peter and Paul.

4. Discuss the death of Peter. Saint Peter's Basilica was built over his tomb at the Vatican. His bones are under the main altar and are a witness to the historicity of our faith.

5. Discuss the Christian persecutions. Christians were persecuted for not worshipping Roman gods (including the emperor). They were accused of cannibalism (eating the body and blood of Christ), and for gathering for rituals in cemeteries and outside of town. Many people were killed for their faith in Christ. This death for the faith is called martyrdom. The text gives the examples of Perpetua and Felicity and mentions Stephen, Linus, Cletus, Clement, Sixtus, Agatha, Lucy, and Cecilia. All the apostles were martyred (except John). Have the students research these witnesses of faith.

6. It is a great gift that anyone can baptize. If you were waiting to be thrown to the lions, you could turn to another prisoner and instruct him to baptize you!

7. Ask your students to imagine they are about to be martyred. Tell them to express in writing their thoughts and feelings, knowing they will die for Christ.

Name:_____

Apostles and Martyrs

Answer the following questions in complete sentences.

1. What happened in the early days of the Church?
   In the early days of the Church the apostles spread the Gospel, carrying out Jesus's command to "make disciples of all nations."

2. What happened to St. Peter?
   St. Peter became the first Pope. After much laboring, suffering, imprisonment and travel for the sake of the Gospel, he was crucified upside down.

3. Who was the greatest missionary in the early Church? What did he do?
   St. Paul was the greatest missionary in the early Church. He traveled and preached the Good News, especially to the Gentiles. Eventually, he also was martyred.

4. What characterized the next 250 years of the Church? Who are the martyrs?
   The next 250 years of the Church are characterized by Church persecution. The martyrs are those who died for their faith.

5. How is it that the "blood of the martyrs is the seed of the Church"?
   The "blood of the martyrs is the seed of the Church" because by their example and redemptive sacrifice, united with Christ, their blood spreads the growth of the Church.

6. How did Saints Perpetua and Felicity witness to their faith?
   Saints Perpetua and Felicity witnessed to their faith by refusing to deny Christ. They put God before their money, their family, and even their own lives.

Faith and Life Series • Grade 8 • Chapter 11 • Lesson 1   41

Reinforce

1. Have the students work *Activity Book*, p. 41.

2. Give the students time to work on the Memorization Questions and Words to Know from this chapter.

3. Tertullian, a Church Father who lived during the Roman persecutions of the late second century, wrote: "The blood of martyrs is the seed of Christians." And Saint Edmund Campion, a Jesuit priest who was martyred in 1581 wrote of the willingness of Jesuits all over the world to go to England and help them return to the Catholic faith: "Either to win you heaven, or to die upon your pikes . . . cheerfully never to despair of your recovery, while we have a man left to enjoy your Tyburn, or to be racked by your torments, or consumed with your prisons. The expense is reckoned; the enterprise is begun; it is of God; it cannot be withstood. So the faith was planted: So it must be restored." What does this mean? How might people be inspired by the martyrdom of a Christian? Would you want to become a Christian, knowing that Christians are being killed? Discuss the importance and value of martyrdom to the Church.

Conclude

1. Teach the students to sing "From all thy saints in warfare," *Adoremus Hymnal*, #592.

2. End class by praying the Nicene Creed.

Preview

In the next lesson, the students will learn about Fathers and Doctors of the Church.

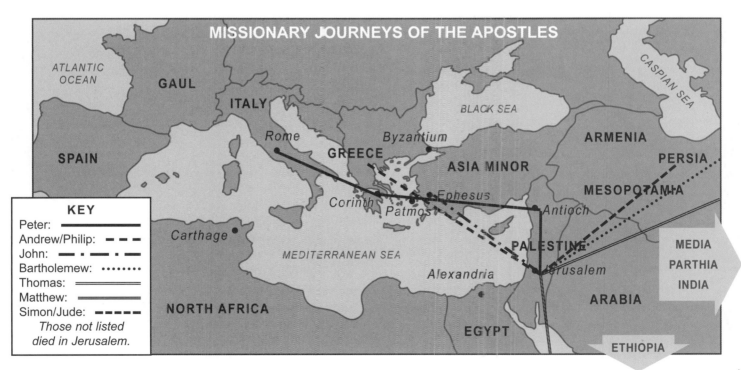

LESSON TWO:
FATHERS AND DOCTORS

Aims

The students will learn that Constantine legalized Christianity and ended Roman persecutions.

They will learn that heresy is the denial of a doctrine of the faith. The early Church faced the problem of heresies such as Arianism.

They will learn that Doctors and Fathers of the Church worked to protect the Church from heresy and error.

Materials

- *Activity Book*, p. 42

Optional:
- "From all thy saints in warfare," *Adoremus Hymnal*, #592

Begin

Instruct the students to go back to Chapter 4 and review what was taught about the Fathers and Doctors of the Church. The list of Fathers and Doctors will be helpful for the students in researching their works.

Be sure the students understand who the Fathers and Doctors of the Church are.

He was martyred under the Roman Emperor Nero around the year 64 or 67 A.D. It is said that when they were crucifying him Peter said he was not worthy to die as his Master had died, and therefore he asked that the crucifix be turned upside down. He was buried on the Vatican Hill. St. Peter's Basilica was later built over his tomb. Pope St. Linus was elected to succeed him.

The greatest missionary of these early days is the apostle St. Paul. From the time of his conversion, which is described in the Acts of the Apostles, St. Paul preached throughout Palestine, Syria, parts of Asia Minor (modern-day Turkey), Greece, and Rome. During four missionary journeys he zealously preached the good news of Jesus Christ to the Jews and to the **gentiles** (non-Jews). In some places he endured bitter opposition—for example, he was stoned and imprisoned—but still he continued to preach.

In the fourteen letters that he wrote to the communities where he preached, as well as in the accounts of his journeys found in the Acts, we can see St. Paul's great devotion to Christ. Because he so fully carried out Our Lord's command to teach *all* nations, he is called the "Apostle to the Gentiles." Like many of the early Christians, St. Paul not only lived for Christ; around 68 A.D. he died for him as well, as a martyr.

Although the Church continued her missionary work, the next 250 years were characterized by the persecution of Christians. As their numbers increased, and Christianity spread throughout the Roman Empire, the Roman government began to fear the Church. Under certain emperors over the next two centuries, many Christians were put to death for their faith in Christ. Those who died giving witness to their faith were called **martyrs**, the Greek word for witness. Many of them were young and only recently baptized, while still

others had only heard and accepted the message but had not yet been baptized. Yet they all had one thing in common: they willingly accepted horrible tortures and death rather than deny Christ or his message.

These martyrs were an inspiration both to their fellow Christians and to many Roman citizens. In fact, many people were drawn to the faith after seeing those who willingly died for it. They realized that the Christian faith must be great if so many Christians were willing to give up their lives for its sake. The rapid growth of the Church during this period led one early Christian writer to remark that the "blood of the martyrs is the seed of the Church."

Among those whose blood nourished the Church were two young women who lived in the early third century, St. Perpetua and St. Felicity. Perpetua, a young married woman, was from a wealthy family in Carthage, North Africa. Felicity was a young servant in her

75

Develop

1. Read paragraphs 14–21 (up to The Monasteries).

2. Teach the students about Emperor Constantine and his mother Saint Helen. After a vision of the Cross leading to a victory, Constantine legalized Christianity, putting an end to the Christian persecutions in the fourth century. His mother, Saint Helen, went to the Holy Land and brought to Rome many of the Church's greatest relics, such as the Holy Cross of Christ, the holy stairs from pilate's praetorium, and the crown of thorns.

3. Define heresy—the denial of a doctrine of the faith. Examples are listed in the box, at right. Often ecumenical councils were called to clarify Church teaching, and to protect God's people from error.

4. Discuss the role of Athanasius in defending the truth. Do we see Arianism today? How can we follow the example of Athanasius?

5. Discuss the life of Saint Augustine. He was a great sinner, but a brilliant man. Through the prayers of his mother and the teaching of Saint Ambrose, Augustine converted and later became a priest and bishop. His works were important in defending the truths taught by the Church. He also wrote important works on the nature of man and his need for Christ.

6. Tell the students to research a Father and a Doctor of the Church. Each student should write a summary paragraph, outlining the lives, teachings, example, and witness to the Faith of his Father and Doctor. The students should be prepared to present their findings or to turn in a typed report.

7. Remind the students that they have an important duty to learn the truths of the faith.

Name:_____

Fathers and Doctors of the Church

Answer the following questions in complete sentences.

1. When and why did the age of martyrdom end?

   The age of martyrdom ended in the fourth century when the Emperor Constantine converted to Christianity and allowed Christians to practice their faith freely.

2. What is heresy? What is a heretic?

   Heresy is the obstinate denial of a truth of the faith. A heretic is one who holds and teaches a heresy.

3. What is Arianism? When was it defined as a heresy?

   Arianism is the heresy that denies that Jesus is God. It was defined as a heresy in 381 A.D.

4. Who is St. Athanasius? What is his significance in the Church?

   St. Athanasius was the Bishop of Alexandria in the fourth century. He was one of the few who affirmed that Jesus is God and fought heresy at the cost of exile and threats to his life.

5. Who is St. Augustine? What is his significance in the Church?

   St. Augustine lived in the fourth century and due to the persistent prayers of his mother, Monica, he converted to Catholicism. Before his conversion, he led a sinful life. After his conversion he became a great teacher, bishop, and theologian and wrote many works. He is a saint and Doctor of the Church.

42   *Faith and Life Series • Grade 8 • Chapter 11 • Lesson 2*

Reinforce

1. Have the students work on *Activity Book*, p. 42.

2. Give the students time to work on the Memorization Questions and Words to Know from this chapter.

3. The students should work on their reports on the Church Fathers and Doctors.

4. The students should discuss why learning about their faith is important. You might consider the necessity of faith (and knowledge of our faith) for salvation.

5. You may review the early Church heresies, and counteract them with the truth. This may be done in a debate format. Have the students defend the true teachings of the Church against the arguments of heretics.

Conclude

1. Lead the students in singing "From all thy saints in warfare," *Adoremus Hymnal*, #592.

2. End class by praying the Nicene Creed.

Preview

In the next lesson, the students will learn about monasticism.

HERESIES RESOLVED BY THE FIRST SEVEN ECUMENICAL COUNCILS

Ecumenical Councils are often called to define the Faith in light of (and in order to counter) specific heresies. The following is a list of early heresies countered by early Councils.

Arianism: Denied the divinity of Jesus. Taught that he was the highest of all created things, but that he was still a created thing who had a beginning in time and was less than the Father.

Macedonian: Known as the *Pneumatomachi*, or "Combators against the Spirit," followers of this heresy denied the divinity of the Holy Spirit, saying he was created and was a ministering angel.

Nestorianism: Denied the substantial hypostatic union and believed that Jesus was a union of two persons, human and divine, with the Son of God dwelling in the man as a man dwells in a house.

Monophysitism: Denied the true humanity of Christ and believed that he had only a divine nature.

Monothelitism: Accepted Jesus's true humanity but denied that he had a human will.

Iconoclasm: Due to a very literal reading of the Old Testament prohibition of images, iconoclats believed that any use of images in worship was idolatrous. Followers of this heresy destroyed many icons and religious images, hence their name, *Iconoclasts*, which means "Image-breakers."

LESSON THREE: MONASTERIES

Aims

The students will learn that monasteries are communities of people committed to serving Christ. Monks are bound by vows of poverty, chastity, and obedience. They are responsible for the spreading of Christianity, Christian education, Christian witness, and prayer.

Materials

- *Activity Book*, p. 43

Optional:
- "From all thy saints in warfare," *Adoremus Hymnal*, #592

Begin

Begin class by explaining the expanse of the Roman Empire and the spread of Christianity. Tell the students about the barbarians, how they invaded and plundered Rome, making their mark on history. They were non-Christians, many of whom converted to Christianity. The Church recognized the need to protect herself from them—and to convert them.

household. Shortly after Perpetua gave birth to a baby, she and other members of her household, including Felicity, were arrested because they were Christians. Despite her family's pleas that she give up her faith and return home to her child, Perpetua refused and remained strong.

Felicity, who was awaiting the birth of her own child, was eager to join Perpetua in facing death for Christ. The Roman law, however, would not allow a woman who was with child to be put to death. Because Felicity's child was born soon after her imprisonment, she was martyred along with her mistress and the others who had been arrested with them. The willingness of both Perpetua and Felicity to die for Christ—even though they were young women with children they loved—shows us that they placed God first in their lives.

We honor the memories of St. Perpetua and St. Felicity when we ask their intercession during the Eucharistic prayer of the Mass. We also invoke the intercession of many of the other martyrs here. Among them are the first martyr, Stephen; several early popes: Linus, Cletus, Clement, and Sixtus; several holy women: Agatha, Lucy, and Cecilia; and the apostles.

In the same way that the early Christians were inspired by the faith of the martyrs, we too look to them as examples of courage. We also can look to the martyrs of our own times. For although the early centuries of the Church were the age of martyrs, we still have many people who have died—and are dying—for their faith.

Fathers and Doctors of the Church

The great age of martyrdom ended in the early fourth century, when the Roman emperor Constantine issued a decree allowing Christians to practice their religion freely. Once this occurred, Christians were able to preach the gospel in the open. Even though the Church was freed from one problem, she soon had to face others. Trouble now came from within the Church in the form of heresies. A **heresy** is a denial of a basic doctrine of the faith. Those who hold and teach heresies are called *heretics*.

At the time when Constantine became emperor, a major heresy was being preached in Egypt by a priest named Arius. Arius taught that Jesus Christ, the Son of God, was not of the same nature as the Father. In other words, he said that Jesus was not God.

Because Arius was a forceful speaker and persuasive writer, his heresy, called the Arian heresy, spread rapidly through the Church and even deceived many bishops and priests. Because this heresy denied one of the most fundamental doctrines of our faith, it had to be stopped. The first step was the Church council that met in Nicaea in 325 A.D.

One of the bishops who fought to defend the truth during and after that council was **St. Athanasius**. Athanasius was the bishop of Alexandria in Egypt, where he defended the teaching of the Church against many Arian forces. He faced several threats to his life and was exiled for his defense of orthodoxy. Despite all of this, he never wavered in defending the truth that the Son of God is "one in being with the Father."

Many of Athanasius' writings concern the doctrine he defended throughout his life. One of his books, *On the Incarnation*, is a treatise on the mystery of the Second Person of the Trinity made flesh. When he died in 373 A.D., Arianism had not been completely conquered. His efforts, however, were not in vain, and Arianism was finally defeated by 381 A.D.

Other heresies, many of which also concerned the nature of Christ, followed the Arian heresy. Saints were raised up to defend the Church against these heresies as well. One of the greatest saints to defend the Church was

76

Develop

1. Read paragraphs 22–26 (up to The Church Faces Problems).

2. Who are monks? Monks are men who live in community to serve Christ. They are bound by vows of poverty, chastity, and obedience. Their communities are called monasteries and those who live in the monastery live by a rule or way of life. Originally, all monasteries were self-sufficient: they grew and cooked their own food, did their own laundry, taught themselves, etc. Many Catholic schools were started as a form of missionary work by the monastic orders. Through their schools, the monks were able to Christianize and educate most of Europe.

3. Benedictines are monks whose daily activities are divided into work and prayer. Saint Benedict was a holy man, known for his power of exorcism. (You may be familiar with the Benedictine Cross or the Saint Benedict medal, which holds a prayer of exorcism and protection against the devil.)

4. Have the students imagine they are monks. How could they live in community and be self-sustaining? Who would be their "father/abbot" or leader? What duties would be assigned? How would they ensure the safety of their community in the time of the barbarians? What would they do to support one another in the faith? Would they want to leave their community—ever? Benedictines took a vow of stability so that they knew they would always be in the same monastery, with the same people. Imagine living that way until your death! What would be life's challenges and blessings in a monastery?

5. The students should research some of the great monastics, such as Saints Benedict, Boniface, and Columban.

Monasteries

Answer the following questions in complete sentences.

1. What happened in the fifth century and why did this challenge the Church?
   In the fifth century, barbarians started to move near and threaten the Roman Empire. This challenged the Church to civilize them and to convert them to Christianity.

2. How did monasteries, with monks and monastic rules, help the Church face this challenge?
   Monasteries, with monks and monastic rules, helped the Church face this challenge because they set up schools and monasteries around Europe. Through their schools, books and prayer they converted and educated many people.

3. Who is St. Benedict and what is his importance to the Church?
   St. Benedict lived in the fifth and sixth century and is called the "Father of Western Monasticism". He founded Monte Cassino and the Benedictine Order. He also wrote the Benedictine Rule, a guide for daily activities of his monks which consisted of prayer and physical work.

4. Who is St. Columban and what is his importance to the Church?
   St. Columban was an Irish missionary monk who preached among the Franks in the sixth century.

Reinforce

1. Have the students work on *Activity Book*, p. 43.

2. Give the students time to work on the Memorization Questions and Words to Know from this chapter.

3. If possible, take the students to visit a local monastery.

4. Study the rule of Saint Benedict.

5. Some of the oldest religious books in the Church were written by monks. It was their work to copy out entire books by hand (this was before the printing press). Monks copied everything from Bibles to announcements for the Church. Have the students do a calligraphy project writing a Christian motto that they want to embrace as their own; e.g., Totus Tuus, Ora et Labora, My Lord and My God, etc.

Conclude

1. Lead the students in singing "From all thy saints in warfare," *Adoremus Hymnal*, #592.

2. End class by praying the Nicene Creed.

Preview

In the next lesson, the students will learn about problems that faced the Church during the first millenium.

EXAMPLES OF WESTERN ORDERS

Benedictine (O.S.B.): Order of St. Benedict. One of the oldest Catholic monastic orders. Governed by the *Rule of St. Benedict*, written by St. Benedict of Nursia in the sixth century. Monks and nuns following the Benedictine Rule live in community, domiciled in abbeys or in monasteries. Their lives are dedicated to prayer, liturgy, and manual labor. The Order also includes extern clergy, extern religious, and lay Oblates.

Cistercian (O.Cist.): Cistercians of the Common Observance. A Benedictine reform, this Order was founded by St. Robert of Molesmes in 1098, at which time it was governed by the original *Rule of St. Benedict*. The Order is composed of monks and nuns.

Trappist (O.C.S.O.): Cistercian Order of the Strict Observance. A Cistercian reform, this Order was founded by Abbot Jean-Armand le Bouthillier de Rancé in the late seventeenth century. The Order is composed of monks and nuns who are governed by the *Rule of St. Benedict*.

Carthusian: This Order was founded by St. Bruno in the eleventh century. Its original community came from the Cistercian of the Common Observance. Carthusian hermits live in austere solitude, silence and contemplative prayer. They are governed by the original *Carthusian Rule*, which has never changed.

LESSON FOUR: PROBLEMS

Aims

The students will learn that other challenges facing the Church included Islam, schism, and corruption of the clergy. Schism is a refusal to submit to the Pope or the Church, which is subject to him.

They will learn that many of the clergy in the Church became corrupt. As the Roman Empire collapsed, the clergy assumed civil responsibility, exercising both spiritual and temporal power.

Materials

- *Activity Book*, p. 44

Optional:
- "From all thy saints in warfare," *Adoremus Hymnal*, #592

Begin

Discuss Islam. It is important that the students understand the main differences between Islam and Christianity. These two religions have clashed throughout history; e.g., in the Crusades. These two religions still clash today. Stress for the students that Catholicism is the one true Church founded by Jesus Christ. Islam, founded upon the teachings of the man Muhammad, rejects the divinity of Christ (this is heresy). Although they believe in God (who they call Allah) their moral system and teachings are different from those of Catholicism.

St. Augustine, who was born near the end of Athanasius' life. Although Augustine became a great bishop, teacher, and **theologian** (someone who studies and teaches about God) in the Church, his early life reminds us that even great sinners who repent can become saints.

Born in North Africa, Augustine was the son of a Roman official and a Christian woman named Monica. During his youth he showed that he had a brilliant mind and was recognized as a great student. In his adolescence, however, he acquired many bad habits and lived a wild life; he seriously broke the Commandment on purity. His mother patiently prayed for him, begging God to give him the grace to accept the faith and reform his life.

Her prayers were answered when, after many years of searching for the truth, Augustine was baptized at the age of thirty-three. Later he became a priest and eventually a bishop. During the remainder of his life he preached many sermons and wrote over one hundred books in defense of the faith. Among these books is his own story of his life and his conversion, *The Confessions*. Another book, which many consider his most famous work, is *The City of God*, which contrasts the life of the Christian with the evils of the world in which we must live. Like St. Athanasius, St. Augustine, who died in 430 A.D., is considered one of the Fathers of the Church.

The Monasteries

Later, in the fifth century, barbarian tribes began to threaten the stability of the Roman Empire. The barbarians were warlike, uncivilized tribes living in northern Europe outside the boundaries of the empire. As they expanded, they moved south and began invading the empire, once even threatening the city of Rome. The Church recognized the need to convert them to Christianity and to civilize them.

Much of this work was performed during the next three centuries by the monks. Monks are men who live a life of poverty, chastity, and obedience together in a community in order to serve Christ. They live according to a specific *rule*, or way of life, in communities called **monasteries** that are often in remote areas. They support themselves through agricultural activity and dedicate their time to God. Gradually they formed schools at their monasteries. It was through these schools and their later missionary work that the monks were able to Christianize and educate much of Europe.

Although there were monks in the Church as early as the third century, the title of "Father of Western Monasticism" is given to **St. Benedict**, who was born in 480 A.D. He established the famous monastery at Monte Cassino in Italy and is the founder of the Benedictine order. He composed a rule, which we call the *rule of St. Benedict* to guide the daily activities of his monks.

Benedict divided the daily activities of his monks into prayer and physical work. This became the motto of all Benedictines: "*Ora et Labora*" (pray and work). The daily prayer consisted of the Divine Office—chanted together at seven specific hours of the day and night—and the daily Sacrifice of the Mass. The labor, which was also considered a form of prayer, was both manual—farming, building, and so on—and intellectual—copying of manuscripts, writing books, educating, and the like.

As time passed, the monasteries were not only centers of learning but also missionary centers, from which monks set out to spread the faith. Among these missionary monks was St. Columban, an Irishman who preached the faith among the Franks (living in the area of modern-day France) during the end of the sixth century. Another great example was St. Boniface, a Benedictine monk from England. In the

77

Develop

1. Read paragraphs 27–30 (to the end of the chapter).

2. Discuss why it was bad for the Church of the East and the Church of the West to be separated. Their communication broke down. The Eastern Church looked for leadership from its bishops and no longer submitted to Rome (and the Pope). These two parts of the empire were already separated by language and culture. In 1054 the Great Schism occurred and the Churches of East and West were separated. This was a tremendous loss for the Church. The Eastern Church had a highly developed sense of mysticism and theology. It had many great saints.

3. Discuss what is meant by the expression that "The Church needs to breathe with both lungs: East and West." To be fully alive, the Church needs the richness, vitality, and spirit of the different traditions. We share the same faith, sacraments, Scripture, Tradition, moral teachings etc.,

and we must recognize and appreciate the goods we share. Some of the Eastern Churches are in union with Rome and some are not (see box at right). Those that are not in union are in dialogue, working toward reunion. You may have the students enter a dialogue to "reunite" the Eastern and Western Churches.

4. Corruption of the clergy was a problem for the Church— it was a great scandal. Many church leaders became corrupted by power, money, and earthly attachments. Fortunately, God called up great saints to purify the Church and to strengthen her against these problems.

5. It is important to know that even though the Church leaders were corrupt, they never taught error, as the Church was protected by the Holy Spirit and the charism of infallibility.

Name:_____

The Church Faces Problems

Answer the following questions in complete sentences.

1. What is Islam?

   Islam is a religion that emerged in Arabia early in the seventh century. Followers of Islam are called Moslems.

2. How did Moslems separate the East from the West and how did this contribute to the schism in 1054?

   Moslems gained control of the Mediterranean Sea. This separated Christians in the East from those in the West and amplified already existing disagreements between the two on the authority of the Pope and specific wording of certain doctrines. This eventually led to the separation of the Church in the East from the Pope.

3. Explain the difficulties that faced the Church from within near the end of the first millennium.

   Toward the end of the first millennium, the Church faced a period of corruption of the clergy. As the Roman Empire collapsed, the Church was the only stable force still remaining. Since mainly the clergy were the most educated, they had to run the government. This became a source of temptation to become too concerned with temporal affairs. Many lost sight of their primary task and led sinful lives, even many popes.

4. Did the Holy Spirit abandon the Church during those years? How can we say the Church is divine when corruption occurs in the Church?

   No. The Holy Spirit did not abandon the Church. We can still say the Church is divine when corruption occurs because although her human members may be corrupt, she herself will never formally teach error and the Holy Spirit still guides her.

44   *Faith and Life Series • Grade 8 • Chapter 11 • Lesson 4*

Reinforce

1. Have the students work on *Activity Book*, p. 44.

2. Give the students time to work on the Memorization Questions and Words to Know from this chapter and to prepare for the quiz.

3. *Discuss the political climate of the early Middle Ages. The Roman Empire was decreasing in size and each country struggled with its own governing. This caused many clergy (who were educated) to take on positions of leadership in society. The question became one of allegiance. To whom should the people be faithful? To their king? To the Pope? Further, the temptations of the world became more available to clergy with wealth, nobility (popularity), power, etc.*

Conclude

1. Lead the students in singing "From all thy saints in warfare," *Adoremus Hymnal*, #592.

2. End class by praying the Nicene Creed.

Preview

In the next lesson, the students' understanding of the material covered in this chapter will be reviewed and assessed.

EASTERN AND WESTERN CHURCHES

Every Church in union with Rome is a Catholic Church. However, there are several churches within the Catholic Church with different liturgies, customs, and traditions. They are all Catholic because they have the same doctrines and they all accept the authority of the Bishop of Rome (the Pope). It is easy to confuse the Eastern Churches with the Orthodox Churches, because they have many of the same liturgies, customs, and traditions. The fundamental difference between the two is that the Orthodox Church does not accept the authority of the Pope. The Eastern Churches show us that we can be unified in belief while having diversity in the way we express those beliefs. It is important to note, however, that these differences are all of apostolic origin. We cannot just create new rites on our own.

NOTES

_____
_____
_____
_____
_____
_____
_____
_____
_____
_____
_____

_____

_____

_____

_____

_____

_____

_____

_____

_____

_____

_____

_____

_____

_____

_____

_____

_____

_____

_____

_____

eighth century he left England for the area of Germany. For many years Boniface preached there, spreading the faith and baptizing many from the Germanic tribes.

The Church Faces Problems

While the monks were busy Christianizing the barbarians in Europe, the Church was faced with other invasions as well. A new religion, Islam, had emerged in Arabia early in the seventh century and was now being spread throughout North Africa and the eastern portion of the old Roman Empire. The followers of Islam, called Moslems, eventually gained control of the Mediterranean Sea. As a result, Christians living in western Europe were physically separated from those in the East.

This event intensified problems that had existed for a long time. Christians in the two parts of the empire were divided by language and culture. There had also been a long-running debate over the wording of certain doctrines and over the authority of the bishop of Rome (the Pope). These problems were finally brought to a head in 1054 A.D. In that year, the Church in the East formally separated herself from the Pope and the Roman Catholic Church. This is known as the Eastern *schism*, or split. Schism is a refusal to submit to the Pope or to the Church, which is subject to him. While *some* of the Eastern Christians have been reunited with the Church—for example,

the Byzantine Catholics—the schism still exists today.

This schism was only one great problem that the Church faced as she completed her first thousand years. A second was the great corruption of the clergy during part of the *Middle Ages*. This period of increased corruption, from about 850–1000 A.D., was the result of the gradual collapse of the old Roman Empire. As the Empire collapsed, the Church was the only stable force remaining in the world. Because few laymen were educated, it was left to the clergy to take up the responsibility of governing civil society. Many Church leaders then exercised not only spiritual but temporal power as well.

After a while many bishops, priests, and monks began to forget their roles as spiritual leaders. Unfortunately they became far too concerned with their temporal affairs or their own possessions and lost sight of their primary task. Sad to say, there were even popes who, though they never taught error, were sinful, corrupt, and worldly. The need for reform of the clergy became more and more urgent. Once again, many saints rose up during the next few centuries to guide the Church through her next crisis.

Words to Know:
    gentiles martyrs heresy
  St. Athanasius St. Augustine St. Benedict
    theologian monasteries

78

_____

_____

_____

_____

_____

_____

_____

_____

_____

_____

_____

_____

_____

Q. 79 *What is a monastery?*

A monastery is a community of those who consecrate their lives to God through vows of poverty, chastity, and obedience, and who together pray the Liturgy of the Hours (CCC 925, 927).

Q. 80 *What is heresy?*

Heresy is the obstinate denial after Baptism of a truth of the Faith which must be believed (CCC 2089).

Q. 81 *What is schism?*

Schism is a refusal to submit to the Pope or to the Church which is subject to him (CCC 2089).

79

CHAPTER ELEVEN
REVIEW AND ASSESSMENT

Aims

The students' understanding of the material covered in this chapter will be reviewed and assessed.

Materials

- Quiz 11, Appendix, p. A-15

Optional:
- "From all thy saints in warfare," *Adoremus Hymnal*, #592

Review

1. The apostles were the first missionaries of the Church. The students should know this and be able to name several places to which the apostles brought the Good News in the early years of the Church.

2. In the first three centuries of the Church, Christians were persecuted and many were martyred. Christianity became legal under Emperor Constantine.

3. The students should understand the problem of heresy in the early Church. Ecumenical councils were needed to clarify Church teaching. The students should know that Church Fathers and Doctors helped the Church overcome heresies and clearly define what the Church believes.

4. The students should understand that monasteries are communities of men who live together to serve Christ, bound by vows of poverty, chastity, and obedience. The monks founded the first Christian schools and became great missionaries.

5. The students should understand the problems of Islam, the Great Schism, and the corruption of the clergy with the fall of the Roman Empire.

Name: _____

Saints in Our History: The First Thousand Years Quiz 11

Part I: Define the following terms.

Gentile: <u>non-Jews</u>

Martyr: <u>a witness to the truth of the Faith, in which the person endures even death to be faithful to Christ</u>

Heresy: <u>a denial of a basic doctrine of the faith</u>

Monastery: <u>the place where men or women live in community with a specific rule or way of life</u>

Arianism: <u>a heresy in the fourth century which denied the divinity of Christ</u>

Part II: Matching.

1. _J_ Founder of Islam
2. _F_ Roman emperor who legalized Christianity
3. _H_ Father of western monasticism
4. _A_ First Pope, Prince of the Apostles
5. _E_ Women martyrs
6. _B_ Convert and apostle
7. _D_ Convert, bishop, and theologian
8. _G_ Denied the divinity of Christ
9. _C_ Fought Arianism
10. _I_ An Irish missionary monk

a. Peter
b. Paul
c. Athanasius
d. Augustine
e. Perpetua and Felicity
f. Constantine
g. Arius
h. Benedict
i. Columban
j. Muhammad

Part III: Choose one of the following saints or pairs of saints and, on the back of this page, write a brief essay on how they contributed to the life of the Church.

Paul, Athanasius, Augustine, Benedict, Perpetua and Felicity

Faith and Life • Grade 8 • Appendix A   *A - 15*

Assess

1. Distribute the quizzes and read through them with the students to be sure they understand the questions.

2. Administer the quiz. As they hand in their work, orally quiz the students on the Memorization Questions from this chapter.

3. After all the quizzes have been handed in, review the correct answers with the class.

Conclude

1. Lead the students in singing "From all thy saints in warfare," *Adoremus Hymnal*, #592.

2. End class by leading the students in the Nicene Creed.

CHAPTER TWELVE
SAINTS: THE SECOND THOUSAND YEARS

Catechism of the Catholic Church References

Atheism: 2123–28, 2140, 2424
Authority in Society: 1897–1904, 1918–23
Christ's Missionary Mandate in the Church: 849–56, 868
Christian Holiness: 2012–16, 2028–29
Communion of Saints: 946–62
Council of Trent: 9
Devotion to the Blessed Virgin: 971
Ecumenical Councils: 884, 891
Evangelical Councils: 915–16, 944, 2052–53, 2103
Fortitude: 1805, 1808–9, 1831, 1834, 1837, 1845
Fruits of Communion: 1391–1401, 1416

Holy Communion: 1355, 1382–90, 1415, 1417
Jesus as Our Teacher and Model of Holiness: 468–69, 516, 519–21, 561
Love for the Poor and the Works of Mercy: 2443–49, 2462–63
Martyrdom: 2473–74, 2506
Poverty of Christ: 517, 520, 525, 1506
Principles of Church and State Relationship: 2244–46
Religious Freedom: 2108–9, 2137
Safeguarding Peace and Avoiding War: 2302–17, 2327–30
Saints as Companions in Prayer: 2683–84, 2692–93

Scripture References

"Blessed are the poor in spirit": Mt 5:3

Camel through eye of needle: Mt 19:24

Summary of Lesson Content

Lesson 1

Holy men like Saint Bernard founded religious orders. Saint Bernard preached all over Europe and rekindled the faith of laity and monks. He encouraged participation in the Second Crusade. Near the end of the eleventh century, Moslems gained control of the Holy Land.

Saint Louis IX was a French king who fought in the Crusades. The Crusades were not successful, but they opened Western Europe to new theories of medicine, philosophy, and navigation.

Lesson 2

New mendicant religious orders, whose members survived by begging, were founded in the thirteenth–fourteenth centuries. Saint Francis of Assisi founded the first of these orders, the Order of Friars (franciscans). Saint Dominic founded the Order of Preachers minor, a mendicant order sent to convert heretics. Saint Thomas Aquinas, the greatest western theologian (Dominicans) was a Dominican. Saint Catherine of Siena, a Doctor of the Church, served the Church and guided the Pope back to Rome.

Lesson 3

The sixteenth century brought the Renaissance and the Protestant Reformation. Several groups rebelled and broke away from the Church, challenging Church teaching. The Council of Trent defended Church teaching against the Protestants.

Saint Ignatius founded the Society of Jesus, known as the Jesuits, which was dedicated to defending the faith and serving the Church in obedience to the Pope. Missionaries from many religious orders went to Asia and the Americas.

Lesson 4

In modern times, the Church defended herself against the heresy of Modernism (which teaches that faith and morals should evolve and that all is relative—there is no truth).

Other challenges to the Church included atheistic, totalitarian governments such as Nazism, communism, and fascism.

Saint Maximilian Kolbe strove to win the world for Mary Immaculate. He was martyred in this pursuit.

LESSON ONE: MIDDLE AGES

Aims

The students will learn that holy men like Saint Bernard founded religious orders. Saint Bernard preached all over Europe and rekindled the faith of laity and monks. He encouraged participation in the Second Crusade. Near the end of the eleventh century, Moslems gained control of the Holy Land.

They will learn that Saint Louis IX was a French king who fought in the Crusades. The Crusades were not successful, but they opened Western Europe to new theories of medicine, philosophy, and navigation.

Materials

- *Activity Book*, p. 45   Optional:
- "From all thy saints in warfare," *Adoremus Hymnal*, #592

Begin

Discuss the state of the Church (from the last chapter). As the Church moved into the eleventh and twelfth centuries, it began an internal reform —holy Popes began to reform the clergy. Holy men began to reform the monasteries. The faith of the laity began to be rekindled through good preachers and the positive changes in the Church.

CHAPTER 12

Saints in Our History: The Second Thousand Years

Having the eyes of your hearts enlightened, that you may know what is the hope to which he has called you, what are the riches of his glorious inheritance in the saints. . . .

Ephesians 1:18

As the Church moved into the eleventh and twelfth centuries, one of her first concerns was reforming the corrupt clergy. Fortunately, the Church was blessed with several holy popes, who were able to begin these reforms.

Other holy men began to reform the monasteries. The most important of these is St. Bernard of Clairvaux. As a young man Bernard joined a new monastic community known as the Cistercians, whose way of life was based on the rule of St. Benedict. But their way of life was simpler and stricter than that in most Benedictine communities of the time.

After he was ordained, Bernard was chosen to begin a new monastery following the Cistercian way of life. Bernard became the abbot of this monastery at Clairvaux and then founded sixty-eight more monasteries according to the same rule. The new generation of monasteries corrected many of the abuses that had crept into monastic life during the Middle Ages, and these monasteries were a great source of hope.

St. Bernard's own holiness was reflected in the life of Clairvaux and the other monasteries. He strengthened the faith by his sermons

about devotion to Jesus and to his Mother. So great were these sermons that people from all over Europe came to hear him. Thus St. Bernard was able to rekindle the faith of the laity as well as that of his monks.

The Crusades

St. Bernard had great influence on other matters in Europe as well. For example, he called for the Second Crusade, encouraging many people in France and Germany to join. The **Crusades** were the response of the Church to a new difficulty that had arisen because of the Moslems.

Toward the end of the eleventh century, the Moslems seized control of the *Holy Land* (Palestine) and persecuted those Christians who traveled on pilgrimages to Jerusalem and the other holy places. The Crusades were military efforts to win back the Holy Land. They were carried on periodically during the next two centuries. The knights and soldiers who fought those battles for the cause of Christ used the Cross as their symbol. Many who

80

Develop

1. Read paragraphs 1–11 (up to New Religious Orders).

2. Discuss Saint Bernard of Clairvaux. He was the second founder of the Cistercians, based upon the original Benedictine Rule. He founded sixty-nine monasteries. Their strict Order corrected abuses that had come into monastic life.

3. Discuss the Crusades. They were holy wars—military efforts to win back the Holy Land, which had been invaded and taken over by the Moslems (followers of Islam). Discuss Saint Louis, who fought in the Crusades. Would we be willing to fight and die for our faith? Is this martyrdom?

4. Discuss the importance of the Holy Land. It is the land of Jesus. It is the land of the Jews. The Moslems had gained control and were assaulting Christian pilgrims. These three religions had struggled for power in the Holy Land for centuries. For each religion, it is a shrine of sanctity—an impor-

tant place for the history of their faith, and a sign that whoever possesses it has the true religion. For the Jews, this land was promised to them by God through Abraham. For the Christians, it is the land where Jesus lived and founded his Church (it is a place where Christians can go to be where Jesus was). For the Moslems, it is the location of one of the most holy shrines founded by Muhammad. It is easy to see why people wanted this land and would die for it in the name of their faith.

5. Discuss what Saint Louis' mother had said to him: "I would rather see you dead at my feet than that you should commit one mortal sin." Wow! What a powerful image. What does this say about sin?

6. Have the students write prayers asking for the grace to be courageous in the faith and to become saints.

Name:_____

The Crusades

Answer the following questions in complete sentences.

1. Who is St. Bernard of Clairvaux? What is his importance to the Church?

St. Bernard of Clairvaux was a monastic reformer of the twelfth century. He established 68 new monasteries which corrected many of the monastic abuses of the day. He also inspired people all over Europe with his beautiful sermons, giving many new hope.

2. What were the Crusades and why were they waged?

The Crusades were a military efforts to win back the Holy Land. They were waged because the Moslems had seized the Holy Land and were persecuting Christians on pilgrimage to the holy shrines.

3. Who is King Louis IX and what is his importance in the Church?

King Louis IX was the king of France and a just and holy man. He was a saint and a wonderful example to the people of France. He also led two major Crusades.

4. Did the Crusaders win the war?

The Crusaders did not win the war, since they did not achieve the objective of freeing the Holy Land from the hands of the Moslems.

5. What was the effect of the Crusades?

The effect of the Crusades was that they strengthened the faith of many and increased devotion to the saints. They also opened the door in areas of knowledge which the Moslems had excelled in such as medicine, philosophy, and navigation.

Reinforce

1. Have the students work on *Activity Book*, p. 45.

2. Give the students time to work on the Memorization Questions and Words to Know from this chapter.

3. *Explain that, today, we live better than royalty in the time of Saint Louis. We have luxuries even the king did not have! We have cars (for him, travel took weeks on horseback); we have air conditioning (he likely had servants with fans). We have rich foods in our refrigerators that we cook quickly on our stoves in our microwaves. Not so the king. Jesus said: "Blessed are the poor in spirit" (Mt 5:3), and "It is easier for a camel to go through the eye of a needle than for a rich man to enter the kingdom of God" Mt 19:24. How can Saint Louis be an example for us to help us get to heaven? Discuss the importance of fear of God (fear of offending him), daily Mass and prayer, charity, teaching others the Faith, etc.*

Conclude

1. Teach the students to sing "From all thy saints in warfare," *Adoremus Hymnal*, #592.

2. End class by praying the Nicene Creed.

Preview

In the next lesson, the students will learn about the Church in the Middle Ages.

THE CRUSADES

- First Crusade, 1095–1101.
- Second Crusade, 1145–47.
- Third Crusade, 1188–92.
- Fourth Crusade, 1204.
- Fifth Crusade, 1217.
- Sixth Crusade, 1228-29.
- Seventh Crusade, 1249-52.
- Eighth Crusade, 1270.

NOTES

_____
_____
_____
_____
_____
_____
_____
_____
_____
_____

LESSON TWO:
SERVE THE CHURCH

Aims

The students will learn that new mendicant religious orders, whose members survived by begging, were founded in the thirteenth–fourteenth centuries. Saint Francis of Assisi founded the first of these orders, the Order of Friars Minor (Franciscans). Saint Dominic founded the Order of Preachers (Dominicans), a mendicant order sent to convert heretics. Saint Thomas Aquinas, the greatest western theologian, was a Dominican. Saint Catherine of Siena, a Doctor of the Church, served the Church and guided the Pope back to Rome.

Materials

- *Activity Book*, p. 46
- List of Popes, Appendix, pp. B-1–B-2

Optional:
- From all thy saints in warfare," *Adoremus Hymnal*, #592

- "The Spirit of Assisi," video, available through Ignatius Press

Begin

Remind the students of the monastic orders that existed in the Church up to this point. Today, we will learn about radical new religious orders—ones that lived poverty in a new way and served the Church outside of their monasteries.

---

either led or fought these Crusades were truly saintly men.

One of these courageous men was King St. Louis IX of France, who led the last two major Crusades. He is noted for being a holy man and a just ruler. His devotion to his faith was instilled in him at an early age by his mother. When he was growing up she often said to him, "I love you, my dear son, as much as a mother can love her child, but I would rather see you dead at my feet than that you should commit a mortal sin." Such lessons never left him, even when he became the king of France.

While he was king, he attended two Masses each day and spent much of his time in prayer. He frequently cared for the poor personally, often having them join his family at meals. And he taught his sons to love their faith as well. In his last words to his eldest son he wrote, ". . . the first thing I would teach thee is to set thine heart to love God."

For St. Louis, as for any saint, love of God came first. Thus, when it seemed necessary to fight a battle for Christ, St. Louis readily responded. He died on his way to fight his second Crusade. His last words echoed those of Our Lord on the Cross, "Into thy hands I commend my spirit."

Despite their great efforts, the Crusaders did not finally achieve their goal. The Holy Land was not freed from the Moslems. The Crusades did, however, strengthen the faith of many in Europe and increase devotion to Christ and his saints. They also opened western Europe to many areas of knowledge in which the Moslems had advanced—for example, navigation, medicine, and philosophy. This provided the basis for many scholarly and scientific achievements during the next few centuries.

The internal reforms of the Church, begun by St. Bernard and others, grew and flourished during the thirteenth century. This was the height of the period known as the **Middle Ages**.

New Religious Orders

During this century, two new religious orders were founded that were dramatically different from the traditional orders. The members of these communities did not live in monasteries isolated from society but lived instead in the towns where they worked. Unlike the monastic communities, which owned large portions of land to support themselves, these new orders depended on the generosity of ordinary people for their basic needs. They are called *mendicant* orders, because they lived by begging. By living simply, these orders reminded Christians that the true role of the religious was to serve God.

The first of these communities was the Franciscan order, which was founded in Italy by **St. Francis of Assisi**. Francis, the son of a wealthy merchant in Assisi, grew up with plenty of money, which he spent recklessly. He wanted to become a knight but realized that Christ was calling him to serve God in the religious life. Francis then decided to live as a poor man, discarding his fine clothes for those of a beggar and caring for the needy and the sick.

He began a life of prayer—preaching and serving the poor. His holiness attracted many young men, who joined him in his work. Eventually Francis wrote a simple rule for his followers. With the Pope's blessing they were established as the Order of Friars Minor ("Little Brothers"). By the time of Francis' death, there were over five thousand Franciscans in Europe.

Men were not the only ones attracted to Francis' way of life. A rich young woman from Assisi also asked to join him, and thus with Francis' help St. Clare established a community for women, the Poor Clares, who also lived according to the Franciscan rule.

Another mendicant order for men was founded by a young Spanish priest, Dominic

81

Develop

1. Read paragraphs 12–25 (up to Protestant Reformation).

2. Discuss the mendicant orders. These orders survived on the charity of the laity, through begging. The first of these communities was the Order of friars minor (Franciscans), founded by Saint Francis of Assisi. He lived a holy life of prayer and served the poor and sick. Soon others gathered with him, discarding wealth for the clothes of a beggar, and caring for the needy and the sick. Francis wrote a rule for the Friars Minor. Women were also attracted to this way of life, and Saint Francis helped Saint Clare found a women's community called the Poor Clares (based upon the rule of Saint Francis). Saint Dominic founded the Order of Preachers (the Dominicans). Their work was to convert heretics living in southern France. They lived simple lives preaching the truth. They emphasized scholarly learning for their members so they could grow in the faith and preach it well. The greatest of the Dominicans was Saint Thomas Aquinas.

3. Although the Church flourished, disagreements between the Popes and the kings of France caused a crisis—the Pope moved to Avignon, France! A devout laywoman, Saint Catherine of Siena, persuaded the Pope to return to Rome. Saint Catherine chose to live a life of prayer and service to others, especially the sick. She is a Doctor of the Church.

4. Saint Peter could have only one successor. The Great Western Schism, a time when two men claimed to be Pope, was a difficult time for the Church. This weakened the role of the Pope (because no one was sure who the real Pope was)! By the time this was resolved, the Church's unity was threatened.

Name:_____

The Middle Ages

Answer the following questions in complete sentences.

1. What two new religious orders were founded during the Middle Ages and how did they differ from monastic orders?

   Two new religious orders founded in the Middle Ages were the Order of Friars Minor (known today as the Franciscans) and the Order of Preachers (known today as the Dominicans). They differed from the previous monastic orders because they lived and relied upon the people for their needs.

2. Who is St. Francis of Assisi and what is his importance to the Church?

   St. Francis of Assisi was a wealthy, reckless Italian youth who had a powerful conversion to Christ. He gave up everything to live as a poor man and follow Jesus. He started the Franciscan Order as well as inspiring St. Clare to found a women's branch, called the Poor Clares.

3. Who is St. Dominic de Guzman, and what is his importance to the Church?

   St. Dominic de Guzman founded the Order of Preachers, known as the Dominican Order. Dominicans are a very scholarly order that is devoted to preaching. St. Dominic was sent to convert the Albigensians (heretics of that day) and promoted devotion to the Rosary.

4. Who is St. Thomas Aquinas and what is his importance to the Church?

   St. Thomas Aquinas was an Italian Dominican who was a brilliant philosopher and theologian. He is a Doctor of the Church and was given the title "The Angelic Doctor" for his brilliant writings and great love of God and neighbor.

5. Who is St. Catherine of Siena and what is her importance to the Church?

   St. Catherine was a holy Italian lay woman. She convinced the Pope, who at the time was living in Avignon, to return to Rome. She also left many spiritual writings and is a Doctor of the Church.

46   *Faith and Life Series • Grade 8 • Chapter 12 • Lesson 2*

Reinforce

1. Have the students work on *Activity Book*, p. 46.

2. Give the students time to work on the Memorization Questions and Words to Know from this chapter.

3. Have the students research Saints Francis, Clare, Dominic, and Thomas. Show a video, such as "The Spirit of Assisi," available through Ignatius Press; 25 minutes.

4. Read some of Saint Thomas' prayers.

5. Using the List of Popes found in Appendix, pp. B-1–B-2, point out where the great western schism occurred.

Conclude

1. Lead the students in singing "From all thy saints in warfare," *Adoremus Hymnal*, #592.

2. End class by praying the Nicene Creed.

Preview

In the next lesson, the students will learn about the Protestant Reformation.

THE CARMELITES

The beginning of the Carmelite Order dates back to the eleventh century. A community of hermits living on Mount Carmel in the Holy Land took their inspiration from the prophet Elijah and strove to live in deep union with God. Due to increased European presence in the Holy Land during the Crusades, some of the Carmelites traveled to Europe, and the order was officially approved by the second council of Lyons in 1247. Carmelites dedicate their lives to contemplation and union with God. Many of the greatest mystics of the Church, such as Saint Teresa of Avila, Saint John of the Cross, and Saint Thérèse of Lisieux were members of this Order.

NOTES

_____
_____
_____
_____
_____
_____
_____
_____
_____
_____
_____
_____
_____

LESSON THREE: REFORMATION

Aims

The students will learn that the sixteenth century brought the Renaissance and the Protestant Reformation. Several groups rebelled and broke away from the Church, challenging Church teaching. The Council of Trent defended Church teaching against the Protestants.

They will learn that Saint Ignatius founded the Society of Jesus, known as Jesuits, which was dedicated to defending the faith and serving the Church in obedience to the Pope. Missionaries from many religious orders went to Asia and the Americas.

Materials

- *Activity Book*, p. 47   Optional:
  - "From all thy saints in warfare," *Adoremus Hymnal*, #592

Begin

Discuss an example to help the students understand the disobedience of the Protestant Reformation. There were many abuses in the Church and Martin Luther (a religious) disagreed with them. Instead of being obedient and working with the Church, he rejected the Church and some of her teachings (e.g., the need for Confession; he believed that the sacraments were not effective, just rituals). He founded the Lutheran Church.

---

de Guzman. This order is known as the Dominicans, or Order of Preachers. As a young priest **St. Dominic** was sent to convert a group of heretics living in southern France, the Albigensians. To help him in this task, he gathered a group of young men who were willing to dedicate themselves to preaching. Like the Franciscans, they lived in simplicity and poverty. They spent their time in teaching and preaching. The Dominicans emphasized scholarly learning for their members, so that they would be able to preach more effectively. Consequently, many of the great university teachers of this age were Dominicans.

St. Thomas Aquinas

The greatest of these Dominican scholars and teachers was **St. Thomas Aquinas**. Thomas was born in Italy in 1225 A.D. and began his education at the Benedictine monastery at Monte Cassino. His wealthy family hoped that one day he would become a Benedictine. Thomas went on to study at the University of Naples, where he first met the Dominicans. Their simple life of poverty and study attracted Thomas, and, despite many vigorous objections from his family, he joined the order.

He studied theology and philosophy with another Dominican, St. Albert the Great, and eventually became a teacher himself at the University of Paris.

Thomas studied the ancient Greek philosopher Aristotle, whose writings were among those brought back to Europe by the Crusaders. St. Thomas used Aristotle's ideas in his own work in theology. He taught that God's revelation to man is not contrary to reason but, rather, that reason is necessary to understand God more completely. While his method was based on Aristotle, his insights were based on the Scriptures and the writings of the Fathers. He wrote a large number of books, but the best known and most important of these is his *Summa Theologiae*. In this famous book he organized, explained, and defended all the doctrines of our faith. Thomas' writings have never been surpassed in the Church and remain today among the most important sources for Catholic theology.

Although Thomas' scholarly works were important to the Church, it was his love of God that made him a saint. His devotion to Christ and the Blessed Sacrament are reflected in some of the beautiful prayers and poems he composed for certain feasts. For example, St. Thomas wrote the beautiful hymn *Pange Lingua* ("Sing My Tongue"), the final verses of which are frequently sung at Benediction. Christ and the Church were the center of St. Thomas' life, and he knew that his writings were unimportant compared to the infinite wisdom of God.

In 1274 A.D. St. Thomas was asked by the Pope to attend the Church council in Lyons,

82

Develop

1. Read paragraphs 26–43 (up to Modern Times).

2. The formation of Protestantism was tragic for the Church. Many of her followers were blindly guided away. With the creation of the printing press, heresy was easily spread and believed. With a sense of distrust in the Church, many turned to the Protestant religion and questioned Church teaching. Because of this, the Church called the Council of Trent (1545–63). The Council of Trent re-asserted Church teaching and the period after the Council was called the Counter-Reformation (an attempt to undo the damage done by the Protestant Reformation). To this day, there are many Protestant denomination throughout the world—united with us in Baptism, but deprived of the fullness of the means of salvation offered in the Catholic Church. We continue to pray for the unity of all Christians.

3. Saint Ignatius of Loyola founded the Jesuits who were soldiers for the Church, obedient to the Pope. They fought heresy. They founded many universities and spread the teachings of the Church.

4. With the Industrial Revolution, travel became easier and missionary work flourished. The Church spread to Asia, India, China, and North America. Spend some time discussing the missionary work in North America, particularly the work of the North American Martyrs (see right).

5. The first American born saint was Elizabeth Ann Seton. She founded the Sisters of Charity, teaching children and caring for the poor.

6. Have representatives from various religious orders visit your class. You might also have the students research the different religious orders on the Internet, and get their contact information.

Name:_____

The Protestant Reformation

Answer the following questions in complete sentences.

1. What is the Protestant Reformation? How did Martin Luther contribute to it?
   The Protestant Reformation refers to the period of history when, due to a misguided effort to reform Church corruption, many broke away from the Church. Martin Luther contributed since he was a key leader in the Catholic Church who was the first among those reformers who broke away from the Church.

2. What is the Council of Trent? Why was this council called?
   The Council of Trent was the Church's response to the Protestant Reformation. The Church did need reform and still needed to clarify many of her doctrines which Protestants were questioning. The Council strengthened the Church and brought some good out of the Reformation.

3. What is the Counter-Reformation?
   The Counter-Reformation is the period after the Council of Trent in which new saints were canonized and religious orders were formed to bring true reform and renewal to the Church.

4. Discuss some of the new religious orders formed to help the Church.
   Answers will vary.

5. Who is St. Ignatius of Loyola and what is his importance to the Church?
   St. Ignatius of Loyola was a Spanish nobleman who founded the Society of Jesus. Known as the Jesuits, their mission is to defend the faith and serve the Church and educate people in the Catholic faith.

6. Who were some of the missionaries to the New World and what did they do?
   Answers will vary, but should be based on text and discussion.

Reinforce

1. Have the students work on *Activity Book*, p. 47.

2. Give the students time to work on the Memorization Questions and Words to Know from this chapter.

3. *Follow the history of the Church using a timeline. Discuss the Protestant churches' origin in the Catholic Church. Protestant churches have divided many times since the initial break with the Catholic Church. With each division, they change their teachings. Help the students to see that the true teachings subsist in the true Church of Christ, demonstrated by the four marks of the Church: one, holy, catholic, and apostolic.*

Conclude

1. Lead the students in singing "From all thy saints in warfare," *Adoremus Hymnal*, #592.

2. End class by praying the Nicene Creed.

Preview

In the next lesson, the students will learn about the Church in modern times.

NORTH AMERICAN MARTYRS

While many settlers, soldiers, and explorers came to the New World with hopes of personal gain, many religious came for a different motive: to evangelize the Indian tribes. A group of eight Jesuits worked among the Hurons in the seventeenth century. They suffered greatly for the faith, facing disease, hunger, torture, and even death. One priest, Saint Isaac Jogues, was once captured by an Iroquois raiding party. They tortured him horrifically and killed some of his Christian Huron companions. Finally Jogues was released, but his hands were so mangled that he was unable to hold the host in the way required to say Mass. He returned to Europe, but rather than living in peace and safety back home, he travelled to Rome and asked Pope Urban VIII for special permission to say Mass. The Holy Father granted him permission, and Jogues returned to the Hurons. After many years of work and hundreds of conversions, all of the Jesuits serving the Huron people were martyred. Along with Isaac Jogues, John de Brébeuf, Antony Daniel, Gabrial Lalemant, Charles Garnier, Noel Chabanel, René Goupil, and John Lalande were all martyred in Iroquois attacks in 1648 and 1649. Many of them died baptizing catechumens and absolving Christians before they, too, were killed. Although these martyrs did not see the fruits of their work, their successors converted all of the tribes that had been in contact with the martyrs.

LESSON FOUR: MODERN TIMES

Aims

The students will learn that, in modern times, the Church defended herself against the heresy of Modernism (which teaches that faith and morals should evolve and that all is relative—there is no truth).

They will learn that other challenges to the Church included atheistic, totalitarian governments such as Nazism, communism, and fascism. Saint Maximilian Kolbe strove to win the world for Mary Immaculate. He was martyred in this pursuit.

Materials

- *Activity Book*, p. 48

Optional:
- "From all thy saints in warfare," *Adoremus Hymnal*, #592

Begin

There have been many advances in the twentieth century, such as computers and technology. Many of these advances are positive. However, as the Church entered modern times, she was faced with the threat of Modernism, a heresy that denies objective revelation. Modernists think that teachings on faith and morals should change and evolve.

France. While on his way he became ill and died on March 7, 1274. Before he died, he displayed his humility and love for God. As he prepared to receive the Eucharist for the last time, he said:

I receive thee, price of my redemption, Viaticum of my pilgrimage, for love of whom I have fasted, prayed, taught, and labored. Never have I said a word against thee. If I have it was in ignorance and I do not persist in my ignorance. I leave the correction of my work to the Holy Catholic Church, and in that obedience I pass from this life.

St. Catherine of Siena

Although the Church flourished in the thirteenth century, she suffered many problems in the centuries that followed. During the fourteenth century debates between the popes and the kings of France created a major crisis. For the first time since St. Peter, the Pope was not in Rome. For seventy years the popes lived in the French city of Avignon. It was a woman from Siena, Italy, who finally persuaded the Pope that he must return to Rome.

St. Catherine of Siena was a young laywoman who had chosen to live a life of prayer and service to others, particularly the sick. Her reputation for holiness spread throughout Italy, and many people turned to her for help and advice.

Several times Catherine went to Pope Gregory XI, urging him to return to Rome for the good of the Church. Finally, she visited him in Avignon, pointing out to him that many of the Church's problems stemmed from the absence of the popes from Rome. Pope Gregory listened to her, returned to Rome, and began to reform the Church. Catherine died only a few years later at the age of thirty-three. Because of her many spiritual writings, Catherine was declared a Doctor of the Church.

Although St. Catherine helped the Church end one crisis, another, even greater, followed almost immediately. For the next forty years there were two men, one in Avignon and one in Rome, who claimed to be Pope. This confusion, known as the **Great Western Schism**, divided the Church and weakened the role of the Pope. By the time it was resolved, the Church's unity was threatened.

Protestant Reformation

The fifteenth century also brought with it many new developments. This age is known as the **Renaissance** (rebirth) because of the renewed interest in the ancient Greek and Roman civilizations. During this time many of the clergy were once again corrupted by money and other luxuries. Also, the invention of the printing press made it possible for new ideas—some heretical—to spread more rapidly. By the beginning of the sixteenth century, the Church was once more in need of reform.

83

Develop

1. Read paragraphs 44–50 (to the end of the chapter).

2. Discuss Pope Saint Pius X. He upheld the truths of the Church against Modernism. He was a great shepherd of the Church. One of his most important teachings was the need for frequent Communion (reception of the Eucharist). He lowered the age for First Communion.

3. Modern times have seen many evils which attack the Church, including evil governments which deny the dignity of man and reject revelation. Included in these are Nazism, communism, and fascism. Our Lady of Fatima warned the world to pray and convert, and especially to beg God for the end of communism.

4. In Poland, Maximilian Kolbe formed a group called the Knights of Mary Immaculate. They began a magazine called the Knight of the Immaculate to spread the truths of Christianity, even against the orders of the Nazis. The Gestapo arrested him and put him in a concentration camp where he died, offering his life in place of another man's.

5. In modern times, the Church continues to spread to places like India, Africa, China, and Russia—to all the ends of the earth.

6. Pope John Paul II called for a New Evangelization. In many countries which were once Catholic, the faith has become weak. Today, we are called to be part of this New Evangelization—bearing witness to the faith, spreading and defending the truth. How can your students participate in the New Evangelization?

7. Discuss the many obstacles the Church has faced, internally and externally. Can we see the guidance of the Holy Spirit? The Church continues on!

Modern Times

Answer the following questions in complete sentences.

1. What are the teachings of Modernism?

   The Modernists think that teachings in faith and morals should evolve and change and that there is no unchangeable, objective revelation from God. They also deny the reality of supernatural events, such as miracles, which support the Christian faith.

2. Who is Pope St. Pius X and what is his importance to the Church?

   Pope St. Pius X was Pope during the beginning of the twentieth century. He wrote two influential encyclicals refuting Modernism. He encouraged frequent reception of Holy Communion and lowered the age at which children could receive Communion. He encouraged the laity to be more involved in charitable works.

3. What is one of the main challenges that the Church and the world have faced in modern times?

   One of the main challenges that the Church and the world have faced in modern times is the spread of atheistic, totalitarian governments such as Nazism, communism, and fascism.

4. Who is St. Maximilian Kolbe and what is his importance to the Church?

   St. Maximilian Kolbe was a Polish Franciscan priest. He was very devoted to Our Blessed Mother and started an organization called "The Knights of Mary Immaculate". He was arrested by the Gestapo and imprisoned in Auschwitz in 1941, where he voluntarily died in place of another man.

Reinforce

1. Have the students work on *Activity Book*, p. 48.

2. Give the students time to work on the Memorization Questions and Words to Know from this chapter and to prepare for the chapter and unit quizzes.

3. Have the students chart out a basic timeline of the Church, adding important events and saints to show the growth of the Church.

4. *Discuss other challenges the Church faces today, e.g., pluralism, the occult, rejection of God in society, Christian persecutions around the world, etc.*

5. Discuss how the Church has grown and continues to spread the truth (e.g., television, papal trips, books, etc.).

Conclude

1. Lead the students in singing "From all thy saints in warfare," *Adoremus Hymnal*, #592.

2. End class by praying the Nicene Creed.

Preview

In the next lesson, the students' understanding of the material covered in this chapter will be reviewed and assessed.

OUR LADY OF FATIMA

From May 13 to October 13, 1917, Mary appeared to three children in Fatima, Portugal. She asked the children to pray the rosary daily, wear the brown scapular, and make acts of penance for sinners. She warned that a time of war and suffering was coming and asked that the Pope consecrate Russia to her Immaculate Heart. She also promised a sign to show that she really had appeared to the children. On October 13, nearly 70,000 people came in the rain to see the promised miracle. Suddenly the clouds broke, the sun appeared and began to dance around the sky and fall to earth before returning to its place. In 1930, the Church affirmed the apparitions to be "worthy of belief."

SAINT MAXIMILLIAN KOLBE

While Maximillian Kolbe was imprisoned in the Nazi concentration camp of Auschwitz, one man escaped. In retaliation, the soldiers decided to starve ten prisoners. They had all the prisoners line up outside as they randomly chose the men who would die. One of the men began to beg for his life, saying he had a family that needed him. The soldiers ignored him, but Kolbe stepped forward, saying that he was a Catholic priest and, therefore, had no family depending on him. He offered his life in place of the other man's. The soldiers agreed and Kolbe was placed in a starvation bunker to die with nine other men. The man Kolbe died to save survived the camp and was released when the war ended.

Unfortunately, some attempts to reform the Church led the "reformers" away from her. This is known as the **Protestant Reformation**. Beginning with Martin Luther, several groups rebelled and broke away from the Church. This was the beginning of the many Christian denominations we see around us today.

This tremendous upheaval was the reason that the Church called the Council of Trent. The Church did need reform, and she also needed to clarify the doctrines that were being challenged by the Protestants. The work of this council strengthened the Church so that she emerged from her latest crisis stronger and more able to face the work ahead.

The period immediately following the council is known as the **Counter-Reformation**. Just as new religious orders had helped the Church to reform during the Middle Ages, likewise new religious orders helped the Church to renew herself at this time. For example, the Ursuline sisters, dedicated to

teaching young women, were formed by St. Angela Merici. The most important of these new communities was the Society of Jesus (the Jesuits), founded by *St. Ignatius of Loyola*.

St. Ignatius of Loyola

St. Ignatius of Loyola was a Spanish nobleman who was trained to be a soldier. During his career, he became noted for his bravery and loyalty to his king. In one battle he was seriously wounded and required several months of rest. During this time he read the only books that were available to him—a life of Christ and some lives of the saints. By the time his leg had healed, his life had changed. St. Ignatius vowed to become a "soldier" in the service of Christ and his Church.

After a time of spiritual retreat, Ignatius began to study theology to prepare himself for his new work. While he was studying at the University of Paris, he was joined by other young men, and together they made their first vows of poverty and chastity. After a few years they formed themselves into an order and offered their services to the Pope.

The special work of the Society of Jesus was to defend the faith and serve the Church in whatever way or place the Pope asked them. At the beginning this took the form of defending the faith against the attacks of the Protestants. For example, many Jesuits were sent to Germany to preach against Lutheranism, and they were successful in bringing many people back to the Church. As time passed, the Society began to establish its own universities, convinced that a strong Catholic education would ensure loyalty to the Church.

The motto of St. Ignatius and his Society is "*Ad Majorem Dei Gloriam*" ("to the greater glory of God"). He really lived only for God's glory, and that eventually made him a saint.

84

Missionaries to the New World

In the centuries that followed, the Church, strong and healthy once more, began to spread even further. The European nations had begun to explore and colonize territories in Asia, Africa, and the Americas. The Church also was active, spreading the faith to the people in these areas. The greatest missionary activity since the early days of the Church followed the Reformation.

One of the greatest missionaries at this time was a Jesuit, St. Francis Xavier. He was among the original members of the Society of Jesus and was chosen by St. Ignatius to be one of the Society's first missionaries. Like the great missionary St. Paul, Francis covered a vast territory in a very short time.

His preaching began in India. From there he traveled through Sri Lanka, Malaysia (Indonesia), and Japan, converting many as he went. He died before he could enter China, but future Jesuits, Franciscans, and Dominicans who continued his work did preach the gospel in China. The work begun by St. Francis Xavier paved the way for later missionaries to the Orient.

Jesuit missionaries from France were among those who brought the message of Christ to the French territories in North America. St. Isaac Jogues and seven others are called the "North American martyrs." They preached among the Indians and suffered martyrdom for their faith.

Spanish missionaries labored in the southwestern and western portions of the North American continent. One of the most notable is the Franciscan priest Fr. Junipero Serra, who founded a series of missions among the Indians in California.

With the work of the missionaries and Catholics who settled in America from Europe, the faith was planted on American soil. The first saint born in the United States was St. Elizabeth Ann Seton, who was born in 1774.

Elizabeth was raised as an Episcopalian and married William Seton, a prosperous merchant from New York. They had five children. When Elizabeth's husband became ill with tuberculosis, they moved to Italy, where he died. In Italy Elizabeth became convinced that the Roman Catholic Church was the true Church.

When she returned home, Elizabeth became a Catholic, despite the strong objections of her family and friends. To support herself and her children she opened a school for other young children in her vicinity and later in Maryland. Her school was unusual because it was intended for any student, not just the children of the rich. This was the beginning of the Catholic school system in the United States.

Other young women joined her. In time this group became a religious community, the Sisters of Charity. Founded in 1809, this was the first religious order to be founded in America.

During this time of missionary expansion, the Church was challenged by the scientific, intellectual, and political revolutions taking place in Europe. The Church was constantly called upon to defend herself but was able to remain strong.

Modern Times

As the Church entered the twentieth century, she was blessed with a saintly Pope, Pius X. A simple country priest, but also a great teacher, Pius was able to help the Church face one of the greatest heresies in her history—**Modernism**. Modernists think that teachings on faith and morals should change and evolve, and that there is no unchangeable, objective revelation from God on which Christianity is based. In addition, modernists deny the reality of supernatural events, such as miracles, which support the Christian faith. Pope Pius X wrote two great encyclicals summarizing and refuting these ideas.

85

NOTES

_____
_____
_____
_____
_____
_____
_____
_____
_____
_____
_____
_____
_____
_____
_____
_____
_____
_____
_____
_____
_____
_____

Pope St. Pius served as a great shepherd of the Church. He encouraged frequent reception of Holy Communion. He reminded Catholics that the Eucharist is our spiritual food. He also lowered the age at which young children may first receive this great sacrament. In addition, Pope Pius X encouraged the Catholic laity to become involved in charitable work among the poor. He died broken hearted as the First World War began, expressing his simplicity in his last will and testament, "I was born poor, I lived poor, I die poor."

Since his death, the Church and the world have faced more challenges—particularly the spread of _atheistic, totalitarian_ forms of government in various nations. The two world wars since the death of Pius X remind us of the terrible evils of _Nazism, communism_, and _fascism_. In opposition to these evils, one of the great saints of this century, St. Maximilian Kolbe, shines forth as an example for our times.

Maximilian was born in Poland near the turn of the century. As a member of the Franciscan order, he devoted much of his time and intelligence to understanding the role of Our Lady in our salvation. Before he was ordained, he organized a group of the friars into what he called the "Knights of Mary Immaculate." Members of this group dedicated themselves to win the whole world for Mary. After his ordination, he also gathered lay people into his group. In order to spread his message further, in the early 1920s he began a magazine called _The Knight of the Immaculate_. He had no financial backing, but the magazine thrived surprisingly, although it continually faced financial difficulties. He also established a community in Nagasaki, Japan, which later miraculously survived the atom bomb.

In 1936, after establishing the community in Japan, Maximilian returned to Poland. At this time Hitler came to power in Germany, and soon his armies invaded Poland. Maximilian was arrested by the Gestapo and imprisoned in Auschwitz in 1941.

Maximilian was immediately a source of strength for all imprisoned with him. Shortly after he arrived, some prisoners escaped from the camp. In retaliation, the Nazis randomly chose ten prisoners to be starved to death. One man who was chosen, Sgt. Francis Gajowniczek, began to cry for his wife and children. At this point Fr. Maximilian asked the guards if he could take the sergeant's place. When asked why he chose to do this, he answered, "I am a Catholic priest." With that Maximilian Kolbe began the road to his martyrdom. He prayed and gave courage to the other nine men in the starvation bunker. To the complete surprise of the Nazi guards, he was still alive after three weeks of neither food nor water, and they finally killed him. St. Maximilian died as he had lived—offering his life to God.

In our times the Church continues to grow, as the faith is spread in places such as India and Africa. After two thousand years we see that the Holy Spirit continues to guide the Church. Christ's promise continues: ". . . the powers of death shall not prevail against it."

Words to Know:
Crusades   Middle Ages
St. Francis of Assisi
St. Dominic   St. Thomas Aquinas
St. Catherine of Siena
Great Western Schism   Renaissance
Protestant Reformation
Counter-Reformation
St. Ignatius of Loyola   Modernism

86

_____
_____
_____
_____
_____
_____
_____
_____
_____
_____
_____
_____
_____

Q. 82 *What is a mendicant order?*
A mendicant order is a religious community which relies on the generosity of others for its basic needs (CCC 927).

Q. 83 *What is a Protestant?*
A Protestant is a Christian who belongs to a church which separated from the Catholic Church in the sixteenth century (CCC 838).

St. Dominic receiving the Rosary from Our Lady.

"Exactly as Christian communion between men on their earthly pilgrimage brings us closer to Christ, so our community with the saints joins us to Christ, from whom as from its fountain and head issues all grace and the life of the People of God itself."

(LG, 50)

87

CHAPTER TWELVE
REVIEW AND ASSESSMENT

Aims

The students' understanding of the material covered in this chapter and unit will be reviewed and assessed.

Materials

- Quiz 12, Appendix, p. A-16
- Unit 3 Test, Appendix, pp. A-17– A-18

Optional:
- "From all thy saints in warfare," *Adoremus Hymnal*, #592

Review

1. Discuss the Crusades and review the involvement of Saint Bernard and Saint Louis.

2. Discuss the Middle Ages. The students should be familiar with the founding of mendicant orders: Franciscans, Poor Clares, and Dominicans.

3. Discuss the role Saint Catherine of Siena played in the Church.

4. Review the Protestant Reformation and the Counter-Reformation.

5. Discuss the missionary work of the Church, including the special work of the Jesuits.

6. What challenges has the Church faced in modern times?

7. How can the students participate in the New Evangelization?

Assess

1. Distribute the quizzes and read through them with the students to be sure they understand the questions.

2. Administer the quiz. As they hand in their work, you may orally quiz the students on the Memorization Questions from this chapter.

3. After all the quizzes have been handed in, review the correct answers with the class. Repeat steps 1–3 for the unit test.

Conclude

1. Lead the students in singing "From all thy saints in warfare," *Adoremus Hymnal*, #592.

2. End class by leading the students in the Nicene Creed.

CHAPTER THIRTEEN
SEPARATED BRETHREN

Catechism of the Catholic Church References

Agnosticism: 2127–28
Atheism: 2123–26, 2140, 2424
Baptism of Blood: 1258, 1281
Baptism of Desire: 1259–60, 1281
Charity: 1822–29, 1844
The Church and Non-Christians: 839–45
Jews: 839

Moslems: 841
Ecumenism: 820–22
Necessity of Baptism for Salvation: 846, 1257
Necessity of the Catholic Church for Salvation: 846–48
Orthodox Church: 838
Polytheism: 2112
Separated Brethren: 817–19

Scripture References

Difficulty Accepting Jesus: John 6:66
Rich Young Man: Mt 19:16–22

Salvation for the Gentiles: Acts 11

Summary of Lesson Content

Lesson 1

All salvation comes from Christ through the Church.

All baptized Christians are united with the Catholic Church by virtue of their Baptism. They share faith in Christ and some degree of his teachings.

Those closest to the Catholic Church are the Orthodox Christians, who share our faith and sacraments, but are separated from the authority of the Church.

Lesson 2

Those who do not believe in Christ, but in one God include the Jews and the Moslems.

The Jews are the ancestors of the Catholic Church, and share the Old Testament. It was through the Jews that God prepared the world for the revelation of Christ. The Jews, however, do not recognize Christ as the Messiah.

Lesson 3

Moslems believe in one God.

Islam developed in Arabia about 600 years after Christ and draws from both Judaism and Christianity. Moslems do not recognize Jesus as the Son of God. They recognize Jesus as one of the prophets.

Lesson 4

Pagans and atheists do not believe in the one true God. Pagans may practice an idolatrous religion or believe in many false gods—polytheism. Animism is the worship of inanimate objects.

Atheism is the denial of the existence of God. Agnostics are those who believe that the existence of God can neither be proved nor disproved.

Ecumenism is promotion of the restoration of unity among all Christians.

LESSON ONE: CHRISTIANS

Aims

The students will learn that all salvation comes from Christ through the Church.

They will learn that all baptized Christians are united with the Catholic Church by virtue of their Baptism. They share faith in Christ and some degree of his teachings. Those closest to the Catholic Church are the Orthodox Christians, who share our faith and sacraments, but are separated from the authority of the Church.

Materials

- *Activity Book*, p. 49

Optional:
- "All people that on earth do dwell," *Adoremus Hymnal*, #622

Begin

Begin this lesson by reviewing the four marks of the Church. Refer to the four marks of the Church in each section of this chapter to show how other religions are connected to and separated from the Church of Christ.

CHAPTER 13

Separated Brethren

"I do not pray for these only, but also for those who believe in me through their word, that they may all be one; even as thou, Father, art in me, and I in thee, that they also may be in us, so that the world may believe that thou hast sent me."

John 17:20–21

The universality of the Church is manifested in our times by the millions of Catholics throughout the world. At the same time, there are still many people who do not belong to the Catholic Church yet are members of various organized religions. Of these people, some believe in Christ, while others do not, even though they believe in the one, true God. There are others who may have some sort of religion but do not believe in the one, true God. All of these people are outside the visible Church, but in varying degrees. In this chapter we will consider their relationship to the Church.

Let us pray for all our brothers and sisters who share our faith in Jesus Christ, that God may gather and keep together in one Church all those who seek the truth with sincerity *(General Intercession from the Liturgy of Good Friday).*

Those closest to the Church are non-Catholic Christians who have been baptized. They are often referred to as our **separated brethren**. They are united in some way to the Mystical Body in virtue of their Baptism. This is because there is but "one Baptism for the

88

forgiveness of sins," as we profess in the Nicene Creed. We are all baptized in Christ. Thus anyone who has received the Sacrament of Baptism has been united to Christ and his Body, the Church. Such a person is put in a certain, although imperfect communion with the Catholic Church.

What divides Christians, however, is the degree to which they possess the teachings and practices handed down through the apostles from Christ. Many elements of truth and holiness exist outside the visible structure of the Catholic Church. These elements include the Bible, the life of grace, and the gifts of faith, hope, and charity. The Holy Spirit uses these elements possessed by non-Catholic churches and communities to bring people to salvation. Christ gives all these gifts of truth and grace to the Catholic Church. These gifts come from Christ and help people to unity in the Catholic Church. At the same time, it is only the Catholic Church that teaches the full message of Our Lord. The divisions in belief and practice among Christians vary by degrees. Those who are closest to the Church are the Orthodox Christians, who possess all of the sacraments

---

Develop

1. Read paragraphs 1–7 (up to the second general intercession from the liturgy of Good Friday).

2. Using the Chalk Talk at right, explain the various degrees of separation from the Roman Catholic Church.

3. Explain that those closest to the Roman Catholic Church are the non-Catholic Christians. They are united with the Catholic Church by virtue of their faith in Christ and by their Baptism. They are separated by their rejection of the authority of the Church and some of her doctrines. What do we have in common?
- *We accept Christ as our Savior*
- *Our faith in the Trinity*
- *The Bible*
- *The life of grace*
- *The gifts of faith, hope, and charity, etc.*

The Holy Spirit uses these elements possessed by non-Catholic Churches and communities to bring people to

salvation. (It is important to note that only the Catholic Church has the full message of our Lord and the fullness of the means of salvation—teaching, moral life, sacraments, and liturgy.)

4. Review the separation of the Orthodox Church from the Catholic Church. We share the same faith, but are separated by their rejection of the legitimate authority of the Church, the Pope.

5. Review also the Protestant Reformation. Many protestant denominations have been formed since the Reformation began. They broke away from the Catholic Church, accepting only parts of her teaching and practices.

Name:_____

Separated Brethren: Orthodox and Protestants

Answer the following questions in complete sentences.

1. Are baptized non-Catholics part of the Mystical Body of Christ? Explain.
   Baptized non-Catholics are part of the Mystical Body of Christ by virtue of the one Baptism which unites us in Christ.

2. Why do we say that the Catholic Church alone is the true Church of Christ?
   We say that the Catholic Church alone is the true Church of Christ because it is the Catholic Church that teaches the full message of Our Lord.

3. How do Orthodox Christians differ from us? What do we have in common?
   Orthodox Christians differ from us because they reject the authority of the Pope. We have many doctrines in common as well as all sacraments.

4. How do the churches who broke away from us in the Reformation relate to the Catholic Church? (What are their similarities? What are their differences?)
   Churches which broke away from us in the Reformation differ from the Catholic Church since they deny the Pope's authority as well as many other doctrines such as the need for the Sacrament of Penance. They are similar to us since they have many doctrines in common with us such as belief in the Trinity and the Incarnation. They also have many of the sacraments.

Reinforce

1. Have the students work on *Activity Book*, p. 49.

2. Give the students time to work on the Memorization Questions and Words to Know from this chapter.

3. Lead the students through a series of ecumenical presentations, covering the different religions mentioned in this chapter. The students should have a basic understanding of the different religions and the ways they relate to Catholicism.

4. Relate Orthodox Christianity and Protestantism to the four marks of the Church.

Conclude

1. Teach the students to sing "All people that on earth do dwell," *Adoremus Hymnal*, #622.

2. Lead the students in praying an Act of Love.

Preview

In the next lesson, the students will learn about Judaism.

CHALK TALK: RELATION TO THE CHURCH

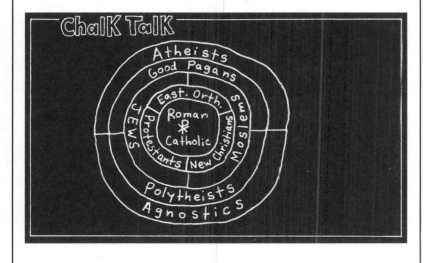

NOTES

_____
_____
_____
_____
_____
_____
_____
_____
_____
_____
_____

LESSON TWO: JUDAISM

Aims

The students will learn that those who do not believe in Christ, but in one God include the Jews and the Moslems.

They will learn that the Jews are the ancestors of the Catholic Church, who share the Old Testament. It was through the Jews that God prepared the world for the revelation of Christ. The Jews, however, do not recognize Christ as the Messiah.

Materials

- *Activity Book*, p. 50

Optional:
- "All people that on earth do dwell," *Adoremus Hymnal*, #622

Begin

Review the special relationship Catholicism has with Judaism. Salvation came from the Jews— Jesus was a Jew. We share the Old Testament. It is through the Old Testament that we see God preparing his chosen people for the coming of the Messiah. In it, we see the prophecies pointing to Christ; we see the typology pointing to Jesus as the Savior and Redeemer. The roots of Christianity are found in Judaism.

---

but who have separated themselves from the authority of the Church. They did this, as we saw, one thousand years ago when they rejected the authority of the Pope.

In the next place are those denominations that broke away from the Church at the time of the Reformation—for example, the Lutherans. In addition to separating themselves from the authority of the Church, these groups also rejected certain teachings and sacraments of the Church. The Lutherans, for example, rejected the need for the Sacrament of Penance and taught that individuals may interpret the Scriptures without the guidance of the Church.

Finally, there are Christian denominations that have broken from these groups, rejecting still more doctrines of our faith. Since the Reformation, new Christian denominations have continued to appear, as people decided to keep certain parts of the message of Christ while rejecting others.

While all of these various Christian groups possess some parts of Christ's gospel, they are still separated from the fullness of his message.

The fullness of unity in the Church requires that all Christians be united again in doctrine and worship. The Church prays for this, especially in the Liturgy of Good Friday. The message of the prayer is that those united to Christ, initially in Baptism, may be fully united with him in faith.

> Almighty and eternal God, long ago you gave your promise to Abraham and his posterity. Listen to your Church as we pray that the people you first made your own may arrive at the fullness of redemption *(General Intercession from the Liturgy of Good Friday)*.

Then there are those people who do not believe in Christ, but who do believe in the one, true God. These are the Jews and the Mos-

lems. The Jews, by virtue of their history, bear a closer relationship with the Church.

The Jews were the first **chosen people**. God first revealed himself to man when he made the Covenant with Abraham. He promised that Abraham's descendants would be his special people and that he would be their God.

Over the centuries God gradually revealed himself to these people, preparing them specially for his spiritual Kingdom, which was still to come. God revealed to his people that salvation would come to the world through them. God promised that he would restore to the world the harmony and closeness to God that had existed before the Fall. This would be accomplished by a descendant of Abraham— the Messiah.

When they had been instructed and formed, the Jews were ready to receive the fullness of God's revelation. They were ready to be transformed into the wholly spiritual people God had intended them to be. And so Jesus Christ, the Son of God, came into the world.

Many of the Jews, however, did not recognize him as the Messiah. Because of this, they are separated from the Church today. They should be members of the Church, for salvation came from them. Jesus himself said to the Samaritan woman at the well, "salvation comes from the Jews" (Jn 4:22). A special bond unites us with them. Jesus sprang from their own stock; he was "Son of David." God still loves them with a special love. We pray that they may recognize in Our Lord their own Messiah promised by God—and thus once more become part of the new People of God, as they had been destined to be.

Like the Jews, the Moslems also believe in the one, true God of Creation. However, unlike Judaism, their religion is not the preparation for Christianity. The Moslem religion—Islam —developed in Arabia about six hundred years after Christ and draws from both Judaism and

89

Develop

1. Read paragraphs 8–13 (up to the section on the Moslems).

2. You may, using a timeline of Salvation History, show the students how much of our faith and history is shared with the Jews. Start with Creation and work toward the present. The separation occurred after the Resurrection of Christ.

3. Discuss how the Old Testament prepared the Jews for the coming of the Messiah:
- *Promise given to Adam and Eve*
- *Covenants established with Noah, Abraham, Isaac, Moses, and David*
- *Prophets*
- *Typologies, etc.*

4. Using the list at right, the students may look up prophecies about the Messiah and find ways that they point to Jesus.

5. Explain how the Jews did not recognize Jesus Christ. We tend to think that it would have been perfectly simple to recognize Jesus as the Christ. On the contrary, he looked like everyone else! He was not a political leader (which was expected). He was not a warrior, and his message was radical (e.g., blessed are the poor). Many had a hard time receiving Jesus' messages. See John 6:66. We have other examples of good practicing Jews who did not follow Christ; e.g., the Rich Young Man: Mt 19:16–22.

6. You may discuss how the first Christians were Jews. In fact, it was presumed that to be Christian you had to be a Jew. It was radical for Peter to proclaim that salvation could be given to the Gentiles (Acts 11).

7. Because Jews do not believe in Christ, they cannot believe in the Trinity. They are not baptized and are still awaiting the coming of the Messiah.

Name:_____

Jews

Answer the following questions in complete sentences.

1. Who are the Jews?
   <u>The Jews are the chosen people to whom God
   revealed himself, beginning with his covenant with
   Abraham. Jews believe in the one true God, but
   do not believe that Jesus is God.</u>

2. How are Catholics connected with the Jews?
   <u>Catholics are connected with the Jews because the Catholic Church
   is the fulfillment of Judaism. Jesus was a Jew and the Messiah
   whom they had been waiting for. However, the Jewish people did
   not recognize him.</u>

3. What did God gradually reveal to the Jews?
   <u>God gradually revealed himself to the Jews. He also
   revealed that salvation would come to the world
   through them and that he would restore the world
   back to God through the Messiah who would be one
   of the descendants of Abraham. He was also preparing the
   Jewish people for the Messiah.</u>

4. Why did some Jews not recognize Jesus as the Son of God and their Messiah?
   <u>Some Jews did not recognize Jesus as the Messiah because they
   were expecting a Messiah who would establish a new kingdom in
   this world. They expected the Messiah to have earthly power
   and success.</u>

5. Why do we pray that they will "arrive at the fullness of redemption"?
   <u>We pray that the Jews will "arrive at the fullness of redemption"
   because we want them to believe in Christ and accept his teaching.</u>

6. How is the Jewish religion the preparation for Christianity?
   <u>Judaism is the preparation for Christianity
   because Christ fulfills the Jewish religion
   and was preparing the Jewish people for himself.</u>

50   *Faith and Life Series • Grade 8 • Chapter 13 • Lesson 2*

Reinforce

1. Have the students work on *Activity Book*, p. 50.

2. Give the students time to work on the Memorization Questions and Words to Know from this chapter.

3. You may discuss the Temple Mount and its importance in history to this very day.

4. Using the four marks of the Church, compare Judaism and Catholicism.

5. *The Jewish holy book is the Old Testament.*

6. *You may discuss the various biblical sects of Judaism: Pharisees, Sadducees, and Essenes.*

Conclude

1. Lead the class in singing "All people that on earth do dwell," *Adoremus Hymnal*, #622.

2. Lead the students in praying an Act of Love.

Preview

In the next lesson, the students will learn about Islam.

MESSIANIC PROPHECIES

Jesus would:
- Be God's Son: Ps. 2:7
- Be God's glory: Hag 2:7
- Be of the line of David: 2 Sam 7:8–16; Ps 89:20–37; 132; Is 9:6–7; Jer: 23:5–6
- Be Emmanuel and born of a virgin: Is 7:14
- Descend from Abraham: Gen 12:2–3; 15:5; 17:1–7; 49:10
- Be born in Bethlehem: Mic 5:2
- Be announced by a star: Num 24:17
- Be given homage by gentiles: Num 24:17; Ps 72:10–11; Is 49:23; 60:5–16
- Come out of Egypt: Hos 11:1
- Be a Suffering Servant: Is 42:1–4; 49:1–6; 50:4–9; 52:13—53:12

NOTES

_____
_____
_____
_____
_____
_____
_____
_____
_____
_____
_____
_____
_____

LESSON THREE: ISLAM

Aims

The students will learn that Moslems believe in one God. Islam developed in Arabia about 600 years after Christ and draws from both Judaism and Christianity. Moslems do not recognize Jesus as the Son of God; they recognize Jesus as one of the prophets.

Materials

• *Activity Book*, p. 51

Optional:
• "All people that on earth do dwell," *Adoremus Hymnal*, #622

Begin

It is important to note that Judaism prepared for Christianity. Islam did not prepare for Christianity. In fact, it is a religion that began about 600 years after the death of Christ. We have already discussed how Islam spread throughout the Mediterranean and took control of the Holy Land.

Christianity. They accept some of the revelation of God to the Jews found in the Old Testament but do not recognize Christ as the Son of God. They see him as one of the prophets, not as the Second Person of the Trinity. We pray that the Moslems, too, may see the truth and one day be fully united to the Church.

Almighty and eternal God, you created mankind so that all might long to find you and have peace when you are found. Grant that, in spite of hurtful things that stand in their way, they may all recognize in the lives of Christians the tokens of your love and mercy and gladly acknowledge you as the one true God and Father of us all *(General Intercession from the Liturgy of Good Friday).*

Then there are those people—both the *pagans* and the *atheists*—who do not believe in the one, true God at all. The pagans are those who do not believe in the only true God but may practice some form of idolatrous religion or even believe in many gods, which is called **polytheism**. The ancient Greek and Roman religions were of this sort. There are also those pagans who practice **animism**, believing that inanimate objects possess supernatural powers and can be controlled by us. The pagans then worship many gods, but not the one, true God.

There are also people who are **atheists**. Strictly speaking, atheism is the denial of the existence of a personal God. In our modern world atheism takes many forms. There are those who expressly deny God's existence. Others maintain that there may be a God but that we can know nothing about him. We call these people **agnostics**. Still other people do not expressly deny God's existence but never take any interest in God or religion. They choose to ignore him and concentrate on mankind and its accomplishments instead.

There can be many obstacles that prevent these people from believing in God. We pray that God will remove these obstacles, so they too may come to believe in him.

As members of the Church we should work toward the reunion of all Christians with the Church and pray that all others outside the Church might fully become members of the Mystical Body. This is what is meant by **ecumenism**. As Catholics we have been given a great gift, and we should have a longing to share this gift with others.

We know that salvation has come into the world through Christ. He left us the Church to distribute to us the graces of salvation and to provide a secure guide for us. We have been blessed with the sacraments that help us on our path to heaven. Christ also left us with a visible representative on earth, so that we might clearly see his message in the world. Those who are outside the Catholic Church do not have these great gifts. Does this mean, then, that those who are outside the visible Church cannot be saved?

The Church teaches that "outside the Catholic Church there is no salvation." What exactly does this mean? The Church is necessary for salvation because Jesus Christ is necessary for

91

Develop

1. Read paragraph 13 (to the next intercession from the liturgy of Good Friday).

2. Islam is a fast-growing religion. In fact, the 1998 World Almanac states that there are 14 million Jews, 1.9 Billion Christians (of which 981 million are Catholic), and 1.1 billion Moslems. You may discuss some reasons why Islam is such a strong religion:
• Often Islamic countries do not separate state from religion; civil law is directed by Islamic law (e.g., it is punishable— sometimes even by death—to convert to Christianity)
• They have large families
• They proselitize, etc.

3. Although Moslems believe in one God, they do not believe that Jesus is the Son of God (and do not believe in the Trinity). They believe that Jesus is one in a line of prophets that ended with Muhammad, the "Seal of the Prophets," who

received the final and full revelation of God. These revelations are written in their holy book called the Koran.

4. Some beliefs Moslems share in common with Christians:
• *There is one God*
• *God created the universe*
• *Abraham, Moses, and Jesus are in the line of prophets*
• *There will be a day of Judgment*
• *Heaven and hell exist (although their view of heaven and hell is very different from ours)*

5. Moslems practice a very disciplined prayer life. Research the pious practices of Moslems.

Name:_____

Moslems

Answer the following questions in complete sentences.

1. Do the Moslems believe in the one true God?
   Yes, Moslems believe in the one true God.

2. How does Islam differ from Judaism?
   Islam differs from Judaism in that it is not a preparation
   for Christianity. Also, God did not establish their religion
   and reveal himself to them.

3. When did Islam begin?
   Islam began in the seventh century.

4. Do Moslems recognize Jesus Christ as the Messiah?
   Moslems do not recognize Jesus Christ as the Messiah,
   but they accept some of the revelation of God to the
   Jews found in the Old Testament. They see Jesus as a
   prophet, not the Second Person of the Blessed Trinity.

Faith and Life Series • Grade 8 • Chapter 13 • Lesson 3   51

Reinforce

1 Have the students work on *Activity Book*, p. 51.

2. Give the students time to work on the Memorization Questions and Words to Know from this chapter.

3. *Compare Islam with Catholicism using the four marks of the Church.*

4. You may research various holy sites of Islam.

5. *You may make a comparative chart on Catholicism, Protestantism, Judaism, and Islam, comparing their religion, worship structure, culture, practices, etc.*

Conclude

1. Lead the class in singing "All people that on earth do dwell," *Adoremus Hymnal*, #622.

2. Lead the students in praying an Act of Love.

Preview

In the next lesson, the students will learn about ecumenism.

NOTES

_____
_____
_____
_____
_____
_____
_____
_____
_____
_____

LESSON FOUR: ECUMENISM

Aims

The students will learn that pagans and atheists do not believe in one God. Pagans may practice an idolatrous religion or believe in many false gods—polytheism. Animism is the worship of inanimate objects. Atheism is the denial of the existence of God. Agnostics are those who believe that God's existence can neither be proved or disproved.

They will learn that ecumenism is promotion of the restoration of unity among all Christians.

Materials

- *Activity Book*, p. 52

Optional:
- "All people that on earth do dwell," *Adoremus Hymnal*, #622

Begin

Explain to the students that the pagans and the atheists do not believe in the one true God. Although there are many obstacles that prevent these people from believing in God, they can still be united with God if they follow the truths they know and try their best to live a good life.

Church Teaching

". . . it is through Christ's Catholic Church alone, which is the universal help towards salvation, that the fullness of the means of salvation can be obtained" (UR, 3).

---

salvation. Jesus and his message are found completely in the Church—his Body.

The Church does not teach, however, that all of those who are outside the visible Church will not be saved. Only those who know that God wants them to be in full communion with the Catholic Church, yet who deliberately choose to remain outside the Church—by willingly rejecting Christ and his message—will not be saved. There are many people, though, who are outside the visible Church through no fault of their own. For example, there are many who have never heard the gospel or may have a distorted picture of it. Even so, lack of the gospel or the fullness of the gospel does not mean that these people are without the grace necessary for salvation. If they seek God with a sincere heart, and moved by grace try to do God's will as they understand it through their consciences, they have the hope of salvation.

But a problem still exists. Our Lord told us that Baptism *is* necessary in order to enter heaven. When he spoke to the Pharisee Nicodemus, he said:

Truly, truly I say to you, unless one is born of water and the Spirit, he cannot enter the kingdom of God (Jn 3:5).

We have already seen that those Christians who are outside the Church are truly baptized in Christ, but what about those who have never been baptized—can they enter into the Kingdom of God?

92

For those who do not know of the sacrament and its importance, or who are unable to receive it before they die, there are two other means of receiving the sanctifying grace necessary to enter heaven. The first is called *Baptism of desire*. This desire for Baptism can be explicit as in the case of someone who is preparing for Baptism but who dies before receiving the sacrament. Or it can be implicit. The desire is implied in those people who *faithfully* and *truly* try to carry out God's will in their lives. Perhaps they do not know of the need for Baptism but would receive it if they did. God, knowing their thoughts and desires, does not punish them for circumstances beyond their control.

The second extraordinary means of receiving the grace necessary for heaven is called *Baptism of blood*. This is the "baptism" granted to those non-Christians who have been martyred for Christ. The fact that they are willing to die for Christ demonstrates their faith and love, and they are welcomed into heaven, even though they have never received sacramental Baptism.

Now that we see the great gift we have been given by being baptized and raised as members of the Catholic Church, we should work to bring others into union with the Church. At the same time we should show respect for the religions of others, leading them with patience and compassion to see the fullness of truth.

We ought to see that we are unworthy to receive such a gift, and not think that this entitles us to feel smug and superior. Indeed we

Develop

1. Read paragraphs 14–27 (to the end of the chapter).

2. Review the Words to Know from this section.

3. Review the meaning of ecumenism. In the Church today, ecumenism refers to the dialogue between Catholics and non-Catholics. Through this dialogue, we hope to unite the non-Catholics with Catholics in the fullness of truth found in the Catholic Church. This is our duty! We have such a great gift in the Catholic Church, that we should have a longing and sense of urgency to share this gift with others.

4. Discuss the statement, "Outside the Catholic Church there is no salvation." This means that the Church is necessary for salvation because Jesus is necessary for salvation. Jesus and his message are found completely in the Catholic Church. We have the fullness of the means of salvation with the Church's teachings, moral life, sacramental life, and liturgy. This does

not mean that unless you are Roman Catholic, you cannot be saved. There are many people who, through no fault of their own, are not Catholic. If, through God's grace, they live a good life and do what God expects, they have the hope of salvation. (Remind the students that what God expects is written in our hearts—it is our conscience. We all have one!)

5. Review the Church's teaching on the necessity of Baptism for salvation. Use the box at right to assist you in this teaching. Clearly explain Baptism of desire and Baptism of blood and how these Baptisms obtain the graces necessary for salvation.

6. Review the important duty to participate in the new evangelization. Discuss ways the students can do this.

Name:_____

Pagans and Atheists

Answer the following questions in complete sentences.

1. What do pagans and atheists have in common?
   <u>Pagans and atheists do not believe in the one, true God.</u>

2. What are the pagan practices of polytheism and animism?
   <u>The pagan practice of polytheism is the idolatrous worship of many gods. The pagan practice of animism is the belief that inanimate objects possess supernatural powers and can be controlled by us.</u>

3. What three ways do modern men deny the existence of God?
   <u>Three ways modern men deny the existence of God are: 1) to deny the existence of God; 2) to claim that God may exist but that we cannot know anything about him; and 3) to take no interest in God or in religion.</u>

4. Explain the phrase: "Outside the Church there is no salvation."
   <u>The phrase "Outside the Church there is no salvation" means that the Church is necessary for salvation because Jesus Christ is necessary for salvation. Jesus and his message are found fully in the Catholic Church. This does not mean that only Catholics are saved, but it does mean that if a non-Catholic is saved, it is through Christ's Church that he is saved.</u>

52   *Faith and Life Series • Grade 8 • Chapter 13 • Lesson 4*

Reinforce

1. Have the students work on *Activity Book*, p. 52.

2. Give the students time to work on the Memorization Questions and Words to Know from this chapter and to prepare for the quiz.

3. Discuss New Age and the occult. Many pagan practices have re-emerged in modern times.

4. The students should research and write a paper on religious freedom.

Conclude

1. Lead the class in singing "All people that on earth do dwell," *Adoremus Hymnal*, #622.

2. Lead the students in praying an Act of Love.

Preview

In the next lesson, the students' understanding of the material covered in this chapter will be reviewed and assessed.

UNDERSTANDING BAPTISM

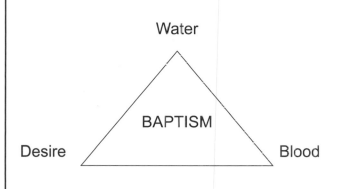

Baptism of desire refers to the Baptism received by those people who do not know about the need for baptism but who would want to receive Baptism if they did know about it. For example, a young person growing up in an atheistic environment, with atheists for parents and teachers, might sincerely be willing to be baptized, if he knew how important Baptism is.

Baptism of blood is the Baptism received by non-Christians who are martyred for Christ. Jesus says, "No one has greater love than this, to lay down one's life for his friends." Someone who dies for Christ receives Baptism of blood.

NOTES

_____
_____
_____
_____
_____
_____
_____
_____
_____
_____
_____
_____
_____
_____
_____
_____
_____
_____
_____
_____
_____
_____
_____
_____

"I, therefore, a prisoner for the Lord, beg you to lead a life worthy of the calling to which you have been called, with all lowliness and meekness, with patience, forbearing one another in love, eager to maintain the unity of the Spirit in the bond of peace."

(Eph 4:1–3)

can learn from so many of our separated brethren.

The Eastern Orthodox venerate tradition. The splendor of their liturgy inspires in us deep reverence for the worship of God. Episcopalians have a great understanding for the beauty of ceremonies. Lutherans, Baptists, and Evangelicals read the Bible and are very familiar with it. Jews have a deep sense of the sacred, love of the Commandments, and the courage to stand up for their beliefs.

We Catholics must live our faith more seriously. Our love must increase, and each of us must personally convert, turn away from sinful ways, and follow Christ.

Words to Know:
separated brethren   chosen people
polytheism   animism   atheists
agnostic   ecumenism

Church Teaching

"For although the Catholic Church has been endowed with all divinely revealed truth and with all means of grace, yet her members fail to live by them with all the fervor that they should. As a result the radiance of the Church's face shines less brightly in the eyes of our separated brethren and of the world at large, and the growth of God's Kingdom is retarded. Every Catholic must therefore aim at Christian perfection and, each according to his station, play his part, that the Church, which bears in her own body the humility and dying of Jesus, may daily be more purified and renewed, against the day when Christ will present her to himself in all her glory without spot or wrinkle" (UR, 4).

93

_____
_____
_____
_____
_____
_____
_____
_____
_____
_____
_____
_____
_____
_____
_____
_____
_____

Q. 84 *Can another church, outside the Catholic Church, be the Church of Christ?*

No church outside the Catholic Church can be the Church of Christ, although other churches can be imperfectly united with the Church of Christ, which exists fully in the Catholic Church alone (CCC 816, 838).

Q. 85 *Is it a serious loss to be outside the Church?*

It is a most serious loss to be outside the Church, because outside one does not have either the means, which have been established, or the secure guidance, which has been set up for eternal salvation, which is the only thing truly necessary for man (CCC 846–48).

94

CHAPTER THIRTEEN
REVIEW AND ASSESSMENT

Aims

The students' understanding of the material covered in this chapter will be reviewed and assessed.

Materials

- Quiz 13, Appendix, p. A-19

Optional:
- "All people that on earth do dwell," *Adoremus Hymnal,* #622

Name: _____

Separated Brethren   **Quiz 13**

Part I: Using your student text, write a short paragraph explaining who the Church considers our separated brethren and how we are all still members of the same Church.

Answers will vary but should be based on the student text.

Part II: Answer in complete sentences.

1. What is the difference between an atheist and an agnostic?
   The difference between an atheist and an agnostic is that an atheist denies God's existence while an agnostic thinks God may exist but that we cannot know anything about him.

2. What is ecumenism and why is it important for the salvation of man?
   Ecumenism is the effort to reunite all those outside the Church to become members of the Mystical Body of Christ.

3. How are animism and polytheism expressions of paganism?
   Animism and polytheism are expressions of paganism because both are forms of idolatry.

Faith and Life • Grade 8 • Appendix A   *A - 19*

Review

1. The Roman Catholic Church is universal. She has the fullness of the means of salvation.

2. There are many people who are outside the Catholic Church. Some groups are further outside the Church than others. Those outside the Church are:
   - Non-Catholic Christians
   - Those who believe in the one true God, but are not Christians
   - Pagans and atheists.

3. The students should know what distinguishes these religions from one another. Using the four marks of the Catholic Church, they should be able to compare these other groups to the Catholic Church.

Assess

1. Distribute the quizzes and read through them with the students to be sure they understand the questions.

2. Administer the quiz. As they hand in their work, you may orally quiz the students on the Memorization Questions from this chapter.

3. After all the quizzes have been handed in, review the correct answers with the class.

Conclude

1. Lead the class in singing "All people that on earth do dwell," *Adoremus Hymnal,* #622.

2. End class by leading the students in praying an Act of Love.

CHAPTER FOURTEEN
THE UNIVERSAL CALL TO HOLINESS

Catechism of the Catholic Church References

Anger and the Desire for Revenge: 2302
Apostolate: 863–64, 900, 905
Capital Sins: 1866
Christian Holiness: 2012–16, 2028–29
Concupiscence: 2514–17
Consequences of Original Sin: 55–58, 399–400, 402–9, 416–19
Covetousness: 2535–37
Envy: 2538–40, 2553–54

Grace of Baptism: 265, 1262–74, 1279–80
Holiness: 2012–15, 2030
Man's Vocation to Beatitude: 1718–24, 1726–29
Passions and the Moral Life: 1763–75
Pride: 2094, 2540
Respect for Health: 2288–91
Sloth: 2094, 2733, 2755
Vices and the Proliferation of Sin: 1865–69, 1876
Vocation: 542–43, 825, 1694

Scripture References

Call to Holiness: Eph 6:10–18; Col 4:2; 3:15–17; 1 Pet 1:13–16; Gal 5:13–26; 1 Jn 3:14–18; 1 Tim 2:1–8; 1 Cor 11:23–26; 13:1–13; Jas 2:14–20

Great Commission: Mt 28:18–20
God's Plan: Mt 25:14–27

Summary of Lesson Content

Lesson 1

Through Baptism every Christian is called to holiness and the apostolate of evangelization (through word and example).

Every person has a particular vocation. God has a plan for every person. We must discern and follow this.

Because of concupiscence, man faces many obstacles to holiness, including vice.

Lesson 2

There are seven capital vices, including:
- Pride, which is an excessive, disordered love of one-self.
- Covetousness, which is avarice or greed. It is an uncontrolled desire for earthly possessions.

Lesson 3

The capital vices include:
- Lust, which is the uncontrolled desired for—or disordered indulgence in—sexual pleasure.
- Anger, which is an uncontrolled expression of displeasure or antagonism, often accompanied by revenge.

Lesson 4

The capital vices include:
- Gluttony, the uncontrolled desire for food and drink.
- Envy, which is discontent at the good fortune or success of others.
- Sloth, which is excessive laziness, especially in the spiritual life.

LESSON ONE: HOLINESS

Aims

The students will learn that, through Baptism, every Christian is called to holiness and the apostolate of evangelization (through word and example).

They will learn that every person has a particular vocation. God has a plan for every person. We must discern and follow this.

They will learn that, because of concupiscence, man faces many obstacles to holiness, including vice.

Materials

- *Activity Book*, p. 53
- Bibles

Optional:
- "Lift high the cross," *Adoremus Hymnal*, #606

Begin

Begin class by presenting the Chalk Talk at right.

With a Bible for each student, direct them to search for passages about the call to holiness. You can organize the students into groups for this project. They should look up references and write explanations. Some suggested passages are as follows: Eph 6:10–18; Col 4:2; 3:15–17; 1 Pet 1:13–16; Gal 5:13–26; 1 Jn 3:14–18; 1 Tim 2:1–8; 1 Cor 11:23–26; 13:1–13; Jas 2:14–20.

CHAPTER 14

The Universal Call to Holiness

You, therefore, must be perfect, as your heavenly Father is perfect.

Matthew 5:48

As members of the Mystical Body we have a general calling, or **vocation**, from God. Each Christian is called to **holiness**, which means that we are each called to follow Christ so that one day we may be with him in heaven for eternity. As St. Paul tells us in his letter to the Christians in Ephesus, God "chose us in him before the foundation of the world, that we should be holy and blameless before him" (Eph 1:4). The vocation of each Christian, then, is to become a saint.

In addition to becoming saints, we are also called by God to spread the faith given at our Baptism. Each of us must be a missionary, or apostle, for Christ, preaching the gospel in whatever way we can, by word and by example. We call this work the **apostolate**.

For each of us, becoming a saint and spreading the faith are done in different ways. This is our *specific vocation*, to which God calls us, according to our own gifts, talents, and circumstances. St. Paul, in his letter to the Romans, reminds us that the Church, like the body, has many members, each of which has its own particular role:

Having gifts that differ according to the grace given to us, let us use them: if prophecy, in proportion to our faith; if service, in our serving; he who teaches, in his teaching; he who exhorts, in his exhortation; he who contributes, in liberality; he who gives aid, with zeal; he who does acts of mercy, with cheerfulness (Rom 12:6–8).

Thus our own particular vocation depends upon the gifts that God has given us.

In discovering our vocation, we cannot simply follow our own desires, for often these may lead us away from God. Nor can we expect God to hand us a detailed list of instructions about how to live our lives. Rather, we should pray for the wisdom to recognize our talents and abilities—as well as our limitations—and to choose our life's work accordingly. We also have to recognize the circumstances we are in, where God has placed us. For instance, a father who has to take care of his family cannot say, "Well, I have a special gift to be an artist [or some other talent], so I ought to pursue that

97

Develop

1. Read paragraphs 1–7.

2. Every Christian is called to holiness. What does this mean? We are called to follow Christ so that we may be with him forever in heaven. This means we must live in the state of grace and strive to know and do God's will. Discuss some basic premises for holiness:
- We must be in the state of grace (we must follow the Ten Commandments and live the moral life).
- We must live a sacramental life (the sacraments are channels of grace).
- We must live in union with Christ on earth so we can be with him in heaven. This means we must worship and pray (faith and hope).
- We must love God and neighbor (charity).

3. Remember the Great Commission (Mt 28:18–20)? We are to share in the mission of bringing the Good News to all

people. We are to be missionaries, sharing in the apostolic work of preaching the gospel. This apostolic work is called an apostolate. An apostolate is a work that brings the Good News to others. We often hear of apostolates as works by the Church; e.g., caring for the elderly, serving the poor, teaching the Faith, etc. Have the students name ways they can live their apostolates at this stage in their lives.

4. God knows each of us and has a plan for each of us—a specific vocation. God has given us gifts and talents and he arranges the circumstances in our lives for our specific vocations. The students may read and discuss Mt 25:14–27.

5. Review the effects of Original Sin. Concupiscence is the tendency to sin. Show how concupiscence leads us to vice—habits of doing bad deeds. Be sure the students understand what vice is. Have them give examples of vice.

Name:_____

Call to Holiness

Answer the following questions in complete sentences.

1. What does it mean to say that each Christian is called to holiness?

   To say the Christian is called to holiness means that we are called to follow Christ so that we will live with him in heaven one day.

2. What is an apostolate?

   An apostolate is the work done to preach the Gospel by word and example.

3. What is a specific vocation?

   A specific vocation is God's specific call to us individually on the manner in which we are to be a saint. This call God designs according to our talents, gifts, and circumstances.

4. How can man's inclination to sin be seen?

   Man's inclination to sin can be seen very easily! Just read any newspaper and you will see evidence of our inclination to sin.

5. Define vice and explain how we acquire it.

   Vice is the habit of doing evil.

6. How can what we know about vice help us to grow in holiness?

   What we know about vice can help us grow in holiness because it is helpful to know what you must overcome, to know your enemy. This way you know what to avoid and look out for.

Reinforce

1. Have the students work on *Activity Book*, p. 53.

2. Give the students time to work on the Memorization Questions and Words to Know from this chapter.

3. Have the students write about their specific vocations. They should list their gifts and talents, as well as their desires and aspirations. They should then write a prayer asking God to show them his will.

4. Discuss vice with the students. They should understand the difference between an amoral habit (brushing teeth), and a sinful habit (lying, gossiping).

Conclude

1. Teach the students to sing "Lift high the cross," *Adoremus Hymnal*, #606.

2. Lead the students in praying an Act of Hope.

Preview

In the next lesson, the students will learn about pride and covetousness.

CHALK TALK: UNIVERSAL CALL TO HOLINESS

NOTES

_____
_____
_____
_____
_____
_____
_____
_____
_____
_____

LESSON TWO:
PRIDE AND COVETOUSNESS

Aims

The students will learn that there are seven capital vices, including pride, which is an excessive, disordered love of oneself, and covetousness, which is avarice or greed. Covetousness is an uncontrolled desire for earthly possessions.

Materials

- *Activity Book*, p. 54

  Optional:
  - "Lift high the cross," *Adoremus Hymnal*, #606

Begin

Review the definition of vice.

Explain that there are seven capital vices. "Capital" means head or source. All sins and vices spring from the capital vices.

Over the next three lessons, we will study the capital vices. The capital vices are major obstacles in our path to holiness and we must learn to recognize and avoid them.

---

instead of the drudgery of my job or the care of my children." In later chapters we will consider the possible states of life to which God may call us.

Obstacles to Holiness

Before considering how to become holy, we shall look first at those things that are obstacles to holiness. We know that all men are born with original sin, and that it is removed through Baptism. After Baptism, however, we are still weak and inclined toward sin. We are still easily tempted, and inclined toward evil, toward disobedience to God and his Commandments.

This inclination to sin can also be seen in the way we often use our natural tendencies. God has placed in all men certain tendencies to help us live here on earth. For example, we have a natural desire for food and drink so that we can survive physically. Because of original sin it is easy for these tendencies to get out of control. When this occurs, they lead us to sin. For example, the desire for food and drink can become excessive, leading a person to gluttony or drunkenness.

If we allow these tendencies to get out of control frequently, they can become *habits*. A **habit** is a way of acting that is acquired by repetition of certain actions. Habits are a familiar part of our daily routine. We brush our teeth, for example, without giving it much thought. Once we have learned to ride a bicycle, we develop the habit and ride without thinking about all the steps we are following. These habits are morally indifferent—that is, they are neither good nor evil. Some habits, however, are sinful. These are acquired by repeatedly doing bad actions and are known as vices.

There are seven principal vices, which are known as the seven **capital sins**. They are called *capital*, from the Latin word for head or source, because they are the source of all other sins and vices. They are not the only vices, just the chief ones from which many more stem. Because these vices are the major obstacles in our path to holiness, we should consider each of them briefly and learn to recognize them.

> *"The beginning of man's pride is to depart from the Lord. . . . For the beginning of pride is sin, and the man who clings to it pours out abominations" (Sir 10:12–13).*

Pride is the chief capital sin, for it is at the root of all the others. It is an *excessive, disordered* love of oneself. This leads us to prefer our own desires to those of God and our neigh-

---

Church Teaching

"It is therefore quite clear that all Christians in any state or walk of life are called to the fullness of Christian life and to the perfection of love, and by this holiness a more human manner of life is fostered also in earthly society. In order to reach this perfection the faithful should use the strength dealt out to them by Christ's gift, so that, following in his footsteps and conformed to his image, doing the will of God in everything, they may wholeheartedly devote themselves to the glory of God and to the service of their neighbor" (LG, 40).

98

Develop

1. Read paragraphs 8–10 (Pride and Covetousness).

2. Have the students define pride: an excessive, disordered love of oneself. Why is extreme love of self wrong? It is wrong because it leads us to prefer our own desires to those of God and our neighbor.

3. Should we be proud of our accomplishments? We can be justifiably proud of our accomplishments when we recognize that they are the result of God's gifts and talents in our lives. However, pride in our accomplishments is sinful if we fail to recognize God's work in our lives and thank him for our talents.

4. Discuss some of the sins of pride. You may use examples of failing to love God and others as we should (because we love ourselves more). Examples might include:

- *Placing our desires before those of God or others*
- *Believing that everything revolves around us (not recognizing the needs of others)*
- *Not being charitable, etc.*

5. Have the students define covetousness: greed or uncontrolled desire for earthly possessions. To what things do we find it easy to be too attached?

- *Money*
- *Power*
- *Popularity*
- *Possessions (e.g., clothes, cars, games, etc.)*

6. How are pride and covetousness like idolatry? Pride and covetousness are like idolatry because they cause us to place ourselves or our things before God. How can we keep God first in our lives? We can keep God first in our lives through prayer, penance, sacrifices, sacraments, etc.

Seven Capital Sins: Pride and Covetousness

Answer the following questions in complete sentences

1. What is pride?

   Pride is an excessive, disordered love of self.

2. Why is pride the chief capital sin?

   Pride is the chief capital sin because it is the root of all other sins.

3. How was pride at the root of the sin of our first parents?

   Pride was at the root of the sin of our first parents because they wanted to be like God and not to be subordinate to their Creator.

4. What is rightful pride?

   Rightful pride is correctly being proud of your accomplishments and having a healthy self esteem. Rightful pride knows that God is the true source of our talents and self-worth.

5. What is covetousness?

   Covetousness means greed. It is an uncontrollable desire for earthly possessions, such as money, clothes, and so on.

6. If material things are good, why is covetousness wrong?

   Covetousness is wrong even though material things are good because it is an improper and uncontrolled desire for material things.

7. How can covetousness lead to other sins?

   Covetousness can lead a man to lie, cheat, steal, or murder in order to possess those things he desires.

Reinforce

1. Have the students work on *Activity Book*, p. 54.

2. Give the students time to work on the Memorization Questions and Words to Know from this chapter.

3. *Discuss examples of pride and covetousness. Give the students scenarios and have them offer suggestions on how to overcome these vices. Discuss lives of the saints and how they overcame attachments to pride and covetousness.*

4. Have the students write down ways they can overcome the vices of pride and covetousness in their lives.

5. We can sin by thought, word, deed, and omission. Discuss how pride and covetousness can lead to further sins.

Conclude

1. Lead the class in singing "Lift high the cross," *Adoremus Hymnal*, #606.

2. Lead the students in praying an Act of Hope.

Preview

In the next lesson, the students will learn about lust and anger.

SAINT FRANCIS OF ASSISI AND COVETOUSNESS

Quite often, before saints become saints, they have to overcome very practical difficulties. For the next several lessons, we will look at specific weaknesses saints have had to overcome on their path to holiness.

Saint Francis of Assisi grew up rich and popular. His father was a successful cloth merchant, and Saint Francis loved to spend his father's money on parties for himself and his friends. When he chose to follow God, though, he left it all behind. In front of his father and the local bishop, Saint Francis returned to his father everything he had been given, even the clothes he was wearing, and happily proclaimed, "Now I can truly say, our Father who art in heaven."

SAINT BERNADETTE AND PRIDE

Bernadette was a common peasant girl who grew up in Lourdes, France. That is, until the Blessed Virgin began to appear to her (see story in Appendix, p. B-6). After the apparitions, she became a sort of celebrity. Many people, both Catholics and non-Catholics, came from all around to see her. Her visitors often offered her money and other goods, but she refused them all. Even when she joined the Sisters of Notre Dame many people came to the convent to meet the sister who had seen Mary. Through all her fame, she was steadfast in simplicity and humility, and although she was always kind to those who came to see her, she tried to avoid any special attention. Her main concern was always the glory of God, never the fame of Bernadette.

LESSON THREE: LUST AND ANGER

Aims

The students will learn that the capital vices include lust, which is the uncontrolled desired for or disordered indulgence in sexual pleasure and anger, which is an uncontrolled expression of displeasure or antagonism, often accompanied by revenge.

Materials

- *Activity Book*, p. 55

  Optional:
  - "Lift high the cross," *Adoremus Hymnal*, #606

Begin

Begin class by reviewing the capital vices (also called the capital sins) and the first two which we have already studied: pride and covetousness. They should be able to discuss definitions, examples, and the means of overcoming capital vices.

---

bors. It is pride that was at the root of the sin of our first parents—their desire to be like God. They did not want to be subordinate, as creatures, to their Creator. We should not confuse this vice with the rightful pride we take in our accomplishments or with a correct sense of self-esteem. These are sinful only if we exaggerate them.

> *"And [Jesus] said to them, 'Take heed, and beware of all covetousness; for a man's life does not consist in the abundance of his possessions' " (Lk 12:15).*

Covetousness, or avarice, means greed. It is an uncontrolled desire for earthly possessions, such as money, clothes, and so on. A certain desire for these things is natural, since they are necessary in order to live in the world. However, we must constantly take care that these desires do not turn to greed, and that we do not put these things first in our lives or ahead of more important values. Not only is covetousness itself wrong, as the Ninth and Tenth Commandments tell us, but greed can easily lead to further sins. For example, the person with this vice may eventually lie, cheat, steal, or even murder, in order to possess those things he desires.

> *"But I say, walk by the Spirit, and do not gratify the desires of the flesh. For the desires of the flesh are against the Spirit, and the desires of the Spirit are against the flesh; . . . Now the works of the flesh are plain: immorality, impurity, licentiousness" (Gal 5:16–17, 19).*

Lust is the uncontrolled desire for or indulgence in sexual pleasure. It should not be confused with the lawful use of our sexual powers within the holy state of marriage. God created human beings with a natural attraction to the opposite sex. As long as this attraction is controlled and ordered finally to Christian mar-

riage, it is healthy and good. This attraction becomes disordered when it is focused on our own pleasure instead of a selfless, true love of another person, and when it is separated from marriage and the purpose of marriage.

> *"Be angry but do not sin; do not let the sun go down on your anger. . . . Let all bitterness and wrath and anger and clamor and slander be put away from you" (Eph 4:26, 31).*

Anger is an uncontrolled expression of displeasure and antagonism, often accompanied by a desire for revenge. This is not the same as the righteous anger spoken of by St. Paul in his letter to the Ephesians or that exhibited by Our Lord when he threw the moneychangers out of the Temple. Anger is the proper response to an injustice—for example, defrauding the poor or abortion—but we must control it and use it properly. If our anger is uncontrolled or if it is bitter and full of hate and we seek only revenge, it has become a vice.

99

Develop

1. Read paragraphs 11–12 (lust and anger).

2. Have the students find the definition of lust: uncontrolled desire for or disordered indulgence in sexual pleasure. What does this mean? Well, first we must understand the proper context for sexual pleasure. Sexual love is only appropriately expressed and shared in marriage. For sex to be truly loving, it must be ordered toward two things (both must be present): sex must be unitive (it unites and expresses the indissoluble union of a man and woman in the context of holy matrimony) and sex must be procreative (this means it is open to life). You may discuss sins against the true goods of sexual desire and matrimony.

Against the Unitive aspect:
- *Fornication (premarital sex)*
- *Masturbation (sexual self-gratification)*
- *Adultery (extramarital sex)*

- *Homosexual activity (sexual encounters between two people of the same gender)*

Against the procreative aspect:
- *Contraception (artificial barriers to pregnancy)*
- *Homosexuality (can never be open to life)*
- *Abortion (the termination of life before birth)*

3. Sexual attraction is powerful and it is ordered toward matrimony. Sexual attraction requires much self-control and sacrificial love. We must respect our bodies and those of others. We must not sin or cause another to sin in selfish desire. We must avoid occasions of sin.

4. Anger is the uncontrolled expression of displeasure, often with the intent of revenge. Proper anger responds to an injustice. Sinful anger is connected with pride, hate, or revenge. Discuss these evils, give examples, and help the students to truly love (and not just tolerate) others.

Name:_____

Seven Capital Sins: Lust and Anger

Answer the following questions in complete sentences.

1. What is lust?
   Lust is the uncontrolled desire for or indulgence in sexual pleasures.

2. How can sexual pleasure be good?
   Sexual pleasure can be good in the context for which God created it: marriage, in which one gives oneself fully to the other in a permanent, committed, fruitful, loving relationship.

3. When does sexual pleasure become disordered?
   Sexual pleasure becomes disordered when it is focused on one's own pleasure instead of selfless true love of another person and when it is separated from marriage and the purpose of marriage.

4. What is anger?
   Anger is an uncontrolled expression of displeasure and antagonism, often accompanied by a desire for revenge.

5. What is righteous anger? How does this differ from sinful anger?
   Righteous anger is the proper response to injustice. It differs from sinful anger because sinful anger is done out of bitterness or hatred and seeks revenge.

6. How does anger become disordered?
   Anger becomes disordered when it is accompanied by a desire for revenge.

Reinforce

1. Have the students work on *Activity Book*, p. 55.

2. Give the students time to work on the Memorization Questions and Words to Know from this chapter.

3. *The students may discuss the challenges that they face in being pure. How can they protect themselves against sins of lust: e.g., dressing modestly, avoiding alcohol, avoiding being alone with a boy/girlfriend (especially late or where there is occasion to sin), doing activities together, such as sports or going out in public, striving to be pure in thought and to foster respect for the other person.*

4. *You may discuss social justice movements. Righteous anger may lead to the welfare of others, protecting their rights and upholding their dignity.*

Conclude

1. Lead the class in singing "Lift high the cross," *Adoremus Hymnal*, #606.

2. Lead the students in praying an Act of Hope.

Preview

In the next lesson, the students will learn about gluttony, envy, and sloth.

SAINT AUGUSTINE AND LUST

"Lord, give me chastity and continence, but not yet." This is the infamous prayer of Saint Augustine before his conversion. After a long and difficult spiritual journey, pressed on by the prayers of his mother, Saint Monica, Saint Augustine was almost ready to accept the truths of the Catholic faith. There was only one problem. He had lived a very licentious youth and the idea of giving up all those worldly pleasures was hard to accept. However, from the prayers of his mother, the prompting of his bishop Saint Ambrose, and the grace of God, Augustine was finally able to choose God. He embraced chastity and continence and became a bishop and one of the greatest theologians of the Church.

NOTES

_____
_____
_____
_____
_____
_____
_____
_____
_____
_____
_____
_____
_____
_____

LESSON FOUR: GLUTTONY, ENVY, AND SLOTH

Aims

The students will learn that the capital vices include gluttony, the uncontrolled desire of food and drink; envy, which is discontent at the good fortune or success of others; and sloth, which is excessive laziness, especially in the spiritual life.

Materials

- *Activity Book*, p. 56   Optional:
  - "Lift high the cross," *Adoremus Hymnal*, #606

Begin

Review pride, covetousness, lust, and anger. Discuss examples of these sins and ways of overcoming them.

You may give the students silent time to pray and make resolutions to overcome their sins with God's grace. Lead the students in praying an Act of Contrition.

"Let your light so shine before men, that they may see your good works and give glory to your Father who is in heaven."

(Matthew 5:16)

"Do not have an insatiable appetite for any luxury, and do not give yourself up to food; . . . Many have died of gluttony, but he who is careful to avoid it prolongs his life" (Sir 37:29–31).

Gluttony is an uncontrolled desire for and indulgence in food and drink. Eating and drinking are intended to be pleasurable and are certainly not sinful in themselves. In fact, they are necessary for our survival. However, like our desire for possessions, these desires can become excessive and be abused by us.

"For where jealousy [envy] and selfish ambition exist, there will be disorder and every vile practice" (James 3:16).

Envy is unhappiness or discontent over the good fortune or success of others. We are envious when we are saddened at another's prosperity or when we rejoice in another's misfortune. This vice is not the same as the ordinary desire or wish we might have to be successful like someone else. Similarly, it is not the wish or desire to possess a certain talent.

"And whatever you do, in word or deed, do everything in the name of the Lord Jesus, giving thanks to God the Father through him."

(Colossians 3:17)

100

"And we desire each one of you to show the same earnestness in realizing the full assurance of hope until the end, so that you may not be sluggish, but imitators of those who through faith and patience inherit the promises" (Heb 6:11–12).

Sloth is excessive laziness or carelessness. It is unlike the other vices, because it is not an ordinary desire that is uncontrolled. It is really a lack of desire to do one's duties, particularly spiritual ones, because of the effort that is involved. It is not the same as a reasonable desire for times of rest or leisure.

We do not all have equal inclinations to these vices. Some of us must struggle more against temptations to envy, while others are more tempted by anger or gluttony. The first step on the path to holiness is to look at ourselves, try to recognize our weaknesses, and try to overcome them with God's help.

In the next chapter we will consider positive steps to holiness. We will study the virtues, what they are and how we can develop them.

Words to Know:
vocation   holiness   apostolate
habit   capital sins

Develop

1. Read paragraphs 13–17 (to the end of the chapter).

2. Have the students define gluttony: uncontrolled desire for and indulgence in food and drink. An obvious example of this includes overeating at Thanksgiving/Christmas/Easter dinner. But, this also includes getting drunk or consuming things that are harmful to the body; e.g., cigarettes, drugs, too much candy, etc. Gluttony includes not wanting others to have food/drink because you want it. Gluttony also includes any over-indulgence in luxury. Gluttony refers to any uncontrolled appetite; e.g., shopping, chocolate, etc.

3. Envy is discontent over the good fortune or success of others. Envy is not just jealousy. Jealousy is wanting what someone else has. Envy is not wanting others to have something good—it is sometimes vengeful. Examples of envious acts include breaking someone else's video game because you don't want him to have it, being angry that another

student was made class president or received an expensive birthday gift, etc.

4. Sloth is laziness or carelessness. It is the lack of desire to do one's duties, especially spiritual ones (such as prayer, going to Mass, doing works of charity, etc.). It is not the same as desire for rest or leisure. It is a negligence. Have the students give examples of sloth.

5. Explain that we all have different dispositions to sin. We each must examine our own conscience and know our own weakness in order to overcome them with God's help. Have the students continue their resolutions. They may record these resolutions in their journals and take them to church for prayer before the Blessed Sacrament. We should ask God to help us overcome our sinfulness.

Name:_____

Seven Capital Sins: Gluttony, Envy, and Sloth

Answer the following questions in complete sentences.

1. What is gluttony?
   <u>Gluttony is an uncontrolled desire for and an indulgence in
   food and drink.</u>

2. When is our desire for food good? When does it become disordered?
   <u>Our desire for food is good when it is controlled and not
   overindulgent. It becomes disordered when we overindulge
   and lose control.</u>

3. What is envy?
   <u>Envy is unhappiness or discontent over the good fortune or
   success of others.</u>

4. Is any act of wishing to be like another a sin of envy? Explain.
   <u>Not any act of wishing to be like another is the sin of
   envy. (We should wish to be like the saints!) But it is envy
   when we are not happy with another's good fortune or if
   we rejoice in his misfortune.</u>

5. What is sloth and how is it unlike the other vices?
   <u>Sloth is excessive laziness or carelessness. It differs from
   the other vices because it is not an ordinary desire that is
   uncontrolled. It is a lack of a desire to do one's duties.</u>

6. How does a desire for rest and leisure become disordered?
   <u>A desire for rest and leisure becomes disordered when it
   becomes excessive and prevents one from doing his
   duties.</u>

Reinforce

1. Have the students work on *Activity Book*, p. 56.

2. Give the students time to work on the Memorization Questions and Words to Know from this chapter and to prepare for the quiz.

3. Have the students discuss examples of gluttony, envy, and sloth. They should list ways of overcoming these sins.

4. Each student should research a saint and his struggle with a capital sin. The brief report should include ways we can follow the saint's example of overcoming sin.

Conclude

1. Lead the class in singing "Lift high the cross," *Adoremus Hymnal*, #606.

2. Lead the students in praying an Act of Hope.

Preview

In the next lesson, the students' understanding of the material covered in this chapter will be reviewed and assessed.

SAINT TERESA OF AVILA AND GLUTTONY AND SLOTH

One of the greatest mystics and spiritual writers of the Church in her later years, Saint Teresa struggled greatly in her early years as a nun. Although she began religious life with strong discipline, high aspirations, and great favors from God, she soon fell away from the spiritual life. Her gluttony was not an inordinate desire for food or drink, but an inordinate desire for frivolous conversation. Her convent was very lax in following its rule and the nuns wasted many hours each day. Writing her autobiography years later, Saint Teresa laments, "I thus began to go from pastime to pastime, from vanity to vanity, from one occasion to another, and to allow my soul to become . . . spoiled by many vanities" (*Life* 7.1). As her sins increased, Saint Teresa faced the sin of sloth as she lost the joy she used to find in virtuous acts, and was tempted to think she was too corrupted for intimate mental prayer. For a time she did not pray mentally at all and only recited her required prayers. After several years of this, she took a holy Dominican priest as her confessor and he began to lead her back to the spiritual life. At first, Teresa was attracted both to the spiritual life and to the joys of the world, and she tried to have both. She soon realized, however, that she must choose, and she set aside the joys of this world to pursue Christ and the joys that transcend this world.

_____

_____

_____

_____

_____

_____

_____

_____

_____

_____

_____

_____

_____

_____

_____

_____

_____

_____

_____

_____

_____

_____

_____

_____

_____

_____

_____

Prayer

"Almighty and eternal God, your Spirit guides the Church and makes it holy. Listen to our prayers and help each of us in his vocation to do your work more faithfully. We ask this through Christ Our Lord. Amen."

(General Intercessions, Holy Week)

". . . but as he who called you is holy, be holy yourselves in all your conduct: since it is written 'you shall be holy, for I am holy.' "

(1 Pet 1:15–16)

Q. 86 *What is vice?*
A vice is a bad habit that is acquired by repeating bad actions (CCC 1865).

Q. 87 *What are the principal vices?*
The principal vices are the seven capital sins of pride, avarice, lust, anger, gluttony, envy, and sloth (CCC 1866).

101

_____

_____

_____

_____

_____

_____

_____

_____

_____

_____

_____

_____

_____

_____

_____

Name:

The Universal Call to Holiness   **Quiz 14**

Part I: Define the following terms.

Holiness: the call of each Christian to follow Christ so that one day we may be with him in heaven for eternity

Apostolate: the work of spreading the Gospel in whatever way we can

Capital Sins: the seven vices which are source of all other vices and sins

Part II: Fill in the chart.

CAPITAL VICE	DEFINITION	EXAMPLE
lust	uncontrolled desire for or indulgence in sexual pleasure	adultery (examples will vary)
anger	uncontrolled expresssion of displeasure and antagonism	beating someone
gluttony	uncontrolled desire for and indulgence in food or drink	drunkenness
envy	unhappiness over the good fortune of others	unhappy when someone gets a better grade than you
sloth	excessive laziness	not doing your chores
covetousness	uncontrolled desire for earthly possessions	stealing
pride	excessive, disordered self-love	putting others down to make yourself look better

A - 20   *Faith and Life • Grade 8 • Appendix A*

Aims

The students' understanding of the material covered in this chapter will be reviewed and assessed.

Materials

- Quiz 14, Appendix, p. A-20

Optional:
- "Lift high the cross," *Adoremus Hymnal,* #606

Assess

1. Distribute the quizzes and read through them with the students to be sure they understand the questions.

2. Administer the quiz. As they hand in their work, you may orally quiz the students on the Memorization Questions from this chapter.

3. After all the quizzes have been handed in, review the correct answers with the class.

Conclude

1. Lead the class in singing "Lift high the cross," *Adoremus Hymnal,* #606.

2. End class with an Act of Hope.

Review

1. The students should understand the universal call to holiness.

2. By virtue of Baptism, the students share in the apostolate of evangelization. They should understand what this means: it is their duty as baptized Christians to spread the Gospel.

3. The students should be able to define capital sin. They should know each of the capital sins and be able to give examples of each.

4. The students should know that they have a specific vocation, which must be discerned.

CHAPTER FIFTEEN
THE LIFE OF VIRTUE

Catechism of the Catholic Church References

Characteristics of faith: 153–65, 176–81
Chastity: 2337–59, 2394–95
Christian Holiness: 2012–16, 2028–29
Grace of Baptism: 265, 1262–73, 1279–80
Jesus as Our Teacher and Model of Holiness: 468–69, 516, 519–21, 561
Man Created in the Image of God: 280–81, 355–57
Moral Virtues/Cardinal Virtues: 1804–9, 1833–39

New Law, or Law of the Gospel: 1965–74, 1977, 1983–86
Theological Virtues: 1812–29, 1840–44
Theological Virtues and Prayer: 2656–58, 2662
Theological Virtues and the First Commandment: 2086–87, 2090, 2093, 2134
Virtue: 1804, 1833–34
Virtue of Religion: 2095–97
Virtues and Grace: 1810–11, 1839

Scripture References

Faith and Virtue: 2 Pet 1:5–7

Great Commandment: Lk 10:25–28

Summary of Lesson Content

Lesson 1

A virtue is an abiding disposition of the soul to do good. Virtue enables a person to do good actions easily and to avoid bad actions.

Lesson 3

The moral virtues stem from the cardinal virtues. The moral virtues help us to counteract the seven capital sins. The moral virtues include humility, liberality, chastity, meekness, moderation, brotherly love, and diligence.

Lesson 2

Cardinal virtues enable us to act rightly in our conduct with other men. The four cardinal virtues are the hinge for all the other moral virtues. The cardinal virtues are prudence, justice, temperance, and fortitude.

Lesson 4

The theological virtues are supernatural virtues that belong to Christians. They are infused by God at Baptism. We exercise these virtues with the help of God through the graces he gives us. The theological virtues come from God and direct us toward God. They are faith, hope, and charity.

LESSON ONE: VIRTUE

Aims

The students will learn that a virtue is an abiding disposition of the soul to do good. Virtue enables a person to do good actions easily and to avoid bad actions.

Materials

- *Activity Book*, p. 57   Optional:
  - "Be thou my vision," *Adoremus Hymnal*, #623

Begin

Review that a vice is an evil inclination of the soul formed by a habit. The opposite of vice is virtue.

Virtue is the disposition of the soul to do good. Like vice, virtue is formed by habit. It must be exercised like a muscle. The more we do virtuous actions, the more they become a part of us; virtue takes root in us. E.g., if we tell the truth one time, it is not virtue, but if we continue to tell the truth, it become easier, and we will want to always be truthful. In this way we acquire the virtue of honesty.

CHAPTER 15

The Life of Virtue

Make every effort to supplement your faith with virtue, and virtue with knowledge, and knowledge with self-control, and self-control with steadfastness, and steadfastness with godliness, and godliness with brotherly affection, and brotherly affection with love.

2 Peter 1:5–7

Just as there are habits that can be obstacles to our pursuit of holiness, there are also habits that can help us. If we consciously and willingly perform a good action frequently, we will be on the right path and acquire a disposition to do it again. Then it becomes more and more

102

part of us. It takes root in us. For example, if we tell the truth, or perform one generous act, we have not yet acquired the virtue of honesty or generosity. But if we repeat it we will be strengthened. The word *virtue* comes from the Latin word for strength.

A **virtue** is an abiding disposition of the soul, or power that enables a person to perform good actions easily and to avoid bad actions. It can be either *natural*—that is, acquired through repeated action, such as the virtue of honesty —or *supernatural*, that is, given to us by God.

The natural virtues in many ways resemble other habits. Take the example of a runner. At first running is difficult and a big effort for him. He endures and overcomes obstacles. Finally he can easily run for miles. He has the strength to do it. And then he even loves running.

So it is with virtues. We make the effort. We conquer the obstacles, and then we grow stronger, it becomes easier, and we finally love it. It is a joy for us. We conquer sin and grow closer to God. (Sinful habits give us a moment of pleasure, but unhappiness and a feeling of sadness in the end.) St. Benedict says that as we progress in virtue "our hearts shall be en-

Develop

1. Read paragraphs 1–4 (up to The Cardinal Virtues).

2. Using the Chalk Talk at right, explain the qualities of a virtue. A virtue is a habit of doing good. A virtue is a habit that has ease, love, and strength. There are natural and supernatural virtues. The natural virtues are acquired by repeated action. The supernatural virtues are given to us by God, but we must practice them in order to grow in them. All virtues require habitual practice in order to acquire the ease, love, and strength necessary to lead a virtuous life.

3. We must recognize opportunities for virtue. Give the students various scenarios and ask them what virtues could be practiced; e.g., you are waiting in line at the grocery store and the person ahead of you is taking an inordinately long time to pay; you broke an expensive lamp and your mother asks you about it; you know your friend cheated on a test; etc.

4. To live the virtuous life, we must make choices. We must choose to do good and to discipline ourselves to make a habit of these good deeds. You may make the parallel between an athlete or a musician. When we begin, virtue is difficult and requires greater effort; with practice, it become easy and enjoyable.

5. Go around the room and ask the students to list one natural virtue. For each, ask, "Why is this a virtue?" and "Why is this virtue natural?"

6. Discuss the need to grow in all the virtues. What good is it to be very patient, but full of sloth? How can we be generous, but full of anger? Suggest a daily self-examination based upon the virtues. Ask the students to write the "ideal" for themselves. Optional: you may discuss the quotation at the beginning of the chapter (2 Pet 1:5–7) and use this as a plan for growing in virtue.

Name:_____

The Life of Virtue

Answer the following questions in complete sentences.

1. What is a virtue?

   A virtue is an abiding habit of the soul to do good.

2. List the two types of virtues and explain how they are acquired.

   The two types of virtues are natural and theological.
   Natural virtue is acquired by repeated action. Theological
   virtue is given to us by God.

3. How does growing in virtue compare to being a runner?

   Growing in virtue is comparable to being a runner because
   at first, running is very difficult and hard work. The runner
   has to work hard consistently to overcome obstacles until
   he can run for a long time and, eventually, even loves
   running.

4. Are virtues easy? Should we find joy in living them?

   Virtues are not easy at first. Like running, practicing
   virtue takes consistent effort and many obstacles must be
   overcome. After a time, it becomes easier and we find
   joy in living the virtuous life.

5. Compare the pleasure of a life of virtue with the pleasure of a life of vice.

   Answers will vary.

Reinforce

1. Have the students work on *Activity Book*, p. 57.

2. Give the students time to work on the Memorization Questions and Words to Know from this chapter.

3. Read 2 Pet 1:5–7. Demonstrate the usefulness of this reading as an outline for growing in virtue by using a specific example; e.g., honesty. We know we should speak the truth because it is the Eighth Commandment, so we should practice this virtue. We should learn about truth and the evils of deceitfulness. We should learn how we practice honesty and why we fail in honesty—and the occasions of our dishonesty. We must commit to being more honest and pray for this virtue. We must grow in love for God and our neighbor.

Conclude

1. Teach the students to sing "Be thou my vision," *Adoremus Hymnal*, #623.

2. Lead the students in praying the Prayer Before a Crucifix.

Preview

In the next lesson, the students will learn about the cardinal virtues.

CHALK TALK: THE VIRTUES

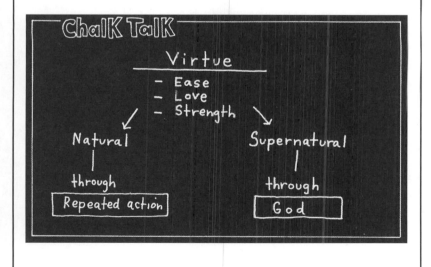

PRAYER BEFORE A CRUCIFIX
by Saint Francis of Assisi
before the Crucifix of San Damiano

Most high, glorious God,
enlighten the shadows of my heart
and grant unto me
a right faith, a certain hope,
a perfect charity, sense and
    understanding
so that I may carry out
your true and holy will.

LESSON TWO:
CARDINAL VIRTUES

Aims

The students will learn that the cardinal virtues enable us to act rightly in our conduct with others. The four cardinal virtues are the hinge for all the other moral virtues. The cardinal virtues are prudence, justice, temperance, and fortitude.

Materials

- *Activity Book*, p. 58

  Optional:
  - "Be thou my vision," *Adoremus Hymnal*, #623

Begin

Explain the definition of "cardinal." Cardinal means hinge or source. Just as the capital vices are the source of other vices, the cardinal virtues are the hinge upon which the other virtues depend.

Note: cardinal virtues are moral virtues—this means that they enable us to live in right conduct with others. We acquire them with practice.

---

larged, and we shall run with unspeakable sweetness of love in the way of God's commandments."

And if one loves righteousness her labors are virtues; for she teaches self-control and prudence, justice and courage; nothing in life is more profitable for men than these (Wis 8:7).

The Cardinal Virtues

The natural, or *moral*, virtues enable us to act rightly in our conduct with other men. The chief moral virtues are the four **cardinal virtues**. They are called cardinal, from the Latin word for hinge, because they are the support or framework for all the other moral virtues. These four—prudence, justice, temperance (self-control), and fortitude (courage)—are the foundation for living a good life.

Prudence is the chief moral virtue, which directs all the others. Also called practical wisdom, this virtue enables us to determine what action is required in a given situation, and it moves us to do the action. The person who acts using good judgment at all times—knowing the right thing to do in every situation—has the virtue of prudence. Prudence requires that we know what to do and that we have the will to do it.

Prudence should be operating in all the decisions we make in our lives. We must learn to examine a situation clearly and to decide on the proper course of action with deliberation. For this to become a habit takes time and a great deal of experience.

Justice is the virtue that prompts us to give to others what is due to them—that is, what they deserve. Justice prompts us to pay debts owed to another, to keep promises that we have made, to obey laws made by those who have the authority, to keep secrets that someone entrusts to us, to play games fairly, and to respect the property of others. Justice directs us to act fairly and honestly toward others; it is commanded by the Seventh Commandment. For those in authority, acting justly sometimes means assigning punishments, since at times they may be deserved.

There are some debts that we can never fully repay—for example, the debts we owe to God who created us, to our parents for giving us life and raising us, or to our country. The respect, love, and loyalty that we show to them are derived from this virtue of justice.

Fortitude is the virtue that enables us to confront difficulties or dangers, perhaps even death, with courage and hope. With fortitude we are able to act calmly and reasonably even in the face of great dangers.

The martyrs of the Church all demonstrated the virtue of fortitude when they chose to remain faithful to Christ, despite the terrible deaths that awaited them. We might never be called upon to die for Christ, yet we need to develop the virtue of fortitude to be able to face the difficult moments in our lives—perhaps refusing to get drunk or use drugs when others encourage us to do this. St. Paul exhorts us to practice the virtue of fortitude when he says, in his letter to the Ephesians:

Take the whole armor of God, that you may be able to withstand in the evil day, and having done all, to stand (Eph 6:13).

Temperance is the virtue that enables us to control our passions and desires. This virtue allows us to act moderately and reasonably, so that we may use our bodies correctly. We often think of temperance as applying particularly to food and drink. This is true, but it also applies to all areas of our lives. The temperate person is one who eats the right amount, exercises the right amount, sleeps the right amount, and so on—that is, he is a person who habitually balances all activities of life.

103

Develop

1. Read paragraphs 5–13 (up to Other Moral Virtues).

2. Discuss each cardinal virtue, including its definition and some examples.

- *Prudence: the chief moral virtue, also called the practice of wisdom. Prudence enables us to determine what action is required in a given situation and moves us to do that action. In other words, prudence is knowing the right thing to do and choosing to do it. E.g., choose not to go to a party where we know there will be alcohol; study before a test, etc.*

- *Justice: prompts us to give others what is due to them. We must evaluate each situation carefully to judge the proper course of action. E.g., give worship to God, play a sport fairly, be honest in dealing with others, etc.*

- *Fortitude: enables us to confront difficulties and dangers (even death) with courage and hope. E.g., we must speak the truth even when it is difficult; faithfulness unto martyrdom; defying negative peer pressure.*

- *Temperance: helps us to control our passions and desires. Temperance allows us to act moderately and reasonably. It helps us to use created goods well (and for their intended purpose). E.g., proper diet and exercise, proper stewardship, not spending too much on unnecessary things, etc.*

3. Have the students research saints and ways they exemplified the cardinal virtues. Discuss how the students see these virtues lived in the world today.

4. The students should write a short prayer, asking God to help them grow in the cardinal virtues.

Name:_____

The Cardinal Virtues

I. Answer the following questions in complete sentences.

1. What are the chief moral virtues?

   The chief moral virtues are prudence, justice, fortitude, and temperance.

2. Why are the chief moral virtues called "cardinal" virtues?

   The chief moral virtues are called "cardinal" virtues because they are the support or framework of the other moral virtues.

II. In the chart below, explain and give examples of the cardinal virtues.

VIRTUE	EXPLANATION AND EXAMPLE
Prudence	Answers will vary.
Justice	
Fortitude	
Temperance	

58   *Faith and Life Series • Grade 8 • Chapter 15 • Lesson 2*

1. Have the students work on *Activity Book*, p. 58.

2. Give the students time to work on the Memorization Questions and Words to Know from this chapter.

3. *The students should write down ways they can improve their practice of the cardinal virtues.*

4. Discuss other moral virtues and how they "hang" upon the cardinal virtues.

5. Have the students create posters depicting the cardinal virtues. They may create symbols of these virtues and explain them to the other students.

Conclude

1. Lead the class in singing "Be thou my vision," *Adoremus Hymnal*, #623.

2. Lead the students in praying the Prayer before a Crucifix.

Preview

In the next lesson, the students will learn about the moral virtues.

SAINT THOMAS MORE: AN EXAMPLE OF PRUDENCE AND JUSTICE

After studying for many years at Oxford, building a reputation as a respected attorney, and authoring widely popular works of political literature, such as his classic, *Utopia*, Saint Thomas More was appointed Lord Chancellor of England by King Henry VIII. When the Protestant Reformation hit England, Saint Thomas More was faced with a choice that forced him to use the virtues of prudence and justice. King Henry VIII wanted to divorce his lawful wife Catherine of Aragorn. The Pope refused to allow it, so, in 1531, King Henry VIII separated the Church in England from that of Rome. He attempted to have himself named "Protector and Supreme Head of the Church of England." In doing so, King Henry broke with the Holy Father and the true Church and demanded that Saint Thomas More do the same. For several years, Saint Thomas More opposed the King's move and finally Henry had him imprisoned in the Tower of London where he stayed for fifteen months. On July 6, 1535, Saint Thomas More was condemned to death for refusing to recognize the King as head of the Church of England. Before losing his head, Saint Thomas declared: "I die the king's good servant, but God's first." In justice Saint Thomas gave God his due over that of the king, and in prudence he did the right thing in the best way possible, even though it led to his death.

LESSON THREE: MORAL VIRTUES

Aims

The students will learn that the moral virtues stem from the cardinal virtues. The moral virtues help us to counteract the seven capital sins. The moral virtues include humility, liberality, chastity, meekness, moderation, brotherly love, and diligence.

Materials

- *Activity Book*, p. 59

  Optional:
  - "Be thou my vision," *Adoremus Hymnal*, #623

Begin

Review moral virtues. They enable us to act rightly in our conduct with other men. Moral virtues are natural virtues. We must acquire moral virtues and grow in them through practice. The cardinal virtues are moral virtues. The moral virtues that we will study today hinge upon the cardinal virtues and are the opposite of the capital vices.

Upon these four virtues hang many other moral virtues. One of these is the virtue of *religion*. Religion is the virtue by which we give to God the worship he deserves. This means that we praise him in a manner that is appropriate to his place as our Creator and Lord. This virtue stems from the cardinal virtue of justice.

Other Moral Virtues

Other moral virtues stemming from the cardinal virtues help us to counteract the seven capital sins. These good habits will replace the bad habits that can so easily develop.

Humility is the virtue opposed to pride. It leads one to have a just opinion of one's self and to give credit for our successes and gifts to God. Humility is related to the virtue of prudence, because it enables us to see the correct way to think about ourselves.

Liberality is the virtue opposed to covetousness. It enables a person to give freely of his money, possessions, talents, and so on to worthy purposes. Stemming from justice, liberality enables one to act fairly with his gifts and to serve the needs of others.

Chastity is the virtue opposed to lust. Chastity should not be seen *only* as self-control, moderation, and balance of sexual inclinations, but more importantly it should be understood in relation to the expression of human love. What does this mean? It means that sex is a great gift which by its nature entails complete donation of one person to another only in marriage. It therefore means abstaining from sex outside of marriage, so that the purest love can be given most completely to the spouse, or, in the case of priests and religious, to God in loving abstinence.

Meekness is the virtue opposed to anger. It is the virtue that enables us to be patient under injury or insult. The meek person is able to control his temper even in a trying or difficult

104

situation. Because this takes a certain amount of spiritual strength or courage, meekness is related to the virtue of fortitude.

Moderation and *sobriety* are virtues opposed to gluttony. They enable one to use food and drink sensibly—enjoying them in the proper amounts and at suitable times. As forms of self-control, they stem from the cardinal virtue of temperance.

Brotherly love is the virtue opposed to envy. This virtue enables one to show true love for one's neighbor—praying for him, doing acts of kindness for him, and helping him in his needs. This virtue stems from the virtue of justice—for we are giving to another what is owed.

Diligence is the virtue opposed to sloth. This virtue enables us to do our work and carry out our religious duties—whatever they may be—with devotion and dedication. It stems from the virtue of prudence, for we see that hard work at our given tasks is the right way to act.

The Theological Virtues

The supernatural virtues are those that belong to us as Christians. Unlike the moral virtues, they cannot be acquired by repetition of certain actions, but are *infused*, given to us, by God. We receive them at Baptism, when we receive sanctifying grace. We exercise these virtues with the help of God, through the actual graces he gives us.

The supernatural virtues are faith, hope, and charity. Because these virtues come from God as well as direct us toward him, they are called *theological* virtues (theological in this sense means pertaining to God).

Faith is the virtue by which we believe all that God has revealed to us through Christ and his Church. The gift of faith is necessary, for it enables us to believe those mysteries—such as the Trinity—that are beyond the grasp of the

Develop

1. Read paragraphs 14–21 (up to Theological Virtues).

2. Review the capital vices: pride, covetousness, lust, anger, gluttony, envy, and sloth. Today we will study the opposites of these vices: the moral virtues.

3. *Explain each of these moral virtues and have the students give examples when they understand them well:*
   - *Humility (opposite of pride): having a just opinion of one's self. Humility enables us to give credit to God for his gifts and our successes. Rooted in truth and justice, humility does not call us to put ourselves down or have a negative opinion of ourselves. (Someone who says he is ugly when he is actually attractive has false humility—it is not based on truth.)*
   - *Liberality (opposite of covetousness): enables a person to give freely of his riches—be they money, talents, etc.—to worthy purposes.*

   - *Chastity (opposite of lust): the genuine and true expression of love—it is self-gift. Chastity recognizes the dignity of the human person and the sanctity of marriage.*
   - *Meekness (opposite of anger): enables us to be patient under insult and injury. Meekness is connected with fortitude—strength in enduring trouble.*
   - *Moderation/sobriety (opposite of gluttony): using goods sensibly (proper amounts at proper times). Moderation is connected to temperance.*
   - *Brotherly love (opposite of envy): desiring the best for our neighbor, brotherly love allows us to show our true love for others.*
   - *Diligence (opposite of sloth): enables us to work efficiently and to fulfill our religious duties with joy and devotion.*

4. Discuss examples of these virtues in the lives of the saints. Do the students see these virtues in their daily lives? How can they grow in these virtues?

Name:_____

Other Moral Virtues

For each of the following virtues, give a definition, an example, and the name of the capital sin they counter.

VIRTUE	EXPLANATION AND EXAMPLE
Humility	Answers will vary.
Liberality	
Chastity	
Meekness	
Moderation and Sobriety	
Brotherly Love	
Diligence	

Reinforce

1. Have the students work on *Activity Book*, p. 59.

2. Give the students time to work on the Memorization Questions and Words to Know from this chapter.

3. Have the students find examples of the moral virtues and discuss how to grow in these virtues. Use specific scenarios to demonstrate the moral virtues.

4. Have the students write down ways they can grow in the moral virtues. They should write a prayer asking for the grace to grow in these virtues.

Conclude

1. Lead the class in singing "Be thou my vision," *Adoremus Hymnal*, #623.

2. Lead the students in praying the Prayer before a Crucifix.

Preview

In the next lesson, the students will learn about the theological virtues.

SAINT MARIA GORETTI: AN EXAMPLE OF TEMPERANCE AND FORTITUDE

Saint Maria Goretti died when she was twelve years old. Shortly before she died, a young man who worked with her family tried to make her commit an act of impurity. When she refused, he stabbed her several times. She died from these wounds shortly after and forgave the man who had killed her. Although she was only twelve, she showed remarkable temperance and incredible fortitude in refusing to be unchaste and carrying that refusal even to death. After her death, the young man was imprisoned and remained unrepentant until, one night, Saint Maria Goretti appeared to him in a dream and gave him some flowers, showing that she had forgiven him. Upon his release nearly thirty years later, he went directly to Saint Maria's mother and asked her to forgive him. Her mother replied that if her daughter could forgive him then she could do the same. In 1950, this man stood in Saint Peter's Square watching as Pope Pius XII canonized Saint Maria Goretti.

LESSON FOUR: THEOLOGICAL VIRTUES

Aims

The students will learn that the theological virtues are supernatural virtues that belong to Christians. They are infused by God at Baptism. We exercise these virtues with the help of God through the graces he gives us. The theological virtues come from God and direct us toward God. They are faith, hope, and charity.

Materials

- *Activity Book*, p. 60

Optional:
- "Be thou my vision," *Adoremus Hymnal*, #623

Begin

Review the difference between the natural and supernatural virtues (see Chalk Talk on p. 187).

We acquire and grow in natural virtues through repetitive action (habit).

Supernatural virtues are a gift from God; we grow in them by exercising them.

---

human mind. We need faith in order to know our goal, which is heaven.

Hope is the virtue by which we trust in God's promises of eternal salvation. With hope we can find comfort in the words of Our Lord: "I am the resurrection and the life: he who believes in me, though he die, yet shall he live . . ." (Jn 11:25–26). Hope tells us that God, who promised us eternal salvation, will also give us the graces that we need to reach heaven.

Charity is the virtue by which we love God above all things for his own sake and love our neighbor as ourselves. The two Great Commandments of which Our Lord spoke to the scribe (Lk 10:25–28) can be summed up in the virtue of charity. This virtue enables us to love God above all, simply because he is good and deserves our love. We love our neighbors, including our enemies, because God loves them and because they, like ourselves, have been created in his image.

So faith, hope, love abide, these three; but the greatest of these is love (1 Cor 13:13).

All three of these virtues are necessary if we are to reach heaven, but charity, which is love in its highest and fullest sense, is the greatest. It is the virtue that unites us most intimately with God and our neighbor. It is through charity that we are moved to obey God's law and to perform good actions. Every virtue we have studied so far becomes radiant, beautiful, and new when infused by this love. As St. Paul says, all things are made new through Jesus Christ (see 2 Cor 5:17).

While the theological virtues cannot be acquired through repetition of certain acts, we can strengthen them by our actions. Through prayer we open ourselves to God's grace so that we can receive these great gifts. If we *really* want them and *really* strive after them, then we

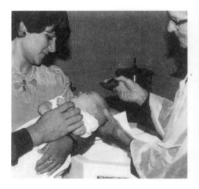

will receive them. Christ says, "Ask, and it shall be given you; . . . knock, and it will be opened to you" (Mt 7:7). Just as our bodies require exercise to remain in shape, so these virtues must be exercised if they are to help us reach heaven. In general, we can develop and exercise these virtues by making acts of faith, hope, and charity.

Faith is strengthened when we profess and defend our faith, and when we study and think about the meaning of the mysteries of the faith. It is also made stronger by the good actions that we do, since ". . . faith apart from works is dead" (James 2:26). We can exercise hope by accepting the will of God, trusting him to care for us as he cares for the birds of the air and the lilies of the field (Lk 12:22–34). By doing so we can avoid becoming unduly anxious or upset by life—even by trials or sorrows. We strengthen the virtue of charity by observing the Commandments, as Our Lord instructed us: "He who has my commandments and keeps them, he it is who loves me. . . . If a man loves me, he will keep my word" (Jn 14:21, 23). We also exercise charity by doing the works of mercy, which we will consider in the next chapter.

105

Develop

1. Read paragraphs 22–31 (to the end of the chapter).

*2. The virtues of faith, hope, and charity are called theological virtues because they are gifts from God that direct us toward God. (*Theos *means God in Greek.)*

3. Help the students to understand the definitions of the theological virtues. Have the students give examples.

- *Faith: the virtue by which we believe all that God has revealed to us through Christ and his Church. E.g., belief in the Holy Trinity, the Incarnation, eternal life, etc.*

- *Hope: the virtue by which we trust in God's promises of eternal salvation. E.g., we hope to be with God forever in heaven—we can trust in his ways for us to grow in holiness.*

- *Charity: the virtue by which we love God above all things, and our neighbor for love of God. This is summarized in the Great Commandment: Lk 10:25–28. In charity, we love God because he is all good and deserving of all of our love. We love our neighbors, including our enemies, because God loves them and they are made in his image.*

4. We can strengthen our theological virtues through prayer (e.g., Acts of Faith, Hope, and Charity) and by our actions (e.g., serving others in need, studying our religion, etc.).

5. Have the students create a chart defining the theological virtues. They should write practical ways to grow in each:
- *Faith: study our faith, pray the creed, etc.*
- *Hope: live the moral life, receive the sacraments, pray, etc.*
- *Charity: worship God, volunteer for a charity, etc.*

Name:_____

The Theological Virtues

I. Answer the following question in complete sentences.

1. What are the supernatural virtues?
   Supernatural virtues are those virtues given to us by God. They are faith, hope, and charity.

2. When do we receive them?
   We receive them at Baptism, when we receive sanctifying grace.

3. How do we exercise them?
   We exercise them through God's help and the actual graces he gives us.

4. Why are they called "theological" virtues?
   They are called "theological" virtues because they pertain to God, and they come from him and direct us to him.

II. In the chart below, explain the theological virtues.

VIRTUE	EXPLANATION
Faith	Answers will vary, but should be based on the student text.
Hope	
Love	

60   *Faith and Life Series • Grade 8 • Chapter 15 • Lesson 4*

1. Have the students work on *Activity Book*, p. 60.

2. Give the students time to work on the Memorization Questions and Words to Know from this chapter and to prepare for the quiz.

3. Discuss charity as the most perfect of the virtues.

4. Play a review game of all the virtues and vices studied in the Chapters 14 and 15. Describe a virtue or vice and have the students compete to answer.

Conclude

1. Lead the class in singing "Be thou my vision," *Adoremus Hymnal*, #623.

2. Lead the students in praying the Prayer before a Crucifix.

Preview

In the next lesson, the students' understanding of the material covered in this chapter will be reviewed and assessed.

UNDERSTANDING THE VIRTUES

There are several distinctions used when discussing the virtues that can cause confusion unless they are properly understood.

The distinction between *natural* and *supernatural* virtues is based on how they are acquired:
- *Natural virtues* are acquired by repeatedly doing good acts.
- *Supernatural virtues* are directly infused by God.

The distinction between *human* and *theological* virtues is based on their end (purpose):
- *Human virtues* help us to lead a morally good life. The cardinal virtues are human virtues.
- *Theological virtues* help us to live in relationship with God.

The *theological* virtues (faith, hope, and love) cannot come about by human action, they must be infused by God. Therefore, *theological* virtues are always *supernatural*. The cardinal virtues, however, can be both *natural* and *supernatural*. They can be acquired by repeated act (natural), and they are infused by God at baptism (supernatural).

_____
_____
_____
_____
_____
_____
_____
_____
_____
_____
_____
_____
_____
_____
_____
_____
_____
_____
_____
_____

Living the virtuous life—practicing these virtues daily—is not easy. It is, in fact, a great challenge. But it is a challenge that we can meet, because we have God's help through prayer and the sacraments. In our struggle we should remember the saints. They are the proof for us that the life of virtue is possible. They also show that virtue will be rewarded by God.

Finally, we should recall the example of Our Lord himself. Christ is both God and man. But he showed us as man the perfect way to live as a human being.

Words to Know:
    virtue   cardinal virtues

Q. 88   *What is a virtue?*
A virtue is an abiding habit of the soul to do good (CCC 1803).

Q. 89   *What are the two kinds of virtues?*
The two kinds of virtues are natural and supernatural virtues. Natural virtues are acquired by repeating good acts. The supernatural virtues (also known as the theological virtues) cannot be acquired or even exercised by our own power. They come to us as gifts from God (CCC 1804, 1812).

Q. 90   *What is a moral virtue?*
A moral virtue (also called a human virtue) is a habit of doing good, acquired by repeatedly doing good acts (CCC 1804).

Q. 91   *What are the principal moral virtues?*
The principal moral virtues are religion, by which we give God the worship owed to him, and the four cardinal virtues: prudence, justice, fortitude, and temperance (CCC 1805).

106

_____
_____
_____
_____
_____
_____
_____
_____
_____
_____
_____
_____
_____
_____

Q. 92 *Why are certain virtues called cardinal virtues?*

Certain virtues are called cardinal virtues because they are pivotal and the support, or framework, for all the other moral virtues (CCC 1805).

Q. 93 *What is the virtue of prudence?*

Prudence is the virtue that directs our actions to the true good in every situation and enables us to choose the right means of achieving it (CCC 1806).

Q. 94 *What is the virtue of justice?*

Justice is the virtue by which we always give to God or our neighbor what is due him (CCC 1807).

Q. 95 *What is the virtue of fortitude?*

Fortitude is the virtue by which we confront with courage any difficulty or danger, even death itself, for the service of God and the welfare of neighbor (CCC 1808).

Q. 96 *What is the virtue of temperance?*

Temperance is the virtue by which we hold our passions and desires, especially the sensual ones, under control (CCC 1809).

Q. 97 *What are the theological virtues?*

The theological virtues are faith, hope, and charity (CCC 1813).

Q. 98 *Why are certain virtues called theological virtues?*

Certain virtues are called theological virtues because they have God himself for their origin, motive, and object (CCC 1812–13).

107

Q. 99 *How do we receive and exercise the theological virtues?*
We receive the theological virtues together with sanctifying grace by means of the sacraments. We exercise them with the hope of actual graces, namely the good thoughts and inspirations with which God moves and helps us in every good act that we do (CCC 2025).

Q. 100 *Which is the most excellent among the theological virtues?*
The most excellent among the theological virtues is charity, which unites us intimately to God and to our neighbor (CCC 1826).

Q. 101 *What is faith?*
Faith is the theological virtue by which we believe what God has revealed as it is taught by the Church (CCC 1814).

Q. 102 *What is hope?*
Hope is the theological virtue by which we trust in God for the graces necessary to obey him and merit eternal life (CCC 1817).

Q. 103 *What is charity?*
Charity is the theological virtue by which we love God above all things for his own sake, and love our neighbor as ourselves because we love God (CCC 1822).

Q. 104 *Why must we love God for his own sake?*
We must love God for his own sake because he is supremely good and the source of every good thing (CCC 2055).

Q. 105 *Why must we love our neighbor?*
We must love our neighbor because God has commanded that we love one another and because every human being has been created in God's image (CCC 1823).

108

Q. 106 *Why are we obliged to love our enemies?*
We are obliged to love our enemies because they are also our neighbors and Jesus Christ explicitly commanded us to love our enemies (CCC 1825, 2303).

Q. 107 *How do we give proof of our faith?*
We give proof of our faith by professing it, defending it, and living according to its teachings (CCC 1816, 2471).

Q. 108 *How do we give proof of our hope?*
We give proof of our hope by living in peaceful acceptance of the promises of Christ (CCC 1817–18).

Q. 109 *How do we prove our charity?*
We prove our charity by observing the commandments of God, living in love, and giving of ourselves for the sake of the Kingdom according to our vocation (CCC 1827–28).

109

CHAPTER FIFTEEN
REVIEW AND ASSESSMENT

Aims

The students' understanding of the material covered in this chapter will be reviewed and assessed.

Materials

- Quiz 15, Appendix, p. A-21

Optional:
- "Be thou my vision," *Adoremus Hymnal,* #623

Review

1. The students should know what a virtue is. They should know the difference between natural and supernatural virtues.

2. The students should be able to define the cardinal virtues and give examples of each. They should know the virtues that oppose the cardinal vices. They should also know the theological virtues.

Assess

1. Distribute the quizzes and read through them with the students to be sure they understand the questions.

2. Administer the quiz. As they hand in their work, you may orally quiz the students on the Memorization Questions from this chapter.

3. After all the quizzes have been handed in, review the correct answers with the class.

Conclude

1. Lead the class in singing "Be thou my vision," *Adoremus Hymnal,* #623.

2. End class with the Prayer before a Crucifix.

CHAPTER SIXTEEN
THE WORKS OF MERCY AND HAPPINESS

Catechism of the Catholic Church References

Beatitudes: 1716–19, 1725, 1820
Charity: 1822–29, 1844
Christian Beatitude: 1720–24, 1728–29
Christian Holiness: 2012–16, 2028–29
Forgiveness: 2842–45, 2862
Jesus as Our Teacher and Model of Holiness: 468–69, 516, 519–21, 561
Love for the Poor, the Works of Mercy: 2443–49, 2462–63

Man's Vocation to Beatitude: 1718–24, 1726–29
Poverty of Spirit: 2544–47, 2556
Prayer for the Dead: 1032, 1055
Purity of Heart: 2517–19, 2531–33
Sickness in Christian Life: 1506–10
Sickness in Human Life: 1500–1501
Works of Mercy: 2447

Scripture References

Sermon on the Mount: Mt 5–7
Beatitudes: Mt 5:3–12

Final Judgment: Mt 25:31–46

Summary of Lesson Content

Lesson 1

Works of mercy express our love for Christ by helping our neighbor.

Man is comprised of body and soul and, therefore, man has physical and spiritual needs. Both of these needs are cared for through the Corporal and Spiritual Works of Mercy.

Lesson 3

The Corporal Works of Mercy are for the physical needs of others. They are: feed the hungry; give drink to the thirsty; clothe the naked; visit the imprisoned; shelter the homeless; visit the sick; bury the dead.

Lesson 2

The Spiritual Works of Mercy are for the spiritual needs of others. They are: admonish the sinner; instruct the ignorant; counsel the doubtful; comfort the sorrowful; bear wrongs patiently; forgive all injuries; and pray for the living and the dead.

Lesson 4

Beatitude is the state of happiness of those who live the Christian life. There are eight Beatitudes, which speak of the blessings for: the poor in spirit; those who mourn; the meek; those who hunger and thirst for righteousness; the merciful; the pure of heart; those who are persecuted for righteousness sake; those who are persecuted on account of Christ.

LESSON ONE: WORKS OF MERCY

Aims

The students will learn that works of mercy express our love for Christ by helping our neighbor.

They will learn that man is comprised of body and soul and, therefore, man has physical and spiritual needs. Both of these needs are cared for through the corporal and spiritual works of mercy.

Materials

- *Activity Book*, p. 61

Optional:
- "Come with us, O blessed Jesus," *Adoremus Hymnal*, #626

Begin

Man is created in the image of God. He has dignity because of this. Does this mean we look like God? No, but man is created as a body and soul unity (see the Chalk Talk at right). The body is our physical being. Through the body we enjoy the senses. Man has a rational soul, which will live forever. Man is a spiritual being because of his soul. This is how he is in God's image. Because of this rational soul, man can learn, love, communicate, and make decisions. Both our bodies and souls need special care.

The Works of Mercy and Happiness

"Blessed are the merciful, for they shall obtain mercy."

Matthew 5:7

We grow in virtue, particularly in practicing the *works of mercy*. In these acts we show our love for Christ by helping our neighbor. Our Lord told us, "Then the just will ask him: 'Lord, when did we see you hungry and feed you or see you thirsty and give you drink? When did we welcome you away from home or clothe you in your nakedness? When did we visit you when you were ill or in prison?' The King will answer them: 'I assure you, as often as you did it for one of my least brothers, you did it for me' " (Mt 25:37–40).

Since we have both bodies and souls—and both require care—the works of mercy are divided into two groups. We care for our neighbors' souls and spiritual needs through the spiritual works of mercy. We care for their bodies and physical needs through corporal works of mercy (the Latin word *corpus* means "body").

Because our souls are the most important part of our human nature—the part by which we can think, know, and freely choose good or evil—the seven spiritual works of mercy are the most important. As we consider each of

them, think of how you can practice these in your life. Remember that the heart and soul of each of these works is love; love is their moving force.

Spiritual Works

Admonish the sinner. Because sin separates one from God, it is truly an act of love to help another person realize the seriousness of sin and the need for forgiveness. This does not mean humiliating someone in public or acting as if we ourselves have never sinned. Rather, we should quietly and tactfully steer our friends away from occasions of sin or encourage those who have sinned to seek forgiveness in the sacrament of Penance, giving them hope that they will be able to overcome sinful ways with the mercy of God.

Instruct the ignorant. Helping a person to learn or understand the truths that God has revealed to us is a second way to nourish another's spiritual life. Our religion teachers and parents, of course, do this for us, but there are also other ways to practice this work of mercy

110

Develop

1. Read paragraphs 1–3 (up to Spiritual Works).

2. Read the entirety of the Mt 25:31–46 (the Final Judgment). The students should be able to discuss the virtues practiced in each of the works of mercy listed by our Lord in his teaching on the Final Judgment. You may note in this passage that we will be judged on the charity we show to others.

3. We sometimes think that, to be Catholic, we should love God in our hearts, but we need not show it in the world. We may create a gulf between the world and our Faith. We are reminded by the works of mercy, that we need to care for both the spiritual and corporal (physical) needs of people— all people, including our enemies.

4. The spiritual works are more important because it is through the spiritual that we know and love God.

5. *Review that we must have grace in order for our good works to be meritorious. Without grace, good acts are merely humanitarian. With grace, they are works of charity and gain us treasure in heaven. We should always do these acts with love as their motivating force.*

6. *In practicing the works of mercy, we grow in virtue. Discuss how the works of mercy provide great opportunities to grow in the natural and supernatural virtues. Using examples of the works of mercy, discuss the virtues we exercise in doing these works.*

7. *Have the students think of modern day works of mercy. These may be the Spiritual and Corporal Works of Mercy, but with modern-day examples; e.g., care for addicts, instructing those who are lukewarm in their faith, etc.*

Name:_____

Works of Mercy

Answer the following questions in complete sentences.

1. How do the works of mercy help us to grow in virtue?
   The works of mercy help us grow in virtue because by practicing them, we begin to form good habits. They also enable us to show our love for God and neighbor

2. Why are there spiritual and corporal works of mercy?
   There are spiritual and corporal works of mercy because man is made up of both body and soul and both require care.

3. Why are the works of mercy most important?
   The works of mercy are most important because they nurture the soul, the highest part of human nature. The soul is that part of us whereby we think, know and, freely choose good and evil.

4. What are we preparing for by living the virtuous life and practicing the works of mercy?
   We are preparing for heaven by living the virtuous life and practicing the works of mercy.

5. What kind of happiness does a virtuous life lead to?
   A virtuous life leads to happiness that does not go away. It leads to the happiness of spiritual blessings which Our Lord refers to in the Sermon on the Mount. If we live a virtuous life, we will be happy in this life and in the next.

Reinforce

1. Have the students work on *Activity Book*, p. 61.

2. Give the students time to work on the Memorization Questions and Words to Know from this chapter.

3. Discuss the difference between good works done with and without grace.

4. *Discuss modern day works of mercy.*

5. *You may discuss ways to care for our bodies and souls.*

Conclude

1. Teach the students to sing "Come with us, O blessed Jesus," *Adoremus Hymnal*, #626.

2. Lead the students in praying an Act of Love.

Preview

In the next lesson, the students will learn about the Spiritual Works of Mercy.

CHALK TALK: MAN THE METAPHYSICAL MIXTURE

Man = body + soul =

NOTES

_____
_____
_____
_____
_____
_____
_____
_____
_____
_____
_____

LESSON TWO: SPIRITUAL WORKS

Aims

The students will learn that the Spiritual Works of Mercy call us to work for the spiritual needs of others. The Spiritual Works of Mercy are: admonish the sinner; instruct the ignorant; counsel the doubtful; comfort the sorrowful; bear wrongs patiently; forgive all injuries; and pray for the living and the dead.

Materials

- *Activity Book*, p. 62

  Optional:
  - "Come with us, O blessed Jesus," *Adoremus Hymnal*, #626

Begin

The Spiritual Works of Mercy call us to care for the spiritual life of others. These works are more important than the Corporal Works of Mercy, since the soul—the spiritual part of man— is eternal. Today, the students will learn more about the spiritual works, and find ways to practice them in life.

as well. There are many people who have not heard the message of the gospel in its fullness. We can often find opportunities to tell them about it, remembering the words of Our Lord:

> No one after lighting a lamp puts it in a cellar or under a bushel, but on a stand, that those who enter may see the light (Lk 11:33).

We have been given the "light of faith" and should not hide it but should let it shine forth. However, we must avoid preaching or acting as if we know all the answers.

Counsel the doubtful. To counsel someone means giving him advice or guidance. Those who most need this counsel are people who are weak in the virtues of faith and hope. For example, someone may reject certain beliefs of the faith—or at least question them—or may fall into despair, doubting that God will forgive him for his sins. These people need loving guidance and encouragement to strengthen them, thus bringing them closer to God once more.

Comfort the sorrowful. Suffering is a part of our life in this world. Indeed, Our Lord told us that those who wish to follow him must first take up their cross, just as he took up his Cross for us. Each of us has our own specific crosses that Our Lord asks us to bear out of love for him. This is not always easy, and this work of mercy reminds us that we should help one another to bear the sufferings in our lives. Sometimes a word of love and understanding can help. Sometimes a kind deed can lighten the burden of someone else's suffering.

111

Develop

1. Read paragraphs 4–10 (up to Corporal Works).

2. Discuss each of the Spiritual Works of Mercy, being sure the students understand them.

- *Admonish the sinner: helping another to realize his sin and to seek forgiveness. Review the horror or sin—it separates us from God and kills the life of grace in our souls (risking hell).*

- *Instruct the ignorant: helping someone understand the truths about God and the faith; nourishing the spiritual life.*

- *Counsel the doubtful: giving advice or guidance—especially to help people to walk in the ways of faith and hope.*

- *Comfort the sorrowful: Suffering is a part of life because of original sin. Those who suffer in union with Christ share in his glory. Sometimes, people need encouragement in their sufferings. We can help others or ease their burdens in their time of suffering.*

- *Bear wrongs patiently: to suffer injustice and accept the wrong done, instead of doing another wrong ourselves.*

- *Forgive all injuries: we must forgive those who injure us, imitating Christ's love and mercy.*

- *Pray for the living and the dead: this is an act of love for other members of the Communion of Saints.*

3. The students should be able to give examples of each of the Spiritual Works of Mercy.

Name:_____

Spiritual Works of Mercy

Explain each spiritual work of mercy.

WORK OF MERCY	EXPLANATION
Admonish the sinner	Tactfully and lovingly show our brothers and sisters the seriousness of sin and the need for forgiveness.
Instruct the ignorant	Helping others learn and understand the truths of God and our faith.
Counsel the doubtful	Lovingly guiding and encouraging those who need it and strengthening their faith and love of God.
Comfort the sorrowful	Helping one another bear the sorrows of life.
Bear wrongs patiently	To be patient and strong when being a victim of injustice.
Forgive all injuries	Forgive wrongs we suffer as we would want the Lord to forgive us.
Pray for the living and the dead	To pray for all the living and dead, even our enemies.

Faith and Life Series • Grade 8 • Chapter 16 • Lesson 2

Reinforce

1. Have the students work on *Activity Book*, p. 62.

2. Give the students time to work on the Memorization Questions and Words to Know from this chapter.

3. *Discuss the scenarios below, applying the Spiritual Works of Mercy. Have the students come up with their own examples.*

4. Find examples of ways the saints practiced the Spiritual Works of Mercy.

Conclude

1. Lead the class in singing "Come with us, O blessed Jesus," *Adoremus Hymnal*, #626.

2. Lead the students in praying an Act of Love.

Preview

In the next lesson, the students will learn about the Corporal Works of Mercy.

SCENARIOS FOR DISCUSSION ON THE SPIRITUAL WORKS OF MERCY

1. Your friend is going to throw a party when his parents are away.
2. Your friend asks about a religious picture in your house.
3. Your friend is angry at God because his relative died.
4. Your friend's boyfriend broke up with her.
5. You are being punished because your friends were caught drinking at a party—but you weren't.
6. Your best friend was talking about you behind your back, and is now sorry because he sees how upset you are.
7. Your uncle does not believe in God.
8. Your grandmother died and it is the anniversary of her death.

NOTES

_____
_____
_____
_____
_____
_____
_____
_____
_____
_____
_____
_____

LESSON THREE:
CORPORAL WORKS

Aims

The students will learn that the Corporal Works of Mercy call us to work for the physical needs of others. The Corporal Works of Mercy are: feed the hungry; give drink to the thirsty; clothe the naked; visit the imprisoned; shelter the homeless; visit the sick; bury the dead.

Materials

- *Activity Book*, p. 63

Optional:
- "Come with us, O blessed Jesus," *Adoremus Hymnal*, #626

Begin

Review the Spiritual Works of Mercy from the previous lesson, discussing examples of each.

Discuss the need to care for the physical well-being of others. Today, we will learn about the Corporal Works of Mercy.

Bear wrongs patiently. It is important to remember that it is better to suffer an injustice than to be guilty of committing one ourselves. In his Sermon on the Mount, Our Lord said:

I say to you. . . . Love your enemies, do good to those who hate you, bless those who curse you, pray for those who abuse you. To him who strikes you on the cheek, offer the other also; and from him who takes away your cloak do not withhold your coat as well (Lk 6:27–29).

This true charity is the mark of the Christian, and we must learn to be patient and strong when we are the victims of injustice. It is by such actions that we may draw others to Christ.

Forgive all injuries. Not only must we patiently bear these wrongs, we must also forgive those who injure us. In the *Lord's Prayer*, which Jesus taught us, we say, "Forgive us our trespasses, as we forgive those who trespass against us" (Mt 6:12). This means the measure by which we forgive will be the measure by which God will forgive us. By forgiving others we imitate the love that Christ shows for us. He offers forgiveness to all—even those who put him to death on the Cross.

Pray for the living and the dead. We have already seen that the Communion of Saints means that we can pray for one another. This act of love is one of the easiest—and one of the most important—ways to help others. We recall that charity toward our neighbor includes our enemies, and our prayers should extend to them as well. When we pray for those who have died, let us remember not only our relatives and friends, but also those souls who are most forgotten.

Corporal Works

The seven corporal works of mercy are those acts of love that Our Lord spoke about

112

when he described the Last Judgment. To those who practice these works Our Lord will say:

Come, O blessed of my Father, inherit the kingdom prepared for you from the foundation of the world; for I was hungry and you gave me food; I was thirsty and you gave me drink; I was a stranger and you welcomed me; I was naked and you clothed me; I was sick and you visited me; I was in prison and you came to me (Mt 25:34–36).

Feed the hungry, give drink to the thirsty, and clothe the naked. Most of us have been greatly blessed by God. Nevertheless, there are many people in the world—even some in our country—who lack many of the basic needs of life. We must not neglect these people. It is an obligation of charity to help them. While we may not be able to help these people directly or dramatically, we can contribute money or possessions to groups whose works are such charitable activities. For example, there may be an organization in your parish—such as the St. Vincent de Paul Society—which carries out these works of mercy.

These works of mercy start in the family. Parents are responsible for seeing that their children are fed and clothed. In the same way, when the children are older they are responsible for taking care of these needs for their aging parents. At this point in our lives we can practice these works of mercy in simple ways. For example, we can prepare lunch for a hungry brother or sister or share some of our clothes with others in our family. Families together can reach out to other poorer families. These acts of mercy will prepare us for greater works as we grow older.

Visit the imprisoned. There are many kinds of people in prison. There is the hardened criminal. Some great conversions have taken place among the most hardened, and perhaps

Develop

1. Read paragraphs 11–19 (up to the paragraphs on the Beatitudes—the last three paragraphs).

2. Discuss each of the Corporal Works of Mercy, being sure the students understand them.

- *Feed the hungry and give drink to the thirsty: every person deserves the necessities of life. We may know of places in the world where people are starving to death. There are people in our own country who go hungry.*

- *Clothe the naked: we must ensure that people have clothes to wear, for protection from weather and abuse.*

(There is an obligation of charity to be sure that all men have what is necessary for life. What charities in your parish or city provide food/drink and clothes for the poor? Have your class do a project to contribute to these charities.)

- *Visit the imprisoned: there are many people in prison and many experience conversion. Prisoners need encouragement to overcome their sins and help to be rehabilitated.*

- *Shelter the homeless: there are many people who are homeless; there are many homeless families. We need to ensure that people have a safe place to rest.*

- *Visit the sick: many people, when they are sick, find it hard to care for all the needs they have; e.g., grocery shopping, cooking, child care, etc. We can encourage them and help them with their recoveries.*

- *Bury the dead: because the body is sacred, it deserves proper burial after death and will one day be resurrected.*

3. Discuss examples of the Corporal Works of Mercy. Have the students work on a project to do these works.

Name:_____

Corporal Works of Mercy

Explain each corporal work of mercy.

WORK OF MERCY	EXPLANATION
Feed the hungry	<u>Answers will vary, but should be</u> <u>based on the student text.</u>
Give drink to the thirsty	
Clothe the naked	
Visit the imprisoned	
Shelter the homeless	
Visit the sick	
Bury the dead	

SCENARIOS FOR DISCUSSION ON THE CORPORAL WORKS OF MERCY

1. Your friend forgot his lunch.
2. The water in a neighborhood is contaminated because of flooding after a big storm.
3. Your neighbors have lost everything they had in a fire.
4. Your aunt just had a baby and has not been able to get out for a long time because of the care the baby needs.
5. There is a beggar on the corner who is homeless.
6. Your grandmother entered a nursing home for long-term care. Your brother has to go to the hospital to have his tonsils out.
7. An old neighbor who had no family has just died.

Reinforce

1. Have the students work on *Activity Book*, p. 63.

2. Give the students time to work on the Memorization Questions and Words to Know from this chapter.

3. Find ways to put the Corporal Works of Mercy into practice.

4. Discuss modern day applications of the Corporal Works of Mercy as age-appropriate and ways to practice them (e.g., it may not be practical for an eighth grade student to visit a prison or invite a homeless person into his home).

Conclude

1. Lead the class in singing "Come with us, O blessed Jesus," *Adoremus Hymnal*, #626.

2. Lead the students in praying an Act of Love.

Preview

In the next lesson, the students will learn about the Beatitudes.

NOTES

_____
_____
_____
_____
_____
_____
_____
_____
_____
_____
_____
_____
_____

LESSON FOUR: BEATITUDES

Aims

The students will learn that beatitude is the state of happiness of those who live the Christian life. There are eight Beatitudes which speak of the blessings for: the poor in spirit; those who mourn; the meek; those who hunger and thirst for righteousness; the merciful; the pure of heart; those who are persecuted for righteousness sake; and those who are persecuted on account of Christ.

The Spiritual Works of Mercy	The Corporal Works of Mercy
Admonish the sinner	Feed the hungry
Instruct the ignorant	Give drink to the thirsty
Counsel the doubtful	Clothe the naked
Comfort the sorrowful	Visit the imprisoned
Bear wrongs patiently	Shelter the homeless
Forgive all injuries	Visit the sick
Pray for the living and the dead	Bury the dead

the grace they received came through the prayers or kindness of people who knew them. There are some who were weak and made mistakes but are now sorry for what they have done. These people need to be encouraged, so that they will continue to reform their lives. Some are innocent. If we are able, we should help them obtain justice. In the meantime, they need our support.

There are still other people who are not in jail, but whose state in life can be like a prison —separating them from other people and the support such contact brings. For example, some who, for a long period of time, must care for a sick relative at home may need our visits to help him accept his present cross.

Shelter the homeless. There are many homeless people in our cities. We should pay attention to their great need. For example, Trevor Ferrell, a twelve-year-old boy in Philadelphia brought the street people blankets from his own home. The word got around and soon the whole neighborhood was helping. Finally they

even rented a house for the homeless. We may not always be able to do much directly for those people who are homeless. However, we can practice this work of mercy by being willing to share our homes with someone in need —for example, a friend whose home has been damaged by a fire or flood. We can also willingly share our own room with a brother or sister if this is needed in our family.

Visit the sick. The sick are often frightened and may be in particular need of encouragement. It is not always easy for us who are healthy to understand the suffering sick people go through. Visiting them may give them the strength they need to bear their cross. Perhaps they may need us in some practical way. Christ can touch them through our acts of love.

Bury the dead. The final act of mercy is mentioned in the Old Testament. The angel Raphael praised Tobias for this charitable act:

And when you buried the dead, I was likewise present with you. When you did

113

Materials

- *Activity Book*, p. 64

Optional:
- "Come with us, O blessed Jesus," *Adoremus Hymnal*, #626

Begin

Review the works of mercy, both corporal and spiritual.

Develop

1. Read paragraphs 20–22 (to the end of the chapter).

2. Discuss the Beatitudes. To beatify means to make happy. A beatitude is a special happiness or blessing of a special nature. The Beatitudes promise happiness for those who follow Christ's example.

3. Go through each of the Beatitudes, explaining them, and how we can follow them as a moral guide to virtues:

Blessed are the poor in spirit, for theirs is the kingdom of heaven.
- *Humility, liberality*

Blessed are those who mourn, for they shall be comforted.
- *Justice, meekness*

Blessed are the meek, for they shall inherit the earth.
- *Meekness, brotherly love*

Blessed are those who hunger and thirst for righteousness, for they shall be satisfied.

- *Diligence, justice, brotherly love*

Blessed are the merciful, for they shall obtain mercy.
- *Justice, brotherly love*

Blessed are the pure in heart, for they shall see God.
- *Chastity, prudence, moderation, brotherly love, temperance*

Blessed are those who are persecuted for righteousness, for theirs is the kingdom of heaven.
- *Fortitude, brotherly love, diligence,*

Blessed are you when men revile you and persecute you and utter all kinds of evil against you falsely on my account. Rejoice and be glad, for your reward is great in heaven.
- *Fortitude, temperance, meekness, humility*

4. Discuss how we can keep the Beatitudes by fulfilling the works of charity (both corporal and spiritual).

5. Discuss how the Beatitudes give a word-picture of Christ.

Name:_____

Beatitudes

Answer the following questions in complete sentences.

1. Write the Beatitudes.
    1. Blessed are the poor in spirit, for theirs is the Kingdom of heaven.
    2. Blessed are the meek, for they shall possess the land.
    3. Blessed are those who mourn, for they shall be comforted.
    4. Blessed are they who hunger and thirst for justice, for they shall have their fill.
    5. Blessed are the merciful, for they shall obtain mercy.
    6. Blessed are the pure of heart, for they shall see God.
    7. Blessed are the peacemakers, for they shall be called the children of God.
    8. Blessed are they who suffer persecution for justice's sake, for theirs is the Kingdom of Heaven.

2. What happiness does Jesus promise to those who live the moral life?
    Jesus promises happiness in the next life and peace and joy in this life.

3. Why does Jesus, contrary to the opinion of the world, call the person who is humble and suffers tribulations happy?
    Contrary to the world's opinion, Jesus calls the person who is humble and suffers tribulation happy because his true joy is the lasting happiness of eternal life.

4. Can they who follow the maxims of the world be truly happy?
    They who follow the maxims of the world cannot be truly happy because there happiness is fleeting and only brings temporary pleasure.

64   *Faith and Life Series • Grade 8 • Chapter 16 • Lesson 4*

Reinforce

1. Have the students work on *Activity Book*, p. 64.

2. Give the students time to work on the Memorization Questions and Words to Know from this chapter and to prepare for the chapter and unit quizzes.

3. Have the students memorize the Corporal and Spiritual Works of Mercy and the Beatitudes.

4. Have the students discuss the promises made in the Beatitudes. Are they attractive to us?

5. Imagine how the Beatitudes would have sounded in the time of Christ. What a difference for the Jews, who had learned the dictum, "an eye for an eye and a tooth for a tooth." The Jewish people were oppressed by the Romans; their history was plagued with exile. The students should compose an essay on the probable Jewish response to Christ's Beatitudes.

Conclude

1. Lead the class in singing "Come with us, O blessed Jesus," *Adoremus Hymnal*, #626.

2. Lead the students in praying an Act of Love.

Preview

In the next lesson, the students' understanding of the material covered in this chapter will be reviewed and assessed.

BEATITUDE SAINT: PIER GIORGIO

Known as "The Man of the Beatitudes," Blessed Pier Giorgio never swerved in his devotion and love for the poor and the sick. Born in 1901 in Turin, Italy, the son of a newspaper publisher and Italian ambassador to Germany, Pier Giorgio was a robust, good humored young man whose favorite pastime was mountain climbing. Despite the privileges he was born to, Pier Giorgio found his greatest joy in the Eucharist and sought to share his love of God with the poor, often giving money or even the coat off his back to people he met on the street. In 1925, at the age of 24, he died of an illness caught while tending the sick. To the surprise of his family, huge crowds filled the streets for his funeral procession.

NOTES

_____
_____
_____
_____
_____
_____
_____
_____
_____
_____
_____

_____

not hesitate to rise and leave your dinner in order to go and lay out the dead, your good deed was not hidden from me (Tob 12:12–13).

By this action we show respect for the body, because it is part of the human being. We can practice this work of mercy by attending a funeral of someone we knew—and offering consolation to those who are bereaved—or by respecting cemeteries, perhaps leaving flowers at the grave site of a relative.

By living the virtuous life and practicing the works of mercy, we will be _happy_ for ever with God in heaven. This is the happiness of which Our Lord spoke in the Sermon on the Mount (Mt 5:3–11). He promised this happiness to those who live the Christian life, which he summarized in the eight _Beatitudes_.

"Beatify" means "to make happy." A beatitude is a special happiness or blessing of a spiritual nature. These eight Beatitudes are the promises for happiness that Christ makes to those who faithfully accept his teaching and follow his example.

The happiness of which Our Lord speaks, however, is not what the world identifies with happiness—money, power, fame, and so on. Even when such things bring us pleasure or happiness, it is fleeting. The happiness that belongs to the _meek, the pure in heart_, and so on is the lasting happiness of eternal life. This happiness brings us true joy and peace even in our life on earth. It is the happiness which no one can take from us. It lasts for ever.

> **Q. 110** _What are the spiritual works of mercy?_
> The spiritual works of mercy are admonish the sinner; instruct the ignorant; counsel the doubtful; comfort the sorrowful; bear wrongs patiently; forgive all injuries; pray for the living and the dead (CCC 2447).
>
> **Q. 111** _What are the corporal works of mercy?_
> The corporal works of mercy are feed the hungry; give drink to the thirsty; clothe the naked; visit the imprisoned; shelter the homeless; visit the sick; bury the dead (CCC 2447).

114

Name:

The Works of Mercy And Happiness   **Quiz 16**

Part I: Match the action with the work of mercy.

1. _A_ Going to the hospital to visit cancer patients
2. _F_ Writing to a lonely person in a nursing home
3. _G_ A friend whose parents are away stays with you
4. _N_ Accepting an unfair group punishment
5. _I_ Praying for the souls in purgatory
6. _D_ Taking old coats to a children's shelter
7. _E_ Helping a convert understand their faith
8. _J_ Teaching your brother his prayers
9. _K_ Cooking for a widow
10. _C_ Telling your friend that his sin offends God
11. _L_ Giving canned goods to the food bank
12. _B_ Going to a funeral
13. _H_ Forgiving someone who bullied you
14. _M_ Your father is working hard outside and you get him a cold glass of water

a. Visit the sick
b. Bury the dead
c. Admonish the sinner
d. Clothe the naked
e. Instruct the ignorant
f. Visit the imprisoned
g. Shelter the homeless
h. Forgive all injuries
i. Pray for the living and dead
j. Comfort the doubtful
k. Comfort the sorrowful
l. Feed the hungry
m. Give drink to the thirsty
n. Bear wrongs patiently

Part II: Fill in the chart.

BEATITUDE	PROMISE
Blessed are the poor in spirit	the Kingdom of Heaven is theirs
Blessed are those who mourn	they shall be comforted
Blessed are the meek	they shall inherit the earth
Blessed are those who hunger and thirst for justice	they shall be satisfied
Blessed are the merciful	for they shall obtain mercy
Blessed are the clean of heart	they shall see God
Blessed are those who are persecuted for rightousness sake	theirs is the Kingdom of Heaven
Blessed are the peacemakers	for they shall be called the children of God

A - 22   *Faith and Life • Grade 8 • Appendix A*

Aims

The students' understanding of the material covered in this chapter and unit will be reviewed and assessed

Materials

- Quiz 16, Appendix, p. A-22
- Unit 4 Test, Appendix, pp. A-23–A-24

Optional:
- "Come with us, O blessed Jesus," Adoremus, 626

Assess

1. Distribute the quizzes and read through them with the students to be sure they understand the questions.

2. Administer the quiz. As they hand in their work, you may orally quiz the students on the Memorization Questions from this chapter.

3. After all the quizzes have been handed in, review the correct answers with the class. Repeat steps 1–3 for the unit test.

Conclude

1. Lead the class in singing "Come with us, O blessed Jesus," *Adoremus Hymnal*, #626.

2. End class with an Act of Charity.

Review

1. The students should know the Spiritual and Corporal Works of Mercy. They should be able to give examples of each.

2. The students should know all of the Beatitudes.

CHAPTER SEVENTEEN
VOCATIONS: RELIGIOUS LIFE AND PRIESTHOOD

Catechism of the Catholic Church References

Christian Holiness: 2012–16, 2028–29
Church's Hierarchical Constitution: 871–96, 934–39
Ecclesial Ministry: 874–79
Evangelical Counsels and Consecrated Life: 914–33, 944–45
Eremitical Life: 920–21
Consecrated Virgins: 922–24
Religious Life: 925–27
Secular Institutions: 928–29

Societies of Apostolic Life: 930
Holy Orders: 1536–1600
Jesus, Our Teacher and Model of Holiness: 468–69, 516, 519–21, 561
Priesthood: 1536, 1562–67
      Celibacy: 1579, 1599
      Obedience to the Bishop: 1567
Sacrifice: 2099–2100
Vocation of the Laity: 782–86, 898–913, 940–43

Scripture References

Poverty: Mt 19:16–30
Chastity: Mt 19:10–12

Obedience: Lk 22:42

Summary of Lesson Content

Lesson 1

All Christians share the call to holiness.

God has a plan for every person. God calls each of us to a vocation. The particular vocations include laity, religious life, and (for men) holy orders. Our vocation allows us to follow Christ most perfectly on earth. We are to seek holiness in the state of life that God calls us to live.

Lesson 2

Religious life is the highest vocation. It consists in following the three evangelical counsels of poverty, chastity, and obedience. Those who live the counsels take vows (free, deliberate promises made to God), which free them to live entirely for God and to serve his Church.

The evangelical counsels, lived in imitation of Christ, are a witness to the eternal state of heaven.

Lesson 3

Religious communities have been instituted throughout history for those called to religious life. There are communities for men and for women. In both, members live by a rule, or way of life.

Contemplative orders spend their days in prayer, withdrawn from the world. Apostolic orders dedicate themselves to active service of God and neighbor through the works of mercy.

Lesson 4

The Sacrament of Holy Orders has three degrees: episcopate, presbyterate, and deaconate.

The priesthood calls a man to live as "another Christ". It is a sacrificial life in service to the life of the Church through the sacraments. Priests promise to pray the Divine Office, obey their bishop, and live a life of celebacy.

Some priests are members of religious communities.

LESSON ONE: VOCATIONS

Aims

The students will learn that all Christians share the call to holiness.

They will learn that God has a plan for every person. God calls each of us to a vocation. The particular vocations include laity, religious life, and (for men) holy orders. Our vocation allows us to follow Christ most perfectly on earth. We are to seek holiness in the state of life that God calls us to live.

Materials

- *Activity Book*, p. 65   Optional:
  - "Of the glorious Body telling," *Adoremus Hymnal*, #392

Begin

God is all knowing. His loving care for man considers each and every one of us. He loves each of us and has a plan for every person. Jesus died for each of us on the Cross (individually and collectively). He wants each of us to be saved. His plan for man is fulfilled through the collective works of individuals. God has something for each of us to do—something that only we can do. It is profoundly important that we discern God's will in our lives.

CHAPTER 17

Vocations: The Religious Life and the Priesthood

Greater love has no man than this, that a man lay down his life for his friends.

John 15:1

"Under the impulse of love, which the Holy Spirit pours into their hearts, they live more and more for Christ and for his Body, the Church. The more fervently, therefore, they join themselves to Christ by this gift of their whole life, the fuller does the Church's life become and the more vigorous and fruitful its apostolate" (PC, 1).

In an earlier chapter we spoke of the vocation that all of us share as Christians—to follow Christ and ultimately to be with God in heaven. Yet, each must pursue this goal differently, according to his own temperament and particular call from God. The vocation of most Christians is the life of a layman or laywoman in the world. For others, though, it will be the priestly or religious life.

We have seen that, from the beginning of Christianity, some in the Church have directly consecrated their lives to God by a vow. Although not everyone is called to this life, Our Lord invites many to follow him in this way. In the Gospels he tells us of the reward that will be given to those who answer this call:

And every one who has left houses or brothers or sisters or father or mother or children or lands for my name's sake, will receive a hundredfold, and inherit eternal life (Mt 19:29).

The call to the priesthood or the religious life is a vocation to follow Christ most perfectly on earth. Once Our Lord was approached by a rich young man who asked what he must do to have eternal life. Our Lord told him:

"If you would enter life, keep the commandments. . . ." The young man said to him, "All these I have observed; what do I still lack?" Jesus said to him, "If you would be perfect, go, sell what you possess and give to the poor, and you will have treasure in heaven; and come, follow me" (Mt 19:17, 20–21).

Here Jesus was speaking of the call to the religious life—following the counsels of perfection.

Although this vocation is the highest call, God does not intend everyone to live the religious life. Each of us must seek holiness in the state that God wants us to live. The consecrat-

115

Develop

1. Read paragraphs 1–4 (up to Religious Life).

2. Discuss how the students may discern their particular callings. First, each must consider the natural:
- *What are his talents and skills?*
- *What is his temperament?*
- *What are his personal longings/goals?*
- *How are events in his life directed? (these are not just coincidences)*

Next, they must consider the supernatural:
- *How can they use these gifts for the Church and for God's greater glory?*
- *How is God calling them? (this can be known by joy, peace, and a sense of rightness)*
- *Do they have a sense of what God wants of them? (an interior sense of direction in their lives)*
- *Prayer—how is God speaking to their hearts?*

Have the students record their discernment in their journals, answering these questions.

3. Review that, with a vow, we are truly freed. Sometimes, we keep too many options open, and are not able truly to commit and serve. A vow, in any state of life, enables one truly to commit and know how to serve God most faithfully, whether it be in loving and serving a family, serving the Church in community, or even individually. We can only be truly happy in our real vocation (e.g., if one is called to be a religious, but gets married, he will not be happy).

4. The religious life and priesthood are the most perfect vocations to follow Christ and serve his Church since those who accept these vocations have made Christ and his Church their first priority and greatest love. They are examples for us and models of the eternal, in which we all live in union with God and one another in the Mystical Body.

Name:_____

Vocations

I. Answer the following questions in complete sentences.

1. What vocation do all of us share as Christians?
   Each of us is called to holiness and to follow Christ so that we might live forever with him in heaven.

2. Why do we also have particular vocations?
   We also have particular vocations because each man pursues the goal of heaven and holiness according to his temperament and particular call from God.

II. Write a brief essay on why the call to religious life is the highest calling. Discuss what Jesus asks of and promises to those who are called; how it allows them to follow Christ more perfectly; and why, if this is objectively a higher call, not everyone is called to it.
   Answers will vary.

_____
_____
_____
_____
_____
_____
_____
_____
_____
_____
_____
_____
_____
_____

Reinforce

1. Have the students work on *Activity Book*, p. 65.

2. Give the students time to work on their Memorization Questions and Words to Know.

3. Have the students take time to discern their call and record their answers to the questions in *Develop 2*.

4. Invite guests to come to the class to discuss the various vocations. Include among these guests religious brothers and sisters, priests, married people, and consecrated singles.

5. The students may break into small groups and discuss their vocational calls.

Conclude

1. Teach the students to sing "Of the glorious Body telling," *Adoremus Hymnal*, #392.

2. End class with a prayer for vocations.

Preview

In the next lesson, the students will learn about religious life.

CHALK TALK: STATES OF LIFE

STATES OF LIFE

consecrated   secular

priesthood   religious life   married   single

NOTES

_____
_____
_____
_____
_____
_____
_____
_____
_____
_____
_____

LESSON TWO: RELIGIOUS LIFE

Aims

The students will learn that religious life is the highest vocation. It consists in following the three evangelical counsels of poverty, chastity, and obedience. Those who live the counsels take vows (free, deliberate promises made to God), which free them to live entirely for God and to serve his Church.

They will learn that the evangelical counsels, lived in imitation of Christ, are a witness to the eternal state of heaven.

Materials

- *Activity Book*, p. 66

Optional:
- "Of the glorious Body telling," *Adoremus Hymnal*, #392

Begin

Review what a vow is. It is a promise made to God. It is binding before God and man. It must be made freely. A vow is truly liberating because it allows us to love and serve God and his Church. Discuss what vows are made in marriage (fidelity and openness to family), religious life (poverty, chastity, and obedience), and holy orders (chastity, obedience to the bishop).

ed life calls for great generosity. Objectively, religious life is the most perfect. This does not mean that a lay person cannot attain perfection. Every vocation leads to holiness. Everyone must try to find out what God calls him to.

Religious Life

The religious life consists in following the three **evangelical counsels**, also known as the counsels of perfection. These are recommendations for perfect love taught and practiced by Christ—poverty, chastity, and obedience. Those who follow these counsels take *vows* (free, deliberate promises made to God) to keep each one. They willingly give up certain good things of this life—money and possessions, marriage, and liberty—in order to devote themselves more completely to loving and serving God and neighbor. These vows set a person free from temporal goods, so that he may freely give himself to love of God and neighbor.

116

The first counsel is poverty. The person who takes this vow gives up his earthly possessions in order to follow Christ. In our modern world, where so much emphasis is placed upon jobs, money, and possessions, this is indeed a sacrifice, even for one who is not rich.

Through religious life Christ calls for a life of total consecration in individual service to God and to one's neighbor. This means that you give to God the highest natural goods. One of these is the loving union with another person in marriage and family life. Human love in marriage is a holy thing, which Our Lord has blessed. Thus the sacrifice involved in giving this up is truly great. By the vow of chastity a person consecrates himself more completely to God, surrendering the good of marriage.

Since one might fulfill the counsels of poverty and chastity but still be filled with love of self, God asks one final sacrifice of the person who dedicates his life to him. He asks that one surrender his own personal preferences and wishes. This is the vow of obedience. The person who follows this path then gives up his liberty, submitting himself completely through his legitimate religious superiors, to the will of God as it is manifest in the Church.

One who enters the religious life, practicing the vows of poverty, chastity, and obedience, does so in imitation of Christ himself. At his death Our Lord had nothing; the soldiers even cast lots for the clothes he had been wearing (Mt 27:35). At one time he said of himself, ". . . . the Son of man has nowhere to lay his head" (Mt 8:20). We know Our Lord never married; he spent his public life preaching and teaching the Good News. Most important, he submitted his will to his Father in heaven. This was particularly demonstrated on the eve of his death, when he prayed in the Garden of Gethsemane. Knowing what lay ahead of him, he said:

Develop

1. *Read paragraphs 1–6 (up to the section on various religious communities).*

2. *Religious life consists in following the three evangelical counsels. They are the way, taught and practiced by Jesus Christ, to achieve perfect love. Look up the following passages:*
   - *Poverty: Mt 19:16–30*
   - *Chastity: Mt 19:10–12*
   - *Obedience: Lk 22:42*
   Discuss these passages and the value of these virtues.

3. Discuss how religious life is a closer imitation of Christ's teaching and example.

4. Should all people live these evangelical counsels? Why or why not? We must act according to our state in life, but all are called to the evangelical counsels.

5. *Discuss the evangelical counsels and copy the Chalk Talk at right.*

6. How are religious to be an example to all people? Discuss the importance of living their vows faithfully (and joyfully).

7. If you have religious in your diocese, take the class to visit their community and learn more about the religious life. Otherwise, have the students write questions for the religious, and ask the religious to respond. This may be better for cloistered communities.

8. *Discuss how, if one feels called to religious life, he can find the right order. He can contact the office of vocations in his diocese, visit communities, do research on the internet.*

Name:_____

Religious Life

Answer the following questions in complete sentences.

1. What are the evangelical counsels and why do religious vow to follow them?
<u>The evangelical counsels are the counsels</u>
<u>of perfection, the recommendations for</u>
<u>perfect love, taught and practiced by</u>
<u>Christ. They are poverty, chastity,</u>
<u>and obedience.</u>

2. What are vows?
<u>Vows are free and deliberate promises</u>
<u>made to God.</u>

3. Explain the vow of poverty.
<u>The vow of poverty is the promise to live a life detached from</u>
<u>earthly possessions in order to better follow Christ.</u>

4. Explain the vow of chastity.
<u>The vow of chastity is where one consecrates himself totally to</u>
<u>God and gives up the good of marriage for the sake of the</u>
<u>Kingdom of Heaven.</u>

5. Explain the vow of obedience.
<u>The vow of obedience is the surrender of one's personal pref-</u>
<u>erences and the promise to obey and submit to his legitimate</u>
<u>religious superiors.</u>

6. Explain how each of the evangelical counsels can help one to conform his life to Christ.
<u>Each of the evangelical counsels helps one conform his life to</u>
<u>Christ by imitating him. Our Lord lived and died as a poor man.</u>
<u>He lived a life of chastity, and he did not do his own will but</u>
<u>the will of his Father.</u>

66   *Faith and Life Series • Grade 8 • Chapter 17 • Lesson 2*

Reinforce

1. Have the students work on *Activity Book*, p. 66.

2. Give the students time to work on their Memorization Questions and Words to Know.

3. Have the students discuss ways they can live poverty, chastity, and obedience according to their state in life.

4. Visit a rectory or convent and assist the religious there by doing yard work, helping with their particular apostolate, or visiting the elderly living there.

5. The students may write letters to religious.

6. Use resources available to find various religious communities from all over your country and around the world.

Conclude

1. Lead the students in singing "Of the glorious Body telling," *Adoremus Hymnal*, #392.

2. End class with a prayer for vocations.

Preview

In the next lesson, the students will learn about religious communities.

CHALK TALK: EVANGELICAL COUNCILS

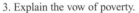

Chalk Talk	Poverty	Chastity	Obedience
Good offered to God	Property	Marriage	Freewill
Benefit	Freedom to be concerned about God's business	Freedom to love God and neighbor more generously	Freedom to do God's will more perfectly

NOTES

_____
_____
_____
_____
_____
_____
_____
_____
_____
_____
_____
_____
_____

LESSON THREE: COMMUNITIES

Aims

The students will learn that religious communities have been instituted throughout history for those called to religious life. There are communities for men and for women. In both, members live by a rule, or way of life.

They will learn that contemplative orders spend their days in prayer, withdrawn from the world. Apostolic orders dedicate themselves to active service of God and neighbor through the works of mercy.

Materials

• *Activity Book*, p. 67   Optional:
　　　　　　　　　　　• "Of the glorious
　　　　　　　　　　　　Body telling," *Adoremus Hymnal*, #392

Begin

If you have done Reinforce 5 from the previous lesson (p. 209), have the students present their findings on various religious communities. If you have not done this, do so now. It is important for the students to understand that there are differences between various religious communities. Minimally, the students should research religious communities in your diocese: Franciscans, Carmelites, Dominicans, Benedictines, and Jesuits.

"Father, in your plan for our salvation you provide shepherds for your people. Fill your Church with the spirit of courage and love. Raise up worthy ministers for your altars and ardent but gentle servants of the gospel. Grant this through Our Lord Jesus Christ, your Son, who lives and reigns with you and the Holy Spirit, one God, for ever and ever. Amen."

(Sacramentary, Mass for Priestly Vocations)

Father, if thou art willing, remove this cup from me; nevertheless not my will, but thine, be done (Lk 22:42).

Those in the religious life are an example to all people. They remind us of the importance of placing God first in our lives. Although we are not all called to sacrifice these goods, even those living in the world are called to place their love of God above the love of possessions, family, and self.

As we have seen, various religious communities have been officially instituted throughout history for those who are called to the religious life. There are communities for men and others for women. In both, members live a community life according to a particular rule. Prayer and contemplation ordered to a more perfect love of God and neighbor are the basic work of all religious communities. For some communities this is their principal work. These members of *contemplative* orders spend their days in prayer, by which they serve God and the entire Church. This is a great work that helps the world tremendously, since there are so many who forget God. The **contemplatives** usually live a *cloistered* life, separated completely from the world and working within their monasteries or convents to support themselves. The Benedictine and Cistercian communities, as well as some Carmelite communities, are examples of the contemplative religious life.

Other religious communities dedicate themselves to a more active service of God and neighbor by engaging in various works of mercy —both corporal and spiritual. These active orders may operate schools, hospitals, or

117

Develop

1. Read paragraphs 7 and 8 (up to Priesthood).

2. You may discuss how a religious community is formed and instituted. You may use the lives of the saints, such as Francis and Clare, as examples.

3. Discuss the benefits of contemplative orders. The Contemplative life is the heart of the Church. These religious live in union with Christ—an intimate union of love. Their greatest work is prayer. We often fail to see the value of this way of life, but prayer is the most important work in the Church—without it, all other works would not be fruitful. Most of these communities live apart from the world; they never leave their communities. In this way, their communities are safe-havens of union with Christ in the world. They are like tabernacles. The cloistered religious live in total service to our Lord, always remaining in his presence.

4. Discuss the benefits of apostolic communities/active orders. These communities dedicate themselves to the active works of God—especially the works of mercy (corporal and spiritual). Many orders serve in schools, hospitals, orphanages, etc. Each community has a particular apostolate (work) that exemplifies their charism. In serving in this work, they serve Christ and bring Christ to the world. It is important to note that even in active orders, the religious must be rooted in prayer.

6. Discuss the attire (habits, cords, veils, scapulars, etc.) of religious. Some religious do not wear clothing to identify them as religious. They must be distinguished and may wear a cross, pin, or something else to identify themselves.

Name:_____

Religious Communities

In the chart below, compare contemplative and active religious communities using your text as a guide.

CONTEMPLATIVE	ACTIVE
<u>Answers will vary.</u>	

Reinforce

1. Have the students work on *Activity Book*, p. 67.

2. Give the students time to work on their Memorization Questions and Words to Know.

3 Make a presentation on the attire of religious.

4. *Have the students write an essay titled "If I were called to religious life I would join an active/contemplative community because . . ." They may choose to write about a specific community if they wish.*

Conclude

1. Lead the students in singing "Of the glorious Body telling." *Adoremus Hymnal*, #392.

2. End class with a prayer for vocations.

Preview

In the next lesson, the students will learn about Holy Orders.

CHALK TALK: CHRIST THE CENTER

Christ's love and love for Christ are the center

Community
community
contemplation
Christ
prayer
life
apostolate

of all the activities of religious life whether contemplative or active

NOTES

_____
_____
_____
_____
_____
_____
_____
_____
_____
_____
_____

LESSON FOUR: HOLY ORDERS

Aims

The students will learn that the Sacrament of Holy Orders has three degrees, or levels: episcopate, presbyterate, and deaconate.

They will learn that the priesthood calls a man to live as "another Christ." It is a sacrificial life in service to the life of the Church through the sacraments. They promise to say the Divine Office, obey their bishop, and live a life of celibacy.

They will learn that some priests are members of religious communities.

Materials

- *Activity Book*, p. 68   Optional:
  - "Of the glorious Body telling," *Adoremus Hymnal*, #392

Begin

Define the Sacrament of Holy Orders for the students.

You may choose to discuss the difference between the lay/common priesthood, in which we all have a share by Baptism, and the ministerial priesthood, in which priests are ordained through Holy Orders.

"If you would be perfect, go, and sell what you possess and give to the poor, and you will have treasure in heaven; then come, follow me."

(Matthew 19:21)

orphanages. There is one community of sisters who both visit and pray for those in prison, helping them to reform their lives. This order has, in fact, many sisters who were once prisoners themselves. Mother Teresa's Missionaries of Charity are an active community who care for those who are dying and perform other active works. This active work, however, must always flow from and be an expression of the prayer life of these religious communities. Prayer, then, even in the active religious life is the basis for all their work.

Priesthood

There is a very special calling of Christ which is of great importance in the Church. It is not something one can simply choose, but something one is called to. It is the priesthood, the sacrament of Holy Orders. This call to exercise the priestly power of Christ and to be "another Christ" is a great honor but also a

great and beautiful sacrifice. Those who have received Holy Orders share most perfectly in the redeeming work of Jesus Christ. They are the ministers of grace to the Church, as they administer the sacraments.

Some priests or clergy are members of a religious community. The **clergy** is made up of deacons, priests, and bishops. Most ordained ministers in the Church have been called to serve Christ as *diocesan clergy*. They are members of a particular diocese, often serving in parish work.

At their ordination the diocesan clergy promise obedience to their bishop, and bishops owe their obedience to the Pope. In the Latin rite the priests do not marry, taking a vow (or promise) of **celibacy**. However, in the Latin rite permanent deacons may be married, and in some Eastern rites priests may be married. Those who are married do promise, however, not to marry again if their spouse dies. Diocesan clergy are not bound to take a vow of

---

Church Teaching

"This then is the primary purpose, this the central idea of Christian virginity: to aim only at the divine, to turn thereto the whole mind and soul; to want to please God in everything, to think of him continually, to consecrate body and soul to him."

(Holy Virginity, Pius XII, March 25, 1954)

118

Develop

1. Read paragraphs 9–12 (to the end of the chapter).

2. Review the three degrees of Holy Orders.
- *Bishops (episcopate): have the fullness of Holy Orders, are successors of the Apostles, and may celebrate all seven sacraments. Their work is to teach, sanctify, and govern a diocese.*
- *Priests (presbyterate): are co-workers of the Bishop, who teach, sanctify, and govern in obedience to the Bishop in a given parish community. They cannot ordain and need faculties to be granted in order to celebrate Confirmation.*
- *Deacons (deaconate): are also co-workers of the Bishop. They may celebrate marriages and Baptism and lead others in worship through the Liturgy of the Word in funerals and prayer services. They may serve at the Altar as Ordinary Ministers of Holy Communion. There are permanent and transitional deacons. Permanent deacons may be married before they are ordained.*

3. Review the ordination rite with the students.

4. Review that men must be called to the priesthood—it is nobody's right to become a priest. The priesthood is a life of sacrifice and service. (You may want to address why the Church does not have women priests.)

5. Discuss the daily lives of priests (they do much more than say Mass). If possible, have a priest visit your class to answer questions. You may want to preview the students' questions.

6. Discuss the differences between religious and diocesan clergy.

7. You may discuss married deacons/priests. Permanent deacons can be married at the time of ordination, but they may not remarry if they are widowed. Eastern rite priests may be married, but may not remarry.

Priesthood

Answer the following questions in complete sentences.

1. Can someone simply choose to become a priest? Explain.

   <u>No, someone cannot simply choose to be a priest. He must be called by God.</u>

2. What does it mean for a priest to be "another Christ"?

   <u>For a priest to be "another Christ" means that he acts in the person of Christ. It is by Christ's power that sins are forgiven in Confession. Christ acts through the priest to change bread and wine into the Body, Blood, Soul and Divinity of Jesus.</u>

3. How do those who have received Holy Orders share most perfectly in the redeeming work of Jesus Christ?

   <u>Those who have received Holy Orders share most perfectly in the redeeming work of Jesus Christ because they are the ministers of grace in the Church and they administer the sacraments.</u>

4. What are the three kinds of clergy?

   <u>The three kinds of clergy are bishops, priests, and deacons.</u>

5. What types of clergy can be married?

   <u>In the Latin Rite, deacons may be married and in some Eastern Rites priests may marry. However, in both rites, if the spouse dies, they may not remarry.</u>

6. What promises do diocesan clergy make?

   <u>Diocesan clergy promise chastity and obedience.</u>

68   *Faith and Life Series • Grade 3 • Chapter 17 • Lesson 4*

Reinforce

1. Have the students work on *Activity Book*, p. 68.

2. Give the students time to work on their Memorization Questions and Words to Know and prepare for the quiz.

3. Invite a priest to class to answer your students' questions about Holy Orders and the priesthood. If he is not able to visit your class, write letters to the priests of your parish.

Conclude

1. Lead the students in singing "Of the glorious Body telling," *Adoremus Hymnal*, #392.

2. End class with a prayer for vocations.

Preview

In the next lesson, the students' understanding of the material covered in this chapter will be reviewed and assessed.

POPE JOHN PAUL II: SACRED ORDINATION

In his 1994 Apostolic Letter *Ordinatio Sacerdotalis*, Pope John Paul II addressed the issue of women's ordination. He wrote: "In order that all doubt may be removed regarding a matter of great importance, a matter which pertains to the Church's divine constitution itself, in virtue of my ministry of confirming the brethren (cf. Lk 22:32) I declare that the Church has no authority whatsoever to confer priestly ordination on women and that this judgment is to be definitively held by all the Church's faithful." This does not mean that women are second-class citizens within the Church. There are many wonderful and important ways that women can serve God—but the priesthood is not one of them.

SUGGESTED READING ON THIS ISSUE

Pope John Paul II. *Mulieris Dignitatem*. On the dignity and vocation of women.

C.S. Lewis. *God in the Dock*.

Manfred Hauke. *Women in the Priesthood?*

poverty. They may own things and usually receive a small salary for their personal expenses. They try to live a simple life in order to imitate Our Lord more closely and to be a witness for Christ to the world.

The Church needs many men and women to follow Christ, answering God's call to the religious life and the priesthood. We should pray to know if this is God's will for us. Even if this is not our vocation, we should pray that those who are called will joyfully respond, for:

The harvest is plentiful, but the laborers are few; pray therefore the Lord of the harvest to send out laborers into his harvest (Mt 9:37–38).

Words to Know:
evangelical counsels
clergy contemplative celibacy

"Father, you call all who believe in you to grow perfect in love by following in the footsteps of Christ your Son. May those whom you have chosen to serve you as religious provide by their way of life a convincing sign of your Kingdom for the Church and the whole world. We ask this through Our Lord Jesus Christ, your Son, who lives and reigns with you and the Holy Spirit, one God, for ever and ever. Amen."

(Sacramentary, Mass for Religious Vocations)

119

Q. 112 *Is the priesthood a great dignity?*

Yes, the priesthood is a great dignity because of its powers to consecrate the Eucharist and to forgive sins. Those who receive this great dignity have the sublime mission of leading men to holiness and the life of the blessed (CCC 1563).

Q. 113 *How may one enter into Holy Orders?*

To enter Holy Orders, one must be called by God and submit his desire to the authority of the Church. He must have the vocation to Holy Orders, with the disposition required by the sacred ministry (CCC 1578).

Q. 114 *What are the evangelical counsels?*

The evangelical counsels are vows of poverty, chastity, and obedience, and are called evangelical because they were given to us by Jesus in the Gospels (CCC 915, 944).

Q. 115 *What is religious life?*

Religious life is a gift of self to God through public profession of the evangelical counsels. The religious life gives witness to Christ's union with the Church (CCC 925).

120

CHAPTER SEVENTEEN
REVIEW AND ASSESSMENT

Aims

The students' understanding of the material covered in this chapter will be reviewed and assessed.

Materials

- Quiz 17, Appendix, p. A-25

  Optional:
  - "Of the glorious Body telling," *Adoremus Hymnal*, #392

Name: _____

Vocations: The Religious Life and the Priesthood **Quiz 17**

Part I: Define the following terms.

Religious: <u>those whose life vocation is to follow Christ most perfectly on earth</u>

Clergy: <u>ordained ministers (bishops, priests, deacons)</u>

Vows: <u>free, deliberate promises made to God</u>

Part II: Answer in complete sentences.

1. Why is religious life/priesthood a higher vocation than marriage?
   <u>The religious life/priesthood is a higher vocation than marriage because it is a call to follow Christ most perfectly on earth. Although this vocation is the highest call, God does not intend everyone to live as religious. Each of us must seek holiness in the state that God wants us to live.</u>

2. What is the difference between a contemplative and an active religious community?
   <u>A contemplative community is cloistered and separated from the world completely, living and working within the monastery. An active religious community engages in works of mercy in the world. This active work, however, flows from their prayer.</u>

Part III: Fill in the chart.

EVANGELICAL COUNSEL	GOOD OFFERED TO GOD	BENEFIT
poverty	money and possessions	detachment from earthly goods
chastity	marriage	more completely consecrated to God
obedience	independence and freedom	complete surrender to God's will

Review

1. The students should understand the importance of discerning their particular call from God—their vocation.

2. The students should know what religious are. They should know the difference between contemplative and apostolic orders.

3. The students should know the evangelical counsels and their importance in the religious life.

4. The students should understand the basics of Holy Orders, including:
   - Matter, form, effects
   - Three degrees, or levels, and their works
   - Differences between diocesan and religious

Assess

1. Distribute the quizzes and read through them with the students to be sure they understand the questions.

2. Administer the quiz. As they hand in their work, orally quiz the students on the Memorization Questions from this chapter.

3. After all the quizzes have been handed in, review the correct answers with the class.

Conclude

1. Lead the students in singing "Of the glorious Body telling," *Adoremus Hymnal*, #392.

2. End class with a prayer for vocations.

CHAPTER EIGHTEEN
THE LAY APOSTOLATE

Catechism of the Catholic Church References

Called to Holiness: 898
Christian Holiness: 2012–16, 2028–29
Grace: 1996–2005, 2021–24
Grace Conferred by the Sacraments: 1127–29, 1131

In the World: 873–75, 897, 913
Lay Apostolate: 897
Vocation of the Laity: 782–86, 898–913, 940–43

Scripture References

Creation: Gen 1—2

Summary of Lesson Content

Lesson 1

Most people are called to serve God in the world as laity. They are called to develop a strong spiritual life, uniting themselves with Christ through work, prayer, and the sacraments.

The laity serve God in the world by bringing the Good News to all people they encounter.

They must bring Christian justice to the world.

Lesson 2

The laity are called to use three goods for the good of the Church: wealth, sexuality, and independence. Most lay people are married.

The lay apostolate encompasses work and leisure.

Lesson 3

The single life is a vocation for those who are called to serve others in the world more fully than they could if they had a family.

Lesson 4

Marriage is a vocation and one of seven sacraments. It was instituted and blessed by God at the creation of the world and elevated to the state of a sacrament by Christ.

As Catholics, we are obliged to have a sacramental marriage, which means our marriages must be blessed by the Church.

LESSON ONE: LAITY

Aims

The students will learn that most people are called to serve God in the world as laity. They are called to develop a strong spiritual life, uniting themselves with Christ through work, prayer, and the sacraments.

They will learn that the laity serve God in the world by bringing the Good News to all people they encounter. They must bring Christian justice to the world.

Materials

- *Activity Book*, p. 69

Optional:
- "Good Christian men, rejoice and sing," *Adoremus Hymnal*, #419

Begin

Review the vocations already covered, namely religious life and the priesthood. Discuss that most people are not called to these vocations; nonetheless, all are called to holiness and perfection as members of the Church.

Discuss who the laity are. Have the students give examples and discuss the important role of the laity in the Church.

CHAPTER 18

The Lay Apostolate

"Go into all the world and preach the gospel to the whole creation."
Mark 16:15

"From the fact of their union with Christ the head flows the laymen's right and duty to be apostles. Inserted as they are in the Mystical Body of Christ by baptism and strengthened by the power of the Holy Spirit in confirmation, it is by the Lord himself that they are assigned to the apostolate." (AA, 3).

While God calls some to serve him in the religious life or the priesthood, he calls most people to serve him in the world. Those members of the Church who are not ordained or do not belong to a religious community are called the **laity**.

The laity share the universal call to holiness with those in religious life. They, like priests, sisters, and brothers, must develop a strong spiritual life, uniting themselves with Christ through prayer, work, and the sacraments. This form of the spiritual life, however, will be different for each group because of their activities and obligations.

In addition to this universal call to holiness, members of the laity are also called to serve the Church in various capacities. This service begins within their individual parish communities. They may also serve the Church at the diocesan, national, or even international levels.

Finally, the laity, like the religious, are called to be witnesses of Christ and his Church. Both by their word and their example, laymen are called to bring Christ's gospel message to the world. Because their manner of life is the same as that of others in the world—raising families, working, and so on—they may at times be more effective witnesses of the gospel than are those in religious life.

121

Develop

1. Read paragraphs 1–6.

2. Review that the laity are members of the Church, who are called to holiness. To fulfill this call, they must live a moral life (keeping the Commandments and precepts of the Church, and living the virtues). The laity must develop a deep spiritual life through prayer, charity, and frequent reception of the sacraments. How each of us lives this, however, differs for every person, based upon his activities, capabilities, and obligations.

3. How can the laity serve in their parish communities? How can they serve the Church? Examples include:
- *Music ministry*
- *Altar society*
- *Teaching the faith*
- *Lector*

How can they serve the members of the Church? Examples include:

- *Caring for the poor and the sick*
- *Charity groups; e.g., Knights of Columbus*
- *Faith-sharing*

4. How can the laity be witnesses of Christ and his Church by word and example? Discuss how this can be done in different stages of life, in various occupations, in married/single life, etc.

5. Review that laity are to live in the world and lead the world to Christ. Christianity should affect every aspect of society, including economics, industry, politics, culture, and recreation. Have the students think of Christian paradigms for each of these. Discuss these paradigms with the class. (See box at right for examples.)

6. Discuss how we can offer the natural to God, so he can bless and sanctify it. We do this in our morning offering. We also do this in ordering all goods to God.

Name:_____

The Lay Apostolate

Answer the following questions in complete sentences.

1. Who are the laity?
   The laity are all the faithful who have been baptized but are not ordained or members of a religious community.

2. What call do the laity share in? How does this make them like those called to the religious life?
   The laity share in the call to holiness, to serve the Church and witness to Christ and his Church. This makes them like those called to religious life because they too must develop a strong spiritual life and unite themselves to Christ through prayer, work, and the sacraments.

3. How is the vocation of the laity different from the vocation of the religious?
   The vocation of the laity differs from that of the religious because they must live in the world and sanctify the world by their state in life. The layman is called to use the goods the religious specifically gives up in order to bring himself and others to Christ.

4. What does it mean to bring Christ's Gospel message to the world? Give an example.
   To bring Christ's Gospel message to the world means to bring Christian justice and charity into all the activities of human life.

5. What does it mean to live in the world, but not of the world? Give an example.
   To live in and not of the world means to renew the temporal order and draw it to God, but to remain detached from worldly corruptions. Examples will vary.

Faith and Life Series • Grade 8 • Chapter 18 • Lesson 1   69

Reinforce

1. Have the students work on *Activity Book*, p. 69.

2. Give the students time to work on their Memorization Questions and Words to Know.

3 Have the students research various Catholic groups in which they can serve the Church using their particular gifts and talents. Discuss parish groups, diocesan groups, etc. They should consider:
   • What work do I want to do for the Church?
   • Who do I want to help? Why?
   • How can I help others?
   • How can I bring Christ to others?

Conclude

1. Teach the students to sing "Good Christian men, rejoice and sing," *Adoremus Hymnal*, #419.

2. End class with a prayer for the laity.

Preview

In the next lesson, the students will learn about using the goods of the laity in service to God.

CATHOLIC CULTURE

As Christians we need to promote a culture that accepts and embraces God and his truth.

We need a culture of life, recognizing God's great gift, protecting it, and regarding it as sacred.

We need a culture where the moral life is expected, and moral disorder is seen as harmful to the common good.

Art, language, music, literature, etc. should give glory to God.

Holy days should be holidays; work should be seen as a good and just opportunity to serve God.

PRAYER FOR THE LAITY
by Pope John Paul II

from Christifideles Laici, *"On the vocation and the mission of the lay faithful in the Church and in the world."*

O Virgin Mother,
Guide and sustain us
so that we might always live
as true sons and daughters
of the Church of your Son.
Enable us to do our part
in helping to establish on earth
the civilization of truth and love
as God wills it for his glory. *Amen.*

LESSON TWO: GOODS FOR GOD

Aims

The students will learn that the laity are called to use three goods for the good of the Church: wealth, sexuality, and independence. Most lay people are married.

They will learn that the lay apostolate encompasses work and leisure.

Materials

- *Activity Book*, p. 70

Optional:
- "Good Christian men, rejoice and sing," *Adoremus Hymnal*, #419

Begin

You may review the story of Creation (Gen 1—2). Note how all created things are "good." In paradise, all goods were used according to God's plan. We refer to this proper ordering and use of creation and the material world as stewardship.

Review that when we are baptized, we share in Christ's threefold ministry as priests, prophets, and kings. Through this union, we can sanctify the world. See the Chalk Talk at right.

Unlike priests and religious, who are called to live *separated from* the world, the laity must live *in* the world. They must "permeate society with the leaven of the gospel." The laity must be the "salt of the earth" (Mt 5:13), drawing the world to Christ. This means that they must try to bring Christian justice and charity into all the activities of human life—social, economic, industrial, political, cultural, and recreational activities.

All of these are temporal (worldly) goods, and it is the specific vocation of the layman to sanctify them. The grace of Christ does not take the place of nature but respects the natural order and perfects it.

The layman is especially called to use the three great goods that religious freely give up—wealth, sexuality, and independence. The laity are called to use their money and possessions for the good of the Church, of their families and of those in need. Most are also called to marry and raise a family, thus bringing new souls to Christ. Finally, they are called to use their freedom to make Christ present everywhere in the world.

Even though the layman's vocation is to live in the world, he must always keep in mind the warning of Our Lord that we live in the world but not be of the world. The laity must work to renew the temporal order, drawing all toward God. But at the same time, they must strive to keep themselves free from the corruptions of the world. St. Paul wrote, "Do not be conformed to this world" (Rom 12:2).

The lay apostolate encompasses both work and *leisure* (those activities that are not work and are done for their own sake). The layman must sanctify himself as well as the world through these activities.

Each person is called to sanctify his ordinary labor, using it as a means of serving God. For you, as students, your principal "work" or duty right now is to study, learning basic skills and preparing yourself for future studies and work. You must, then, use your studies and

> "Help me spread your fragrance everywhere. Flood my soul with your spirit and life. Penetrate and possess my whole being so utterly that all my life may be a witness, a radiance of yours. Shine through me and be so in me that every soul I come in contact with may be aware of your presence in me. Let them look up and see no longer me, but only you, Lord Jesus."
>
> (Cardinal Newman)

122

Develop

1. Read paragraphs 7–10.

2. Review the goods that religious sacrifice in the world and why. Laity, on the contrary, are called to use these goods for Christ and his Church. How can this be done?
- Money and possessions: *these goods can be used to help the poor, support the Church and her missions, and support religious (especially the cloistered). Think of all the things we need as laity and must pay for: housing, utilities, health care, food, clothes, etc. All these things are needed by members of the Church who do not have resources.*
- Sexuality: *Sexuality is a good ordered to marriage. In marriage, sexuality is a good that brings new members into the Church through children and unites spouses in love..*
- Freedom: *The laity are free to serve the Church in her various needs; e.g., caring for their families. Various particular needs that may not be met through apostolates;*

e.g., helping a friend in need, helping people internationally. Essentially, where and when a need is seen, the laity may see the opportunity to serve Christ.

3. The lay apostolate encompasses work and leisure. How can the lay person sanctify the world in work and leisure?
- Work: *do our work in justice and for the good of others; e.g., be a doctor to care for the sick, a lawyer to protect the rights of people, a teacher to help others learn what is necessary for a good life, a truck driver to bring goods to people where they are needed, etc.*
- Leisure: *using leisure for the good of the body—we need rest and exercise to promote unity and charity; e.g., relaxing together and building strong relationships.*

4. Discuss how the students can (at this stage in their lives) sanctify the world as laity and as students, in their extracurricular activities, in their families and friendships, in their leisure, etc.

Sanctifying the World

Answer the following questions in complete sentences.

1. To what must the laity bring Christian justice and charity? Why?

The laity must bring Christian justice and charity to all human activities because they are called to "permeate society with the leaven of the Gospel".

2. What three goods are the laity especially called to use? Explain.

The laity is especially called to use wealth, sexuality, and independence. The laity are called to use their wealth for the good of the Church. Most are called to marriage and to raise a family. They also should use their freedom to spread the Gospel everywhere.

3. How is St. Paul's admonition in Romans 12:2 particularly important for the laity?

St. Paul's admonition in Rom 12:2 is particularly important for the laity because it warns us that although the laity must live in the world and sanctify it, they must be on guard to not be conformed to the world.

4. How can we sanctify our ordinary labor?

We can sanctify our ordinary labor by using it as a means to serve God.

5. As students (who are laity), how can you sanctify your work?

Answers will vary.

6. As laity, how can you bring Christ's Gospel message to the world and be his witness?

Answers will vary.

70   *Faith and Life Series • Grade 8 • Chapter 18 • Lesson 2*

Reinforce

1. Have the students work on *Activity Book*, p. 70.

2 Give the students time to work on their Memorization Questions and Words to Know.

3. Have the students write about their duties/obligations to the world. In fulfilling these, they faithfully serve God. What does this leave time for? What gifts and talents can they nurture to help promote the life of the Church?

4. Have the students write an essay titled "As a lay person, I can serve the Church by . . ." They should include in this essay ways they can prepare to serve the Church better (e.g., learn more about the faith nor receive training to do a particular work).

Conclude

1. Lead the students in singing "Good Christian men, rejoice and sing," *Adoremus Hymnal*, #419.

2. End class with a prayer for the laity.

Preview

In the next lesson, the students will learn about the vocations of the laity.

CHALK TALK: PRIEST, PROPHET, AND KING

Priest	Prophet	King
sanctification of work and leisure	witness of Christian justice and charity	service of church and world (bringing others to Christ)

NOTES

_____
_____
_____
_____
_____
_____
_____
_____
_____
_____
_____
_____

LESSON THREE: LAY VOCATIONS

Aims

The students will learn that the single life is a vocation for those who are called to serve others in the world more fully than they could if they had a family.

Materials

- *Activity Book*, p. 71

Optional:
- "Good Christian men, rejoice and sing," *Adoremus Hymnal*, #419

Begin

Review that there are two lay vocations: married life and single life. Today, we will focus on the single life.

Present three objects to the class: e.g., three different balls (basketball, soccer ball, and baseball). Tell the students they must choose one and renounce the two others. Some may have a hard time choosing one and some may find it easy. It is important to note that they all choose one, even if it is by rejecting the other two. We must all choose our vocations. Some know clearly, others go through a process of elimination. Sometimes not choosing is a choice!

---

homework to praise God. This means beginning now to do the best you can in your schoolwork, so that it may be a fitting offering to God. The same is true of any duties you may have at home —for example, doing the dishes, caring for the yard—or at a job. The layman is also called to sanctify his leisure—serving God through excellence in art, music, athletics, and the like.

The lay vocation embraces both the married and the unmarried life. Both are called to live chastity in different ways, according to their state. While most of the laity are called to the married state, there are some lay people who live the lay life as unmarried persons. These people continue to live in the world and have no intention of entering a religious community. While this calling may not be for many, those who are called to the single life in the world are given the graces they need to become holy through the sacrament of Confirmation. They also gain strength from the sacraments of Penance and the Eucharist.

The single state may be chosen by some people who desire to serve others in the world more fully than they could if they had a family. For example, it was common in our country in the nineteenth century for women teachers to remain unmarried, so that they could devote themselves more fully to educating others. Others may remain unmarried because obligations in justice or charity require it. For example, one might remain single in order to be able to care for aged parents or other relatives who need one's care.

Most lay people however, live the married life. This state is a great vocation, instituted and blessed by God at the Creation of the world. We will consider the married state in the next chapter.

Words to Know:
laity

> **Q. 116 Who are the laity?**
> The laity are all the faithful people who have been baptized, and therefore are members of the Church, but are not clergy or members of a religious community. The laity participate in the priestly, prophetic, and kingly ministry of Christ in the world (CCC 897).

123

Develop

1. Read paragraphs 11–12.

2. Discerning our vocation may be easy or it may be very difficult. Once we know to what state in life we are called, there is often further discernment (e.g., what order, which spouse, etc.).

3. To be called to the single life is a holy call. The single life is for those who choose to be in the world and have no intention of marrying or entering a religious community. These people are called to ministry and are strengthened for this state in life by their Confirmation, in which they are given all the graces necessary for this state in life.

4. The consecrated single life (also called consecrated virginity) is a special call for those who are single and want to be bound more perfectly to Christ through vows of poverty, chastity, and obedience. They take these vows to their local ordinary

(bishop) and live in the world, serving the Church. Consecrated singles must support themselves financially in their work and are free to serve the Church in whatever need arises.

5. One must choose the single life as a vocation—it should not be a state in life by default. It is possible that one realizes his vocation through the circumstances and events in his life, which directs him to the single state, but one must freely choose this state in order for it to be a vocation. The single vocation is a great gift that allows individuals to serve others in the world more fully than they could if they had a family. The single life allows one to teach, to care for elderly/sick relatives, to do Church work, etc.

6. What about single people who do not want to be single? They should discern their calling and follow it.

Name:_____

The Single Life

Answer the following questions in complete sentences.

1. What graces do those who live the single state receive?

   Those who live the single state receive the graces they
   need to become holy.

2. How do both married and unmarried people live chastity?

   Married and unmarried people live chastity according to
   their state in life.

3. How can the single life be a path to holiness? Give an example.

   The single life can be a path to holiness by choosing to live
   for others and devoting oneself entirely to Christ and
   neighbor more fully than one could do in the married state.
   Not being a religious enables the single person to reach
   people where religious cannot.

4. What does it mean to remain single because of obligations in justice or
   charity? Give an example.

   To remain single because of obligations in justice or charity
   means to forego marriage or religious life in order to fulfill
   one's obligations.

Reinforce

1. Have the students work on *Activity Book*, p. 71.

2. Give the students time to work on their Memorization Questions and Words to Know.

3. Have the students consider the need to discern their vocations. They should include among their choices the married and single states.

4. If there is a consecrated single person in the parish, have him visit your class and discuss his particular vocation, how he knew his call, and what he does in service to the Church.

Conclude

1. Lead the students in singing "Good Christian men, rejoice and sing," *Adoremus Hymnal*, #419.

2. End class with a prayer for the laity.

Preview

In the next lesson, the students will learn about Matrimony.

THE *CATECHISM OF THE CATHOLIC CHURCH* ON THE CONSECRATED LIFE

"From apostolic times Christian virgins, called by the Lord to cling only to him with greater freedom of heart, body, and spirit, have decided with the Church's approval to live in a state of virginity 'for the sake of the Kingdom of heaven.'

"'Virgins who, committed to the holy plan of following Christ more closely, are consecrated to God by the diocesan bishop according to the approved liturgical rite, are betrothed mystically to Christ, the Son of God, and are dedicated to the service of the Church.' By this solemn rite (*Consecratio Virginum*), the virgin is 'constituted . . . a sacred person, a transcendent sign of the Church's love for Christ, and an eschatological image of this heavenly Bride of Christ and of the life to come.'

"'As with other forms of consecrated life,' the order of virgins establishes the woman living in the world (or the nun) in prayer, penance, service of her brethren, and apostolic activity, according to the state of life and spiritual gifts given to her. Consecrated virgins can form themselves into associations to observe their commitment more faithfully."

—CCC 922–924

LESSON FOUR: MATRIMONY

Aims

The students will learn that Marriage is a vocation and one of the seven sacraments. It was instituted and blessed by God at the creation of the world and elevated to the state of a sacrament by Christ.

They will learn that, as Catholics, we are obliged to have a sacramental marriage, which means our marriages must be blessed by the Church.

Materials

- *Activity Book*, p. 72

Optional:
- "Good Christian men, rejoice and sing," *Adoremus Hymnal*, #419

Begin

Review that there are two lay vocations: married life and single life. Today, we will focus on the married life. Because this is the more common state of the laity, this chapter will also focus on how the laity can sanctify the world.

Begin the class by defining Matrimony. It is the sacramental union between a man and a woman who freely bind themselves together for the goods of faithful unity and procreation of children.

Develop

1. Read paragraph 13 with the students (to the end of the chapter).

2. Sacramental Matrimony needs four things:
- a baptized man and woman (who are the ministers of the sacrament) and the matter of the sacrament
- freedom to enter marriage (no constraint, no impediments by natural or church law)
- public ratification (expression of consent) before a priest or deacon and two witnesses (we are obliged to be married in the Catholic Church); this consent includes:
  - unity (intention of faithful love)
  - indissolubility (permanence—until death)
  - openness to life (openness to children)
- consummation (conjugal love)

3. The vows of marriage allow spouses to give themselves freely to each other and to help one another serve God faithfully in the world.

4. Laity can serve God in communities, as well. There are many lay organizations that allow the lay faithful to serve the Church. Some are clubs, such as the Knights of Columbus, the Catholic Women's League, Blue Army, pro life groups, etc. There are also lay apostolates and institutions, which provide formation in a way of life that helps the lay person to grow in holiness and serve the Church. Examples of these include Opus Dei, Regnum Christi, Youth Apostles, etc.

5. Lay persons are called to sanctify the world as priests, prophets, and kings, through the graces they receive in Baptism and Confirmation. They are called to bring Christian charity and justice to society. Discuss ways single and married persons can do this.

Name:_____

In the World...

Explain how the laity can bring justice and charity to the following areas of human life.

Social: Answers will vary.

Economic:

Industrial:

Political:

Cultural:

Recreational:

Educational:

72   *Faith and Life Series • Grade 8 • Chapter 18 • Lesson 4*

Reinforce

1. Have the students work on *Activity Book*, p. 72.

2. Give the students time to work on their Memorization Questions and Words to Know and to prepare for the quiz.

3. Discuss how various groups, organizations, apostolates, and institutions allow the laity to bring Christ more fully into the world. How do these groups help the laity to grow in holiness?

4. Have the students research various groups, organizations, lay apostolates, and institutions and make presentations for each other.

Conclude

1. Lead the students in singing "Good Christian men, rejoice and sing," *Adoremus Hymnal*, #419.

2. End class with a prayer for the laity.

Preview

In the next lesson, the students' understanding of the material covered in this chapter will be reviewed and assessed.

THE *CATECHISM OF THE CATHOLIC CHURCH* ON LAY APOSTOLATES AND INSTITUTIONS

"'A secular institute is an institute of consecrated life in which the Christian faithful living in the world strive for the perfection of charity and work for the sanctification of the world especially from within.'

"By a 'life perfectly and entirely consecrated to [such] sanctification.' the members of these institutes share in the Church's task of evangelization, 'in the world and from within the world,' where their presence acts as 'leaven in the world.' 'Their witness of a Christian life' aims 'to order temporal things according to God and inform the world with the power of the gospel.' They commit themselves to the evangelical counsels by sacred bonds and observe among themselves the communion and fellowship appropriate to their 'particular secular way of life.'

"Alongside the different forms of consecrated life are 'societies of apostolic life whose members without religious vows pursue the particular apostolic purpose of their society, and lead a life as brothers or sisters in common according to a particular manner of life, strive for the perfection of charity through the observance of the constitutions. Among these there are societies in which the members embrace the evangelical counsels' according to their constitutions." —CCC 928–930

CHAPTER EIGHTEEN
REVIEW AND ASSESSMENT

Aims

The students' understanding of the material covered in this chapter will be reviewed and assessed.

Materials

- Quiz 18, Appendix, p. A-26

Optional:
- "Good Christian men, rejoice and sing," *Adoremus Hymnal,* #419

Review

1. The students should understand the role and work of the laity.

2. The students should understand the two forms of the lay vocation: marriage and single life.

3. The students should understand how they can use the goods of the world to glorify God.

4. The students should know that the laity must discern their vocations.

5. The students should be familiar with groups, organizations, lay apostolates, and institutions.

Name:

The Lay Apostolate   Quiz 18

Part I: The laity are to sanctify the world. Explain how you can do this in the following situations.

In your family: <u>Answers will vary.</u>

In your classroom:

As a member of a sports team:

At a party:

When a friend is ill:

Part II: Answer in complete sentences.

1. Who are the laity?
   <u>The laity are all the faithful people who have been baptized, and therefore are members of the Church, but they are not clergy or members of a religious community.</u>

2. How are laity to grow in holiness?
   <u>The laity are to grow in holiness by uniting themselves to Christ through prayer, work, and the sacraments; serving the Church; and being witnesses to Christ.</u>

3. In what way can the laity use the goods sacrificed in the evangelical counsels for the glory of God and his Church?
   <u>The laity can use the goods sacrificed in the evangelical counsels for the glory of God and his Church by giving their money to the Church, raising a family, and making Christ present everywhere.</u>

4. How does Cardinal Newman's prayer, "Help me spread your fragrance everywhere. . ." sum up the lay vocation?
   <u>Answers will vary.</u>

A - 26   *Faith and Life • Grade 8 • Appendix A*

Assess

1. Distribute the quizzes and read through them with the students to be sure they understand the questions.

2. Administer the quiz. As they hand in their work, orally quiz the students on the Memorization Questions from this chapter.

3. After all the quizzes have been handed in, review the correct answers with the class.

Conclude

1. Lead the students in singing "Good Christian men, rejoice and sing," *Adoremus Hymnal,* #419.

2. End class with a prayer for the laity.

CHAPTER NINETEEN
MARRIAGE AND THE FAMILY

Catechism of the Catholic Church References

Duties of Children Toward Parents: 2214–20, 2247–48, 2251
Duties of Parents: 2221–31, 2252–53
Equality and Difference between Men and Women: 369–73, 383
Family and Society: 2207–13, 2250
Family in God's Plan: 2201–6, 2249
Jesus as Our Teacher and Model of Holiness: 468–69, 516, 519–21, 561
Love of Spouse: 2360–79, 2397–99
Man Created in the Image of God: 355–57, 380–81
The Sacrament of Marriage: 1601–58, 1659–66

Marriage in the Plan of God: 1602–20, 1659–60
Celebration of Marriage: 1621–24, 1663
Matrimonial Consent: 1625–37, 1662
Effects of the Sacrament of Marriage: 1638–43, 1661
Exclusivity of Marriage: 2335
Goods and Requirements of Conjugal Love: 1643–54, 1664–65
Indissolubility of Marriage: 1648
Domestic Church: 1655–58, 1666
Virginity and Celibacy: 1620

Scripture References

"Be Fruitful and Multiply" Gen 1:28
Creation of Woman: Gen 2:18–24

Wedding at Cana: Jn 2:1–11
Indissolubility of Marriage: Mt 19:6, 9

Summary of Lesson Content

Lesson 1

The two vocations of love are marriage and virginity or celibacy. Marriage is the vocation specific to human love.

Marriage is ordered to the creation of new life. Therefore, spouses must be open to the gift of life, of having children.

Lesson 2

Marriage is ordered to the unity of the spouses. This unity must be exclusive and lifelong. The bond of this unity is the mutual love and support of the husband and wife. Marital unity requires the sacrifice of independence by the individual spouses for the greater good—the family.

The unity of marriage is a unity of body and soul. Bodily unity is expressed in conjugal love.

Lesson 3

The first miracle of Jesus was at the Wedding at Cana. The marriage was blessed by Christ's presence. When a baptized man and woman unite in Matrimony, they receive from Christ the graces that they need to live this life. The husband and wife help each other to grow closer to Christ and are dedicated to each other's sanctification.

Sacramental marriage is indissoluble until death.

Lesson 4

A husband and wife form a new community: a family.

The obligations of marriage include openness to life, caring for children, and raising children in the faith.

Children are bound by filial piety. Filial piety requires children to honor their parents, their siblings, and authorities placed over them by their parents.

LESSON ONE: MARRIAGE

Aims

The students will learn that the two vocations of love are marriage and virginity or celibacy. Marriage is the vocation specific to human love.

They will learn that marriage is ordered to the creation of new life. Therefore, spouses must be open to the gift of life, of having children.

Materials

- *Activity Book*, p. 73

Optional:
- "O Lord, the Giver of all life," *Adoremus Hymnal*, #609

Begin

Review the teachings on Matrimony from Chapter 18, Lesson 4. These include the matter, form, and all that is necessary for a sacramental marriage.

You may list these on the board for reference throughout this chapter.

CHAPTER 19

Marriage and the Family

". . . What therefore God has joined together, let no man put asunder."
Matthew 19:6

"God created man in his own image and likeness: calling him to existence through love, he called him at the same time for love" (FC, 11).

There are two main vocations to love: marriage and virginity or celibacy. The vocation to marriage is a vocation to a specific kind of human love (conjugal love), blessed by God and instituted by him at the creation of the world. In the first two chapters of Genesis we read about the creation of the world and the institution of married life.

In the above quote, the Pope refers to the words of Genesis 1:27 telling us that God made man and woman in his own image. This means that they are different from everything else in the world that God had created until then. They have an intellect and free will as God has. They are persons, a man and a woman, equal in dignity—"male and female he created them." God is love, and since they were made in his image they were made to love God and each other. The words of Genesis continue, "God blessed them." Thus they formed the first community of love, an image of the Trinity, which is the divine community of love.

Then God said to them, "Be fruitful and multiply, and fill the earth . . ." (Gen 1:28).

This tells us that God meant this community of love, which is marriage, to bear fruit. He gave them a share in his act of creation. The fruit of marriage is children. This is its first purpose. God intended that through the loving union of man and woman in marriage, children be brought forth. They are its crowning glory.

In the second chapter of Genesis we read more about the vocation of marriage:

The Lord God said, "It is not good that the man should be alone; I will make him a helper fit for him" . . . and the rib which the Lord God had taken from the man he made into a woman and brought her to the man. Then the man said, "This at last is bone of my bones and flesh of my flesh. . . ." Therefore a man leaves his father and mother and cleaves to his wife, and they become one flesh (Gen 2:18, 22–24).

Here God reveals to us that marriage, which by its nature is a union of love, has as a second purpose *mutual love* and *support* of the husband and wife. The man and woman united in marriage are to support one another in life. They are to help one another in their tasks on earth—primarily raising their children. Through marriage they become *one* and are no

124

Develop

1. Read paragraphs 1–3.

2. Marriage is a vocation of love. Today, there is much confusion about love. We love our parents and family; we love things in our lives (pets, food, clothes, a present, etc.); and we love our friends. We may have a loyalty in these loves ("I will always love pizza or chocolate"). Marriage is a vocation ordered to a specific human love—conjugal love. Marriage is the sacrament in which this love is blessed by God and made holy. We are specifically speaking of the exclusive and faithful love of a man and woman that is open to the blessing of children.

3. It is important to note that men and women are equal in dignity but different in their roles. We see this in the natural world: men cannot have babies, women tend not to be as physically strong as men. Men and women share the great dignity of being made in the image of God—they have intel-

lects, free wills, and rational souls. Men and women also have a complementarity. Together, a man and woman can share in the beauty of the co-creation of human life with God. (This cannot happen between two men or two women.)

4. In the story of creation in Genesis, God blessed the union of man and woman, making it holy. They became models of the Holy Trinity, which is the divine community of love. God said, "Be fruitful and multiply." This means that God intended for this community of love (marriage) to be open to life—one of the fruits of marriage is children. See the Chalk Talk at right.

5. Marital love is to be exclusively for marriage, and any violation of that particular expression of love is a lie and a mortal sin. These include: masturbation, fornication, adultery, and homosexual acts.

Name:_____

Marriage and Family

Answer the following questions in complete sentences.

1. What are the two vocations of love? What kind of love is marriage ordered to?

   The two vocations of love are marriage and virginity or celibacy. Marriage is ordered to conjugal love.

2. How are men and women different from everything else in the world that God created?

   Men and women are different from everything else in the world that God created because they are made in his image and likeness with an intellect and free will.

3. What does it mean for the family to be a community of love? Compare the family to the Trinity.

   For the family to be a community of love means the family should bear fruit and live in love. Both the Trinity and the family are communities of love.

4. What did God command men and women?

   God commanded men and women to be fruitful and multiply.

5. What then, is the first purpose of marriage?

   The first purpose of marriage is to have children.

Faith and Life Series • Grade 8 • Chapter 19 • Lesson 1 73

Reinforce

1. Have the students work on *Activity Book*, p. 73.

2. Give the students time to work on the Memorization Questions and Words to Know.

3. Discuss the importance of chastity. How can we live chastity in a world that is so obsessed with sex? Discuss the importance of modesty, avoiding occasions of sin, respecting one another in relationships, and holding marriage and marital love sacred.

4. Boys and girls may be separated by gender to discuss their questions about human sexuality. Find a group leader that is of the same gender as the group having the discussion. This should be arranged by the principal/DRE, and parents should be informed beforehand.

Conclude

1. Teach the students to sing "O Lord, the Giver of all life." *Adoremus Hymnal*, #609.

2. End class with a prayer for families.

Preview

In the next lesson, the students will learn about the unity of marriage.

CHALK TALK: BIG TRINITIES AND LITTLE TRINITIES

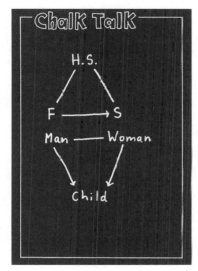

PRAYER FOR FAMILIES
by Mother Teresa

Heavenly Father,
you have given us a model of life
in the Holy Family of Nazareth.
Help us, O loving Father,
to make our family another Nazareth,
where love, peace, and joy reign.

May it be deeply contemplative,
intensely eucharistic,
and vibrant with joy.
Help us to stay together
in joy and sorrow
through family prayer. *Amen.*

LESSON TWO:
UNITY OF MARRIAGE

Aims

The students will learn that marriage is ordered to the unity of the spouses. This unity must be exclusive and lifelong. The bond of this unity is the mutual love and support of the husband and wife. Marital unity requires the sacrifice of independence by the individual spouses for the greater good—the family.

They will learn that the unity of marriage is a unity of body and soul. Bodily unity is expressed in conjugal love.

Materials

- *Activity Book*, p. 74

  Optional:
  - "O Lord, the Giver of all life," *Adoremus Hymnal*, #609

Begin

Read Gen 2:18–24 and discuss the following questions:
- Why did God want Adam to have a helper?
- Why is it not good for man to be alone? What about priests and religious?
- Describe the love of the man for the woman. How should people who get married love one another?
- Why does it say the man cleaves to his wife? (It expresses an exclusive and intimate union.)
- How are they one flesh? Can this be separated?

longer simply individuals. They are called to sacrifice some of their individual freedom for the sake of a greater good—the new family they have formed.

We also learn from the above quote that the man and woman shall become one flesh—that is, the union in marriage is one of body as well as of soul. There is a total giving, under God, of the whole person to the other. There can be no total conjugal self-giving apart from marriage. Total self-giving means giving of oneself, until death, exclusively to one person. You enter freely and consciously into marriage. You make a public promise in front of witnesses which, once made, you are no longer free to take back. You even give up the right to decide otherwise in the future. Total giving of self also means accepting all the consequences, which includes openness to the gift of life.

Since bodily union is an expression of the total self-giving of two persons, it is a lie if it takes place between two unmarried persons. If your body expresses, "I am yours for ever," but your mind knows that is not true, then you are lying. That is why sex outside of marriage is a lie. It is also, of course, fornication or adultery.

The Sacrament of Marriage

The married state has been blessed by Our Lord as well. At the beginning of his public life, Our Lord attended a wedding feast where he worked his first miracle (Jn 2:1–11). By his presence at this wedding, Christ blessed the vocation of marriage. He also raised marriage above the natural level to the dignity of a sacrament. Thus, the baptized man and woman who unite themselves in marriage receive from Christ the graces that they need to live this life. These are special graces to help them overcome obstacles, bear their crosses, and become better spouses and parents.

For the Christian the natural ends, or pur-

poses, of marriage are raised to a supernatural level. The bearing and raising of children are not simply for life here on earth. Christian parents raise children that they may eventually be united for ever with God in heaven. Similarly, the Christian husband and wife not only support one another in mutual love but, even more importantly, must help one another to know, love, and serve God so that they may reach heaven. This is called the *mutual sanctification* of the spouses.

Christ also emphasized the *indissoluble* nature of marriage. He taught us that the union of husband and wife is a lifelong union, which ends only with death. On one occasion, when Our Lord was questioned by the Pharisees about divorce, he quoted the passage from the second chapter of Genesis and then said:

125

Develop

1. Read paragraphs 4–6 (up to The Sacrament of Marriage).

2. What is mutual love? This means the man and the woman love each other. Can a person be forced into marriage? No, the man and woman must freely consent to marriage.

3. Marital love is exclusive. This means spouses must be faithful to one another. They promise this in their vows. (Imagine the hurt and destruction infidelity brings to a marriage.) A person's marriage vows are a sacrifice of individual freedom for the greater good of the marriage and family.

4. What support do a husband and wife need? Marriage is difficult. The man and woman are two individuals with different backgrounds who come together. They must both make sacrifices and work hard at having a good marriage. Mutual support is needed to raise children, fulfill household duties, etc.

5. The mutual love of the man and woman is that of body and soul. A husband and wife must carefully nurture one another emotionally, spiritually, and physically. How is this done?
- *Emotionally: communication, affection, charity, etc.*
- *Spiritually: prayerful support, living virtuous lives, etc.*
- *Physically: sexual union, care for the other in illness, etc.*

6. The marital union is indissoluble. A vow cannot be taken back. Therefore, a couple is married until death. This means, in good times and in bad, in sickness and in health, etc. Suggest scenarios that will help the students understand the gravity of marriage; e.g., care for a chronically ill spouse, inability to have children, not getting along, etc.

Name:_____

Marriage: Husband and Wife

Answer the following questions in complete sentences.

1. What is the second purpose of marriage and what does the Bible tell us about it?

   The second purpose of marriage is the mutual love and support of husband and wife. The Bible tells us that it is not good for man to be alone and that a married couple becomes "one flesh".

2. How does the second purpose of marriage help with the first purpose of marriage?

   The second purpose of marriage helps the first purpose because their love and support of one another help in the raising of children.

3. What is total self-giving and how does it relate to marriage?

   Total self-giving is the giving of oneself exclusively until death. It relates to marriage because total conjugal self-giving does not exist outside of marriage and both husband and wife must give themselves entirely to the other.

4. Why does marriage require sacrifice? Read Ephesians 5:21–33 to see who we can imitate.

   Marriage requires sacrifice because one cannot totally give of oneself without sacrifice. Love is putting the other first and that requires sacrifice. Also many sacrifices are demanded in the raising of children.

Faith and Life Series • Grade 8 • Chapter 19 • Lesson 2

Reinforce

1. Have the students work on *Activity Book*, p. 74.

2. Give the students time to work on their Memorization Questions and Words to Know.

3. *Discuss that, in modern times, many people do not marry until later in life. Discuss the importance of preparing for a holy marriage and the need to develop good communication skills, etc.*

4. *Discuss healthy dating tips. Date in public, in groups, etc. Also, discuss ways to end unhealthy relationships (often youth stay in bad relationships because they are afraid to hurt the other).*

5. Emphasize the students' need for self-esteem.

Conclude

1. Lead the students in singing "O Lord, the Giver of all life," *Adoremus Hymnal*, #609.

2. End class with a prayer for families.

Preview

In the next lesson, the students will learn about the Sacrament of Matrimony.

SAINT GIANNA MOLLA

Gianna was born into a loving Catholic family on October 4, 1922 in Milan, Italy. When Gianna was twenty, her mother died and her father followed less than five months later. Soon after, Gianna began studies at the University of Milan to become a doctor and graduated in 1949. She opened a clinic in Mesero, a small city near Milan, in 1950 and, in 1955, married Pietro Molla. They lived together happily until, in 1961, Gianna became pregnant with their fourth child. At the same time, they found that she had an ovarian cyst. The only way to save Gianna's life was an operation that would result in the death of her unborn child. Being a doctor, Gianna knew what would happen if she accepted the surgery. However if she did not have the surgery, she would sacrifice her own life. Her words at this time were: "I trust in God, but now it is up to me to fulfill my duty as a mother. I renew the offering of my life to the Lord. I am ready for anything as long as my baby is saved." She refused the surgery—knowing that she would die, but her baby would live. Their daughter, Gianna Emanuala, was born on Holy Saturday, April 21, 1962. One week later, Gianna Molla died. Pietro relates that, as she lay on her death bed, Gianna repeated many times "Jesus, I love you. Jesus, I love you." On May 16, 2004, Pope John Paul II canonized Saint Gianna Molla, and prayed: "Through the example of Gianna Beretta Molla, may our age rediscover the pure, chaste and fruitful beauty of conjugal love, lived as a response to the divine call!"

LESSON THREE: SACRAMENT

Aims

The students will learn that the first miracle of Jesus was at the Wedding at Cana. The marriage was blessed by Christ's presence. When a baptized man and woman unite in Matrimony, they receive from Christ the graces that they need to live this life. The husband and wife help each other to grow closer to Christ and are dedicated to each other's sanctification.

They will learn that sacramental marriage is indissoluble until death.

Materials

- *Activity Book*, p. 75

- Rite of Marriage, Appendix, pp. B-10–B-11.

Optional:
- "O Lord, the Giver of all life," *Adoremus Hymnal*, #609

Begin

In modern times, divorce is very common. In fact, as many as half of all marriages end in divorce. This is tragic. Divorce is hurtful to the family, and it is hurtful to society. Explain the difference between separation, divorce, and annulment.

What therefore God has joined together, let no man put asunder. . . . I say to you: whoever divorces his wife . . . and marries another, commits adultery; and he who marries a divorced woman, commits adultery (Mt 19:6, 9).

Thus did Our Lord make clear that marriage must be a permanent state on earth. He himself taught this on his authority as Son of God, for even in the Gospels we see that his contemporaries accepted divorce. Because the indissolubility of marriage is often rejected in today's world as well, the Christian must be an example and witness to the world.

The New Testament also teaches us about the supernatural element of marriage. In his letter to the Christian community in Ephesus, St. Paul reminds us of the mutual obligation of husbands and wives to love one another: "Husbands, love your wives, as Christ loved the church . . . and let the wife see that she respects her husband" (Eph 5:25, 33). Thus, we are to love one another with Christ himself as our model.

The Family

As we have seen, husband and wife unite in marriage to form a new community—the family. The family is the basic unit of society. It is in the family that new human beings are brought into the world. It is here that we first learn how to live in society. And it is in the family that children are first taught and prepared for their place in the Church and in society. There are then obligations for both parents and children in the family.

In addition to helping one another to serve God and neighbor and thus reach heaven, the state of marriage places other obligations and responsibilities on the husband and wife in their roles as parents.

126

1. The first obligation is that they must be open to the gift of life. This means that they must accept children as coming from God and destined for God. While it is true that not all marriages will be blessed with children, this openness to children must always be present. In childless marriages the couples can glorify God through their union of love and their mutual sanctification. They are called to be spiritually fruitful through works of mercy such as, for instance, adoption or foster care of children.

2. The second obligation of parents is to care for those children whom God has given them. The basic needs of life must be met first. Satisfying physical needs, however, is not sufficient for preparing children for the world or for eternal life.

3. The third obligation of parents is to educate and form their children so that they will be able to lead good and useful lives on earth and, finally, to attain salvation in heaven. Naturally, parents must see to the basic instruction of their children—reading, mathematics, and the like. More importantly, parents are responsible for their moral and religious education. They must care for the spiritual needs of their children—not simply their physical needs. One of the first duties of Christian parents, for example, is to have their children baptized.

Since moral, religious, and intellectual education begin very early in life, parents are the first teachers of their children, by both word and example. They are also the *primary* educators of their children. This means that the obligation for educating their children belongs first to the parents. Even though most parents eventually delegate their role of educator to the school, they should not abandon their role as the primary educators. Parents must continue to teach their children and help to form their moral characters.

Develop

1. Read paragraphs 7–10 (up to The Family).

2. Since Creation, marriage was a natural union between a man and a woman blessed by God. Our Lord sanctified marriage with his presence, as seen at the Wedding at Cana (Jn 2:1–11). Read this passage with the students. Furthermore, Jesus declared marriage indissoluble in Mt 19:6, 9. In these ways, Jesus elevated marriage to the level of a sacrament. No longer was it a natural union, but a sacramental union in which a man and woman are bound together until death and blessed by the presence and love of Christ.

3. Marriage as a sacrament needs matter, form, and ministers. The matter in the marriage is the man and the woman (not the rings). The form is the mutual consent of the man and woman. This sacrament is unique in that the minister of this sacrament is not a priest or deacon (who are necessary by Church law to witness the exchange of consent); the ministers are the man and woman!

4. Every sacrament confers grace; in marriage, the grace perfects the spouses in their love for one another, strengthens them in their unbreakable unity, and sanctifies them on their way to eternal life.

5. As a project, have the students research and plan a wedding liturgy. Use Appendix, pp. B-10–B-11 for the rite and a list of possible readings. Borrow hymnals from your church and have the students work independently. They may go so far as to plan an entire wedding day, make a budget, and create a scrap book of ideas and dreams.

6. Have the students write an essay comparing the importance of the wedding to that of the marriage. (One is a day, the other a lifetime—often this focus is lost in real planning.)

Name:_____

The Sacrament of Marriage

Answer the following questions in complete sentences.

1. When did marriage become a sacrament?
   Marriage became a sacrament when Jesus blessed marriage
   by his presence at the wedding at Cana.

2. What graces does Christ bestow on marriage?
   Christ bestowed on marriage the graces that married people
   need in order to live the married life. He grants special
   graces to overcome obstacles, bear crosses, and become
   better spouses and parents.

3. What does it mean to say that the bearing and raising of children has been raised
   to a supernatural level?
   To say that the bearing and raising of children has been
   raised to a supernatural level means that it has a supernatural end: the sanctification of the family members and
   for them to live forever in heaven.

4. What does mutual sanctification mean?
   Mutual sanctification means that husband and wife support
   one another in love and also help one another love and serve
   God in order to live in heaven.

5. What does "indissoluble" mean? How did Jesus apply it to marriage?
   "Indissoluble" means "the union of husband and wife is a lifelong union which ends only in death". Jesus applied it to
   marriage when he said "What God has joined together, let
   no man put asunder".

6. Why is infidelity contrary to marriage? Marital infidelity is a sin against which
   commandments and cardinal virtues?
   Infidelity is contrary to marriage because you cannot completely
   give yourself to more than one person. Marital infidelity is a
   sin against the sixth commandment and against the virtue of
   temperance.

Faith and Life Series • Grade 8 • Chapter 19 • Lesson 3   75

Reinforce

1. Have the students work on *Activity Book*, p. 75.

2. Give the students time to work on their Memorization Questions and Words to Know.

3. Have the students work on their wedding plans.

4. The students should write about the qualities they would seek in a spouse in order to have a holy marriage.

5. Give the students time to work on their essays.

Conclude

1. Lead the students in singing "O Lord, the Giver of all life," *Adoremus Hymnal*, #609.

2. End class with a prayer for families.

Preview

In the next lesson, the students will learn about families.

NOTES

_____
_____
_____
_____
_____
_____
_____
_____
_____
_____
_____

LESSON FOUR: FAMILY

Aims

The students will learn that a husband and wife form a new community: a family.

They will learn that the obligations of marriage include openness to life, caring for children, and raising children in the faith.

They will learn that children are bound by filial piety. Filial piety requires children to honor their parents, their siblings, and authorities placed over them by their parents.

Materials

- *Activity Book*, p. 76

Optional:
- "O Lord, the Giver of all life," *Adoremus Hymnal*, #609

Begin

Review that when a man and woman are married, they form a new community—no family. The family is the basic unit of society. It is into a family that babies are born. It is here that we first learn how to live in society and, more importantly, how to be Catholics. Having a family is a great responsibility for both parents and children. Today, we will learn about these responsibilities.

Filial Piety

Children also have obligations and duties within the family, and must develop the virtue known as **filial piety**. This is the virtue of giving honor and respect to our parents, who are immediately responsible for our existence and well-being. Like the virtue of religion, filial piety is a part of justice and is an acknowledgement of the debt that we owe to our parents.

Filial piety requires us to obey our parents since they have been given authority from God to raise us. In this we can model ourselves on Jesus, who was obedient to Mary and Joseph. "And he went down with them and came to Nazareth, and was obedient to them" (Lk 2:51). This obligation is proper to us until we reach adulthood and are responsible for our own lives.

Filial piety, however, does not end with our maturity. We are still obliged to honor and respect our parents. We must recognize the great work they have undertaken with God and should show them esteem and gratitude. That is what the Fourth Commandment is all about.

Finally, filial piety requires us to care for our parents in their old age or infirmity. The Word of God in the book of Sirach reminds us of this duty: "O son, help your father in his old age, and do not grieve him as long as he lives" (Sir 3:12).

Behold, how good and pleasant it is when brothers dwell in unity! (Ps 133:1).

Children also have the duty within the family to love and respect their brothers and sisters. This charity should be offered to everyone, but since we share a more intimate bond with the members of our family, it is even more important there. Often this is difficult to achieve, but we must each work to make our homes centers of Christian charity and unity.

Finally, children also have an obligation to respect the authority belonging to those who teach them. Since parents may delegate some of their authority to the school, just as they respect, honor, and obey their parents, children must respect, honor, and obey those who teach them. We recognize this special role of the school as taking the place of our parents temporarily when we call the school our *alma mater*, which means "loving or nourishing mother." Truly we are nourished by the school as we are nourished by our parents.

In addition to this, as children grow older, they must take upon themselves more and more responsibility for their education. This is particularly important in our religious education. Often people study their faith during their youth, are confirmed, and then do not pay any further attention to their religious development. Our knowledge of our faith does not end with our Confirmation. Rather, we must, as adults in the Church, take charge of our religious development and continue to grow in the knowledge and love of God.

The married state, through family life, prepares us for our place in society. In the next chapter we will examine the role of the Christian in the state and the world.

Words to Know:
   filial piety

127

Develop

1. Read paragraphs 11–16 (up to Filial Piety).

2. The primary work of the vocation of marriage is to help one another to serve God and neighbor (and therefore reach heaven). In marriage, there are grave responsibilities:
- *The husband and wife must be open to God's gift of new life. While it is true that God does not bless all marriages with children, it is true that all marriages are to share life—the life of grace. This being said, all marriages must be open to children and must not prevent their conception (through artificial contraception) or birth (through abortion).*
- *The husband and wife must care for the children God has given them. If a husband and wife foresee an inability to provide for the basic needs of children, they may cooperate with God through natural means (periods of abstinence) to space out the births of their children, but they must accept any children with which God blesses them.*

- *The parents are obliged to educate and form their children so that they will be good Catholics, leading good and useful lives on earth and, finally, attaining heaven.*

3. Read paragraphs 17–24 (to the end of the chapter).

4. Children have duties within the family:
- *Children must honor their parents, especially through obedience.*
- *Children must care for their aged and infirm parents and family members after they have reached an age of maturity.*
- *Children must respect and love their brothers and sisters.*
- *Children must respect the authorities their parents have placed over them (e.g., teachers, priests, etc.).*
- *As they mature, children must work toward their education.*

Name:_____

The Family and Filial Piety

Answer the following questions in complete sentences.

1. Why is the family the basic unit of society?
   The family is the basic unit of society because it is in the family where new life is brought into the world, where human beings learn to live in society, and where they are prepared and formed for their place in the society and the Church.

2. What is the first obligation of the husband and wife? How can childless marriages give glory to God?
   The first obligation of husband and wife is to bring new life into the world. Childless marriages give glory to God through their mutual love and sanctification and by bearing spiritual fruit.

3. What is the second obligation of parents? Why is this insufficient?
   The second obligation of parents is to provide and care for their children. However, simply providing for the body is not sufficient since the soul also needs care.

4. What is the third obligation of parents? What is the most important part of this obligation?
   The third obligation of parents is to form and educate their children so they can lead good and fruitful lives on earth and attain salvation. The most important part of this obligation is to form children spiritually and religiously.

5. What is the virtue of filial piety and why is it part of the virtue of justice?
   The virtue of filial piety is the virtue of children giving honor and respect to their parents. It is part of the virtue of justice because it is an acknowledgement of the debt we owe our parents.

6. What does filial piety require of us?
   Filial piety requires that we obey our parents, show them esteem and gratitude, and care for them in their old age.

7. Other than their parents, who must the children love and respect?
   The children must also love and respect their siblings and those in authority.

8. Why must you eventually take responsibility for your education in the faith?
   You must eventually take responsiblity for your own education because it must become your own faith and you must nurture it.

76   *Faith and Life Series • Grade 8 • Chapter 19 • Lesson 4*

Reinforce

1. Have the students work on *Activity Book*, p. 76.

2. Give the students time to work on their Memorization Questions and Words to Know and to prepare for the quiz.

3. Discuss that, in the family, it is important to respect the marriage of the parents. It is not good to try to come between the parents, or turn one against the other. The union of the parents is sacred and will be present after the children leave the home.

4. Discuss the importance of respecting parents. Discuss typical family issues; e.g., teenagers feel parents are embarrassing or nosy. Review the need for parents to care for their children and ensure their safety. Parents have more experience. They see the dangers of the world and know what is best for their children.

Conclude

1. Lead the students in singing "O Lord, the Giver of all life," *Adoremus Hymnal*, #609.

2. End class with a prayer for families.

Preview

In the next lesson, the students' understanding of the material covered in this chapter will be reviewed and assessed.

NOTES

_____
_____
_____
_____
_____
_____
_____
_____
_____
_____
_____

_____

Q. 117 *What happens in the Sacrament of Matrimony?*
In the Sacrament of Matrimony, a man and a woman are united indissolubly as Jesus Christ and his Spouse, the Church, are united. Through the sacrament they are given special graces to live in a holy way and to raise and educate their children in a Christian manner (CCC 1601).

Q. 118 *What duties do the spouses assume?*
The spouses assume the duties of living together in a holy way helping each other with unfailing affection in their temporal and spiritual necessities, and raising their children in the Catholic faith (CCC 1641).

"God created man in his own image and likeness: calling him to existence through love, he called him at the same time for love."

(FC, 11)

128

Name:

Marriage and the Family   Quiz 19

Part I: Define the following terms.

Conjugal love: <u>the total self-giving expressed in bodily union in the vocation of</u> <u>marriage</u>

Indissolubility: <u>the union of husband and wife is a lifelong union, which ends only</u> <u>in death</u>

Mutual Sanctification: <u>the call for spouses to help one another to know, love, and</u> <u>serve God so that they may reach heaven</u>

Divorce: <u>a rejection of the indissoluble nature of marriage, which should be a</u> <u>permanent state on earth</u>

Part II: Answer in complete sentences.

1. What are the duties of parents in the family?
   <u>The duties of parents in the family are 1) to be open to the gift of</u>
   <u>life, 2) to care for their children's bodily needs and, 3) to educate and</u>
   <u>form their children so that they will be able to lead good and useful</u>
   <u>lives on earth and attain salvation in heaven.</u>

2. What are the duties of children in the family?
   <u>The duties of children are to obey their parents, show them esteem</u>
   <u>and gratitude, and care for them in their old age.</u>

3. What are the duties of the husband and the wife towards one another?
   <u>The man and the woman are to support one another in life, help one</u>
   <u>another in their tasks on earth, help one another raise the children,</u>
   <u>and sacrifice their individual freedom for the sake of a greater good.</u>

4. How can we honor and protect the sanctity of marriage in society today?
   <u>Answers will vary.</u>

Faith and Life • Grade 8 • Appendix A   *A - 27*

Aims

The students' understanding of the material covered in this chapter will be reviewed and assessed.

Materials

- Quiz 19, Appendix, p. A-27

Optional:
- "O Lord, the Giver of all life," *Adoremus Hymnal,* #609

Assess

1. Distribute the quizzes and read through them with the students to be sure they understand the questions.

2. Administer the quiz. As they hand in their work, orally quiz the students on the Memorization Questions from this chapter.

3. After all the quizzes have been handed in, review the correct answers with the class.

Conclude

1. Lead the students in singing "O Lord, the Giver of all life," *Adoremus Hymnal,* #609.

2. End class with a prayer for families.

Review

1. Review that marriage is a vocation and sacrament of human love.

2. The students should understand the two goods of marriage: procreation and unity.

3. The students should understand the Sacrament of Marriage—matter, form, minister, grace conferred, etc.

4. The students should understand the duties of parents and children to the family.

CHAPTER TWENTY
THE CHRISTIAN IN THE WORLD

Catechism of the Catholic Church References

Attributes of God Shown in and through Creation: 293–95, 315, 341
Authorities in Civil Society: 1897–1904, 1918–23, 2234–46, 2254–57
Civil Laws: 1904
Duties of Civil Authorities: 2235–37, 2254
Duties of Citizens: 2238–43, 2255–56
The Common Good: 1905–12, 1924–26
The Dignity of the Human Person: 1700–1712
Equality and Differences among Men: 1934–38, 1944–46

God as Creator of Heaven and Earth: 279–81, 325–27
God Created and Ordered a Good World: 299
God Creates out of Nothing: 296–98, 317–18
Love for the Poor; the Works of Mercy: 2443–49, 2462–63
Man Created in the Image of God: 355–57, 380–81
Respect for the Human Person: 1929–33, 1943–44
Respect for the Integrity of Creation: 2415–18, 2456–57
Responsibility and Participation in Society: 1913–17
Safeguarding Peace and Avoiding War: 2302–17, 2327–30
State for Common Good: 1905–12, 1927

Scripture References

Creation: Gen 1—2
Saul: 1 Sam 9:15—10:1

David: 1 Sam 16:1–13

Summary of Lesson Content

Lesson 1

The family is the basic unit of society. Families come together to form societies. Civil societies belong to an order established by God to promote and ensure the common good of every man.

Civil authorities must make just laws to regulate and govern their citizens.

Lesson 2

God's laws come first. The state has legitimate authority only under God. Therefore, the state does not have the right to demand something that violates God's laws.

To exercise its authority, the state must promote the common good through morally acceptable means.

Lesson 3

We are not bound to obey unjust laws. We are bound to obey all laws which conform to God's laws.

Citizens have a duty to promote patriotism.

Citizens have a duty to use their influence to make their nation just. They must support the government through taxes and be willing to defend their country against unjust aggression. We must also pray for our country.

Lesson 4

God created the world out of nothing, giving man dominion over the created world. This dominion is to be exercised through stewardship—caring for the created world and using it according to God's plan.

LESSON ONE: SOCIETY

Aims

The students will learn that the family is the basic unit of society. Families come together to form societies. Civil societies belong to an order established by God to promote and ensure the common good of every man.

They will learn that civil authorities must make just laws to regulate and govern their citizens.

Materials

- *Activity Book*, p. 77

Optional:
- "All the world is God's own field," *Adoremus Hymnal*, #570

Begin

Review how the family is the primary unit of society. What happens in a family?
- Children are born
- Children are raised to contribute to the good of society
- Children receive a moral formation
- Children are raised to be responsible—first to their families, then to society
- Children learn to respect all authorities legitimately placed over them

---

CHAPTER 20

The Christian in the World

By me kings reign, and rulers decree what is just; by me princes rule, and nobles govern the earth.

Proverbs 8:15–16

Just as men and women naturally come together to form families, human beings also join together to form larger societies. Not only are we members of a family, but we are citizens of a city or town, state, and a nation. Just as our parents have legitimate authority over us in the family, so do the officials of the civil government. St. Paul reminds us that their authority, like that of our parents, comes from God:

Let every person be subject to the governing authorities. For there is no authority except from God. . . . Therefore he who resists the authorities resists what God has appointed. . . (Rom 13:1–2).

Human nature, as God created it, calls human beings to form civil societies. Civil society belongs to an order established by God. The purpose of civil society is to promote and ensure the **common good** of its members. The common good is the welfare of the whole community, not just an individual. The common good includes everything in society that helps people, either as groups or individuals, to reach more easily their fulfillment as human beings. In order to promote the common good of the whole community the state has the authority to make just (fair) laws and regulations to govern its citizens. And citizens have an obligation to

obey and respect these laws. Our Lord taught us the importance of recognizing civil authority when he was asked about the lawfulness of paying tribute to Caesar, "Render to Caesar the things that are Caesar's, and to God the things that are God's" (Lk 20:25). It is important to remember that in this passage Our Lord gives two commands. As Christians we must first of all obey the laws of God. Then, as citizens, we must obey the laws of society. Society, on the other hand, should promote citizens' exercise of virtue. It should foster appropriate values and establish the conditions for the proper exercise of freedom.

God's Laws Come First

Civil government is sometimes called "the state." The state, like every social organization, should protect and promote the dignity and rights of the human person. While the state has legitimate authority, it does not have the right to demand something which violates God's law. In order to exercise legitimate authority, the state must promote the common good through morally acceptable means. For example, no government has the right to command willful murder, since this is a violation of God's law. When such laws are made, citizens are not

129

Develop

1. Read paragraphs 1 and 2 (up to God's Laws Come First).

2. What societies do we belong to?
- The family
- The Church
- Various organizations (e.g., sports teams)
- Local municipal community (city, town, etc.)
- Regional community (state or province, etc.)
- Federal/national community (country)
- International community (world)

3. What is the common good? It is the welfare of the whole community in which the goods of society flow back to each individual. How do various societies promote the common good? (Look at examples of the home, the Church, and the government.)

4. Men naturally seek to live in society with others. Discuss

our need for society.

5. What does the state do to promote the common good? It creates fair laws to govern its citizens. Give examples. We must obey the civil authority in all that is good and just. We must first obey the laws of God and then the laws of society.

6. In a Christian society, the laws of God would be the laws of society. Some civil laws obey God's laws; e.g., do not kill, do not steal. Some civil laws are not mentioned in God's laws (e.g., traffic laws). These we should obey. However, some civil laws permit things that are contrary to God's laws; abortion, contraception, etc. We are bound first to God. Even if these immoral actions are permitted, we must never commit them, for they offend God and violate his laws (which are of greater importance and consequence than civil laws).

7. How can a society promote Christian virtues? Discuss.

Name:_____

The Christian in the World

Answer the following questions in complete sentences.

1. What (or who) is the source of all authority?
   God is the source of all authority.

2. What is the purpose of civil society?
   The purpose of civil society is to promote and ensure the common good of its members.

3. What is the common good?
   The common good is the welfare of the whole community, not just an individual.

4. Who taught us the importance of recognizing civil authority? How did he do this?
   Jesus taught us the importance of recognizing civil authority. He did this by his preaching. Civil authorities are legitimate and God-given and should be obeyed as long as they do not go against God's laws.

5. What two sets of laws must we obey, and in what order?
   The two sets of laws that must be obeyed are God's laws and civil laws. They must be obeyed in that order.

6. What three things should the laws of society promote?
   Three things the laws of society should promote are exercising virtue, fostering appropriate values, and establishing the conditions for the proper exercise of freedom.

Faith and Life Series • Grade 8 • Chapter 20 • Lesson 1   77

Reinforce

1. Have the students work on *Activity Book*, p. 77.

2. Give the students time to work on their Memorization Questions and Words to Know.

3. The students should research their society. How can they promote a Christian society?

4. *Discuss how laws lead to freedom. (Many people think they take freedom away.) Without laws, we would live in chaos. There would be no structure and, consequently, no real freedom. True freedom is found in the assent to that which is true and good.*

Conclude

1. Teach the students to sing "All the world is God's own field," *Adoremus Hymnal*, #570.

2. End class with a prayer for one's country.

Preview

In the next lesson, the students will learn about the priority of God's laws.

CHALK TALK: LAW

THE *CATECHISM* ON THE COMMON GOOD

The common good comprises "the sum total of social conditions which allow people, either as groups or as individuals, to reach their fulfillment more fully and more easily" (*Gaudium et Spes* 26.1).

"The common good consists of three essential elements: respect for the promotion of the fundamental rights of the person; prosperity, or the development of the spiritual and temporal goods of society; the peace and security of the group and of its members."

—CCC 1924–1925

LESSON TWO: GOD FIRST

Aims

The students will learn that God's laws come first. The state has legitimate authority only under God. Therefore, the state does not have the right to demand something that violates God's laws.

They will learn that to exercise its authority, the state must promote the common good through morally acceptable means.

Materials

- *Activity Book*, p. 78

Optional:
- "All the world is God's own field," *Adoremus Hymnal*, #570

- "A Man for all Seasons," video, available through Ignatius Press; 168 minutes

Begin

Is there a hierarchy of societies? Which ones have the greatest priority in our lives? To which do we give the most time, dedicate the most submissiveness, etc.?
- God's family
- Our family
- Others

130

Develop

1. Read paragraphs 3–6 (up to Civil Laws).

2. Discuss the duties of the state. It should protect and promote the dignity and rights of persons and the common good through moral means. Discuss ways the state does the following:
Protect and promote the dignity and rights of person:
- *Social aide programs*
- *Anti-discrimination laws*
- *Promote a fair and just society*
- *Protect life*

Protect and promote the common good:
- *Military efforts*
- *Legal/justice systems*
- *Health care*

Using moral means:
- *Respect freedom of people (no forced labor or involuntary medical treatments)*
- *Allows for freedom of religion*

3. The authority of the state comes from God. For it to have legitimate authority, the state must use its authority according to God's will. (You may review the first two kings of Israel, Saul, who lost authority and favor with God, and David, who served God. See 1 Sam 9:15—10:1 and 1 Sam 16:1–13.)

4. Watch the video "A Man for all Seasons." Discuss the life and the choices of Saint Thomas More. Discuss:
- Whose authority is greater, God's or man's?
- How did Saint Thomas More die as the king's good servant, when he did not do what the king wanted?

5. What are some modern day examples of how we must choose God's laws over man's laws. If a society does not have the right to command something against God's laws, how should we respond to these commands? What if a society allows something against God's laws?

Name:_____

God's Laws Come First

Answer the following questions in complete sentences.

1. Why are we not bound to obey laws that contradict God's laws?

   We are not bound to obey laws that contradict God's laws because the state has its authority from God and does not have the right to demand something which violates God's laws.

2. How is the state violating its authority if it demands something contrary to God's law?

   The state is violating its authority if it demands something contrary to God's law because the state receives its authority from God and is there to promote the common good through morally acceptable means. It is never morally acceptable to violate God's laws.

3. Explain the difficulty St. Thomas More faced and how it led to his martyrdom. What can we learn from the stand he took?

   Answers will vary.

Reinforce

1. Have the students work on *Activity Book*, p. 78.

2. Give the students time to work on their Memorization Questions and Words to Know.

3. Show the video "A Man for all Seasons," available through Ignatius Press, or study the life of Saint Thomas More.

4. Write letters to your government leaders, asking that civil laws obey God's laws. Topics might include:
• *Life issues (e.g., abortion)*
• *Social justice (e.g., care for elderly and the poor)*
• *Freedom of religion (e.g., praying in public, displaying nativity scenes in public, or religious slogans, such as "In God We Trust," on public buildings)*

Conclude

1. Lead the students in singing "All the world is God's own field," *Adoremus Hymnal*, #570.

2. End class with a prayer for one's country.

Preview

In the next lesson, the students will learn about the duties of citizens.

LAW

ETERNAL LAW

PHYSICAL LAWS
Laws for matter

MORAL LAWS
Laws for human wills

LAWS FROM GOD

LAWS FROM MEN

NATURAL LAW
Laws in nature

REVEALED LAW
Positive laws from God

ECCLESIASTICAL LAW
Made by the Church

CIVIL LAW
Made by competent civil authority

NOTES

_____
_____
_____
_____
_____
_____
_____
_____
_____
_____
_____
_____
_____

LESSON THREE: DUTIES OF CITIZENS

Aims

The students will learn that we are not bound to obey unjust laws. We are bound to obey all laws which conform to God's laws.

They will learn that citizens have a duty to promote patriotism. Citizens have a duty to use their influence to make their nation just. They must support the government through taxes and be willing to defend their country against unjust aggression. We must also pray for our country.

Materials

- *Activity Book*, p. 79

Optional:
- "All the world is God's own field," *Adoremus Hymnal*, #570

Begin

Being a citizen of a just society is a privilege. There are various forms of governments in the world, and some are unjust. As a citizen, we must develop the virtue of patriotism, which is rightly ordered love for one's country. This is not merely an emotional reaction but a deep sacrificial love. Patriotism prompts us to dedicate ourselves to promoting those things which are good for our country and its citizens. Today, we will discuss how we can exercise a healthy patriotism.

---

bound to obey them. In fact, in some sense they are not really laws. In such a situation we should think of the words of St. Peter to the Sanhedrin, "We must obey God rather than men" (Acts 5:29).

To illustrate this point—that God's law is above the law of the state—we can look at the life of St. Thomas More. Thomas More was a great lawyer and statesman in England at the beginning of the sixteenth century. He was a layman who dedicated himself to serving his country and his king. He rose to prominence during the reign of his friend King Henry VIII and was eventually appointed Chancellor of England, second in power to the king.

In order to divorce his wife, King Henry declared himself to be the supreme head of the Church in England. All of his subjects were then required to take an oath acknowledging this and declaring their primary allegiance to the king. Thomas More knew that he could not take this oath, for that would mean denying God's law.

On July 6, 1535, Thomas More was beheaded—by order of the king and his court—for refusing to sign the oath. Before he died, he reminded us that God's law is supreme: "I die the king's good servant, but God's first."

Civil Laws

Although we are not bound to obey such unjust laws, we are bound to obey all laws which conform to God's laws. For example, we must obey laws regarding the property rights of others. In addition to obeying just laws, there are several other duties which we have as citizens.

As citizens we must develop the virtue of **patriotism**, which is love of one's country. It is natural and good for us to love our native land. Patriotism is not merely the emotional reaction we may have when we sing our na-

tional anthem or see our nation's flag. This emotional reaction may be the beginning. However, patriotism is actually a deep love for our country which prompts us to dedicate ourselves to promoting those things which are good for our country and its citizens.

At the same time, we must avoid that excessive love of country which can result in the error of excessive *nationalism*. This can result from a love which is blind to the defects of one's nation. One must also avoid the opposite error which is a lack of love for one's country which can lead one to despise and turn against one's own country. The actual betrayal of one's country is known as *treason*.

The Christian citizen must use his influence to help make his nation just. This is an area in which the laity are especially called to bring Christ to the world. We must work to promote just and moral laws, in keeping with God's law. When there are unjust laws, we must work to change them. We must work to change harmful attitudes such as racism and lack of respect for human beings, including the unborn and the poor, by conforming our own attitudes to justice, truth, and love. In a democratic nation, the Christian, then, has a particular duty to take part in the government of his country—voting for good leaders or perhaps even running for office himself.

Duties of Citizens

There are also other duties which we have as citizens. We must support the government through the payment of taxes and we should, if necessary, be willing to defend our country against unjust aggression. Finally, as Christians we have a particular obligation to pray for our leaders and our country.

Besides being citizens of our nation, we are also members of the larger society of the world. We cannot isolate ourselves in our own nation,

131

Develop

1. Read paragraphs 7–12 (up to The Christian View of Creation).

2. Discuss the difference between patriotism and nationalism. See the box at right.

3. A Christian citizen has a greater duty than other citizens, for we are placed in our societies by God and must conform ourselves and these societies to his will. Therefore what are some things that Christians can do as citizens to promote a nation that is in accordance with God's will?
- *Use his influence to make his nation just*
- *Bring Christ to his society—be a witness of the faith*
- *Promote moral and just laws (in accord with God's laws) and fight against unjust laws*
- *Promote social justice*
- *Christians have a duty to vote when they can. We must vote for good leaders and even consider running for office.*

4. Other duties as citizens of our country include:
- *Pay taxes*
- *Defend our country against unjust aggression*
- *Pray for our country and our leaders*

5. How should we act as citizens of the world?
- *Be concerned for all peoples*
- *Support the missions*
- *Work for peace and justice in the world*
- *Corporal and Spiritual Works of Mercy*
- *Promote the goods of the entire human family*

6. Discussion questions for the students:
- Is it a sin to cheat on your taxes?
- Is it good to support the military? What about joining?
- What should you do if there are two candidates in an election and there are good and bad things about both? Who do you vote for?

Name:_____

Civil Laws

Answer the following questions in complete sentences.

1. Which civil laws are we bound to follow? Give an example of such a law.
   <u>We are bound to obey all civil laws which do not violate God's laws.</u>

2. What is patriotism?
   <u>Patriotism is a deep love for our country which prompts us to dedicate ourselves to promoting those things which are good for our country and its citizens.</u>

3. How are nationalism and treason disordered ways of loving one's country?
   <u>Nationalism is disordered because it is blind to the country's defects. Treason is disordered because it is a hatred of country that leads one to betray his country.</u>

4. List and explain the four duties we owe to our country as Christians.
   <u>The Christian must: 1) work to promote just and moral laws; 2) work to change unjust laws; 3) work to change harmful attitudes and 4) vote.</u>

5. How and why must we work for the common good beyond our nation? Give some examples of this need from recent news.
   <u>We must work for the common good beyond our nation because we are also members of the entire human family. We can do this by being concerned for all people and doing what we can to help them.</u>

Reinforce

1. Have the students work on *Activity Book*, p. 79.

2. Give the students time to work on their Memorization Questions and Words to Know.

3. The students may write prayers for their political leaders.

4. Have the students research the beliefs of various political parties. They should be able to debate key issues, such as social justice, life issues, and education. You may hold a mock election and then discuss why people voted for various candidates.

5. Collect goods for a mission church in a foreign country.

Conclude

1. Lead the students in singing "All the world is God's own field," *Adoremus Hymnal*, #570.

2. End class with a prayer for one's country.

Preview

In the next lesson, the students will learn about stewardship.

PATRIOTISM

Treason	Patriotism	Nationalism
"I hate my country, I wish I had never been born here!"	"This is my country, land that I love. May God heal the flaws in her."	"My country right or wrong!"

NOTES

_____
_____
_____
_____
_____
_____
_____
_____
_____
_____
_____

LESSON FOUR: STEWARDSHIP

Aims

The students will learn that God created the world out of nothing, giving man dominion over the created world. This dominion is to be exercised through stewardship—caring for the created world and using it according to God's plan.

Materials

- *Activity Book*, p. 80

Optional:
- "All the world is God's own field," *Adoremus Hymnal*, #570

Begin

Begin class by reading the story of creation (Gen 1–2). Diagram the creation of the world. Create story boards, a mural, or a dramatization of Creation. Discuss various principles that are important, using these questions:
- *Who created? (All persons of the Trinity were present in creation)*
- *From what did God create? (from nothing)*
- *Was all creation good?*
- *What role did man have in creation?*
- *What role does man still have in creation?*

---

but we must be concerned about all peoples. As Christians we have a responsibility to serve others—particularly those whose rights and human needs are not recognized. We must work for peace and justice in the world, practicing the corporal works of mercy wherever we can. Aside from the common good of a particular society, there is also a universal common good of the whole human family. This good requires an organization of the community of nations, which respects and promotes the rights of all peoples.

The Christian View of Creatures

In the first chapter of Genesis we read of the creation of the world. Out of nothing God brought into existence all the creatures of our world. First he created many inanimate objects—the sun, the moon, the mountains, and the seas. Then he made the various plants and the many animals—birds, fish, insects, and the beasts of the earth. Finally, as the pinnacle of his creation on earth, God created man and woman and said to them:

> Fill the earth and subdue it; and have dominion over the fish of the sea and over the birds of the air and over every living thing that moves upon the earth (Gen 1:28).

When God created the world he gave human beings *dominion* over his creation. This means that God made the earth and all of the creatures on it—animals, plants, mountains,

rivers, etc.—for us. They were made, first of all, to glorify God and to remind us of him and lead us to himself—as does, for example, a magnificent sunset. But these things were also made to give us joy.

Because we are the highest creatures on earth, we have been entrusted with a great responsibility to exercise **stewardship** over creation. This means that we must take care of creation and use wisely the many gifts God has given us. We must not waste or abuse any of God's creation. We should care for creation so that future generations can share in what God has given us. Man depends on air, water, forests, plants, and animals for his life, food, and clothing. Stewardship does not mean that we cannot kill animals for these purposes, but we must use them for our needs, not wastefully. Nor should we cause animals any unnecessary suffering but treat them kindly.

St. Francis of Assisi can be an example for us of the care we should have for all God's creatures. Francis loved not only the poor of this world but all of God's creatures as well—animals and all of nature. He saw all of creation as traces and reflections of God. His tenderness for and his gentle sway over animals were often noted by his companions. He spoke of animals and indeed, all creatures, as his "brothers" and "sisters." His beautiful "Canticle of the Sun" illustrates this reverence for God's work.

Words to Know:
common good   patriotism
stewardship

"Let every person be subject to the governing authorities. For there is no authority except from God, and those that exist have been instituted by God. . . . for he [in authority] is God's servant for your good."

(Rom 13:1–4)

132

Develop

1. Read paragraphs 13–16 (to the end of the chapter).

2. Why did God create? All creation gives glory to God. It reflects his beauty, order, majesty, etc. Creation should remind us of God and lead us to him. However, God also created out of love. He loved so greatly that this love was generous and life-giving. He created man in his image and gave dominion to man over all creation—in this way, creation is a gift to man to be used to unite man with God.

3. What is stewardship? It is the care of the created world. We must use creation according to God's plan and, through the wise use of creation, glorify God and tend to the needs of creatures (e.g., agriculture, medicine, etc.).

4. What are ways man wastes or abuses creation? Why is this wrong?

5. What responsibility do we have to preserve creation for the good of man and future generations? What would happen if we depleted the world's supply of fresh water? What if we no longer had fuel for energy? What if we destroyed the habitats of animals and the playgrounds for children? What if we allowed the industry of agriculture to be destroyed? What can we do to be good stewards?

6. How should we treat animals? Should all animals be domesticated (made into pets)? Is it ever good to kill an animal (hunting, farming)? What about torturing and abusing animals? Should animals have as many rights or more rights than humans?

7. Study the life of Saint Francis. How did he exemplify good stewardship? We often think of Saint Francis as the friar who loved nature and animals. Is this the only way we should see him? What other things did he do?

Name:_____

The Christian View of Creatures

Answer the following questions in complete sentences.

1. Explain man's dominion over creation. What sort of rights and responsibilities does it give us?
   Man's dominion over creation means that God made the earth, animals, plants, etc., to serve man's needs. This gives man the right to use all these things responsibly to serve himself. It gives man the responsibility to care for the earth and not to be wasteful or abusive of this great gift.

2. How do we exercise stewardship over creation?
   We exercise stewardship over creation by caring wisely for the earth and not being wasteful.

3. Give some examples of modern-day stewardship.
   Answers will vary.

4. What can we learn from St. Francis of Assisi's love of nature?
   Answers will vary.

Faith and Life Series • Grade 8 • Chapter 20 • Lesson 4

Reinforce

1. Have the students work on *Activity Book*, p. 80.

2. Give the students time to work on their Memorization Questions and Words to Know and to prepare for the chapter and unit quizzes.

3. Study the life of Saint Francis of Assisi.

4. Do a class project that reflects what the students have learned about stewardship; e.g., a recycling project, planting trees, adopting an abused pet for the classroom, etc.

5. Research and discuss the distribution of the world's natural goods/resources. How is this connected to social justice?

Conclude

1. Lead the students in singing "All the world is God's own field," *Adoremus Hymnal*, #570.

2. End class with a prayer for one's country.

Preview

In the next lesson, the students' understanding of the material covered in this chapter will be reviewed and assessed.

CREATION

Day 1: creates light; separates light from dark	Day 4: creates sun, moon, and stars
Day 2: creates sky; separates waters above from waters below	Day 5: creates water creatures and birds
Day 3: separates water and dry land; creates vegetation	Day 6: creates land animals and man

NOTES

_____

NOTES

_____

_____

_____

_____

_____

_____

_____

_____

_____

_____

_____

_____

_____

_____

_____

_____

_____

_____

_____

_____

_____

_____

Q. 119 *Why must we obey those in authority?*
We must obey those in authority because this authority comes from God, and to oppose it is to oppose the authority of God (CCC 2197, 2234, Rom 13:1–2).

Q. 120 *What is the duty of a citizen?*
The duty of a citizen is to contribute to the common good in a spirit of truth, justice, solidarity, and freedom. We are to love and serve the community, pay taxes, vote, and defend our country (CCC 2239–40).

Q. 121 *What must we do if those in authority command us to violate God's law?*
If those in authority command us to violate God's law, we must obey God rather than men (CCC 2242, Acts 5:29).

133

_____

_____

_____

_____

_____

_____

_____

_____

_____

_____

_____

_____

_____

Name: _____

The Christian in the World   **Quiz 20**

Part I: Define the following terms.

Common Good: <u>the welfare of the whole community, not just an individual</u>

Stewardship: <u>the call to take care of creation and use wisely the many gifts</u>
<u>God has given us</u>

Patriotism: <u>love of one's country</u>

Nationalism: <u>disordered love of country, which is blind to the defects of the</u>
<u>country</u>

Part II: Answer in complete sentences.

1. What duties does a Christian have to society?
<u>Christians should pray for their country and serve others, particularly</u>
<u>those whose rights and human needs are not recognized.</u>

2. What does a good society do?
<u>A good society promotes citizens' exercise of virtue, fosters</u>
<u>appropriate values, and establishes the conditions for the proper</u>
<u>exercise of freedom.</u>

Part III: On the back of this page, write an essay on the following topic.

In this country, the government has said it is legal to have an abortion. It is not forced upon people, but is provided upon request and is supported by government money. As a Christian, what are you morally obliged to do? (Consider whether you must obey this law, whether you can make changes to this law, and how you can promote a Christian society.)

Aims

The students' understanding of the material covered in this chapter and unit will be reviewed and assessed.

Materials

- Quiz 20, Appendix, p. A-28
- Unit 5 Test, Appendix, pp. A-29–A-30

Optional:
- "All the world is God's own field," *Adoremus Hymnal,* #570

Review

1. The students should understand that they are members of various societies. They should see that they are connected with others in society.

2. The students should understand what the common good is and how it should be promoted and protected, especially by the Church and the state.

3. The students should understand that in the hierarchy of authority, God's laws always come first.

4. The students should understand the duties of citizens.

5. The students should understand stewardship and be able to give practical examples of stewardship.

6. The students should be able to discuss the lives of Saint Thomas More and Saint Francis of Assisi.

Assess

1. Distribute the quizzes and read through them with the students to be sure they understand the questions.

2. Administer the quiz. As they hand in their work, orally quiz the students on the Memorization Questions from this chapter.

3. After all the quizzes have been handed in, review the correct answers with the class. Repeat steps 1–3 with the unit test.

Conclude

1. Lead the students in singing "All the world is God's own field," *Adoremus Hymnal,* #570.

2. End class with a prayer for one's country.

CHAPTER TWENTY-ONE
LAW AND CONSCIENCE

Catechism of the Catholic Church References

Choices Presented to the Conscience: 1786–89, 1799–1800, 1806
Civil Law: 1904
Conscience: 1776–1800
Divine Law: 707–10, 1953, 1970
Ecclesial Law: 1951, 2180, 2641–43
Erroneous Judgment: 1790–82, 1795–97
Formation of Conscience: 1783–85, 1789, 1971
God Creates an Ordered and Good World: 299

Jesus and the Law: 574–82, 592, 2052–55, 2075
Moral Law: 1950, 1984
Natural Moral Law: 1954–60, 1978–79
Old Law: 1961–64, 1975, 1980–82
New Law, or Law of the Gospel: 1965–74, 1977, 1983–86
Precepts of the Church: 2041–43
Revealed Law: 1962
The Commandments as Light and Foundation of Conscience: 1962

Scripture References

God's Loving Providence: Lk 12:4–7; 22–32; Mt 6:25–33

Natural Law Written on the Hearts of Men: Rom 2:15

Summary of Lesson Content

Lesson 1

God's providence governs all things.

The eternal law governs all creatures on earth. Eternal law has two parts: physical laws (also called laws of nature) and moral laws (which direct our wills toward the good). Eternal law cannot be repealed.

Lesson 2

The natural law is the basic moral law which God has placed in human nature and which we discover through reason.

Positive revealed law includes God's Commandments. The first stage of revelation (the Decalogue) by itself is imperfect. Revealed precepts confirm natural law. Natural law and the old revealed law were perfected in the revelation of Christ, who gave us the command to love. The Church is the authentic interpreter of the law.

Lesson 3

Many moral laws are made by humans. These laws are called human laws. Human laws are divided into civil and ecclesiastical.

The precepts of the Church are examples of ecclesiastical laws.

Human laws that repeat divine law are not human laws, but divine laws.

Lesson 4

Every man has a conscience—the internal guide to help him determine which actions are good and which are bad. Conscience is the capacity to judge an act in a given situation. It is an act of our reason, or intellect.

We must follow our conscience.

We are obliged to form our conscience properly.

LESSON ONE: PROVIDENCE

Aims

The students will learn that God's providence governs all things.

They will learn that the eternal law governs all creatures on earth. Eternal law has two parts: physical laws (also called laws of nature) and moral laws (which direct our wills toward the good). Eternal law cannot be repealed.

Materials

- *Activity Book*, p. 81

Optional:
- "Lead, kindly Light," *Adoremus Hymnal*, #578

Begin

Read Lk 12:4–7; 22–32 and Mt 6:25–33. These passages reveal God's loving providence for all of his creation, especially for man. Discuss the ways that God provides for our needs (directly and indirectly):

Directly:
- *Natural—food, water, sun, plants, etc.*
- *Supernatural—grace, sacraments, prayer, virtue, etc.*

Indirectly:
- *Parents who provide for our needs, etc.*

CHAPTER 21

Law and Conscience

They show that what the law requires is written on their hearts, while their conscience also bears witness and their conflicting thoughts accuse or perhaps excuse them.

Romans 2:15

"The law is holy, and the commandment is holy and just and good" (Rom 7:12).

When we look at the world we see that everything operates according to a certain plan or order. For example, rivers flow toward the sea, birds build nests each spring for their young, and when we drop a stone it falls to the ground. As Creator of the world, God has provided for all of his creatures. In his *providence* he governs all things, directing and ordering each to its proper end or purpose. This is the **eternal law** of God which encompasses all creatures on earth.

The chart on page 136 shows that all laws come from God, the Eternal Law. Let us examine each of these sorts of law.

Physical Laws

God's eternal law is first divided into *physical laws* and *moral laws*. Physical laws, also called *laws of nature*, are those which govern the nature and operation of all material things and natural forces. The law of gravity or other laws of physics and chemistry are examples of physical laws. The instincts of animals, which cause them to act in particular ways, are also

134

physical laws. The laws which govern the physical world can neither be disobeyed nor repealed.

The laws which direct our will toward the good are called **moral laws**. Since human beings have free wills, the laws which guide our actions can be broken. We are always free to choose good or evil. Such laws help us to direct our wills toward their proper purpose—perfection on earth and, finally, happiness in heaven.

Blessed are those whose way is blameless, who walk in the law of the Lord! . . . who also do no wrong, but walk in his ways! (Ps 119:1, 3).

The entire moral law comes to us from God. Part of it comes directly from him, but another part of it comes indirectly from him through a human lawgiver. The first part, **divine law**, is divided into two sorts—*natural law* and *revealed law*.

Divine Law

Natural Law

The **natural law** is the basic moral law which God has placed in human nature and

---

Develop

1. Read paragraphs 1–5 (up to Divine Law).

2. Review the chart on p. 243 showing the levels of law.

3. Discuss the eternal law with the students. The eternal law includes both physical and moral laws. God sustains the eternal law and, in this way, directs all of creation according to his plan.

4. Discuss the physical eternal laws. Have the students give examples, such as: birds flying south every winter, spiders building webs, spring always following winter, etc. Have the students think of how God directs the natural laws in both big ways and small ways. Consider the vast expanse of the universe, the laws of nature (e.g., gravity), etc. Consider also the tiniest details of God's creation, which he also cares for and directs; e.g., colonies of ants, the workings of a cell and microscopic organisms, etc. Finally, consider man—the

greatest of all creatures. A single man is more important than all the animals and stars. Man has an eternal soul, which is of great value to God—we know this because he sent his Son, Jesus Christ, to suffer and die so that we might have life and be united with God forever.

5. Discuss the eternal moral laws with the students. Man has free will, which means he can choose to do good or evil. The moral laws direct man to choose the good. What are some of the goods that moral law directs us to do? The goal of moral law is to unite man with God for eternity in heaven.

6. Explain that, unlike plants, animals, planets, etc., we can freely choose to disobey God's law. However, if we fail to obey God's law, we cause disorder. Use the example of a symphony. A composer writes the music, but the musicians can choose to play any notes they want. Would the music be beautiful if the musicians chose not to obey the composer?

Name:_____

Eternal Law

Write a brief essay about the two divisions of God's eternal law. Describe and give examples of each type of law, and answer the following questions: What is their purpose? Can they be disobeyed? Can they change?

Physical Laws:

<u>Answers will vary.</u>

_____
_____
_____
_____
_____
_____
_____
_____
_____
_____

Moral Laws:

<u>Answers will vary.</u>

_____
_____
_____
_____
_____
_____
_____
_____
_____

Faith and Life Series • Grade 8 • Chapter 21 • Lesson 1　　　81

Reinforce

1. Have the students work on *Activity Book*, p. 81.

2. Give the students time to work on the Memorization Questions and Words to Know from this chapter.

3. Have the students write about a time in their lives when God's providence could be seen. Perhaps they did not clearly see the hand of God at the time, but now that they have had a chance to look back, they can see that God was indeed there at all times.

4. Give the students silent time to pray and praise God for his providence in each of their lives.

Conclude

1. Teach the students to sing "Lead, kindly Light," *Adoremus Hymnal*, #578.

2. End class by leading the students in the Prayer before Confession.

Preview

In the next lesson, the students will learn about divine law.

EXAMPLES OF THE PHYSICAL ETERNAL LAW

Macro examples: the universe, planetary alignments, the rotation of the earth, the tides, gravity, etc.

Micro examples: single cell organisms, the circulatory system and instincts of an animal, the structure of an atom, etc.

Human examples: the development of a person from conception to adulthood and the nervous system.

NOTES

_____
_____
_____
_____
_____
_____
_____
_____
_____
_____

LESSON TWO: DIVINE LAW

Aims

The students will learn that the natural law is the basic moral law which God has placed in human nature and which we discover through reason.

They will learn that positive revealed law includes God's Commandments. The first stage of revelation (the Decalogue) by itself is imperfect. Revealed precepts confirm natural law. Natural law and the old revealed law were perfected in the revelation of Christ, who gave us the command to love. The Church is the authentic interpreter of the law.

Materials

- *Activity Book*, p. 82

Optional:
- "Lead, kindly Light," *Adoremus Hymnal*, #578

Begin

Review examples of providence.

Review the eternal law. Eternal law includes the physical laws and the moral laws. Have the students give examples of each. The moral laws are subdivided into the divine laws and the human laws. Today we will learn about the divine moral laws.

---

which we discover through reason. This law is written in the hearts of men, and its most basic principle is "Do good and avoid evil." However, because of original sin, which has clouded our intellects, we do not always recognize what is good and what is evil. Most people, even pagans, can easily see that certain things, like murder, stealing, or lying are wrong. However, it is not so easy to see that at times it can be wrong to say something which is actually true. For example, spreading facts that would deliberately harm or embarrass another person might be seriously wrong.

Revealed Law

Because human beings often find it difficult to know what is right and wrong on their own, God has also revealed certain commandments to us. This is what we call *positive* or *revealed law*. These are the commandments which are contained in the Old Law given through Moses at Mount Sinai and the New Law given by Our Lord when he was on earth. The Old Law was given by God in the Old Testament—for example, the Ten Commandments. This law was the first stage of God's revelation and by itself is incomplete. This law was perfected in the New Testament. Our Lord said: "Think not that I have come to abolish the law and the prophets; I have come not to abolish them but

to fulfill them" (Mt 5:17). Our Lord tells us to keep his law out of love rather than out of fear (Jn 14:15). While the Ten Commandments are examples of revealed laws given in the Old Testament, the forbidding of divorce by Jesus (Mt 19:1–9) is an example of a revealed law from the New Testament. It is important to recall that the Church's magisterium is the authentic interpreter of divine law, that is, of both the natural law and positive revealed law.

Many of the revealed precepts repeat and confirm points in the natural law which men might discover on their own. God repeats these —for example, "Thou shalt not kill," "Thou shalt not steal"—because of their importance. Other precepts require God's revelation if we are to know them. Thus, for example, God tells us that we are to worship him on a particular day each week.

Human Laws

Many moral laws are made by humans themselves and are called *human laws*. Human laws are divided into *civil laws* and *ecclesiastical* (Church) *laws*. **Civil laws** are those made by the civil authorities. Laws regarding the payment of taxes or traffic laws are examples.

Ecclesiastical laws are those made by the Church. There are many ecclesiatical laws, and they are contained in the book of Canon

> ### Church Teaching
>
> ". . . In forming their consciences the faithful must pay careful attention to the sacred and certain teaching of the Church. For the Catholic Church is, by the will of Christ, the teacher of truth. It is her duty to proclaim and teach with authority the truth which is Christ and, at the same time, to declare and confirm by her authority the principles of the moral order which spring from human nature itself" (DH, 14).

135

Develop

1. Read paragraphs 6–8 (up to Human Laws).

2. Discuss the ways that God communicates with us. He sometimes (but rarely) directly speaks to us—as he did to Moses; God spoke through Jesus Christ, and he speaks in mystical ways, through apparitions/visions/locutions. Usually God's communication is a gentle, quiet voice that we must follow in our lives. God also communicates with us indirectly—through others. Some examples of indirect communication might include your teacher of religion, who is passing on God's teaching, the priest, who confers the grace of Christ in the sacraments, and family and friends, who share the love of Christ with us. Have the students give examples.

3. Today, we will speak about God's direct communication of the moral law: the divine law. Divine law includes both natural and revealed law.

- *Natural law: The basic moral law, which God has placed in human nature and which we discover through reason. Natural law is written on the hearts of man (Rom 2:15). It states: do good; avoid evil. Sometimes this is not clear because of the effects of original sin.*
- *Revealed law: Revealed or positive law was given to man because it is difficult for man to know what is right and wrong on his own. Out of mercy, he gave us his law in the Ten Commandments (Decalogue). This law was perfected by Jesus, who taught us to live the law of God in love. Many of the teachings in the revealed law repeat what is known in the natural law: e.g., do not kill. Other precepts require God's revelation if we are to know them; e.g., honor the Lord's Day.*

4. The divine moral law is binding upon all people.

Name:_____

Natural and Revealed Moral Law

Write a brief essay comparing natural and revealed moral law using the information given in your student text. Be sure to include the source of each and to explain why we need both.

Natural Law:

Answers will vary.

_____

_____

_____

_____

_____

_____

_____

_____

_____

_____

Revealed Law:

Answers will vary.

_____

_____

_____

_____

_____

_____

_____

_____

_____

_____

82   *Faith and Life Series • Grade 8 • Chapter 21 • Lesson 2*

1. Have the students work on *Activity Book*, p. 82.

2. Give the students time to work on the Memorization Questions and Words to Know from this chapter.

3. Have the students look for Bible verses that reflect the natural laws.

4. Lead the students in an age-appropriate examination of conscience, based upon the Ten Commandments. (The students need to understand that each commandment forbids a multitude of sins.) You may wish to review mortal and venial sin.

Conclude

1. Lead the students in singing "Lead, kindly Light," *Adoremus Hymnal*, #578.

2. End class by leading the students in the Prayer before Confession.

Preview

In the next lesson, the students will learn about human law.

SAINT THOMAS AQUINAS

Saint Thomas Aquinas, the Angelic Doctor, is one of the greatest theologians of the Church. Although he lived in the thirteenth century, his philosophical and theological writings are still held in high esteem. During the Council of Trent (sixteenth century), the council fathers laid his books on the altar along with the Scriptures, and recently the writers of the new *Catechism of the Catholic Church* followed his schema of discussing man's ultimate end, the virtues, and then the Commandments when presenting the moral teachings of the Church (Part Three of the *Catechism*). In 1879, Pope Leo wrote an encyclical encouraging a revival of Thomistic studies, saying: "It has come to light that there were not lacking among the leaders of heretical sects some who openly declared that, if the teaching of Thomas Aquinas were only taken away, they could easily battle with all Catholic teachers, gain the victory, and abolish the Church. A vain hope, indeed, but no vain testimony" (*Aeterni Patris* 23). Because of his intellectual brilliance, it is easy to see Saint Thomas as no more than a philosopher, but we must remember that he was first and foremost a saint. This means that he lived what he taught. He wrote many theological works, Scriptural commentaries, and Eucharistic hymns and spent many hours in prayer between writing. Three months before he died, he was caught up into a sort of rapture while celebrating Mass. After that, he spoke little and wrote nothing, saying that, after what God had shown him, all he had written seemed as chaff.

LESSON THREE: HUMAN LAW

Aims

The students will learn that many moral laws are made by humans. These laws are called human laws. Human laws are divided into civil and ecclesiastical.

They will learn that the precepts of the Church are examples of ecclesiastical laws. Human laws that repeat divine law are not human laws, but divine laws.

Materials

- *Activity Book*, p. 83

Optional:
- "Lead, kindly Light," *Adoremus Hymnal*, #578

Begin

Review the eternal law: physical and moral. The moral law is divided into divine and human law. In the last lesson, the class learned how the divine law was divided into natural and revealed law. They should be able to give examples of each.

Today, the students will learn about human law.

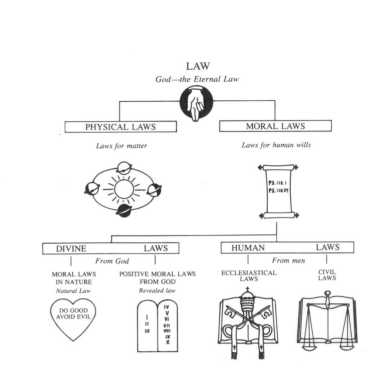

Law. They are particularly important for all Catholics and we should know them. These are the precepts of the Church:

Precepts of the Church

1. "You shall attend Mass on Sundays and on holy days of obligation and rest from servile labor." The first precept requires us to keep holy the day of the Lord's Resurrection; to worship God by participating in Mass every Sunday and holy day of obligation; to avoid those activities that would hinder renewal of soul and body on the Lord's day.

2. "You shall confess your sins at least once a year." The second precept requires us to lead a sacramental life; to receive the Sacrament of Penance regularly—minimally, to receive the Sacrament of Penance at least once a year (annual confession is obligatory only if serious sin is involved) in preparation to receive Holy Communion.

3. "You shall receive the Sacrament of the Eucharist at least during the Easter Season." The third precept requires us to receive Holy Communion frequently; minimally, to receive Holy Communion once during the Easter Season.

136

Develop

1. Read paragraphs 9–21 (including the Precepts of the Church, up to Conscience).

2. Human law is divided into two categories: civil (state) and ecclesiastical (Church).

3. The civil laws receive their authority from God. To be binding, human laws must cooperate with God's laws. This means a law that is contrary to divine law is not binding. For example, if the state made a law requiring people to worship the president, this law would not be binding, since it violates the First Commandment. Civil laws are enforced by state agencies; e.g., traffic laws, taxes, etc.

4. The ecclesiastical laws are made by the Church. You may review that the Catholic Church finds her authority in Jesus Christ himself.

5. The ecclesiastical moral laws are recorded in the code of Canon Law. These are rules for the governing of the Church, and are binding. Part of these rules, which must be known and practiced by all Catholics, are the Precepts of the Church. Review the Precepts, listed on pp. 136-37 of the student text.

6. Sometimes human laws repeat divine laws. These are not equal. When something is repeated in human law, it is simply reaffirming the more important divine law. An example is the civil law against murder—this simply repeats the Fifth Commandment, which is more important and of greater consequence. (Note: divine laws cannot be changed by men.)

7. Discuss the need to follow both the letter and spirit of the law. The letter of the law refers to the actual words of the law; the spirit refers to the understanding behind the law.

Name:_____

Ecclesiastical Laws

Answer the following questions in complete sentences.

1. What are the ecclesiastical laws, who makes them, and where are they found?
   Ecclesiastical laws are Church laws. They are made by Church officials and are found in the Code of Canon Law.

2. What are the seven precepts of the Church?
   The seven precepts of the Church are 1) to keep holy Sundays and Holy Days of Obligation; 2) to lead a sacramental life; 3) to study Church teaching; 4) to observe the marriage laws of the Church; 5) to strengthen and support the Church; 6) to do penance and 7) to join the missionary spirit and apostolate of the Church.

3. What is the "spirit" and the "letter" of the law and how can charity keep us from excessive legalism?
   The "spirit" of the law is the understanding behind the law and the "letter" of the law is the actual word. Charity can keep us from excessive legalism because the highest law is the law of love and all other laws are subordinate to that.

THE PRECEPTS OF THE CHURCH

1. Attend Mass on Sundays and holy days of obligation.

2. Receive the Sacrament of Penance at least once a year in the case of grave sin.

3. Receive the Sacrament of the Eucharist at least once a year during the Easter Season.

4. Observe the days of fasting and abstinence established by the Church.

5. Provide for the needs of the Church.

See CCC 2042–43.

Reinforce

1. Have the students work on *Activity Book*, p. 83.

2. Give the students time to work on the Memorization Questions and Words to Know from this chapter.

3. The students must memorize the Precepts of the Church.

4. *Discuss the authority of the Church. Authority was given to the Church by Christ himself. This authority rests upon the apostles and their successors, the bishops.*

5. Have the students play a review game, strengthening their grasp of the Decalogue, the Precepts, and other laws they should know.

Conclude

1. Lead the students in singing "Lead, kindly Light," *Adoremus Hymnal*, #578.

2. End class by leading the students in the Prayer before Confession.

Preview

In the next lesson, the students will learn about conscience.

NOTES

_____
_____
_____
_____
_____
_____
_____
_____
_____
_____
_____
_____
_____
_____

LESSON FOUR: CONSCIENCE

Aims

The students will learn that every man has a conscience—the internal guide to help him determine which actions are good and which are bad. Conscience is the capacity to judge an act in a given situation. It is an act of our reason, or intellect.

They will learn that we must follow our conscience. We are obliged to form our conscience properly.

Materials

- *Activity Book*, p. 84

Optional:
- "Lead, kindly Light," *Adoremus Hymnal*, #578

Begin

Begin class with a review game. Review the definitions of the various types of law, the Decalogue, precepts of the Church, and examples of the various types of law.

The students should have the precepts of the Church memorized.

---

4. "You shall observe the days of fasting and abstinence established by the Church." The fourth precept requires us to do penance, including abstaining from meat and fasting from food on the appointed days.

5. "You shall help to provide for the needs of the Church." The fifth precept requires us to strengthen and support the Church—one's own parish community and parish priests, the worldwide Church, and the Pope.

(CCC 2042–43)

Sometimes the government and the Church repeat and reaffirm divine laws. For example, a state may have laws against murder or stealing, and the Church also teaches us that these actions are wrong. Such laws, though repeated by men, are *not* human laws. They are *divine laws*. It is important to understand this because these laws cannot be changed by men.

We must also realize that there is a hierarchy among laws; for example, God's laws are higher than man's. Thus if a law of man is in conflict with or contradicts a law of God, we must follow God's law. This was what Thomas More did, as we saw in the last chapter.

When we speak of laws we speak of both the *spirit* and the *letter* of the law. The spirit is the understanding behind the law and the letter is the actual words of the law. In following these laws we must follow both the spirit and the letter.

There is a clear difference between the law and legalism. Christ said, "It is easier for heaven and earth to pass away, than for one dot of the law to become void" (Lk 16:17). On the other hand, he severely rebuked the Pharisees for their legalism. They had forgotten all about the spirit behind the law, while holding fast to the letter. Thus they made the law void. For instance, there was a tradition among them that

if you said to your parents that you were dedicating your goods to God, then you were no longer obliged to help and honor them. Jesus said, "So for the sake of your tradition, you have made void the word of God. You hypocrites! Well did Isaiah prophesy of you, when he said: 'This people honors me with their lips, but their heart is far from me'" (Mt 15:6–9). Time and again Christ showed that the law of charity is supreme. It does not void the law but fulfills it. St. Paul reminds us: "Above all these put on love" (Col 3:14).

Conscience

Besides the external guide of the moral law, God has also given us an internal guide to help us determine which actions are good and which are bad. This is known as our **conscience**. Many of us may think of our conscience as a 'little voice'—like Jiminy Cricket—which tells us what to do or scolds us when we do wrong.

137

Develop

1. Read paragraphs 22–25 (to the end of the chapter).

2. Define the term "conscience." It is a judgment of reason whereby we recognize the morality of an act. Emphasize that right conscience is informed and reasonable. Conscience speaks with reason, not with feeling or emotion. We use our conscience in any given situation, when we judge an action to be right or wrong.

3. Ask the students to give descriptions of conscience. Examples might include: a friendly warning, an encouraging voice, a pleading force, God's voice/messenger.

4. Every person is obliged to follow his conscience—even if it is malformed! Imagine if your conscience told you it was right to steal and that if you did not steal you would be sinning. Because a malformed conscience is so dangerous, it is of great importance to form our conscience properly. We are obliged to form our conscience properly, using the

divine and human law (see Chalk Talk on p. 259, at right).

5. We must never act on a doubtful conscience. If we are not sure whether something is right or wrong, we must find out before we act. Where can we find answers to our questions? (Read the Bible, ask a priest, read the Catechism, look in Canon Law, etc.) It is important to form our conscience well and to listen to our conscience. Conscience can become lax through lack of education and through sin (this is why when we tell one lie, it is easier to tell another).

6. Some people choose not to know the truth—they are failing in the duty of forming their conscience.

7. A scrupulous conscience is one that magnifies the gravity of sin or sees sin where there is none.

Name:_____

Conscience

Answer the following questions in complete sentences.

1. What is the conscience and what does it do?

   The conscience is our God-given internal guide which helps us determine which actions are good and which are bad.

2. Is the conscience in the intellect, will, or passions (emotions)? Explain.

   The conscience is an act of the intellect because it is an application of certain moral principles to specific, concrete moral situations.

3. Why is it so important that a conscience be correctly formed and how are we to be sure it is correctly formed?

   It is so important that a conscience be correctly formed because we are obliged to follow our conscience. If we have a well-formed conscience and make correct judgments, then we will have a true conscience. If not, we will have a false conscience and will still suffer the consequences of our actions.

5. Explain the difference between true, lax, and scrupulous consciences.

   A true conscience is when a well-formed conscience makes a correct judgment. A lax conscience is an incorrect judgment which fails to see sin where sin actually exists. A scrupulous conscience is an incorrect judgment which sees sin where sin does not exist.

Reinforce

1. Have the students work on *Activity Book*, p. 84.

2. Give the students time to work on the Memorization Questions and Words to Know from this chapter and to prepare for the quiz.

3. Discuss the lives of saints who followed their consciences. Include Saint Maria Goretti, who denied the advances of Alexander, etc.

4. Review, if you have not already, mortal and venial sin.

5. Give your students an opportunity to receive the Sacrament of Penance.

Conclude

1. Lead the students in singing "Lead, kindly Light," *Adoremus Hymnal*, #578.

2. End class by leading the students in the Prayer before Confession.

Preview

In the next lesson, the students' understanding of the material covered in this chapter will be reviewed and assessed.

CHALK TALK: HOW TO FORM YOUR CONSCIENCE

NOTES

_____
_____
_____
_____
_____
_____
_____
_____
_____
_____
_____
_____

Church Teaching

"It is through his conscience that man sees and recognizes the demands of the divine law. He is bound to follow this conscience faithfully in all his activity so that he may come to God, who is his last end. Therefore he must not be forced to act contrary to his conscience. Nor must he be prevented from acting according to his conscience, especially in religious matters" (DH, 3).

This is a false understanding of conscience.

Conscience is a specific action of our reason, or intellect, by which we judge the rightness or wrongness of a particular action. It is not a feeling or emotion. Conscience is the application of certain principles—found in the moral law—to a specific, concrete moral situation.

In order to be of any use to us, our conscience must be correctly *formed* or taught. We are obliged to follow our conscience, but we are also obliged to make sure that our conscience is properly formed.

When our conscience is correctly formed and the judgments which we make are correct, we have a *true* conscience. If our judgments are incorrect we have a *false* conscience. A false conscience is lax if it fails to see sin where sin actually exists. For example, our conscience is lax if we do not think deliberately missing Mass on Sunday is a serious sin. A false conscience is scrupulous if it magnifies the gravity of sin or finds sin where there really is none. For example, our conscience is scrupulous if we think that missing Sunday Mass when we are very ill is a sin. Such false consciences have not been correctly formed.

To form our conscience we must look to the Church, which speaks the Word of God to us today, and we must listen to her voice. At the same time we should try to understand these laws of God so that we may be better able to follow them.

Words to Know:

eternal law   moral law   divine law
natural law   civil law
ecclesiastical law   conscience

Q. 122 *What is mortal sin?*
Mortal sin is an act of disobedience to the law of God in a serious matter, done with full knowledge and deliberate consent (CCC 1857).

Q. 123 *Why is serious deliberate sin called "mortal"?*
Serious deliberate sin is called mortal because it takes divine grace away from the soul, which is its life, and it makes the soul worthy of everlasting punishment and eternal death in hell (CCC 1855, 1861).

138

Q. 124 *What is venial sin?*

Venial sin is an act of disobedience to the law of God in a lesser matter, or in a matter that is serious, but done without full knowledge or consent (CCC 1862).

Q. 125 *What is an occasion of sin?*

An occasion of sin is any person, circumstance, or thing that puts us in danger of sinning (CCC 1865–69).

Q. 126 *Are we obliged to avoid the occasions of sin?*

Yes, we are obliged to avoid the occasions of sin because we are obliged to avoid sin itself (CCC 1451).

Q. 127 *Why does the Church have the authority to make laws and precepts?*

The Church has the authority to make laws and precepts because she has received this authority from Jesus Christ through his apostles (CCC 2035–38).

Q. 128 *Must the members of the Church obey the precepts of the Church?*

Yes, members of the Church must obey the precepts of the Church (CCC 2037).

Q. 129 *What is conscience?*

Conscience is the use of the reason or intellect in a person to judge the rightness or wrongness of an action. It is the application of certain principles (in the moral law) and must be formed correctly, for man is obliged to follow it (CCC 1777–78, 1783).

139

CHAPTER TWENTY-ONE
REVIEW AND ASSESSMENT

Aims

The students' understanding of the material covered in this chapter will be reviewed and assessed.

Materials

• Quiz 21, Appendix, p. A-31

Optional:
• "Lead, kindly Light," *Adoremus Hymnal*, #578

Review

1. The students should understand providence.

2. The students should be able to define each of the following and give examples:

Eternal Law:
• Physical law
• Moral law
    • Divine law
        • Natural law
        • Revealed law
    • Human Law
        • Ecclesiastical law
        • Civil law
• Conscience:
    • True conscience
        • Natural law
        • Revealed law
        • Ecclesiastical law
    • False Conscience
        • Lax conscience
        • Scrupulous conscience

Name: _____

Law and Conscience   **Quiz 21**

Part I: Explain the source, purpose, and characteristics of the following types of law.

Physical laws: <u>the laws which govern the nature and operation of all material things and natural forces</u>

Moral laws: <u>the laws which direct our wills toward the good</u>

Civil laws: <u>the laws made by civil authorities</u>

Natural laws: <u>the basic moral law, which God has placed in human nature and which we discover through reason</u>

Revealed laws: <u>the laws given to us by God</u>

Ecclesiastical laws: <u>ecclesiastical laws are Church laws made by Church officials</u>

Part II: Answer in complete sentences.

1. What is a conscience?
<u>A conscience is our God-given internal guide, which helps us determine which actions are good and which are bad.</u>

2. Why must a conscience be correctly formed? How does one form a conscience?
<u>A conscience must be formed correctly because we are obliged to follow our conscience and it guides our actions. In order to form one's conscience well, one should look to the Church for guidance and try to understand her teachings.</u>

3. Can a well-formed conscience ever lead one to disobey Church teaching?
<u>No. A well-formed conscience would never lead one to disobey Church teaching.</u>

4. Explain, using examples, a true conscience, a lax conscience, and a scrupulous conscience.
<u>A true conscience is when a well-formed conscience makes a correct judgment. A lax conscience is an incorrect judgment, which fails to see sin where sin actually exists. A scrupulous conscience is an incorrect judgment, which sees sin where sin does not exist. Examples will vary.</u>

Faith and Life • Grade 8 • Appendix A   *A - 31*

Assess

1. Distribute the quizzes and read through them with the students to be sure they understand the questions.

2. Administer the quiz. As they hand in their work, orally quiz the students on the Memorization Questions from this chapter.

3. After all the quizzes have been handed in, review the correct answers with the class.

Conclude

1. Lead the students in singing "Lead, kindly Light," *Adoremus Hymnal*, #578.

2. End class by leading the students in the Prayer before Confession.

CHAPTER TWENTY-TWO
THE CHURCH AND THE SOCIAL ORDER

Catechism of the Catholic Church References

Dignity of the Human Person: 1700–1712
Economic Activity and Social Justice: 2426–36, 2459–60
Equality and Differences among Men: 1934–38, 1944–46
Human Life: 2258–2330
Justice and Solidarity among Nations: 2437–42, 2461
Love for the Poor; the Works of Mercy: 2443–49, 2462–63
Man Created in the Image of God: 355–57, 380–81

Principles of Church and State Relationship: 2244–46
Respect for Human Life: 2259–83, 2319–25
Respect for the Human Person: 1929–33, 1943–44
Safeguarding Peace and Avoiding War: 2302–17, 2327–30
Social Justice: 2420–2425
Social Teaching of the Church: 2419–25, 2458

Scripture References

Four Sins that Cry Out to Heaven for Justice:
    Murder: Gen 4:19
    Sodomy: Gen 18:20; 19:1–23
    Oppression of the Poor: Ex 3:7–10; Deut 24:14–15
    Unjust Wage: Jas 5:4

Great Commission: Mt 28:19–20

Summary of Lesson Content

Lesson 1

The Great Commission tells us to spread the Gospel and form Christian nations. We are obliged to help shape society so that the public morality will be Christian morality.

Encyclicals include matters of Church social teaching. These are letters by the popes to all the bishops. They discuss various matters of Church teaching, including her social teaching.

Lesson 2

Man has a duty to protect human life. Willful murder is a sin that cries out to God.

Abortion is the murder of unborn babies (in the wombs of their mothers).

Euthanasia is the murder of the elderly or physically impaired.

Lesson 3

The Church teaches that man may protect himself (and his nation) from unjust aggression. Protecting oneself is self-defense.

The Church has guidelines for just war. For a war to be just, all avenues for peace must be exhausted and a proportionate response must be used.

Lesson 4

Justice is giving everyone what is due to him. Social justice establishes conditions in society that allow individuals or groups to obtain their due. Social justice often addresses economic or civil matters.

Christians are obliged to care for the unfortunate and underprivileged among us (worldwide).

Aims

The students will learn that the Great Commission tells us to spread the Gospel and form Christian nations. We are obliged to help shape society so that the public morality will be Christian morality.

They will learn that encyclicals are letters by the popes to all the bishops. They discuss various matters of Church teaching, including social teaching.

Materials

- *Activity Book*, p. 85
- *Bible*
- *Paper and pen*

Optional:
- "I heard the voice of Jesus say," *Adoremus Hymnal*, #579

Begin

Begin class by handing out bibles, pencils and paper to all the students. Have them find the four sins that cry out to God (these are also in the text):

- Gen 4:19 (murder)
- Gen 18:20; 19:1–23 (homosexuality, rape)
- Ex 3:7–10 (slavery, oppression)
- Deut 24:14–15 (slavery, oppression)
- Jas 5:4 (unjust wage)

Discuss these passages.

CHAPTER 22

The Church and the Social Order

For God sent the Son into the world, not to condemn the world, but that the world might be saved through him.

John 3:17

Immediately before the Ascension, Our Lord stood on the mountain in Galilee and said these words to his apostles: "Go therefore and make disciples of all nations, baptizing them in the name of the Father and of the Son and of the Holy Spirit, teaching them to observe all that I have commanded you. . ." (Mt 28:19–20). This final command tells us of the duty to spread the gospel to every man. But Our Lord meant more than baptizing individuals. He told the apostles to baptize all nations. This means to infuse society with the message of the gospel —to *form Christian nations*.

The Church's duty then extends beyond drawing individuals to Christ. The Church must also help to shape society so that the public morality will be Christian. In this way the Church "baptizes" the social order, so that all things may be renewed in Christ.

In Scripture we find mentioned four sins which "cry to heaven for vengeance." They are sodomy (perverse sexual behavior), willful murder, oppression of the poor, and defrauding the laborer of his just wage. These sins do not "cry to heaven" because they are the most serious sins. Idolatry and blasphemy, for ex-

ample, are even worse. These four sins, however, are all injustices which undermine the fundamental order of society—particularly the family, the basic unit of society. Because of their effect on society, the Church, over the centuries, has often addressed these matters in her social teachings.

Much of the Church's social teaching may be found in the *encyclicals* of the popes. These letters addressed to all the bishops and the entire Church are also a means of instructing the world and bringing the gospel to all nations. As we consider the last three of the sins which cry out to heaven, we will mention some of these encyclicals. Because they are addressed to the entire Church, they were written originally in the universal language of the Church — Latin. Below, the Latin title of each encyclical is given with the English title in parentheses.

Protection of Human Life

"Cain rose up against his brother Abel, and killed him. Then the Lord said to Cain, 'Where is Abel your brother? . . .

141

Develop

1. Read paragraphs 1–4 (up to Protection of Human Life).

2. Review the Great Commission: Mt 28:19–20. Jesus called the Apostles to baptize and teach all nations—to spread the Good News and form Christian nations.

3. The Church has a duty to bring people to Christ. How do we do this? How can you do this? How can the students share their faith and invite others to Catholicism?

4. The Church must help to shape society so that the public morality will be Christian. Review the four sins that cry to heaven for justice. These sins undermine the fundamental order of society, especially the family. How do each of these sins undermine the family? Discuss this with the students.
- *Murder: Murder is the taking of innocent life. All innocent life is a blessing, building up society and giving glory to God.*

- *Oppression of the Poor: Some people are successful by preventing others from being successful. The poor are dearly loved in God's eyes. We should see Christ in every person, especially the poor. Oppression is a way of degrading the value of a person. Some people are oppressed because of their gender, color, race, religion, etc.*
- *Sodomy (perverse sexual behavior): We must love the sinner, but hate the sin. Perverse sexual behavior attacks the sacred marital union and the security of the family.*
- *Defrauding the laborer of a just wage: A just wage is the amount needed to support a family.*

5. Encyclicals are letters of the popes, addressed to all the bishops of the Church. They are a way of instructing the faithful and bringing the Christian message to the world.

Name:_____

The Church and the Social Order

Answer the following questions in complete sentences.

1. How does Jesus' last command to his apostles require more than individual baptisms?

   Jesus' last command to his apostles required more than individual baptisms because Jesus said to "baptize all nations" and so we must infuse the society with Christianity.

2. What does it mean to form a Christian nation?

   To form a Christian nation means that we need to shape society so that public morality will be Christian.

3. Which four sins cry out to heaven? What is significant about these four sins?

   Four sins which cry out to heaven are sodomy, murder, oppression of the poor, and defrauding the laborer of his just wage. They cry out to heaven because they undermine the fundamental order of society, in particular, the family.

4. What are encyclicals and why are they important?

   Encyclicals are papal letters addressed to the bishops and the entire Church to express Church teaching on an important matter. They are important because they often address current issues and help clarify the Church teaching on them.

Reinforce

1. Have the students work on *Activity Book*, p. 85.

2. Give the students time to work on the Memorization Questions and Words to Know from this chapter.

3. *Discuss the privilege of being a Catholic. We should have great enthusiasm for our faith, and should desire to share it with others. How can we do this?*

4. You may want to discuss the topic of homosexuality. Review the Church's teaching that sexual powers are ordered to marriage, which is a life-long union between a man and a woman for the goods of children, unity, and mutual sanctification. Homosexual activity cannot do this. We should, however, love the sinner, and hate the sin. Homosexual orientation is not a sin, but homosexual activity is, just as premarital or extramarital sex is a sin.

Conclude

1. Teach the students to sing "I heard the voice of Jesus say," *Adoremus Hymnal*, #579.

2. End class by leading the students in a prayer for social justice.

Preview

In the next lesson, the students will learn about the protection of human life.

PAPAL ENCYCLICALS THAT ADDRESS THE FOUR SINS THAT CRY TO HEAVEN

- Pope Leo XIII, *Rerum Novarum*, "On Capital and Labor"
- Pope Pius XI, *Quadragesimo Anno*, "On Reconstruction of the Social Order"
- Pope John XXIII, *Mater et Magistra*, "On Christianity and Social Progress"; and *Pacem in Terris*, "On Establishing Universal Peace"
- Pope Paul VI, *Humanae Vitae*, "On the Regulation of Births"; and *Popularum Progressio*, "On the Development of Peoples"
- Pope John Paul II, *Ecclesia in America*, "On the Church in America"; *Evangelium Vitae*, "On the Value and Inviolability of Human Life"; and *Sollicitudo Rei Socialis*, "For the Twentieth Anniversary of *Populorum Progressio*"

NOTES

_____
_____
_____
_____
_____
_____
_____
_____
_____
_____
_____

LESSON TWO: LIFE IS SACRED

Aims

The students will learn that man has a duty to protect human life. Willful murder is a sin that cries out to God.

They will learn that abortion is the murder of unborn babies (in the wombs of their mothers). Euthanasia is murder of the elderly or the physically impaired.

Materials

- *Activity Book*, p. 86   Optional:
  - "I heard the voice of Jesus say," *Adoremus Hymnal*, #579

Begin

Review that God is the author of all life. He gives life, and he alone has the authority to take life away. In fact, at every moment of our existence, God is sustaining us and giving us life. He could withdraw life at any time. It is amazing and wonderful to know that God is holding us in existence at each and every moment of our lives because he loves us.

Throughout Scripture, life is shown to be a blessing from God—it is sacred. But throughout history we have valued luxury more than people. This is an unhealthy view of life and love. Love is not having more things, but being in relationship with people—in life!

What have you done? The voice of your brother's blood is crying to me from the ground' " (Gen 4:8–10).

Murder was the first sin committed after the Fall. God, in speaking to Cain, tells us of the grave injustice which has been done. Yet, we know that not all killing is necessarily wrong. If Abel had killed Cain in self-defense this would not have been murder. Murder is the unjust taking of innocent life, which is what Cain did. This is also what is meant by the Fifth Commandment "Thou shalt not kill."

In modern times one of the most serious forms of willful murder is the killing of unborn children in the wombs of their mothers—**abortion**. This is the destruction of the most innocent and helpless human life. It destroys the future of our families and society. Abortion is certainly a sin which cries out to heaven.

Through her teachings the Church has always tried to protect human life from such injustices. During the twentieth century, when the practice of abortion spread to many nations—including our own—the popes frequently addressed the world on this matter. They have proclaimed the sacredness of human life from conception until natural death and the importance of the family, where new life begins and is nurtured. Three important social encyclicals which speak on these matters are *Casti Connubii* (Christian Marriage) by Pope Pius XI, *Humanae Vitae* (Of Human Life) by Pope Paul VI, and *Evangelium Vitae* (The Gospel of Life) by Pope John Paul II.

War and Peace

The Church has always taught that just as it is licit for a person to defend himself or his family or defenseless persons against attack, so it is licit for nations to defend themselves or help others defend themselves against unjust aggression. This is what is known as a **just war**. Of course, first, other avenues for stopping the attack must be considered and used, if possible and effective. Also, the response to an attack must not be out of proportion. The moral principle used is: "preserving the moderation of blameless defense."

The Second Vatican Council taught:

Every act of war directed to the indiscriminate destruction of whole cities or vast areas with their inhabitants is a crime against God and man, which merits firm and unequivocal condemnation (GS, 80).

As far as nuclear deterrence is concerned Pope John Paul II stated that:

under present conditions, deterrence based on equilibrium—certainly not as an end in itself, but as a stage on the way to progressive disarmament—can still be judged to be morally acceptable. How-

---

Church Teaching

"The Church makes a judgment about economic and social matters when the fundamental rights of the person or the salvation of souls requires it. She is concerned with the temporal common good of men because they are ordered to the sovereign Good, their ultimate end" (CCC, 2458).

142

Develop

1. Read paragraphs 5–7 (up to War and Peace).

2. Murder is the taking of an innocent life. Distinguish this from self-defense (in which a life is taken), capital punishment, accidents, etc. Review that all life is sacred, but not all life is innocent. The Fifth Commandment refers to the taking of innocent life—thus it could read: thou shalt not murder.

3. In modern times, there have been serious atrocities committed again innocent human life. One of these atrocities is abortion. Abortion is a form of murder. It is the killing of an unborn baby in the womb of its mother. Abortion is legal in many countries, but it is contrary to God's law. We must remember that no matter how a life is conceived, a baby is a gift from God and should be embraced and loved. Other topics relating to abortion that you may want to address are:
- *Contraception: many forms of contraception; e.g., the birth control pill, IUD, birth control patch, are abortifacients (means of abortion). Some forms of contraception*

are advertised as "morning after pills," or RU486. These all end pregnancy very early on by aborting human life.
- *Abortion in the case of violence. Rape is a horrendous crime. Often the trauma and treatment for the trauma will not allow the conception of a child; however, should a child be conceived, we must value that child as a precious gift from God.*

4. Just as innocent life must be protected from the moment of conception, so too life must be protected until natural death. Euthanasia is the wilful taking of the life of an elderly, infirm, or diseased person. This may be called "mercy killing," but man is not the author of life. In treating these people, there is not a need for extraordinary measures to be taken (e.g., life support) but ordinary necessities of life (e.g., nutrients—food).

Name:_____

Protection of Human Life

Answer the following questions in complete sentences.

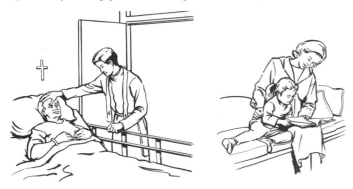

1. Is all killing necessarily wrong? Use the example of self-defense.
   Killing is not wrong if a person or nation must defend himself or itself.

2. What is meant by the Fifth Commandment?
   The Fifth Commandment means that it is a sin to take a life unjustly.

3. What is abortion? Is this always wrong?
   Abortion is the willful murder of an unborn child in its mother's womb. Abortion is always wrong.

4. Give the names and authors of three encyclicals which have defended the right to life.
   The names of three encyclicals defending life are Humanae Vitae by Pope Paul VI, Evangelium Vitae by Pope John Paul II and Casti Connubii by Pope Pius XI.

Reinforce

1. Have the students work on *Activity Book*, p. 86.

2. Give the students time to work on the Memorization Questions and Words to Know from this chapter.

3. Have the students do a project to benefit a pregnancy crisis center, the elderly in a nursing home, a neo-natal unit in a hospital, etc.

4. Have a pro-life speaker come in to speak to your class. He may show a video of an ultrasound. Be sure he does not show graphic images to the students.

5. *Discuss the importance of a loving home for a family. What responsible decisions should we make to achieve this? We should be chaste, loving, and capable of providing for the needs of children.*

Conclude

1. Lead the students in singing "I heard the voice of Jesus say," *Adoremus Hymnal*, #579.

2. End class by leading the students in a prayer for social justice.

Preview

In the next lesson, the students will learn about war and peace.

CAPITAL PUNISHMENT

The Church has always understood capital punishment to be morally licit under certain circumstances. This is not an exception to the fifth commandment. The fifth commandment forbids the taking of innocent life, but there are times when the legitimate authority may take the life of a guilty person for the defense of the common good. The *Catechism* teaches, "Legitimate defense can be not only a right but a grave duty for one who is responsible for the lives of others" (CCC 2265). Two criteria must be met if capital punishment is to be licit: the person's "identity and responsibility have been fully determined" and it must be the "only possible way of defending human lives against the unjust aggressor" (CCC 2267). The Holy Father has recently taught that, given modern laws and technology, cases in which capital punishment is absolutely necessary are now "very rare, if not practically non-existent" (*Evangelium Vitae* 56). However, he does not teach that it is an offense against the fifth commandment as are abortion, euthanasia, and homicide. Arguments about the necessity of capital punishment do not change the fact that, in object, capital punishment can be a good and just act on the part of the state if the above conditions are met. The *Catechism* also teaches that, when punishment "is willingly accepted by the guilty party, it assumes the value of expiation" (CCC 2266). A classic example of such a case is the good thief who died with Jesus. He accepted his punishment as just, asked for the mercy of God, and was promised Paradise (Lk 23:39–43).

LESSON THREE: JUST WAR

Aims

The students will learn that the Church teaches that man may protect himself (and his nation) from unjust aggression. Protecting oneself is self-defense.

They will learn that the Church has guidelines for just war. For a war to be just, all avenues for peace must be exhausted and a proportionate response must be used.

Materials

- *Activity Book*, p. 87   Optional:
   - "I heard the voice of Jesus say," *Adoremus Hymnal*, #579

Begin

War is a tragic violence that causes suffering to both the good and the bad. Often, we think of war as a video game because of the technologies we see on television. Special-guided bombs, amazing technology, and video footage that does not show the death and destruction make us overlook the tragedy of war. The Church is concerned about all human life—the people on both sides of a war. We also know that there have been times the Church led wars (the Crusades). Therefore there must be some principles for a "just war." We will address these today.

---

ever, to insure peace it is indispensable not to be content with a minimum which is always fraught with a real danger of explosion (Message to the United Nations, June 1982).

Several national bishops' conferences have issued Pastoral Letters on the question of war and peace, for instance, the U.S. bishops and the French bishops. They agree on the basic principles, but also agree that the practical application may differ because prudential judgments are involved. Unjust war is contrary to God's plan for the human family. God's will is that men ought to be united among themselves. Indeed, there is a similarity between the unity of the three Persons in God and the unity God wills men to establish among themselves.

Social Justice

"You shall not wrong a stranger or oppress him . . . you shall not afflict any widow or orphan. If you do afflict them, and they cry out to me, I will surely hear their cry. . . (Ex 22:21–23).

"Behold, the wages of the laborers who mowed your fields, which you kept back by fraud, cry out; and the cries of the harvesters have reached the ears of the Lord . . ." (James 5:4)

Justice means giving a person what is due to him. Social justice means establishing conditions in society that allow individuals and groups to obtain their due. Such conditions require respect for the human person and for the rights that come from human dignity. This includes the basic equality of all human beings as being made in God's image.

The material goods of this worlds were given to man by God. Every human being

should have what is necessary to live a decent human life.

Oppressing the poor, the widowed, the orphaned, etc., and defrauding the laborer of his wage are also sins which directly harm society. These two evils are the basis of the Church's teaching on economic and civic matters. The Church reminds all people and nations of their obligations in justice to care for the unfortunate among us. Almsgiving to the poor expresses the charity that God expects of his followers. Almsgiving is also an act of justice that pleases God. Thus, the Church teaches us of the evils of economic systems that exploit the poor. Human dignity requires that we try to eliminate sinful, excessive economic and social inequalities.

The Church also teaches us of the importance of paying the laborer a fair wage. Families cannot survive unless the heads of households are paid enough to provide for their basic needs—food, clothing, and shelter. The moral law also forbids enslaving human beings, or buying and selling human beings like merchandise. The basic equality of all men means that all men are to be respected as other "selves."

These teachings on economic issues have been particularly emphasized during the last one hundred years. The popes have written a number of important encyclicals on these topics. The first, in 1891, which is the basis for all those which followed, was *Rerum Novarum* (The Condition of Labor) by Pope Leo XIII. A more recent one, called *Laborem Exercens* (The Dignity of Labor), was written by Pope John Paul II.

In our concern for the promotion of the dignity of man, we must note that not every movement, ideology, or form of government which claims to benefit man or the poor does so. Certain movements in the twentieth century have been condemned by the Church. Com-

143

Develop

1. Read paragraphs 8–9 (up to Social Justice).

2. If a person broke into your house and showed a weapon, you would have the right to defend yourself (even if it meant shooting the aggressor); similarly, a country has the right to protect itself from an unjust aggressor. This is called a just war. The Church has very strict criteria to determine if a war is just. It is a legitimate defense if:
- *The damage caused by the aggressor is lasting, grave, and certain.*
- *All other means of putting an end to the aggression must have been shown to be impractical or ineffective. (We've tried talking, we've tried treaties, others have tried to intercede to prevent war, sanctions will not work, etc.)*
- *There must be a serious prospect of success. (We cannot go to war without a chance of winning. The cost of innocent life would be too great. If a war is to be just, we must be convinced that it will end well.)*

- *The use of arms must not produce evils or disorders graver than the evil to be eliminated. (We cannot retaliate in a way that is far greater than the damage caused to us. For example, if they kill ten men, we cannot kill one hundred thousand. We must not attack innocent civilians.)*
- *The decision of whether or not a war is just falls to those who have the responsibility to the common good. (A president and his advisors can determine if a war is just. Also, the Pope will advise if a war is just.)*

3. Peace is more than the absence of war or violence. Discuss true peace. True peace is found in the security of the necessities of life, in faith, in loving relationships, etc. How can others have peace? What about someone who has been abused or is depressed?

Name:_____

War and Peace

Answer the following questions in complete sentences.

1. Can war ever be just? Explain.

Yes. War may be just when a nation must defend itself from an aggressor. But a nation must first try other avenues, if that is possible and effective.

2. Give the two conditions for just war found in your student text.

Two conditions for just war are the threat of an unjust aggressor and that all other avenues for stopping an attack have been considered and used, if possible and effective.

3. What type of actions in war can never be just?

In war it is never just to destroy indiscriminately whole cities or areas.

4. How is unjust war contrary to God's plan?

Unjust war is contrary to God's plan because God's will is that men be united among themselves.

Faith and Life Series • Grade 8 • Chapter 22 • Lesson 3 87

Reinforce

1. Have the students work on *Activity Book*, p. 87.

2. Give the students time to work on the Memorization Questions and Words to Know from this chapter.

3. Look at various examples of war in our history. Using the Catholic criteria, determine whether or not they were just wars. Why or why not?

4. *Discuss how the students can support peace.*

5. Have the students create patriotic posters or bumper stickers.

Conclude

1. Lead the students in singing "I heard the voice of Jesus say," *Adoremus Hymnal*, #579.

2. End class by leading the students in a prayer for social justice.

Preview

In the next lesson, the students will learn about social justice.

QUOTATIONS ON PEACE

"We do not seek peace in order to be at war, but we go to war that we may have peace. Be peaceful, therefore, in warring, so that you may vanquish those whom you war against, and bring them to the prosperity of peace."
　　　　　　　　—Saint Augustine of Hippo

"Those who wage war justly aim at peace."
　　　　　　　　—Saint Thomas Aquinas

"Nothing is lost by peace; everything may be lost by war."
　　　　　　　　—Pope Pius XII

PEACE

Following Jesus, "the Prince of Peace," the Church urges all men to seek peace (Is 9:6). Even in cases where war is just, the ultimate goal must be peace. But "peace is not merely the absence of war" (CCC 2304). Pope John XXIII writes, "peace is but an empty word" unless it is "founded on truth, built up on justice, nurtured and animated by charity, and brought into effect under the auspices of freedom" (*Pacem in Terris* 167). True peace requires justice, charity, and respect for the rights and dignity of all men.

LESSON FOUR:
SOCIAL JUSTICE

Aims

The students will learn that justice is giving everyone what is due to him. Social justice establishes conditions in society that allow individuals or groups to obtain their due. Social justice often addresses economic or civil matters.

They will learn that Christians are obliged to care for the unfortunate and underprivileged among us (worldwide).

Materials

- *Activity Book*, p. 88   Optional:
  - "I heard the voice of Jesus say," *Adoremus Hymnal*, #579

Begin

Imagine Jesus has decided to come to earth right now and he chooses to come to our town. What concerns do we think Jesus would have? Jesus was always helping people. Whom would he help at our school, in our town, in the world today? What if he saw the evening news? How would he answer the needs of our society? How might Jesus answer the problems of poverty, abortion, oppression, war, etc.?

---

munism, while claiming to be for the oppressed classes in society, actually exploits them and suppresses basic human rights. National Socialism (Nazism) claimed the superiority of one race, and the Nazis brutally enslaved and persecuted others, even committing mass genocide. Any form of racism is condemned by the Church, since we are all created in God's image and Christ died for each one of us. Consequently, the Church has taught about the evils of these systems. Pope Pius XI wrote two encyclicals on these matters—*Mit Brennender Sorge* (Against the Nationalist State) and *Divini Redemptoris* (On Atheistic Communism).

These social teachings remind us of our Christian call to live in the world without adopting the ways of the world. At various times in history, people have ignored the Church's guidance and lived in ways contrary to the gospel. Our task is to reshape the values of society, if we can. At all times, even if the world is against us, we must listen to and follow the Church.

Words to Know:
> just war   abortion

Q. 130 *Is all human life sacred?*
Yes, all human life is sacred and must be protected from conception to natural death (CCC 2270, 2277).

Q. 131 *What is the goal of social justice?*
The goal of social justice is for man to live in justice and peace according to divine wisdom (CCC 2419).

Q. 132 *Is war always forbidden?*
No, war is not always forbidden. All are obliged to work for avoidance of war, but some wars are just (CCC 2307–8, 2312).

144

Develop

1. Read paragraphs 10–16 (to the end of the chapter).

2. Discuss the definition of social justice. Have the students give you a definition. Social justice is the establishment of conditions in society that allow individuals and groups to obtain what is due to them; e.g., dignity, a living wage, equal protection under law, etc. Have the students give examples.

3. What are some of the evils that directly harm society?
- *Oppression of various groups of people*
- *Sins against life and family*
- *Poverty/defrauding people, etc.*

4. We have a duty to care for the unfortunate among us. Who are some of these people? (Be specific.)
- *People at a local homeless shelter*
- *The abused*
- *Those who are poor, etc.*

5. How can we care for the underprivileged in a way that respects their dignity? It is wrong to make people feel bad about receiving charity. How can we give charity and help the recipients feel dignity? How can we help people to overcome their unfortunate condition? (Some ideas might include training centers, giving them employment, etc.)

6. Is it sinful to have material wealth? How should we use our wealth?

7. Sometimes we are limited in the ways we can help others; e.g., we do not have anything to give, it might not be safe to help some people (for instance, by bringing a homeless stranger into your home), they might use money we give for drugs or alcohol, etc. What can we do to care for these people? Have the students give age-appropriate examples.

Name:_____

Social Justice

Answer the following questions in complete sentences.

1. Define justice and social justice.

   <u>Justice is giving a person what is</u>
   <u>due to him. Social justice is</u>
   <u>establishing conditions in society</u>
   <u>which allow individuals and groups</u>
   <u>to obtain their due.</u>

2. Which sins form the basis of the Church's economic teaching? Why?

   <u>The sins of oppressing the poor</u>
   <u>and downtrodden and defrauding</u>
   <u>laborer his due wages are the</u>
   <u>sins which form the basis of the Church's economic teaching.</u>
   <u>They do so because society's duty is to protect the down-</u>
   <u>trodden and the laborer and doing so must always be the</u>
   <u>basis of economic systems.</u>

3. What is a "fair wage" and why is it a matter of justice?

   <u>A "fair wage" is giving the laborer his due and that is why</u>
   <u>it is a matter of justice.</u>

4. Name some encyclicals that have been written on social justice.

   <u>Some encyclicals that have been written on social justice</u>
   <u>are Rerum Novarum and Laborem Exercens.</u>

5. Why have certain forms of government been condemned by the Church?

   <u>Certain forms of government have been condemned by the</u>
   <u>Church because they oppress the poor and exploit the</u>
   <u>laborer.</u>

88   *Faith and Life Series • Grade 8 • Chapter 22 • Lesson 4*

Reinforce

1. Have the students work on *Activity Book*, p. 88.

2. Give the students time to work on the Memorization Questions and Words to Know from this chapter and to prepare for the quiz.

3. Spend some time discussing discrimination and tolerance. This is often a timely issue at this age. Often youths have not been exposed to people who are different from them. This is also a very competitive age-group, in which the non-athletic might be persecuted or a person might be bullied or picked on because he is not attractive, wealthy, etc. Remind the students that, as Catholics, we are called to do more than just tolerate others. Jesus did not say: "Tolerate one another as I have tolerated you." We are called to love our neighbors in imitation of Christ.

Conclude

1. Lead the students in singing "I heard the voice of Jesus say," *Adoremus Hymnal*, #579.

2. End class by leading the students in a prayer for social justice.

Preview

In the next lesson, the students' understanding of the material covered in this chapter will be reviewed and assessed.

IDEOLOGIES THAT ARE HARMFUL TO MAN: COMMUNISM AND FASCISM

The fundamental problem with both ideologies is that are entirely materialistic in outlook. They deny that man has an immortal soul and see him as a merely material being. This leads them to deny man's inherent dignity and to set up ideals at odds with man's true end.

Communism offers liberation by eliminating class distinctions, creating equality, and bringing all men together into a unified whole. However, communist theory denies transcendence and cannot see the individual as a person. Therefore, the individuals who make up the state are not persons but members of the whole, and the freedom offered is a freedom of the whole, not of the individual. Hence the greatest common good communism offers is great economic production. The nation as a whole must be well off, whatever the consequences for the individuals who make up that whole.

Fascism arose against communism, but ultimately degrades man in the same way. This theory embraces inequality as inevitable and bases human dignity on race or nationality (e.g. the Nazi master race) rather than on human nature alone. Fascism exalts the state and, just like communism, sees the individuals who make it up not as persons, but as material individuals whose rights and freedoms are subordinate to the good of the state.

CHAPTER TWENTY-TWO
REVIEW AND ASSESSMENT

Aims

The students' understanding of the material covered in this chapter will be reviewed and assessed.

Materials

- Quiz 22, Appendix, p. A-32

Optional:
- "I heard the voice of Jesus say," *Adoremus Hymnal*, #579

Review

1. Review Christ's desire, expressed in the Great Commission, for the formation of Christian nations.

2. Review the four sins that cry out to heaven.

3. The students should know what an encyclical is.

4. The students should know that human life is sacred and must be protected, especially against the sins of abortion and euthanasia.

5. The students should understand the principles of a just war.

6. The students should understand our duty as Catholics to promote social justice and to care for the underprivileged.

7. As Catholics, we are called to love all other people.

The Church and the Social Order   Quiz 22

Part I: Explain how each of the things listed below attack the good of society.

Oppression of the poor: <u>This exploits the poor and effects all the "classes" of society.</u>

Defrauding the laborer of a just wage: <u>This makes it difficult for individuals and families to survive. Families are the basic unit of society.</u>

Abortion: <u>Abortion destroys families and affects all of society in a very negative manner.</u>

Part III: Answer in complete sentences.

1. Can war ever be just? Explain.
   <u>Yes, war may be just when a nation must defend itself from an aggressor. But a nation must first try other avenues, if that is possible and effective.</u>

2. Is killing someone in self-defense murder? Explain.
   <u>No, killing someone in self-defense is not murder because murder is the unjust taking of an innocent life and in this case the one murdered is neither innocent nor just.</u>

3. Can abortion ever be morally good acts? Explain.
   <u>No, abortion can never be a morally good act because it is always the unjust taking of an innocent life. Abortion is always intrinsically evil.</u>

Assess

1. Distribute the quizzes and read through them with the students to be sure they understand the questions.

2. Administer the quiz. As they hand in their work, orally quiz the students on the Memorization Questions from this chapter.

3. After all the quizzes have been handed in, review the correct answers with the class.

Conclude

1. Lead the students in singing "I heard the voice of Jesus say," *Adoremus Hymnal*, #579.

2. End class by leading the students in a prayer for social justice.

CHAPTER TWENTY-THREE
PRAYER

Catechism of the Catholic Church References

Childlike Trust in Prayer: 2734–41, 2756
Christian Holiness: 2012–16, 2028–29
Eucharist: 1322–1405, 1419
Forgiveness: 2842–45, 2862
Holiness of God's Name: 2142–45, 2160–61
Jesus at Prayer: 2598–2606, 2620
Jesus Hears and Answers Prayers: 261, 2616
Jesus Teaches Us How to Pray: 2607–15, 2621
Liturgy of the Hours: 1174–78, 1196
Lord's Prayer: 2777–2865
Lord's Prayer as Summary of the Whole Gospel: 2761–76

Meditation on the Rosary: 2705–8, 2723
Prayer: 2777–88
Prayers of Blessing and Adoration: 2626–28, 2647
Prayers of Intercession: 2634–36, 2647
Prayers of Petition: 2629–33, 2646
Prayers of Praise: 2639–43, 2649
Prayers of Thanksgiving: 2637–38, 2644
Rosary: 971, 2678, 2708
What Is Prayer?: 2559–65, 2590, 2644
Worship: 2096–97, 2135–36

Scripture References

Jesus in Prayer:
    Up the Mountain: Mk 6:46; Mt 14:23; Lk 6:12
    With Children: Mt 19:13
    Agony in the Garden: Mt 26:36-46
    Transfiguration: Lk 9:28-37
    Sending the Holy Spirit: Jn 14:16

A Prayer of Christ: Jn 17
Prayer of the Proud/Humble: Mt 6:5–8; Lk 18:10–14
Teaching the Our Father: Mt 6:8–15
Persistence: Lk 18:1–8
Pray in Faith: Lk 11:9–13

Summary of Lesson Content

Lesson 1

As Christians we are called to unite ourselves with Christ. The two principle means of uniting ourselves with Christ are the sacraments and prayer.

Prayer is the lifting of our minds and hearts to God. Jesus taught about the necessity of prayer. The five steps to prayer are preparation, humility, faith, resignation, and perseverance.

Lesson 2

The two forms of prayer are mental and vocal prayer. Mental prayer is that which is said interiorly. During such prayer, we unite our hearts with God and meditate upon his truths. Vocal prayer is prayer spoken aloud, either alone or with others.

Formal prayers are those which follow a set pattern. Informal prayers are those we pray with our own words.

Lesson 3

Prayers may be said for four reasons: adoration, thanksgiving, contrition, and petition.

Adoration acknowledges God's greatness; thanksgiving recognizes God's gifts; contrition recognizes our failings before God and asks for his forgiveness, and petition is when we ask for God's blessings for ourselves or others.

Lesson 4

The liturgy is the Church's public worship. The most important prayers, namely the Mass and the Liturgy of the Hours, are part of the Church's liturgy.

The Mass is the supreme act of worship, as it is the offering of Christ to the Father. The Liturgy of the Hours is the prayer of the Church said throughout the day to sanctify it. Other formal prayers include the Our Father and the Rosary.

LESSON ONE: PRAYER

Aims

The students will learn that, as Christians, we are called to unite ourselves with Christ. The two principle means of uniting ourselves with Christ are the sacraments and prayer.

They will learn that prayer is the lifting of our minds and hearts to God. Jesus taught about the necessity of prayer. The five steps to prayer include: preparation, humility, faith, resignation, and perseverance.

Materials

- *Activity Book*, p. 89

Optional:
- "Come down, O Love divine," *Adoremus Hymnal*, #440

Begin

The students should think of their best friends. They want to spend time with their friends and get to know them better. They talk to each other all the time—why? Because of love and friendship. Now imagine they never talk or spend time with their best friends. Would this harm their friendship? Of course it would. So it is with God. We must spend time with him in prayer; we must raise our hearts and minds to God—speak with him and listen to him. This will make our relationship strong. Why should we pray? God loves us and invites us to love him in return. We should pray because we love and need God.

146

Develop

1. Read paragraphs 1–5 (up to There are two forms of prayer—mental and vocal).

2. Read the following passages about Jesus at prayer:
- *Jesus went up the mountain to pray (alone, all night): Mk 6:46; Mt 14:23; Lk 6:12*
- *Jesus prayed with children: Mt 19:13*
- *The Agony in the Garden: Mt 26:36-46*
- *The Transfiguration: Lk 9:28-37*
- *Sending the Holy Spirit: Jn 14:16*
- *A prayer of Christ: Jn 17*
What do we learn from Jesus' examples above?

3. What did Jesus teach us about prayer? Look up these passages:
- *Prayer of the Proud/Humble: Mt 6:5–8; Lk 18:10–14*
- *The Our Father: Mt 6:8–15*
- *Persistence: Lk 18:1–8*

- *Pray in faith: Lk 11:9–13*
Have the students find other teachings on prayer. Discuss these passages. What can we learn from them?

4. Discuss the dispositions we should have to prayer (the steps to prayer):
- *Preparation: We must turn our thoughts toward God and not allow ourselves to be distracted. We might need to be alone or focus with the aide of a sacred image or in front of the Blessed Sacrament.*
- *Humility: We should not be proud. God answers all prayers and we owe everything to God.*
- *Faith/Confidence: God answers our prayers (sometimes the answer is "no" or "not now"). He hears our prayers and gives us what we need.*
- *Resignation: We should desire and submit ourselves to God's will.*
- *Perseverance: We must be dedicated in our prayers.*

Prayer

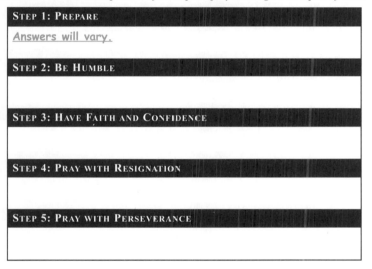

I. Answer the following questions in complete sentences.

1. What is prayer?
   <u>Prayer is the uplifting of our minds and hearts to God.</u>

2. Why is prayer essential to our spiritual lives?
   <u>Prayer is essential to our spiritual lives because it is how we speak to God.</u>

3. What did Jesus teach about prayer?
   <u>Jesus taught us to pray always.</u>

4. How are we to deal with distractions in prayer?
   <u>We should fight off distractions during prayer but not let distractions tempt us to stop praying.</u>

II. In the chart below, explain the five steps to prayer and give examples of each.

STEP 1: PREPARE
<u>Answers will vary.</u>

STEP 2: BE HUMBLE

STEP 3: HAVE FAITH AND CONFIDENCE

STEP 4: PRAY WITH RESIGNATION

STEP 5: PRAY WITH PERSEVERANCE

Faith and Life Series • Grade 8 • Chapter 23 • Lesson 1   89

Reinforce

1. Have the students work on *Activity Book*, p. 89.

2. Give the students time to work on the Memorization Questions and Words to Know from this chapter.

3. Help the students to pray with Jesus in the prayers listed in Develop 2 and in the box, "The Seven Last Words of Christ," at the bottom of this page.

4. *Discuss the difficulties we face in prayer. Offer suggestions to help the students develop their prayer lives; e.g., the use of sacramentals, prayer books, finding a good time for prayer, etc.*

Conclude

1. Teach the students to sing "Come down, O Love divine," *Adoremus Hymnal*, #440.

2. End class by leading the students in the Our Father.

Preview

In the next lesson, the students will learn about the forms of prayer.

THE SEVEN LAST WORDS OF CHRIST

1. "Father, forgive them; for they know not what they do" (Lk 23:34).

2. "Woman, behold, your son... Behold, your mother" (Jn 19:26-27).

3. "I thirst" (Jn 19:28).

4. "Today you will be with me in Paradise" (Lk 23:43).

5. "My God, my God, why hast thou forsaken me?" (Mt 27:46; Mk 15:34).

6. "It is finished" (Jn 19:30).

7. "Father, into thy hands I commit my spirit" (Lk 23:46).

NOTES

_____
_____
_____
_____
_____
_____
_____
_____
_____
_____

LESSON TWO:
FORMS OF PRAYER

Aims

The students will learn that the two forms of prayer are mental and vocal prayer. Mental prayer is prayer said interiorly. During such prayer, we unite our hearts with God and meditate upon his truths. Vocal prayer is prayer either spoken aloud, alone or with others.

They will learn that formal prayers are prayers which follow a set pattern. Informal prayers are prayers we pray with our own words.

Materials

- *Activity Book*, p. 90

Optional:
- "Come down, O Love divine," *Adoremus Hymnal*, #440

Begin

Review the definition of prayer and the examples of Jesus' prayers. What did Jesus teach us about prayer?

The students may share their positive experiences of prayer. When do they pray best? What helps them to pray well?

CHAPTER 23

Prayer

Likewise the Spirit helps us in our weakness; for we do not know how to pray as we ought, but the Spirit himself intercedes for us with sighs too deep for words.

Romans 8:26

As Christians we are called to sanctify our lives and unite ourselves with Christ. The two principal means for accomplishing this are *prayer* and the *sacraments*.

Prayer is the lifting up of our minds and hearts to God. Just as the spoken word is our way of communicating with friends, so prayer is our way of conversing with God. Every thought of God—short or long—can be a prayer. We are called to "Pray at all times in the Spirit, with all prayer and supplication" (Eph 6:13). For example, we might acknowledge the sovereignty of God or express gratitude to him for blessings he has given us. Or we might simply express our love for him. All of these are prayers.

Prayer is essential to our spiritual lives, as we can see from the Gospels. During his public life Our Lord often prayed. For example, he prayed in the desert before beginning his public ministry, he prayed on the mountain before he was transfigured, and he prayed in the Garden of Gethsemane on the night before he died. By these actions he taught us the importance of prayer.

I beseech you, O Lord, that the fiery and honey-sweet strength of your love

may free my soul from all that is under heaven, that I may die out of love for you, who deigned to die out of love for me. *Amen.*

Prayer of St. Francis

But Jesus did not only teach us by example; he frequently spoke to the apostles about the necessity of prayer. At one point he told the apostles that they ". . . ought always to pray and not lose heart" (Lk 18:1). Here he told us that we need to pray—even when it is difficult. There are times, for example, when various thoughts may distract us from our prayer. Such distractions may discourage us and tempt us to quit, but Jesus tells us that we should continue. Although these distractions are not always our fault, we should still work to draw our thoughts back to God as a sign of our love for him.

How should we pray? First, before we pray we should *prepare* ourselves to turn our thoughts to God. We should try to dismiss all other thoughts from our minds and direct our attention to God. Sometimes visible reminders—such as statues or paintings—will help us to concentrate on God. Next, we should pray with *humility*, like the tax collector in one of

147

Develop

1. Read paragraphs 6–9 (up to Prayers are said for four reasons).

2. Discuss the two forms of prayer: mental and vocal.
- *Mental prayer: the interior prayer which unites our hearts with God while we meditate upon his holy truths. It usually begins with meditation (see the box at right for methods of prayer).*
- *Vocal prayer: prayer said aloud—alone or with others. Words alone are not prayer; we must join our hearts and minds to our words to make a prayer.*

3. Discuss formal prayers with the students. It is likely that these are the only prayers they know. These prayers follow a set pattern, or formula. They are usually composed by someone else, and can be said in a group. Formal prayers can help us to communicate our thoughts to God. They give us a good example of prayer and help us to lift our hearts and

minds to God. Have the students give examples of formal prayers: e.g., Our Father, Hail Mary, etc.

4. Discuss informal prayer—prayer in our own words. These prayers are very intimate, for they are our own. Sometimes we may not know what to say to God. Speak to him as your dearest friend and love. Discuss the things we can speak to God about; we can tell God about our day, what interests us, our needs and those of our loved ones, etc.

5. Give the students a formula to help them meditate:
- *Recall God's presence*
- *Call upon God (and the saints) and ask for help meditating*
- *Reflect upon a topic of meditation*
- *Talk to God heart to heart*
- *Consider how this meditation is to be lived in your life*
- *Resolve to live what you learned in prayer*

Name:_____

Methods of Prayer

Answer the following questions in complete sentences.

1. What is mental prayer?

   Mental prayer is interior prayer. It is when our hearts speak to God without words and we meditate on his holy truths.

2. What is vocal prayer?

   Vocal prayer is spoken prayer with our hearts and minds united with the words.

3. What is the difference between formal and informal vocal prayer?

   Formal prayer is a prayer that follows a set pattern or formula while informal prayer is when we use our own words and spontaneously speak to God.

4. How can the Bible be a source of prayer?

   The Bible can be a source of prayer because it is God's word and can inspire us and be the source of much meditation.

5. Why is Mass the perfect prayer?

   Mass is the perfect prayer because it is the offering of Christ to his Father. It is the same sacrifice as that of Calvary and so is the means to make satisfaction for sins perfectly, thank God, and petition him.

6. Why is the Liturgy of the Hours an important prayer?

   The Liturgy of the Hours is an important prayer because it is a prayer of praise by which we can sanctify our day. It is the prayer of the Church.

90   *Faith and Life Series • Grade 8 • Chapter 23 • Lesson 2*

Reinforce

1. Have the students work on *Activity Book*, p. 90.

2. Give the students time to work on the Memorization Questions and Words to Know from this chapter.

3. *Using the principles of meditation in Develop 5, have the students meditate upon one of the following Scripture passages for ten minutes:*
- *God's eternal providential love for me: Ps 23; Ps 139:1–10; Lk 12:22–32*
- *My sins before God: Is 63:7–19; Lk 13:34; 15:11–32; 19:41–44; Mk 3:1–6*
- *The reality of heaven and hell: Mt 25:31–46; Lk 16:19–31; Mk 9:43–48*
- *The Our Father: Mt 6:7–15*
- *The Passion of Christ: Mt 26–27; Mk 14:32—15:39; Lk 22:39—23:49; Jn 18–19*

Conclude

1. Lead the students in singing "Come down, O Love divine," *Adoremus Hymnal*, #440.

2. End class by leading the students in the Our Father.

Preview

In the next lesson, the students will learn about the reasons for prayer.

METHODS OF PRAYER

Vocal: prayers based on actual words. Because we are body and spirit, vocal prayers have both an external, bodily expression—they are said, either privately or in groups—and an internal, spiritual expression—the heart and mind must be aware of the God to whom we pray. The most perfect example of vocal pray is the Our Father.

Meditative: wholly internal prayer in which we focus our "thought, imagination, emotion, and desire," on God (CCC 2707). People often use books, especially Scripture, icons, crucifixes, or other sacred things to help them. Rather than praying specific words as in vocal prayer, we must direct our thoughts to God, reflecting on him, and attentively waiting for him to speak to us. Classic examples of this type of prayer are the Rosary and *lectio divina*.

Contemplative: the highest and simplest type of prayer. It has been described as a gaze of faith and love, fixed on God. Unlike the other types of prayer, contemplative prayer is not the result of our action. We can make ourselves available, but it is purely a matter of God touching us when and how he chooses.

LESSON THREE: REASONS FOR PRAYER

Aims

The students will learn that prayers may be said for four reasons: adoration, thanksgiving, contrition, and petition.

They will learn that adoration acknowledges God's greatness; thanksgiving recognizes God's gifts; contrition recognizes our failings before God and asks for his forgiveness, and petition is when we ask for God's blessings for ourselves or others.

Materials

- *Activity Book*, p. 91
- Missals

Optional:
- "Come down, O Love divine," *Adoremus Hymnal*, #440

Begin

Review the definitions of prayer, the kinds of prayer, and the differences between formal and informal prayer.

You may lead the class in a short meditation. The students should close their eyes. Read a Scripture passage to the students. Have them share some of their meditations if they wish.

---

the parables told by Jesus (Lk 18:9–14). In addition, we should have *faith* and *confidence* that God will hear our prayer. As Our Lord said to his disciples at the Last Supper:

> Truly, truly, I say to you, if you ask anything of the Father, he will give it to you in my name (Jn 16:23).

Fourth, we should pray with *resignation* to the will of God, as Our Lord did on the eve of his death. That means that we accept how he answers our prayers. Finally, we should pray *with perseverance*. This means that we should keep on praying even if it seems as if God has not heard our prayer. To illustrate this point, Our Lord told the following parable:

> Which of you who has a friend will go to him at midnight and say to him, "Friend, lend me three loaves; for a friend of mine has arrived on a journey, and I have nothing to set before him"; and he will answer from within, "Do not bother me; the door is now shut, and my children are with me in bed; I cannot get up and give you anything"? I tell you, though he will not get up and give him anything because he is his friend, yet because of his importunity [persistence] he will rise and give him whatever he needs (Lk 11:5–8).

There are two forms of prayer—*mental* and *vocal*. **Mental prayer** is that which is said interiorly. Such prayer unites our hearts with God while we meditate on his holy truths. It usually begins with meditation—for example, on a passage from Scripture or one of the mysteries of our faith—which stirs our hearts to love God and unite ourselves with him. A good opportunity to pray in this manner is after we receive Our Lord in Holy Communion.

Vocal prayer is said by spoken words—alone or with others. However, the words alone

148

are not prayer, as the prophet Isaiah reminded the people of the Old Testament:

> This people draw near with their mouth and honor me with their lips, while their hearts are far from me (Is 29:13).

We must join our hearts and minds to the words that we speak.

Vocal prayer may be *formal* or *informal*. Formal prayers are those that follow a set pattern or formula. These prayers use words composed by someone else—for example, Our Lord, the angel Gabriel, or one of the saints. The Our Father, the Hail Mary, the Memorare, and the Act of Contrition are all examples of formal prayers. The Psalms of the Old Testament, written by David and inspired by God, are also formal prayers. There are many times when such prayers help us to communicate our thoughts to God. They show us how we ought to pray. They lift our minds and hearts and fill us with heavenly desires and right attitudes. These prayers also unite us with other members of the Body of Christ, who pray the same prayers.

At other times it is good to use our own words to pray. This is called informal prayer. It allows us to talk to God sincerely about ourselves, offering to him our particular joys and sorrows and asking him for the special help we need.

Prayers may be said for four reasons: adoration, thanksgiving, contrition, and petition. Prayers that primarily acknowledge God's greatness and our dependence on him are prayers of *adoration*. While all of our prayers should begin as prayers of praise, some, such as the *Sanctus* (Holy, Holy, Holy) of the Mass are solely prayers of adoration.

The second reason for prayer is to give thanks to God for the blessings he has given us. These are prayers of *thanksgiving*. We are reminded of the importance of giving thanks

Develop

1. Read paragraphs 10–13 (up to Let us now consider some of the formal prayers).

2. Prayers can be said for four reasons. We will discuss each:

Blessing and Adoration:
- *Blessing is an encounter between God and man; it is man receiving God's gifts and responding to them*
- *Adoration is recognition before the Creator that man is a creature; man is in wonder and awe of God*

Thanksgiving:
- *We are united with Christ in offering thanksgiving, which is done perfectly in the Eucharist*
- *We should offer prayers of thanksgiving for all God's gifts*

Contrition:
- *Sorrow for our sin is a recognition of ourselves before God; we see our sinfulness and failings in God's plan*

- *We ask God for his forgiveness, expressing our sorrow and remorse for our sins, knowing they offend God and neighbor*
- *This is a prayer of humility*

Petition and Intercession:
- *By petition, we express awareness of our relationship with and dependence upon God*
- *Intercession is when we imitate Christ in prayer, praying to the Father on behalf of others.*

3. Have the students give examples of each of these prayers.

4. Using missals, have the students find examples of each type of prayer from the Mass.

Name:_____

Reasons for Prayer

Prayers may be said for four reasons. Give a description of each reason and an example prayer that expresses each one.

ADORATION
Answers will vary.

THANKSGIVING

CONTRITION

PETITION

Reinforce

1. Have the students work on *Activity Book*, p. 91.

2. Give the students time to work on the Memorization Questions and Words to Know from this chapter.

3. Have the students write prayers to God. These prayers should include all four reasons for prayer.

4. Give the students time for meditation before the Blessed Sacrament.

5. Have the students research prayers written by various saints. What do the students appreciate most in these prayers?

6. Have each student chose a psalm and write a meditation upon that psalm.

Conclude

1. Lead the students in singing "Come down, O Love divine," *Adoremus Hymnal*, #440.

2. End class by leading the students in the Our Father.

Preview

In the next lesson, the students will learn about formal prayer.

FROM THE CATECHISM

"The heart is the dwelling-place where I am, where I live; according to the Semitic or Biblical expression, the heart is the place 'to which I withdraw.' The heart is our hidden center, beyond the grasp of our reason and of others; only the Spirit of God can fathom the human heart and know it fully. The heart is the place of decision, deeper than our psychic drives. It is the place of truth, where we choose life or death. It is the place of encounter, because as image of God we live in relation: it is the place of covenant.

"Christian prayer is a covenant relationship between God and man in Christ. It is the action of God and of man, springing forth from both the Holy Spirit and ourselves, wholly directed to the Father, in union with the human will of the Son of God made man."

—CCC 2563–2564

LESSON FOUR:
FORMAL PRAYER

Aims

The students will learn that the liturgy is the Church's public worship. The most important prayers, namely the Mass and the Liturgy of the Hours, are part of the Church's liturgy.

They will learn that the Mass is the supreme act of worship, as it is the offering of Christ to the Father. The Liturgy of the Hours is praise said throughout the day to sanctify it. Other formal prayers include the Our Father and the Rosary.

Materials

- *Activity Book*, p. 92

Optional:
- "Come down, O Love divine," *Adoremus Hymnal*, #440

Begin

The Church is a community that prays together. Prayer may be part of the liturgy (the public worship of the Church community) or it may be private devotion. However, it is important for the Church to have formal prayers for a group of people to pray together. Formal prayers help us to unite our hearts and minds to God in the prayer of the Church as a whole. Ask the students to give examples of the Church praying together in liturgy and in private devotion.

---

during each Mass. Before the Eucharistic Prayer the priest proclaims "Let us give thanks to the Lord our God," to which we reply, "It is right to give him thanks and praise."

Contrition is the third reason for prayer. In a prayer of contrition we acknowledge our sins and pray to obtain forgiveness from God. When we say the *Confiteor* (I Confess) at the beginning of Mass we are saying a prayer of contrition.

The last reason for prayer *is petition*. This is the most common prayer; in fact, many people only remember to pray to God when they need something. Prayers of petition are those in which we ask God for blessings for ourselves and others. It is fitting that we should ask for God's help, since we do need it for our life on earth and in order to reach heaven. The *Prayers of the Faithful* during Mass are examples of prayers of petition.

Let us now consider some of the formal prayers that are important in the Catholic Church.

First in importance are those prayers that are part of the Church's liturgy—the Mass and the Liturgy of the Hours. The Mass is the perfect prayer, because it is the offering of Christ to his Father in heaven. The Mass is also the supreme act of worship, by which we thank God. Because the Mass is the same sacrifice as that of Calvary, it is the perfect means of making satisfaction for our sins. Since the Mass is in memory of the Resurrection, it is a prayer of thanksgiving. Finally, since the Mass is the perfect sacrifice, it is the best way of petitioning God.

The Liturgy of the Hours is also an important prayer. It is a prayer of praise, by which we can sanctify our entire day. As we have seen, certain members of the Church—priests and religious—are required to pray the **Divine Office** each day. But we also are invited by the Church to join in this prayer.

One day the disciples said to Jesus, "Lord, teach us to pray," and he taught them the *Our Father*, or *Lord's Prayer*. This prayer contains an outline of all the qualities that should be present in our prayers and all those things that we should ask of God. Hence, it is not just a wonderful prayer, it is also a model for all of our prayers. It is so rich in meaning that we could meditate on it all our lives. Let us briefly examine the statements found in the Our Father.

Our Father, who art in heaven,

We begin this prayer by placing ourselves in the presence of God, recognizing him as our Father, but also as God.

hallowed be thy name,

Next we adore God, as we ask that his name be made holy and honored on earth.

thy Kingdom come,

We pray that his Kingdom—the Kingdom of Christ, the Church—may grow and be spread throughout the earth.

thy will be done on earth as it is in heaven

We end the first half of this prayer asking that God's will—not ours—be done. To all three of these first petitions we add *"on earth as it is in heaven,"* for God's name is honored in heaven; in heaven his Kingdom has been spread; and finally, in heaven his will is done.

Give us this day our daily bread,

We pray now for ourselves, asking God to give us the things we need—both physical and spiritual.

149

Develop

1. Read paragraphs 14–19 (including the meditation on the Our Father, to the end of the chapter).

2. Discuss the Mass with the students. They should be familiar with the prayers of the Mass from the work done for Develop 4 in Lesson 3 of this chapter. Questions:
- *How is the Mass the perfect prayer?*
- *How is the Mass the supreme act of worship?*
- *In the Mass, how do we use vocal and meditative prayer?*
- *In the Mass, where do we see the four ends/reasons for prayer?*

3. Show the students a copy of the Liturgy of the Hours. If possible, have a priest, deacon, or religious come and explain this prayer to the students (and possibly lead them in one of the hours). They should know what the Liturgy of the Hours, or the Divine Office, is.

4. Jesus taught us to pray the Our Father. We pray this prayer during the Mass. It is an important model for prayer. The Our Father includes all that should be present in our prayer; further, it tells us what we should ask of God. Re-read the Our Father line-by line and discuss each line with the students. Ask them what each line means and how it applies to their lives.

5. The Our Father is the summary of the Gospels. Have the students write a meditation upon this theme.

6. Another important prayer of the Church is the Rosary. The Rosary is vocal—formal prayers are recited. This is why it is good to pray in groups. The Rosary is also meditative, for with each decade of Hail Marys we are to meditate upon mysteries of the lives of Jesus and Mary. Make rosaries, teach the students how to pray them, and have them memorize the twenty mysteries.

The Our Father

Write a meditation on the Our Father, or explain the prayer line by line.

Answers will vary.

Our Father, Who art in heaven,

hallowed be Thy Name,

Thy Kingdom come,

Thy will be done

on earth, as it is in heaven.

Give us this day our daily bread,

and forgive us our trespasses as we forgive those who trespass against us

and lead us not into temptation

but deliver us from evil.

AMEN.

92   *Faith and Life Series • Grade 8 • Chapter 23 • Lesson 4*

Reinforce

1. Have the students work on *Activity Book*, p. 92.

2. Give the students time to work on the Memorization Questions and Words to Know from this chapter and to prepare for the quiz.

3. *Have the students create meditation books for the Rosary. They may go through examples of religious art and select an image for each mystery. Additionally, the students should write a brief reflection on each mystery beside the picture.*

4. Have the students make rosaries. Take these rosaries to a priest to have them blessed.

5. *Discuss the need to develop a prayer life in order to fulfill our call to holiness.*

Conclude

1. Lead the students in singing "Come down, O Love divine," *Adoremus Hymnal*, #440.

2. End class by leading the students in an Our Father.

Preview

In the next lesson, the students' understanding of the material covered in this chapter will be reviewed and assessed.

POPE JOHN PAUL II: *ROSARIUM VIRGINIS MARIAE*

On October 16, 2002, the beginning of the 25th year of his pontificate, Pope John Paul II wrote an Apostolic Letter on the Rosary. His purpose in writing it was to remind Catholics of the beautiful prayer of the Rosary and to encourage a revival of this age-old prayer. "A prayer so easy and yet so rich truly deserves to be rediscovered by the Christian community." Focusing on the Rosary as a fundamentally Christocentric (Christ-centered) prayer, the Holy Father suggested a new set of mysteries: the Mysteries of Light. These Luminous Mysteries are an optional addition to the Rosary which allow us to meditate on the ministry of Christ from his Baptism to the eve of his Passion.

"I look to all of you, brothers and sisters of every state of life, to you, Christian families, to you, the sick and elderly, and to you, young people: *confidently take up the Rosary once again.* Rediscover the Rosary in the light of Scripture, in harmony with the liturgy, and in the context of your daily lives."

—Pope John Paul II, *Rosarium Virginis Mariae*

_and forgive us our trespasses as we
forgive those who trespass against us._

We acknowledge our sins and ask that God
in his mercy forgive us in the same measure as
we have forgiven those who offend us.

_Lead us not into temptation,
but deliver us from evil._

We end the prayer asking God to help us in
times of temptation and to strengthen us when
we face occasions of sin.

Another great prayer that the Church especially recommends is the _Rosary_. This prayer
has been part of the spiritual life of many
Catholics—mainly in the Latin rite—for about
eight centuries. The Church has encouraged us
to say this beautiful prayer by dedicating one
month—October—to the Rosary. The Rosary
combines both mental and vocal prayer. It is
divided into fifteen mysteries, or episodes,
from the lives of Jesus and Mary. As we recite
the vocal prayers—one Our Father, ten Hail
Marys, and one Glory Be for each mystery—
we meditate on the various events from the
lives of Our Lord and his Mother.

It is important to develop times for prayer in
our lives, so that we may fulfill our call to
holiness. In the next chapter we will consider
the sacraments that further nourish our spiritual life.

Words to Know:
    mental prayer   vocal prayer
          Divine Office

150

Q. 133 *What is prayer?*
Prayer is the lifting of the mind and heart to God, in order to know him better, to adore him, to thank him, and to ask him for what we need (CCC 2559, 2590).

Q. 134 *How many forms of prayer are there?*
There are two forms of prayer: mental and vocal (CCC 2700–24).

Q. 135 *What is mental prayer?*
Mental prayer is that which is offered with the mind and heart alone (CCC 2708).

Q. 136 *What is vocal prayer?*
Vocal prayer is that prayer which is expressed by spoken words with the participation of the mind and heart (CCC 2700).

Q. 137 *How should we pray?*
We should pray humbly, attentively, and devoutly (CCC 2559).

Q. 138 *Why is it necessary to pray?*
It is necessary to pray in order to grow in our faith in God, in our hope in him, and in our love for him, and in this way to receive the grace necessary to be united with him in heaven (CCC 2558).

151

CHAPTER TWENTY-THREE
REVIEW AND ASSESSMENT

Aims

The students' understanding of the material covered in this chapter will be reviewed and assessed.

Materials

- Quiz 23, Appendix, p. A-33

Optional:
- "Come down, O Love divine," *Adoremus Hymnal*, #440

Review

1. The students should be able to give examples of Jesus praying and know what he taught us about prayer.

2. The students should know the five steps to prayer.

3. The students should know the two kinds of prayer.

4. The students should know the difference between formal and informal prayer.

5. The students should know the four reasons for prayer.

6. The students should know the formal prayers of the Church, especially the Liturgy of the Hours, the Mass, and the Rosary.

Name: _____

Prayer   Quiz 23

Part I: Answer in complete sentences.

1. What is prayer?
   Prayer is the lifting of the mind and heart to God, in order to know him better, to adore him, to thank him, and to ask him for what we need.

2. What are the two kinds of prayer? Describe them.
   The two kinds of prayer are mental and vocal. Mental prayer is prayer offered with the mind and heart alone. Vocal prayer is the prayer which is expressed by spoken words with the participation of the mind and heart.

3. What are the five steps of prayer? Give examples of each
   The five steps of prayer are to prepare oneself to turn to God, to humble oneself, to have faith and confidence, to resign oneself to God's will and to persevere.

4. What is the difference between formal and informal prayer?
   Formal prayer is a prayer that follows a set pattern or formula while informal prayer is when we use our own words and spontaneously speak to God.

5. What are the four reasons for prayer?
   The four reasons for prayer are adoration, thanksgiving, contrition, and petition.

6. What is liturgy? Give two examples.
   Liturgy is the Church's official public worship. Examples can vary.

Assess

1. Distribute the quizzes and read through them with the students to be sure they understand the questions.

2. Administer the quiz. As they hand in their work, orally quiz the students on the Memorization Questions from this chapter.

3. After all the quizzes have been handed in, review the correct answers with the class.

Conclude

1. Lead the students in singing "Come down, O Love divine," *Adoremus Hymnal*, #440.

2. End class by leading the students in an Our Father.

CHAPTER TWENTY-FOUR
THE SACRAMENTAL LIFE

Catechism of the Catholic Church References

Efficacious Signs: 1127–28
Forgiveness: 2839–45, 2862
Grace: 1996–2005, 2021–24
Grace Conferred by the Sacraments: 1127–29, 1131

Baptism: 1213–84
Penance: 1420–98
Eucharist: 1322–1419
Benediction: 1088, 1373–78, 1418

Scripture References

Baptism: Mt 28:18–20; Jn 3:5
Confirmation: Jn 20:21–22; Acts 2:1–4; 8:14–17
Eucharist: Mt 26:26–28, Mk 14:22–25, Lk 22:7–20;
24:13–53; Jn 6:25–71

Penance: Jn 20:19–23; Mt 16:13–19
Anointing of the Sick: Jas 5:13–16; Jn 9:1–7; Mk 2:1–12
Holy Orders: Lk 22:19; Heb 5:1–10
Matrimony: Mt 19:3–12; Eph 5:25–32; 1 Cor 12–16

Summary of Lesson Content

Lesson 1

A sacrament is an outward sign instituted by Christ which gives us grace. Christ instituted the sacraments to give us a share in his life of grace.

The sacraments make us holy by giving us grace or by restoring or increasing the life of grace in us.

Lesson 3

The steps to a good confession are examination of conscience; contrition; amendment; sacramental confession; and acceptance of penance.

Lesson 2

Penance is the sacrament by which sins committed after Baptism are forgiven.

Mortal sin kills the life of grace in the soul. This life is restored in the Sacrament of Penance. In the Sacrament of Penance, the penitent is given grace to overcome future sin.

Lesson 4

The Eucharist is the Sacrament in which our Lord is present, Body, Blood, Soul, and Divinity, under the appearances of bread and wine. The Eucharist is a means of grace and, at the same time, a source of grace.

The steps to a worthy reception of Communion are covered in this lesson. Spiritual Communion is also covered.

Catholics may adore the Eucharist, which is Christ, really and truly present.

LESSON ONE: SACRAMENTS

Aims

The students will learn that a sacrament is an outward sign instituted by Christ, which gives us grace. Christ instituted the sacraments to give us a share in his life of grace.

They will learn that the sacraments make us holy by giving us grace or by restoring or increasing the life of grace within us.

Materials

• *Activity Book*, p. 93

Optional:
• "O Lord, I am not worthy," *Adoremus Hymnal*, #512

Begin

Begin class by defining the word sacrament. A sacrament is an outward sign instituted by Christ, which confers grace.

Review that the grace conferred through the sacraments was won by Jesus Christ by his suffering and death on the Cross and his Resurrection from the dead. He instituted the sacraments as the ordinary means of grace. The sacraments are distributed through his Church, which was founded upon Peter and the Apostles.

152

Develop

1. Read paragraphs 1–6 (up to The Sacrament of Penance).

2. Review each sacrament:
• *Baptism: washes away all sin and pours the life of grace into the soul. Matter: threefold pouring or immersion with water. Form: the words "I baptize you in the name of the Father, and of the Son, and of the Holy Spirit." Scripture: Mt 28:18–20; Jn 3:5.*
• *Confirmation: an outpouring of the Holy Spirit and his gifts and a maturation of faith for full initiation into the Church. Matter: laying of hands and anointing with chrism. Form: "Be sealed with the gift of the Holy Spirit." Scripture: Jn 20:21–22; also, Acts 2:1–4; Acts 8:14–17.*
• *Eucharist: the presence of Christ, Body, Blood, Soul, and Divinity, made present in the Sacrifice of the Mass. Matter: bread and wine. Form: the words "This is My Body . . . This is the cup of My Blood." Scripture: Mt 26:26–28; Mk 14:22–25; Lk 22:7–20; Jn 6:25–71; Lk 24:13–53.*

• *Penance: through the confession of sins to a priest, absolution is given for the forgiveness of sins committed after Baptism. Matter: contrition, confession, and satisfaction. Form: the words "I absolve you from your sins in the name of the Father, and of the Son, and of the Holy Spirit." Scripture: Jn 20:19–23; Mt 16:13–19.*
• *Anointing of the Sick: through the anointing and prayers of a priest, a person receives healing of soul and possibly of body and is prepared for union with God. Matter: anointing with oil and laying of hands. Form: Prayer of anointing. Scripture: Jas 5:13–16; Jn 9:1–7; Mk 2:1–12.*
• *Holy Orders: a man is ordained to ministry for the Church as a deacon, priest, or bishop. Matter: laying of hands. Form: prayer of ordination. Scripture: Lk 22:19; Heb 5:1–10.*
• *Matrimony: a man and woman are united for life for the goods of marriage. Matter: man and woman consent. Form: vows. Scripture: Mt 19:3–12; Eph 5:25–32; 1 Cor 12–16.*

Name:_____

The Sacramental Life

Answer the following questions in complete sentences.

1. Define sacrament.
   A sacrament is an outward sign instituted by Christ to give us grace.

2. Who gave us the sacraments and why did he give them to us?
   Jesus gave us the sacraments so that we could share in his life and be nourished by it, and so that we would have a sure way to receive the grace he won for us by his death and resurrection.

3. What is the difference between a sign and an efficacious sign?
   The difference between a sign and an efficacious sign is that an efficacious sign brings about what it represents. A sign simply represents something else.

4. Why did Jesus give us the sacraments as sensible means to receive his grace?
   Jesus gave us the sacraments as sensible means to receive his grace because he knows that man is made up of body and soul and comes to learn through his senses and the material world around him. Thus, the best way to instruct man is through his senses and the material world. Jesus gave us sensible means to know that grace is active in our lives.

5. Using Baptism as an example, show the sign and the effects of the sacrament.
   Answers will vary.

1. Have the students work on *Activity Book*, p. 93.

2. Give the students time to work on the Memorization Questions and Words to Know from this chapter.

3. *The students should research each of the passages on the sacraments. They should write a paragraph on each sacrament, explaining each as they would to a non-Catholic friend.*

4. Review the need for grace in order to live forever with God in heaven. The sacraments are an ordinary means of grace and a sure help for salvation.

Conclude

1. Teach the students to sing "O Lord, I am not worthy," *Adoremus Hymnal*, #512.

2. End class by leading the students in the *Anima Christi*.

Preview

In the next lesson, the students will learn about Penance.

THE TRIDENTINE RITE

The tridentine rite is the rite that was in use before the Second Vatican Council. Some parishes still use it and several priestly orders and societies, such as the Priestly Fraternity of Saint Peter, are dedicated to preserving this beautiful liturgy. The following quotations are English translations of prayers from the solemn Holy Thursday Mass of the tridentine rite:

"And now, O Lord, we thy servants and with us all thy holy people, calling to mind the blessed Passion of this same Christ, thy Son, our Lord, and also his Resurrection from the dead, and finally his glorious Ascension into heaven, offer to thy supreme majesty, of the gifts bestowed upon us, the pure Victim, the holy Victim, the all-perfect Victim: the holy Bread of life eternal and the Chalice of perpetual salvation."

"I will take the Bread of Heaven, and I will call upon the Name of the Lord. Lord I am not worthy that though shouldst enter under my roof, but only say the word and my soul will be healed. What return shall I make to the Lord for all he has given me? I will take the chalice of salvation, and I will call upon the Name of the Lord. Praising will I call upon the Lord and I shall be saved from my enemies. May the blood of our Lord Jesus Christ preserve my soul to life everlasting."

"May Thy Body, O Lord, which I have eaten, and thy Blood which I have drunk, cleave to my very soul, and grant that no trace of sin be found in me, whom these pure and holy mysteries have renewed."

LESSON TWO: PENANCE

Aims

The students will learn that Penance is the sacrament by which sins committed after Baptism are forgiven.

They will learn that mortal sin kills the life of grace in the soul. This life is restored in the Sacrament of Penance. In the Sacrament of Penance, the penitent is given grace to overcome future sin.

Materials

- *Activity Book*, p. 94

Optional:
- "O Lord, I am not worthy," *Adoremus Hymnal*, #512

Begin

Review why we need to receive the Sacrament of Penance. It is in this sacrament that the sins we commit after Baptism are forgiven.

Review the Church's precepts on the Sacrament of Penance. A Catholic must receive the Sacrament of Penance at least once a year if he is in mortal sin. In order to receive Communion, one must be free from mortal sin. This means that, if one has committed a mortal sin, he must receive the Sacrament of Penance before he may receive Communion. It is advisable to receive this sacrament regularly (e.g., once a month).

CHAPTER 24

The Sacramental Life

But one of the soldiers pierced his side with a spear, and at once there came out blood and water.

John 19:34

In addition to prayer, Christ has given us a wonderful means to become holy. The *sacraments* were given to the Church by Jesus Christ to sanctify us. They are the means by which we receive the "living water" of which Our Lord spoke. Water in this sense signifies the life of God called *sanctifying grace.*

A **sacrament** is an outward sign instituted by Christ to give us grace. A *sign* is a thing that stands for, or represents, something else. For example, our national flag represents our country; smoke indicates the presence of fire. We are all familiar with the signs in the sacraments. The water in Baptism, for example, indicates our death to sin, the cleansing of the soul, and the new life which is given by God. But the sacraments are more than ordinary signs. They are *efficacious* signs. This means that they actually bring about what they represent.

To understand this better, think about the ordinary stop sign. This sign indicates to the driver that he should stop at an intersection. But it cannot *make* him stop; he must stop himself. The sacraments are different. In Baptism when the water is poured and the words "I baptize you . . ." are spoken, the soul is actually cleansed and the new life of **grace** is actually infused. This is the great power that Our Lord gave to these simple signs.

Christ himself gave us the sacraments so that we could share in his life and have that life nourished in us. He gave us these sacraments so that we would have a certain, or sure, way to receive the grace he won by dying on the Cross for us. But why did he choose to give us this grace through the sacraments?

As human beings we learn through *corporeal*, material, things around us. Thus, to learn we depend on our senses—sight, hearing, touch, taste, and smell. Our Lord gave us the sacraments as *sensible* means—means that can be sensed—for us to know that grace is active in our lives. At Baptism, when we see the water being poured and hear the words, we know that God's life now dwells in the soul of the person baptized. We are certain of this. In the same way, when we hear the priest in Confession say that our sins are forgiven, we *know* that God has forgiven our sins.

All of the sacraments make us holy by giving us grace or by restoring or increasing the life of grace in us. Thus all of the sacraments nourish and strengthen our spiritual life and help us draw closer to God. However, two of the sacraments are our "lifelines" to grace—Penance and the Holy Eucharist.

153

Develop

1. Read paragraphs 7–10 from the student text.

2. Review the definitions of mortal sin and venial sin:
- *Mortal sin is a sin that is serious, we know it is serious and is committed with full knowledge and consent. Mortal sin kills the life of grace in our soul. The life of grace is necessary for union with God in heaven.*
- *Venial sin is less serious sin. It may be serious, but done without full knowledge or free will, or it may be less serious, but done with knowledge and intention. Venial sin does not kill the life of grace in the soul, but wounds it and creates a disposition to commit further (and more grave) sins.*

3. The effects of the Sacrament of Penance include:
- *Reconciliation with God by which sanctifying grace is recovered*
- *Reconciliation with the Church*

- *Remission of eternal punishment*
- *Remission (at least partially) of temporal punishment due to sin*
- *Peace is restored to the soul*
- *Strength to overcome sin and to live the life of grace and virtue*

4. Review the seal of the confessional. Anything that is said to a priest in the Sacrament of Penance is bound by this seal. The priest can never reveal what you said—ever.

5. You may discuss why we need to go to a priest for Confession. Explain that Jesus gave the power to forgive sins to his apostles and that this power has been passed down through Holy Orders. The priest acts in the person of Christ in the sacrament and, thus, it is Jesus who forgives our sins.

Name:_____

The Sacrament of Penance

Answer the following questions in complete sentences.

1. How did Jesus institute the Sacrament of Penance?
   Jesus instituted the Sacrament of Penance by breathing on his apostles the night of his Resurrection and giving them the Holy Spirit and the power to forgive and retain sins.

2. If original sin is removed in Baptism, why do we need the Sacrament of Penance?
   We need the Sacrament of Penance because even with Baptism we still have the strong inclination to sin and are very weak and fall often into sin.

3. What are the sacramental graces of Penance?
   The sacramental graces of Penance are our sins are forgiven and we are restored to friendship with God. We are strengthened to avoid sin, and God increases his life in us.

4. How does the Sacrament of Penance draw us closer to God?
   Penance draws us closer to God because we are taking a step to be reconciled with him and to be friends with him again. He honors that and returns the friendship.

94   *Faith and Life Series • Grade 8 • Chapter 24 • Lesson 2*

Reinforce

1. Have the students work on *Activity Book*, p. 94.

2. Give the students time to work on the Memorization Questions and Words to Know from this chapter.

3. Have your students do a thorough examination of conscience and prepare to receive the Sacrament of Penance. Arrange for a priest to be available to hear the students' confessions.

4. You may define and explain general confession. Sometimes, when a person is preparing to enter his vocation (e.g., religious life, the priesthood, or marriage) he may make a general confession. This is a thorough confession which covers all the sins they recall from their life.

Conclude

1. Lead the students in singing "O Lord, I am not worthy," *Adoremus Hymnal*, #512.

2. End class by leading the students in the *Anima Christi*.

Preview

In the next lesson, the students will learn the proper way to receive the Sacrament of Penance.

SAINT MATEO CORREA MAGALLANES: MARTYR OF CONFESSION

During the 1920s and 30s, the Catholic Church in Mexico faced severe persecution. Many priests and religious were killed and others were forced to flee to the United Stated and Europe. Several Carmelite monasteries in California owe their founding to sisters who survived the persecutions and escaped. One of the priests who gave his life for the faith is Saint Magallanes. In 1927, as he was bringing the Eucharist to a sick woman, he was caught by the police and imprisoned. On February 5, 1927, Saint Magallanes was ordered to hear the confessions of the other prisoners. He gladly heard them and encouraged the prisoners to keep their faith and hope and die in a state of grace. After he had heard their confessions, the general in charge of the prison, who had ordered Saint Magallanes to hear their confessions, ordered him to reveal everything they had confessed. Saint Magallanes refused. The general threatened to kill him if he did not reveal what the prisoners had confessed, but still Saint Magallanes refused. The next day, a group of soldiers took Saint Magallanes to a cemetery outside the city and killed him. On May 21, 2000, Pope John Paul II canonized Saint Magallanes and twenty-six other Mexican saints. In his homily, the Holy Father said, "They did not stop courageously exercising their ministry when religious persecution intensified in the beloved land of Mexico, unleashing hatred of the Catholic religion. They all freely and calmly accepted martyrdom as a witness to their faith, explicitly forgiving their persecutors."

LESSON THREE: CONFESSING

Aims

The students will learn that the steps to a worthy reception of the Sacrament of Penance are examination of conscience; contrition; amendment; sacramental confession; and acceptance of penance.

Materials

- *Activity Book*, p. 95

  Optional:
  - "O Lord, I am not worthy," *Adoremus Hymnal*, #512

Begin

You may teach the students the various titles for the Sacrament of Penance:

- Sacrament of Penance
- Sacrament of Reconciliation
- Sacrament of Confession
- Sacrament of Conversion
- Sacrament of Forgiveness

Discuss these titles with the students. Upon which aspect of the sacrament does each title focus?

The Sacrament of Penance

On the evening of the Resurrection, Our Lord appeared to the apostles in the upper room. He said to them, "Receive the Holy Spirit. If you forgive the sins of any, they are forgiven; if you retain the sins of any, they are retained" (Jn 20:22–23). Christ gave the apostles and their successors the power to forgive sins, thus instituting the Sacrament of Penance, or Reconciliation.

Although original sin is removed through the sacrament of Baptism, we know that we are still in a weakened state. We have a strong inclination to sin, and we do, in fact, easily fall into sin. Our Lord knew that even after Baptism Christians could still sin. He gave us the Sacrament of Penance, or Reconciliation, so that we could receive God's forgiveness frequently.

The sacrament of Penance, then, is a great gift by which the sins we commit after Baptism are forgiven. If we have committed a mortal sin, God restores to our soul his life which had been lost. God increases his life within us and strengthens our friendship with him when we confess our venial sins. In addition, through the actual or sacramental graces which we receive, God helps us to avoid sin in the future. For example, if you confess that you have lied, God will give you strength and help you be truthful in the future.

The sacrament of Penance can help us draw closer to God and make us better and stronger Christians. For this reason, it is good to receive this sacrament often—even when we have not committed any mortal sins.

To make a good Confession and worthily receive the sacrament we must do five things:

1. Before receiving the sacrament you must examine your conscience. You should ask God to help you recognize your sins since your last confession.

2. You must have true sorrow, *contrition*, for your sins. This contrition is based on our love of God, sorrow for having offended him, and hatred of our sins.

3. You must have a firm commitment not to sin again. This means that you must resolve to do all you can to avoid sin and the occasions of sin in the future. If you do not intend to give up your sinful ways, God cannot forgive you. You would not be truly sorry.

4. You must confess your sins honestly to the priest. This means that you should not conceal any mortal sins. Neither should you try to hide anything out of shame or embarrassment. The priest, taking the place of Christ, is there to give you forgiveness and not to rebuke you unnecessarily. He may, however, give you some advice or guidance to help you overcome your sins.

5. You must be willing to perform the

"I am the bread of life; he who comes to me shall not hunger, and he who believes in me shall never thirst."

(John 6:35)

154

Develop

1. Read paragraph 11 (up to The Holy Eucharist).

2. The Sacrament of Penance was initiated by Jesus. Penance calls for an interior conversion. It is initiated by a work of God's grace. Through this grace, we experience a discovery of the great love of God. Next we experience sorrow for sin and for offending God and being separated from him.

3. There are five formal steps to the Sacrament of Penance:
- *Examination of conscience: requires the penitent to know his sins. He will need to confess his mortal sins and their number or frequency since his last good confession. The Ten Commandments, the virtues, Works of Mercy, Precepts of the Church, Beatitudes, law of love, seven deadly sins, etc., may be of assistance in an examination of conscience.*
- *Contrition: the penitent must have contrition, or sorrow for sin. There are two types of contrition: attrition (imperfect contrition)—we are sorry for our sins because we fear*

God's just punishment due to them; and contrition (perfect contrition)—we are sorry for our sins because they offend God, who deserves all our love.
- *Amendment: the penitent must decide not to sin again and to avoid occasions of sin.*
- *Sacramental Confession of sins: the penitent must confess his mortal sins and their number. It is also beneficial to confess venial sins.*
- *You must receive and perform the penance, which is a sign of unifying oneself with Christ, who paid the price for our sins by his suffering and death.*

Name:_____

Five Steps to a Good Confession

In the chart below, explain the five steps to a good confession and why we must do each step.

| 1. Examination of Conscience |
| Answers will vary. |

| 2. Contrition |
| |

| 3. Firm commitment not to sin again |
| |

| 4. Confess your sins |
| |

| 5. Perform the penance |
| |

Reinforce

1. Have the students work on *Activity Book*, p. 95.

2. Give the students time to work on the Memorization Questions and Words to Know from this chapter.

3. The students may write about the merciful love of God that they have experienced in the Sacrament of Penance.

Conclude

1. Lead the students in singing "O Lord, I am not worthy," *Adoremus Hymnal*, #512.

2. End class by leading the students in the *Anima Christi*.

Preview

In the next lesson, the students will learn about the Holy Eucharist.

RIGHT TO ANONYMITY

Often, the Sacrament of Penance is celebrated face to face. While some people prefer this method, others desire anonymity. Anonymous confession through a screen is still a valid and acceptable option. See the *Code of Canon Law*, canon 964.2.

THE SEAL OF CONFESSION

A priest can never talk about another's confession or make use of what he hears in confession in any way. A confession is between the penitent and God, so whatever is confessed is kept absolutely confidential. This is called the seal of the confession. See the *Catechism of the Catholic Church*, number 1467.

NOTES

_____
_____
_____
_____
_____
_____
_____
_____
_____
_____
_____

LESSON FOUR: EUCHARIST

Aims

The students will learn that the Eucharist is the sacrament in which our Lord is present, Body, Blood, Soul, and Divinity, under the appearances of bread and wine. The Eucharist is a means of grace and, at the same time, a source of grace.

They will learn that Catholics adore the Eucharist, which is Christ, really and truly present.

Materials

- *Activity Book*, p. 96

Optional:
- "O Lord, I am not worthy," *Adoremus Hymnal*, #512

Begin

Review that the Eucharist is the Body, Blood, Soul, and Divinity of Jesus Christ, the Son of God, truly present under the appearances of bread and wine. It is food for our souls and the strength of the saints. The Eucharist does not only confer grace, it is the source of grace.

The Eucharist is called Holy Communion, since the Eucharist puts us in intimate union with our Lord. His sacramental presence remains as long as the species is within us—roughly 10–15 minutes.

"... This is the bread which comes down from heaven, that a man may eat it and not die."

(John 6:50)

penance which the priest gives you and then to do it.

The Holy Eucharist

"Truly, truly, I say to you . . . he who eats my flesh and drinks my blood, has eternal life. . ." (Jn 6:53–54).

The **Eucharist** is the sacrament in which Our Lord is present—Body and Blood, Soul and Divinity—under the appearances of bread and wine. Just as our bodies need physical nourishment in order to live, our souls also must be nourished. The Eucharist is this spiritual food.

The Eucharist is a means of receiving grace and, at the same time, is the source of grace—Jesus, himself. The Eucharist is thus the most important sacrament and the fountain from which all grace flows.

In receiving the Eucharist—called Holy Communion—we become united to Christ. This union nourishes us by helping us to become more like Christ. Through reception of Communion the life of God is increased in our souls, bringing us closer to him. Just as food strengthens our bodies for difficult physical tasks, this great Sacrament helps us to become spiritually stronger.

To benefit from the graces of the Eucharist we must prepare ourselves to receive it worthily. These are the things we must do:

1. We must be in the state of grace when we receive Holy Communion. This means that if we have committed a mortal sin we

must first go to Confession before receiving Our Lord. St. Paul told the Christians at Corinth: "Whoever . . . eats the bread or drinks the cup of the Lord in an unworthy manner will be guilty of profaning the body and blood of the Lord" (1 Cor 11:27). To receive Our Lord in the state of serious sin is a sin of sacrilege.

2. To receive the Eucharist worthily we must believe that Jesus Christ is truly present in the sacrament. Again St. Paul reminds us: ". . . anyone who eats and drinks without discerning the body eats and drinks judgment upon himself" (1 Cor 11:29). We must, then, prepare our-

Soul of Christ, sanctify me.
Body of Christ, save me.
Blood of Christ, inebriate me.
Water from the side of Christ, wash me.
Passion of Christ, strengthen me.
O Good Jesus, hear me.
Within thy wounds, hide me.
Suffer me not to be separated from thee.
From the malicious enemy, defend me.
In the hour of death, call me.
And bid me come to thee, that with thy saints I may praise thee for ever and ever. *Amen.*

155

Develop

1. Read paragraphs 12–15 (to the end of the steps of a worthy Communion).

2. To benefit from the graces of Holy Communion, we must worthily receive our Lord. The steps to a worthy Communion are:

- *We must be in the state of grace. This means we must be free from mortal sin. If one is in need of grace, he must receive the Sacrament of Penance before receiving Communion, lest he commit the sin of sacrilege.*
- *We must know whom we are about to receive. We must truly believe that Jesus is present in the Eucharist.*
- *We must observe the Eucharistic fast (only water or medicine for an hour before Communion). This helps us to prepare to receive our Lord—to hunger for him.*
- *We must receive our Lord reverently. This requires our preparation at home (praying before coming to Mass, striving to grow in the life of virtue daily, dressing modest-*

ly and appropriately for Mass, etc.), as well as our reverence at Mass. We are to make a gesture of reverence before receiving our Lord (such as a profound bow) and then reverently receive on the tongue or in the hand.

3. Read paragraphs 16–21 (to the end of the chapter).

4. Teach the students how to make a spiritual communion. A spiritual communion is a prayer inviting Jesus into one's heart when one cannot receive the Eucharist. For example: "My Lord, as I cannot receive you now in the Most Holy Sacrament of the Altar, I ask you to come, nevertheless, into my heart and render it like unto thine own."

5. Review adoration and benediction with the students. If possible arrange for your class to go to adoration.

Name:_____

The Sacrament of the Holy Eucharist

Answer the following questions in complete sentences.

1. What is the Eucharist?
   The Eucharist is the Sacrament in which Jesus is present—Body, Blood, Soul, and Divinity—under the appearances of bread and wine.

2. Why do we call the Eucharist the source of grace?
   of grace because it is Jesus himself, the source of all grace.

3. Why do we call it our spiritual food?
   We call the Eucharist spiritual food because it is the food that nourishes our soul and strengthens us.

4. Why do we call it Holy Communion?
   We call the Eucharist Holy Communion because through it we are united to Christ in a physical and spiritual way.

5. List and explain the four steps to a worthy reception of Holy Communion.
   The four steps to a worthy reception of Holy Communion are 1) we must be in a state of grace and not be in a state of mortal sin; 2) we must believe and recall that Jesus is truly present in the Sacrament; 3) we must observe the Eucharistic one-hour fast and 4) we must spend time in thanksgiving to Jesus afterward.

6. Choose one of the quotations of the saints in this chapter, by St. Francis de Sales, St. Teresa of Avila, or St. Bonaventure, and explain what it tells you about the Eucharist.
   Answers will vary.

96   *Faith and Life Series • Grade 8 • Chapter 24 • Lesson 4*

Reinforce

1. Have the students work on *Activity Book*, p. 96.

2. Give the students time to work on the Memorization Questions and Words to Know from this chapter and to prepare for the chapter and unit quizzes.

3. Have the students write a prayer to help them prepare for Communion. They should also compose a prayer of thanksgiving for after Communion.

4. Take the class to Adoration and Benediction.

5. Review the beauty of daily Mass and its benefits to the spiritual life. You may use the saints as examples.

Conclude

1. Lead the students in singing "O Lord, I am not worthy," *Adoremus Hymnal*, #512.

2. End class by leading the students in the *Anima Christi*.

Preview

In the next lesson, the students' understanding of the material covered in this chapter will be reviewed and assessed.

ADORATION AND BENEDICTION

Eucharistic Adoration is when the Blessed Sacrament is exposed in a monstrance for public worship. This may be accompanied with songs, litanies, and other prayers, or it may be a time for silent prayer. Some parishes have Perpetual Adoration, in which the Blessed Sacrament is exposed twenty-four hours a day. There must always be at least one person present while the Blessed Sacrament is exposed, so in such parishes someone is always present, praying before Jesus. Another devotion is the Holy Hour, in which people are encouraged to spend one hour a week, or a day, in prayer before the Blessed Sacrament. Adoration often ends in benediction, a service in which a priest blesses the people by making the sign of the cross with the monstrance before them.

NOTES

_____
_____
_____
_____
_____
_____
_____
_____
_____
_____
_____

_____

_____

_____

_____

_____

_____

_____

_____

_____

_____

_____

_____

_____

_____

_____

_____

_____

_____

_____

_____

_____

_____

_____

_____

"According to the riches of his glory he may grant you to be strengthened with might through his Spirit in the inner man, and that Christ may dwell in your hearts through faith; that you, being rooted and grounded in love, may have power to comprehend with all the saints what is the breadth and length and height and depth, and to know the love of Christ which surpasses knowledge, that you may be filled with all the fulness of God."

(Ephesians 3:16–19)

selves to receive Communion by remembering that we are about to receive the Body and Blood of Our Lord.

3. We must observe the Eucharistic fast. The Church gives us this law—no food or drink (except water or medicine) for one hour before receiving Communion —out of reverence so that we may prepare ourselves to receive our great Lord and King. This small sacrifice reminds us of what we are about to do. (The sick and those who care for them are exempt from this fast.)

4. After we receive Our Lord, we should spend time in _thanksgiving—thanking_ him for coming to us and asking Jesus to help us. The following prayer, called the _Anima Christi_, might help us meditate on the great gift we receive. Many people recite this prayer after Communion.

Because the Eucharist is our source of spiritual nourishment, it is good to receive this sacrament frequently. By attending Mass each Sunday we are able to receive Holy Communion at least once a week. However, realizing the greatness of this sacrament, we should try to receive Our Lord even more often—even daily—by attending Mass during the week. St. Francis de Sales, in his _Introduction to the_

Devout Life reminds us of this.

Two classes of people should communicate often, the perfect because, being well prepared, they would be very wrong not to approach the fountainhead of perfection; and the imperfect, that they might preserve their strength; the weak that they might become strong; the sick that they might find a cure; the healthy, that they might be preserved from sickness.

Even when we are unable to attend Mass we can make a _spiritual communion_ in which we ask Our Lord to come to us and dwell in us in a special way.

When we pray, "Give us this day our daily bread," we include asking to receive the Eucharist. When we realize the extreme love for us which Jesus showed in establishing a way to stay with us on earth, we will long to receive him as often as possible. He was the delight of the saints. St. Teresa of Avila prayed that "though our bodily eyes cannot feast themselves on the sight of him since he is hidden from us, he may reveal himself to the eyes of the soul and may make himself known to us as another kind of food, full of delight and joy, which sustains our life."

St. Bonaventure prays: "Grant that my soul may hunger after you . . . upon whom the angels desire to look, and may my inmost soul

156

_____

_____

_____

_____

_____

_____

_____

_____

_____

_____

_____

_____

_____

_____

_____

_____

be filled with the sweetness of your savor; may it ever thirst for you, the fountain of life, the foundation of wisdom and knowledge, the fountain of eternal light, the torrent of pleasure, the richness of the house of God."

In addition to the reception of Our Lord in the Eucharist, we can adore him and draw closer to him through adoration of the Blessed Sacrament. The *Real Presence* of Christ in the Eucharist remains after Mass. Therefore consecrated Hosts are reserved in the tabernacle in the church. Because Christ is truly present in our churches and chapels, we should try to spend time adoring him, thanking him, and talking to him about our needs. If we cannot get to daily Mass, perhaps we can make a daily visit to Our Lord in the Blessed Sacrament.

Besides such visits, there are sometimes special devotions to the Blessed Sacrament in which we can participate. We may go to church for **Benediction**. The Eucharist is placed in a special container called a **monstrance**, so that we may see and adore the Body of Christ. The priest holds up the monstrance and blesses us with Christ himself. Sometimes the Host in the monstrance will be exposed on our altars for a period of time so that we may pray to Our Lord in a special way.

These devotions remind us of Christ's presence in the Eucharist and help us draw closer to him. We can deepen our union with Christ by receiving Communion often and visiting him in the Blessed Sacrament.

Words to Know:
sacrament grace Eucharist
Benediction monstrance

Prayer After Communion

"My Lord Jesus Christ, I believe that you are truly within me with your Body, Blood, soul and divinity; humbled in my nothingness, I adore you profoundly as my God and my Lord."

". . . Whoever drinks of the water that I shall give him will never thirst; the water that I shall give him will become in him a spring of water welling up to eternal life."

(Jn 4:14)

157

Q. 139 *What are sacraments?*
Sacraments are outward signs instituted by Jesus Christ to give us grace and to make us holy (CCC 1115–16).

Q. 140 *What are the seven sacraments?*
The seven sacraments are Baptism, Confirmation, Holy Eucharist, Penance, Anointing of the Sick, Holy Orders, and Matrimony (CCC 1113).

Q. 141 *What is the Sacrament of Penance?*
The Sacrament of Penance (also called confession and reconciliation) is the sacrament instituted by Jesus Christ to forgive those sins committed after Baptism (CCC 1425).

Q. 142 *What five things are required to make a good confession?*
The five things required to make a good confession are: 1) examination of conscience; 2) contrition; 3) the intention not to sin again; 4) the accusation of our sins to a priest; 5) reception of absolution and penance (CCC 1451, 1454–55, 1459).

Q. 143 *How is an examination of conscience made?*
An examination of conscience is made by recalling the sins we have committed in thought, word, act, or omission against the Commandments of God, against the Precepts of the Church, or against the obligations to our state in life, since our last good confession (CCC 1454).

Q. 144 *In the examination of conscience should we seek to know the number of our mortal sins?*
In the examination of conscience we should seek with diligence to know the number of our mortal sins (CCC 1456).

Q. 145 *What is contrition?*
Contrition is sorrow of the soul and hatred for the sins we have committed, which brings us to form the intention not to sin again (CCC 1451–53).

158

Q. 146 *Is it necessary to have contrition for all the sins we have committed?*

It is necessary to have contrition for all the mortal sins we have committed, and it is fitting to have sorrow also for our venial sins (CCC 1452–53).

Q. 147 *When is it fitting to do the penance given in the Sacrament of Penance?*

It is fitting to do the penance given in the Sacrament of Penance as soon as possible, unless the confessor has assigned a particular time for it (CCC 1460).

Q. 148 *What effects does the Eucharist produce in him who receives it worthily?*

In him who receives it worthily, the Holy Eucharist produces and increases grace, the life of the soul, wipes away venial sins, preserves us from future mortal sin, and gives spiritual joy and consolation by increasing the hope of eternal life, of which it is the pledge (CCC 1392, 1394, 1402).

Q. 149 *What is transubstantiation?*

Transubstantiation is the change of bread and wine into the Body, Blood, Soul, and Divinity of our Lord Jesus Christ, which occurs at Consecration (CCC 1376).

Q. 150 *What sin does a peron commit if he deliberately receives Holy Communion in the state of mortal sin?*

Sacrilege is the sin a person commits who receives Holy Communion in the state of mortal sin (CCC 1385).

159

NOTES

CHAPTER TWENTY-FOUR
REVIEW AND ASSESSMENT

Aims

The students' understanding of the material covered in this chapter and unit will be reviewed and assessed.

Materials

- Quiz 24, Appendix, p. A-34
- Unit 6 Test, Appendix, pp. A-35–A-36

Optional:
- "O Lord, I am not worthy," *Adoremus Hymnal*, #512

Review

1. The students should know the seven sacraments, their matter, form, and institution by Christ.

2. The students should thoroughly understand Penance and Eucharist.

3. The students should know how to prepare for and receive Penance and Eucharist.

4. The students should understand the seal of the confessional.

5. The students should be familiar with Eucharistic devotions, including spiritual communion, adoration, and benediction.

Name: _____

The Sacramental Life　　　　　　　　　　　　**Quiz 24**

Part I: Answer in complete sentences.

1. What are the seven sacraments?
   The seven sacraments are Baptism, Confirmation, Holy Eucharist, Penance, Anointing of the Sick, Holy Orders and Matrimony.

2. What is the Sacrament of Penance?
   The Sacrament of Penance is the sacrament istituted by Jesus Christ to forgive those sins committed after Baptism.

3. Why do we confess our sins to a priest?
   We confess our sins to a priest because Christ gave the apostles and their successors the authority to forgive sins.

4. What is contrition?
   Contrition is sorrow for one's sins.

5. What are the five things required to make a good confession?
   The five things required to make a good confession are: 1) examination of conscience; 2) contrition; 3) the intention not to sin again; 4) the accusation of our sins to a priest and 5) reception of absolution and penance.

6. Why is the Eucharist the source and summit of our Christian faith?
   The Eucharist is the source and summit of our Christian faith because it is a means of receiving grace and the source of grace, Jesus, himself.

7. How do we worthily receive Holy Communion?
   To receive Holy Communion worthily we must be in a state of grace, we must believe that Jesus is truly present in the Sacrament, we must observe the Eucharistic fast, and we should spend time in thanksgiving.

8. What is transubstantiation?
   Transubstantiation is the change of bread and wine into the Body, Blood, Soul and Divinity of Jesus Christ, which occurs at Consecration.

A - 34　　　　　　　　　　*Faith and Life • Grade 8 • Appendix A*

Assess

1. Distribute the quizzes and read through them with the students to be sure they understand the questions.

2. Administer the quiz. As they hand in their work, orally quiz the students on the Memorization Questions from this chapter.

3. After all the quizzes have been handed in, review the correct answers with the class. Repeat steps 1–3 for the unit 6 test.

Conclude

1. Lead the students in singing "O Lord, I am not worthy," *Adoremus Hymnal*, #512.

2. End class by leading the students in the *Anima Christi*.

CHAPTER TWENTY-FIVE
DEATH AND PARTICULAR JUDGMENT

Catechism of the Catholic Church References

Angels: 328–36, 350–52
Beatific Vision: 1028
Christian Beatitude: 1720–24, 1728–29
Christian Holiness: 2012–16, 2028–29
Fall of the Angels: 391–95, 414
Heaven: 1023–29, 1053
Hell: 1033–37, 1056–57

Individual Judgment: 1021–22, 1051
Man as Body and Soul: 362–68, 382
Preparation for a Happy Death: 1014
Purgatory: 1030–32, 1054
To Die in Christ Jesus: 1005–14, 1018–20, 1052
Separation of Body and Soul: 400-403, 1005, 1007, 1016, 1020

Scripture References

Original Sin: Gen 3
Life after Death: Mt 4:12–17; 16:18; 19:16–21; 28:1–9
    Jn 3:15–16; 5:24; 6:35–54, 68; 11:17–44
Holy Death: Sir 1:11

Man Dies (Denial of Reincarnation): Heb 9:27
The Beatitudes: Mt 5:1–12
Heaven: Mt 13:44–52

Summary of Lesson Content

Lesson 1

Death is the separation of body and soul. The body will die and decompose. The soul has eternal life.

Death is a consequence of original sin.

Death is the gateway to eternal life with God. We do not know the time of our death.

Lesson 2

We should prepare ourselves for death. The best preparation is to live our lives according to God's will, developing ourselves spiritually, morally, and sacramentally.

Mary can pray for us at the hour of our death.

We should receive the Sacrament of Anointing of the Sick when we are seriously ill or dying.

Lesson 3

At the moment of death, we will receive particular judgment. We will be judged on what we thought, said, did, and failed to do.

Hell is the just reward of those who have died in the state of mortal sin, rejecting God. Purgatory is a transitional state of purification leading to heaven. Heaven is the eternal reward of those who have died and are prepared to see God face to face.

Lesson 4

Heaven is the end for which we were made. We should long for heaven and live in hope of this reward.

We should pray for the grace of a happy death.

LESSON ONE: DEATH

Aims

The students will learn that death is the separation of body and soul. The body will die and decompose. The soul has eternal life.

They will learn that death is a consequence of original sin.

They will learn that death is the gateway to eternal life with God. We do not know the time of our death.

Materials

- *Activity Book*, p. 97

Optional:
- "Help, Lord, the souls that thou has made," *Adoremus Hymnal*, #571

Begin

Read Gen 3. It is important for the students to know that death and decay (corruption of the body) are consequences of original sin. In Creation, God breathed into the man he formed from the dirt. The dirt represents the body, and the breath the eternal soul. Man was created for eternal life. Had he not sinned, man would live forever and never experience sickness or suffering. However, because man sinned and we all inherit the effects of original sin, we will all experience death.

162

Develop

1. Read paragraphs 1–4 (up to How can we prepare ourselves).

2. Define death. Death is the separation of the the finite body from the eternal soul. It is the end of earthly life.

3. Discuss how people view death and how they feel about it. It is normal for us to mourn the loss of a loved one, because we will miss his earthly presence. Review the Christian view of death. We hope for everlasting life with God forever in heaven. Read the following passages from Scripture:
Mt 4:12–17; 16:18; 19:16–21; 28:1–9
Jn 3:15–16; 5:24; 6:35–54, 68; 11:17–44

4. Because of Christ, Christian death is a positive event. In death, God calls man to himself. Christ can transform our death into an act of obedience and love for the Father, after the example of Christ. To rise with Christ, we must die with Christ. Because Christ transformed death from a curse to a

blessing by his self-sacrifice, we can joyfully anticipate the eternal glories to come.

5. The Communion of Saints is reminded of its duty to pray for the dead. We can also pray for the intercession of the saints in heaven and the holy souls in purgatory. Review that we are united with the entire Communion of Saints in Holy Communion, for in Communion we are more closely bound to the Mystical Body of Christ, of which Christ is the head.

6. It is sinful to participate in seances and occult practices, which encourage communication with the dead. Wilful participation in such activities is a mortal sin.

7. Catholics do not believe in reincarnation (Heb 9:27). At the end of our earthly lives, we shall not return to other earthly lives. Our life does not end—it is changed and glorified.

Name:_____

Death

Answer the following questions in complete sentences.

1. Why must we die?

   We must die because death is one of the consequences of
   the Fall.

2. Explain the phrase: "death is not the end of life, but only the end of this life."

   Answers will vary.

3. What sort of attitude should we have toward death? What does our faith tell us?

   We should realize that we are mortal and that death can
   come at any time. We should prepare for death by living
   good lives and by praying for a holy death. We should not
   view death as the end of life but as the beginning of our
   life with God. Our faith tells us that death is simply a
   transition to a new life.

Reinforce

1. Have the students work on *Activity Book*, p. 97.

2. Provide time for the students to work on the Memorization Questions and Words to Know from this chapter.

3. The students should compose a meditation upon Christian death.

4. Discuss funeral etiquette. How should the students extend condolences to those who mourn? What constitutes proper behavior and Catholic custom? (E.g., it is proper to have a Mass said for the deceased, etc.)

Conclude

1. Teach the students to sing "Help, Lord, the souls that thou has made," *Adoremus Hymnal*, #571.

2. End class with a prayer for a happy death.

Preview

In the next lesson, the students will learn how to prepare for death.

SAINT THOMAS MORE ON DEATH

The following quotations are from the play *A Man for All Seasons* by Robert Bolt about the life and martyrdom of Saint Thomas More. Although it is a play, it is historically accurate. Some of the dialogue from the play's trial comes from official records of the real trial.

"Death comes for us all, my lords, yes, even for kings he comes, to whom amidst all their royalty and brute strength he will neither kneel nor make them any reverence nor pleasantly desire them to come forth, but roughly grasp them by the very breast and rattle them until they be stark dead! So causing their bodies to be buried in a pit and sending them to judgment . . . whereof at their death their success is uncertain."
—Saint Thomas More in *A Man for All Seasons*

"For our own deaths . . . dare we for shame enter the kingdom with ease when Our Lord himself entered with so much pain?"
—Saint Thomas More in *A Man for All Seasons*

"Death comes for us all; even at our birth, death does but stand aside a little. And every day he looks towards us and muses to himself whether that day or the next he will draw nigh. It is the law of nature and the will of God."
—Saint Thomas More in *A Man for All Seasons*

LESSON TWO: PREPARING FOR DEATH

Aims

The students will learn that we should prepare ourselves for death. The best preparation is to live our lives according to God's will, developing ourselves spiritually, morally, and sacramentally.

They will learn that Mary can pray for us at the hour of our death.

They will learn that we should receive the Sacrament of Anointing of the Sick.

Materials

- *Activity Book*, p. 98

Optional:
- "Help, Lord, the souls that thou has made," *Adoremus Hymnal*, #571

Begin

"With him who fears the Lord it will go well at the end; on the day of his death he will be blessed" Sir 1:11

The way we live our lives determines our final reward, which will be given at our particular judgment at the moment of death. How should we prepare for a good death and a positive judgment? Discuss this with the students.

CHAPTER 25

Death and the Particular Judgment

"Truly, I say to you, today you will be with me in Paradise."

Luke 23:43

Each year on Ash Wednesday we hear the words: "Remember, man, that you are dust and to dust you will return" to remind us of our mortality. Each of us will eventually die. This is one of the consequences for all living, material creatures. Plants and animals eventually die; even inanimate, non-living, objects do not last for ever. Human beings, since we are mortal, must eventually die, a result of original sin.

Although the separation of body and soul—death—is inevitable, we know that there is life beyond the grave. Human beings have a mortal body but an *immortal* soul. **Immortal** means living forever. Because of this we see that death is not really the end of life but only the end of this life. In the Preface used at Masses for the dead we are reminded that for the Christian "life is not ended but merely changed."

Our faith tells us that death is the gateway to life with God. In the Gospel, Martha, the sister of Lazarus, showed us how Christians ought to understand death. When Our Lord came to Bethany after Lazarus' death, Martha said to Him: "I know that [my brother] will rise again in the resurrection at the last day" (Jn 11:24).

Since death will come for each of us, what should be our attitude toward it? Our Lord tells us that we should prepare ourselves for death. We should remember the parable about the servants who are awaiting their master's return. Since they do not know exactly when he will come, they must prepare themselves. We must also be prepared:

Watch therefore—for [you] do not know when the master of the house will come, in the evening, or at midnight, or at cockcrow, or in the morning. . . (Mk 13:35).

How can we prepare ourselves for death? We prepare throughout our lives by growing in faith and love. The best preparation for death is to live according to God's will, developing our spiritual lives through prayer and the sacraments. Whenever we pray the Hail Mary we ask our Mother in heaven to pray for us "now and at the hour of our death." Following our vocation and generously serving God will prepare us for death and our meeting with Christ.

163

Develop

1. Read paragraph 5 (up to the section on the particular judgment).

2. We can prepare for a holy death by living a holy life. We can:
- *Learn about God and love him faithfully*
- *Follow God's laws*
- *Pray*
- *Receive the sacraments, etc.*

3. A vital aide for Catholics is the Anointing of the Sick.
- *Matter: anointing with oil and laying on of hands by a priest*
- *Form the words: "Through this holy anointing, may the Lord in his love and mercy help you with the grace of the Holy Spirit. Amen. May the Lord who frees you from sin save you and raise you up. Amen."*
- *Effects: unites the sick and suffering with Christ in his Passion in his death and in his Resurrection; gives peace and strength to endure suffering and illness; forgives sins; restores health if it is God's will; prepares for the passage to eternal life.*

4. If one is conscious when he receives the Anointing of the Sick, he can receive the Sacraments of Penance and the Eucharist. If he receives the Eucharist for the last time before his death, this Communion is called viaticum, *food for the journey. It sustains the soul and strengthens it for eternal union with God. If a one is unconscious, he may still receive the Anointing of the Sick and also receive apostolic pardon. Should he regain consciousness, he should avail himself of the Sacrament of Penance.*

5. Review that Anointing of the Sick may be received by anyone who is gravely ill and may be received more than once.

Name:_____

Preparing for Death

Answer the following questions in complete sentences.

1. Explain how the following things can help you to prepare for death.

   The Sacraments of Baptism and Confession:
   Answers will vary.

   The Sacrament of the Holy Eucharist:

   Following God's laws:

   Virtue:

   The Sacrament of the Anointing of the Sick:

2. Why can we have faith and hope?
   Answers will vary.

3. How can we grow and exercise faith and hope?
   Answers will vary.

Reinforce

1. Have the students work on *Activity Book*, p. 98.

2. Provide time for the students to work on the Memorization Questions and Words to Know from this chapter.

3. Have a priest come in to explain the Sacrament of Anointing of the Sick. Show the oil of the sick and discuss what is usually needed; e.g., candles, crucifix, etc.

4. The students may write prayers asking for the grace of a happy death.

5. Each student should create an "action plan" for his life, in order to prepare for death.

Conclude

1. Lead the students in singing "Help, Lord, the souls that thou has made," *Adoremus Hymnal*, #571.

2. End class with a prayer for a happy death.

Preview

In the next lesson, the students will learn about the particular judgment.

SAINT JOSEPH, PATRON OF A HAPPY DEATH

Saint Joseph, husband of Mary and foster-father of Jesus, is the patron of the Universal Church and of a happy death. The Gospel of Matthew tells us that Joseph was "a just man" (Mt 1:19). It also tells us of Joseph's love for Mary and that he travelled all the way to Egypt at the word of an angel to protect Jesus. There is a tradition in the East that Jesus and Mary were both present at Joseph's death. With that company, his death must have been a happy one. Although we cannot have Mary and Jesus physically with us, we can receive Jesus in *viaticum* and, through the other sacraments, our prayers, and the intercession of Saint Joseph and Mary, we, too, can have a happy death.

PRAYER TO SAINT JOSEPH FOR A HAPPY DEATH

Sweet Saint Joseph be thou near me,
when my soul is called away,
from this earth so dark and dreary,
to the bright eternal day.

Bring with thee my dearest Jesus,
in whose wounds I fain would hide,
and with Mary my sweet mother,
come dear father to my side.

LESSON THREE: PARTICULAR JUDGMENT

Aims

The students will learn that, at the moment of death, we will receive particular judgment. We will be judged on what we thought, said, did, and failed to do.

They will learn that hell is the just reward of those who have died in the state of mortal sin, rejecting God. Purgatory is a transitional state of purification leading to heaven. Heaven is the eternal reward of those prepared to see God face to face.

Materials

- *Activity Book*, p. 99

- The Dream of Gerontius, Appendix, pp. B-12–B-14

Optional:
- "Help, Lord, the souls that thou has made," *Adoremus Hymnal*, #571

Begin

Read Jn 6:47 and Mt 19:16–21. The first passage states we must have faith to have eternal life. The second states we must follow God's holy laws to have eternal life. Are these exclusive of one another? Of course not. If we truly believe in Christ, we will follow God's laws. However, we should not merely go through the motions of following the law, but have faith in and love of God.

"Everyone who sees the Son and believes in him should have eternal life and I will raise him up at the last day"

(John 6:40)

We should pray that we may receive the sacraments before our death. By the sacrament of Anointing, dangerously ill persons are commended to the Lord, that he may support and save them. Hopefully, we will also be able to receive the sacrament of Penance and the Eucharist as Viaticum.

When we die we will meet Our Lord and be judged by him. The **particular judgment** occurs at the moment of our death and will be based on those things which we did or neglected to do in this life. At this judgment we will see ourselves as we are—our sins and failings, as well as our virtues. We will also see the perfect justice of God's judgment. For this reason it is extremely important to develop the habit of appealing to God's mercy for us sinners. This appeal, made habitually, will bring down his mercy on us and others for that moment when we so critically need it. By remembering what St. Paul said we will prepare for this great moment:

> He will render to every man according to his works: to those who by patience in well-doing seek for glory and honor and immortality, he will give eternal life; but for those who are factious and do not obey the truth, but obey wickedness, there will be wrath and fury (Rom 2:6–8).

At the particular judgment those who have died in the state of mortal sin—without repenting—will be separated from God for ever. They will suffer eternal punishment because

164

of their own actions and choice. In the parable of the rich man (Dives) and Lazarus Our Lord reminded us of the permanence of this state (Lk 16:19–31). Once one is in hell, there is no chance for repentance. While the souls of the damned suffer sensible pain, the greatest suffering in hell is the loss of God. They will be without hope, knowing that their own rejection of God is the cause of their damnation.

It is good to remember that God does not want anyone to suffer in hell. In fact, he did not create hell for man. The angels who rebelled were banished from God's sight and this is hell. God created man, like the angels, with a free will. Thus, if we should turn away from him, we will join the fallen angels in suffering this eternal punishment.

Some who die are not in the state of mortal sin, but still have venial sins which they have not fully repented of or done adequate penance for. Because these people have not completely separated themselves from God, they will not go to hell. They will go first to *purgatory*. Here they will be prepared for heaven. The doctrine of purgatory is very consoling since, because of God's mercy, we can be saved even though we are not perfect. We can go through a time of purification. Even though it is a painful suffering, we are full of hope.

Other people whose love for God is perfect will go straight to heaven. The reward for the just is *eternal life* in which they will enjoy the vision of God. This is called the **Beatific Vision**. In heaven "we shall see [God] as he is"

Develop

1. Read paragraphs 6–11 (up to Since we cannot really understand much of what heaven is like).

2. Define the particular judgment. We will see ourselves with all our faults, failures, and sins. We will, therefore, realize the justice of God's judgments. Also, seeing the perfection of God and our own imperfection, we will not want to be in the presence of God until we are cleansed of our sins and failures. Be sure the students understand the need for the life of grace; dying without grace merits eternal damnation.

3. Define hell. Outline the pain of hell:
- *Pain of loss—there is no hope of seeing God; this is the greatest suffering*
- *Pain of sense—there will be a material or external cause for spiritual and physical pain in hell*
- *Eternal pain—have the students recall the worst pain they have suffered. Imagine that same pain lasting forever!*

4. Define purgatory. Outline the suffering of purgatory:
- *Suffering is different for each person, depending upon his faults and sins*
- *Suffering can be lessened by the prayers and sacrifices of those on earth*
- *There is certainty of reaching heaven*
- *At the end of the world, the souls still in purgatory will go to heaven and purgatory will end*

5. Define heaven. Outline the joys of heaven:
- *Joy of seeing and loving God perfectly*
- *Joy of seeing and loving family members, friends, saints, and angels*
- *Joy in heaven is always full but our capacity for joy depends on the degree of love we had for God on earth*

Name:_____

The Particular Judgment

Answer the following questions in complete sentences.

1. Explain the particular judgment, including when we face it, how we will see ourselves, and what will happen to our soul afterwards.

   <u>The particular judgment will happen when we die and</u>
   <u>face Our Lord. He will judge us on all that we did or neg-</u>
   <u>lected to do in our life. We will see ourselves as we really</u>
   <u>are, as God sees us. Afterwards our soul will go either to</u>
   <u>heaven, hell, or purgatory.</u>

2. What enables the soul to go to heaven, hell, or purgatory?

   <u>The soul is enabled to go to heaven, hell, or purgatory by</u>
   <u>its actions and choices in life.</u>

3. If God does not want people to go to hell, why is it possible for us to end up there?

   <u>It is possible for people to go to hell because he respects</u>
   <u>our free choice. He does not want to force himself on us.</u>
   <u>He wants us to love him and in order for love to be love,</u>
   <u>it must be free.</u>

4. Explain how purgatory is an example of God's perfect justice and mercy.

   <u>Purgatory is an example of God's perfect justice and mercy</u>
   <u>because his justice demands that the soul be purified</u>
   <u>before it enters heaven. But his mercy allows the soul an</u>
   <u>opportunity to be purified and does not insist on perfection</u>
   <u>at death in order to eventually enter heaven.</u>

Faith and Life Series • Grade 8 • Chapter 25 • Lesson 3   99

Reinforce

1. Have the students work on *Activity Book*, p. 99.

2. Provide time for the students to work on the Memorization Questions and Words to Know from this chapter.

3. Review that, by our lives on earth, we determine our eternal state. Hell is the state for those who die in the state of mortal sin, rejecting God's mercy. Heaven is for those who die in the state of grace, sharing in God's life and in loving friendship with God—free from all sin (mortal and venial) and all stain from sin. Purgatory is a transitional state for those who die in the state of grace, but must be purified from venial sin or the punishment due to sins (including mortal sins that have been forgiven).

4. Each student should meditate upon his particular judgment.

Conclude

1. Lead the students in singing "Help, Lord, the souls that thou has made," *Adoremus Hymnal*, #571.

2. End class with a prayer for a happy death.

Preview

In the next lesson, the students will learn about the beatific vision.

THE DREAM OF GERONTIUS

Discuss "The Dream of Gerontius" by Venerable John Henry Newman, a short play which portrays a soul on its way to judgment. Throughout the play the soul walks with his guardian angel and speaks impatiently of the coming vision of God. However, once the soul sees God, he sees all his imperfections and cries to the angel, "Take me away." Use the questions provided in the Appendix or simply discuss the idea of this play, noting that we choose our own eternal reward: heaven or hell.

See Appendix, pp. B-12–B-14 for passages and questions from "The Dream of Gerontius".

NOTES

_____
_____
_____
_____
_____
_____
_____
_____
_____
_____
_____
_____

LESSON FOUR:
BEATIFIC VISION

Aims

The students will learn that heaven is the end for which we were made. We should long for heaven and live in hope of this reward.

They will learn that we should pray for the grace of a happy death.

Materials

- *Activity Book*, p. 100

- Rite of Christian Funeral, pp. B-15–B-17

Optional:
- "Help, Lord, the souls that thou has made," *Adoremus Hymnal*, #571

Begin

Read Mt 5:1–12, the Beatitudes. They are also in the student text.

If heaven is the greatest consolation and reward for the blessed then what might heaven be like? You may read other Scripture passages on heaven, Mt 13:44–52.

(1 Jn 3:2). It is this which gives us true happiness. In heaven, we will know God as completely as we can:

Now we see in a mirror dimly, but then face to face. Now I know in part; then I shall understand fully. . . (1 Cor 13:12).

Here we will be able perfectly to love God and others.

We know that heaven will bring us great joy, and yet it is difficult for us to grasp what it is really like. St. Paul tells us:

No eye has seen, nor ear heard, nor the heart of man conceived, what God has prepared for those who love him (1 Cor 2:9).

Heaven will be far greater than anything we can imagine. It will encompass all those things which are truly good.

Besides the great joy of the Beatific Vision, there will be other joys in heaven. In heaven there will be no sorrow or pain as St. John tells us in the book of Revelation:

He will wipe away every tear from their eyes . . . neither shall there be mourning nor crying nor pain any more. . . (Rev 21:4).

There will also be no more sin or temptation in heaven. The struggle will be over and peace will remain. We will be united with the angels, the saints, and those we have known and loved on earth.

Since we cannot really understand much of what heaven is like, we may sometimes be tempted to think that it will be boring. Yet boredom is an imperfection of life on earth and cannot be part of life in heaven. If boredom is a part of life after death, it is part of life in hell, not heaven. Although the many particulars of life in heaven are unknown, we should remember the words of St. Paul—heaven is beyond our wildest dreams!

We should begin now by preparing ourselves for the day when Christ will call us to come home and be with him. We want to be able to say the words which St. Paul wrote near the end of his life, in a letter to Timothy:

For I am already on the point of being sacrificed; the time of my departure has come. I have fought the good fight, I have finished the race, I have kept the faith. Henceforth there is laid up for me the crown of righteousness, which the Lord, the righteous judge, will award to me on that Day, and not only to me but also to all who have loved his appearing (2 Tim 4:6–8).

Words to Know:
immortal
particular judgment   Beatific Vision

165

Develop

1. Read paragraphs 10–13 to the end of the chapter. (Note: paragraph 10 is re-read.)

2. Discuss the beatific vision. The beatific vision is the eternal joy of heaven, in which the elect will enjoy the vision of God. What does this chapter teach us about heaven? Heaven is the most wonderful state that can be attained.

3. Since we cannot really understand the glory of heaven, we can only speak of it in analogy:
 • Heaven is more beautiful than _____ .
 • Heaven is more perfect than _____ .
 • Heaven makes me happier than _____ .
The students should create analogies to speak of the glories of heaven. These analogies should truly attempt to convey the beatific vision.

4. Review ways that the students can prepare themselves for heaven.

5. Discuss the reality that heaven is made present at Mass. At Mass, Jesus is made present, and he comes to us in a way that foretells heaven. When we receive our Lord, we become living tabernacles. At Mass, the Communion of Saints worship around the altar—it is as though heaven has descended to earth, or we have been elevated to heaven.

6. Have the students review the rite of Christian Funerals, Appendix, pp. B-15–B-17. Now that they understand the Christian view of death and the glories that await the faithful, have each student plan his own funeral, choosing the readings, hymns, and rituals that he would want. This exercise will help the students to communicate their understanding of the mystery of death and eternal life.

Name:_____

A Happy Death

Write a letter or a prayer to God, praying for the graces necessary for a happy death.

<u>Answers will vary.</u>

_____

_____

_____

_____

_____

_____

_____

_____

_____

_____

_____

_____

_____

Reinforce

1. Have the students work on *Activity Book*, p. 100.

2. Provide time for the students to work on the Memorization Questions and Words to Know from this chapter and to prepare for the quiz.

3. *The students should prepare a funeral liturgy.*

4. Have the students write an essay on the glories of heaven, which are present at Mass.

Conclude

1. Lead the students in singing "Help, Lord, the souls that thou has made," *Adoremus Hymnal*, #571.

2 End class with a prayer for a happy death.

Preview

In the next lesson, the students' understanding of the material covered in this chapter will be reviewed and assessed.

MARY, QUEEN OF HEAVEN AND EARTH: OUR ESCHATOLOGICAL ICON

"Then God's temple in heaven was opened, and the ark of his covenant was seen within his temple; and there were flashes of lightning, loud noises, peals of thunder, an earthquake, and heavy hail. And a great portent appeared in heaven, a woman clothed with the sun, with the moon under her feet, and on her head crown of twelve stars; and she was with child and she cried out in her pangs of birth, in anguish for delivery. . . . She brought forth a male child, one who is to rule all the nations with a rod of iron, but her child was caught up to God and to his throne."

—Rev 11:19—12:5

INTERPRETATION

The images of the ark and the woman have traditionally been understood in two ways. Christ dwells within the Church as the ark, and the Church brings Christ forth into the world as the woman in labor. So both the ark and the woman represent the Church. According to another interpretation, they represent Mary, in whom Christ dwelt (the Litany of Loreto refers to Mary as "Ark of the Covenant"), and Mary, of course, bore Christ for the world. However, these two interpretations are not contradictory, for Mary herself is often seen as an image of the Church. This is an example of the many layers of meaning in Scripture.

_____
_____
_____
_____
_____
_____
_____
_____
_____
_____
_____
_____
_____
_____
_____
_____
_____
_____
_____
_____
_____
_____
_____

Q. 151 *What is the Sacrament of the Anointing of the Sick?*
The Sacrament of the Anointing of the Sick is given to Christians who are gravely ill for their spiritual and bodily strengthening (CCC 1499).

Q. 152 *Who is the minister of the Sacrament of the Anointing of the Sick?*
The minister of the Sacrament of the Anointing of the Sick is a priest: the pastor of the parish or another priest who has his permission (CCC 1519).

Q. 153 *How does the priest administer the Sacrament of the Anointing of the Sick?*
The priest administers the Anointing of the Sick by anointing the forehead and the hands of the sick person with the oil blessed by the bishop or priest and by saying: "Through this holy anointing may the Lord in his love and mercy help you with the grace of the Holy Spirit. Amen. May the Lord, who frees you from sin, save you and raise you up. Amen." (CCC 1517–19).

Q. 154 *When can the Sacrament of the Anointing of the Sick be given?*
The Sacrament of the Anointing of the Sick can be given whenever a person is in a dangerous condition of health, either on account of an illness serious in itself, a serious injury, or on account of old age (CCC 1514).

Q. 155 *What happens to each of us at the end of life?*
At the end of life each of us will die, our body and soul will be separated, and we will face a particular judgment (CCC 1005, 1022).

Q. 156 *On what will Jesus Christ judge us?*
Jesus Christ will judge us on the good and evil that we have done in life, including our thoughts, and things we failed to do in response to God's grace (CCC 1021).

166

_____
_____
_____
_____
_____
_____
_____
_____
_____
_____
_____
_____
_____
_____
_____
_____

Q. 157 *What happens to each man after the particular judgment?*
After the particular judgment, those who love God and are perfectly holy go immediately to heaven to be with him. Those who love God but still need purification go to purgatory until they are ready to be with God in heaven. Those who have rejected God through dying in mortal sin go to hell (CCC 1022).

Q. 158 *What is hell?*
Hell is the eternal suffering of separation from God (CCC 1033–35).

Q. 159 *How long will heaven and hell last?*
Heaven and hell will last forever (CCC 1022, 1033).

167

CHAPTER TWENTY-FIVE
REVIEW AND ASSESSMENT

Aims

The students' understanding of the material covered in this chapter will be reviewed and assessed.

Materials

- Quiz 25, Appendix, p. A-37

Optional:
- "Help, Lord, the souls that thou has made," *Adoremus Hymnal*, #571

Review

1. The students should understand the concept of death. Death is a consequence of original sin.

2. The students should understand the particular judgment. Upon what will they be judged in the particular judgment?

3. The students should know what heaven, hell, and purgatory are.

4. The students should be familiar with funeral etiquette and the preparation of a funeral liturgy.

Name: _____

Death and the Particular Judgment   Quiz 25

Part I: Define the following terms.

Particular Judgment: the judgment every person will face at death when Our Lord will judge us on all that we did or neglected to do in our life, and we will see ourselves as we really are, as God sees us

Heaven: eternal life and the enjoyment of the vision of God

Hell: eternal suffering of separation from God

Purgatory: a state after death of temporary suffering that cleanses the soul and makes it worthy to see God

Part II: Answer in complete sentences.

1. What can we do during our lives to prepare for death?
   We should prepare for death by living good lives, taking advantage of the sacraments, particularly Confession and the Eucharist, and by praying for a holy death.

2. What does the Church offer to help us before we die?
   The Church offers us the Sacrament of the Anointing of the Sick to help us before death, as well as Confession and Holy Communion.

3. What is the Christian understanding of death?
   We should realize that we are mortal and that death can come at any time. We should not view death as the end of life but as the beginning of our life with God. Our faith tells us that death is simply a transition to a new and eternal life.

4. Comment on the statement "life is not ended but merely changed."
   Answers will vary.

Faith and Life • Grade 8 • Appendix A   *A - 37*

Assess

1. Distribute the quizzes and read through them with the students to be sure they understand the questions.

2. Administer the quiz. As they hand in their work, orally quiz the students on the Memorization Questions from this chapter.

3. After all the quizzes have been handed in, review the correct answers with the class.

Conclude

1. Lead the students in singing "Help, Lord, the souls that thou has made," *Adoremus Hymnal*, #571.

2. End class with a prayer for a happy death.

CHAPTER TWENTY-SIX
THE TRUMPET SHALL SOUND

Catechism of the Catholic Church References

Christ's Resurrection and Ours: 992–1004, 1015–17
Christian Beatitude: 1720–24, 1728–29
Heaven: 1023–29, 1053
Hell: 1033–37, 1056–57

General Judgment: 678–79, 681–82, 1038–41, 1051–52, 1059
Resurrection of the Body: 988–91
Second Coming: 671

Scripture References

Ascension and Second Coming: Acts 1:1–12
Signs of the Times: Mk 13:1–37
General Judgment: Mt 24:29–51; 25:31–46
Resurrection: Mt 28:1–20; Mk 16:1–20; Lk 24:1–53;
    Jn 20:1–31; 21:1–15

Transfiguration: Lk 9:28–36
Creation: Gen 1—2
Creation Transformed: Rom 8:19–23

Summary of Lesson Content

Lesson 1

Jesus will come again to judge the living and the dead. This is the Second Coming of Christ.

The time of the Second Coming is unknown, but the signs that tell of the Second Coming are known. The Second Coming will signify the end of the world.

Lesson 2

At the end of the world, Jesus will judge the entire human race. This is called the General Judgment. Jesus will judge those who are alive and those who have already died.

Purgatory will cease to exist at the Second Coming. Man will either be in union with God or condemned forever.

Lesson 3

At the General Judgment, our bodies will be reunited with our souls and glorified. Our bodies will share in our eternal reward (heaven or hell).

The glorified body has four qualities: impassibility, subtlety, agility, and clarity.

Lesson 4

The earth will be transformed to a state of perfection.

These promises will be fulfilled. We must keep the end in mind and live in a manner that is pleasing to God.

LESSON ONE: SECOND COMING

Aims

The students will learn that Jesus will come again to judge the living and the dead. This is the Second Coming of Christ.

They will learn that the time of the Second Coming is unknown, but the signs that tell of the Second Coming are known. The Second Coming will signify the end of the world.

Materials

- *Activity Book*, p. 101

  Optional:
  - Day of wrath! O Day of mourning!"
    Adoremus Hymnal, #576

Begin

Recite the Creed (Apostles or Nicene). As Catholics, we believe that Christ will come again! What does this mean? How did we come to this belief? Jesus told us he would return. The angel at the Ascension also told us this. Read Acts 1:1–12. What did the angel tell us about the Second Coming of Christ? The angel told us that Christ will come in glory! The students should share ideas about how the glorious Second Coming might appear.

CHAPTER 26

The Trumpet Shall Sound— The End of the World

"Tell us, when will this be, and what will be the sign of your coming and of the close of the age?"

Matthew 24:3

At the Ascension of Our Lord into heaven, two angels spoke to the apostles saying:

"Why do you stand looking into heaven? This Jesus, who was taken up from you into heaven, will come in the same way as you saw him go into heaven" (Acts 1:11).

In the Nicene Creed we say that Jesus "will come again in glory to judge the living and the dead." When Christ first came among us, he came in poverty, humility, and weakness. He was born in a stable fit for animals, not a King. He was God, but he took on human nature and began his life in the most humble state—as a baby. He was God, but he took on the weaknesses of human nature—except sin—in order to teach us. When Christ comes again—the **Second Coming**—at the end of the world, he will come in triumph, as the King and Judge of the world. He will come in glory and be recognized by all men as Christ the King.

The time when this Second Coming will occur is unknown. When the apostles asked Our Lord about the end of the world (Mt 24), he spoke of various signs and warnings which

168

would precede the event. He said that there would be wars and rumors of wars, famines, false prophets, and persecutions. All of these, however, have occurred at various times in history. And many individuals in the past (as well as the present) have mistaken the troubles of their own times as signs of the end of the world. But they neglected Our Lord's final words about the end, which are the most important:

But of that day and hour no one knows, not even the angels of heaven . . . the Father only. . . (Mt 24:36).

Just as we do not know when the world will end, we do not know exactly how it will end either. It is possible that the end of the world will be caused by humans, for example through war or the misuse of natural resources. But it is also possible that God will directly bring about the end of the world. However, it will not take place until God wills it.

At the end of the world Our Lord will judge the entire human race. This is known as the **General Judgment** and is described by Our Lord in the Gospel of Matthew (Mt 25). At that

Develop

1. Read paragraphs 1–3 (up to "At the end of the world Our Lord will judge").

2. We do not know the day or the hour that our Lord will return. He did, however, tell us to watch for signs. What are these signs? Read: Mk 13:1–37 on the signs of the times. List the signs:
- *Temple destroyed*
- *Many come saying they are Christ or a prophet*
- *Wars: nation against nation*
- *Earthquakes*
- *Famines*
- *Christians delivered to councils, beaten, and tortured on behalf of Christ; family members will turn against each other*
- *Gospel must first be preached to all nations*
- *People will flee, leaving everything*
- *Stars fall from heaven*

- *Sun dark, moon gives no light*
- *Son of Man (Jesus) coming on the clouds; angels gather the elect.*

3. Many of these signs have occurred at different times throughout history. Some people have expected the Second Coming and it did not happen. Should we pretend the Second Coming will never happen? Rather, should we prepare ourselves for this to happen at any time?

4. Do we know how the world will come to an end? No. We do not know if this will be a man-made end or if God will directly bring the world to an end. We know that the end of the world will not occur until God wills it.

5. Have the students reflect on the awe and majesty of the Second Coming of Christ. Are they ready? Are they excited for this great event?

Name:_____

The Second Coming

Answer the following questions in complete sentences.

1. What does the Nicene Creed teach about the Second Coming?

   The Nicene Creed teaches that when the Second Coming occurs, Jesus will judge the living and the dead and will appear in glory and power.

2. Compare Jesus' first coming and his Second Coming.

   Jesus' first coming was humble, poor, weak, lowly and he hid his power and glory. He was not recognized by most as God. In the Second Coming, Jesus will appear with power, glory and as King and Judge of the world and will be recognized by all men.

3. What signs will precede the Second Coming (see Matthew 24)? Using these signs, can we know for sure when the world will end?

   The signs that will precede the Second Coming are wars, false prophets, persecutions, and famine. We cannot know for sure when the world will end since that has not been revealed to us and only the Father knows.

4. Should we look forward to the Second Coming? Why or why not?

   We should look forward to the Second Coming because then the reign of God will be complete. Jesus will be fully glorified and evil will be completely overcome.

Reinforce

1. Have the students work on *Activity Book*, p. 101.

2. Provide time for the students to work on the Memorization Questions and Words to Know from this chapter.

3. The students should write prayers asking God to prepare them for the Second Coming of Christ.

Conclude

1. Teach the students to sing "Day of wrath! O Day of mourning!" *Adoremus Hymnal*, #576.

2. End class with the Apostles' Creed.

Preview

In the next lesson, the students will learn about the General Judgment.

WATCH AND PRAY

After explaining the signs that will come before the Second Coming, Jesus says: "But of that day or that hour no one knows, not even the angels in heaven, nor the Son, but only the Father. Take heed, watch and pray; for you do not know when the time will come. It is like a man going on a journey, when he leaves home and puts his servants in charge, each with his work, and commands the doorkeeper to be on watch. Watch therefore—for you do not know when the master of the house will come, in the evening or at midnight, or at cockcrow, or in the morning—lest he come suddenly and find you asleep. And what I say to you I say to all: Watch" (Mk 13:32–37).

We are the servants our Master has left in charge. We cannot predict when he will return, so we must always be ready. Our Lord's exhortation to "watch and pray" foreshadows his words to the apostles in Gethsemane (Mk 14:38). We know that trials and temptations will come, but we do not know when they will come or when we will be delivered from them. We must always pray and keep watch, anxiously awaiting the moment when we will meet our Lord, be it at the particular judgment with our death, or the General Judgment of the Second Coming.

LESSON TWO:
GENERAL JUDGMENT

Aims

The students will learn that, at the end of the world, Jesus will judge the entire human race. This is called the General Judgment. Jesus will judge those who are alive and those who have already died.

They will learn that purgatory will cease to exist at the Second Coming. Man will either be in union with God or condemned forever.

Materials

- *Activity Book*, p. 102

- Picture of *The Last Judgment* by Michelangelo

Optional:
- "Day of wrath! O Day of mourning!" *Adoremus Hymnal*, #576

Begin

Read Matthew's account of the General Judgment (Mt 24:29–51; Mt 25:31–46).

We know that we will be judged upon our thoughts, words, deeds, and omissions. In the readings above, upon what especially will we be judged? We will be judged especially on our charity.

time Christ will judge both those who are alive at the end and those who have already died. All of our deeds—even secret ones—will be made known. Everyone will recognize the holiness of the just and understand why they have been rewarded. We will also see God's justice in the condemnation of unrepentant sinners who will be banished for eternity to hell. There will be no changes in the judgment for those who have already died. But now, however, their judgment will be made known to all.

The *Dies Irae* (which means "day of wrath") is a Latin poem which was written many centuries ago and sung on All Souls' Day and at Masses for the dead. It reminds us of this day of final judgment. Below are two verses which illustrate what will occur at the last judgment:

Then the volume shall be spread
And the writing shall be read
Which shall judge the quick and dead.
When the Judge his place has ta'en
All things shall be made plain
Nothing unavenged remain.

Those who have loved God and served him on this earth will stand on his right. They will be rewarded with heaven. Those who have turned away from God will stand on the left and will be banished for ever to hell. There will no longer be any need for purgatory at the end of the world. Those souls who are in purgatory at the end will go to heaven. All the wisdom, justice, mercy and loving kindness of God in his dealings with men will be made known. Our Lord Jesus Christ will be fully glorified. He will appear in splendor and triumph. Evil will be completely overcome. The reign of God will be complete.

We shall not all sleep, but we shall all be changed, in a moment, in the twinkling of an eye, at the last trumpet. For the

169

Develop

1. Read paragraphs 4–6 (up to At the end of the world).

2. Look at the image of *The Last Judgment* by Michelangelo. Discuss this image. Point out:
- Christ is in the center as judge
- Mary is pleading for our souls at Jesus' right hand
- Various martyrs and apostles are around Christ, each having some symbol of his life or death
- The elect are on either side of Christ, embracing one another as they enter into the joy of heaven
- In the two lunettes above, angels are carrying the instruments of the passion and death of Jesus
- Angels of the resurrection are in the middle section, blowing their trumpets
- To the left of the angels are the saved souls, to the right are the damned
- Among the damned, a soul in despair is being dragged to hell

- In the middle of the lowest section, there is a cavern of flames and a group of mocking demons
- To the left of the cavern are souls rising from the dead, regaining their bodies
- To the right are sinners being taken to hell

What else do the students notice in this image? (E.g., people from every state in life are in heaven and in hell, etc.)

3. At the Last Judgment, in the presence of Christ, the truth of each man's relationship with God will be laid bare. The Last Judgment will reveal the good and evil that each man has done. The Last Judgment will reveal God's infinite justice and glorify him. All will see that God's love is stronger than death.

4. The Last Judgment is a call to conversion. We should answer this call while God still gives us time to turn to him.

Name:_____

The General Judgment

Answer the following questions in complete sentences.

1. Who will be judged at the General Judgment?
   At the General Judgment all men who ever lived will be judged.

2. What will be made known?
   All of our deeds will be made known and the judgment the Lord has made in our regard will be known to all. Also God's wisdom, love, mercy and justice in dealing with men will be made known.

3. Will there be a need for purgatory? What will happen to the souls there?
   There will not be a need for purgatory and all the souls in purgatory will go to heaven.

4. What will happen to evil?
   Evil will be completely overcome.

Reinforce

1. Have the students work on *Activity Book*, p. 102.

2. Provide time for the students to work on the Memorization Questions and Words to Know from this chapter.

3. *Discuss that, at the Last Judgment, all our actions and omissions will be revealed before Christ. We will not be concerned about what other people think. We will only be concerned about God and his justice.*

Conclude

1. Lead the students in singing "Day of wrath! O Day of mourning!" *Adoremus Hymnal*, #576.

2. End class with the Apostle's Creed.

Preview

In the next lesson, the students will learn about the resurrection of the body.

ON THE HYMN, *DIES IRAE* ("DAY OF WRATH")

The suggested hymn for this week is an English translation of the ancient *Dies Irae*. It is briefly described in this chapter of the student text. We do not know its source definitively, but evidence suggests this hymn was written by a Franciscan friar in the thirteenth century. The man most commonly credited as author is Thomas of Celano, a Franciscan and a friend and biographer of Saint Francis of Assisi. The beginning of this hymn seems to come from Zeph 1:15 and 16.

Suggestion: Many great composers have put this hymn to music. You may find a recording of the *Dies Irae* from Mozart's "Requiem in D Minor" or Verdi's "Requiem" and play it for the class.

NOTES

_____
_____
_____
_____
_____
_____
_____
_____
_____
_____
_____

LESSON THREE:
RESURRECTION OF THE BODY

Aims

The students will learn that, at the General Judgment, our bodies will be reunited with our souls and glorified. Our bodies will share in our eternal reward (heaven or hell).

They will learn that the glorified body has four qualities: impassibility, subtlety, agility, and clarity.

Materials

• *Activity Book*, p. 103

Optional:
• "Day of wrath! O Day of mourning!" *Adoremus Hymnal*, #576

Begin

Read from the Gospels the Resurrection accounts of Christ: Mt 28:1–20; Mk 16:1–20; Lk 24:1–53; Jn 20:1–31; 21:1–15.

The students may study these passages in small groups and then discuss the resurrected Christ.

---

trumpet will sound, and the dead will be raised imperishable, and we shall be changed. For this perishable nature must put on the imperishable, and this mortal nature must put on immortality (1 Cor 15:51–53).

At the end of the world, also, our human natures will once again be complete. Our bodies will be reunited with our souls, because man is both body and soul. This is called the *resurrection of the body*. We will enjoy the glories of heaven or suffer the pains of hell as a complete human being—body and soul.

The bodies of the just will be glorified in heaven. This means that our bodies will be perfected as was Our Lord's body after the Resurrection. Theologians have distinguished four properties or gifts which will belong to the glorified body. The glorified body will be incapable of physical suffering and will be free from death. This is known as *impassibility*, which comes from the Latin word "to suffer." Our bodies will have the property of *subtlety*, which means that our spiritual nature will shine through the body instead of being hidden by it. Thirdly, the glorified body will possess *agility*, which means that the body will be able to obey the soul with great ease and speed. This was manifested by the risen Christ, who quickly disappeared from the midst of the apostles (Jn 20:19, 26). Finally our resurrected bodies will have *clarity*. They will be free from all deformities—even minor ones—and will be filled with beauty.

Even the earth will be transformed in some way. St. John had a vision of the transformation of all things which he tells us in the book of Revelation:

Then I saw a new heaven and new earth; for the first heaven and the first earth had passed away, and the sea was no more. And I saw the holy city, new

170

Jerusalem, coming down out of heaven from God . . . and I heard a great voice from the throne saying, "Behold, the dwelling of God is with men. He will dwell with them, and they shall be his people. . ." (Rev 21:1–3).

All of this is the perfect happiness which awaits us. God has prepared this for us. We must spend our lives preparing for this so that we may enjoy the blessings of heaven for eternity.

"When the Son of man comes in his glory, and all the angels with him, then he will sit on his glorious throne. Before him will be gathered all the nations. . . . Then the King will say to those on his right hand, 'Come, O blessed of my Father, inherit the kingdom prepared for you from the foundation of the world; for I was hungry and you gave me food, I was thirsty and you gave me drink, I was a stranger and you welcomed me, I was naked and you clothed me, I was sick and you visited me, I was in prison and you came to me.' . . . Then he will say to those on his left hand, 'Depart from me you cursed, into the eternal fire prepared for the devil and his angels; for I was hungry and you gave me no food, I was thirsty and you gave me no drink. . . .'"
(Matthew 25:31–36, 41–42)

Words to Know:
Second Coming   General Judgment

Develop

1. Read paragraphs 7–8 (up to Even the earth will be transformed).

2. At death, the body and the soul are separated. However, God created man as a body and soul unity. At the end of the world, the body will be raised from the dead and reunited with the soul. Our bodies will share in our eternal reward—either the glories of heaven or the sufferings of hell.

3. There are four qualities to the resurrected body:
• *Impassibility: the body will be incapable of suffering and death (it will not die again).*
• *Subtlety: our spiritual nature will shine through the body instead of being hidden by it. Read the story of the Transfiguration from Lk 9:28–36. How did Jesus appear? Some mystics stated that if we could see a soul in the state of grace, we would think it divine! This is what our bodies will reflect when they rise from the dead.*

• *Agility: the body will be able to obey the soul with great ease and speed. The body will perfectly conform to the will. Similar to the resurrected Christ, a resurrected body will be able to pass through substances and travel at the speed of thought.*
• *Clarity: the resurrected body will be perfected. It will be free from all deformities (even minor ones) and filled with radiance and beauty.*

4. Each will have the same body he had on earth, though it will be perfected and glorified when reunited with his soul. Review that Christ showed his wounds to the apostles.

5. Remind the students that the qualities of the glorified body are reserved for those who are saved. The bodies of the damned will not be glorified when reunited with the soul.

Name:_____

Resurrection of the Body

Answer the following questions in complete sentences.

1. Will our bodies be reunited with our souls? Why?
   Yes. Our bodies will be reunited with our souls because man is both body and soul.

2. What does it mean for our bodies to be glorified?
   For our bodies to be glorified means that our bodies will be perfected like Jesus's was after the Resurrection.

3. What are four properties of the glorified body? Explain them.
   1. Our bodies will be impossible which means that they will be incapable of suffering and free from death.

   2. Our bodies will have subtlety which means our spiritual nature will not be hidden but will shine through.

   3. Our bodies will have agility which means that the body will obey the soul with ease and speed.

   4. Our bodies will possess clarity which means they will be beautiful and free of deformities.

4. What will happen to the earth at the General Judgment?
   At the General Judgment the earth will be transformed.

5. What awaits us after all this comes to pass?
   After all this comes to pass, eternal and perfect happiness in heaven awaits us.

Faith and Life Series • Grade 8 • Chapter 26 • Lesson 3   103

Reinforce

1. Have the students work on *Activity Book*, p. 103.

2. Provide time for the students to work on the Memorization Questions and Words to Know from this chapter.

3. The students should write about their hopes for the resurrection of the body.

4. *Discuss how the wounds of Christ were glorified (and not removed) in his resurrected body. Why? The wounds of Christ are a great treasure, from which flowed the Blood of our salvation.*

5. Some writers have said that our scars and wounds are reminders of how we can share in Christ's passion.

Conclude

1. Lead the students in singing "Day of wrath! O Day of mourning!" *Adoremus Hymnal*, #576.

2. End class with the Apostles' Creed.

Preview

In the next lesson, the students will learn about the transformation of heaven and earth.

THE ASSUMPTION OF MARY

At the General Judgment, our souls will be reunited with our bodies, which will be resurrected and glorified. Man is a union of body and soul so it is fitting that, ultimately, our bodies will share in the joys of heaven, or the sufferings of hell, with our souls. But there are, in fact, two bodies in heaven already. Jesus rose from the dead and ascended to heaven with a glorified body, and we know that Mary, at the end of her earthly life, was taken up into heaven body and soul (Pope Pius XII, *Munificentissimus Deus*). As a humble, faithful, sinless lover of God, Mary is an example to us of what we are all called to be, and her Assumption is a sign of hope for us of what awaits those who live in the love of God.

NOTES

_____
_____
_____
_____
_____
_____
_____
_____
_____
_____
_____
_____

LESSON FOUR: TRANSFORMED!

Aims

The students will learn that the earth will be perfected at the end of time.

They will learn that the eschatological promises of the Second Coming and the Last Judgment will be fulfilled. We must keep the end in mind and live in a manner that is pleasing to God.

Materials

- *Activity Book*, p. 104

Optional:
- "Day of wrath! O Day of mourning!" *Adoremus Hymnal*, #576

Begin

Review that the Garden of Eden was paradise on earth. There were no natural disasters or disorder until sin entered the world. At the end of the world the Kingdom of God will come in its fullness.

You may read Gen 1—2, and meditate upon the goodness of creation at the beginning and its perfection at the end of time.

Q. 160 *Will Jesus Christ visibly return to earth?*
Yes, Jesus Christ will visibly return to earth to judge the living and the dead at the end of the world, at the General Judgment (CCC 671).

Q. 161 *What awaits us at the end of the world?*
The resurrection of the body and the General Judgment await us at the end of the world (CCC 678).

Q. 162 *Will Jesus Christ wait until the end of the world to judge us?*
Jesus Christ will not wait until the end of the world to judge us, he will judge each one of us immediately after death. This is called the particular judgment (CCC 1021–22).

Q. 163 *What does "resurrection of the body" mean?*
The "resurrection of the body" means that our bodies will be transformed by the power of God and reunited with our souls, so that we will share in the eternal reward or punishment we have merited (CCC 988, 997–98).

171

Develop

1. Read paragraphs 9 and 10 (to the end of the chapter).

2. In the Catechism of the Catholic Church, we read: "The Church . . . will receive her perfection only in the glory of heaven, when will come the time of the renewal of all things. At that time, together with the human race, the universe itself, which is so closely related to man and which attains its destiny through him, will be perfectly re-established in Christ" (CCC 1042). Discuss this passage with the students.

3. In the new universe, the heavenly Jerusalem, God will have his dwelling among men. How is this like Eden?

4. Read Rom 8:19–23. What is this passage saying? Why will creation be transformed at the end of time? The restored world will be at the service of the just.

5. If the earth and the body are so important that God will renew them at the end of time, how should we care for them?
- Care for the body: proper exercise, nutrition, and hygiene. Do not corrupt the body (e.g., tattoos, intentional deformation, etc.). We must care for the body in death, which is why we bury the dead. What other ways to care for the body can the students name?
- Care for the earth: Christians are called to be stewards over the earth. How can we do this? We can care for the earth by recycling, preserving nature, controlling pollution and exploitation of the earth's natural resources, etc.

6. It is important for us always to recognize what God's plan is and to pursue it. Even in an imperfect world, we should strive to leave things better than we found them and thereby give glory to God. We must care for all that is entrusted to us—the world, the body, and especially the soul.

Name:_____

Be Prepared

Read the Bible passages below and explain how each shows us how to be prepared for Jesus' Second Coming.

Matthew 24:36–42, The Need to Be Prepared:

<u>Answers will vary.</u>

_____

_____

_____

_____

_____

Matthew 25:1–13, The Parable of the Virgins:

_____

_____

_____

_____

_____

_____

Matthew 25:31–26, The Last Judgment:

_____

_____

_____

_____

_____

_____

Reinforce

1. Have the students work on *Activity Book*, p. 104.

2. Provide time for the students to work on the Memorization Questions and Words to Know from this chapter and to prepare for the quiz.

3. The students may create images of the new heaven and the new earth.

4. The class should take part in a project to exercise Christian stewardship.

5. The students should write essays on the glories of the eternal life after the resurrection of the body and the transformation of heaven and earth.

Conclude

1. Lead the students in singing "Day of wrath! O Day of mourning!" *Adoremus Hymnal*, #576.

2. End class with the Apostles' Creed.

Preview

In the next lesson, the students' understanding of the material covered in this chapter will be reviewed and assessed.

A NEW HEAVEN AND A NEW EARTH

Man's ultimate end is the vision of God in heaven. That is what we were created for and it is the only thing that can bring us true happiness and fulfillment.

"No eye has seen, nor ear heard,/ nor the heart of man conceived,/ what God has prepared for those who love him."
—1 Cor 2:9

"'Behold, the dwelling of God is with men. He will dwell with them, and they shall be his people, and God himself will be with them; he will wipe away every tear from their eyes, and death shall be no more, neither shall there be mourning nor crying nor pain any more, for the former things have passed away.'"
—Rev 21:3–4

"There we shall rest and see, see and love, love and praise. This is what shall be in the end without end. For what other end do we propose to ourselves than to attain to the kingdom of which there is no end?"
—Saint Augustine, *City of God*, XXII, 30

"The summit of man does indeed touch the base of the angelic nature, by a kind of likeness; but man does not rest there as in his last end, but reaches out to the universal fount itself of good, which is the common object of happiness of all the blessed, as being the infinite and perfect good."
—Saint Thomas Aquinas, *Summa Theologica*, II-II, 2, 8

CHAPTER TWENTY-SIX
REVIEW AND ASSESSMENT

Aims

The students' understanding of the material covered in this chapter will be reviewed and assessed.

Materials

- Quiz 26, Appendix, p. A-38

Optional:
- "Day of wrath! O Day of mourning!" *Adoremus Hymnal*, #576

Review

1. The students should know that Jesus Christ will come again in glory to judge the living and the dead.

2. The students must know and understand what the General Judgment is.

3. The students should know the qualities of the resurrected body.

4. The students should know that the heavens and the earth will be transformed at the end of time.

The Trumpet Shall Sound: The End of the World Quiz 26

Part I: At the end of time, our bodies will be raised and reunited with our souls. Complete the chart below explaining the glorified body.

QUALITY	DESCRIPTION
impassible	incapable of suffering and free from death
subtlety	spiritual nature will not be hidden but will shine through
agility	the body will obey the soul with ease and speed
clarity	the body will be beautiful and free of deformity

Part II: Answer in complete sentences.

1. What is the Second Coming? What do we know about it?
   The Second Coming is Jesus's coming to earth at the end of time. He will appear with power, glory, and as King and Judge of the world and will be recognized by all men.

2. Describe the General Judgment.
   At the General Judgment all men who ever lived will be judged. All of our deeds will be made known and the judgment the Lord has made in our regard will be known to all. Also God's wisdom, love, mercy, and justice in dealing with men will be made known.

3. What does "resurrection of the body" mean?
   "Resurrection of the body" means that after death our bodies will be transformed by the power of God and reunited with our souls, so that we will share in the eternal reward or punishment we have merited.

Assess

1. Distribute the quizzes and read through them with the students to be sure they understand the questions.

2. Administer the quiz. As they hand in their work, orally quiz the students on the Memorization Questions from this chapter.

3. After all the quizzes have been handed in, review the correct answers with the class.

Conclude

1. Lead the students in singing "Day of wrath! O Day of mourning!" *Adoremus Hymnal*, #576.

2. End class with the Apostles' Creed.

Faith and Life series: *Our Life in the Church*
Appendices

APPENDIX A: QUIZZES AND UNIT TESTS

APPENDIX B: STORIES, GAMES, CRAFTS, AND SKITS

Name:

Christ's Abiding Presence

Quiz 1

Part I: Answer in complete sentences.

1. How do we know that Jesus intended to found the Church? Why did he found the Church?

2. How is the Church human?

3. How is the Church divine?

4. How is Christ present in the Church?

5. What is your role in the life of the Church?

The Birth of the Church

Quiz 2

Part I: Define the following terms.

Deposit of grace:

Deposit of faith:

Pentecost:

Vicar:

Ekklesia:

Part II: Explain how God established the Church during each of the three stages listed below.

1. Old Testament:

2. Life and death of Jesus Christ:

3. New Testament days of the apostles unto the present:

The Nature of the Church

Quiz 3

Part I: Explain the four marks of the Church using examples.

One:

Holy:

Catholic:

Apostolic:

Part II: Explain how the Church is the Mystical Body of Christ.

Name: _____

The Teaching Church

Part I: Matching.

1. ___ Men personally taught by the Apostles
2. ___ Letter written by the Pope about Church teaching
3. ___ Communication by God to humanity
4. ___ Growing in our understanding of God's revelation
5. ___ The written Word of God
6. ___ Teachings of Jesus passed on to his followers
7. ___ The Teaching Church
8. ___ Testimony of what Christ's followers have believed for centuries
9. ___ Holy teachers/theologians of Christian doctrine
10. ___ Christian writers of the early days of the Church

a. Revelation
b. Scripture
c. Tradition
d. Apostolic Fathers
e. Doctors of the Church
f. Fathers of the Church
g. encyclical
h. *sensus fidei*
i. development of doctrine
j. Magisterium

Part II: Answer in complete sentences.

1. Why do we need Sacred Scripture, Tradition, and the Magisterium?

2. Who are the Fathers and Doctors of the Church? Name one Father or Doctor and explain what he has done for the Church.

3. What is an ecumenical council? Why are they important? Give the name, date, and significance of two ecumenical councils.

Name: _____

Unit 1 Test   Chapters 1 – 4

Part I: On a separate piece of paper, write an essay on *one* of the following topics:

a) What did Jesus mean when he said, "I will not leave you desolate; I will come to you" (Jn 14:18)? How is he still present?
b) How is the Church like an orchestra?

Part II: Answer in complete sentences.

1. How is the Church human? How is the Church divine?

2. Briefly explain the four marks of the Church.

Part III: Explain how God prepared for and established his Church in the following events of salvation history.

Adam and Eve after the Fall:

Noah:

Abraham and Isaac:

Moses:

The Levitical Priesthood:

David:

The Prophets:

Jesus Christ:

"You are Peter":

The Last Supper:

"Whose sins you forgive are forgiven them":

The Great Commission:

Pentecost:

Authority in the Church: Teaching and Governing Quiz 5

Part I: Using the definitions below, write in the correct term.

1. _____   Said of the Pope when he speaks "from the chair" to bind the whole Church in matters of faith and morals.

2. _____   This word means to be without sin.

3. _____   The extraordinary and ordinary teaching of the Church.

4. _____   This man is the successor of the Apostle Peter and the representative of Jesus Christ on earth.

5. _____   The various levels of authority in the Church.

6. _____   The meeting of some bishops with the Pope.

7. _____   The "Shepherd" of a geographical area called a diocese.

8. _____   A protection from teaching error in matters of faith and morals.

9. _____   A universal gathering of bishops with the Pope to define Church teaching.

10. _____   Submission to the authorities of the Church in matters of doctrine and discipline.

Part II: Answer in complete sentences.

1. Explain what true freedom is. Does submitting to Church authority enhance or restrict our freedom?

2. Can a bishop alone teach infallibly? Explain.

Name:

The Visible Hierarchical Church

Part I: Define the following terms.

Diocese:

Monsignor:

Cardinal:

Curia:

Bishop:

Priest:

Vicar of Christ:

Part II: Explain why the apostles selected other apostles/bishops. How was Matthias chosen?

Name:

The Church Sanctifying: Sacraments of Membership **Quiz 7**

Part I: Fill in the chart.

SACRAMENT	MATTER	FORM	MINISTER	EFFECTS
Baptism				
Confirmation				
Eucharist				

Part II: The following sentences describe aspects of Baptism, Eucharist, and Confirmation. Indicate the sacrament described by each sentence.

1. _____ This is the very first sacrament a person receives.

2. _____ In this sacrament, we become Spirit-filled soldiers of Christ.

3. _____ This sacrament is food for the soul, without which it would die of spiritual starvation.

4. _____ Through the water and words of this sacrament, we become brothers and sisters of Jesus Christ.

5. _____ When we receive this sacrament, we are said to have become adult or more mature Christians.

6. _____ This sacrament is the "gateway" to all the other sacraments.

7. _____ This sacrament is unique in that it is Jesus truly present Body, Blood, Soul and Divinity.

8. _____ This sacrament brings with it a special responsibility to witness to Jesus and the Gospel, and to defend our faith.

9. _____ This sacrament does not put an indelible mark on your soul.

Part III: Briefly describe some of the similarities and differences between the Eastern and Western Rites.

The Church Sanctifying: Worship **Quiz 8**

Part I: Answer in complete sentences.

1. What is liturgy?

2. List and explain the three elements of liturgy:
   1.

   2.

   3.

Part II: Fill in the chart describing the use and symbolism of the liturgical colors.

	GREEN	RED	WHITE	PURPLE	ROSE
Used for (masses and seasons)					
Symbolizes					

Part I: Define the following terms.

Diocese:

Cardinal:

Curia:

Bishop:

Priest:

Magisterium:

Ex Cathedra:

Infallibility:

Part II: Fill in the chart.

SACRAMENT	MATTER	FORM	MINISTER	EFFECTS
Baptism				
Confirmation				
Eucharist				

Part III: Answer in complete sentences.

1. Explain what true freedom is. Does submitting to Church authority enhance or restrict our freedom?

2. Explain why the apostles selected other apostles/bishops. How was Matthias chosen?

2. What is liturgy?

3. List and explain the three elements of liturgy:

    1.

    2.

    3.

Part IV: Put the following dates in order according to the Liturgical Year.

_____	Lent	_____	Baptism of Jesus
_____	Palm Sunday	_____	Christmas
_____	Holy Week	_____	Epiphany
_____	Triduum	_____	Advent
_____	Easter	_____	Christ the King
_____	Ascension Thursday	_____	Pentecost
_____	All Souls' Day	_____	Ash Wednesday
_____	All Saints' Day		

Name: _____

Mary—Mother of the Church **Quiz 9**

Part I: Define the following terms.

Annunciation:

Fiat:

Immaculate Conception:

Perpetual Virginity:

Part II: Answer in complete sentences.

1. Do Catholics pray to Mary? Do we worship her? Explain.

2. Choose and explain a title of Mary.

Part III: Fill in the blanks and true or false.

1. Mary is called the new _____ just as Jesus is called the new _____.

2. When Jesus said, "Behold your son," he made Mary our spiritual _____.

3. Mary has been called our sure _____ to Jesus, and she will help us reach heaven by her _____.

4. _____ The phrase "Immaculate Conception" refers to the time when Jesus first began to live within the womb of Mary.

5. _____ Mary's "Assumption" means that she is now in heaven with both her body and her soul.

The Communion of Saints   **Quiz 10**

Part I: Define the following terms.

Communion of Saints:

Pilgrim Church:

Canonized Saint:

Intercessory Prayer:

Purgatory:

Part II: Answer in complete sentences.

1. How is the communion of saints a community of prayer?

2. How can you honor or venerate a saint?

3. Why should you pray for the dead?

4. What is the Church Militant fighting?

Saints in Our History: The First Thousand Years **Quiz 11**

Part I: Define the following terms.

Gentile:

Martyr:

Heresy:

Monastery:

Arianism:

Part II: Matching.

1. ____ Founder of Islam	a. Peter
2. ____ Roman emperor who legalized Christianity	b. Paul
3. ____ Father of western monasticism	c. Athanasius
4. ____ First Pope, Prince of the Apostles	d. Augustine
5. ____ Women martyrs	e. Perpetua and Felicity
6. ____ Convert and apostle	f. Constantine
7. ____ Convert, bishop, and theologian	g. Arius
8. ____ Denied the divinity of Christ	h. Benedict
9. ____ Fought Arianism	i. Columban
10. ____ An Irish missionary monk	j. Muhammad

Part III: Choose one of the following saints or pairs of saints and, on the back of this page, write a brief essay on how they contributed to the life of the Church.

Paul, Athanasius, Augustine, Benedict, Perpetua and Felicity

Saints in Our History: The Second Thousand Years Quiz 12

Part I: Define the following.

Crusades:

Protestant Reformation:

Counter-Reformation:

Modernism:

Part II: Matching.

1. ___ Holy king, husband and father	a. St. Bernard of Clairvaux
2. ___ Italian woman devoted to the Church	b. St. Francis of Assisi
3. ___ First American-born Saint	c. St. Thomas Aquinas
4. ___ Began the Protestant Reformation	d. St. Catherine of Siena
5. ___ Monk who spread the Cistercian way of life	e. St. Maximilian Kolbe
6. ___ Great missionary in Asia	f. St. Louis IX of France
7. ___ Lived a holy life of poverty	g. St. Pius X
8. ___ Knight of the Immaculata	h. St. Dominic
9. ___ Twentieth century Pope	i. St. Ignatius of Loyola
10. ___ Soldier of Christ, founded the Jesuit order	j. St. Francis Xavier
11. ___ Founder of the Order of Preachers	k. St. Elizabeth Ann Seton
12. ___ Dominican priest, great theologian	l. St. Clare of Assisi
13. ___ Founded women's order with Francis	m. Martin Luther

**Part III: Choose one of the following saints and, on the back of this page,
             write a brief essay on how they contributed to the life of the Church.**
*Maximilian Kolbe, Francis of Assisi, Dominic, Thomas Aquinas,
Catherine of Siena, Louis IX, Ignatius of Loyola, Bernard of Clairvaux*

Name:

Part I: Matching.

1. ___ First American-born Saint	a. St. Bernard of Clairvaux
2. ___ Began the Protestant Reformation	b. Martin Luther
3. ___ Great missionary in Asia	c. St. Paul
4. ___ Father of Western Monasticism	d. Pope Gregory XI
5. ___ Soldier of Christ, founded the Jesuit order	e. Sts. Felicity and Perpetua
6. ___ Knight of the Immaculata	f. St. Catherine of Siena
7. ___ Mothers and Martyrs	g. St. Athanasius
8. ___ Dominican priest, great theologian	h. St. Francis of Assisi
9. ___ Holy king, husband and father	i. St. Augustine
10. ___ Lived a holy life of poverty	j. St. Thomas Aquinas
11. ___ Greek philosopher	k. St. Louis IX of France
12. ___ Converted by Jesus after the Resurrection	l. St. Pius X
13. ___ Was told to return to Rome	m. St. Dominic
14. ___ Twentieth century Pope	n. St. Ignatius of Loyola
15. ___ Italian woman devoted to the Church	o. St. Francis Xavier
16. ___ Founder of the Order of Preachers	p. St. Elizabeth Ann Seton
17. ___ Founded women's order with Francis	q. St. Clare of Assisi
18. ___ Bishop, converted by his mother's prayer	r. Aristotle
19. ___ Monk who spread the Cistercian way of life	s. St. Maximilian Kolbe
20. ___ Holy bishop who fought heresy	t. St. Benedict

Part II: Choose a saint studied in this chapter. On a separate sheet of paper write an essay on why you admire this saint.

Part III: Define the following terms.

Fiat:

Immaculate Conception:

Perpetual Virginity:

Communion of Saints:

Martyr:

Heresy:

Monastery:

Arianism:

Crusades:

Protestant Reformation:

Counter-Reformation:

Modernism:

Part I: Using your student text, write a short paragraph explaining who the Church considers our separated brethren and how we are all still members of the same Church.

Part II: Answer in complete sentences.

1. What is the difference between an atheist and an agnostic?

2. What is ecumenism and why is it important for the salvation of man?

3. How are animism and polytheism expressions of paganism?

The Universal Call to Holiness **Quiz 14**

Part I: Define the following terms.

Holiness:

Apostolate:

Capital Sins:

Part II: Fill in the chart.

CAPITAL VICE	DEFINITION	EXAMPLE
lust		
anger		
gluttony		
envy		
sloth		
covetousness		
pride		

The Life of Virtue

Quiz 15

Part I: Define the following terms.

Virtue:

Cardinal Virtue:

Moral Virtue:

Theological Virtue:

Prudence:

Justice:

Fortitude:

Temperance:

Part II: Fill in the chart.

THEOLOGICAL VIRTUE	DEFINITION	HOW TO GROW IN THIS VIRTUE
faith		
hope		
love		

Name: _____

The Works of Mercy And Happiness

Part I: Match the action with the work of mercy.

1. ___ Going to the hospital to visit cancer patients
2. ___ Writing to a lonely person in a nursing home
3. ___ A friend whose parents are away stays with you
4. ___ Accepting an unfair group punishment
5. ___ Praying for the souls in purgatory
6. ___ Taking old coats to a children's shelter
7. ___ Helping a convert understand their faith
8. ___ Teaching your brother his prayers
9. ___ Cooking for a widow
10. ___ Telling your friend that his sin offends God
11. ___ Giving canned goods to the food bank
12. ___ Going to a funeral
13. ___ Forgiving someone who bullied you
14. ___ Your father is working hard outside and you get him a cold glass of water

a. Visit the sick
b. Bury the dead
c. Admonish the sinner
d. Clothe the naked
e. Instruct the ignorant
f. Visit the imprisoned
g. Shelter the homeless
h. Forgive all injuries
i. Pray for the living and dead
j. Comfort the doubtful
k. Comfort the sorrowful
l. Feed the hungry
m. Give drink to the thirsty
n. Bear wrongs patiently

Part II: Fill in the chart.

BEATITUDE	PROMISE
Blessed are the poor in spirit	
	they shall be comforted
	they shall inherit the earth
Blessed are those who hunger and thirst for justice	
Blessed are the merciful	
	they shall see God
Blessed are those who are persecuted for rightousness sake	
	for they shall be called the children of God

Name:

Unit 4 Test   # Chapters 13 – 16

Part I: Define the following terms.

Apostolate:

Capital Sins:

Ecumenism:

Virtue:

Cardinal Virtue:

Theological Virtue:

**Part II: Using your student text, write a short paragraph explaining who the
Church considers our separated brethren and how we are all still
members of the same Church.**

Unit 4 Test *(continued)*

Part III: Answer.

1. How are natural and supernatural virtues acquired?

2. Can someone who does not believe in God have the cardinal virtues? Can he have the theological virtues? Explain.

3. How does the happiness offered in the Beatitudes differ from the happiness offered by the world?

Part IV: Fill in the chart with the opposing moral virtues and give examples.

CAPITAL VICE	EXAMPLE	MORAL VALUE	EXAMPLE
pride			
anger			
lust			
gluttony			
covetousness			
envy			
sloth			

Name: _____

Vocations: The Religious Life and the Priesthood Quiz 17

Part I: Define the following terms.

Religious:

Clergy:

Vows:

Part II: Answer in complete sentences.

1. Why is religious life/priesthood a higher vocation than marriage?

2. What is the difference between a contemplative and an active religious community?

Part III: Fill in the chart.

EVANGELICAL COUNSEL	GOOD OFFERED TO GOD	BENEFIT
poverty		
chastity		
obedience		

The Lay Apostolate   **Quiz 18**

Part I: The laity are to sanctify the world. Explain how you can do this in the following situations.

In your family:

In your classroom:

As a member of a sports team:

At a party:

When a friend is ill:

Part II: Answer in complete sentences.

1. Who are the laity?

2. How are laity to grow in holiness?

3. In what way can the laity use the goods sacrificed in the evangelical counsels for the glory of God and his Church?

4. How does Cardinal Newman's prayer, "Help me spread your fragrance everywhere. . ." sum up the lay vocation?

Marriage and the Family

Quiz 19

Part I: Define the following terms.

Conjugal love:

Indissolubility:

Mutual Sanctification:

Divorce:

Part II: Answer in complete sentences.

1. What are the duties of parents in the family?

2. What are the duties of children in the family?

3. What are the duties of the husband and the wife towards one another?

4. How can we honor and protect the sanctity of marriage in society today?

The Christian in the World

Quiz 20

Part I: Define the following terms.

Common Good:

Stewardship:

Patriotism:

Nationalism:

Part II: Answer in complete sentences.

1. What duties does a Christian have to society?

2. What does a good society do?

Part III: On the back of this page, write an essay on the following topic.

In this country, the government has said it is legal to have an abortion. It is not forced upon people, but is provided upon request and is supported by government money. As a Christian, what are you morally obliged to do? (Consider whether you must obey this law, whether you can make changes to this law, and how you can promote a Christian society.)

Unit 5 Test   **Chapter 17 – 20**

Part I: Define the following terms.

Evangelical Counsels:

Poverty:

Chastity:

Obedience:

Sacrament of Matrimony :

Divorce:

Part II: Fill in the chart.

EVANGELICAL COUNSEL	GOOD OFFERED TO GOD	BENEFIT
poverty		
chastity		
obedience		

Unit 5 Test *(continued)*

Part III: Answer in complete sentences.

1. Why is religious life/priesthood a higher vocation than marriage?

2. How are laity to grow in holiness?

3. What are the duties of parents and children in the family?

4. What duties does a Christian have to society?

5. What does a good society do?

Law and Conscience **Quiz 21**

Part I: Explain the source, purpose, and characteristics of the following types of law.

Physical laws:

Moral laws:

Civil laws:

Natural laws:

Revealed laws:

Ecclesiastical laws:

Part II: Answer in complete sentences.

1. What is a conscience?

2. Why must a conscience be correctly formed? How does one form a conscience?

3. Can a well-formed conscience ever lead one to disobey Church teaching?

4. Explain, using examples, a true conscience, a lax conscience, and a scrupulous conscience.

Name:

The Church and the Social Order   **Quiz 22**

Part I: Explain how each of the things listed below attack the good of society.

Oppression of the poor:

Defrauding the laborer of a just wage:

Abortion:

Part III: Answer in complete sentences.

1. Can war ever be just? Explain.

2. Is killing someone in self-defense murder? Explain.

3. Can abortion ever be morally good acts? Explain.

Prayer   **Quiz 23**

Part I: Answer in complete sentences.

1. What is prayer?

2. What are the two kinds of prayer? Describe them.

3. What are the five steps of prayer? Give examples of each.

4. What is the difference between formal and informal prayer?

5. What are the four reasons for prayer?

6. What is liturgy? Give two examples.

The Sacramental Life **Quiz 24**

Part I: Answer in complete sentences.

1. What are the seven sacraments?

2. What is the Sacrament of Penance?

3. Why do we confess our sins to a priest?

4. What is contrition?

5. What are the five things required to make a good confession?

6. Why is the Eucharist the source and summit of our Christian faith?

7. How do we worthily receive Holy Communion?

8. What is transubstantiation?

Unit 6 Test   **Chapters 21 – 24**

Part I: Diagram the hierarchy of law as in your student text. Include:
Eternal law, Moral law, Physical law, Divine law, Human law, Civil law, Natural law, Ecclesiastical law, Revealed law.

Part II: Answer in complete sentences.

1. What is a conscience? How does one form a conscience?

2. Explain, using examples, a true conscience, a lax conscience, and a scrupulous conscience.

3. Can war ever be just? Explain.

4. What is prayer?

5. What is liturgy?

6. Why is the Eucharist the source and summit of our Christian faith?

Part IV: Explain each line of the Our Father.

Our Father, who art in heaven.

Hallowed be thy Name.

Thy Kingdom come.

They will be done on earth as it is in heaven.

Give us this day our daily bread.

And forgive us our trespasses as we forgive those who trespass against us.

And lead us not into temptation, but deliver us from evil.

Amen.

Death and the Particular Judgment

Part I: Define the following terms.

Particular Judgment:

Heaven:

Hell:

Purgatory:

Part II: Answer in complete sentences.

1. What can we do during our lives to prepare for death?

2. What does the Church offer to help us before we die?

3. What is the Christian understanding of death?

4. Comment on the statement "life is not ended but merely changed."

The Trumpet Shall Sound: The End of the World Quiz 26

Part I: At the end of time, our bodies will be raised and reunited with our souls. Complete the chart below explaining the glorified body.

QUALITY	DESCRIPTION
impassible	
subtlety	
agility	
clarity	

Part II: Answer in complete sentences.

1. What is the Second Coming? What do we know about it?

2. Describe the General Judgment.

3. What does "resurrection of the body" mean?

The Papacy

1. St. Peter (Simon Bar-Jona): d. 64 or 67.
2. St. Linus: 67–76.
3. St. Anacletus (Cletus): 76–88.
4. St. Clement: 88–97.
5. St. Evaristus: 97–105.
6. St. Alexander: 105–115.
7. St. Sixtus I: 115–125.
8. St. Telesphorus: 125–136.
9. St. Hyginus: 136–140.
10. St. Pius I: 140–155.
11. St. Anicetus: 155–166.
12. St. Soter: 166–175.
13. St. Eleutherius: 175–189.
14. St. Victor I: 189–199.
15. St. Zephyrinus: 199–217.
16. St. Callistus I: 217–222.
17. St. Urban I: 222–230.
18. St. Pontian: 230–235.
19. St. Anterus: 235–236.
20. St. Fabian: 236–250.
21. St. Cornelius: 251–253.
22. St. Lucius I: 253–254.
23. St. Stephen I: 254–257.
24. St. Sixtus II: 257–258.
25. St. Dionysius: 259–268.
26. St. Felix I: 269–274.
27. St. Eutychianus: 275–283.
28. St. Caius: 283–296.
29. St. Marcellinus: 296–304.
30. St. Marcellus I: 308–309.
31. St. Eusebius: 309–310.
32. St. Melchiades: 311–314.
33. St. Sylvester I: 314–335.
Most of the popes before Saint Sylvester I were martyrs.
34. St. Marcus: 336–336.
35. St. Julius I: 337–352.
36. Liberius: 352–366.
37. St. Damasus I: 366–384.
38. St. Siricius: 384–399.
39. St. Anastasius I: 399–401.
40. St. Innocent I: 401–417.
41. St. Zosimus: 417–418.
42. St. Boniface I: 418–422.
43. St. Celestine I: 422–432.
44. St. Sixtus III: 432–440.
45. St. Leo I (the Great): 440–461.
46. St. Hilary: 461–468.
47. St. Simplicius: 468–483.
48. St. Felix III (II): 483–492.
49. St. Gelasius I: 492–496.
50. Anastasius II: 496–498.
51. St. Symmachus: 498–514.
52. St. Hormisdas: 514–523.
53. St. John I, Martyr: 523–526.
54. St. Felix IV (III): 526–530.
55. Boniface II: 530–532.
56. John II: 533–535.
57. St. Agapitus I: 535–536.
58. St. Silverius: 536–537.
59. Vigilius: 537–555.
60. Pelagius I: 556–561.
61. John III: 561–574.
62. Benedict I: 575–579.
63. Pelagius II: 579–590.
64. St. Gregory I (the Great): 590–604.
65. Sabinian: 604–606.
66. Boniface III: 607–607.
67. St. Boniface IV: 608–615.
68. St. Deusdedit: 615–618.
69. Boniface V: 619–625.
70. Honorius I: 625–638.
71. Severinus: 640–640.
72. John IV: 640–642.
73. Theodore I: 642–649.
74. St. Martin I: 649–655.
75. St. Eugene I: 654–657.
76. St. Vitalian: 657–672.
77. Adeodatus II: 672–676.
78. Donus: 676–678.
79. St. Agatho: 678–681.
80. St. Leo II: 682–683
81. St. Benedict II: 684–685.
82. John V: 685–686.
83. Conon: 686–687.
84. St. Sergius I: 687–701.
85. John VI: 701–705.
86. John VII: 705–707.
87. Sisinnius: 708–708.
88. Constantine: 708–715.
89. St. Gregory II: 715–731.
90. St. Gregory III: 731–741.
91. St. Zachary: 741–752.
92. Stephen II (III): 752–757.
93. St. Paul I: 757–767.
94. Stephen III (IV): 768–772.
95. Adrian I: 772–795.
96. St. Leo III: 795–816.
97. Stephen IV (V): 816–817.
98. St. Paschal I: 817–824.
99. Eugene II: 824–827.
100. Valentine: 827–827.
101. Gregory IV: 827–844.
102. Sergius II: 844–847.
103. St. Leo IV: 847–855.
104. Benedict III: 855–858.
105. St. Nicholas I (the Great): 858–867.
106. Adrian II: 867–872.
107. John VIII: 872–882.
108. Marinus I: 882–884.
109. St. Adrian III: 884–885.
110. Stephen V (VI): 885–891.
111. Formosus: 891–896.
112. Boniface VI: 896–896.
113. Stephen VI (VII): 896–897.
114. Romanus: 897–897.
115. Theodore II: 897–897.
116. John IX: 898–900.
117. Benedict IV: 900–903.
118. Leo V: 903–903.
119. Sergius III: 904–911.
120. Anastasius III: 911–913.
121. Landus: 913–914.
122. John X: 914–928.
123. Leo VI: 928–928.
124. Stephen VII (VIII): 928–931.
125. John XI: 931–935.
126. Leo VII: 936–939.
127. Stephen VIII (IX): 939–942.
128. Marinus II: 942–946.
129. Agapitus II: 946–955.
130. John XII: 955–964.
131. Leo VIII: 963–965.

The Papacy *(continued)*

132. Benedict V: 964–966.
133. John XIII: 965–972.
134. Benedict VI: 973–974.
135. Benedict VII: 974–983.
136. John XIV: 983–984.
137. John XV: 985–996.
138. Gregory V: 996–999.
139. Sylvester II: 999–1003.
140. John XVII: 1003–1003.
141. John XVIII: 1004–1009.
142. Sergius IV: 1009–1012.
143. Benedict VIII: 1012–1024.
144. John XIX: 1024–1032.
145. Benedict IX: 1032–1044.
146. Sylvester III: 1045–1045.
147. Benedict IX: 1045–1045.
148. Gregory VI: 1045–1046.
149. Clement II: 1046–1047.
150. Benedict IX: 1047–1048.
151. Damasus II: 1048–1048.
152. St. Leo IX: 1049–1054.
153. Victor II: 1055–1057.
154. Stephen IX (X): 1057–1058.
155. Nicholas II: 1059–1061.
156. Alexander II: 1061–1073.
157. St. Gregory VII: 1073–1085.
158. Bl. Victor III: 1086–1087.
159. Bl. Urban II: 1088–1099.
160. Paschal II: 1099–1118.
161. Gelasius II: 1118–1119.
162. Callistus II: 1119–1124.
163. Honorius II: 1124–1130.
164. Innocent II: 1130–1143.
165. Celestine II: 1143–1144.
166. Lucius II: 1144–1145.
167. Bl. Eugene III: 1145–1153.
168. Anastasius IV: 1153–1154.
169. Adrian IV: 1154–1159.
170. Alexander III: 1159–1181.
171. Lucius III: 1181–1185.
172. Urban III: 1185–1187.
173. Gregory VIII: 1187–1187.
174. Clement III: 1187–1191.
175. Celestine III: 1191–1198.
176. Innocent III: 1198–1216.

177. Honorius III: 1216–1227.
178. Gregory IX: 1227–1241.
179. Celestine IV: 1241–1241.
180. Innocent IV: 1243–1254.
181. Alexander IV: 1254–1261.
182. Urban IV: 1261–1264.
183. Clement IV: 1265–1268.
184. Bl. Gregory X: 1271–1276.
185. Bl. Innocent V: 1276–1276.
186. Adrian V: 1276–1276.
187. John XXI: 1276–1277.
188. Nicholas III: 1277–1280.
189. Martin IV: 1281–1285.
190. Honorius IV: 1285–1287.
191. Nicholas IV: 1288–1292.
192. St. Celestine V: 1294–1294.
193. Boniface VIII: 1294–1303.
194. Bl. Benedict XI: 1303–1304.
195. Clement V: 1305–1314.
196. John XXII: 1316–1334.
197. Benedict XII: 1334–1342.
198. Clement VI: 1342–1352.
199. Innocent VI: 1352–1362.
200. Bl. Urban V: 1362–1370.
201. Gregory XI: 1370–1378.
202. Urban VI: 1378–1389.
203. Boniface IX: 1389–1404.
204. Innocent VII: 1404–1406.
205. Gregory XII: 1406–1415
206. Martin V: 1417–1431.
207. Eugene IV: 1431–1447.
208. Nicholas V: 1447–1455.
209. Callisius III: 1455–1458.
210. Pius II: 1458–1464.
211. Paul II: 1464–1471.
212. Sixtus IV: 1471––484.
213. Innocent VIII: 1484–1492.
214. Alexander VI: 1492–1503.
215. Pius III: 1503–1503.
216. Julius II: 1503–1513.
217. Leo X: 1513–1521.
218. Adrian VI: 1522–1523.
219. Clement VII: 1523–1534.
220. Paul III: 1534–1549.
221. Julius III: 1550–1555.
222. Marcellus II: 1555–1555.
223. Paul IV: 1555–1559.

224. Pius IV: 1559–1565.
225. St. Pius V: 1566–1572.
226. Gregory XIII: 1572–1585.
227. Sixtus V: 1585–1590.
228. Urban VII: 1590–1590.
229. Gregory XIV: 1590–1591.
230. Innocent IX: 1591–1591.
231. Clement VIII: 1592–1605.
232. Leo XI: 1605–1605.
233. Paul V: 1605–1621.
234. Gregory XV: 1621–1623.
235. Urban VIII: 1623–1644.
236. Innocent X: 1644–1655.
237. Alexander VII: 1655–1667.
238. Clement IX: 1667–1669.
239. Clement X: 1670–1676.
240. Bl. Innocent XI: 1676–1689.
241. Alexander VIII: 1689–1691.
242. Innocent XII: 1691–1700.
243. Clement XI: 1700–1721.
244. Innocent XIII: 1721–1724.
245. Benedict XIII: 1724–1730.
246. Clement XII: 1730–1740.
247. Benedict XIV: 1740–1758.
248. Clement XIII: 1758–1769.
249. Clement XIV: 1769–1774.
250. Pius VI: 1775–1799.
251. Pius VII: 1800–1823.
252. Leo XII: 1823–1829.
253. Pius VIII: 1829–1830.
254. Gregory XVI: 1831–1846.
255. Blessed Pius IX: 1846–1878.
256. Leo XIII: 1878–1903.
257. St. Pius X: 1903–1914.
258. Benedict XV: 1914–1922.
259. Pius XI: 1922–1939.
260. Pius XII: 1939–1958.
261. John XXIII: 1958–1963.
262. Paul VI: 1963–1978.
263. John Paul I: Aug. 26, 1978 to Sept. 28, 1978.
264. John Paul II: Oct. 16, 1978.

Vestments

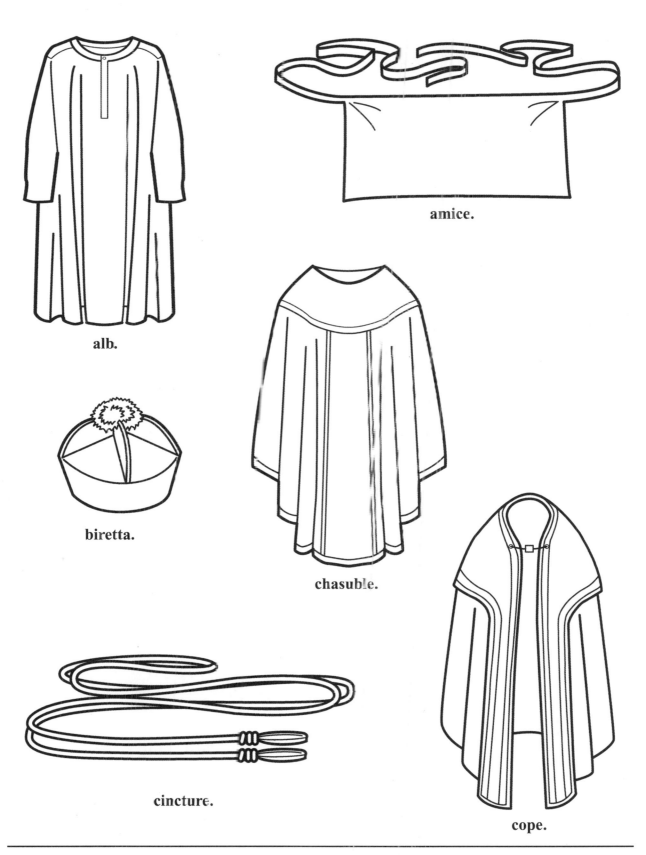

alb.

amice.

biretta.

chasuble.

cincture.

cope.

Vestments *(continued)*

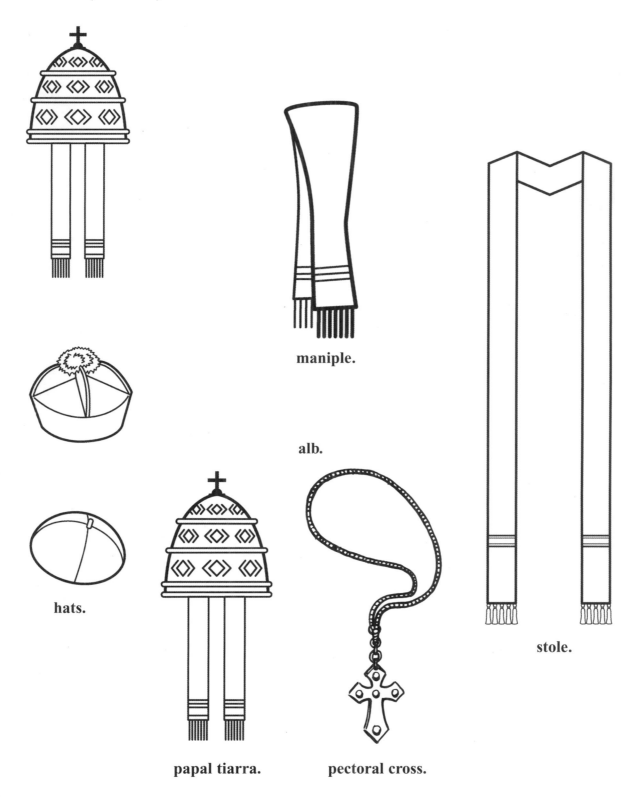

maniple.

alb.

hats.

papal tiarra.

pectoral cross.

stole.

Icons

Our Lady of Lourdes

Every year, millions of pilgrims travel to Lourdes, France, to pray at Our Lady's grotto and to bathe in the famous spring which is credited with miraculous healings of tumors, cancer, blindness, and deafness, just to name a few.

The story of the grotto begins with a ninteenth century french girl, Bernadette Soubirous. On February 11, 1858, when Bernadette was fourteen, she, her sister Marie, and their friend Jeanne passed by a grotto near Lourdes on their way to pick up wood for a fire. As they passed the grotto, Bernadette saw a beautiful girl dressed in white and blue holding a large rosary. The girl smiled at Bernadette and gestured towards her rosary. Bernadette knelt and prayed the rosary, and when they had finished five decades, the woman vanished.

At first, few believed that Bernadette had seen anything, and those who did thought she had seen a soul from purgatory, but Bernadette continued to visit the grotto. A few days after the first apparition, the woman appeared again. She smiled at Bernadette but still said nothing.

On February 18, the woman appeared again and finally spoke. She told Bernadette that she would not make her happy in this life, but would do so in the next. Then she asked Bernadette to visit her everyday for a fortnight. As word spread, many people came to watch Bernadette during the apparitions. First small crowds, then five hundred, then several thousand people came. The local authorities were concerned about the large numbers and told her not to go to the grotto, but Bernadette continued nonetheless.

One week into the apparitions, on February 25, the lady showed Bernadette the famous spring. When she appeared, she told Bernadette to drink and wash in the spring. Bernadette went to a nearby stream to drink, but the lady told her that was not what she meant. Instead, she guided Bernadette to a muddy pool of water. In front of the huge crowd and in obedience to the lady, Bernadette drank the muddy water. This must have seemed ridiculous to Bernadette and the crowd, but later that day a steady stream of water began to flow from the place where Bernadette had drunk. In a week the stream had grown and 27,000 gallons of water gushed forth daily. The spring continues to flow at the same rate today.

Another important apparition occured on March 2. The lady asked Bernadette to have a chapel built at the grotto. Bernadette passed this message on to her local priest, but he refused. Two days later, the fortnight had passed and the apparitions ended. But on March 25, the feast of the Annunciation, Bernadette returned to the grotto and the lady appeared to her again. Bernadette asked the lady for her name and she replied, "Que soy era Immaculado Conceptiou." Then she repeated her request for a chapel.

Bernadette did not know what these words meant, but she went to her priest and repeated them to him. He was amazed. The lady had told Bernadette, "I am the Immaculate Conception." Pope Pius IX had defined the doctrine of the Immaculate Conception just four years earlier.

Two more apparitions followed, and after that Mary appeared to Bernadette no more. In 1866 Bernadette joined the sisters of Notre-Dame de Nevers, where she was known for her humility and patience, despite poor health and a steady stream of visitors wishing to ask her about the apparitions. The local bishops soon approved the apparitions and a chapel was built. Bernadette, however, did not attend the concecration of the chapel, choosing to stay within the convent. She died when she was thirty-five, and was canonized in 1933.

Saint Catherine Labouré

In the year 1830, Mary appeared several times to a young French nun by the name of Sister Catherine Labouré. Catherine had been born in 1806 and joined the Sisters of Charity in 1830. The first of her miraculous visions occured on July 18.

Catherine was awakened that night by what she described as a shining child. This child led her to the chapel, where she saw a beautiful woman waiting for her. This woman was the Blessed Virgin Mary. Mary told Catherine that she had an important but difficult mission for her and pointed to the altar as a sure source of consolation in times of trial.

Our Lady appeared to Catherine again on November 27. This time, as on another apparition a short time later, Catherine saw an image of Mary standing on a globe with light shining from her outstretched hands. This image was framed by the words, "O Mary, conceived without sin, pray for us who have recourse to thee." As Saint Catherine saw this image, she heard a voice telling her to have a medal made bearing the image she saw. Mary promised many graces and her intercession for those who wore the medal.

Catherine spoke to her confessor, Father Aladel, about the apparitions and, with the approval of the Archbishop of Paris, he had the medal made. These medals, now known as miraculous medals, were distributed throughout Paris and were credited with many miracles and conversions.

The apparitions ceased after the medal had been made, and Catherine lived the quiet life of a religious sister until her death on December 31, 1876. It is said that a crippled child was cured at her grave soon after her burial. Use of the miraculous medal continued to spread, and Catherine was canonized in 1947.

Litany of the Saints

Lord, have mercy on us.
   Christ, have mercy on us.
Lord, have mercy on us. Christ, hear us.
   Christ, graciously hear us.
God, the Father of Heaven,
   have mercy on us.
God the Son, Redeemer of the World,
   have mercy on us.
God the Holy Spirit,
   have mercy on us.
Holy Trinity, one God,
   have mercy on us.

Holy Mary,
   pray for us.*
Holy Mother of God,
Holy virgin of virgins,
St. Michael,
St. Gabriel,
St. Raphael,
All you Holy Angels and Archangels,
All you Holy Orders of Blessed Spirits,
St. John the Baptist,
St. Joseph,
All you Holy Patriarchs and Prophets,
St. Peter,
St. Paul,
St. Andrew,
St. James,
St. John,
St. Thomas,
St. James,
St. Philip,
St. Bartholomew,
St. Matthew,
St. Simon,
St. Thaddeus,
St. Barnabas,
St. Luke,
St. Mark,
All you Holy Apostles and Evangelists,
All you Holy Disciples of Our Lord,
All you Holy Innocents,
St. Stephen,

St. Lawrence,
St. Vincent,
Ss. Fabian and Sebastian,
Ss. John and Paul,
Ss. Cosmos and Damian,
Ss. Gervase and Protase,
All ye Holy Martyrs,
St. Sylvester,
St. Gregory,
St. Ambrose,
St. Augustine,
St. Jerome,
St. Martin,
St. Nicholas,
All you Holy Bishops and Confessors,
All you Holy Doctors,
St. Anthony,
St. Benedict,
St. Bernard,
St. Dominic,
St. Francis,
All you Holy Priest and Levites,
All you Holy Monks and Hermits,
St. Mary Magdalen,
St. Agatha,
St. Lucy,
St. Agnes,
St. Cecilia,
St. Catherine,
St. Anastasia,
All you Holy Virgins and Widows,

All you Men and Women, Saints of God,
   intercede for us.

Be merciful,
   Spare us, O Lord!
Be merciful,
   Graciously hear us, O Lord!

*Pray for us is repeated after each invocation.

Litany of the Saints *(continued)*

From all evil,
    *O Lord, deliver us.**
From all sin,
From thy wrath,
From a sudden and unprovided death,
From the deceits of the devil,
From anger, hatred, and all ill will,
From the spirit of fornication,
From lightning and tempest,
From the scourge of earthquake,
From pestilence, famine, and war,
From everlasting death,
Through the mystery of thy holy incarnation,
Through thy coming,
Through thy nativity,
Through thy baptism and holy fasting,
Through thy cross and passion,
Through thy death and burial,
Through thy holy resurrection,
Through thine admirable ascension,
Through the coming of the Holy Ghost, the
    Paraclete,

In the day of judgment,
    *We beseech thee, hear us.***
That you would spare us,
That you would pardon us,
That you would vouchsafe to bring us to true
    penance,
That you would vouchsafe to govern and preserve
    your holy church,
That you would vouchsafe to preserve our
    apostolic prelate and all ecclesiastical
    orders in holy religion,
That you would vouchsafe to humble the enemies
    of thy holy church,
That you would vouchsafe to give peace and true
    concord to Christian kings and princes,
That you would vouchsafe to grant peace and
    unity to all Christian people,

That you would vouchsafe to bring back to the
    unity of the Church all those who have
    strayed away, and lead to the light of the
    Gospel all unbelievers,
That you would vouchsafe to confirm and
    preserve us thy holy service,
That you would lift up our minds to heavenly
    desires,
That you would render eternal blessings to all
    our benefactors,
That you would deliver our souls and those of
    our brothers, relatives, and benefactors
    from eternal damnation,
That you would vouchsafe to give and preserve
    the fruits of the earth,
That you would vouchsafe to give eternal rest to
    all the faithful departed,
That you would vouchsafe graciously to hear us,
Son of God.

Lamb of God, who takes away the sins of the
    world, *spare us, O Lord.*
Lamb of God, who takes away the sins of the
    world, *graciously hear us, O Lord.*
Lamb of God, who takes away the sins of the
    world, *have mercy on us.*

Christ, hear us.
    Christ, graciously hear us.
Lord, have mercy on us.
    Christ, have mercy on us.
Lord, have mercy on us.
    Our Father . . .

* *O Lord, deliver us* is repeated after each invocation.
** *We beseech thee, hear us* is repeated after each invocation.

Rite of Marriage

The Liturgy of the Eucharist proceeds as usual. After the homily, the Rite of Marriage begins.

QUESTIONS
After the Liturgy of the Word, the Rite of Marriage beings. The priests asks the couple:
N. and N., have you come here freely and without reservation to give yourselves to each other in marriage? R/ *Yes.*

Will you love and honor each other as man and wife for the rest of your lives? R/ *Yes.*

Will you accpet children lovingly from God, and bring them up acording to the law of Christ and his Church? R/ *Yes.*

CONSENT
The priest says to the couple:
Since it is your intention to enter into marriage, join your right hands, and declare your consent before God and his Church.

The couple joins hands and the bridegroom says:
I, N., take you, N., to be my wife. I promise to be true to you in good times and in bad, in sickness and in health. I will love you and honor you all the days of my life.

The bride says:
I, N., take you, N., to be my husband. I promise to be true to you in good times and in bad, in sickness and in health. I will love you and honor you all the days of my life.

The priest says:
You have declared your consent before the Church. May the Lord in his goodness strengthen your consent and fill you both with his blessings.
R/ *Amen.*

BLESSING OF RINGS
Priest:
Lord, bless these rings which we bless + in your name.
Grant that those who wear them
may always have a deep faith in each other.
May they do your will
and always live together
in peace, good will, and love.
We ask this through Christ our Lord.
R/ *Amen.*

EXCHANGE OF RINGS
The bridegroom places the bride's ring on her finger and says:
N., take this ring as a sign of my love and fidelity. In the name of the Father, and of the Son, and of the Holy Spirit.

Rite of Marriage *(continued)*

The bride places the bridegroom's ring on his finger and says:
N., take this ring as a sign of my love and fidelity. In the name of the Father, and of the Son, and of the Holy Spirit.

The Liturgy of the Eucharist is celebrated.

NUPTIAL BLESSING
After the Our Father, the priest prays:
**My dear friends, let us turn to the Lord and pray
that he will bless with his grace this woman
now married in Chist to this man
and that through the sacrament of the body and blood of Christ,
he will unite in love the couple he has joined in this holy bond.**

**Father, by your power you have made everything out of nothing.
In the beginning you created the universe
and made mankind in your own likeness.
You gave man the constant help of woman
so that man and woman should no longer be two, but one flesh,
and you teach us that what you have united
may never be divided.**

The rest of the Mass is celebrated.

SOLEMN BLESSING
Before the final blessing of the people, the priest gives the couple a special blessing:
May God, the almighty Father, give you His joy and bless you in your children. R/ *Amen.*

May the only Son of God have mercy on you and help you in good times and in bad. R/ *Amen.*

May the Holy Spirit of God always fill your hearts with his love. R/ *Amen.*

And may almighty God bless you all, the Father, and the Son, + and the Holy Spirit. R/ *Amen.*

SUGGESTED READINGS		
Old Testament	*New Testament*	*Gospel*
Gen 1:26–28, 31	Rom 12:1–2, 9–18	Mt 5:1–12
Gen 2:28–24	1 Cor 13:1–13	Mt 5:13–16
Gen 24:48–51, 58–67	Eph 5:21–32	Mk 10:6–9
Tob 7:9–10, 11–15	Col 3:12–17	Jn 2:1–11
Tob 8:5–10	1 Pet 3:1–9	Jn 15:9–12
Song 2:8–14	1 Jn 3:18–24	Jn 15:12–16
Sir 26:1–4	1 Jn 4:7–12	Jn 17:20–26

The Dream of Gerontius

Materials: copies of this worksheet.

Aim: to imagine death and the particular judgment.

What to Do and Say

"The Dream of Gerontius" is a poem by Venerable Cardinal Newman. It portrays a soul on his way to judgment.

The soul walks with his guardian angel and speaks impatiently of the coming vision of God. However, when the soul sees God, he sees at once all his imperfections and cries to the angel, "Take me away."

Direct the students to read the selected passages from "The Dream of Gerontius" and to comment on these passages, explaining them in their own words. Definitions are given for some of the more difficult words, and there are questions for the students to consider. Pass out copies of the worksheet, and direct the students to write their explanations on a separate sheet of paper, numbering their commentaries to correspond with the numbers of the passages on the worksheet.

This worksheet can be used for classwork, group discussion, or homework.

The Dream of Gerontius *(continued)*

> *"The Dream of Gerontius" is a poem by Venerable Cardinal Newman. It portrays a soul on his way to judgment. The soul walks with his guardian angel and speaks impatiently of the coming vision of God. However, when the soul sees God, he sees at once all his imperfections and cries to the angel, "Take me away." Read the poem. Then, on a separate sheet of paper, explain each section of the poem (I-V) in your own words. The questions in the margin are to help you with your comments.*

The Dream of Gerontius
BY VENERABLE JOHN HENRY NEWMAN

I. *Reality of Death*

1. What is the Venerable Newman describing?

SOUL
So much I know, not knowing how I know,
That the vast universe, where I have dwelt,
Is quitting me, or I am quitting it.

II. *The Difference between Earthly Time and Eternal Time*

ANGEL
Thou art not let; but with extremest speed

2. Whom is the soul hungering to see?

Art hungering to the Just and Holy Judge:
For scarcely art thou disembodied yet.

3. What is the angel trying to show the soul by asking him to "Divide a moment, as men measure time, /Into its million-million-millionth part"?

Divide a moment, as men measure time,
Into its million-million-millionth part,
Yet even less than the interval
Since thou didst leave the body, and the priest
Cried "Subvenite,"* and they fell to prayer;
Nay, scarcely yet have they begun to pray.

For spirits and men by different standards mete*
The less and greater in the flow of time.

III. *No Fear at Judgment for a Holy Soul*

SOUL

4. Why was the soul afraid of death while he lived on earth?

Dear Angel, say,
Why have I now no fear at meeting him?
Along my earthly life, the thought of death
And judgment was to me most terrible.
I had it aye before me, and I saw
The Judge severe e'en in the Crucifix.
Now that the hour is come, my fear is fled;

*subvenite: the first word of a Latin prayer for the death, meaning "come to his assistance."

*mete: measure

The Dream of Gerontius *(continued)*

And at this balance of my destiny,
Now close upon me, I can forward look
With a serenest joy.

ANGEL
                                It is because
Then thou didst fear, that now thou dost not fear.

IV. *Christ's Piercing Look at the Particular Judgment*

ANGEL (speaking of the choirs of angels)
They sing of thy approaching agony,
Which thou so eagerly didst question of:
It is the face of the Incarnate God
Shall smite thee with that keen and subtle pain;
And yet the memory which it leaves will be
A sovereign febrifuge* to heal the wound;
And yet withal it will the wound provoke,
And aggravate and widen it the more.

V. *The Encounter with Christ at the Particular Judgment*

SOUL
I go before my Judge. Ah! . . .

ANGEL
                                . . . Praise to his Name!
The eager spirit has darted from my hold,
And, with the intemperate energy of love,
Flies to the dear feet of Emmanuel;
But, ere it reaches them, the keen sanctity,
Which with its effluence,* like a glory, clothes
And circles round the Crucified, has seized,
And scorched, and shrivelled it; and now it lies
Passive and still before the awful Throne.
A happy, suffering soul! for it is safe,
Consumed, yet quickened, by the glance of God.

SOUL
Take me away, and in the lowest deep
There let me be.
And there in hope the lone night-watches keep,
Told out for me.
There, motionless and happy in my pain,
Lone, not forlorn,
There will I sing my sad perpetual strain,
Until the morn.

5. Why would the face of the Incarnate God "smite" the soul and its memory be a "febrifuge"?

6. Why does the angel describe the soul as "happy, suffering"?

7. Why does the soul say, "Take me away"?

febrifuge: a remedy to remove or mitigate a fever

effluence: outflow, emanation

Rite of Funerals

INTRODUCTORY RITES

GREETING
May the God of hope give you the fullness of peace, and may the Lord of life be always with you.
R/ *And also with you.*

OPENING HYMN
Choose an appropriate song.

INVITATION TO PRAYER
My brothers and sisters, we believe that all ties of friendship and affection which knit us as one throughout our lives do not unravel with death.

Confident that God always remembers the good we have done and forgives our sins, let us pray, asking God to gather N. to himself.

Pause for silent prayer.

OPENING PRAYER
**O God,
glory of believers and life of the just,
by the death and resurrection of your Son. we are redeemed:
have mercy on you servant N.,
and make him/her worthy to share the joys of paradise,
for he/she believed in the resurrection of the dead.
We ask this through Christ our Lord.**
R/ *Amen.*

LITURGY OF THE WORD

FIRST READING
Have one of the students read 2 Corinthians 5:1, 6–10.

RESPONSORIAL PSALM
Have one of the students read Psalm 27.
Between each stanza, all respond: *The Lord is my light and my salvation.*

GOSPEL
Read Luke 12:35–40.

HOMILY
At this point, the priest or deacon would give a homily.

Rite of Funerals *(continued)*

PRAYER OF INTERCESSION

LITANY
Let us turn to Christ Jesus with confidence and faith in the power of his Cross and Resurrection:

Risen Lord, pattern of our life for ever: Lord, have mercy.
R/ *Lord, have mercy.*

Promise and image of what we shall be: Lord, have mercy.
R/ *Lord, have mercy.*

Son of God who came to destroy sin and death: Lord, have mercy.
R/ *Lord, have mercy.*

Word of God who delivered us from the fear of death: Lord, have mercy.
R/ *Lord, have mercy.*

Crucified Lord, forsaken in death, raised in glory: Lord, have mercy.
R/ *Lord, have mercy.*

**Lord Jesus, gentle shepherd who brings rest to our souls, give peace to N. for ever:
   Lord, have mercy.**
R/ *Lord, have mercy.*

**Lord Jesus, you bless those who mourn and are in pain. Bless N.'s family and friends who gather
   around him/her today: Lord, have mercy.**
R/ *Lord, have mercy.*

THE LORD'S PRAYER
With God there is mercy and fullness of redemption; let us pray as Jesus taught us:
All: *Our Father . . .*

CONCLUDING PRAYER
**Lord God,
you are attentive to the voice of our pleading.
Let us find in your Son
comfort in our sadness,
certainty in our doubt
and courage to live through this hour.
Make our faith strong
through Christ our Lord.**
R/ *Amen.*

At this point, a friend or family member would say a few words about the deceased.

Rite of Funerals *(continued)*

CONCLUDING RITE

BLESSING
Blessed are those who have died in the Lord; let them rest from their labors for their good deeds go with them.

Eternal rest grant unto him/her, O Lord.
R/ *And let perpetual light shine upon him/her.*

May he/she rest in peace.
R/ *Amen.*

If a priest or deacon is present, they will conclude with these prayers:
May the peace of God,
which is beyond all understanding,
keep your hearts and minds
in the knowledge and love of God
and of his Son, our Lord Jesus Christ.
R/ *Amen.*

May almighty God bless you, the Father, and the Son, and the Holy Spirit.
R/ *Amen.*

If a priest or deacon is not available, a lay minister concludes:
May the love of God and the peace of the Lord Jesus Christ
bless and console us
and gently wipe every tear from our eyes.
in the Name of the Father,
and of the Son, and of the Holy Spirit.
R/ *Amen.*

CLOSING HYMN
Choose an appropriate song.